Schoenberg's New World

SCHOENBERG'S NEW WORLD
THE AMERICAN YEARS

Sabine Feisst

OXFORD
UNIVERSITY PRESS

Oxford University Press, Inc., publishes works that further
Oxford University's objective of excellence
in research, scholarship, and education.

Oxford New York
Auckland Cape Town Dar es Salaam Hong Kong Karachi
Kuala Lumpur Madrid Melbourne Mexico City Nairobi
New Delhi Shanghai Taipei Toronto

With offices in
Argentina Austria Brazil Chile Czech Republic France Greece
Guatemala Hungary Italy Japan Poland Portugal Singapore
South Korea Switzerland Thailand Turkey Ukraine Vietnam

Published by Oxford University Press, Inc.
198 Madison Avenue, New York, New York 10016

www.oup.com

Library of Congress Cataloging-in-Publication Data
Feisst, Sabine.
Schoenberg's new world : the American years / Sabine Feisst.
p. cm.
Includes bibliographical references and index.
ISBN 978-0-19-537238-0
1. Schoenberg, Arnold, 1874–1951. 2. Composers—Biography. I. Title.
ML410.S283F45 2011
780.92—dc22
[B]
2010013245

Publication of this book was supported by the AMS 75 PAYS Publication Endowment Fund of the American Musicological Society.
1 3 5 7 9 8 6 4 2

For Don

About the Companion Web site

www.oup.com/us/schoenbergsnewworld

Access with username Music3 and password Book3234

Schoenberg's New World features a password-protected companion web site. A supplemental chronology guides the reader through Schoenberg's American years and important events in the reception of his work in the United States. Rare photographs, audio tracks of Schoenberg's American works, and video clips illustrate the content of the book. The reader is encouraged to take advantage of these additional resources.

Contents

Preface

Like countless refugees from Nazi Europe, Arnold Schoenberg, pioneer of musical modernism and polarizing figure in twentieth-century music, spent a significant part of his career in the United States. During his American years from 1933 to his death in 1951, he produced a rich body of works, distinguished himself as an influential teacher, and made a strong and lasting impact on American musical life. Yet while his European career and works, especially his innovative twelve-tone technique, have received significant scholarly attention, research on his American years has achieved neither depth nor breadth commensurate with the importance of this period in his career. Little has been written about his works composed in the United States, his interactions with Americans and with other émigrés, or the performance, publication, and reception of his music in this country. The existing literature is fraught with misinformation and misunderstandings, and lacks substantive discussion of biographical, cultural, and sociohistorical contexts. No full-length account of his life and work in America has yet been written, a fact all the more unusual given this topic's significance.

My intention with this volume is to fill crucial gaps in the Schoenberg literature and dispel various myths by drawing on new information and offering new perspectives and scholarly approaches. In reexamining Schoenberg's American career, I draw on the vast Schoenberg correspondence, much of which has remained unpublished and is only recently being made easily available through the Arnold Schönberg Center in Vienna. I consider little-known writings by Schoenberg and a variety of primary sources by figures associated with him. Manuscripts of finished and unfinished works Schoenberg composed in America are reconsidered in new contexts. Much of this material is located at the Arnold Schönberg Center (formerly Arnold Schoenberg Institute, Los Angeles), the Library of Congress, and the New York Public Library. I also make use of numerous interviews with émigré and American musicians in the oral-history archives at Yale University and several West Coast libraries, and interviews I conducted with Schoenberg students, some of whom have since passed away: the late Patricia Carpenter, Frank Glazer, the late Lou Harrison, the late Leon Kirchner, the late Dika Newlin, the late David Raksin, the late Leonard Rosenman, the late Leonard Stein, and other adherents, as well as his family members and critics. All these investigations yielded much new information.

In an effort to gain new perspectives and overcome the narrow hagiographic and Eurocentric outlook of existing narratives of Schoenberg's American years, I draw on a variety of approaches to biography (including David Riesman's concepts of "inner" and "other directed" biographical narratives) and writings on other émigrés, as well as on ethnomusicological ideas about music migration. I take into account the new tendencies in exile scholarship since the 1990s (by Martin Jay and others); texts on the history, politics, and culture of twentieth-century America; and ideas of cultural theory, aiming at a holistic and broad-based discussion of Schoenberg in America.

With this background I traced and analyzed treatments of this subject in international Schoenberg literature, exile studies, and reference works from a historiographic standpoint, seeking to identify clichés, omissions, shifting perspectives, and authors' agendas. In addition, I researched the reception of Schoenberg in America, systematically reading through major music periodicals, newspaper reviews, and scholarly publications from the 1910s through the end of the twentieth century, and studied circumstances of performances and Schoenberg's impact on the American music scene, along with scholarly commentary.

This volume is not a chronological survey with systematic musical analyses of all Schoenberg's American works, and it does not aim at comprehensive coverage of the topic. Instead, it focuses on a selection of pertinent issues hitherto neglected in the Schoenberg literature. Although the equation of "America" with "the United States" is a touchy matter in certain disciplines and the book does not cover Schoenberg reception in South America and Canada, I will, for pragmatic reasons, use the terms "America" and "United States" interchangeably throughout.

The book falls into seven chapters. The opening chapter illuminates influential yet often negatively flavored interpretations of Schoenberg's émigré personality, his American compositions, and his experience as a teacher and influence in America as expounded in the existing Schoenberg literature. Disclosing the myths, gaps, and changing trends in these views sets the stage for the following discussions.

The second chapter explores the reception of Schoenberg in America before 1933, tracing performances of his works in the United States and the audience and journalistic responses since 1913. I review the dissemination of his ideas in scholarly venues and among American composers in the 1920s and early 1930s, and analyze the role of early Schoenberg enthusiasts in America. Schoenberg's views of America before his emigration are discussed as well.

The third chapter focuses on Schoenberg's socialization in America. Here I will challenge the notion of Schoenberg as an isolated figure unwilling to adapt to American life and show how he came to terms with his Austrian-German, Jewish, and American identities socially, intellectually and culturally. Light is cast on his interactions with other émigrés and Americans, and on the complex nature of his manifold musical and nonmusical activities by reverting to such concepts as acculturation. I also call into question the static view of Schoenberg's American years as a time of "exile," and show that during his eighteen years in America, Schoenberg's status, like that of many others from Nazi Europe, changed from "refugee" to "exile" and "immigrant." He became an American citizen in 1941 and never returned to Europe again.

The traditional view that Schoenberg's music was "practically not performed" in America is disputed in the fourth chapter. This misconception stems in part from Schoenberg's own worries about his legacy and his lack of awareness of the scope of his work's reception. The fifth chapter, on the publication of Schoenberg's works, examines how American publishers (and other institutions) directed his creative activities by commissioning works from him and initiating arrangements of earlier compositions; it also shows how they sometimes forced him to redirect his compositional projects. This study illuminates why he dealt with so many different publishers, and how they helped overcome public resistance to his works or, in some cases, hindered the dissemination of his music.

The sixth chapter, "Schoenberg's Teaching Career and His Students," questions the negative impression emerging from most accounts of Schoenberg's American teaching activities—that he was, due to unfavorable teaching conditions and an elitist attitude, a dissatisfied teacher. My investigation of his university and private teaching, and discussion of his teaching methods and materials, elucidates Schoenberg's considerable efforts to adjust to the needs and expectations of the American educational system. I also look at his interactions with such American students as John Cage, Patricia Carpenter, Lou Harrison, Earl Kim, and Dika Newlin, along with pupils from the film industry who had distinguished careers as composers, performers, and teachers, but whose names, if mentioned at all, occur only in passing in most accounts of Schoenberg's American years.

The seventh chapter, concerning Schoenberg's reception in America after 1945, examines the impact of his music and ideas on American composers, which was not limited to representatives of high modernism, serialism, and complexity. Many Stravinsky adherents, experimentalists, and jazz and film composers were equally indebted to Schoenberg. This is often overlooked in the aesthetic controversies about the complex music of academy-affiliated, "uptown" Manhattan composers versus the often more accessible music of experimentalist "downtown" composers. Further, I investigate the impact of Schoenberg's ideas on music theory and education through the efforts of figures such as Milton Babbitt, George Perle, Allen Forte, and David Lewin, whose analytic tools, theories, and new terminology for serial and atonal music greatly advanced music theory in American academia. Finally, I show that Schoenberg's music, although never achieving mass appeal and never failing to provoke music critics, has always succeeded in attracting champions in America: performers, conductors, composers, and musicologists. This volume closes with an assessment of the significance of Schoenberg's work and ideas in America today, since the Schoenberg Institute's relocation from Los Angeles to Vienna.

This project has been personally very rewarding, in that it has allowed me to come to terms with the exceptionally difficult period in the (music) history of my native country, Germany, and chosen homeland, the United States. Having lived in two of Schoenberg's countries, I have gained a better sense of some of the challenges he had to face more than seven decades earlier. I hope this book will lead to a new and deeper understanding of a crucial period in Schoenberg's life and that it will be a valuable source of information not just for Schoenberg specialists, music scholars, and critics, but also for readers with an interest in twentieth-century music, culture, and history, as well as music students, musicians, scholars, and readers with a general interest in migration and exile topics, the history of the twentieth century, and cultural sociology.

Acknowledgments

This book was a long time in the making and it could not have been completed without the help of my friends, colleagues and family.

I began research for this volume under a generous two-year grant from the Deutsche Forschungsgemeinschaft, which enabled me to do extensive work in many American archives and libraries, and to conduct interviews with Schoenberg students and adherents in America. I also benefited greatly from a fellowship from the National Endowment for the Humanities, and research grants from the Avenir Foundation and my home institution, the Herberger Institute of Design and the Arts at Arizona State University. The American Musicological Society provided generous financial support to facilitate the publication of this book.

My heartfelt thanks go to Lawrence and Anne Schoenberg, Nuria Schoenberg-Nono, Ronald and Barbara Schoenberg, E. Randol Schoenberg, and Mischa Seligmann for their generous support and permission to use published and unpublished materials, and for untiringly answering my many questions about Arnold Schoenberg.

I am very indebted to the staff of the former Arnold Schoenberg Institute in Los Angeles, especially to the archivist Wayne Shoaf, who provided invaluable information and sources and countless photocopies, and also to research assistants Marilyn McCoy, Deborah How, and Camille Crittenden for their generous assistance. I am immensely grateful to the Arnold Schönberg Center in Vienna, to its director Christian Meyer for his support, and to the archivists Therese Muxeneder and Eike Feß for their excellent and kind assistance and for enormously facilitating my research. I also want to acknowledge Julia Bungardt, Eike Rathgeber, and Nikolaus Urbanek, the team preparing the *Gesamtausgabe der Schriften Schönbergs* at the Schönberg Center.

My thanks go to the numerous librarians and archivists who assisted me with the location of sources. They include Wayne Shirley at the Music Division of the Library of Congress; George Boziwick, Karen Burke, and Bob Kosovsky at the New York Public Library; Vivian Perlis at Yale University (Oral History of American Music Archives); Barbara Wolff at the Houghton Library, Harvard University; Kristie French at California State University at Long Beach (Oral History of the Arts Archive); and Devin Burnworth at the American Symphony Orchestra League. I am grateful to the staff at the Pierpont Morgan Library and at the libraries and special collections of the University of California, University of Southern California, University of Michigan, University of Pennsylvania, City College of the City University of New York, Columbia University, New York University, American Music Center, Boston Public Library, Free Library of Philadelphia, Leo Baeck Institute, and New School for Social Research.

I owe much to composers Milton Babbitt, Leslie Bassett, Hays Biggs, William Bolcom, Evan Chambers, John Evans, Kyle Gann, Pia Gilbert, Mark N. Grant, Ursula

Mamlok, James Newton, Frank Oteri, the late George Perle, Roger Reynolds, Harold Seletsky, Bruce Taub, Richard Teitelbaum, Joan Tower, Marina Voyskun, and Charles Wuorinen, with all of whom I had conversations about Schoenberg. Special mention goes to Schoenberg's American students for sharing with me their recollections of him: the late Patricia Carpenter, Frank Glazer, the late Lou Harrison, Richard Hoffmann, the late Leon Kirchner, Scott Merrick, the late Dika Newlin, the late Roger Nixon, the late David Raksin, the late Leonard Rosenman, and the late Leonard Stein. I am grateful to Elisabeth Pease, daughter of Roger Sessions; Electra Yourke, daughter of Nicolas Slonimsky; and Martha and Christian Hinrichsen, daughter and grandson of Walter Hinrichsen, for giving me helpful materials and permission to use them.

For permission to quote from published and unpublished sources, I thank Tom Artin (Mark Brunswick estate), Theresa Barnett (UCLA Library Center for Oral History Research), Gene Caprioglio (C. F. Peters, New York), Aida Garcia-Cole (G. Schirmer), Robert Craft, Patti Davis (Patricia Carpenter estate), Samuel Elliott (David Diamond estate), Charles Hanson (Lou Harrison estate), Robert Kessler (Pendragon Press), Martha Potter Kim (Earl Kim estate), Laura Kuhn (John Cage Trust), Felix Meyer (Sacher Foundation, Basel), Deborah North (Leonard Stein estate), Michael Owen (Ira and Leonore Gershwin Trust), Nicole Pace (Musical America Archives), Susan Snyder (Bancroft Library, University of California, Berkeley), Vivian Perlis (Oral History of American Music, Yale University), Rachel Steuermann (Edward Steuermann estate), Richard Teitelbaum (Henry Cowell estate), Marilyn Vespier (Edgar Varèse estate), and Richard Workman (Harry Ransom Center, University of Texas at Austin).

Warm thanks go to my friends and colleagues in Schoenberg scholarship, Joseph Auner, David Bernstein, Steven Cahn, Joy Calico, Esther Da Costa Meyer, Walter Frisch, Christopher Hailey, Ethan Haimo, Elizabeth Keathley, Severine Neff, Bruce Quaglia, Jennifer Shaw, and Amy Wlodarski, for their encouragement, insight, and helpful suggestions. My deep appreciation goes to the musicologists Sally Bick, Jon Burlingame, Austin Clarkson, Mimi Daitz, Tina Frühauf, Nicole V. Gagné, William B. George, the late H. Wiley Hitchcock, Howard Pollack, my former dissertation adviser and mentor Albrecht Riethmüller, the late Catherine Parsons Smith, Steven Whiting, and Susan Youens, and to the literary biographer Kenneth Silverman, for their unwavering support and invaluable commentary. I am also indebted to Brian Brandt and Sime Viduka, who helped me with graphic aspects of my work.

My heartfelt thanks go to my exceptionally supportive colleagues in the School of Music at Arizona State University: Wayne Bailey, Glenn Hackbarth, Benjamin Levy, Kimberly Marshall, Richard Mook, Kay Norton, Robert Oldani, Jody Rockmaker, Catherine Saucier, Teodore Solís, and Madeline Williamson. I would like to thank the librarians, Christopher Mehrens, Brian Doherty, and Linda Elsasser, and the staff of the Music Library at Arizona State University, who helped me locate materials. I owe much to the students in my seminars on Schoenberg and Exiled Composers in America at Arizona State University for broadening my perspective on this project.

I am very grateful to Suzanne Ryan, executive editor at Oxford University Press, for taking this book project under her wing and guiding it enthusiastically and expertly through production and distribution. I am also indebted to her assistant Madelyn Sutton and editor Norman Hirschy for their excellent assistance, and to OUP's anonymous readers for their thoughtful comments on my manuscript.

My warmest thanks and love go to my family: my parents Gisela and Hermann Feißt, and siblings Ursula Lavori, Ute Steinam, and Martin Feißt, and above all to my husband Don Gillespie who had endless patience with me, provided the greatest encouragement and support, and untiringly assisted me with comments on my manuscript.

Schoenberg's New World

1 Rethinking Myths of Schoenberg's American Years

When we think of Schoenberg in America, we often envision him as a controversial figure displaced in a culturally alien environment, disadvantaged, neglected, and disillusioned. We have received this negative view in many discussions of Schoenberg's American career: He has been pitied and America blamed for its "commercially" oriented institutions that hindered his productivity and the reception of his music. But Schoenberg himself has also been criticized for being elitist and unwilling to adapt to American life; and conversely, he has been rebuked for his attempts to accommodate to America by sometimes compromising his progressive compositional approach.

Biographers have often been heavily influenced by Schoenberg's sometimes pessimistic perspectives. His own preference for biographies stressing discussions of his works, along with his strong opinions and his (European) students' worshipful attitude toward him, has led to hagiography-like portraits that suggest the image of Schoenberg as a strong and incorruptible musical prophet.[1] Thus most biographies, especially in their treatment of Schoenberg's American period, distinguish themselves by a strong focus on his works, but at the cost of a comprehensive investigation of his personality. Primarily written by German and Austrian Schoenberg adherents with a skewed understanding of American cultural life, these texts are still widely used, shaping a Eurocentric outlook that tends to flavor our view today of Schoenberg in America. As a result, concerns with Schoenberg's threatened yet unshakeable artistic identity and American philistinism are prominent, and a successful European career is thereby pitched against a disappointing American period. Schoenberg's changes in artistic attitude have been predominantly interpreted from the point of view of European left-wing scholars as character weakness—a perspective that has also been misleadingly applied to Béla Bartók, Kurt Weill, and others.

The myth of a superior European and inferior American period in the careers of Bartók and Weill, however, has already been successfully debunked.[2]

This chapter traces the origin, perpetuation, and occasional revision of these perspectives, emphasized in discussions of Schoenberg's personality, health, finances, Jewish identity, politics, late works, teaching, and influence in America. It seeks to expose clichés, gaps, changing trends, and the agendas of Schoenberg specialists reflected in specialized literature concerning this composer, exile studies, and reference works. It reveals the domination of a Eurocentric perspective and a bias toward pro-European and anti-American scholarship among both Europeans and North Americans who have internalized and replicated this viewpoint.

SCHOENBERG'S PERSONALITY

Central to many accounts of Schoenberg's American years is the pejorative image of him as a European in exile, an outsider in Southern California, a snob, an untouchable icon with a forbidding and hermetic aura. Jan Meyerowitz, an émigré composer (without ties to Schoenberg) declared that Schoenberg "was not in the least Americanized."[3] Jost Hermand, a German-born, German-literature specialist, emphasized the incompatibility of Schoenberg's strong interest in Zionism and his "nonconformist" and elitist attitude toward art music with his chosen place of residence, Los Angeles—a commercial and hedonistic environment that was not immune to xenophobia or anti-Semitism.[4] American composer David Schiff described Schoenberg as "disoriented by his new cultural surroundings," and American writer Anthony Heilbut pointed out, "Schoenberg's American career was plagued by disappointment and inattention."[5] American historian Kevin Starr conveyed a particularly unbalanced and negative image: "Despite his long residence in Los Angeles, from 1934 to 1951 . . . Schoenberg remained a figure so detached, so alienated, as to seem not to exist in Los Angeles at all, or at the least, not to derive much satisfaction from his life there."[6] Malcolm MacDonald, a British writer on music, noted that "for most of his time in America he felt isolated and bypassed by the musical world, little performed and little understood in a comparative cultural backwater."[7] Yet Schoenberg had also been a nonconformist and outsider in Europe. How did these and other writers arrive at such views?

Given Schoenberg's personality—a mixture of hypersensitivity, vulnerability, authoritarianism, pride, idealism, gratitude, and kindness—it is not surprising that he made many conflicting statements during this particularly trying period in his life. Thus previous Schoenberg commentators, whether aiming at a negative or a positive portrait, could always substantiate their views by using appropriate quotations from primary sources, and perpetuate a largely biased and negatively flavored impression of his American years. Biographers generally omit in-depth discussions of his acculturation—his embrace of the English language and American culture and myriad social interactions with Americans—and support the thesis of Schoenberg as an elitist and outsider. More often they stress his contact with other émigrés, portraying him as a so-called "bei-uns-ki" (German exiles who socialized among themselves and complained "bei uns daheim war alles besser / Back home in Europe everything was better"). The early, influential monographic studies by Hans Heinz Stuckenschmidt and Willi Reich, students of Schoenberg, Alban Berg, and Anton Webern, are prime examples. Stuckenschmidt and Reich, who both stayed in Nazi Europe, offered a mostly Eurocentric outlook that advances the image of Schoenberg as the "suffering hero."[8] The much-quoted collection of

Schoenberg correspondence (1958) selected and compiled by European Schoenberg student Erwin Stein presents mostly pejorative letters from the American period, reinforcing the picture of dissatisfaction and disappointment.[9] Most "America" chapters in later Schoenberg monographs are heavily modeled on these publications.[10]

There are, however, also occasional attempts, mostly by American writers, to humanize and popularize the "American" Schoenberg. Walter Rubsamen, an American musicologist and Schoenberg's colleague at UCLA, gave an account of his American years that discussed, along with Schoenberg's professional occupations, his relations with numerous musicians and friends (going far beyond the usual references to his friendly relationships with George Gershwin and Oscar Levant), his extraordinary hospitality and frequent parties, his leisure activities, and even his superstitions.[11] Dika Newlin deconstructed the image of Schoenberg as a "disembodied historical force" and aloof authority in her Schoenberg articles and her book *Schoenberg Remembered,* a frank memoir of her experience as his student at UCLA.[12] She discussed, for instance, his secret weakness for film and television—anathema to most Schoenberg biographers, who prefer to focus on his criticisms of the Hollywood film industry.[13] Yet Rubsamen's and Newlin's efforts have been condemned and Newlin's book has even been derisively dubbed "Schoenberg Dismembered."[14] More recently Matthias Henke and Allen Shawn "humanized" Schoenberg in their short biographies. They presented him in a new and more positive way by elaborating on his manifold nonmusical creative activities in America, including his designs of toys for his children, his interest in bookbinding, and his casual interactions with family and friends.[15] Although Shawn's endeavor received some negative responses,[16] some writers bravely continue to challenge the Eurocentric biases of Schoenberg scholarship. American exile specialist Laura Fermi remarked, "Schoenberg too benefited from his transplantation to American soil. He became more human, entering into closer contact with the contemporary world."[17] MacDonald correctly pointed out that Schoenberg wrote and spoke English as much as possible and "made it almost as flexible and vivid (if somewhat idiosyncratic) a medium of self-expression as his German."[18] And the American Schoenberg scholar Alexander Ringer wrote that "American thought and behavior" gained a hold on Schoenberg through his soon "thoroughly Americanized young family" (his two youngest sons were born in the United States).[19]

MISCONCEPTIONS ABOUT SCHOENBERG'S HEALTH AND FINANCES IN AMERICA

The majority of European Schoenberg commentators, among them Stuckenschmidt, Eberhard Freitag, Manuel Gervink, and MacDonald (as well as authors of encyclopedia articles), posit a stark contrast between his seemingly prosperous European and depressing American years, and in support of this they tend to focus on Schoenberg's health and financial problems in America. These writers nourish the idea that America treated badly an artist of such an eminent stature, suggesting what Malcolm Gillies has termed (in reference to Bartók) an "American guilt" theory.[20] They emphasize his initial discomfort with the debilitating weather, his asthma attacks, and the stressful conditions of low-level teaching in the Northeast, along with increased (age-related) health problems later on in California. But they neglect to note that Schoenberg, who had suffered from asthma and other health problems in Europe, spent about twelve (out of eighteen) years of his American career in relative good health and happiness. Igor Stravinsky's commentators, by comparison, generally refrain from discussing that composer's many debilitating illnesses. Many writers opine that Schoenberg's heart attack in 1946, among several other ailments, drove him into a five-year-long agony and pushed him even further into isolation. In the *New Grove Dictionary of American Music* Schoenberg is said to have "led the withdrawn existence of an invalid."[21] This point of view certainly supports the "isolation" and "agony" theories, but it contradicts Schoenberg's busy social and work schedules during that period: private gatherings, lessons in composition, and lectures and courses at the University of Chicago, the Music Academy of the West in Carpinteria, California, and at his home. The notion of Schoenberg as an invalid is challenged by his creative achievements during and after 1946: the String Trio (1946), *A Survivor from Warsaw* (1947), *Phantasy for Violin with Piano Accompaniment* (1949), several vocal works, numerous writings, and the textbook *Structural Functions of Harmony* (1947).

Schoenberg's "financial misery" is another much discussed and distorted subject in the majority of European accounts of the composer's American years. Most biographers have blamed financial issues (and thus American institutions) for Schoenberg's limited compositional output and unfinished works. Meyerowitz claimed that "financial misery did much harm to his creative work."[22] Wilhelm Sinkovicz opined that "during his emigration years, Schoenberg was never able to devote himself in peace to tasks which he would have liked to solve."[23] Other commentators have dwelled upon the financial insecurity induced by Schoenberg's mandatory retirement from the University of California in 1944 at age seventy, which yielded a pension averaging forty dollars per month (for an eight-year tenure).[24] More rarely mentioned is that, in Schoenberg's case, the university extended the retirement age by five years. Stuckenschmidt described this financial situation, as well as the rejection of Schoenberg's application for a Guggenheim fellowship in 1945 (for which the applicants' age limit was forty years), as "embarrassing."[25] Other authors dramatically claimed that Schoenberg was "suddenly forced into deep poverty" and that "Arnold Schoenberg was starving."[26] But despite the Great Depression, Schoenberg enjoyed a comfortable middle-class life with an income drawn from university teaching, lectures, private lessons, conducting, commissions, and royalties. From 1936 through 1944 he could rely on a yearly income of between $4,800 (equal to almost $74,000 in 2009) and $5,400 (due to inflation worth less, around $65,500 in 2009) from UCLA. He lived in a Spanish Colonial house in a fancy neighborhood, Brentwood Park, which he had bought for $18,000 in 1937.[27] Schoenberg was even able to afford housekeeping help to maintain the home. Furthermore, he generously supported his relatives back in Europe when he should have perhaps put the money aside for a rainy day. After 1944 Schoenberg had to cut back financially, teach private students, sell manuscripts to the Library of Congress, and accept lucrative commissions, but he never came close to starving. How else could he have afforded to send regular CARE packages to Europe after the end of the war, buy his son Georg a motor vehicle, and donate money to charitable organizations in 1950?[28] During this period Schoenberg had his greatest financial success in the United States: Antony Tudor's choreographed version of *Verklärte Nacht, The Pillar of Fire,* which has been performed many times since 1942.[29] ASCAP granted him an annual allowance of $1,500 in addition to royalties, friends raised money for him, and the National Institute of Arts and Letters awarded him $1,000 in 1947.[30] More details on Schoenberg's lifestyle and finances will be discussed in the following chapters.

SCHOENBERG'S JEWISHNESS AND POLITICS

In contrast to Schoenberg's personality, health, and finances, his intense involvement in the Jewish national cause (especially from 1933 to 1939 and during his last years) received little or no attention in the early Schoenberg literature. Yet Schoenberg invested much time and energy in Jewish matters. He wrote prolifically about them, composed Jewish-themed works, and even made public speeches for Jewish organizations. Schoenberg's intense preoccupation with such activities outside of music may explain in part why he did not compose or complete more works during his American years. His early biographers Meyerowitz, Reich, and Freitag discussed Schoenberg's Jewishness only in relation to religiously oriented works, such as his *Kol nidre* setting (1938) and *A Survivor from Warsaw* (1947).[31] Stuckenschmidt, in his 500-page Schoenberg monograph, dedicated little more than a page to Schoenberg's engagement with Judaism.[32] Similarly, MacDonald touches only briefly on this subject.[33]

Yet the path-breaking articles and books on Schoenberg and Judaism by Ringer and Michael Mäckelmann undoubtedly influenced some of the more recent Schoenberg publications and encouraged further specialized studies on this subject.[34] Ringer and Mäckelmann cast light on Schoenberg's complex attitude toward the conventions of his Jewish faith (which he never practiced in a conventional way, as his wife and children remained Catholic). They also discussed his views about assimilation and anti-Semitism, his fight for unanimity among Jews, his attempts to establish a Jewish Unity Party, and his idiosyncratic approach to Zionism (involving the establishment of an independent Jewish state through uncompromising and militant means). More recently, however, Schoenberg biographers such as Gervink, Ringer, Shawn, and Hartmut Krones have begun to incorporate into their work discussions of Schoenberg's public speeches (for instance, "The Jewish Situation," 1933) and his most substantial essay on Jewish politics, his "Four-Point Program for Jewry" (1933–38).[35] While these writers mostly refrain from a critical assessment of the antidemocratic and authoritarian positions that mark Schoenberg's polemics, Richard Taruskin, Bluma Goldstein, and Klára Móricz, among others, accuse Schoenberg of sympathizing with fascism.[36] Yet these writers tend to downplay or ignore the roots of Schoenberg's views: his indebtedness to the former Habsburg monarchy, which offered Austrian Jews and artists like Schoenberg more protection than the fragile Weimar democracy and its populist politics.

Besides Schoenberg's preoccupation with Jewish matters, his peculiar attitude toward politics in general throughout his American years deserves more elaboration and clarification, beyond his politically motivated settings of Byron's *Ode to Napoleon* (1942) and *A Survivor from Warsaw*. This research was omitted from the early literature on Schoenberg.[37] German biographies and exile studies from 1993 through 2002, however, have dedicated more attention to his mostly private opinions about politics, granting more insight into his sometimes contradictory ideas, such as his strong and continuous rejection of communism and fascism, his reservations about democracy, his concern with the rights of minorities, and his preference for monarchy.[38] Mäckelmann, Albrecht Dümling, Gervink, and Ringer, among others, explain Schoenberg's caution in politics (as opposed to his political activism in Jewish matters) and his long-term resistance to open criticism of Hitler as a measure to protect his family and friends in Nazi Europe.[39] But this attitude, which will be addressed in detail in chapter 3, could also be viewed as a form of adaptation to American politics and an instance of what Martin Jay has termed "deradicalization."[40]

CONTROVERSIES ABOUT SCHOENBERG'S LATE WORK

In 1954 music philosopher Theodor W. Adorno expressed his belief that the problems Schoenberg poses are no longer objective, "but a product of public opinion, which keeps ready so many clichés for his work."[41] This is especially true for Schoenberg's works composed in the United States. By the time he came to America, he was already notorious as a radical and nonconformist composer of structurally complex and aesthetically challenging works. He was considered the "avatar of twelve-tone music."[42] However, the works that Schoenberg promoted and composed in America often contradicted this image. Soon commentators remarked on the different nature of his "American" works, pitting the steadily progressive "European" Schoenberg against the eclectic and retrogressive "American" Schoenberg, despite his claim that he was unaware of any changes caused by his immigration.[43]

The Accusation of Heterogeneity

Many early Schoenberg biographers, most notably Stuckenschmidt and Reich, included very favorable descriptions of Schoenberg's American compositions. Yet their commitment did not prevent various other commentators from viewing his "American" oeuvre as more eclectic and heterogeneous than his European output. In their eyes, Schoenberg seemed to sacrifice his former stringent "l'art pour l'art" principles by using both tonal and twelve-tone elements and by composing utilitarian, sacred, and politically engaged music. Adorno considered his late works as "fragmentary" and "catastrophes" in which the compositional procedure means everything and the musical material has no significance.[44] He criticized Schoenberg's mixing of old and new compositional techniques in *Ode to Napoleon* and his Piano Concerto (1942) as "forced" and "impure."[45] Pierre Boulez, representative of the European postwar serialist movement, went even further, declaring this approach bluntly as vain and flawed:[46]

> But what are we to think of Schoenberg's American period, during which the greatest disarray and most deplorable demagnetization appeared? How could we, unless with a supplementary—and superfluous—measure, judge such lack of comprehension and cohesion, that reevaluation of polarizing functions, even of tonal functions? Rigorous writing was abandoned in those works. In them we see appearing again the octave intervals, the false cadences, the exact canons at the octave. Such an attitude attests to maximum incoherence—a paroxysm in the absurdity of Schoenberg's incompatibilities.[47]

With research on the majority of his American works having been limited for so long, these verdicts have significantly influenced Schoenberg scholarship.[48] More recently, however, new and positive interpretations of the disparate tendencies in Schoenberg's late works have appeared. His efforts are now also understood as "processes of disjuncture and disruption," marked by "radically dissimilar elements that refuse assimilation."[49] Other commentators, including musicologist Joseph Auner, drew attention to Schoenberg's anticipation of "the broad availability of historical styles and self-conscious manipulation of earlier music in the output of composers we do not normally associate with Schoenberg, such as Crumb, Foss, Berio, and Rochberg."[50] They also emphasized that most of Schoenberg's European works revealed conflicting tendencies as well—rigorous modernism and elements referring to the past.[51]

Schoenberg's Controversial Return to Tonality

The most puzzling and controversial aspect of Schoenberg's American works was his more frequent and emphatic consideration of tonality in works like his Suite in G for String Orchestra (1934) and Theme and Variations for Wind Band (1943). They indeed reveal an unmistakably retrospective quality. The premiere of Schoenberg's first American work, his Suite in G, triggered, for instance, the following response by *New York Times* critic Olin Downes: "Only one thing more fantastical than the thought of Arnold Schönberg in Hollywood is possible, and that thing has happened. Since arriving there about a year ago, Schönberg has composed in a melodic manner and in recognizable keys. That is what Hollywood has done to Schönberg. We may now expect atonal fugues by Shirley Temple."[52] Following many attempts to prevent speculations about an alleged capitulation with regard to twelve-tone composition, Schoenberg published the article "On revient toujours" in the *New York Times* (December 19, 1948), defending his continuous "longing to return to the older style" and his occasional decision to "yield to that urge."[53] While Schoenberg himself classified his Suite in G and Band Variations as "Nebenwerke" (secondary or minor works) and utilitarian or pedagogical music, and ranked through the assignment of opus numbers most of his tonal American works with his nontonal works, Adorno spoke of the "long list of 'secondary works'" ("parerga"), including such compositions as the *Second Chamber Symphony* (1939) and *Kol nidre* (1938).[54] Comparison of these works with his major American twelve-tone compositions still sparks controversy. This is perhaps due to the deep-rooted view—drawn from Schoenberg's unfinished opera *Moses und Aron* (1932)—of Schoenberg as "Moses," the abstract thinker, when during his American years he had a greater affinity with "Aron," the eager communicator.

Adorno, Hanns Eisler, and others did not overlook the fact that these works were more accessible for audiences.[55] Adorno claimed that Schoenberg's audience-friendly music was written for a "false society": "His inexorable music represents social truth against society. His conciliatory music recognizes the right to music which, in spite of everything, is still valid even in a false society—in the very same way that a false society reproduces itself and thus by virtue of its very survival objectively establishes elements of its own truth."[56] Eisler's attitude was similar to Adorno's. After remigrating to East Germany in 1948, Schoenberg's rebellious student Eisler declared that his teacher "fell prey to the delusions that accompany capitalist culture."[57] Schoenberg himself firmly maintained in 1950 that he had "made no concessions to the market," yet young composers in Darmstadt, including Boulez, followed in Adorno's and Eisler's footsteps and accused Schoenberg of adapting to the new cultural situation with retrogressive compositions.[58] According to avant-gardist and leftist perspectives, the tonal or audience-friendly works of Schoenberg—as well as Bartók's, Erich Korngold's, and Weill's—exemplify "deradicalization" and thus are of "slight importance."[59] This view can still be found in some exile narratives of the 1990s where authors emphasize the "adversarial energy of émigrés" and state that the "artistically significant works, which came forth . . . owe nothing to their adaptation to the new circumstances, but everything to their opposition."[60]

Less negative interpretations emerged occasionally in America in the 1970s and have burgeoned recently in both American and European narratives. Schoenberg commentators now tend to see tonal and other retrospectively marked works more positively, as a reflection of his émigré experience rather than a compromise of the composer's integrity: "for the exile his past is almost everything and the present is like a bottomless night."[61] In this sense Schoenberg's tonal works are viewed as his "anchors to a more solid past to which he remained actively connected in a way that Webern and even Berg and succeeding generations did not."[62] In this view, his tonal music as well as his arrangements of his own and classical works of the past appear as sincere attempts to reach out to American publishers, conductors, performers, and audiences, out of a desire or necessity to communicate with the new environment.[63] They are thus "responses to the unfamiliar culture," directed by outer circumstances such as commissions and encouragement from publishers or performers, or works "influenced by the pragmatic atmosphere of the United States."[64] Alan Lessem interestingly viewed Schoenberg's tonal pieces as "public" and his dodecaphonic compositions as "private" works.[65] Others believe that the exile status freed Schoenberg from the pressure to stay the modernist course and enabled him to handle compositional materials more flexibly, granting an interaction between law and freedom.[66]

In contrast, certain writers have continued to stress that Schoenberg resisted adaptation to American culture. Advancing an "isolation" theory, these commentators deny instances of acculturation and conformist tendencies in Schoenberg's artistic output after 1933. They either praise Schoenberg for challenging American culture or criticize him for exhibiting European cultural superiority.[67] Freitag stated that "in the USA Schoenberg remained nonconformist, an outsider, not least because he did not subordinate himself to the mechanisms of the market."[68] Dorothy Crawford similarly asserted that the "American idea of market force—which necessarily lowers the aspirations of the individual in order to satisfy the greatest number of consumers—remained alien to him."[69] Hermand insisted that Schoenberg never changed his elitist attitude that art was not mass entertainment, that he composed "German" music, and that his late works, including his tonal works, remained complex and incomprehensible to a general audience.[70] Other authors elaborated on the new, more sophisticated, and freer kind of tonality Schoenberg used in his American works, and on the (supposedly) great contrast between such retrospective works as the Suite in G and neoclassical compositions by Stravinsky.[71]

Debates about the Politically Engaged American Works

Unlike most of Schoenberg's European works, *Ode to Napoleon* (1942) and *A Survivor from Warsaw* (1947) mark more than any other of his late compositions an unusual change in his artistic approach and have given rise to controversy, despite successful performances. Not only did Schoenberg use the English language in these works, but he also embraced the concept of politically engaged art, an idea that was very topical among his compatriots, American composers Marc Blitzstein, Aaron Copland, Elie Siegmeister, and others in the 1940s. In these vivid musical indictments of Hitler, Nazism, and the Holocaust, Schoenberg seems to have contradicted his own ideals of autonomous music. (He once objected to Berg's *Wozzeck* [1922] on the grounds that "music should rather deal with angels than with officer servants," and in the 1920s rejected out of hand Eisler's engaged music.)[72] Purists such as Adorno questioned whether these works belonged to the aesthetic realm.[73] Yet some scholars maintain that Schoenberg's engaged music did not sacrifice, but rather enlarged, the concept of autonomous art.[74] While most Schoenberg biographers described his politically inspired works in very positive terms and compared them to masterpieces of the past, including Beethoven's opera *Fidelio,* some scholars took exception to the Napoleon-Hitler parallel invoked by Schoenberg's setting of Lord Byron's *Ode to Napoleon* and the "super-topicality" of *Survivor.*[75] The latter work in particular, inspired by dancer Corinne Chochem and commissioned by the Koussevitzky Music Foundation, has inspired a wide variety of interpretations. It has been considered a "testament to Schoenberg's own spiritual struggle," a "personal parable of his experiences as a Jew," a manifestation of "political eschatology" and a modern "Ode to Joy."[76] It has also been viewed as a reflection of Schoenberg's alienation, anger and withdrawal from German music, as well as a work whose "impetus came more from immediate external circumstances than from an intrinsic imperative to create such a piece."[77] *Survivor* has also been rejected as "embarrassing" and "abominably banal" by some scholars and even dismissed as Hollywood kitsch.[78] *Survivor* and other works are discussed in greater detail in the third chapter.

The Question of Schoenberg's Compositional Productivity in America

Further misconceptions pertaining to Schoenberg's American works arise from speculations about the reason for their limited number. During his eighteen years in America, Schoenberg completed fifteen original compositions, in addition to many occasional canons and six arrangements of his own and other composers' works. He also started but left unfinished numerous pieces, including works for piano, organ, string quartet, chorus, and a large-scale programmatic symphony based on Jewish themes. Yet because he was unable to bring to completion his oratorio *Jakobsleiter* (begun in 1917) and opera *Moses und Aron* (begun in 1930), many commentators have suggested that his burdened mental state, heavy teaching load, and financial struggle in America prevented him not only from composing more works but from finishing others. Some biographers have seen the Guggenheim Foundation's denial of a grant to Schoenberg in 1945 as being more or less responsible for foiling his completion of *Jakobsleiter* and *Moses.*[79] Often American society itself takes the blame for his meager creative output:[80] "The United States was not the place where Schoenberg's ideas could fall on fertile ground," stated Sinkovicz.[81] Lessem viewed the relative "unresponsiveness of publishers, performers, and audiences" in America as having inhibited Schoenberg's artistic productivity.[82]

In this respect most scholars (with exceptions such as Henke and Shawn) fail to consider his many nonmusical interests and activities: political, religious, and social engagements; extensive writing (theory books, poems, essays, correspondence); painting; handcraft; sports, card, and chess playing; and dedication to his young family, relatives, and countless friends.[83] These activities, which at times became his priority and undoubtedly took away time from composing, could explain at least in part why Schoenberg was not a prolific composer—either in America or in Europe. Schoenberg's biographers tend to take his own words at face value (to the detriment of a more critical perspective), yet they seem to have overlooked his comments on this issue: "Maybe I would have written more when remaining in Europe, but I think: nothing comes out, what was not in. And two times two equals four in every climate." In 1948 he noted that "to compose the final act [of *Moses und Aron*] I have not yet found the right mood."[84]

SCHOENBERG—THE TEACHER AND HIS STUDENTS

Most accounts of Schoenberg's American teaching career give the impression that he was dissatisfied with the teaching conditions—the teaching load, educational system, and students—in America. Most biographers buttress this by quoting and generalizing critical remarks Schoenberg made about teaching in the United States: "Unfortunately the material [students] I get has had such an inadequate grounding that my work is as much a waste of time as if Einstein were having to teach mathematics at a secondary school."[85] However, at other places Schoenberg remarked that he "was not enthusiastic about German teaching either" and that "American young people's intelligence is certainly remarkable."[86] Furthermore, biographers tend to focus on his first and most stressful teaching job at the branches of the Malkin Conservatory in Boston and New York, and sparsely cover his eight-year tenure at UCLA, where the teaching conditions were more favorable. Detailed information on his private composition lessons and seminars, and elaborate discussions of the nature of his teaching activities, are generally omitted.[87] Such a perspective certainly underscores the image of Schoenberg as a European elitist but does a disservice to his unwavering idealism in the face of adversity, as well as his pragmatism and adaptability. It is an indisputable fact that Schoenberg, a passionate and devoted teacher throughout his life, quickly adjusted to the needs and expectations of the American educational system by providing a high-minded and rigorous teaching approach (the preferred approach of his time in academia).[88] The legacy of his teaching in America can be found not only in his textbooks on harmony, counterpoint, and composition tailored to the needs of American students, but also in his numerous articles on music education and proposals for music schools.

While much has been made of his European students in Schoenberg monographs, little has been said about his American students. Most biographers generally accuse Schoenberg's students of lacking qualification, perseverance, and a thorough knowledge of the musical canon.[89] Composers from the Hollywood film industry, who studied with Schoenberg, come off even worse as they are charged with superficial curiosity, wanting to learn only a few tricks in a little time.[90] This distorted view was furthered by Oscar Levant in his more entertaining than accurate 1940 satirical memoir *A Smattering of Ignorance*: "There is rarely a period in Hollywood when all the orchestrators and most of the movie composers are not studying with one or another of the prominent musicians who have gone there to live recently. At one time the vogue was for Schoenberg, who came with a great reputation, of course, as a teacher. However, most of the boys wanted to take a six weeks' course and learn a handful of Schoenberg tricks."[91] Yet Schoenberg surely would have enjoyed working with such talented composers from the film industry as Levant, Alfred Newman, Ralph Rainger, and David Raksin, because in most cases this was not limited to a six-week-long encounter.[92] While less happy about offering courses to music minors, he would have liked teaching numerous gifted and prepared students such as Wayne Barlow, John Cage, Patricia Carpenter, Lou Harrison, Richard Hoffmann, Earl Kim, Leon Kirchner, Dika Newlin, Leonard Ratner, Leroy Robertson, Leonard Rosenman, William Russell, Leonard Stein, and Gerald Strang, all of whom had distinguished careers as composers, performers, scholars, and teachers. These student names are absent from the majority of biographical accounts. Cage, Levant, and Schoenberg's teaching assistants at UCLA, Stein, Strang, Newlin, and Hoffmann, generally receive only passing mention.[93] Their voices have been neglected, too, although we stand to learn much from an in-depth study of their accounts and notes. Thus the impression arises that Schoenberg's American students could not withstand comparison to his European disciples—a view reinforced by such statements as this: "Strangely enough, only very few out of the hundreds of musicians who studied with Schoenberg at UCLA have become composers of some reputation: Gerald Strang, Leon Kirchner, Simon Carfagno, Earl Kim, Dika Newlin, and Don Estep."[94] This observation, based on a remark by Schoenberg himself, was later topped by Meyerowitz's assertion that "among the hundreds of American students Schoenberg taught there is not one composer worth mentioning."[95] By the 1960s Cage and Harrison had gained international recognition as composers, and Hoffmann, Kirchner, Kim, and Newlin had established themselves as composers and become professors of composition at prestigious colleges and universities. One might want to add that few of Schoenberg's many European students—Berg, Webern, Eisler, Roberto Gerhard, and Nikos Skalkottas—became well known composers.

Only in the past few years have some scholars begun to cast a different, more positive light on Schoenberg's teaching activities in America.[96] A few have embarked upon more detailed studies of Schoenberg's teaching methods in America and his development of textbooks tailored to the needs of American students.[97] Yet studies focusing on Schoenberg's interactions with his students are still rare.[98] Such investigations could in part illuminate reasons for his immense popularity with younger generations of composers and his great influence on American academia after his death, a subject to be explored later in this book.

INFLUENCE AND RECEPTION IN AMERICA

The common perception that "Schoenberg's ideas could not fall on fertile ground," that there was no "productive preoccupation" with his work, and that his music was "practically not performed" in America is also a myth inviting scrutiny.[99] Undoubtedly this misconception grew out of Schoenberg's own professed worries about his legacy and the dissemination of his music, concerns that contradict the assumption that he was not interested in the music market. His concern about being neglected was prompted in part by what his fellow émigré Ernst Krenek called the "echolessness of the vast American expanses"—implying that artists, for lack of feedback, were often unaware of the full scale of the reception of their work in this large country.[100]

While many Schoenberg commentators stress that he was first of all a highly popular and influential teacher who elevated academic standards, they do not mention that his innumerable American students advanced his legacy in manifold ways. Such pre-1933 Schoenberg students as the American composer Adolph Weiss were already spreading his gospel in America in the late 1920s. This, as well as the general topic of the reception of his music in the United States before 1933, has been neglected in Schoenberg scholarship. European biographers report on the revival of his music in Europe after World War II, yet tend to overlook how his presence in the United States nurtured interest in modernism among the young artists who did not even study with him, including Milton Babbitt, Elliott Carter, Robert Craft, George Perle, and George Rochberg.[101] In the 1950s and 1960s Schoenberg's compositional ideas became important and much respected subjects of study in academia, while at the same time atonality and serialism came to be the preferred compositional techniques for many American composers. Throughout his American years, Schoenberg gained visibility in the press through his own articles and letters to the editors of various publications, and these regularly provoked invigorating discussions and debates about modernism by others.

The much-deplored "small number" of American performances that Schoenberg received before 1933 and between 1933 and 1951, which after all amounted to hundreds of events, also has to be considered in relative terms. The limited number before 1933 must be gauged in the light of the different musical infrastructure and political changes resulting from World War I. The frequency of Schoenberg performances after 1933 must be seen against the background of a country coping with the Great Depression, the presence of countless other struggling American-born and immigrant composers in the 1930s, and the economic burden caused by World War II in the 1940s. Thus it is not surprising that during these years populist leanings dominated concert programming and that, if Schoenberg's music was performed in large concert halls, his most accessible works were given preference. The number of Schoenberg performances also needs to be compared with the much smaller number of performances of modernist works by such fellow émigrés as Bartók, Krenek and Edgar Varèse or American-born composers including John Becker, Henry Cowell, Ruth Crawford, Charles Ives, Wallingford Riegger, Carl Ruggles, and Roger Sessions.

It is high time to reassess Schoenberg's American career. His later years were far from "la douloureuse période américaine" that some have made them out to be.[102] As we shall see in subsequent chapters, Schoenberg's life in America is more complex and colorful than suggested by most previous commentators.

2 Schoenberg and America: Early Rapprochements

In 1933, in the wake of Hitler's rise to power, Schoenberg settled in the United States, where he would spend the rest of his life. Yet the story of Schoenberg in America does not start with the composer's emigration. The notion that he was unknown in America before his emigration, and that his music went largely unperformed there, are myths. Long before 1933, Schoenberg had important performances and advocates in America. Furthermore, from the early 1910s onward, his works and aesthetics were a frequent topic of discussion in American musical and intellectual circles, more so than those of most native composers. Even adverse reactions to Schoenberg's music tended to keep his name very much in the American public eye. And as we shall see, Schoenberg himself had well-formed, if idiosyncratic, notions about America, and what opportunities America should bestow upon him, years before he ever set foot there.

DISCOVERING SCHOENBERG THROUGH REPORTS FROM ABROAD

Because classical music programming in America had an overwhelming bias toward European composers, Schoenberg was regularly performed in American concert halls and much discussed in the American press long before he arrived in this country. Between 1907 and 1913 American music lovers attained a first impression of his music by way of journalistic reports from Europe. As his notoriety grew, foreign correspondents of journals such as *Musical America, Musical Courier,* and *Musical Leader,* and newspapers, including the *New York Times* and *Christian Science Monitor,* increasingly reported on early European performances of such works as the First Chamber Symphony, op. 9 (Vienna, 1907); Second String Quartet, op. 10 (Vienna,

1908); *Pelleas und Melisande*, op. 5 (Munich, 1910); and Three Piano Pieces, op. 11 (Berlin, 1911). Yet predictably, these critics, like their European colleagues, gave attention only to the most sensational and entertaining aspects of these events, namely, the music's unfamiliar sounds and the mostly negative and turbulent audience reactions. Schoenberg was portrayed as "arch cacophonist," and anarchist, and labeled an exponent of "musical occultism" and "aural chaos."[1] One critic described the premiere of the First Chamber Symphony as follows:

> A symphony for fifteen soloists is no ordinary work. Nor was the music ordinary. That use of fifteen solo instruments is a proclamation that the composer is a disciple of Mahler in the instrument idea. Whether Schoenberg deliberately sought the chaotic or whether the chaos is the result of his hopelessness, cannot be determined. In either case, each instrument wandered its own silly, themeless way. Mahler was present, and although he tried to hide his thoughts, he looked his feelings. The music caused hysterics in the audience. Many left before the end, others hissed, but there was applause as well.[2]

These reporters encouraged unfavorable prejudices and slogans among Americans who had not had the chance to hear any of Schoenberg's works, yet they also provoked a good measure of curiosity.

Critics and the rest of the American music world seemed puzzled over Schoenberg. "What is Arnold Schönberg? An altruist laboring for the second and third generation or a colossal joker?" asked one journalist.[3] Some American commentators compared Schoenberg with such older modernists as Strauss, Reger, Debussy, Scriabin, and Mahler, because their works had already been heard in the United States. Others emphasized his difference from this generation and his more extreme aesthetic stance, calling him an ultrist, ultra-modern, cubist, and futurist. The famous and controversial "Armory Show" or "International Exhibit of Modern Art" that opened in February 1913 in New York, featuring cubist and futurist art by Pablo Picasso and Marcel Duchamp, among others, might have provided the context for some of these epithets.[4] Schoenberg's name, unlike Stravinsky's, was on everyone's lips. Headlines like "Russia's Schoenberg, Latest of Modernists" and "Truly Is Stravinsky on the Way to Be the Schoenberg of Western Europe" document that until 1913 Stravinsky was an unknown quantity in the United States.[5]

However, American writers soon began to take a stand in favor of Schoenberg. On the occasion of the world premieres of the Five Orchestral Pieces under Henry Wood in London in 1912 and the massive *Gurrelieder* under Franz Schreker in Vienna in 1913, favorable and even enthusiastic reviews appeared in the American press for the first time. The Five Orchestral Pieces were described as "certainly the most startling of the season's novelties at the Queen's Hall Promenade Concerts" and "music well put together," documenting a "deliberate logic," "unsurpassed sheer technical skill," and "the composer's command of color."[6] The *Gurrelieder* were praised as a "great marvel to hear," which revealed "great lyrical beauties" and "extraordinary imaginative power."[7] Positive feature articles on Schoenberg were published by Karleton Hackett, music critic of the *Chicago Evening Post*; Ernest Newman, the renowned English music critic and contributor to the *Boston Evening Transcript*; and Philip Clapp, a young composer and Harvard graduate who authored a dissertation on "Modern Tendencies in Musical Form" in 1911. Hackett declared Schoenberg to be "the most striking figure in the world of music at this particular moment" and "thoroughly trained in the structure of music according to the old models."[8] Newman pointed out that Schoenberg was "not a mere fool or madman," but "a man of undoubted gifts." And Clapp considered him "a creative artist of rank whose point of view is unusual but eminently worthwhile."[9]

Such appraisals alternated with dismissive and sensational reviews on the occasion of early European performances of *Pierrot lunaire* and the notorious Viennese "Scandal Concert" of 1913, which sparked violent audience reactions. Prominent critic and essayist James Huneker's 1913 *New York Times* article "Schoenberg, Musical Anarchist Who Has Upset Europe" is perhaps the most famous and most quoted of the many vigorous American press reactions on early *Pierrot* performances. It was the largest piece on Schoenberg to have appeared in the *New York Times* up to that point, illustrated with a photo, a score excerpt from *Verklärte Nacht*, and Schoenberg paintings. While Huneker had no doubts about Schoenberg's authority and earnestness, he wrote: "Schoenberg is the cruelest of all composers, for he mingles with his music sharp daggers at white heat, with which he pares away tiny slices of his victim's flesh. Anon he twists his knife in the fresh wound and you receive another horrible thrill." Fearing the future acceptance of Schoenberg's music, he stated, "If such music making is to become accepted then I long for Death the Releaser."[10] Death actually released Huneker from witnessing the American *Pierrot* premiere in 1923, as he passed away in 1921.

THE FIRST SCHOENBERG PERFORMANCES IN AMERICA

Having read about Schoenberg's music for some years, Americans finally got to hear some of his works in their own country for the first time. Between October 1913 and April 1917 (when the United States entered World War I) multiple performances of three major orchestra works, two early chamber compositions, and the piano pieces opp. 11 and 19 were given in all the major cities from coast to coast.

Renditions of Schoenberg's orchestral works were limited to America's chief orchestras (many symphonic institutions, such as those of Houston, Baltimore, Detroit, and Los Angeles, had not been founded yet). Thus his larger works received first hearings in Chicago, Boston, Philadelphia, New York, and Cincinnati. Interestingly, his works were presented in an anachronistic order, with the Five Orchestral Pieces, his most progressive orchestral work at that time, performed first; the First Chamber Symphony was presented second, and the early tonal *Pelleas* played last.

In October 1913, the Chicago Symphony Orchestra under Frederick Stock gave the American premiere of the atonal Five Orchestral Pieces—only a year after its very first performance. It was one of the season's most anticipated events. One excited journalist even hoped for tumultuous circumstances, which might evoke those of the recent "Scandal Concert" in Vienna:

> Now no metropolis has ever been able to write its title clear as an art center which had not at least to its credit one riot, while the older and more important the city, the longer the list of riots to which it could point with pride. What better opportunity could we ever expect to have, one more in keeping in tradition of the art-loving cities of the old world, than the first performance in America of a symphony by . . . Schoenberg, for the inauguration of our music riots?[11]

The two concerts were virtually sold out. Yet instead of riots, there were only a few hisses, some laughter and irritation, but also astonishment, interest, fascination, and applause. Nonetheless, the critics caused a verbal turmoil, describing the sounds they heard as "a congress of polecats," "stuff as awful as an overripe and energetic durian fruit," "fowls and other domestic animals beginning their racket at the midday meal," "a ghastly banshee," and "a pandemonium of cross-eyed devils playing a big score."[12] Critics blamed the audience for pressuring Stock with their "lusting after novelties like a baby crying for a lighted match."[13] Stock they rebuked for having been fascinated with Schoenberg's work for some time, for wasting money and talent, and for desecrating the concert hall by programming this "Shame-berg Suite." Some proposed curing him with the "regenerative properties of boiling oil," while others suspected that Stock might have produced a Halloween joke.[14] A few positive comments pointed out Schoenberg's "remarkable technical acumen," and the work's "moments of strange beauty," "subtle dynamic effects," "stupendous detail," and "variety of fantasy surpassing the imagination of scholarship."[15] But such complimentary remarks were submerged in a flood of invective.

In comparison, the reactions to the Boston premiere of the Five Pieces, with the Boston Symphony Orchestra under Karl Muck a year later in December 1914, were much less vehement.[16] Reports about the favorable reception of this work's second London performance under Schoenberg, long and informative pre-concert newspaper articles, and a detailed program book helped shatter some prejudices. These texts included thorough descriptions of structural details and musical examples based on Arthur Eaglefield-Hull's published analysis of the Five Orchestral Pieces.[17] The conduct of the audience was "highly creditable to Boston. There was smiling, there was giggling at times, there was applause," though some concertgoers seem to have concentrated more on reading the program notes than on listening to the new sounds.[18] The reviews were mixed, but generally more polite than those of the Chicago critics. Boston journalists thanked Muck for enabling them to hear this work despite Muck's professed skepticism toward Schoenberg. Renowned critic Henry Taylor Parker, whose initials H.T.P. were often thought to stand for "Hard To Please," surprisingly wrote a sympathetic review; so did eminent music critic Philip Hale, who found the work "extraordinary" and praised Schoenberg as "a man of unusual knowledge, force and originality."[19] John N. Burk, a Harvard student at the time and later author of books on Beethoven, Mozart, and Clara Schumann, published the most glowing review of the event. Schoenberg owned a copy of it and underlined the most flattering passages: "What Schönberg has accomplished requires superhuman technical ability, and superhuman creative, and imaginative power. Schönberg is no raving maniac, but the conceiver of an entirely new plan of things. Aside from the question of genius, or even of beauty, he is certainly a composer of broad and expansive mind; a creator on a large scale."[20] The performance also impressed other Harvard students, including members of the poet group "Harvard Aesthetes," e. e. cummings, and S. Foster Damon. In his commencement address entitled "The New Art" (1915), e. e. cummings, whose experimental poetry became strongly influenced by such concepts as Schoenberg's *Klangfarbenmelodie* (sound color melody), spoke about Schoenberg, Henri Matisse, Gertrude Stein, and other figures. Damon, who later became an important William Blake scholar, vividly recalled the performance of the Five Orchestral Pieces in a 1915 article entitled "Schönberg, Strindberg and Sibelius."[21]

In the fall of 1915 the legendary conductor Leopold Stokowski, who developed into a staunch Schoenberg supporter and conducted many American and world premieres of his works, introduced the First Chamber Symphony to Americans with members of the Philadelphia Orchestra (Figure 2.1). He presented this work in his own way, taking some liberties with Schoenberg's instrumentation by enhancing the

This Week's Concert

The Philadelphia Orchestra

LEOPOLD STOKOWSKI, Conductor

The FOURTH PAIR *of* SYMPHONY CONCERTS *of* THE SEASON *of* 1915-1916

Friday Afternoon at 3.00 Saturday Evening at 8.15
November 5 and 6, 1915

Soloist: MISCHA ELMAN, Violinist

Program

Overture, "Benvenuto Cellini" — Hector Berlioz 1803-1869

Kammer-Symphonie — Arnold Schönberg 1874-
(*First time at these concerts*)

INTERMISSION
Of ten minutes' duration at evening concert only

Violin Concerto in A minor — Carl Goldmark 1830-1914
I. Allegro moderato
II. Air: Andante
III. Moderato; Allegretto
MISCHA ELMAN

Carnival Overture — Anton Dvorak 1841-1904

The war in Europe having prevented the arrival of Mr. Rosenthal, his place on the program for next week will be filled by Mr. Ernest Hutcheson.

Because of the entity of a symphonic program, and that its continuity may be preserved, no encores can be permitted.

Patrons who are obliged to leave the auditorium before the concert is over are asked to withdraw before the last number begins.

It is earnestly hoped that the women patrons of the Orchestra will remove their hats during the performance.

FIGURE 2.1.
Program of the Philadelphia Orchestra under Leopold Stokowski.

soloistically conceived string section. Since Philadelphians at this point had heard only Schoenberg's First String Quartet and *Verklärte Nacht,* Stokowski took several precautions to avoid antagonism from concertgoers and critics.[22] The audience received, in addition to detailed program notes with music examples compiled by Philip Goepp, a red slip with notes by Stokowski. And before taking up his baton he delivered further explanatory remarks about Schoenberg's work and why he chose to perform it. One critic observed that after such preparations "the audience settled back with the expectant expression of patients in dentist chairs."[23] After the hearing, however, concertgoers and the majority of critics were pleasantly surprised and amazed about the mildness of the dissonances and the lack of "big crashes of vociferous discord."[24] A week later Stokowski also introduced the First Chamber Symphony in a semi-private performance at the Ritz-Carlton Hotel to New Yorkers, who for the first time could hear an "orchestral" work of Schoenberg. This work received another rendition in 1916 with the New York Symphony under Walter Damrosch; the only orchestral work of Schoenberg played that year, it was accompanied by such headlines as "Musicians Wage War of Sounds."[25]

The third and longest orchestra work, *Pelleas*, was also introduced in two cities: New York and Cincinnati. Its American premiere with the New York Philharmonic under Josef Stransky took place in November 1915 at Carnegie Hall. Both scheduled performances were sold out, and the lights were dimmed to enhance the tone poem's somber atmosphere. The audience apparently listened attentively and applauded cordially, but the critics were divided. Some praised the work's "masterly orchestration," its "beautiful themes," and "skillful development," while others opined that Schoenberg "boxed the ears of his hearers with some extremely rude and loud dissonances."[26] Some reviewers contentedly thought that Schoenberg "cannot now be said to languish unappreciated in New York for lack of a hearing," while others regretted New York's "blissful ignorance" regarding "the undiluted 'third [atonal] period' Schönberg."[27] In 1917 the Cincinnati Symphony under Ernst Kunwald performed this work for the first time in Cincinnati. But it was the only American performance of an orchestral work by Schoenberg that year and the last rendition of one of his orchestral pieces before the end of World War I. In 1917 the Austrian and German conductors Kunwald and Muck became enemy aliens and soon thereafter were imprisoned until the end of the war.

Schoenberg's songs and early chamber music also began to be introduced in October 1913. The baritone Reinald Werrenrath programmed three early tonal songs, "Dank," "Wie Georg von Frundsberg," and "Warnung," from opp. 1 (1898) and 3 (1899–1903) for a concert in New York. This event of October 23, 1913, was the very first Schoenberg to be heard in America, Werrenrath felt that he had to assure the rather nervous New Yorkers in advance that concerning dissonance there was no cause for worries.[28] Although the reviewers expressed relief at these pieces' "mercy on the performers and listeners," they also revealed some disappointment that those early songs "failed to show any startling measure of tonal anarchy."[29] In the following years these and other songs could be heard in further public and semi-private recitals in New York.

In 1914 the prominent Flonzaley Quartet premiered Schoenberg's lengthy First String Quartet in D minor, op. 7 (1905) in New York, Boston, Chicago, and Philadelphia, and attracted much press attention before and after the events. Schoenberg's great supporter Busoni had introduced the quartet's leader Adolfo Betti to this work during his American concert tour in 1910–11. The performance in January was not only this work's American premiere, but also New York's first hearing of a substantial (though early) Schoenberg piece. Up to this point New Yorkers had listened only to some of his earliest songs. To prepare the concertgoers for this event, the Flonzaley Quartet offered two open rehearsals, one of which was introduced by the director of New York's Schola Cantorum, Kurt Schindler, a German immigrant who knew Schoenberg. Schindler's talk, soon to be published as a pamphlet complete with an index of musical themes, included remarks on Schoenberg's distinguished endorsers Busoni, Mahler, and Richard Strauss; Schoenberg's career; and the structural features of the First Quartet.[30] While the large audience received the work with "rapt attention" and much applause, the critics offered lukewarm assessments.[31] They admitted that the work contained "many moments of beauty," but regretted that "they were fleeting."[32] And most commentators seem to have concluded that this work was "music for the head" and that "listening to it comprehendingly is an intellectual feat."[33] Schindler's careful explanation of the work's logic of construction, intended to prevent denunciations of the music as "aural chaos," seems to have backfired. However, this work was much more kindly greeted by the large Boston audience and press a few days later. It received positive responses by the majority of reviewers, including Olin Downes, who worked for the *Boston Post* until 1924; Downes, as *New York Times* critic, would later tear many of Schoenberg's works to pieces.[34] While the Quartet had the poorest reception in Philadelphia, it arguably received the best response in Chicago. Both audience and critics vividly remembered the recent performance of Five Orchestral Pieces from a few months ago and were now pleasantly surprised to discover a very different side of Schoenberg.

Schoenberg's most popular work, the tonal string sextet *Verklärte Nacht*, op. 4, was introduced in America at the annual meeting of the American Guild of Violinists in 1914 in St. Louis, although this event took place almost unnoticed. The New York–based Kneisel Quartet, famed in America and Europe for its first-rate chamber music performances, introduced this work in 1915 to audiences in Chicago, Philadelphia, New York, and Boston. As it was received with enthusiasm in all cities, the group kept playing it until they disbanded in 1917. This work led conservative critics, including Richard Aldrich, Henry Krehbiel (both New York), Henry T. Parker (Boston), and Maurice Rosenfeld (Chicago), to praise Schoenberg as a "remarkable Viennese genius" and "supreme melodist."[35] Needless to say, *Verklärte Nacht* soon became Schoenberg's most performed work in America.

Most often performed works in America before World War I were the atonal Piano Pieces, opp. 11 (1909) and 19 (1911). Pianists including Harold Bauer, Ossip Gabrilowitsch, Charles Griffes, Charles Hambitzer, Katherine Heyman, Leo Ornstein, Rudolph Reuter, Leo Sowerby, and T. Carl Whitmer presented them in such cities as Boston, New York, Poughkeepsie, Pittsburgh, Cleveland, Grand Rapids, Chicago, San Francisco, and Portland, Oregon.[36] Thanks to their brevity they could be easily presented in small venues and offer increasingly curious audiences a taste of Schoenberg's latest style.

Sowerby, a nineteen-year-old student at the American Conservatory in Chicago and later one of the most prominent American composers of church and organ music, gave in May 1914 what was arguably the American premiere of the first two movements (the second in Busoni's arrangement) from Opus 11 in his hometown, Grand Rapids, Michigan. The "modernist" program given at the St. Cecilia Society also featured works by Debussy, Ravel, Korngold, and Reger. According to the chronicler of the *Grand Rapids Herald*, the Schoenberg selections were representative of what Sowerby tried to accomplish as a composer at that time.[37]

Of the many pianists performing Schoenberg in America before World War I, the young, magnetic Ukrainian-American virtuoso pianist and composer Leo Ornstein drew perhaps the most attention to Schoenberg with his "piano recitals of modern and futuristic music." In these concerts given between 1914 and 1917 Ornstein regularly programmed opp. 11 and 19 along with works of Debussy, Ravel, Albéniz, Scriabin, and effective modernist compositions of his own including *Wild Men's Dance* (1915), *Dwarf Suite* (1915), or *Impressions de Notre Dame* (1914). He startled large audiences in such cities as New York, Boston, Cleveland, and San Francisco, and thereby nurtured the controversy between conservative and progressive musicians and critics. In New York in two recitals at the Bandbox Theatre in 1915, he took credit for introducing the public to Schoenberg's "third style," and was well received by enthusiastic concertgoers and several open-minded critics. Some of them thanked Ornstein "for giving New York its first taste of the real Schoenberg" and declared the pieces "splendid mood pictures" that were "most interesting and impressive."[38] Other critics compared Schoenberg's music with Ornstein's, and claimed that Ornstein "outdid Schoenberg with impunity"; to them Schoenberg's music sounded comparatively "tame" and "anemic."[39] Ornstein must have welcomed such views, because with these novel recital programs he not only filled a gap as a performer, but also launched his own career as a composer by aligning himself with the foremost modernists of the day. Yet Ornstein ran the risk of being seen as an imitator of Schoenberg, a perception he dismissed by asserting that he was completely unacquainted with any new music when he conceived his own adventurous compositions.[40] (Yet how could he have been unaware of contemporary works, having been in Europe in the early 1910s and having met the composer Busoni and critic Michel Dimitri Calvocoressi among others?) After 1917 Ornstein dropped Schoenberg's works from his programs, rejecting him on the grounds that he was "working out his theory before working out his art."[41]

ORCHESTRAL PERFORMANCE AFTER WORLD WAR I

Just as Schoenberg's music and thoughts had started to gain ground in the United States, America's entry into World War I triggered attacks against Austro-German musicians and against these countries' most recent musical tendencies. The result was an eventual boycott of most German and Austrian music until the end of the war. In 1916 the number of Schoenberg performances dropped dramatically. In November 1917 the Metropolitan Opera firmly prohibited productions of German operas. The American symphony orchestras banned the works of living German, Austrian, and Hungarian composers, and drastically reduced the repertoire of deceased composers from these countries in concerts given between 1916 and 1919. Unavoidably, Schoenberg performances came to a complete halt in the fall of 1917.

The new political alliances resulting from World War I, especially America's close diplomatic relations with France, noticeably marked American musical life in the first years after the war. Many performers, particularly those of French origin, such as Pierre Monteux, conductor of various orchestras in New York and Boston between 1917 and 1924, and E. Robert Schmitz, pianist and founder of the Pro Musica Society, categorically refused to play Austro-German music. Schmitz described the work of German composers as follows: "With Weber, Strauss, and Schoenberg comes the worship of the Kolossal [*sic*] that is the religion of Germany's ruinous Kultur . . . the gradual deformation started with Luther . . . Schoenberg is an absolute reflection of this contemporary Germany . . . Schoenberg's music is 'metallic Cubisme,' it is 'heavier than art.'"[42]

As a consequence more music of French and Russian composers regularly appeared on American concert programs. Such American composers as John Alden Carpenter, George Whitefield Chadwick, Edward McDowell, Arthur Foote, Rubin Goldmark, and Edgar Stillman Kelley were increasingly featured as well. The patriotism of the war years led to a serious reconsideration of America's own neglected composers and musical resources. Even critics reminded their audience, "Now is the time to shake our music free, to relieve us from the arrogant and narrow notion that all music made in Germany is divine."[43]

In the early 1920s anti-German feeling declined, and once again the works of living Austro-German composers received attention. In the realm of orchestral music, conductors Willem Mengelberg, Stokowski, and even Monteux started to champion Schoenberg again in 1921. In the course of the 1920s and early 1930s, Walter Damrosch, Arthur Fiedler, Gabrilowitch, Rudolph Ganz, Eugene Goossens, Serge Koussevitzky, Mengelberg, Monteux, Eugene Ormandy, Fritz Reiner, Artur Rodzinski, Walter Rothwell, Nicolas Slonimsky, Alexander Smallens, Stock, Albert Stoessel, Stokowski, Stransky, Arturo Toscanini, Henri Verbrugghen, Ignatz Waghalter, and Bruno Walter all programmed Schoenberg's music. Among these figures, Mengelberg, Reiner, Slonimsky, Stokowski, and Stransky gave world and American premieres of seven works for orchestra (and voices) composed before 1933.[44]

In 1921 Mengelberg and the National Symphony offered a successful American premiere of Schoenberg's 1917 arrangement of *Verklärte Nacht* for string orchestra in New York, whereupon this version entered the repertoire of many other American orchestras. A year later Stransky and the New York Philharmonic mounted the world premiere of a Schoenberg work in America: his orchestral arrangements of the Bach chorales "Komm Gott, Schöpfer, heiliger Geist" (BWV 631) and "Schmücke Dich, o liebe Seele" (BWV 654). While the audience greeted the pieces warmly, New York critics were divided. Some thought that the works were "genuinely refelt" and "bathed in [Schoenberg's] own instrumental magic," but others were disappointed about these transcriptions' lack of futuristic effects.[45] They also queried the "tentativeness and incertitude" of the work's execution.[46] Despite the mixed reactions, these arrangements, along with Schoenberg's 1928 transcription of Bach's Prelude and Fugue in E flat major (BWV 552), introduced in America by the Cincinnati Symphony under Reiner in 1930, also regularly appeared on many American orchestra programs. Besides *Verklärte Nacht* and the Bach arrangements, Schoenberg's Five Orchestral Pieces, his First Chamber Symphony, and *Pelleas* also received multiple hearings (and mixed responses) in the 1920s and early 1930s.

Of all the above-mentioned conductors, Stokowski performed Schoenberg most often and gave the most American premieres of his works before 1933 (Figure 2.2). After performing *Pelleas* with the Philadelphia Orchestra in Philadelphia in 1921, he presented the Five Pieces in Philadelphia and on a tour of five major American cities: New York, Washington, Baltimore, Harrisburg, and Pittsburgh. Stokowski conducted the work from memory and prefaced each of the eight performances with his customary informative remarks about the music. Since most of these cities were hearing this work and, for that matter, Schoenberg's music for the first time, the numerous reactions ranged from acknowledgment and fascination to bewilderment and rejection, though the positive responses were in the minority. In 1923 Stokowski gave the first American performance of the 1922 orchestral version of Schoenberg's First Chamber Symphony.

Most important, in the early years of the Great Depression, Stokowski gave American premieres of three of Schoenberg's most significant large-scale works in Philadelphia. In 1929 he presented the Orchestral Variations, op. 31, Schoenberg's first dodecaphonic work for large forces just a year after its completion and world premiere. In 1930 he offered the first American performance of the expressionistic stage work *Die glückliche Hand* of 1913, and in 1932 he introduced the massive *Gurrelieder* for voices and orchestra to American audiences. The Variations, reflecting Schoenberg's most recent compositional approach, drew the most negative responses, while the two earlier works generated more favorable reactions.

The premiere of the Orchestral Variations prompted, as one might expect, considerable resistance from audience and press. All three performances in Philadelphia and New York were greeted with hisses and some applause, perhaps inspired by Downes's flimsy and acerbic program notes (the orchestra's competent program annotator,

FIGURE 2.2.
Stokowski Portrait by Edward Steichen (1927). Courtesy Joanna T. Steichen and the Smithsonian National Portrait Gallery.

Lawrence Gilman, had fallen ill). However, the performances did not lead to noisy demonstrations, as was the case in Berlin the year before. In New York, where the hissing was strongest, Stokowski rebuked the concertgoers, declaring: "As long as I am conductor of this orchestra, or any other orchestra, I intend to perform the greatest music of the past and the best music of the present . . . America is a country liberal in ideas, broad in thought, we should permit free expression in music and free right to hear such music."[47]

While critics covering performances of dodecaphonic works had heretofore rarely mentioned the twelve-tone concept, reviewers now spun out their own confusing definitions of dodecaphony grounded in Downes's imprecise and misleading description of the technique. In his program notes and review Downes claimed that the work was based on the "twelve-tone scale" and that "different notes of that scale are arranged in basic shapes or 'ground forms' of which a composition may have one or more. The ground shapes can be 'inverted'—turned upside down—or reversed horizontally." He added that the scale is subjected to "very geometrical, almost algebraical" devices and asked if this is "to be called music or musical mathematics."[48] Most critics built on Downes, invoked the "twelve-tone scale," condemned the work as "machine-made music," and deprecated its "labyrinthine structure," "mechanical abstraction," and "threat of mechanization."[49] Schoenberg was labeled a "mathematician," "arch-geometrician," and "musical engineer."[50]

Equally bold and ambitious was Stokowski's premiere of *Die glückliche Hand*, cosponsored by the League of Composers and presented both in Philadelphia and New York. Paired with the ballet version of Stravinsky's *Le Sacre du printemps*, the production was lavishly staged by Rouben Mamoulian and Robert Edmond Jones, and featured

Doris Humphrey and Charles Weidman among the dancers. Schoenberg's composition in its unique concept seemed to open up new horizons of American opera production. And Olin Downes even found Schoenberg's work more attractive than Stravinsky's: "undeniably atmospheric and original in its combination of music, color and other theatrical ingredients."[51] Yet typically there were also critical voices. The staging was queried because of the disregard of Schoenberg's detailed lighting instructions due to the lack of adequate technical production. And a few traditionalist critics dismissed the opera as "pessimistic," "decadent," and "acrid."[52] Yet even though Schoenberg was proving to be by and large a divisive figure, the critical reactions to this and other atonal works were less hostile than the responses to his twelve-tone music.

Gurrelieder, Schoenberg's largest and most popular tonal work, ironically had to wait almost twenty years for its first American performance. This was not the fault of Stokowski and other conductors, such as Artur Bodanzky, Reiner, and Stock. They all tried in vain to perform the work in the 1920s. Indeed, Stokowski had desired to conduct the work for a long time. Having heard two performances under Schoenberg in Vienna in 1920, he purchased the *Gurrelieder* score and unsuccessfully tried to meet the composer to discuss his intention. Stokowski even left Schoenberg a check for over $500 after learning about his financial problems from Schoenberg's publisher Universal Edition.[53] Yet Schoenberg kept holding the rights of *Gurrelieder*'s U.S. premiere.

Stokowski had been studying *Gurrelieder*'s score since 1920, "whenever [he] had leisure," and eventually he succeeded in mounting the work's first complete American performance, despite the economic constraints brought on by the Great Depression.[54] The performance involved the Philadelphia Orchestra augmented to 123 musicians; 400 singers from the Princeton, Fortnightly, and Mendelssohn Clubs; and six soloists, including Jeanette Vreeland, soprano, Rose Bampton, contralto, and Paul Althouse, tenor. The work impressed and pleasantly surprised the many conservative concertgoers and critics who greeted it with much applause and praise. Critics acclaimed *Gurrelieder*'s "glowing lyricism," "rapturous richness of musical material," "extraordinary instrumentation," and the "originality" of the work's vocal lines.[55] Negative voices were few and typically included that of Downes who considered *Gurrelieder* to be "music by the pound and the yard" and "cumbersome, swollen, disproportionate."[56]

In addition to four renditions at Philadelphia's Academy of Music and New York's Metropolitan Opera House, *Gurrelieder* also received exposure through radio and recording: one of the three Philadelphia performances was broadcast, and all three were recorded live without retakes. RCA Victor released this recording in 1932 on a set of fourteen twelve-inch discs, one of which offered spoken remarks by Stokowski and music examples played on the piano by Sylvan Levin. Special in many ways, it was not only the work's premiere recording and the first American recording of a Schoenberg composition, but also then the largest piece ever featured on records, and the release created great excitement in the music world. This recording remained that work's only recording for twenty-one years and became a collectors' item when it was removed from the catalog.[57] Schoenberg found it "in some respects very good, but in others a little poor." He conveyed in a letter to conductor Thor Johnson that "Stokowsky [*sic*] is generally a little too free with violent changes of tempi, and some of the tempi he takes do not agree with my music. The orchestra plays very fine, but almost all of the soloists are rather poor."[58]

Schoenberg was not happy about Stokowski's *Gurrelieder* performance for two reasons. Stokowski managed to program the work without his consent, even though he had reminded Stokowski in the fall of 1931 about his own rights and intention to conduct the work himself in the United States. He was also disappointed that Stokowski refrained from giving the first American performance of his tricky twelve-tone opera *Von heute auf morgen* (*From Today to Tomorrow*, 1929). Although Stokowski rejected any blame, he let his orchestra's business manager Arthur Judson obtain the rights for the premiere from Universal Edition's American representative, Associated Music Publishers. Universal Edition, however, finally admitted that it had ceded the rights to the Philadelphia Orchestra on the assumption that Schoenberg would have been unable to tour the United States in the foreseeable future. Schoenberg's disappointment about his lost opportunity lingered. One and a half years later he grumbled in a letter to Stokowski:

> Your performance of my *Gurrelieder* has been a wrong by Hertzka who had broken the contract which had assured me the first performance in America and the fees for it and also my rights of disks! And further you know that a composer of my rank has no advantage from a performance, for the paid sums are minimally and only for conducting is to get some honorar [*sic*]. Also in this case the reproducer is better treated than the producer.[59]

The last important premiere of one of Schoenberg's orchestral works in America before his arrival there was Slonimsky's performance of *Begleitmusik für eine Lichtspielszene* (*Accompaniment to a Film Scene*), op. 34 in Los Angeles in July 1933. Having successfully premiered this recently composed dodecaphonic work two months earlier in Cuba, Slonimsky included it on one of the Hollywood Bowl concert programs, where he was hired as conductor for the summer season. For the Los Angeles Philharmonic and the Hollywood Bowl audience, it was their first encounter with twelve-tone music (though not their first taste of atonality, Schoenberg's Five Pieces having received a hearing there in 1929), and Slonimsky met with harsh resistance. Having featured mainly modernist works by Ives, Varèse, and others on previous programs, he was fired after the Schoenberg performance. The *Los Angeles Times* abstained from reviewing the concert and instead published an article on the day of the concert, which questioned the conductor's ability and his programming of "ultra-modern" compositions.[60] In presenting Schoenberg's music for an imaginary film scene in the film capital, however, Slonimsky couldn't have imagined that Hollywood would become Schoenberg's new hometown within about a year and that he would soon be a sought-after teacher by numerous film composers.

MODERN-MUSIC SOCIETIES CHAMPION SCHOENBERG'S CHAMBER MUSIC

Interest in modern music in America grew substantially in the 1920s. This fact is reflected in the establishment of contemporary-music societies (perhaps indebted to Schoenberg's Society of Private Musical Performances, 1918–21), new-music journals such as *Modern Music* (1924–46) and *Pro-Musica Quarterly*, and the publishing venture *New Music Quarterly* (1927–58). Especially active in furthering Schoenberg's reception in the 1920s were the Pro-Musica Society (1920–32) organized by Schmitz, the International Composers' Guild (ICG, 1921–27) established by Varèse and Carlos Salzedo, the League of Composers initiated by music patroness Claire Reis among others, and the California-based New Music Society (1925–36) founded by composer Henry Cowell. Since these institutions displayed much openness toward new musical tendencies, but had generally small budgets at their disposal, they focused on the presentation of Schoenberg's most advanced chamber, piano, and vocal music.

Among the above-mentioned societies, Varèse and the ICG take credit for producing American premieres of four important atonal and twelve-tone chamber and vocal works by Schoenberg. The most important was the memorable introduction of *Pierrot lunaire* in February 1923 in New York. Although *Pierrot* could then no longer be considered a novelty, its American premiere took place only a year after its first French performance under Darius Milhaud and a year before its British and Italian debuts under Milhaud and Alfredo Casella, respectively. (For that matter, Stravinsky's *Rite of Spring* was still awaiting its American premiere in 1924.) Many friends of new music, but most of all Varèse, the event's main organizer, and Louis Gruenberg, the conductor, anticipated the *Pierrot* performance with excitement, as they both had witnessed rehearsals and concerts of *Pierrot* and a special private rendition of it at Busoni's home in Berlin in June 1913. Yet Varèse and Gruenberg struggled with several problems. When Varèse invited Schoenberg in August 1922 to become a board member of the ICG, Schoenberg refused on the grounds that German composers were underrepresented on the ICG programs. And when he learned about Varèse's scheduling of a *Pierrot* performance, he was offended that he had not been consulted about the enterprise. He worried that Varèse would underestimate the work's difficulty and not have apt performers and enough rehearsals.[61]

As Schoenberg had feared, the preparation of the premiere turned out to be difficult, and the performance scheduled for January 1923 had to be pushed forward to

FIGURE 2.3.
Rehearsal of *Pierrot lunaire* for the American premiere with Greta Torpadie, voice; Louis Gruenberg, conductor; Jacob Mestechkin, violin; Leroy Shield, piano; William Durieux, cello; George Possell, flute; and Robert Lindemann, clarinet. *MA*, 20 January 1923. Courtesy Musical America Archives.

February. Instead of the planned fifteen rehearsals, the ensemble needed twenty-two (Figure 2.3). Eva Gauthier, the "High Priestess of Modern Song," who had performed early songs by Schoenberg since 1920 and who was first engaged to perform the *Sprechstimme* part, cancelled. So did the singer Mimine Salzedo (Carlos's wife), who was eventually replaced by the Swedish-American soprano Greta Torpadie. However, the efforts paid off. Thanks to numerous press announcements and much publicity by ICG executive director Reis and Minna Lederman, the future editor of *Modern Music*, this performance was sold out and hundreds of concertgoers had to be turned way. The illustrious audience included the poet Amy Lowell; the musicians Gautier, Mengelberg, and Stokowski; and the composers Marion Bauer, Casella, Georges Enesco, George Gershwin, Milhaud, Carl Ruggles, and Lazare Saminsky.[62] Preceded by works of Charles Koechlin, Erik Satie, and Milhaud, and an insightful pre-concert lecture by German-American musicologist Carl Engel, the *Pierrot* performance was a great success. As was to be expected, it produced a big stir and split the audience and reviewers in two camps. Reactionary critics, including Richard Aldrich, Henry T. Finck, and Henry Krehbiel, dismissed the work as iconoclasm and "dreary musical tomfooleries."[63] In contrast, the younger and more open-minded generation of reviewers, such as Paul Rosenfeld, Pitts Sanborn, and Emilie Bauer, considered it "sensuous," "thrilling," and "one of the most typical and significant compositions of one of the most important living composers."[64]

In the following years, *Pierrot* was being presented in major American cities (New York, 1925; Chicago, 1925; Boston and New York, 1928; Philadelphia, 1929; San Francisco, 1930) (Figure 2.4). Because of the plea for a repeat performance, *Pierrot* actually led to a split of the ICG, whose mission was to give exclusively premieres. The disagreement ended with the founding of the League of Composers, which two years later presented the second American *Pierrot* performance under the baton of Howard Barlow and with Torpadie as vocalist.

Meanwhile the League competed with the ICG, organizing American premieres of Schoenberg's Second String Quartet (1908) in 1924, the Woodwind Quintet (1924) in 1926, and *Die glückliche Hand* (1913) in 1930. Until its disbanding in 1927, the ICG gave the U.S. premieres of *Herzgewächse* (1911) in 1923, *Das Buch der hängenden Gärten* (The Book of the Hanging Gardens, 1909) in 1924, and the Serenade in 1925. The New Music Society in Los Angeles and San Francisco produced, in addition to multiple renditions of Schoenberg's Piano Pieces, opp. 11 and 19, the American premiere of the Five Piano Pieces, op. 23 (1923) in 1926, the California premieres of the Woodwind Quintet in 1927, and as mentioned, *Pierrot* in 1930.

Of the novelties offered, *Das Buch* and *Herzgewächse* were overwhelmingly well received. *Herzgewächse*, featuring soprano Eva Leoni and conductor Salzedo, had to be repeated upon popular demand. Gilman described the work as an "iridescent web of delicate and poignant beauty" and commended Leoni's beautiful voice.[65] The three songs from *Das Buch* performed by Marya Freund, the Polish mezzo-soprano and celebrated vocalist of European *Pierrot* performances, were greeted with enthusiasm and called "delicately harmonized specimens."[66] Yet the premiere and two further performances of the Second String Quartet by the Lenox and Pro Arte Quartets with American vocalist Ruth Rodgers and English soprano Dorothy Moulton in 1924 and 1929 drew mixed reactions. Downes, who reviewed the American premiere, perceived "flashes of true beauty" and a "constructive scheme planned before and not after the composer put pen to paper,"

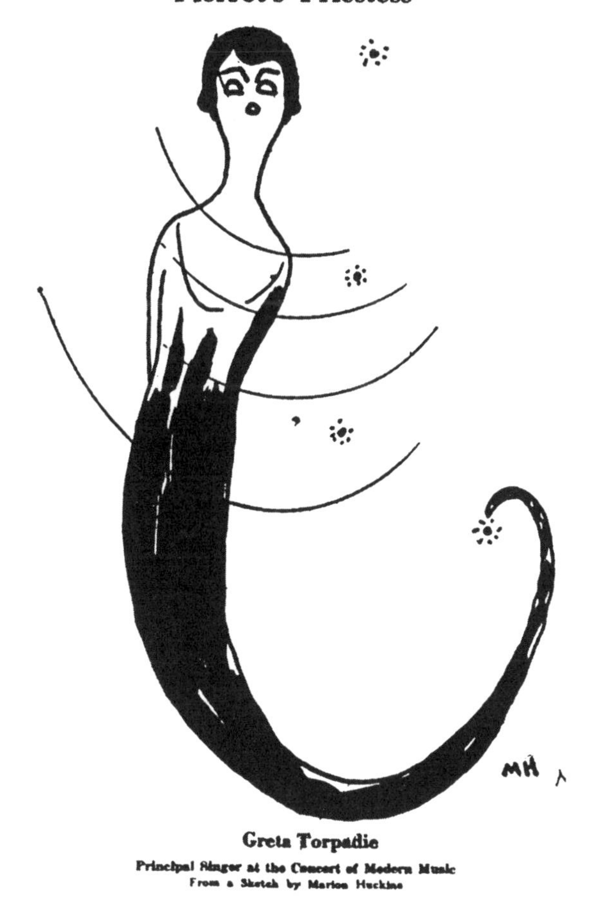

FIGURE 2.4.
Pierrot's Priestess: Caricature of Greta Torpadie as vocalist in a *Pierrot* performance under Richard Burgin in Boston in 1928. *Boston Evening Transcript*, 24 October 1928.

but considered the work in general "labored," "naïvely pretentious," and "self-tortured."[67] At this quartet's second hearing, at the Berkshire Chamber Music Festival in Pittsfield later that year, the audience and critics were split as well. But for many of them this performance seems to have been their first encounter with Schoenberg's music, as they spoke of "strange and unfamiliar worlds."[68] Moulton's unconvincing vocal performance apparently contributed to the tepid reception of the quartet as well.

Thanks to American contemporary-music societies, most of Schoenberg's European twelve-tone works were programmed in America even before his arrival in the United States. In 1925, only a year after its world premiere, the Serenade was presented in an ICG concert: the very first twelve-tone work heard in America. Members of the Philadelphia Orchestra under Stokowski performed the work. For lack of a guitarist, Salzedo played the guitar part on the piano. As with previous performances of Schoenberg's progressive works in America (and in Europe), the dodecaphonic Serenade was accepted by some who "understood it, and loved it, for they shouted for more." And it was rejected by others, who found it "excessively fussy, mannered and dry of genuine emotional quality."[69] Interestingly, none of the 1925 Serenade premiere reviewers mentioned the twelve-tone technique.

Following the ICG performance of the short and serene Serenade, the first American hearing of Schoenberg's lengthy and austere dodecaphonic Woodwind Quintet (1924), initiated by the League in 1926, marked a change in American Schoenberg reception. It sparked overwhelmingly antagonistic reactions. The League audience, generally sympathetic toward modern music, was either puzzled or opposed, "gasping for fresh air."[70] Rosenfeld commented that "no work by Schoenberg makes following more difficult."[71] With only rudimentary technical knowledge, generally open-minded critics and American composers rejected the quintet vigorously. Marion Bauer, for instance, criticized the quintet as "music of geometric design," "excessively dissonant," and found that the "registers and [instrument] combinations were most unhappily antagonistic."[72] Cowell, however, boldly included the Woodwind Quintet in a program of the New Music Society in San Francisco the following year, and thanks to his captivating pre-concert talk and educational program notes, the work received somewhat friendlier responses from the audience and press.

The American premiere of Schoenberg's dodecaphonic Third String Quartet, given by the Gordon Quartet at the Berkshire Festival of Chamber Music in Pittsfield, Massachusetts, in 1928, was another significant event. The work was commissioned by and dedicated to the American art patroness and initiator of the annual Berkshire Festivals in 1918, Elizabeth Sprague Coolidge, who had already programmed Schoenberg's Second Quartet there in 1924. This commission, along with Schoenberg's acquaintance with Coolidge (brought about by Hans Kindler, cellist of the *Pierrot* world premiere and conductor in America), proved most beneficial for his present and future career.[73] In Germany, where the quartet was formerly performed, critics were impressed by Coolidge's sponsorship of modern music: "There lives in America a quite extraordinary woman, a Maecenas of music—Mrs. Elizabeth Sprague Coolidge . . . And since in our own Germany we have no Maecenas like Mrs. Coolidge, no one who assists at the birth of new music, we have to thank this woman for the first interesting concert of our musical season in Berlin."[74] First presented by the Kolisch Quartet in Vienna, Prague, and Berlin, the work earned a number of favorable reviews. And these reactions, reprinted in the American press, apparently influenced American critics who reported on the work's performance in Pittsfield. European critics praised his quartet, though with some exaggeration, as an "unqualified triumph," and found it certainly more accessible than his Woodwind Quintet. They also acknowledged its craftsmanship, clarity, and economy, even claiming that "the spirit of the later Beethoven shines through it." Above all, they felt that atonality was used "in a more positive sense."[75] Similarly, American critics commended the "artistic integrity," lucidity, and beauty of the second and fourth movements, also evoking an affinity with Beethoven.[76] Some detractors, however, found Schoenberg's new musical language "still strange and forbidding" and dismissed the fusion of dodecaphony with devices of the past.[77]

Schoenberg's twelve-tone piano works, the Five Piano Pieces, op. 23 and Suite, op. 25 (both of 1923), received regular hearings within and outside American contemporary-music institutions starting in 1926. Pianists who specialized in this repertoire included Dene Denny, Celius Dougherty, Hortense Monath, and Oscar Ziegler. Denny, a Californian pianist and co-founder of the Carmel Music Center in 1926, may have given the American premiere of the Five Pieces in a concert of the New Music Society in Los Angeles in 1926. Ziegler, a Swiss musician, may have played the first American performance of the Suite at the New School for Social

Research in 1928. Yet there could have been earlier public performances of both pieces, which escaped the attention of the music press. At the same time pianists such as the Californians Richard Buhlig, Winifred Hooke, and Wesley Kuhnle (a Buhlig student), along with Jesús Sanromá, a renowned pianist from Puerto Rico, and others, eagerly promoted the Piano Pieces, opp. 11 and 19, even though the public and critical response to Schoenberg's piano oeuvre remained mixed. Schoenberg was not the sole representative of atonal and twelve-tone music on American concert programs in the late 1920s and early 1930s. Also performed on a regular basis were Adolph Weiss's twelve-tone Second String Quartet (1926), Piano Preludes (1927), Sonata da Camera (1929), and Piano Sonata (1932); Wallingford Riegger's dodecaphonic Three Canons for Woodwinds (1931) and *Dichotomy* (1932); and Ruth Crawford's proto-serial *Diaphonic Suite* (1931). Even Aaron Copland, whose fascination with jazz in the mid-1920s yielded to an interest in leaner and more abstract compositional approaches later in that decade, freely experimented, consciously or not, with ideas of serialism in such works as the "Poet's Song," a setting of an e. e. cummings poem composed in Germany in 1927, and, more important, his Piano Variations (1930).[78] "Poet's Song" was not performed until 1935, but the Piano Variations, premiered in 1931 by Copland himself, regularly figured on new-music programs. Such compositions often appeared on programs with other nonserial dissonant and abstract works by various progressive American composers, including Cowell, Charles Ives, and Ruggles.

SCHOENBERG EXPLAINED AND CONTEXTUALIZED

Aside from performances and concert reviews, from 1914 Schoenberg was much discussed in America in feature articles and, in the context of modernism, in national newspapers, professional journals, and books. As a representative of modernism, Schoenberg pointed to major cultural changes in American life, which in the 1910s and 1920s began to radically undermine the lifestyles, beliefs, and aesthetics marked by American Victorianism. Conservative Americans indebted to such Victorian perspectives as virtuousness and a belief in unshakable universal truths often struggled against the modernist fascination with uncertainty, irrationality, raw emotion, immorality, mechanization, complexity, and new art forms.[79] Consequently they rejected Schoenberg's works, which embodied some of these new phenomena, as a manifestation of cultural decay. Supporters of modernism, however, countered such viewpoints and often enthusiastically endorsed his music.

Among the many opponents of Schoenberg and modernism was Huneker who, however, expressed both aversion and admiration in the Schoenberg chapter of his 1915 book *Ivory Apes and Peacocks*. Conservative New York critic Henry T. Finck published in the widely read *Nation* the malevolent Schoenberg feature "The Musical Messiah—or Satan?" in which he called Schoenberg "the representative of German musical frightfulness."[80] Distinguished old-school composer Arthur Foote and pianist-composer Henry Holden Huss denounced Schoenberg's most recent music as "monstrous crimes against beauty" in articles entitled "Will the Music of Ultra-Modernists Survive?" and "The Anarchic Element in Some Ultra-Modern Futurist Music."[81] And the British composers and critics William Hadow, John Runciman, and Frederick Corder condemned modern music, including Schoenberg's, in their 1915 *Musical Quarterly* articles. Corder also made use of wartime and anti-German rhetoric, expressing his belief that he could now speak his mind about Schoenberg because "the public has plunged into a hysterical fit of hatred of everything

German." He stated: "To pretend that the clotted nonsense of Schönberg and Bartók *must* mean something merely because it is printed in Germany is an insult to humanity." He continued feverishly that "it almost reconciles one to the awful catastrophe of this European war to think that it will at least sweep away these cobwebs from people's brains."[82]

Such negative voices notwithstanding, numerous young American composers and musical thinkers, including Marion Bauer, Philip Clapp, Edward Burlingame Hill, Edward Kilenyi, Sr., A. Walter Kramer, Hiram Moderwell, Roger Sessions, and, as mentioned above, e. e. cummings and S. Foster Damon, concurrently defended Schoenberg's works.

The same year that Corder's denunciations appeared, Moderwell, the young music and drama critic, published an enthusiastic survey of Schoenberg's music in the widely circulated *New Republic*. He pleaded with the public to consider Schoenberg's latest works with open-mindedness, and garnered several responses, including one from Paul Rosenfeld, soon to become an important Schoenberg critic. The writer Carl Van Vechten urged: "Go hear the new music; listen to it and see if you can't enjoy it . . . Your ears will make progress in spite of you and I shouldn't wonder at all if five years more would make Schoenberg and Stravinsky and Ornstein a trifle old fashioned."[83] Kramer, a composer-critic for *Musical America*, wrote his own passionate essay "This Man Schönberg! A Word of Warning to the Unwise," in which he fervently praised him as "the man of the hour" and stressed the need for "Schoenberg champions."[84] Marion Bauer, who owed much of her knowledge about Schoenberg to Eugene Heffley, a prominent New York piano teacher, published interviews with a variety of musicians who expressed their views about Schoenberg's music.[85]

In his positive and detailed review of Schoenberg's *Harmonielehre* (1911), the young Hungarian-American composer Kilenyi praised Schoenberg's "clear and novel explanations" of old phenomena, such as parallel fifths, doubling of intervals, the diminished seventh chord, and the relationship of consonance and dissonance. He also commended Schoenberg's discussion of new types of chords and chord progressions.[86] Reprinted in extracts in the *Musical Observer*, Kilenyi's article provoked criticism from the conservative music pedagogues Percy Goetschius and Daniel Gregory Mason, who found Schoenberg's approach to tonality "very superficial compared with d'Indy's."[87] Undeterred, Kilenyi soon introduced his music-theory student George Gershwin to *Harmonielehre*.[88]

Before the U.S. entry into World War I, the former Schoenberg student Egon Wellesz published what was perhaps the most comprehensive article on Schoenberg to date in the newly founded *Musical Quarterly*. In this essay he provided information about Schoenberg's biography, teaching methods, compositions, and paintings, and advised listeners about how to approach Schoenberg's music.[89]

Throughout the 1920s and early 1930s Schoenberg was seriously and critically discussed in specialized journals, such as *Modern Music*, the *Musical Quarterly*, and *Pro-Musica Quarterly*, and in books on modern music and harmony; two monographs exclusively dedicated to his life and work also appeared in English. The authors of these writings can be divided into four groups: first, Schoenberg's European students and adherents, including Theodor W. Adorno, Alban Berg, Paul Pisk, Willi Reich, Josef Rufer, Paul Stefan, Erwin Stein, and Egon Wellesz, who devotedly conveyed information about their idol to Americans; second, important European composers, musicologists, and critics, such as Casella, Hugo Leichtentritt, Milhaud, Eaglefield-Hull, Edward Dent, Cecil Gray, Rollo Myers, Percy Scholes, and Boris de

Schloezer, who investigated Schoenberg questions; third, eminent American writers on music, including Carl Engel, Frederick Martens, Otto Ortmann, Rosenfeld, Charles Seeger, and Joseph Yasser, who explained Schoenberg's music and ideas to the public; fourth, numerous American composers, such as Bauer, Cowell, Gruenberg, Dane Rudhyar, Lazare Saminsky, and Adolph Weiss, who came to terms with his work. Last but not least, Schoenberg himself emerged with three contributions in the *Etude* ("Aphorisms" and a response to a survey about the future of music, 1923) and the *Christian Science Monitor* ("Tonality and Form," 1925).

The most comprehensive coverage of Schoenberg's career was offered in Martens's monograph *Schönberg* (1922) and Wellesz's 1925 biography *Arnold Schönberg* (originally published in a shorter version in German in 1921).[90] Martens, who had authored a book on Ornstein in 1918, largely built his short volume on the writings of Wellesz and Eaglefield-Hull and on *Harmonielehre*. Rather than focusing on psychological interpretations of Schoenberg's life and art, Martens concentrated on his works up to the unfinished oratorio *Jakobsleiter* (1917–22) which he divided into three periods and described in a nontechnical language. He also commented on the riotous audience reactions and on Schoenberg's growing influence on other composers, avoiding an overly apologetic or polemic tone. He borrowed this approach from Wellesz, whose 1921 monograph was the earliest Schoenberg biography. Written under Schoenberg's supervision, Wellesz's volume was the more comprehensive, offering, besides chapters on his life and teaching, a large section with detailed commentaries on his works, featuring numerous music examples. In the 1925 edition, embracing some 150 pages, Eaglefield-Hull added some information on several early twelve-tone works and a rather spurious explanation of dodecaphony. Both the German and English editions of Wellesz's biography resonated strongly in the American music press, generating book reviews, book chapters, and biographical articles, some of which were also tributes to Schoenberg's fiftieth birthday in 1924.[91]

Among the few worthwhile early essays dedicated to specific Schoenberg works are Engel's essay "Schönberg lunaire," based on his lecture for *Pierrot*'s American premiere, Leichtentritt's analysis of the Six Little Piano Pieces, and Stefan's two surveys of Schoenberg's operas.[92]

Schoenberg was also elevated to a prime position among modernists by composer-writers on music. Among the many new musical tendencies, the influential French-American composer Rudhyar distinguished three major directions represented by Scriabin, Schoenberg and Stravinsky. He asserted that "it is no longer the famous three B's, but the three S's in European music." While he characterized Schoenberg as a revolutionary, who first engaged in "pure self-expression" and later in "neo-scholasticism," he typified Stravinsky as a "neo-primitivist," who musically combined "cerebrality" and "animality." Scriabin he called a "transformer of Europeanism" who "regenerated romanticism, transfiguring its emotional vagaries into mystic ecstasies." Of the "three S's," he considered Stravinsky to be the most successful, yet least individualistic modernist.[93] American music pedagogue Ortmann divided modernists into two schools. The first was the so-called "sensorial school," oriented toward simplicity and primitivism, which included composers using tone clusters (Cowell), noise (Francesco Pratella), and electro-acoustic sounds (Leon Theremin); the other was the "intellectual school," which strove for complexity and embraced Schoenberg. Milhaud and Casella, who both explored polytonal techniques, compared their approach with Schoenberg's atonality. While Milhaud declared both techniques as equally valid tonal expansions and showed intersections between them, Casella found atonality, "the most venturesome of post-Debussyan problems," disquieting. He was disturbed that "all ties with the idea of tonality" were cut.[94]

American composers compared their own creative activities with Schoenberg's, yet their relationship to influential European modernists was not a simple one. Many had developed their own concepts of modernity and dissonant counterpoint, and repudiated the notion of being imitators of European modernists. They attempted in different ways to stake out their positions within the international modern-music scene. Cowell, who had been a friend of Schoenberg since his 1932 Berlin visit, performed and published Schoenberg's music and defended him as the "greatest living composer."[95] Explaining the foundation of dissonant writing with his overtone-series theory, Cowell illustrated how European and American composers, such as Schoenberg, Bartók, Hába, Ruggles, Varèse, and himself, approached dissonance in their works in different ways.[96] He often stressed that some of his compatriots were on a par with the Europeans: "The American composer, Charles Ives, used the materials back in 1901 and 1902 which are supposed to have originated with Schönberg and Stravinsky. I don't mean to infer that Ives influenced them. Stravinsky and Schönberg merely had the same idea years later."[97] And Polish-American theorist Yasser, speculating that future music would be based on an equal-tempered nineteen-tone "supra-diatonic" scale, argued that Schoenberg's atonal melodies were merely a preparatory step toward his own nineteen-tone concept.[98]

Schoenberg also figured prominently in American discussions of dissonant counterpoint. Rudhyar, whose compositions show a kinship with Scriabin, compared Schoenberg's atonal counterpoint to "musical bread-lines" established by Schoenberg in *Pierrot* to control "tonal anarchy." Rudhyar believed that in 1923 Schoenberg's approach to counterpoint was already bearing fruit in France and America, yet he pitched Ruggles's "spiritual and pure" polyphony against Schoenberg's "dry and intellectual" polyphony.[99] Similarly, Cowell weighed Schoenberg against Ruggles, whose exploration of dissonant counterpoint and controlled pitch repetition revealed an affinity with Schoenberg's techniques. Cowell opined that "Ruggles has at least one advantage over Schönberg—that of a long melodic line, giving him a greater flow. And in his choice of the 'right note' he reaches a perfection of technic suggested by Schönberg, but I think, never attained by him."[100] Seeger, who avidly embraced new musical tendencies and theories, was even more critical. He categorized Schoenberg's atonal contrapuntal techniques as unsystematic forms of "dissonant counterpoint," in which the occasional inclusion of consonances seemed wrong.[101]

Twelve-tone music was mentioned in the American press as early as 1924, in connection not with Schoenberg, but with his Austrian rival Josef Matthias Hauer.[102] Foreign correspondents wrote about Hauer's "keyless" "twelve-tone music" on the occasion of the world premiere of his First String Quartet, op. 30 (1924) at the Donaueschingen Music Festival, at which Schoenberg's twelve-tone Serenade, op. 24 (1923) also received its first performance. Though not labeled "twelve-tone" yet, the Serenade, in contrast to Hauer's work, got many sympathetic reviews. Critics remarked positively on Schoenberg's use of classical forms, eccentric yet somewhat "tuney" melodies, "rhythmic springiness," and "scarcely perceptible bits of jazz."[103] Similarly, none of the reviewers of the Serenade's American premiere in 1925 mentioned the work's twelve-tone technique. Later that year, however, César Saerchinger pointed out that the Serenade is "twelve-tone music," and awkwardly explained this phenomenon. He described it as "the absolute emancipation from diatonalism by the substitution of a new, as it were, chromatic key, and the vertical-horizontal exploitation of tone groupings and combinations in diabolically ingenious ways."[104]

Explanations of the twelve-tone technique used in Schoenberg's Woodwind Quintet added to the confusion. Gruenberg heard this work in a 1926 performance under Webern's baton in Zurich and suggested in a report that because "Schoenberg composes now-a-days by a chart, according to reports from those near to him, . . . the greatest service they can possibly do to the fast-dwindling fame of this extraordinarily stubborn but great musician is to burn the chart."[105] Marion Bauer spoke of the dodecaphonic quintet as "music of geometric design," and W. H. Haddon Squire opined that it was "constructed on a series of 'note-circles.'"[106] Leichtentritt maintained that in twelve-tone music, the "twelve-tone scale furnishes the harmonic basis of the composition" and that the main feature of this "scale" "lies in the fact that the semi-tones are reached not by alterations of the existing chord combinations; they are independent entities by themselves, as it were, and lead a life by themselves irrespective of their neighbor fellows." Twelve-tone music, according to him, "contains no melody which does not embody in itself—or in its accompaniment—all the twelve tones of this scale."[107]

Members of the Schoenberg circle increasingly contributed to a better understanding of this compositional technique. Schoenberg student Pisk, a composer-musicologist who would later settle in America, was one of the first to convey the difference between Hauer's and Schoenberg's approaches. In his 1926 essay in *Modern Music*, he distinguished between Hauer's limited concept of the twelve-tone trope, a specific sequence of twelve tones repeated throughout a piece, frequently involving tonal elements, and Schoenberg's more sophisticated technique. He explained Schoenberg's use of an ordered pitch sequence as the main structural element, from which one or more motives can be obtained. Pisk further pointed out that Schoenberg derived from that basic pitch sequence three other row forms (inversion, "crab," and inversion of the "crab") and that all row variants can be transposed to other pitch levels and used simultaneously and interchangeably.[108] Stein, another Schoenberg student and prolific writer on his teacher's music, published three articles on this subject between 1928 and 1930: "Schönberg's Third String Quartet," "Twelve-Tone Music," and most important, "Schoenberg's New Structural Form" (published in *Modern Music* in 1930).[109] Stein limited himself to discussing the Third Quartet's salient formal and morphological features in his first essay, and revealed important serial principles along with the quartet's twelve-tone row in his second article, but he delved into the quartet's structural details and dodecaphony in general in the third text, going far beyond Pisk's explanations. Significantly, he defined the twelve-tone series as a "tone complex" that "determines the melodic and harmonic structure of a composition," but which "is by no means identical with the idea of 'theme.'"[110] Analyzing the third quartet, he presented the principal set and its transformations, explained the concept of octave displacement, and demonstrated linear presentations of row forms as well as the segmentation and partitioning of sets into several voices, all illustrated by music examples.

Later articles by Schoenberg students—Reich's "Schönberg's New Männerchor" and Weiss's "The Lyceum of Schönberg," both published in *Modern Music* in 1932—built on Stein's discussion but did not add substantially new information. Whether Pisk, Stein, Reich, or Weiss had Schoenberg's approval to reveal dodecaphony's technical details in print is unclear. In a letter to his brother-in-law and leader of the Kolisch Quartet, Rudolf Kolisch, Schoenberg famously disapproved of Kolisch's analysis of the Third String Quartet and warned that such a procedure will only reveal how the work is "done," but not what it "is."[111] Yet these revelations of Schoenberg's students were much appreciated by professional musicians in America.

Schoenberg's disciples attempted to position him in the American press as the leader of modern Austro-German music—at a time when he was ever more frequently attacked by European anti-Semitic critics. In his essay "Schoenberg and the German Line," Stein explained that his teacher's works were rooted in Wagner's and Brahms's music, that his feeling for structure was "well-disciplined," that "order dominates his work," and that therefore the "German tradition still lives in him."[112] He also showed how the "German line" continued with Schoenberg's disciples Berg and Webern. Similarly, Leichtentritt declared Schoenberg to be "one of the most powerful forces as regards the influence exerted by him on the efforts of the youngest generation" in Germany.[113]

Rosenfeld, a renowned writer and champion of musical modernism, was among the American critics who shared this view with Schoenberg's European advocates: "It is in Arnold Schoenberg that we feel the one great force in German music capable of dominating the situation as Strauss once dominated it . . . he is the composer of the one German music that shows the art has retained something of its old power—the power it once had of indefinitely renewing itself."[114] But Rosenfeld and Saminsky, themselves of Jewish origin, also interpreted Schoenberg's works from a Jewish viewpoint. In one of his earliest reviews Rosenfeld critically observed that Schoenberg's piano pieces "smell of the synagogue as much as they do of the laboratory. Beside the Doctor of Music there stands the Talmudic Jew, the man all intellect and no feeling, who subtilizes over musical art as though it were the Law." Yet soon thereafter he wrote much more positively about Schoenberg's music, stating that "the modern orientation has been particularly inviting to the Jewish temperament."[115] Saminsky, a Russian-American composer who used Hebrew elements in his music, characterized Schoenberg "with all his extremism as a typical representative of the western, that is continental European Jewry, hysterical neurotic, assimilating and accentuating ideas and feelings adapted from its neighbors."[116] American critics generally abstained from anti-Semitic diatribes against Schoenberg.

SCHOENBERG'S EARLY IMPRESSIONS OF AMERICA

Before Schoenberg set foot on American soil, he obtained a sense of this country through various media, including writings, silent film, and popular music, and through accounts from acquaintances who had traveled or were born there. In the early 1910s he met, among others, the American-born pianist Richard Buhlig, American composer-pianist Louis Gruenberg (both Busoni protégés), and the New York–based Flonzaley Quartet, one of the most significant early quartets in America. Notwithstanding the daunting portrayals of Schoenberg in the American press, these artists sought out his company, surely informing him about America, as they became important international promoters of his music. Buhlig, who premiered the Three Piano Pieces in Great Britain in January 1912, was recognized as being one of the first Americans to perform Schoenberg.[117] Soon thereafter Gruenberg participated in a partial performance in Berlin of the Five Orchestral Pieces, op. 16, arranged for two pianos and eight hands.[118] The Flonzaleys performed Schoenberg's First String Quartet in Berlin in 1913 in his presence and gave its Leipzig and American premieres in 1913 and 1914. Buhlig and Gruenberg became lifelong friends of Schoenberg.

Soon after these encounters Schoenberg made plans to travel to the United States even though it was wartime. He hoped for a speedy victory for Germany and Austria-Hungary, with America on the side of the Central Powers, and encouraged his friends, including Alma Mahler, to send "official reports about German victories" and "accounts of the outbreak of the war, Russia's deception, England's cheating, etc." to all their American acquaintances in order to influence American public opinion.[119] After his brief stint in the Austrian army, Schoenberg was apparently little concerned about America's growing animosity toward the Central Powers since the sinking of the *Lusitania* by a German submarine in 1915. Envisioning a three-month visit to conduct five performances of *Gurrelieder,* he began negotiations with his publisher and its American representative Breitkopf & Härtel in the fall of 1916. Schoenberg, who struggled financially, demanded a sum of $1,000 (about $19,500 in 2009) for each performance to be sent to him in advance, plus money for travel and lodging expenses for him and his family.[120] Yet just as Breitkopf could promise him ten performances at $500 each, the U.S. declaration of war on the Central Powers thwarted his grand plans. American music critics had "declared a war zone around Arnold Schönberg's compositions" for quite some time.[121]

Three years after the war Schoenberg began to make plans for yet another trip to the United States.[122] Determined to attain fame and fortune with the introduction of two of his most popular works, *Pierrot* and *Gurrelieder,* he took into service the New York–based concert manager Lucy Bogue to arrange concert engagements in North America for him.[123] Yet again nothing came of this plan. As mentioned above, *Pierrot* received its American premiere in 1923 without Schoenberg's active involvement. In 1924 he suggested presenting *Gurrelieder* in New York, Chicago, Cincinnati, and Detroit during the season of 1925–26, and asked his publisher to negotiate a compensation of up to $10,000 (about $124,400 in 2009) from the conductors Bodanzky, Stokowski, Stock, and Gabrilowitsch in case the enterprise did not materialize. But this plan failed too. In 1928, as more and more conductors voiced interest in premiering *Gurrelieder* in the United States, he insisted: "If America wants the *Gurrelieder,* she must accept me."[124] He believed that he could achieve his biggest success in America with a composition for large forces, as he emphasized: "Without America we Europeans would be ready to write only for small or chamber orchestra. But in nations with a younger culture, coarse nerves ask for monumentality: whatever might not compel the listener to feel something has to be at least big, then one has something to look at."[125] With Stokowski mounting the American premiere of *Gurrelieder* in 1932, as mentioned above, that dream was destroyed as well.

Thereafter Schoenberg made two more futile attempts to visit America. In 1932 he applied for a position as guest conductor of the New York Philharmonic, but the orchestra's conductor Toscanini unsurprisingly preferred Respighi and Beecham, who had been interested in this post as well.[126] In the same year Schoenberg asked the New York physician Joseph Asch to organize for him a yearly stipend of $2,000–$4,000 (about $31,120–62,240 in 2009) so that he would not have to remain in Berlin, a city he felt was populated with too many Hitlerites (*Hakenkreuzler*) and pogromists.[127]

Even though Schoenberg failed to visit the United States in the 1920s and early 1930s, he closely followed American culture and its growing influence on European societies. He was critical of capitalism, consumerism, and short-lived fashions, yet seemed to enjoy jazz, especially as a form of popular music.[128] He frequented bars and cafés featuring live jazz and modern American dance music, and was once seen listening "with rapture to a set of American jazz records" at a meeting with Hindemith.

On this occasion he reportedly remarked: "Jazz is amusing. I like it in some moods, and I think it has its place."[129]

Although he naively suggested that he had pioneered the instrumentation of jazz orchestras in one of his *Brettl-Lieder* (Cabaret Songs, 1901) and subtly alluded to jazz in his Serenade, op. 24, Suite, op. 29, and comic opera *Von heute auf morgen*, he did not favor the overt mixing of jazz and "serious" music and felt that jazz had not influenced his own work, "except perhaps in a very minor degree."[130] He warned that through the use of jazz, a "mechanical cliché is imposed upon art" which could blur the lines between "music of value and inferior kitsch."[131] This position clearly allowed Schoenberg to distance himself from such jazz-inspired neo-classical composers as Hindemith, Milhaud, and Weill. A generous inclusion of jazz and folk elements seemed incompatible with his purist idea of "German music":

> As long as there is German music and one rightly understands what that has meant up to now, jazz will never have a greater influence on it than did Gypsy music in its time. The occasional use of several themes and the addition of foreign color to several phrases have never changed the essential: the body of ideas and the technique of its presentation. Such impulses can be compared to a disguise. Whoever dresses up as an Arab or a Tyrolean intends to appear this way only externally and temporarily, and as soon as the fun of the masquerade is over, he wants once again to be the person he was before.[132]

Schoenberg's critical view of jazz-influenced art music sheds light on his self-assessment as the most important representative of "German" music of his time and on his belief in a still unbroken superiority of German music, which he held throughout the 1920s and early 1930s.[133] As he remarked in 1931: "Remarkably, nobody has yet appreciated that my music, produced on German soil, without foreign influences, is a living example of an art able most effectively to oppose Latin and Slav hopes of hegemony and derived through and through from the traditions of German music."[134] Keenly aware of the ever-increasing anti-Semitism, he sensed the reason for the futility of his ambitious artistic goals and noted in frustration:

> If one had a hint of common sense in Germany, one would understand that the fight against me means more or less the intention to break down its hegemony in music. Because through me alone and through what I produced on my own, which has not been surpassed by any nation, the hegemony of German music is secured for at least this generation. But I am a Jew! Of course, what else should I be, since I want to give something, which one is unable to accept?[135]

TWO AMERICAN SCHOENBERG STUDENTS IN BERLIN: ADOLPH WEISS AND MARC BLITZSTEIN

Despite the failure of his travel plans and his critical views of American culture, Schoenberg enjoyed direct contact with a growing number of young Americans who sought him out as a teacher, despite the popularity of the Paris-based composition teacher and Stravinsky promoter Nadia Boulanger. American Schoenberg students of the 1920s included Mark Wessel, a composer and teacher from Michigan (1922); Arthur Starbird (c. 1923); Lema Davis from Rockford, Illinois (c. 1923–24); Milton Rush, a composer and teacher from Milwaukee (1926); and the better known composers Adolph Weiss and Marc Blitzstein, who had strongly opposing reactions to their teacher.

Encouraged by Varèse, Weiss, an established thirty-four-year-old bassoonist with more than ten years of compositional experience, began his studies with Schoenberg in Mödling near Vienna in 1925. When Schoenberg moved to Berlin a few months later to succeed Busoni as a professor of composition at the Prussian Academy of Arts, Weiss followed him. Yet in order to be admitted to Schoenberg's master class, he first needed to take classes in strict counterpoint with Schoenberg's assistant Josef Rufer. At first Weiss also struggled with Schoenberg's focus on motivic development and variation in his musical analyses of classical works and student compositions. He soon seemed to thrive, sending an enthusiastic report to the *Musical Courier*: "Schönberg's insight into the formal construction of musical compositions stamps him as a genius. In harmony and counterpoint he is painfully exacting to the most complicated polyphonic structures. Indeed in Europe he is accepted as one of the greatest authorities on all musical forms, contrapuntal, harmonic, ancient and modern."[136]

Weiss particularly enjoyed the interaction with Schoenberg's other students from all over Europe: "We all had our own ideal about music. Schoenberg encouraged us to review and even severely criticize one another's works. He would be the final arbiter."[137] Weiss also learned about the twelve-tone technique. Schoenberg had developed this groundbreaking compositional approach after World War I and officially announced it to Rufer in 1921 and to a wider student circle in 1923. Weiss even gained knowledge of the twelve-tone matrix, or magic square, a device of ordering the four forms of a twelve-tone set and their transpositions. Under Schoenberg's supervision, Weiss completed two twelve-tone works, his First and Second String Quartets dating from 1925 and 1926, and a non-dodecaphonic Chamber Symphony for ten instruments (1926) based on the intervals of the augmented fourth and minor seventh. Privately Weiss was also on good terms with Schoenberg, and took pleasure in playing tennis and chess with him.[138] Schoenberg loved to hear from Weiss about life in America.

When Weiss returned to the United States in 1927, he was arguably the first in the nation to teach and disseminate twelve-tone technique, and his dodecaphonic works soon received American premieres and appeared in print. Buhlig gave the first performance of his serial Twelve Preludes for piano (1927) in San Francisco in 1928, and a year later Cowell published six of them, together with analytical explanations of the various uses of dodecaphony, in the *New Music Quarterly*—the first American publication of a twelve-tone composition. On Weiss's initiative, Cowell soon published two further serial works: Webern's *Volkstext*, op. 17, no. 2 (1930) and Schoenberg's Piano Piece, op. 33b (1932). Webern's and Schoenberg's editions, however, did not include any commentary. Schoenberg had requested that Cowell "not publish either biographical notes or musical explanations concerning his work, since both he and his musical viewpoint are well known."[139] The publication of Weiss's Piano Preludes with brief analyses of serial procedures prompted and prepared American composers to experiment with those new techniques. One notable example is Wallingford Riegger, who began to use dodecaphony, though very freely, in Three Canons for Woodwinds (1931) and *Dichotomy* (1932), one of his first significant dodecaphonic orchestral works.

An effective intermediary between American and European composers in the 1920s and 1930s, Weiss brought Cowell and Schoenberg together. During his 1932 Berlin sojourn, Cowell occasionally sat in on Schoenberg's master classes and became his tennis partner. Weiss translated and authored several articles about Schoenberg, including "The Lyceum of Schoenberg," a detailed account of his musical principles and techniques, published in *Modern Music* in 1932.[140] Weiss's reputation in the United States was undoubtedly stamped by his affiliation with Schoenberg. Rosenfeld, for instance, stressed that his music is "fuller of crabs than Chesapeake Bay."[141] Yet only about a third of his works are atonal or serial, and most of Weiss's "twelve-tone" compositions are not strictly serial. He often changed the pitch order of a set, repeated notes, interpolated additional pitches, and used diagonal pitch orders within a twelve-tone matrix. One of his best known works is *American Life* (1928), a scherzo "jazzoso" for orchestra. Built on an augmented fourth, it toys with elements of jazz, and features muted trumpets, saxophones, brushed snare drum, and syncopated rhythms. This is perhaps why Schoenberg questioned "his own right to claim this talented American as a disciple, granting him independence of method not frequently found or easily tolerated in his group."[142]

Unlike Weiss, Blitzstein studied with Schoenberg for only a short period of time (Figure 2.5). A composer who gained significance for his socially conscious theatrical works and later translation of Brecht's libretto for Weill's *Three-Penny Opera*, he had then just completed studies with Schoenberg's rival Boulanger. Failing to get along with his new teacher, he attended Schoenberg's courses at the Academy of the Arts in Berlin only for the spring semester of 1927. At age twenty-two the rebellious Blitzstein had already encountered difficulties with Boulanger; he also disliked Schoenberg's teaching methods and aesthetic, and in the American music press he made no secret of his negative impressions: "Now I am hard at work with Schoenberg. I think I

FIGURE 2.5.
Marc Blitzstein in Salzburg (1929). Courtesy Stephen Davis and Wisconsin Center for Film and Theatre Research.

disagree with him entirely. His is a totally scientific aesthetic; his principles are based upon a masterly knowledge of the machinery of Beethoven and Brahms; but he does not hear, he does not know the quality or projectivity of sound."[143] The chemistry between Schoenberg and Blitzstein seemed bad. Even though Schoenberg must have thought highly of Blitzstein's musical abilities. Blitzstein surely would have played for him some of his recently completed Walt Whitman settings (1925–27), which Schoenberg probably later remembered as "excellent compositions."[144] Schoenberg also appreciated his pianistic talent, as he depended on students to perform music examples in his classes. Thus Blitzstein, unlike Weiss, was admitted to Schoenberg's master class promptly and without any difficulties. However, Schoenberg must have resented Blitzstein's having received instruction from Boulanger, as he teased him with remarks like, "Go ahead, you write your Franco-Russian *Hübschmusik* [pretty music]," and "It is only since the war that you American composers have been cut off from your source of supply, which is Germany, and have been writing Franco-Russian music. Ten years from now you will all be writing German music again."[145]

Blitzstein's impressions of Schoenberg were equally mixed. He admired Schoenberg's intellectual facility, but did not think that the fervent study of strict counterpoint and meticulous musical analyses of classical works could advance him as a composer. Blitzstein esteemed Schoenberg's insistence on perfection and genius in his composition lessons, and declared that the "world will be cluttered up with less bad music."[146] Yet he found this method, in which Schoenberg "approaches every work of his pupils with scissors" to achieve a "perfect piece of design," stifling.[147] In Berlin Blitzstein indeed composed little music. He completed a setting of Whitman's poem "As Adam early in the morning" and made sketches for his short, one-movement Piano Sonata. Furthermore, Blitzstein saw a contradiction between Schoenberg the teacher, whom he viewed as a "die-hard traditionalist," and Schoenberg the composer, whom he called an "extreme radical." He also perceived a conflict in Schoenberg's music: "This distinct non-classicist externally has been using the very forms of classicism: we find fugues, passacaglias, all manner of canons, crab canons, cancrizons and the like in his work."[148] While he had a high regard for Schoenberg's early atonal works, such as the Second String Quartet and *Pierrot*, he dismissed his dodecaphonic techniques with its "*Zwölftonreihe*, with its *Zauberquadrat*, with its charts, its vigilance over the single note, its new *Verboten*!"[149]

When Blitzstein returned to the United States, he paid tribute to Schoenberg in his own way, always expressing both admiration and criticism. He discussed his music in his essays, reviews for *Modern Music*, lectures, and lecture-recitals on musical modernism, and he participated as a pianist in the Philadelphia *Pierrot* premiere in 1929. Involved with left-wing issues, Blitzstein attempted to reach the masses in the mid-1930s through politically tinged theatrical works that were musically accessible. He wrote the radio-song play *I've Got the Tune* (1937) and parodied the idea of art for art's sake, *Pierrot*, and art patronage. His art patroness Madame Arbutus recites in *Sprechstimme*: "The moon is a happy cheese tonight, I swoon! . . . It is so grand to be so bored! You can afford the kind of music you can not stand." Many of his music theater works, including *The Cradle Will Rock* (1936), feature vocal styles alluding to *Sprechstimme*. Surprisingly, Blitzstein also made use of serial techniques in such works as the unfinished *Discourse* for clarinet, cello, and piano (1930) and *Idiots First* (1963), a one-act opera based on a short story by Bernard Malamud. In the latter work, written shortly before his death, Blitzstein depicts Ginzberg, the angel of death, with two twelve-tone rows while portraying the other characters with modal and folk-like music.[150]

TOWARD SCHOENBERG'S ARRIVAL IN AMERICA IN 1933

Although Schoenberg never had the chance to visit the United States before 1933, he had managed to build a network of strong supporters there. By the time he emigrated to the United States, Americans had heard hundreds of performances of his music, including nearly all of his works composed up to that time. Predictably, the renditions of his tonal works outnumbered the performances of his dissonant works. Schoenberg's tonal compositions were received without much fuss, but his dissonant music, which often caused a stir, seemed to have a stronger impact on the American music scene. As conservative critics dismissed Schoenberg's progressive works, their often younger and more broad-minded colleagues generally acknowledged them. Significant writers from Europe, among them several Schoenberg disciples, influenced American reception of Schoenberg with several monographs and important articles in major American periodicals. But Schoenberg's musical ideas were discussed by American writers as well. Schoenberg had become, for all the controversy, a household name in the American classical-music world.

As American music journalists followed the rapid and massive cultural changes in Hitler's Germany, they expressed concern about the escalating chauvinism and anti-Semitism affecting Jewish artists such as Schoenberg. In April 1933 Leonard Liebling, critic and editor of the *Musical Courier*, pondered the fate of music in Germany and that of Jewish musicians:

> It would be a huge joke on Germany if the new order of things were to result in choking off all elevated musical effort and no first-class musicians were to materialize after the present non-Jewish crop passes on. Meanwhile the present Jewish ones might emigrate to some neighboring country and build up a musical life that would dwarf that of Germany. Switzerland, Denmark, Holland, Sweden, Norway, Belgium could use a few Blechs, Klemperers, Walters, Weills, Schönbergs, and other music makers of their brand of temperament and talent.[151]

FIGURE 2.6.
Gertrud, Nuria, and Arnold Schoenberg arriving in New York City. *MA*, 10 November 1933. Courtesy Musical America Archives.

Liebling could not anticipate that Klemperer, Walter, Weill, and Schoenberg would all soon enrich the musical life of the United States. In late May 1933, only a week after Schoenberg's official ousting from his prestigious position in Berlin, the *New York Times* reported: "Professor Arnold Schoenberg, Austro German composer, has received an indefinite leave of absence as director of the master composition class of the Prussian Academy of Arts."[152] Joseph Malkin, a Russian-American cellist who had met Schoenberg thirty years earlier in Berlin and who had just founded a small conservatory of music in Boston, must have taken note of this announcement. Two weeks later, in mid-June, he approached Schoenberg, now temporarily residing in Paris, about joining his institution's faculty. Schoenberg soon accepted Malkin's job offer, although it was not on a par with his former position.

Schoenberg finally reached America via the luxury liner S.S. *Ile de France* in October 1933. He was never to return to Europe (Figure 2.6). He was received with considerable publicity and greeted with several welcoming recitals and receptions at such institutions as the Library of Congress, Yale, and Harvard. in November the League of Composers organized an "All Schoenberg" concert and a reception in New York, which was attended by over fifty composers and musicians, including Marion Bauer, John Becker, Ernest Bloch, Copland, Gershwin, Percy Grainger, Riegger, Sessions, and Varèse. But the United States was struggling with the Great Depression and had to cope with its own innumerable unemployed musicians, plus an increasing number of asylum-seeking musicians from Nazi-plagued Europe. At the same time American composers were striving more than ever for the performance and appreciation of their own, still neglected music. When Varèse attended the League's Schoenberg reception, he laconically remarked on Schoenberg's career prospects to his composer colleague Becker: Schoenberg had arrived "fifteen years too late."[153]

Yet at almost sixty years of age, Schoenberg quickly adapted to American culture, while at the same time coming to terms with his Jewish and Austrian-German identities. And unlike Varèse's compositional voice, his own never fell silent.

3 Negotiating Three Identities: Schoenberg's Socialization and Creative Work in America

After arriving in the United States in the fall of 1933, Schoenberg lived in Boston, New York City, and Chautauqua. He relocated to Los Angeles the following year and resided there until his death in 1951. Schoenberg pursued a busy professional schedule as a composer, writer, conductor, composition teacher, and guest lecturer. At the same time, even as he helped support his relatives and friends in Nazi Europe and tended to his young family, he built a new circle of international friends in America with whom he enjoyed many leisure-time activities. Yet some scholars have persistently and one-sidedly depicted him as a lonely "finished product from the old world," disinclined to adjust to his new environment, while others have painted him as an opportunist eager to compromise his European ideals in America.[1] Such biased, simplistic views ignore Schoenberg's complex struggles with multiple identities, which are manifest in all of his pursuits in America. Schoenberg ultimately found ways to come to terms with his Austrian-German, Jewish, and American identities in their social, intellectual, and cultural contexts. Such concepts as identity, acculturation, assimilation, dissimilation, and exile are key to understanding Schoenberg's life and work in America.

IDENTITY AND ACCULTURATION

Identity, whether personal, sociocultural, national, or religious, is a complex and multidimensional concept depending on a variety of contexts. Evolving over time, it may be understood as a multifaceted historical process.[2] Although the national and racial identifications of people are a common practice, one must bear in mind that such identities are constructions. Therefore, it would be misleading to view Schoenberg's identities—or those of anybody else—as clear-cut and fixed states.

Schoenberg grappled with two identities from his earliest years. Born in 1874 into a Jewish family in Vienna, he was given the German name Arnold Franz Walter Schönberg; at his circumcision seven days after his birth, he received the Hebrew name Avraham ben Shmuel ("Abraham, son of Samuel," after his grandfather's and father's names).[3] Perhaps because he received little religious education thereafter, Schoenberg did not show very much self-identification as a Jew. Attracted to German culture, he converted to Protestantism at age twenty-four, consciously affirming his German cultural identity. This decision, however, does not necessarily imply that he ever rejected his Jewish identity entirely, even though he once described himself as a one-time "Assimilant."[4] As Paul Mendes-Flohr pointed out, "Jews laid claim not only to German Kultur, and thus identity, but also to the right to maintain their Jewish identity (as either a subsidiary or a parallel identity, be it conceived in ethnic, religious, and cultural terms, or as a combination thereof)."[5]

Contrary to his self-identification as an Austrian or German, however, Schoenberg never possessed Austrian or German citizenship. He only held "Heimatrecht" (right of domicile) in Bratislava (Slovakia), which he inherited from his father. Unlike many other Viennese Jews, the Schoenbergs never considered obtaining "Heimatrecht" for Vienna. Yet "Heimatrecht" in Vienna was not identical with Austrian citizenship; after World War I the Treaty of Saint-Germain-en-Laye (1919) proscribed Jews who came from such East European countries as Slovakia from obtaining citizenship. Hence Schoenberg was regarded as a Czechoslovakian citizen after the war.[6]

Schoenberg became eligible for German citizenship in 1925, upon his appointment at the Berlin Academy, but he eschewed the opportunity—perhaps because of the relentless growth of anti-Semitism in Germany at the time. He had already begun to identify with his Jewish heritage and explore it more deliberately, especially after 1921 when he was expelled from the Austrian lakeside resort Mattsee for anti-Semitic reasons. His conscious rapprochement with Judaism is reflected not only in his correspondence and political statements, but also in musical and literary works, including *Jakobsleiter* (Jacob's Ladder, 1917–22), *Der biblische Weg* (The Biblical Path, 1926) and *Moses und Aron* (1930–32). Yet at the same time, he saw himself as a rightful heir of and innovator in the German music tradition, and even suggested that his newly developed twelve-tone technique could secure the supremacy of German music.[7] After Hitler's rise to power, Schoenberg left Germany and moved to France, where he reconverted to Judaism in the Paris Union Libérale Israëlite in July 1933.[8] A few months later he emigrated with his family to America, where he would attain U.S. citizenship and achieve a third identity as an American while continuously grappling with his Jewish roots and Austrian-German past.

Schoenberg's three identities in America—German, Jewish, and American—left a mark on his life and work, reflecting manifold forms of acculturation—a term that needs some clarification. Processes of adaptation have often been called "assimilation" and "acculturation."[9] Assimilation means the rapprochement of cultures and styles through their sustained contact and interaction, often implying a loss of features. It generally refers to the emancipation of European Jews before 1933 and their adoption of certain traits of the dominant group. Acculturation, however, has become the preferred concept for discussing many complex cultural changes based on the interaction of different cultures.[10] Understood as a process or the result of processes, acculturation implies a range of forms that vary from complete identification with the dominant culture to its total rejection. These forms include the concept of dissimilation, a process whereby one segment avoids taking on the traits of an adjacent segment.[11] Dissimilation therefore refers to poly-cultural and hybrid phenomena. Zionists, critical of assimilation in view of growing anti-Semitism in Europe, were among the first to promote dissimilation.[12] Dissimilation furthered individualism and pluralism, allowing manifold combinations of elements from Jewish and non-Jewish cultures. Dissimilation became, before and after 1933, an important strategy for many Jews, Schoenberg among them.

In considering Schoenberg's three identities and acculturation to America, one must reconsider his classification as an exile or refugee as well. From a Jewish perspective, Schoenberg could be viewed as an exile because he always lived outside the Holy Land. In 1951, shortly before his death, on his appointment as honorary president of the Israel Academy of Music, he said how much he cherished the creation of the state of Israel and that he wished to reside there.[13] It would, however, be wrong to simply label him an "exile" in America as a contrast to his European years. In Austria, Germany, Spain, and France, he had felt increasingly homeless in the face of anti-Semitism. The term "exile"—defined as "state of banishment" and "process of forced expatriation"—obscures Schoenberg's socialization and acculturation during his eighteen years in America.[14] A more appropriate way to look at Schoenberg's life in America, as proposed by Bruno Nettl for the study of displaced musicians, is to recognize his "change from refugee to exile to immigrant."[15]

In May 1933 Schoenberg became a refugee. Forced to leave home, he fled to places of safety: starting with Paris and Arcachon in France, by October he had emigrated to the United States. During his first few years there, however, he remained a refugee in that he possessed return tickets to Europe for his whole family and lived in different places: Boston, New York City and Chautauqua.[16] Uncertain about his situation in America, he pondered a move to Italy and even to the Soviet Union, upon the invitation of Hanns Eisler.[17] When his visa expired one year after he had settled in Los Angeles, he thought about going to England. But despite this and other inconveniences, he was able to continue his professional activities—composing, performing, writing, teaching, and winning new supporters of his music. From 1936 on, he put down roots in Los Angeles. That year he was appointed professor of music at the University of California, Los Angeles, and moved into a house in Brentwood Park, which he bought a year later. In 1937 and 1941 he and his wife had two more children, and in the latter year the adult Schoenbergs became American citizens. Austria's Anschluss and the beginning of the war consolidated his status as an exile. Expelled from his native country for the time being, he could only hope to return home someday, while retaining elements of his old culture in the new environment.[18] After 1945 Schoenberg and his family decided not to return to Europe, although he was appointed an honorary citizen of Vienna and was invited by its mayor in 1946 to contribute to the reconstruction of the city. Schoenberg was then in his seventies, and his way of living, feeling, and thinking had changed. American thought and behavior had also gotten a hold on his family. The Schoenbergs had become immigrants. This progression from refugee to exile to immigrant helps illuminate the narrative that follows, which does not proceed in chronological order.

SCHOENBERG'S GERMAN IDENTITY

The German Perspective

It is often said that in America Schoenberg continued to think like a German, speaking German and composing "German" music.[19] Yet the question of his

German identity, reflected by his Protestant German name Arnold Franz Walter Schönberg, is more complex than that.[20] To be sure, countless non-Germans and many of his non-Jewish and Jewish followers have identified him as German. His disciple Alban Berg emphasized in 1933 that "there is only one description for Schoenberg's musical work, and that is German."[21] And Schoenberg's American publisher Carl Engel stated in 1937, "his musical speech—as his best prose writing—represents . . . the sum total of German logic, German rigor, and unavoidably, German sentiment."[22] However, numerous German Gentiles and anti-Semites, unwilling to recognize the extraordinary contributions of Jews to their culture, did not consider Schoenberg and his art to be German. Schoenberg himself became ever more uncertain about his German identity, especially after settling in the United States.

In America his German identity took on a new meaning, as he was now situated in a German (and Jewish) Diaspora, separated from many family members, friends, colleagues and students, and disconnected from his original cultural environments and inspirational sources. He became nostalgically grounded in "a place and life once lived," even though he had never felt firmly rooted in Vienna, Mödling, or Berlin, all places that he had once called home.[23] Certainly his rhetoric in America sometimes suggested that his past was "almost everything" and his present a "bottomless night."[24] Yet he was never fixated on Germany. He never made statements in the vein of his fellow émigrés Thomas Mann who claimed, "Where I am there is Germany," and Mann's brother Heinrich, who felt he represented the other, "better Germany."[25] But as is characteristic of individuals within diasporas who grapple with forced displacement and loss, Schoenberg sometimes was incapable of fully accepting America or of being fully accepted by his new homeland. For this reason he developed "strategies of adaptation and resistance," insofar as he replaced and marginalized previously made experiences and "selectively accommodated to political, cultural, commercial and everyday life forms" of the new society.[26] Schoenberg's activities and work in America reflect what Lydia Goehr termed a "condition of doubleness," combinations of dissimilar behaviors, languages, and emotions ("melancholy mixed with relief in leaving, happiness mixed with guilt for surviving, excitement mixed with trepidation for the new life to be lived").[27] Schoenberg straddled two worlds: "the experiences of separation and entanglement and of living here and remembering/desiring another place."[28]

Schoenberg's Initial Impressions of America from a German Perspective

An astute observer of American society, Schoenberg commented on many of its idiosyncrasies. His impressions, which he often shared with his family and friends from Europe, frequently reflect the new world and its inhabitants as the Other. Although many of his statements disclose various degrees of exaggeration, generalization, and prejudice, they are typical of a diasporic consciousness and evolved over time. They represented a step in Schoenberg's adjustment to his new home country, reflecting in James Clifford's words "cultures in collision and dialogue" and a freedom of cultural identification and disidentification.[29]

While he missed such German courtesy gestures as obligatory handshakes, Schoenberg grappled with American manifestations of politeness and political correctness uncommon in his previous environment. He theorized, "Americans still practice the same form of politeness which they had to apply as pioneers for whom impoliteness implied the necessity to shoot."[30] He marveled at the high level of civility and advised his son-in-law:[31] "Here [in America] they go in for much more politeness than we do . . . Everything must be said amiably, smiling, always with a smile."[32] Yet he found: "Beneath everything that appears to us sickly, or hypocritical, or superficial or even trite, virtue and merits are hidden which correspond to those that are hidden beneath German roughness, unfriendliness and loyalty."[33] Moreover, he found it strange that in America "everything is supposed to be praised: *marvelous, very nice, beautiful.* As if to say: I also won't tolerate criticism, because it bores me and because I believe I can manage everything so *it is all right.*" Consequently he deemed it bizarre that frankness was often inappropriate and warned a friend: "You have certainly already noticed that on no account may one speak the truth here—even when one knows it; even when the other does not know it; even when the other wants to know it: for that is the game. I have only understood this incompletely, and still have scarcely learned it. But I have already come to appreciate how damaging the opposite is."[34] And Schoenberg could not fathom that, "above all, one never makes a scene; one never contradicts . . . Differences of opinion are something one keeps entirely to oneself."[35]

He clearly struggled to adapt to American-style courtesy: "I know for myself how hard it is to fit in here. We are all a bit *Boches* [the unflattering French moniker for Germans], that is, we let people feel how deeply we despise them, so it is difficult for us to smile incessantly (*keep smiling*) when we would like to spit fire."[36] And he confessed to a friend that in the first years in America, the example of "Goethe's Götz could not prevent him from making enemies of, on top of everything, important people, who could have done me greater favors than those which Götz had not received either."[37] Yet despite his determination to overcome his Boche-style frankness and to avoid "falling into the European error and only complain," he was not always successful.[38]

Formerly unfamiliar with unabashed advertising and aggressive sales tactics, Schoenberg noted with shock: "There's a picture of a man who has run over a child, which is lying dead in front of his car. He clutches his head in despair, but not to say anything like: 'My God, what have I done!' For there is a caption saying: 'Sorry, now it is too late to worry—take out your policy at the XX Insurance Company in time.'"[39] And he cautioned one relative: "It is especially bad that one is constantly offered goods for sale and that the agents give long-lasting lectures and pretend highest humaneness with a scientific touch, greatest kindness and helpfulness and cannot be easily turned away. There is only one thing you should say, *'I am very, very sorry, but I do not need it!'*"[40] He advised another one: "Don't let anybody get money out of you. Not even if you are promised great or small golden mountains. Don't be influenced by somebody's nice, kind and pleasant appearance. All Americans look honest and are charming and helpful, but almost all of them are charlatans and immediately identify a greenhorn! Taking in a greenhorn is not seen as dishonorable, but as *smart.*"[41]

His sober assessment of America's labor market and working conditions betrays his and his circle's previously naïve vision of the United States as the land of unlimited opportunities. "America is no longer a land of gold," he reported to his son-in-law, "and for a long time, but evidently at least since the Great Depression starting in 1929, all Americans live economically and modestly and think ten times about every cent before they spend it."[42] To a friend he wrote that he "did not need to have phantastic [*sic*] ideas about American salaries, even though they [the ideas] are widespread in Europe. Americans know excellently how to exploit our unfavorable situation and derive more pleasure from the cheapness of a thing than from its actual value."[43] He suggested to an Austrian violinist to "1) be patient; 2) take anything that, in whatever way, will earn you a living; 3) and above all, never lose heart, because 4) you will find something, even if it takes one or two years or longer."[44] He warned that "in America every job can end suddenly and unexpectedly" and emphasized that "it is necessary to have enough savings to get through this period."[45] Schoenberg could not understand the American fetish for guns and was appalled about a sign on a house stating, "If you want to shoot, do it now, or else you will never shoot again!"[46]

Schoenberg, however, liked the American landscapes and comforts that he initially saw through European eyes: "You have no idea how beautiful it is here! This is Switzerland, the Riviera, the Wienerwald, the Salzkammergut, Spain, and Italy—everything together in one place. There is rarely a day—supposedly also in winter—without sun."[47] In a letter to his students he wrote with enthusiasm that "here one is in the lap of luxury," and raved about the "many comforts practically unknown in Europe, which are customary here."[48]And to his brother-in-law Zemlinsky he wrote that "in America one has to work very hard for one's daily bread, but it comes with very much and very good butter."[49]

Preserving German Identity Through Creating a New Home

Schoenberg's German identity is perhaps most clearly reflected in his concern for and interactions with his family. Despite a stressful initial work schedule at Malkin Conservatory's Boston and New York branches, he found comfortable places to live for his young family: his thirty-five-year-old wife Gertrud, his one-year-old daughter Nuria, and the dog Witz. The family resided for the first three months in one of Boston's most modern and luxurious apartment houses, Pelham Hall on Beacon Street. Its furnished apartments had porter and laundry service, a maid, and telephone. The Schoenbergs moved to New York City, staying at the Park Central Hotel before settling into a large apartment at the Hotel Ansonia. That residence boasted, according to one of his students, a "spacious and comfortable furnished music room with three enormous windows overlooking the roofs of the city," and made Schoenberg "appreciate the beauty and vigor of the city."[50] The summer was spent in Chautauqua in western New York state, known for its Chautauqua Institution, which hosted summer courses in education and the arts, and a series of concerts. A visit to Niagara Falls in August was among the highlights of this relaxing family vacation.

In late September 1934 the Schoenbergs settled in Los Angeles where the climate relieved Schoenberg's asthma. They first lived in a furnished rental home on Canyon Cove in Hollywood for nearly two years, and during that time they solved their visa problems.[51] In the summer of 1936 they rented a comfortable two-story colonial-style house with a white stucco exterior, a red-tile roof, a lovely long garden, and a large fenced yard (Figure 3.1). It featured central heating and comprised three bedrooms, two dining rooms, a large living room, two rooms used as studio and library, rooms for servants, and three bathrooms. They soon filled the large house with their own furniture as it arrived from Paris.[52] Located on North Rockingham Avenue in Brentwood, the house stood in a beautiful residential area with acacias and blue wild lilacs, close to UCLA, Schoenberg's new workplace. The area was also popular

FIGURE 3.1.
Arnold, Gertrud, and Nuria Schoenberg; Henrietta Kolisch (Arnold's mother-in-law); their Irish setter Roddie; and their La Salle automobile in front of their home in Brentwood Park. Courtesy Arnold Schönberg Center.

with Hollywood celebrities, and Shirley Temple and Cole Porter were among his neighbors.

Schoenberg created a new "home away from home" with this place, which he bought in May 1937.[53] Until 1942 the Schoenbergs had domestic help, as they had had in Europe. The composer's young family soon grew, and his sons Ronald and Lawrence were born in 1937 and in 1941, respectively (Figure 3.2).[54] As the family adapted to their new environment, they held on to several typically German or European customs, such as the celebration of St. Nicholas Day on December 6.[55] They communicated bilingually, with Schoenberg and his wife generally speaking German to each other, but conversing in English with their children.[56] A dedicated and creative father, Schoenberg spent much time with the children.[57] He fixed

FIGURE 3.2.
Lawrence, Arnold, Gertrud, Nuria, and Ronald Schoenberg (1940s). Courtesy Arnold Schönberg Center.

breakfast and packed lunchboxes, and invented imaginative fairy tales, which he told during meals with the stipulation to present the stories in their entirety only if everybody finished their vegetables. For his son Lawrence, he even recorded one of the tales about a grumbling, tennis-playing princess and her dopey servant.[58] Schoenberg also built a variety of elaborate toys, including a woodblock puzzle, a miniature electric traffic light, and a violin, and constructed such games as Tiddlywinks, a number puzzle, and pocket chess games for his children and grandchildren.[59]

Schoenberg and his wife had enjoyed traveling in Europe, so the couple bought their first car in September 1934, and continued this passion. With Gertrud behind the wheel, since Schoenberg did not drive, the family took many trips and visited cities from San Diego to San Francisco. The Schoenbergs also had had a common interest in sports, especially tennis, since the mid-1920s, and they continued this hobby in America. In the 1930s Schoenberg played tennis twice a week, and he fostered his children's involvement in the sport (Figure 3.3) When he had to give up tennis for health reasons in the mid-1940s, he remained a frequent visitor to tennis courts. His son Ronald emerged as a tennis champion, and Schoenberg developed a notation system to transcribe his son's tennis games (1947–48) (Figure 3.4).[60]

Descriptions of the Schoenberg household have been contradictory. The Thomas Manns, who socialized with the Schoenbergs in the 1940s, thought that the children

FIGURE 3.3.
Lawrence, Ronald, Nuria, and Arnold Schoenberg at the tennis court, 1940s. Courtesy Arnold Schönberg Center.

were "terribly ill-behaved." Mann's wife was bothered because "there was always a chance that they would come downstairs in their nightshirts when their parents had guests for dinner and say, 'We want to have something too.'"[61] Hanns Eisler, another frequent guest at the time, jokingly dubbed the home a "twelve-tone hell."[62] But other visitors, including Alma Mahler-Werfel and Paul Dessau, thought that the Schoenbergs had "fine children."[63]

In his new private sphere, Schoenberg also resumed such previously treasured leisure activities as bookbinding and designing everyday items. He invested less and less time in painting, after having dedicated so much time to it back in Europe. The extant works that he created in America comprise fifteen self-portraits (mostly in watercolor or pencil on paper, 1935–44), a portrait of a man (pencil on paper, August 1937), caricatures of himself (after 1933) and of ten American and émigré friends (May 1935).[64]

In the course of the 1930s and 1940s Schoenberg's American family circle widened as more of his European relatives immigrated to the United States, among them his mother-in-law Henrietta Kolisch; his brother-in-law, the violinist Rudolf Kolisch; his sister-in-law Maria (Mitzi) Seligman with her son; his daughter from his first marriage Gertrud (Trudi) Greissle with her husband Felix and their two sons; and his brother-in-law from his first marriage Alexander von Zemlinsky. Before and after their immigration, Schoenberg especially supported Trudi's family. Prior to 1938 he regularly provided money, clothes, well-paid work through his American publisher G. Schirmer, and affidavits.[65] After their arrival, he helped Felix

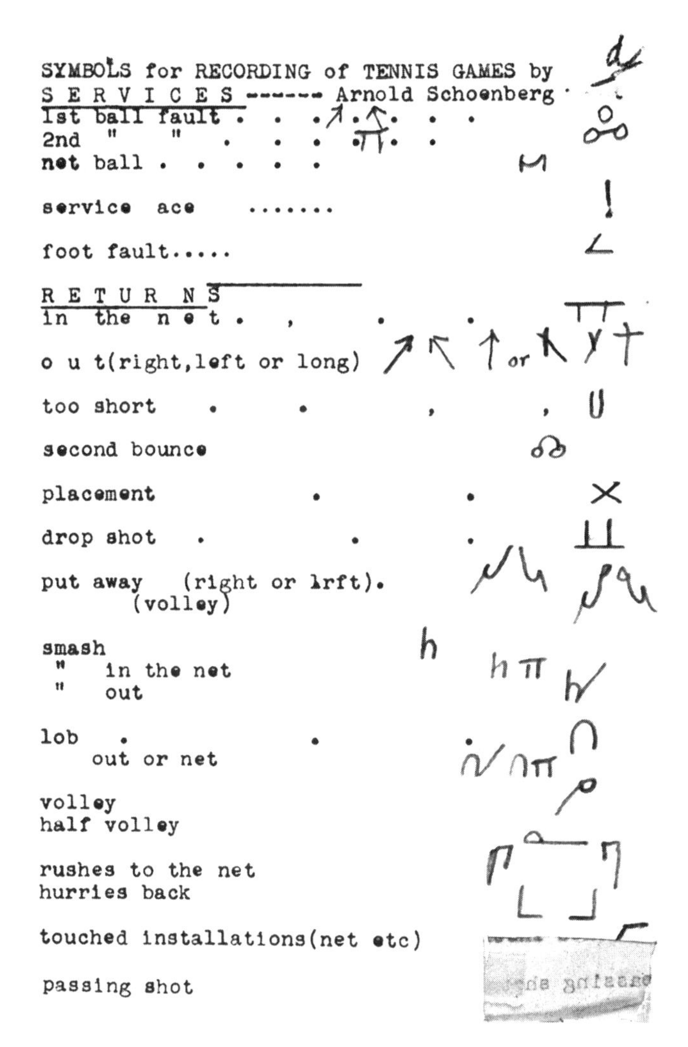

SYMBOLS for RECORDING of TENNIS GAMES by
SERVICES ------ Arnold Schoenberg
1st ball fault
2nd " "
net ball
service ace
foot fault
RETURNS
in the net
out(right,left or long)
too short
second bounce
placement
drop shot
put away (right or lrft). (volley)
smash
" in the net
" out
lob
out or net
volley
half volley
rushes to the net
hurries back
touched installations(net etc)
passing shot

FIGURE 3.4.
Schoenberg's tennis symbols. Courtesy Belmont Music Publishers.

find a job and pay for their trip to Cuba to solve their visa problems.[66] Schoenberg had less contact with Zemlinsky and saw him only once, on his 1940 trip to New York, before Zemlinsky died in March 1942. Yet the two composers, who had been alienated from each other since the mid-1920s over differences of opinion regarding the twelve-tone technique, became closer again in America. When Schoenberg learned that Zemlinsky had fallen seriously ill in December 1938, he cheered him up and sent him a congratulatory note upon listening to a radio broadcast of his *Sinfonietta* for orchestra (1934).[67]

Rescue and Relief Missions

Schoenberg also had other relatives, who never managed to leave Europe and relied heavily on his help. This was particularly true of his difficult oldest son Georg (Görgi), who refused to leave Austria, even though Schoenberg tirelessly offered him affidavits, generous amounts of travel money, and job possibilities in music publishing.[68] Georg and his family were struggling to survive, and Schoenberg not only shared his European royalties with him, but also sent him a monthly allowance of about fifty dollars along with clothes and other gifts. Georg's occasional unreliability notwithstanding, Schoenberg also provided him with lucrative work as a music copyist.[69] After the war Schoenberg supplied Georg with monthly care packages, money for coal, and, as late as August 1950, $250 (about $2, 200 in 2009) for the purchase of a motorcycle.[70] Furthermore, as the geographically divided family drew closer together spiritually, Schoenberg selflessly provided affidavits or tried to find sponsors and other support for such cousins as Anna Berend (née Waitzner); Melanie Feder; Heinrich Goldschmied; Margarete Jontof; Hans, Josef Felix, and Walter Nachod; Emil Neruda; and the Arthur Schönbergs.[71] After the war he sent his relatives care packages.[72] Several relatives, however, including his brother Heinrich, niece Inge Blumauer and her husband, cousin Arthur Schönberg and his wife, and other members of his extended family, unfortunately did not survive the Holocaust.[73]

Schoenberg was just as concerned about the welfare of his German nonmusician and musician friends, especially his former students. They, too, were in a sense part of his extended family, and he missed them just as he did his relatives. Though some of his former students, including Paul von Klenau, Fried Walter, Josef Rufer, and Winfried Zillig, more or less opportunistically adjusted their careers to the Nazi environment, others essentially lost their livelihoods, among them Alban Berg, Josef Polnauer, Anton Webern, and Norbert von Hannenheim. In 1934 Schoenberg helped Berg sell the manuscript of his *Wozzeck* score to the Library of Congress to ease his financial problems.[74] Some of Schoenberg's friends died due to illness: the composers Franz Schreker (1934), Berg (1935), and von Hannenheim (1943), and the writer Karl Kraus (1936). Others were tragically killed during the war: his students Peter Schacht (1941), Viktor Ullmann (1944), and Webern (1945).

Many members of his German circle, however, attempted to flee the Nazis on racial or political grounds and approached Schoenberg for affidavits, career guidance, recommendations, and petitions. He successfully intervened for musicians who were interned during the war: his pupils Karl Alfred Deutsch, Rudolf Goehr, Karl Rankl, and two artists he did not even know at the time, composer-conductor René Leibowitz and pianist Peter Stadlen (both later to become Schoenbergians). He was, however, unable to bring astrologer Oskar Adler, musicologist David Bach, music theorist Josef Polnauer, and conductor Rankl, among others, to America. Yet Schoenberg stayed in touch with these and other friends, who remained in Vienna or settled in England, and supported them, like his relatives, with thoughtful letters and, after the war, with care packages.

A considerable part of his German circle, however, joined him in the United States. These included composers Hanns Eisler, Hugo Kauder, Ernst Krenek, Alma Mahler-Werfel, Julius Schloss, Ashley Vernon (formerly Kurt Manschinger), and Karl Weigl; conductors Walter Herbert (formerly Walter Herbert Seligmann), Fritz Jahoda, Heinrich Jalowetz, Fritz Mahler, Josef Schmid, Fritz Stiedry, and Fritz Zweig; pianists Paul Aron, Rudolf Goehr, Rudolf Serkin, Edward Steuermann, and Moritz Violin; string performers Stefan Auber, Marcel Dick, Kurt Frederick, Kolisch Quartet members, Adolf Rebner, and Julius Toldi; singer Erika Stiedry-Wagner; musicologists Frederic Dorian (formerly Friedrich Deutsch) and Paul Pisk; and the renowned caricaturist Benedict Fred Dolbin.[75] Schoenberg was in touch with many of them and was often able to help them out, even though he could not always take full credit for bringing them to America. As the need for affidavits rose after 1938, his assets were not sufficient for the great number of cases, and he focused on the search for affidavit sponsors. But wealthy sponsors sometimes refused to stand surety for refugees for fear that the revelation of their financial position would entail tax problems, so Schoenberg also worked closely with the Emergency Rescue Committee and the Placement Committee for German and Austrian Musicians (1938–43), founded and headed by American composer Mark Brunswick.[76] Brunswick, who had lived in Europe from 1925 to 1938 and socialized with members of the Viennese Schoenberg circle, secured many affidavits and coached Schoenberg on how to write effective letters on behalf of his friends. For instance, when Schoenberg prepared a recommendation in support of Goehr, Brunswick pointed out that, rather than argue from the standpoint of a German music teacher, Schoenberg needed to emphasize that his student was in danger because he was a "very courageous, upright man of strong democratic convictions"; he also suggested that Schoenberg "might even go beyond the strict bounds of truth" in his assessment of his student's artistic promise.[77] Under Brunswick's supervision, Schoenberg prepared letters for such musicians as Otto Besag, Goehr, and Jalowetz. Schoenberg developed a warm friendship with Brunswick, one of many friendships that he formed with Americans, as discussed later in this chapter.

Besides the provision of affidavits, Schoenberg recommended Eisler, Jalowetz, Kolisch, Schmid, Steuermann, and Violin for teaching jobs at such institutions as the University of Chicago, Black Mountain College, and the St. Louis Institute of Music.[78] He wrote general job recommendations for Schloss and Weigl.[79] He recommended Goehr as an orchestra librarian and substitute teacher in Colorado Springs; and he introduced Toldi to film composer Franz Waxman and Violin to conductor Alfred Hertz in San Francisco.[80] He helped Rebner and the Stiedrys, among others, with general advice on immigration to and life in the United States.[81] In turn, many of these musicians served as advocates for his music. Thus Schoenberg was able to re-create a network of mutual support with old acquaintances residing all over the United States.

Rebuilding a Social Life: The Transplanted "Weimar" Perspective

While fighting for the survival of family members, friends, and students in Nazi Europe and creating a new home for his transplanted family, Schoenberg rebuilt his social life as well. He maintained a sense of connection to his former homeland by continuing certain customs that were typical of Germany, and he greatly expanded his circle of friends. He resumed old friendships and made many new acquaintances, among them the numerous European immigrants who formed the "Weimar on the Pacific."

One of the old customs that the Schoenbergs resumed was to attend opera and concert performances, although they went less frequently than they had in Europe. The American musical infrastructure was different, with fewer prestigious venues and pricier admissions. As a result, they also spent some of their leisure time at the movies and discovered the convenience of radio, often listening to broadcasts of classical music at home. Despite the lack of an opera house in Los Angeles during Schoenberg's time, he followed opera performances by the San Francisco Opera at the 6,300-seat Shrine auditorium in Los Angeles. Although he did not find the space very satisfactory, he commented favorably on such productions as Mozart's *Le Nozze di Figaro* and Wagner's *Walküre*.[82] In addition, the Schoenbergs enjoyed the

Metropolitan Opera radio broadcasts on Saturday afternoons, and once they were observed listening to Wagner's *Meistersinger von Nürnberg*, according to Schoenberg's then sixteen-year old student Dika Newlin, whose composition lessons were scheduled on Saturdays. Newlin reported: "To the accompaniment of the *Dance of the Apprentices* turned full blast, Ronnie and Nuria were scampering about the floor shrieking and yelling, Nuncie [Newlin's pet name for Schoenberg] dancing with his wife all over the room with the greatest abandon and singing all the choral parts with much gusto."[83] Among the concerts the Schoenbergs attended were events with the Pro Arte Quartet with Kolisch as the first violinist, performances of contemporary chamber music at the Evenings on the Roof series, chamber concerts at local clubs and in Pasadena, and orchestra concerts featuring Mahler's Eighth and Beethoven's Ninth Symphonies, Gershwin's music, and works conducted by Alfred Newman at Philharmonic Auditorium or the Hollywood Bowl.[84] Schoenberg attended Klemperer's performance of Mahler's Second Symphony in 1935 and rehearsals and concerts of *Das Lied von der Erde* in 1937. Sometimes, however, he stayed away from the Philharmonic concerts in protest over the orchestra's conservative programming. Later in life he preferred listening to the radio, not only because he had to stay home for health reasons, but also because he could follow the music with his own scores. Listening to the radio allowed him to keep up to date with contemporary music. Emigré writer Bertolt Brecht recalled in his diary Schoenberg's comments on Shostakovich's programmatic Seventh Symphony of 1941: "He does not care much for Shostakovich's 'Leningrad' Symphony which was recently on the radio here, all too long, 35 minutes with material for 12 minutes."[85]

Other old-world habits that the Schoenbergs continued in the new world included the hosting of elaborate birthday parties and other get-togethers, as well as salons.[86] Some of these events may have replaced the European coffeehouse scene. Schoenberg's birthday was generally honored as an elaborate social event. Only his sixtieth birthday on September 13, 1934, was a quiet occasion, with the family then in Chautauqua, preparing for their move to California. Yet despite the small gathering, which included Schoenberg's student Dorothea Kelley and her husband, Schoenberg's wife prepared gifts and cooked a seven-course, European-style dinner complete with a Sachertorte, a famous multi-layered Viennese cake.[87] Schoenberg's subsequent birthday celebrations in California featured fine European foods, and live music performances, and typically included numerous guests. At his sixty-sixth birthday, for instance, such émigrés and immigrants as the Kolisches, the Seligmanns, Klemperer, Felix Khuner, Ernst Krenek, Emanuel Feuermann, Steuermann, and Alexander Schreiner were present. American friends and colleagues and students from UCLA were also among the guests, and Newlin, who was one of them, described the sumptuous European dishes and drinks that were served: "There was coffee with whipped cream (lots), and six or seven kinds of sandwiches made with cheese, liverwurst, and such good things, whole platefuls of rich little pastries, coffee-cake, chocolate raisin cake, peach cake and orange cake. This, keep in mind, was just a little light afternoon tea. The real feast of the day, the birthday dinner, hadn't arrived yet, nor had the birthday drinks."[88] At this birthday celebration, Steuermann, Khuner, Newlin, and Leonard Stein performed Schoenberg's First Chamber Symphony in four-hand and two-hand arrangements, Six Little Piano Pieces and Piano Suite, and Mahler's Sixth Symphony arranged for piano four hands by Alexander Zemlinsky.

While some of Schoenberg's parties centered on musical events—informal performances and dress rehearsals of Schoenberg's works, including the Fourth Quartet and *Pierrot* as well as compositions by students—others were informal Sunday-afternoon gatherings, salons, where relatives, friends, colleagues, and students dropped by, played ping-pong (a game Schoenberg enjoyed playing), and were served Viennese coffee and pastry specialties.[89] The European-born guests who frequented Schoenberg's home at these gatherings represented an impressive cross-section of composers, performers, writers, playwrights, film directors, actors, and architects, and they in turn invited the Schoenbergs to their own homes, and offered them advice on immigration and other professional and everyday matters.

Besides showcasing Schoenberg's hospitality and joie de vivre, these frequent social gatherings also dispel the myth that he was a loner and outsider. The Schoenbergs never socialized exclusively with Europeans, preferring to share their lifestyle with Americans. Several of their American friends, encountering unfamiliar German customs, have vividly described and treasured the *Gemütlichkeit* at these events.[90] The language at these gatherings was typically a hybrid of German and English.

People from the film industry, such as the Viennese-born violinist and opera conductor Hugo Riesenfeld and his wife Mabel, were frequent guests at Schoenberg's parties. In the 1890s Riesenfeld and Schoenberg had played quartets together, but they had lost contact when Riesenfeld moved to the United States in 1907 to make a career, conducting, arranging, and composing music for the movies.[91] When the two met again in Los Angeles in 1934, Riesenfeld was general music director at United Artists, and he helped Schoenberg find his first house in Hollywood. Riesenfeld even tried to secure ASCAP membership for Schoenberg, but was unsuccessful at that time; in 1934 ASCAP did not admit composers of serious music. Not until 1939 did Schoenberg become an ASCAP member, thanks to the efforts of Oscar Levant.[92] In gratitude for Riesenfeld's help, Schoenberg gave him as a Christmas present in 1934 a manuscript of his transcription of Reger's *Romantic Suite* and soon thereafter immortalized him in one of his caricatures.[93]

Like Riesenfeld, William and Charlotte Dieterle, having settled in Hollywood in 1930, were established figures in the film industry, and they were among Schoenberg's earliest and closest acquaintances there. An actor and director, Dieterle worked for Warner Brothers and RKO, and specialized in screen biographies of such figures as Pasteur, Zola, Juárez, and Wagner. He also won acclaim with *A Midsummer Night's Dream*, which he co-directed with Max Reinhardt (1935), and is best remembered for having directed Charles Laughton in *The Hunchback of Notre Dame* (1939). His wife was the co-founder of the European Film Fund and an occasional playwright.[94] Having just completed a screenplay for a Beethoven film, she invited Schoenberg to arrange music by Beethoven for it. Although he declined the offer, he proposed to conceive the score as "a symphonic-dramatic fantasy that would necessarily have the same artistic justification as if I were to write variations on a theme of Beethoven's." He considered Klemperer, and having just given him composition lessons, thought that the conductor, a Beethoven expert, could compose the score—promising that, if need be, he would support him "in stylistic-compositional questions."[95] In addition he recommended the actor Peter Lorre, another Hollywood friend of his, for the role of Beethoven, but the film never materialized. The Dieterles assisted the Schoenbergs in getting U.S. citizenship and helped them in immigration matters.[96] In 1935, as a token of friendship, Schoenberg dedicated to Charlotte a contrapuntal four-part piece in mirror form for string quartet, which he inscribed with the brief text "Man mag über Schönberg denken wie man will [Let people think what they want of Schoenberg]" and "Credit may sometimes be based on a statement like that. Creed and credit."[97] The Dieterles shared with Schoenberg a strong belief in astrology and numerology. In 1941 they apparently influenced the naming of the composer's youngest son as Lawrence Adam instead of Roland. Roland would have been, like Ronald, an anagram of Arnold. But according to the Dieterles, Roland would have been an unlucky name.[98]

The Schoenbergs also socialized with the Korngolds whom they had known in Vienna. Gertrud had become friends with Erich when she was in her teens. His father Julius, although a detractor of Schoenberg's music as critic for the Viennese *Freie Presse*, had advised Gertrud's brother Rudolf to take lessons with Schoenberg, which resulted in Rudolf introducing Gertrud to Schoenberg.[99] Korngold came to Hollywood in 1934 to arrange Mendelssohn's music for the Reinhardt and Dieterle adaptation of *A Midsummer Night's Dream*—an exceptional film that the Schoenbergs may have seen. Korngold proved an extraordinary talent as a film composer; thanks to an exclusive contract with Warner Brothers, he was able to bring his family to Los Angeles after the *Anschluss*, where he made a more comfortable living than the Schoenbergs did. The Korngolds frequented Schoenberg's Sunday-afternoon parties and exchanged birthday greetings with him, and the children of the two families also became friends. In California, Korngold's father apparently revised his unflattering view of Schoenberg, speaking of him as "amiable," a "bourgeois husband and tender father," who had "grown tolerant, very tolerant, and tolerance is not one of the characteristics of a real revolutionary."[100]

Franz Waxman had come to Hollywood in the same year as Schoenberg, and he immediately hit his stride by scoring the famous horror classic *Bride of Frankenstein* (1935). Waxman interacted with Schoenberg in various ways, not only frequenting his parties, but also studying composition and playing tennis with him. Due to his association with the music departments at United Artists, MGM, and Warner Brothers, Waxman was also an important contact for Schoenberg when he sought film industry jobs for his friends.[101] Musically, Schoenberg must have appreciated Waxman's generous use of dissonance in many of his film scores, although he did not seem to be fond of his music for Alfred Hitchcock's *Rebecca* (1940). Schoenberg's student Dika Newlin recounted that one of her classmates asked Schoenberg if he had seen the movie, whereupon he "replied, his voice pregnant with meaning, 'I started to!'"[102] After Schoenberg's death Waxman paid tribute to him by using twelve-tone elements in his score for *The Nun's Story* (1959) and in concert works such as *The Song of Terezin* (1965), and he also featured Schoenberg's music in concerts of his Los Angeles Music Festival (1947–67).

In Los Angeles Schoenberg also became reacquainted with his former pupil Hanns Eisler (1898–1962) (Figure 3.5). The two saw each other quite regularly, and their once frosty relationship warmed. Political and artistic disagreements had estranged the student and his teacher in the mid-1920s: Eisler, an advocate of communism, had rejected Schoenberg's *l'art pour l'art* approach to music and his twelve-tone technique; Schoenberg, a political conservative, had dismissed both communism and Eisler's exploration of engaged art. In the 1930s and 1940s, however, they grew closer again, and in 1934 even discussed plans for a music institute in Russia.[103] Eisler began to use twelve-tone principles again in such works as his Prelude and Fugue on B-A-C-H (1934), his String Quartet (1938), and his scores for Joris Ivens's experimental film *Rain* (1941) and Fritz Lang's dramatic feature *Hangmen Also Die* (1943). At the same time Schoenberg explored engaged art in his *Ode to Napoleon* and *A Survivor from Warsaw*.

Financially, Eisler had more success than Schoenberg did, because he was able to wed his communist and artistic beliefs with American capitalism. Before settling in

FIGURE 3.5.
Hanns Eisler (1948). Bettmann Archive.

Hollywood in 1942 to make a living as a film composer and music professor at the University of Southern California, he spent four years in New York City, where he worked at the New School for Social Research and completed a film-music project that was generously funded by the Rockefeller Foundation.[104] Eisler shared $300 (about $3,900 in 2009) of his grant money with Schoenberg when he learned of his former teacher's struggle to pay for his son Ronald's expensive surgery. Eisler decided to declare Schoenberg as one of his film-project consultants in the final grant report after Schoenberg rejected his idea to use the amount toward further lessons. Schoenberg, who had taught the penniless Eisler for free in the 1920s, joked, "If you haven't learnt it yet I can't teach you any more."[105] In 1943 Eisler coached Basil Rathbone, Hollywood's unforgettable Sherlock Holmes, who was briefly considered for the narrator's part of Schoenberg's newly composed *Ode to Napoleon*.[106] In 1944 Eisler dedicated *Fourteen Ways to Describe Rain* to Schoenberg in celebration of his seventieth birthday. The work features twelve-tone technique, the instrumentation of *Pierrot*, and an introductory "Anagram" section in which Schoenberg's initials A-S-C-H are spelled out musically. In turn Schoenberg discussed Eisler's *Fourteen Ways* in one of his university lectures and recommended him for a teaching job at the University of Chicago, praising him as one of his most talented students.[107] He also initiated Eisler into the secret program of his String Trio (1946), in which details of Schoenberg's heart attack and recovery are musically depicted.

Eisler's and Schoenberg's political convictions, however, remained incompatible. On his first trip to the United States in 1935, Eisler described Schoenberg to the American Marxist magazine *The New Masses* as the "greatest bourgeois composer" whose "music does not sound beautiful [to the uninitiated listener] because it mirrors the capitalist world as it is without embellishment and because out of his work the face of capitalism stares directly at us."[108] Eisler never changed this view.[109] By the same token, Schoenberg never accepted Eisler's political beliefs and for this reason occasionally distanced himself from Eisler. In1940 he wrote to the director of the St. Louis Institute of Music: "Hanns Eisler: He would be grand as a musician and as an intelligence. But I don't want to recommend him because of his political implication."[110] Even though Eisler had abstained from political activism in the United States, in 1947 his views brought him before the hearings of the House Un-American Activities Committee and, a year later, led to his deportation. Such figures as Leonard Bernstein, Charlie Chaplin, Aaron Copland, Thomas Mann, and Stravinsky protested against Eisler's treatment, but Schoenberg categorically refused to support his case.[111] Instead he expressed his frustration about Eisler's politics: "If I had any say in that matter I'd turn him [Eisler] over my knee like a silly boy and give him 25 of the best and make him promise never to open his mouth again but to stick to scribbling music."[112]

Eisler worked with many illustrious figures in the film industry whom he entertained at his house in Santa Monica, and it was through him that Schoenberg encountered a multitude of filmmakers, actors, writers, and musicians, including Adorno, Charlie Chaplin, Harold Clurman, Dessau, Lion Feuchtwanger, Greta Garbo, Ava Gardner, Heinrich Mann, Clifford Odets, Jean Renoir, and Artie Shaw. Also through Eisler, Schoenberg got to know the Marxist poet and playwright Bertolt Brecht, who resided in Los Angeles from 1941 to 1947. Brecht had never met Schoenberg before, and he urged his old friend Eisler to bring them into contact. On the occasion of their first meeting in the summer of 1942, Eisler apparently was panic-stricken because he feared that the unruly Brecht might provoke the touchy Schoenberg with inappropriate remarks about music. Brecht had roguishly attacked Schoenberg's music just a few months earlier, when he and Eisler were at Adorno's house. He disliked emotionally intense music for "raising the temperature of the human body," as well as the "unnatural declamation of texts by the school of Schoenberg."[113] Moreover Brecht ridiculed Eisler's deference to his teacher, his "worries about his tie being straight or arriving 10 minutes too early."[114] Eisler was also afraid that Schoenberg might irritate Brecht with offensive comments on socialism.[115] The meeting, however, seemed enjoyable for all. First the two attended one of Schoenberg's university lectures on modern composition and then visited him at his home. Brecht not only liked Schoenberg's "very lively" teaching style and polemical attitude, but he also seemed to like him as a person. He described him as a "rather bird-like man who has great charm, and is agreeably dry and sharp with it."[116] A few months later, upon the occasion of Schoenberg's sixty-eighth birthday, Brecht gave him a copy of the poem "Und in eurem Lande?" which he inscribed "in admiration." Through this text Brecht poetically wished Schoenberg luck, for any good and honest person needs it in view of the reigning injustice, capitalism, carelessness, and hypocrisy in "our country." Brecht seemed to be criticizing American society, yet the poem was written during his exile in Denmark in 1935.

In the following years, Brecht encountered Schoenberg at various dinners and even in a drugstore where Schoenberg complained to him about the unfairness of copyright laws.[117] Brecht remained fascinated with Schoenberg's personality. After a dinner in October 1944 he described him as "astonishingly lively," "Gandhi-like," and a "mixture of genius and craziness."[118]

Schoenberg never discussed Brecht in his writings, and one can only speculate on what he may have thought of him. Both were influential artists with critical minds, who held views in common and created a variety of myths about their personalities, taking pleasure in viewing themselves as penniless and ignored figures. Politically and artistically, however, they had little common ground. Schoenberg seems to have been the less disgruntled of the two. Unlike Brecht, he did not segregate himself from the English-speaking community, and he became more deeply rooted in his new surroundings. Brecht used the English language as little as possible and remained in a ghetto-like, German-speaking community until his return to Europe after hearings before the House Un-American Activities Committee in 1947.

In 1941 Schoenberg's long-term confidante, the composer and author Alma Mahler-Werfel, and her third and last husband, poet and novelist Franz Werfel, joined the émigré community in Los Angeles (Figure 3.6).[119] The international success of Werfel's novel *The Song of Bernadette* (1942) and its film version (1943) soon enabled them to purchase a luxurious home in Beverly Hills, where Alma re-created her Viennese salon. At the Werfels' parties Schoenberg encountered many writers, among them Alfred Döblin, Lion Feuchtwanger, Bruno and Leonhard Frank, Thomas Mann, and Friedrich Torberg, as well as such musicians as Korngold, Lotte Lehmann, and Klemperer. He may, however, have skipped the gatherings at which the Werfels' friends Stravinsky and Bruno Walter were present, as he avoided both of them. With a few exceptions, such as Werfel's translators Gustave Arlt and S. N. Behrman, these parties included no Americans, perhaps because of Mahler-Werfel's reluctance to speak English.

The Schoenbergs and Werfels also interacted in other ways. Werfel attended Schoenberg's Research Lecture on "Composition with Twelve Tones" at UCLA in March 1941.[120] Schoenberg briefly planned an opera based on one of Werfel's novels and hoped Werfel could help him turn his own drama *Der biblische Weg* (1927) into a performable stage work.[121] In December 1943 Mahler-Werfel heard Steuermann's and Leonard Stein's private performance of Schoenberg's new Piano Concerto arranged for two pianos, on which occasion Schoenberg reportedly remarked that it

FIGURE 3.6.
Alma Mahler and Franz Werfel aboard the S.S. *Ile de France* in New York. Bettmann Archive.

took him "forty-five rehearsals to get to know the work."[122] The Werfels supported Schoenberg's music with contributions to festschrifts and anthologies in 1934, 1937, and 1949, and Schoenberg paid tribute to them musically,[123] supervising student settings of five Werfel poems, two of which were performed at a celebration of Werfel's fiftieth birthday in January 1941 at the Los Angeles Community College.[124] He also composed a four-part canon at the octave in C major to honor Mahler-Werfel's seventieth birthday in August 1949. The canon's text, "Gravitationszentrum eigenen Sonnensystems, von strahlenden Satelliten umkreist, so stellt dem Bewunderer dein Leben sich dar [Center of Gravitation of its own solar system which is circled by radiant satellites, this is how your life appears to the admirer]," reveals his regard for her.[125] Both couples also supported each other in times of crisis. The Schoenbergs consoled Mahler-Werfel when her husband died in 1945, at age fifty-five, and attended his funeral (even though Stravinsky was also there). Mahler-Werfel consoled Gertrud Schoenberg after her husband's death, and her daughter Anna, a talented sculptor, made Schoenberg's death mask.

Perhaps the most illustrious German emigrant with whom Schoenberg fraternized in Los Angeles was Thomas Mann. Schoenberg and Mann had only occasionally corresponded before they met for the first time at the Beverly Hills home of writer Vicky Baum in 1938.[126] They saw each other again in September 1940 at a musical soirée at Salka Viertel's, where Schoenberg conducted a *Pierrot* performance featuring the vocalist Erika Stiedry-Wagner with Viertel's brother Edward Steuermann at the piano.[127] They became better acquainted when the Manns, after occasional stays in California, settled into a comfortable house in Pacific Palisades in 1941. In the following years, they met at the homes of Arthur Rubinstein, the Werfels, and film director and producer Gottfried Reinhardt, and also invited each other to dinner and birthday parties, with the Manns attending Schoenberg's sixty-ninth birthday celebration.[128] They exchanged letters and gifts. In 1943 Mann gave Schoenberg his novel *Der Zauberberg* (1924), and Schoenberg sent him the libretto of *Jakobsleiter* and *Harmonielehre*.[129] In 1944 Mann sent Schoenberg flowers for his seventieth birthday; in 1945 Schoenberg honored Mann's seventieth birthday with an infinite double canon with retrograde elements in all four parts.[130] Schoenberg wrote in his birthday greeting, "it is not without (honest) egotism, that I wish that we both will remain good contemporaries of one another for many years."[131] In 1946 the Schoenbergs wished Mann a speedy recovery after his surgery for lung cancer, and the Manns congratulated Schoenberg on his seventy-sixth birthday in 1950.[132]

Yet despite their regular contact and exchange of polite gestures, the two men never became true friends. Mann did not care for Schoenberg's work, considering *Verklärte Nacht* "insubstantial," the piano works "extreme," *Pierrot* "antiquated modern," and the *Jakobsleiter* text "half-baked"; *Harmonielehre* he found unique and captivating, but also a "strange mixture of pious tradition and revolution."[133] Mann's wife Katia did not regard Schoenberg a "very winning man," and she "took an immediate dislike to his wife."[134] The true motivation for Mann's interest in frequent meetings with Schoenberg was his new novel *Doctor Faustus*, which he had begun in spring 1943. It featured as its protagonist a fictional modernist German composer akin to Schoenberg, and he was determined to use every opportunity to "pump him [Schoenberg] a great deal on music and the life of a composer," without initiating him into the project before its completion in 1947.[135]

The reasons for Mann's secrecy lay in his novel's dark plot and the protagonist Adrian Leverkühn's sinister character. Leverkühn owes his visionary invention of dodecaphony to a Faustian pact with the devil, for which he must ultimately pay with his life, dying of a Nietzschean syphilis infection. Mann's novel critiques Schoenberg's *l'art pour l'art* approach, dodecaphony, and even his religious works, suggesting that the cultism, constructivism, and aestheticism of Leverkühn's music indicated a crisis in contemporary German art and a lack of freedom, thus paving the way for the political decay, fascism, and barbarism of Nazi Germany.[136] Mann knew that Schoenberg would dislike his novel's implications: "Now on the one hand his [Schoenberg's] name is, however, not mentioned (which was impossible), and on the other hand the serial technique is presented as an invention of diabolic coldness. He has to get into a huff—like some others."[137]

Schoenberg unsuspectingly provided Mann with valuable information. The two men conversed, sometimes in the presence of Eisler, about Wagner, *Parsifal*, and "archaic forms of variation."[138] Mann thought it was "strange, how much appreciation and reverence, even love these modern composers [Neutöner] retain for the old, the whole world of harmony and even of romanticism."[139] Hence Mann let Leverkühn combine old and new compositional devices and use variation technique.[140] Mann discussed with Schoenberg the potential use of a nontempered scale in a choral work, since he was pondering possibilities to lend Leverkühn's first major, "very German" work, an oratorio, a "satanically religious" touch by conceiving something "scarcely executable": an "a-cappella chorus to be sung in a nontempered tuning system with almost no pitch or interval to be found on the piano." "Schoenberg said he would not do it, but that it was possible theoretically." Thus Mann dropped this idea.[141] Intrigued by Schoenberg's statement that, despite the degenerate-art campaign, dodecaphonic music was still tolerated in Nazi Germany, Mann noted:[142] "Take this into account. Relationship of nation to Leverkühn's music can be ambivalent like that to Nietzsche."[143] And Mann modeled the description of Leverkühn's chamber music as "impossible, but rewarding" on a comment Schoenberg made about his String Trio's nearly impossible execution, yet rewarding sonorities.[144] Mann also drew on *Harmonielehre* and *Jakobsleiter*.

Many of the novel's references to Schoenberg's music, however, stemmed from such musical consultants as the German-born musicologists Gerhard Albersheim and Alfred Einstein, Otto Klemperer, Mann's musical son Michael, Ernst Toch, Stravinsky, and Walter, who were all more or less critical of Schoenberg's work. Mann's most important adviser by far was the German-born philosopher and musician Theodor W. Adorno, who settled in Los Angeles in 1940. Although a former student of Berg and a scholar of Schoenberg's music since the 1920s, Adorno never became very friendly with Schoenberg. Mann noticed that despite their proximity in California, the two men tended to avoid each other, and speculated that "the old man sensed the critical note within his disciple's respect."[145] Schoenberg had ambiguous feelings about Adorno and disliked his supercilious personality, suspecting him of miserliness; he also distrusted Adorno's secondhand knowledge of dodecaphony and loathed his convoluted prose. Yet in 1940 Schoenberg recommended him, though not very enthusiastically: "Mr. Wiesengrund is a composer, who has been played internationally. He is also a philosopher and an important theorist (musicologist) and has published interesting essays."[146] In California Schoenberg saw Adorno occasionally at his own Sunday-afternoon parties, but more often at his friends' houses where he often participated in battles of words with him.[147] Mann became more closely acquainted with Adorno, although their relationship was perhaps not as harmonious as some commentators have suggested.[148] The two probably met each other through Max Horkheimer in early summer of 1943. For Mann it was quite convenient to find an expert on (contemporary) music of Adorno's stature in his neighborhood, who was willing to work with him on his novel behind Schoenberg's back. For Adorno, who was unknown at the time, collaborating with Mann was prestigious and exciting. Moreover, he himself was working on projects that intersected with some of Mann's ideas about music and politics: his *Philosophy of Modern Music* (to be published in 1948) and the essay "The Musical Climate for Fascism in Germany" (1945).[149] Adorno was very generous with his advice and even lent Mann published and unpublished writings of his, including his essays on Berg and the first part of his *Philosophy* manuscript, which focused on Schoenberg.[150] As is well known, Mann incorporated portions from the latter source verbatim in his novel, thereby appropriating Adorno's dialectic interpretation of music history and criticism of dodecaphony's dogmatism. In a letter to Adorno of December 1945, Mann defended his uncredited borrowings as a "montage" technique while at the same time demanding a more intensive collaboration with him.[151] Adorno helped Mann imagine such details as Leverkühn's alleged compositional development in works from his modernistic apocalyptic oratorio through his last achievement, the dodecaphonic cantata *The Lamentation of Doctor Faustus*.

Published in German and English in 1948, *Doctor Faustus*, though controversial in Germany, was nevertheless successful in the United States, despite its complexity and the mixed reviews. A Book-of-the-Month Club selection, the novel boasted a first printing of more than 100,000 copies. Ironically, it made both Schoenberg and Adorno livid.[152] Although Mann immortalized Adorno at various places in his novel and had inscribed his *Faustus* copy "To my privy councilor," Adorno had expected greater recognition. Mann was able to avoid a dispute over matters of intellectual property with his *Story of a Novel: The Genesis of Doctor Faustus* (published in 1949), in which he gave Adorno some if not all the credit he deserved for his "conceptual and creative contribution to Leverkühn's work and his aesthetics."[153] Schoenberg's reaction to *Faustus*, however, was beyond Mann's control.

In January 1948 Mann had sent Schoenberg the novel with the dedication "Dem Eigentlichen [To the real one]." Due to poor eyesight, Schoenberg was unable to read the entire book. Excerpts, however, were read aloud to him by his wife and recorded onto a Dictaphone by his assistant Richard Hoffmann. He also received summaries of its content from Mahler-Werfel and others. While Schoenberg was amazed by Mann's expert description of his compositional technique and Leverkühn's works, he categorically rejected Mann's uncredited appropriation of his twelve-tone technique in this context. Worried about his legacy, Schoenberg mailed Mann a curious satirical document entitled "Text from the Third Millennium," which he had written under the pseudonym Hugo Triebsamen (a conflation of the names of two musicologists, Hugo Riemann and Walter Rubsamen). The text dating from "2048" conveys that, according to an article from a 1988 *Encyclopedia Americana*, the true inventor of dodecaphony was Mann, who temporarily permitted Schoenberg, a teacher, theorist, and "scrupulous exploiter of other people's ideas," to use this method.[154] After the fictive quarrels of these two men, Mann took his musical property back from Schoenberg and assigned it to an imaginary character, thus influencing the course of American music.

The *Faustus* controversy, at first a private matter, soon grew into a cause célèbre, with letters of Schoenberg and Mann featured in the *Saturday Review of Literature*. Thanks to Mahler-Werfel's intervention, Mann felt compelled to appease Schoenberg and made the following statement:[155]

It does not seem supererogatory to inform the reader that the form of musical composition delineated in Chapter XXII, known as the twelve-tone or row system, is in truth the intellectual property of a contemporary composer and theoretician, Arnold Schönberg. I have transferred this technique in a certain ideational context to the fictitious figure of a musician, the tragic hero of my novel. In fact, the passages of this book that deal with musical theory are indebted in numerous details to Schönberg's *Harmonielehre*.[156]

Yet Schoenberg was unhappy about the "hidden" placement of the note and took offense at being called "*a contemporary* composer and theorist," reasoning: "Of course in two or three decades, one will know which of the two was the other's contemporary."[157] But as he insisted on due credit for his intellectual property, he was all the more troubled by Mann's portrayal of his twelve-tone method as the product of a corrupt, syphilitic character. Schoenberg protested in the *Saturday Review of Literature*: "I am seventy-four and I am not yet insane, and I have never acquired the disease from which this insanity stems."[158] And Mann claimed: "There is no point of contact, not a shade of similarity, between the origin, the traditions, the character and the fate of my musician, on the one hand, and the existence of Arnold Schoenberg on the other." Mann regretted that Schoenberg depended too much on the "gossip of meddling scandal mongers," an allusion to Mahler-Werfel's role in this debate. Mann exaggeratingly asserted that he had hoped Schoenberg would receive his "book with a satisfied smile as a piece of contemporary literature that testifies to his tremendous influence upon the musical culture of the era."[159]

It seems, however, that Schoenberg's strongest resentment was directed at Adorno and his clandestine participation in the novel. He believed that Adorno, the "informer," misunderstood the nature of his dodecaphonic method by interpreting it as a rigid "system" rather than a flexible creative "method."[160] He dismissed Adorno's primitive use of dodecaphony in Leverkühn's *Lamentation of Doctor Faustus*, proposing that the work be subtitled "Twelve-tone Goulash."[161] As Schoenberg revealed to friends, he might have been able to furnish Mann's fictitious composer with more adequate skills: "If Mann had only asked me, I'd have invented a special system for him to use!"[162] Schoenberg and Mann reconciled in January 1950. "Even if you insist on being my enemy," wrote Mann to Schoenberg, "you will not succeed in turning me into yours," whereupon Schoenberg replied: "If the hand I believe I see held out is the hand of peace . . . then I shall be happy to grasp it immediately."[163] Schoenberg and Adorno, however, never made peace. A year after *Faustus*, Adorno's *Philosophy* was published, further irritating Schoenberg by categorizing him as the progressive composer and pitching him against Stravinsky, the retrogressive composer.[164] As he did with *Faustus*, Schoenberg condemned Adorno's book after having read only "parts of scattered pages" and reviews of it sent to him by friends. He disapproved of Adorno's "blathering jargon" and dismissed the fact that his "middle period" was "played against his presumably last period."[165] He found Adorno's assessment of Stravinsky's music "disgusting."[166] Having invested much energy into Schoenberg studies, Adorno must have been astonished when he discovered that before his death Schoenberg had decided to deny him access to his papers.[167]

The interactions among Schoenberg, Mann, Adorno, Mahler-Werfel, and others point to the complicated relationships and struggles among the German-speaking émigré community in Los Angeles. How unfortunate that Mann, who was regarded as the "legitimate representative of German culture and the 'better Germany,'" cast aspersions on Schoenberg's German identity in making him *Faustus*'s secret protagonist.[168] Leverkühn, Schoenberg's *Doppelgänger*, stands for the blinded German people, and his compositional development parallels his country's catastrophic course toward fascism. Schoenberg's German identity made him the representative of the evil Germany. We may note also Steven Schwarzschild's critical observation: "Leverkühn, 'der deutsche Tonsetzer,' is in significant part the Jew Schoenberg (when he is not Nietzsche!)," and thus, "as Mann treats Jews and Germans as one, so the German and the Jewish catastrophes of 1945 are then really one."[169]

The notorious public debate between Schoenberg and Mann unfortunately exposed the vulnerabilities, hypersensitivity, and feelings of neglect and persecution that marked Schoenberg's last few years, when he also suffered health problems that frequently prevented him from participating in social activities. But then that once dense cluster of displaced Europeans, the "New Weimar," had itself begun to diminish in the late 1940s and early 1950s, as such exiles as Mann and Adorno returned to Europe.

Schoenberg and the Idea of German Music

Of all his life's activities Schoenberg's work in music reflects perhaps most strongly "the place and a life once lived."[170] As a teacher, he passed on his European musical heritage to innumerable American students, and as a composer, he suggested that his American works remained influenced by the German cultural tradition. When asked whether music could manifest a racial quality, he replied:

> The musical culture of a nation certainly takes on a racial or at least a national style. Here am I, educated in music from the German standpoint. I cannot think music in some other way—in the way that Bizet thought music from France or a Verdi from Italy. I have been trained in another way and have grown up in it. Therefore the German culture certainly tinges my music. I feel from Americans a different musical attitude or instinct toward harmonic relations than my own. I confess to you that I can feel this difference more readily than I can define it. It is something to be studied, and it should mean something to music.[171]

Despite the elusiveness and ideological implications of such categories as "German," "French," "Italian," or "American" music, Schoenberg held on to them in America.[172] He continued to believe that such aspects of German music as feeling, thoroughness, depth (versus superficiality), sincerity, altruism, and strength in counterpoint are quintessentially German.[173] He continued to stress his indebtedness to German composers from Bach to Wagner, not only to establish his own place in history and legitimize his compositional techniques, but also to call attention to his cultural roots.

Yet Schoenberg left off calling his own music assertively German. He no longer felt the desperation to convince German anti-Semites that his music was "produced on German soil, without foreign influences," that it was "derived through and through from the traditions of German music," and that it was "a living example of an art able most effectively to oppose Latin and Slav hopes of hegemony."[174] He no longer strove to be the leader of German music—a goal that had already begun to lose its viability before his emigration. In 1931 he decided to "increase the distance between me and it [German music] until any relatedness is eliminated," in the fear that "German music will not follow my path, which I have shown her."[175] Schoenberg's most important reason for minimizing the German quality of his music in America, however, may have been that the Nazis had perverted the idea of "German music" and incorporated it into their racist ideology.[176]

After 1933 Schoenberg generally portrayed himself as heir to the "classical" tradition, while instilling his American works with references to his distinctly German musical genealogy. He orchestrated Brahms's Piano Quartet No. 1 in G minor, op. 25, explicitly honoring this German master, and paid tribute to German folk music in his Three Folksongs, op. 49. He evoked his chosen musical ancestors through the use of eighteenth- and nineteenth-century genres and classical forms and techniques. He also adhered to principles he had derived from German music and developed further: the concepts of the musical idea and logic, developing variation, organicism, the restriction of ornamentation, the belief in art for art's sake, the increased use of dissonance, and the twelve-tone technique, which had put him in the forefront of modernism in Europe.[177] Yet such references to his musical past surely took on a new meaning and occurred in new contexts. They helped Schoenberg to "articulate the continuity [he] needed to feel across the radical rupture [he] had experienced," and to prove that music, while perhaps bound to a nation, did not necessarily have to be bound to a place.[178]

Despite Schoenberg's allusions to the German music tradition, it would be wrong to view him as composing music that defied his Jewish identity or his Americanization. Even though he claimed, "If America changed me—I am not aware of it," his experience of racial persecution and displacement, and his encounters with his new homeland's culture, all left their mark on his music as well.[179] Cut off from previous performers, publishers, audiences, and other backers of his music, he had to create a new musical support system in a large country where the modernist musical community was more geographically spread out than in Europe. He also had to make new creative decisions. For instance, his remark that Germany left him not only "homeless, but speechless, languageless," may well explain why he wrote more instrumental than vocal works, and why he did not finish the large German text–based works *Moses und Aron* and *Jakobsleiter*.[180] While he "brought his roots with him," he "remained faithful to them not by making museum-pieces of them, but by testing and quickening his powers of expression on the new stuff of life."[181] Thus his works after 1933 display dissimilation thanks to multiple loyalties, a greater variety of influences, combinations of old and new or familiar and unfamiliar elements, private and public aspects, and an adaptation and resistance to expectations from audiences and critics.

In the following sections, those tonal and nontonal compositions are discussed in which Schoenberg accentuates his German identity and only subtly hints at his Jewish roots and/or American influences.

Schoenberg's Arrangement of Brahms's Piano Quartet

Composed between May 2 and September 19, 1937, Schoenberg's arrangement of Brahms's Piano Quartet in G minor, op. 25 demonstrates both his roots in German music and consideration of his new environment.

Schoenberg loved to arrange works of the past, and he chose this project for several reasons.[182] He deemed Brahms one of his most important musical forebears, and specifically liked this piano quartet. It reminded him of his youth, when he "played it as violist and cellist numerous times." He regretted that it was only rarely presented and that, if performed, the piano often dominated the strings.[183] Upon completing this work's orchestration, Schoenberg documented his fondness of it in a sardonic pun on Brahms's famous remark about Johann Strauss's *Blue Danube*, "leider nicht von Johannes Brahms." On a piece of paper, he notated the first measures of Brahms's piano quartet and added: "Leider von Johannes Brahms, only orchestrated by Arnold Schoenberg."[184]

Yet Schoenberg's Brahms orchestration was also motivated by other factors. Planning a Brahms cycle for the 1937–38 Los Angeles Philharmonic season, Klemperer proposed this arrangement to Schoenberg, who had conducted this orchestra in a 1935 performance of Brahms's Third Symphony. Schoenberg happily embraced the suggestion, recognizing that the project would be beneficial for him in numerous ways. He could create an aesthetically pleasing new orchestral work in a short time period, which would not only enjoy numerous performances, visibility, and public recognition, but also would yield extra revenue—something Schoenberg needed to pay off the mortgage on his house, support his two European children's families, and be able to issue affidavits for relatives and friends.[185] The work also points to Schoenberg's acculturation: He wanted to make an accessible contribution to the American concert repertoire and introduce American audiences to a relatively little known old-world work. As one of the "musicians educated in his [Brahms's] environment," who "knew all the laws which Brahms obeyed," he could assume the role of a "cultural ambassador."[186] Yet he also seized on the opportunity to guide his listeners toward his own more advanced music by adding modernist touches to the arrangement. Schoenberg confidently claimed that he did "not go farther than he [Brahms] himself would have gone if he lived today."[187]

Schoenberg jokingly called his arrangement "Brahms's Fifth." Yet he used an orchestrational approach that was very different from that of Brahms, closer to his own dodecaphonic Orchestral Variations than to Brahms's symphonies. Schoenberg availed himself of such instruments as the E-flat and bass clarinets, glockenspiel, xylophone, tambourine, and snare drum, and instrumental combinations that Brahms never used in his symphonies. His imaginative mixtures of a wide array of instruments recall his concept of *Klangfarbenmelodie*. Schoenberg created new foreground and background effects, revealed previously hidden motivic relationships among other structural details, and emphasized the process of developing variation through timbral differentiation and layering. This individualization of elements is particularly apparent at the beginning of the first movement's development (mm. 130ff.), where Schoenberg assigned the motivic material, originally presented by piano and strings in dialogue form, to many different instruments, thus heightening the drama of this passage. In subdividing the musical lines timbrally, he rendered the acoustic information much more complex. Yet he sometimes limited the color palette: In the middle section of the third movement "Andante con moto," he stressed the ominous emotional qualities latent in the march-like chamber textures with garish and thick brushstrokes to produce massive effects. Schoenberg's severe treatment of this section not only recalls Mahler's gloomy marches, but also hints at the relentless goose-stepping of Hitler's soldiers at that time.[188]

The transcription process, involving a projection of a small number of parts onto twenty-four voices, sometimes necessitated the composition of new lines derived from existing parts and the increased use of octave doublings, atypical of both Brahms's works and Schoenberg's dodecaphonic music. It also led to nonidiomatic instrumental writing and a more difficult execution of the parts than Schoenberg had typically used to challenge the performers of his music.

Schoenberg created a hybrid work, which subtly fuses familiar and unfamiliar elements and demonstrates his adaptation and resistance to expectations. When Klemperer premiered the Piano Quartet on May 7, 1938, with the Los Angeles Philharmonic, he fulfilled Schoenberg's wish "to hear everything" in this work.[189]

Klemperer himself found the arrangement "magnificent" and even confessed to Peter Heyworth: "one does not want to listen to the original quartet anymore."[190] Schoenberg's student, composer Lou Harrison, praised it as "perhaps the most penetrating, emphatic, and beautiful orchestration (as such) ever made."[191] Other reactions were less enthusiastic, deploring the transcription's "loss of concentration of utterance," lack "of many of the finest effects of the original," and "elephantiasis."[192] In addition to Klemperer and Schoenberg himself, Artur Rodzinski, Frederick Stock, Leon Barzin, Richard Burgin, and Charles Munch conducted this work during Schoenberg's lifetime. In 1966 George Balanchine choreographed the work and premiered it with the New York City Ballet, where it has remained in active repertory. The Brahms arrangement was Schoenberg's last completed orchestration of a classical work.

Three Folksong Settings, Opus 49

In 1948 Schoenberg, aged seventy-four, arranged three German folksongs for mixed choir a cappella. One of the very few American Schoenberg compositions to feature the German language, it was his last completed tonal work and unquestionably emphasizes his German identity, suggesting nostalgia as a reason behind these settings. Schoenberg was quite fond of folk music, as Hanns Eisler remembered:

> Folk music gave Schoenberg a good deal of pleasure. His arrangements of folk songs are outstanding. He also arranged waltzes by Johann Strauss and wrote variations on the song 'Es ist ein Ros' entsprungen' . . . In his original works, however, he could do nothing with folk music. He considered folk music, by comparison with classical music, to be a primitive early form, which the classical composers had already assimilated in any case. And so he attached himself to the classicists. Yet one hears popular elements, and indeed Viennese ones, in the melodic structure of even his most advanced works. It sounds as though the ghosts of departed folksongs are invoked, which after all the catastrophes that one has suffered appear pale and distraught.[193]

The origin of these folksong settings, however, was pragmatic. Schoenberg's son-in-law Felix Greissle, the head of the "Serious Music Department" at E. B. Marks since 1946, initiated this work for his new Arthur Jordan Conservatory of Music Choral Series after other possible projects had failed.[194] At first Schoenberg intended to republish his Three Folksong Movements for mixed choir from 1929, and to implement, on Greissle's advice, small changes in the existing settings since their copyright was not protected.[195] But he chose instead to newly arrange for six voices three of his four 1929 folksong settings for voice and piano: "Es gingen zwei Gespielen gut," "Der Mai tritt ein mit Freuden," and "Mein Herz in steten Treuen."[196]

As in his earlier settings, Schoenberg integrated the modal and metrically ambivalent melodies from the fifteenth and sixteenth centuries, in modal and tonal, and double and triple metric textures. Yet the new arrangements are overall more tonal and structurally less complex for at least two reasons. The pieces had to be appropriate for high school choirs. Greissle even advised him to limit the pitch range.[197] Schoenberg himself wanted to explore a new compositional problem: "the aspect between a choral harmonization and a chorale prelude."[198] After the completion of two settings in June 1948, he happily wrote Greissle: "You will probably be surprised about the compass of my new versions. Two of the pieces are more than mere harmonizations or counterpointal [*sic*] elaborations. They are almost independent compositions using the *Volkslieder* as their material. But they are not dissonant but strictly tonal and very close to the stile [*sic*] of the period."[199] All three settings achieve a balance between homophonic and polyphonic textures, and exhibit a greater transparency than his 1929 settings. In all three arrangements major and minor tonality prevails, and modality functions as a color. For this reason, however, Schoenberg's settings do not approach pre-seventeenth-century styles. The first and most sophisticated piece of the group, "Es gingen zwei Gespielen gut," even reveals one of Schoenberg's trademark principles: developing variation. All six stanzas form a unit and, with the exception of the first, develop through growing variation. The other two song settings are simpler and use the same harmonic and textural treatment for every stanza.

Perhaps because of market considerations, the work's chosen title, Three Folksongs, does not emphasize the songs' German identity. From the outset, a bilingual edition with English translations was planned. The songs have English titles: "Two Comely Maidens," "Now May Has Come with Gladness," and "To Her I Shall Be Faithful." The texts seemed to play a secondary role anyway. Schoenberg did the German text underlay at the end of the compositional process and even wondered if the translator could tweak the translation of the upbeat lyrics of "Der Mai tritt ein mit Freuden" to fit the sad character of his setting.[200] Another market-oriented thought was dropped. Initially Schoenberg and Greissle pondered titles or subtitles such as "in Medieval Style," "in Ancient Style," and "in Old Style," to stress the work's tonal character. Yet ultimately Schoenberg recommended including this information in a blurb so that "in order to appease the consumer, he need not be afraid it is in twelve tones."[201] The pieces were advertised as "three easy choral compositions especially written for school choirs."

Unusually, Schoenberg assigned this work an opus number even though none of his other folksong settings and arrangements of classical works possesses one. The idea occurred to him after the work was already published and after he had finished the choral setting of the poem "Dreimal tausend Jahre [Gottes Wiederkehr]" from Dagobert Runes's *Jordan Lieder* (1948). He planned to set one or two more poems from this collection and intended to classify the folksongs as opus 49a and the Runes choruses as opus 49b. Soon, however, his plans changed, and the Runes setting became opus 50a. Even though these arrangements took him ten times longer than he had expected, they were an opportunity to earn an advance against royalties of $300 (about $2,640 in 2009).[202] American music critic Cecil Smith called these settings "ardent," "eloquent," and "supremely singable" and included them "among the few really first-rank contemporary examples of choral technique and expression." He claimed: "I would not trade these songs for a bale of the pallid, pseudo-Elizabethan madrigals and motets most British composers can turn out by the gros."[203] The Masterworks Chorale under Allen Lannom premiered the Folksongs in Los Angeles in June 1949. Other early performances included renditions by Frederick Dorian at Carnegie Tech in Pittsburgh in May 1950 and by the Columbia University Chorus under Jacob Avshalomov in New York in December 1950.

Second Chamber Symphony, Opus 38

Completed in 1939, the Second Chamber Symphony was Schoenberg's fifth original work composed in the United States. Begun in Vienna in 1906 (the year of his First Chamber Symphony's completion) and revisited in 1911 and 1916, the work undoubtedly connects to his Austro-German past. His émigré friend Fritz Stiedry, conductor of The New Friends of Music Orchestra in New York, suggested Schoenberg finish it and convinced the founder of The New Friends of Music, Ira Hirschmann, to recompense the composer for the task.[204] Although Schoenberg did not have to start from scratch to produce this original orchestral work, he was initially reluctant to interrupt his current work on a counterpoint book, and for this reason preferred to transcribe his twelve-tone Suite, op. 29 or Woodwind Quintet, op. 26. Thanks to Stiedry's urging, Schoenberg eventually decided to finish the Second Chamber Symphony.

This work in E-flat minor falls into a period in which Schoenberg produced several tonal works: the Suite in G (1935), *Kol nidre* (1938), and *Variations on a Recitative* (1941). As mentioned earlier, the fact that he composed tonal music at that point in his career has caused more puzzlement and outright criticism than delight. There were many reasons why Schoenberg pursued this direction. In addition to exploring new technical dimensions, his use of tonality points to a nostalgic bond to olden times in his former homeland, and to his continuous and manifold preoccupation with tonality before and after 1933.[205] Schoenberg himself explained that he had always yearned "to return to the older style" and that he "had to yield to that urge."[206] The "musical idea"—an abstract concept underlying all his works—arguably mattered more to him than external stylistic considerations.[207] Thus his employment of tonality also reflects a freedom to resist certain critics' expectations as well as a concern with the tastes of American audiences. Beyond these factors, the prospect of the monetary benefits and public exposure to be garnered from orchestral performances surely must have been an impetus as well.

For Schoenberg, reworking his fragmentary composition was a challenge. Confronting him were 143 measures of a slow ternary first movement in E-flat minor; 86 measures of a quasi-complete exposition of a fast G major sonata-form movement; additional sketches for the development, recapitulation, and transition to the coda; plus Schoenberg's poem "Wendepunkt [Turning Point]," which he may have wanted to set as a melodrama in another section. Not surprisingly, he was left wondering, "What did the author mean here?"[208] Moreover, the "very good, expressive, rich and interesting" material lent itself to a treatment more akin to his Second Quartet than to his current approach. Schoenberg eventually decided to aim at a reconciliation of his former "sense of form" with his present "far-reaching requirements of visible logic."[209]

In the end he finished only two movements, and needed to assure the work's commissioner that it was "not an Unfinished (chamber) Symphony."[210] He made small changes in the first movement's draft and added a coda. For the second movement, he composed a development, recapitulation, and a long coda, which cyclically reinstates thematic material and the first movement's key (E-flat minor), thus rounding off the work. New sketches for a third movement were abandoned. Harmonically, Schoenberg built on the extended tonality of earlier drafts. He combined remotely related tonal triads and quartal harmonies through stepwise motion in the parts, but used more dissonant chordal juxtapositions and disjointed textures in the newly composed portions. He concluded both movements with the same unusual chord progression of #IV-I, as Severine Neff has shown.[211] Moreover, he subjected trichords of the first movement's main theme to serial permutations. Thus he not only hinted at dodecaphony, but also foreshadowed his subsequent fusions of twelve-tone technique and tonal elements in such works as the *Ode* and the Piano Concerto.

Although there is no evidence that this work has a secret program, the content of his poem "Wendepunkt," which Schoenberg had decided to abandon, still resonates with the successions of moods expressed in the two movements. The poem could therefore, as Neff has suggested, be interpreted as a "post festum program."[212] It describes a soul's spiritual journey from mourning and joy to desperation and sadness, with the implication of hope for salvation. The dark first movement and the second movement's coda relate to the soul's repeated states of sadness, and the beginning of the second movement has a cheerful character. Schoenberg himself pointed to this aspect when he mentioned to Stiedry the "exhaustive presentation of musical and *psychic* problems" in the work's two movements.[213] Moreover, he considered "the part immediately before the coda-like epilogue, as anti-climax, expressing a failure."[214] The poem's assertion that luck can be transitory, and that the experience of misfortune and collapse can signify a new beginning, would have had spiritual and historical meaning for Schoenberg. As the work neared completion, Hitler invaded Poland, marking the beginning of World War II.

Initially conceived for eighteen solo instruments and soon thereafter planned for a mid-sized orchestra, the finished Chamber Symphony reflects the size of Stiedry's symphony orchestra, including twenty-eight strings, eight woodwinds, two horns, and two trumpets. Schoenberg regretted, however, that he could not include parts for a bass clarinet, trombone, and tuba.[215] He also reworked the instrumental groupings to suit his current ideas. Instead of heterogeneous instrumental pairings, he opted for the combination of strings, woodwinds, and brass in separate groups. Influenced by his serial writing, he emphasized single lines and shunned octave doublings. In addition to the orchestra version, Schoenberg created an arrangement for two pianos in 1942 to make the work available for chamber-music venues. Stiedry successfully premiered the Chamber Symphony—the first of Schoenberg's late tonal works to receive an opus number—at New York's Carnegie Hall on December 15, 1940. Virgil Thomson found the performance "graceful and clean," the work's harmony "ingenious and intelligent," and its orchestration "unmistakably the work of one of the most profound auditive imaginations in the world." But he considered its "melodic material" despite "a certain meditative intensity . . . on the whole weak."[216] Olin Downes deemed the first movement "beautiful in its formative way, poetic in mood, and admirably worked out," but disliked the second movement.[217] Soon other conductors, including Bernard Herrmann, Klemperer, Monteux, and Stokowski, performed it as well. Herrmann conducted the work in New York for CBS and shared its (noncommercial) recording with Schoenberg, who deemed his rendition "very good, very convincing and expressive."[218] In 1950 the renowned Mexican dancer-choreographer José Limón based his dance "The Exiles" (with a plot about Adam and Eve's flight from Paradise) on this work.[219] Schoenberg's Chamber Symphony follows the trend of many American and émigré composers to expand the symphonic repertoire with such major contributions as Barber's First (1936), Harris's Third (1938), Bernstein's First "Jeremiah" (1942), and Copland's Third Symphony (1946).

Variations on a Recitative for Organ, Opus 40

Variations on a Recitative for Organ of 1941 is another tonal work that unites Schoenberg's German musical heritage with his current compositional interests and the American performers and audiences. Commissioned by William Strickland, editor of the Contemporary Organ Series for music publisher H. W. Gray, it is his last and largest solo work for keyboard and his only completed composition for organ. Although Schoenberg had always had reservations about the organ's great timbral variety and limited capacity for dynamic differentiation, this commission inspired him to begin immediately making sketches for a dodecaphonic organ sonata. Yet after only a few weeks he broke off this project and followed his publisher's wish for a set of variations.

As to the work's retrospective implications, Schoenberg revealed in 1947: "The organ piece represents my *French* and *English Suites*, or, if you want, my *Meistersinger*-Quintet, my *Tristan*-Duet, my Beethoven and Mozart Fugues (who were homophonic-melodic composers), my pieces in Old Style."[220] Beginning with a declamatory eleven-measure theme, followed by ten variations, a cadenza, and a final mirror fugue, the work evokes—thanks to the use of developing variation and complex and cumulative textures—variation sets by Beethoven and Brahms: The concluding fugue specifically recalls Beethoven's "Eroica" and "Diabelli" Variations, as well as Brahms's Variations and Fugue on a Theme of Handel. Schoenberg also evokes Bach through his use of counterpoint and fugue, and his quotation of the "B-A-C-H" motif (transposed a half-step down) in the third exposition of the fugue. Moreover the monophonically stated theme in the bass alludes to the passacaglia principle, and the written-out cadenza hints at the great tradition of organ improvisation.

The treatment of this work's tonality suggests a bow to the conventional tastes of church-music traditions and American audiences. Schoenberg felt that it still offered "many unused possibilities" and that, with this work specifically, he was indeed able to "fill out the gap between my Kammersymphonies [*sic*] and the 'dissonant' music."[221] Perhaps because of the work's profuse chromaticism and constant nonfunctional harmonic changes, he refrained from assigning it a key signature. Its tonality gravitates toward D minor and the work ends on D major, but it is infused with fourth chords (particularly in variations I, VIII, and the cadenza) and serial devices. The recitative-like theme not only includes twelve chromatic pitches, but its units recall the trichordal and hexachordal divisions of twelve-tone rows.[222] Moreover this untransposed and passacaglia-like theme permeates every variation, recalling Schoenberg's use of the basic twelve-tone set in his dodecaphonic Orchestral Variations.[223]

Although Schoenberg may have intended to portray himself as a cultural mediator through this work, it was neither written for a specific American performer nor tailored to an American organ.[224] As it was not a very idiomatically written organ work, Schoenberg authorized renowned organist Carl Weinrich, music director of the Princeton University Chapel, to edit it. He was dissatisfied with the result, however, and later distanced himself from that edition, in which the timbrally rich registration and manual compass reflect the Princeton University Chapel's large organ, rather than his vision of textural transparency.

Although Schoenberg had hoped that soon thousands of American organists would perform the work, both he and his publisher made this goal difficult to achieve. Schoenberg wrote a technically very difficult and lengthy (fifteen-minute) work, and Gray, who had promised a speedy publication in lieu of a commission fee, took six years to make it commercially available.[225] Weinrich's world premiere of the work at the Church of Saint Mary the Virgin in New York on April 10, 1944, prompted good reviews. Virgil Thomson found that "harmonically and contrapuntally it is full of fancy."[226] Other American organists quickly included it in their repertoire, such as Lawrence Petran; Marilyn Mason, who sought Schoenberg's advice on registration issues and made the first recording; H. Endicott Hanson, who performed it on Hammond Organ; Max Miller; and Ludwig Altmann.[227] Schoenberg, along with Copland, Cowell, Piston, Quincy Porter, and Sessions, among others, might not have contributed important works to the American organ repertoire in the 1940s if not for Gray's efforts. With the exception of such composer-organists as Virgil Thomson and Leo Sowerby, few American composers were interested in writing for this instrument at that time. To make the piece more widely available Schoenberg also had it published and performed in an arrangement for two pianos.[228]

The Violin and Piano Concertos

Completed in 1936 and 1942, respectively, the Violin and Piano Concertos, opp. 36 and 42 (Figure 3.7) were the last two of Schoenberg's four concertos. While his first two concertos, one for cello and one for string quartet, are arrangements of compositions by Monn and Handel, which predate his emigration, the Violin and Piano Concertos are original works featuring dodecaphony.[229] Some scholars have argued that they could "in principle have been written in a Nazi-free Germany."[230] However, these pieces, like his other American works, underscore Schoenberg's wistful connection to the German music tradition, while hinting at his Jewish identity and experience of displacement and disclosing his adaptation to his American surroundings.

Both concertos formally and structurally reflect Schoenberg's German musical roots. The Violin Concerto follows the traditional three-movement pattern, with sonata-allegro-form outer movements framing an Andante middle movement, while the Piano Concerto's four-part structure specifically relates to Liszt's First Piano Concerto in E-flat and Brahms's Second Piano Concerto in B-flat, with its four movements played attacca. Both Schoenberg concertos also share with Brahms's work the inclusion of a scherzo. Schoenberg's Piano Concerto, just like Brahms's, features a scherzo as second movement, and his Violin Concerto displays a little scherzo within the first movement (mm. 93–162) and a scherzando section in the second movement (mm. 344–63). Furthermore, the evocation of military marches in both concertos, and the Piano Concerto's allusions to the waltz (first movement's first theme) and the gavotte (fourth movement) seem to recall the bygone musical life in Vienna—specifically, Mahler's marches and Bach's suites. Bach is also summoned in the Piano Concerto in that his name is inscribed in the first, third, and fourth movements by means of the German musical alphabet.[231] Beyond such references, the Violin Concerto, with its four timpani beats at the first movement's final cadence, cites the opening of Beethoven's Violin Concerto, while its exclusion of an orchestral exposition points to Mendelssohn's Violin Concerto. The piano solo opening of his Piano Concerto, a device relatively rare in the literature, brings to mind Beethoven's Fourth Piano Concerto.

Schoenberg's use of dodecaphony—the Violin Concerto was the second and the Piano Concerto the fourth twelve-tone work that he completed in the United States—can be interpreted as both accepting and resisting external pressures. With these very public works, he not only defied rumors about his potential opportunism and capitulation as a dodecaphonist, but also opposed the enemies of modernism in demonstrating his creative freedom. As he deemed the twelve-tone technique his most important contribution to "German music," its use in the concertos can be read as attesting to his German identity. However, dodecaphony can also be interpreted as a reflection of his Jewish identity (a topic discussed later in this chapter) in

FIGURE 3.7.
Piano Concerto Autograph, mm. 325–34. Courtesy Belmont Music Publishers.

that his concern with one overriding musical idea, such as a twelve-tone row underpinning an entire work, coincides with the Jewish concept of "ethical monotheism."[232]

Both concertos belong to Schoenberg's mature twelve-tone oeuvre, as they are based on one single referential twelve-tone set featuring hexachordal inversional combinatoriality (whereby the set's two halves are inversionally related). Schoenberg used the set in linear statements and often let melodic units coincide with the spelling-out of twelve-tone rows, in an effort to achieve clarity and make dodecaphony go hand in hand with his classically oriented phrasing. He also treated hexachords as harmonic entities with the referential hexachord functioning as a tonic. Yet these works sound quite dissimilar, because of their sets' very different intervallic make-up. While the Violin Concerto's row includes mostly semitones and tritones, conditioning dissonant and sharper sonorities, the Piano Concerto's basic row contains several minor and major thirds, alluding to B-flat major, F-sharp minor, and C major.[233] Additionally, the Piano Concerto, unlike the Violin Concerto, features textures with abundant rhythmic-metrically emphasized consonant sounds as well as tonal implications inherent in the work's horizontal and vertical structure, and orchestrational octave doublings.

Both concertos can also be interpreted as reflections of Schoenberg's fate as a German Jew in the wake of Hitler's rise to power. Yet in the case of the Violin Concerto, one can only speculate about the meaning of the sigh-like figures in the outer movements and the fierce march sections and poignant final outburst of the finale. Schoenberg left no other clue than the possibility of a secret program. "For sometime I have not been against program music," he told American composer Marion Bauer in 1934. "I feel that it is impossible for anything to come out of a composer that is not within that composer, and in that way there is a place for romanticism and the program."[234] For the Piano Concerto, however, Schoenberg provided programmatic hints. The first lyrical movement in a free sonata or strophic form is characterized by a phrase alluding to the pre-1933 era, "Life was so easy." The second and third movements, an aggressive scherzo and a lament-like adagio, vividly illustrate the dire consequences of Hitler's aggressions with the respective mottos "Suddenly hatred broke out" and "A grave situation was created." The phrase for the gavotte-like final rondo, "But life goes on," alludes to those who after escaping Nazi Europe were able to continue their lives elsewhere.[235] Schoenberg backed this program with semantically relevant themes and motives including the opening "Viennese waltz" theme, marking the first movement, and a dotted motif labeled "Hatred," which appears in the course of the first movement and figures prominently in the second movement (Figure 3.8).[236]

Moreover, musicologist Peter Petersen has shown that the Piano Concerto's twelve-tone set may specifically refer to Schoenberg's Jewish identity. According to Petersen, the concerto's row reveals a kinship to the *Kol nidre* melody, which Schoenberg had employed in his *Kol nidre* setting four years earlier (this work emphasizing his Jewish identity is discussed later).[237] The *Kol nidre*'s motives, G–F-sharp–D and D–F-sharp–G are intervallically mirrored in the first hexachords of P-4 and I-9 (Figure 3.9) and their transpositions.

Finally, these concertos, although devoid of any overt "Americanisms," also exhibit Schoenberg's distinctive response to his new environment. In choosing to write solo concertos, a genre showcasing performance virtuosity, he may have wanted to reach out to the largely performer-centered American concertgoers. He may also have calculated that solo-concerto performances in large venues would yield more revenues and more attention from the press than would renditions of intimate chamber works. For the Violin Concerto he possibly had Jascha Heifetz in mind; for the Piano Concerto, his American student, the brilliant Gershwin-pianist Oscar Levant. Neither of these plans materialized, however. Heifetz's alleged reason for refusing to perform the work—namely, that he needed to grow a sixth finger on his left hand—points to the difficulty of the writing for violin and the idiosyncratic way in which Schoenberg treated the role of the soloist. The concertante principle, which often implies decorative nonthematic passagework for virtuosity's sake, was incompatible with Schoenberg's aversion to ornament and fondness for sophisticated motivic-thematic integration, developing variation, and counterpoint. Thus, in the Violin Concerto, the solo part is laced with many small and large cadenzas, yet largely integrated in the motivic-thematic fabric of the orchestra. The types of virtuosity, such as the use of multiple stops, harmonics, arpeggios, octaves, and

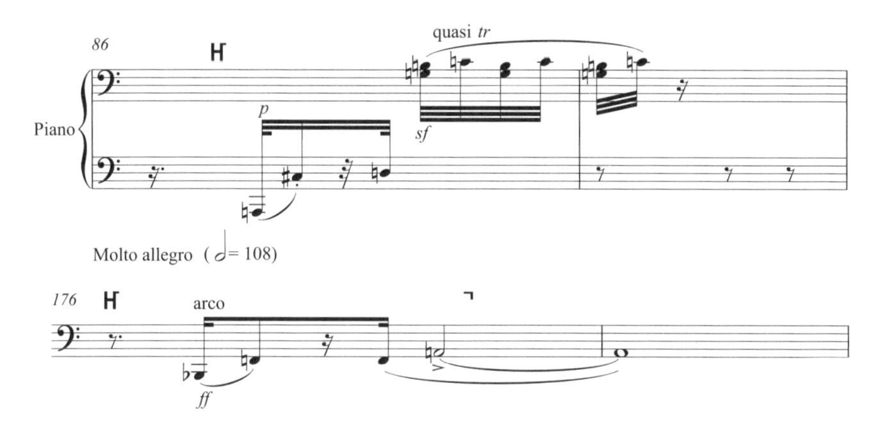

FIGURE 3.8.
Piano Concerto, "Hatred Motif," movement 1, mm. 86–87, and movement 2, mm. 176–77. Courtesy Belmont Music Publishers.

FIGURE 3.9.
Kol nidre opening (version of Baruch Schorr) and Piano Concerto, tone row P-4: 1–6 and I-0: 7–12. Courtesy Belmont Music Publishers.

percussive effects, although extremely difficult, are neither theatrical and flashy, nor always sonically lush. In contrast, the Piano Concerto allows for more artistic brilliance with a more dramatic interaction of soloist and orchestra, and features more playful, virtuosic, and not always thematically integrated repetitive configurations (rapidly alternating chords, arpeggios, trills, tremolos, octave passages). This approach to virtuosity is one of the reasons why the Piano Concerto, despite its structural sophistication, is aurally more accessible and pleasing than his Violin Concerto. Levant did not perform this work, although he inspired Schoenberg to write it. Having asked for a short piano piece, Levant withdrew from the commission when the piece grew into a concerto and the fee increased from $100 to $1,000 (about $1,300–13,000 in 2009). Henry Clay Shriver took over the commission and became the work's dedicatee.

Dedicated to Webern and published in 1939, the Violin Concerto was premiered in 1940 by the Philadelphia Orchestra under Stokowski with Louis Krasner as soloist. The orchestra, audience, and critics overwhelmingly responded with fierce resistance. It was deemed "disagreeable and displeasing even to those well-accustomed and hardened to the harmonic acerbities, jerky rhythms, and ungracious melodic lines of much 'modern' music."[238] The work had been somewhat neglected until Hilary Hahn's recent ear-opening and award-winning recording of the work lent it new appeal.

Premiered in 1944 by the NBC Orchestra under Stokowski with Steuermann as soloist, the Piano Concerto initially received mixed responses and later was dismissed by progressives as a betrayal of modernism and by conservatives as being too advanced.[239] Yet such critiques undoubtedly ignore the fact that this concerto in particular reflects Schoenberg's three identities. In defiance of all the negative verdicts, however, the work has, according to Alfred Brendel, found "a firm place in the repertory" and "has held its own whilst most piano concertos of the Schoenberg generation have paled."[240]

The String Trio, Opus 45 and *Phantasy for Violin with Piano Accompaniment*, Opus 47

The String Trio and *Phantasy for Violin with Piano Accompaniment* are Schoenberg's last two chamber works and his last purely instrumental compositions written after World War II. They evoke his past and present in imaginative ways, but unlike the concertos, these two highly expressive dodecaphonic works have a private and very unconventional character.

Schoenberg composed the Trio in the summer of 1946 in response to a commission from Harvard University's music department, earning him a fee of $750 (about $8,150 in 2009). He began making sketches in June, but the compositional process was interrupted in early August when he suffered a severe heart attack and cardiac arrest. Saved by an adrenalin injection directly into his heart and over one hundred subsequent penicillin injections, he resumed work on the Trio three weeks later. While being cared for around the clock by a male nurse—"an enormous person, a former boxer, who could pick me up and put me down again like a sofa cushion"—he finished the work from his bed and armchair in late September.[241] As Schoenberg confided to Eisler, Thomas Mann, Leonard Stein, and Adolph Weiss, among others, his Trio was programmatic, for he musically depicted his illness and specific medical procedures. Yet ultimately he refrained from sharing the work's program with the general public and providing any further clues.

Like most of Schoenberg's other American works, the Trio refers to his German musical past in various ways. The references, however, are very different here. The one-movement form, with its three so-called "actions" and two connecting "episodes," contains allusions to the sonata, scherzo, waltz, traditional period structure, sonata-form principle, fugue, and recitative.[242] But such suggestions are now more fleeting and only vaguely reminiscent of late Beethoven and Brahms. In the Trio's recapitulative last part, Schoenberg even undermined one of his most important principles, the necessity of constant and developing variation, when he almost literally repeated the first part. The most striking feature of the Trio, however, is its heterogeneous and fragmented musical surface, brimming with impetuous outbursts, jagged contours, manifold colors, and abrupt, sharp contrasts—an approach unmistakably reminiscent of his pre–World War I expressionist style. Yet unlike its early expressionist equivalents, the Trio combines immediate expressivity with sophisticated dodecaphonic procedures that involve, quite unusual for Schoenberg, two basic combinatorially interrelated sets that are very flexibly treated. One is a twelve-tone set falling into two hexachords, the other an eighteen-note set divided into three hexachords.[243]

The Trio's appearance as a "broken" sonata; its tension between adherence to and freedom from Schoenberg's compositional precepts; its conflict between spontaneity and construction; its abrupt combination of agitated and serene gestures; its constant destabilizing of stabilizing processes; its juxtaposition of perfect triads, dissonance, and even noise-like sonorities (produced through such extended techniques as *col legno battuto* and *tratto* and *sul ponticello* played not near, but on the bridge); and its unsettling ending (mm. 292–93): all these can be related to Schoenberg's distinct biographical circumstances.[244] The vacillation between turmoil, trauma, repose, and peace in this radically individualistic work not only points to his delirious experience between life and death, but also to his agony as a surviving German Jew who tried to cope with the horrific revelations emerging from the Nazi concentration camps.[245] Note that Schoenberg completed *A Survivor from Warsaw* just a year after his Trio.

Certain aspects of the Trio arguably imply American influences. Its conception in one movement came about in response to the commissioner's request for a twenty-minute-long work, for Schoenberg found that this length was "too short for three or four movements."[246] Schoenberg did not find it too mundane to pay tribute to his American physician, Dr. Lloyd Jones, and his heavyweight nurse, as indicated in the Trio's program. Thus in one radical step he reduced the gap between ordinary life and highbrow art (an approach later explored in depth by his student John Cage). One may also speculate whether the montage-like juxtaposition of contrasting musical events, the pointed use of caesuras, and the temporal design in the Trio are indebted to film-editing techniques. Arnulf Mattes drew attention to Schoenberg's precise time chart for the Trio, which indicates, just as in filmic editing, the breakdown of the timing for each event (Figure 3.10).[247]

The Walden Quartet gave the Trio's world premiere (along with Walter Piston's Third and Bohuslav Martinů's Sixth String Quartets) on the occasion of a symposium on music criticism at Harvard University in May 1947. Among the small but distinguished audience was John Cage, Chinese-American composer Chou Wen-chung, Robert Mann from the Juilliard Quartet, Eugene Lehner from the former Kolisch Quartet, and "Schoenberg-minded" members of the Boston Symphony.[248] The critical response was mixed. One reviewer insisted, "Had the symposium done nothing but produce this Trio, it would have been amply justified"; another, however, felt that the Trio's alleged lack of "connecting tissue" was "alien to Schoenberg's methods."[249] Published in 1950, the virtuoso score included several *ossia* versions to make it more performable. Before Schoenberg's death the Trio also received performances by the Koldofsky Trio in Los Angeles and by the Pro Arte Quartet in Madison and Chicago, and was presented in radio broadcasts.

Schoenberg had been pleased by the Koldofsky Trio's West Coast premiere of his String Trio in 1948, and violinist Adolf Koldofsky, an Ysaÿe student, commissioned the *Violin Phantasy*. Composed in 1949 and dedicated to Koldofsky, this concise nine-minute work shares several features with the String Trio. It is cast in one movement, and, with its expository opening, slow lyrical section, brief scherzo, and compressed recapitulation, it fleetingly suggests such traditional structural principles as sonata and sonata form. It also nostalgically summons the Viennese waltz and the Austrian Ländler in passing gestures throughout, especially in the grazioso section. Like the Trio, the *Phantasy* combines a highly expressive kaleidoscopic musical surface with a twelve-tone foundation marked by hexachordal inversional combinatoriality, the use of ordered and unordered hexachords, and tonal implications.

Since Schoenberg chose "Phantasy" as the work's title, he may have wanted to underscore connections to Bach's Chromatic Fantasy and Fugue, C. P. E. Bach's work (which Koldofsky extensively explored in the 1940s), Mozart's C minor Fantasia, K. 475, Beethoven's Phantasie, op. 77, or even Beethoven's Sonatas quasi una fantasia, op. 27.[250] More explicitly, the title highlights his music's "unhindered flow" that "can not be traced back to any kind of formal theories," including some of Schoenberg's own previously established compositional principles.[251] It also points

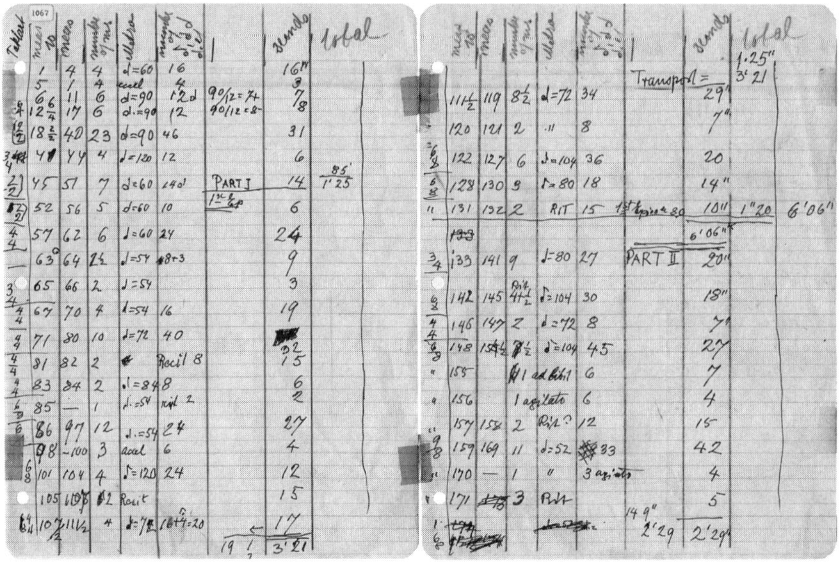

FIGURE 3.10.
Timing chart for String Trio, excerpt. Courtesy Belmont Music Publishers.

to the work's tension between formal disintegration and coherence, and justifies the work's unusual instrumentation for solo violin with a secondary, purely accompanimental piano part, composed after the completion of the violin part.

Although the *Phantasy* is not as dramatic and overtly autobiographical as the String Trio, it allows similar readings. The *Phantasy's* fragments of a "broken" sonata and splinters of waltzes and Ländler may be seen as nostalgic symbols of a European culture shattered by the Nazis. Moreover, the *Phantasy*, coincidentally or not, points to Schoenberg's Jewish identity and spiritual quest at that time. As Mattes discovered, Schoenberg included in the *Phantasy's* lento section an ethereal violin passage (mm. 40–51) with a remarkable affinity to the opening off-stage violin solo of *Jakobsleiter*'s "Great Symphonic Interlude" (the movement following "The Dying One").[252] He contemplated this oratorio's completion in the 1940s and pondered the preparation of a performable version in the early 1950s when he knew he would not finish it (Figure 3.11).

The *Phantasy* also bears the stamp of America. It was initiated by a Canadian musician, who settled in Los Angeles in 1945 and performed in the RKO Studio Orchestra. Schoenberg gave his work an English title, which allows for a broader range of interpretations than its German equivalent does. It not only connotes a musical genre, and an imaginative or wild and visionary fancy, but also (unreal) mental images with blurred continuity, as in a daydream. The *Phantasy* shares the Trio's montage-style juxtaposition of musical units, underscored by the broad spectrum of instrumental colors—a phenomenon associated with film. However, the *Phantasy* is more accessible than the Trio and thus seems to reach out to American audiences. Not only are its sections short and clearly articulated, but its musical texture also alludes to G minor and major keys and other consonant harmonies. Schoenberg, who cautioned that "composing with twelve tones is not nearly as forbidding and exclusive a method as is popularly believed," had become less dogmatic. To those who doubted if some of his works were "pure twelve-tone or twelve-tone

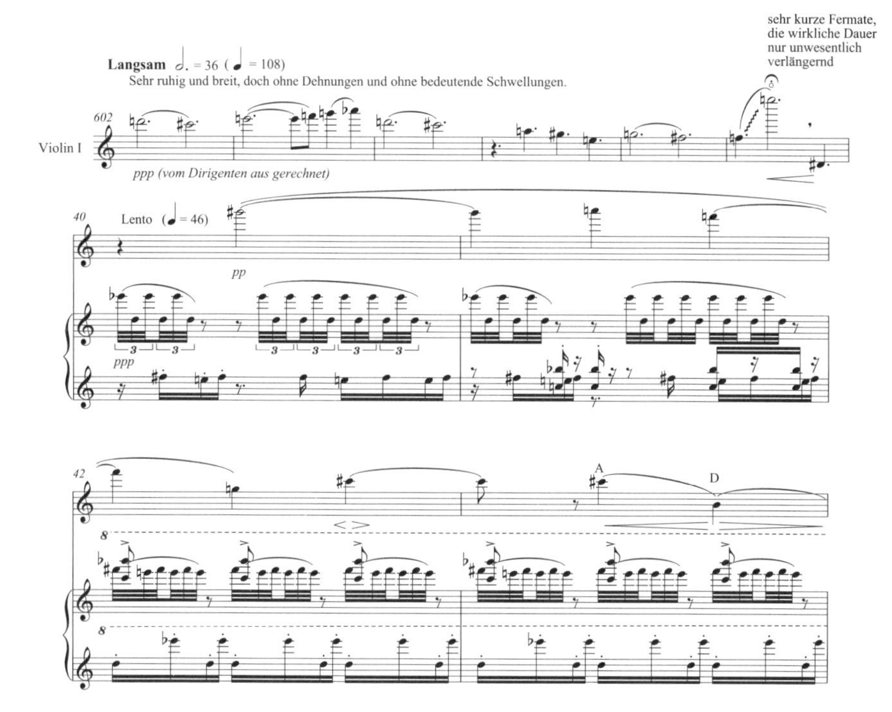

FIGURE 3.11.
Jakobsleiter, mm. 602–7, and *Phantasy for Violin*, mm. 40–44. *Jakobsleiter* courtesy Belmont Music Publishers; Phantasy © 1952 Henmar Press Inc., all rights reserved, used by permission.

at all," he replied: "Whether certain of my compositions fail to be 'pure' because of the surprising appearance of some consonant harmonies—surprising even to me—I cannot, as I have said, decide. But I am sure that a mind trained in musical logic will not fail even if it is not conscious of everything it does."[253]

After Schoenberg's assistants Richard Hoffmann and Leonard Stein had played through the virtuoso *Phantasy* to ensure its "feasibility," Koldofsky and Stein premiered it as part of an all-Schoenberg concert of the International Society for Contemporary Music in Los Angeles on September 13, 1949, Schoenberg's seventy-fifth birthday. Schoenberg praised Koldofsky's "convincing performance" and "deep understanding and feeling of the meaning and expression" of the work.[254] The first audience and critics' responses were equally positive.[255] Before the *Phantasy*'s publication in 1952, Koldofsky and pianist Edward Steuermann gave the work's New York premiere and recorded it. Violinist Nathan Rubin and composer-pianist Earl Kim also performed the *Phantasy* for Schoenberg and in West Coast recitals.

SCHOENBERG'S JEWISH IDENTITY

Just as Schoenberg's German identity was manifest during his American years, his sense of Jewishness was evident as well.[256] Shortly before his immigration to the United States, he emphatically reaffirmed his Jewish identity. He stated: "I have been prepared for fourteen years for what has happened now . . . I have definitely separated myself from whatever binds me to the Occident. I have long since been resolved to be a Jew."[257] Elsewhere he remarked, "We are Asians and nothing essential binds us to the West. We have our [biblical] promise, and no other temptation can more honor us! . . . our essence is not Western; the latter is only an external borrowed one. We must return to our origins, to the source of our strength, to the place where our toughness originates and where we shall rediscover our ancient fighting spirit."[258] When he arrived in America, his Jewish consciousness deepened, perhaps because, as the Israeli sociologist Shmuel Noah Eisenstadt stated, in the United States "a Jew could be, or at least aspire to be, accepted as part of the American collectivity without giving up some type of Jewish collective identity and activities."[259] Even though America was not immune to anti-Semitism, it allowed Schoenberg to gain his self-esteem as a Jew and to come to terms with his Jewish identity in new ways.[260] In a 1934 speech he proclaimed: "I was driven into paradise!"[261] Like many other Jewish emigrants, he shaped his Jewish identity in response to contemporary events and his specific environment, and in accordance with his own idiosyncratic ideas.[262] Schoenberg even classified Jewry into twenty-seven groups, identifying a variety of ethnic, religious, and political categories, perhaps in an effort to discover to which kind he belonged (Figure 3.12).[263] Yet it seems that he himself could not fit easily into any of his own established groupings. Schoenberg manifested his Jewish identity in some of his views, his political activism, and his interactions with Jewish thinkers, writers, and artists, as well as in his music.

Schoenberg's Jewish Perspective

Many of Schoenberg's perceptions, activities, and statements during his American years can be understood from the viewpoint of his experience as a German Jew and his emphatic self-identification as a Jew.[264] Unlike the identities of traditionally religious

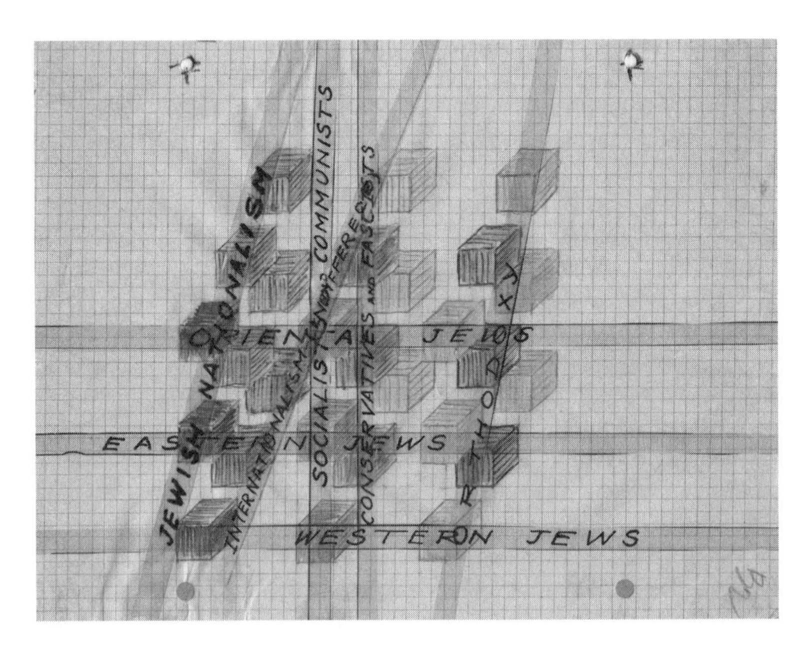

FIGURE 3.12.
Schoenberg's classification of Jewry, excerpt. Courtesy Belmont Music Publishers.

Jews, which are defined by an unwavering faithfulness to the Torah, Schoenberg's identification with Jewishness was strongly affected by the secularization of the Jewish tradition. As a result, he freely selected and reinterpreted Jewish ideas and contributed to what has been termed the Jewish "cultural memory" of secular Jews. Rooted in "fateful events in the past," cultural memory is a self-reflexive and dynamic form of knowledge "specific to a particular group, and by means of which the group bases its consciousness of its unity and specificity."[265]

Much of Schoenberg's rhetoric is marked by a "lachrymose" perspective, which was strongly influenced by the way many Jews have perceived Jewish history and their role as outsiders within host societies.[266] "For the religious thinker," Steven Cahn explained, "the entire period since the destruction of the Temple and subsequent exile is one of unrelieved sorrow that awaits redemption."[267] Religious and secular Jews alike struggled with the feeling of "Jewish pariahism and homelessness which the emancipation had failed to resolve."[268] Schoenberg came to terms with pariahism by "removing all conspicuous features" through a conformation to European lifestyles and change of religion. However, he "became more conspicuous through very special achievements" in the arts that brought him a measure of fame and acceptance in the cultural elite: "a secular version of the chosen people" in society.[269] Schoenberg felt he was chosen to counter the prevailing musical conservatism in his exploration of musical truth and logic (rather than beauty), and he became a highly individualistic and controversial outsider rather than a widely accepted member of the cultural elite. The heavy burden of this role is reflected in his lachrymose rhetoric in both Europe and America, as in the following statement: "Nationalistic musicians regard me as *international*, but abroad my music is regarded as too *German*. National Socialists regard me as a *cultural Bolshevik*, but the communists reject me as *bourgeois*. Anti-Semites personify me as a Jew, my direction as Jewish, but almost no Jews have followed my direction."[270]

Schoenberg often evoked the Judaic notion of chosenness, which became a dominant issue in religious and secular contexts of American Jewry from the 1940s on. Arnold Eisen argued that the "conviction of election enabled relatively secular American Jews . . . to weave a definition of self from the fabric of tradition."[271] Inspired by the biblical figure of Moses, Schoenberg saw himself as elected against his will to the role of the leading pioneer of musical modernism. After Hitler's accession to power, Schoenberg planned to sacrifice his art. Propelled by a prophetic vision, he believed that it was his "duty as a Jew" to initiate and temporarily lead a Zionist mission in the United States and save God's chosen people from their plight in Europe. He stated: "let people follow me until someone else turns up. In the meantime, no one is going to stop me."[272] In 1946 he imagined himself as the chosen "president of the government in exile of the Jewish nation on a ship."[273] Schoenberg's belief in elitism and chosenness, and his aspiration toward leadership, however, provoked controversy and the reproach of snobbery and racial chauvinism.[274] Not surprisingly, this role left him feeling misunderstood and isolated—"no less lonely than Moses after Sinai."[275] In his 1937 speech "How One Becomes Lonely" he poignantly stated: "I had to fight for every new work; I had been offended in the most outrageous manner by criticism . . . I stood alone against a world of enemies. Alone, with one exception: that small group of faithful friends, my pupils."[276] Schoenberg elaborated on his loneliness throughout his career, although his perception was often out of touch with reality.

While his rhetoric in America frequently reflects his general sense of artistic solitude, it also points to his forced separation from his former cultural environment. In

1939 he satirized Rudolf Sieczyński's famous song "Wien, Du Stadt meiner Träume (Wienerlied)" (Vienna, City of My Dreams—Vienna Song), rewording its refrain as follows: "Vienna, Vienna, you alone have to be despised by everyone! Others may possibly be forgiven, but you will never be free from guilt. You must perish, only your shame shall endure! You are stigmatized for all eternity by falseness and hypocrisy."[277] Dika Newlin reported that Schoenberg and his friends performed the song at his sixty-sixth birthday party and drank whiskey "to the doom of Vienna!"[278] Ten years later Schoenberg pondered about his former Austro-German compatriots in an even graver tone:

> You, who hate us, watch out . . . We lived with you for two thousand years and we got to know you. We know all your weaknesses, we know which unworthiness you value. We brought you culture . . . We brought you ethics, justice and law through our ten commandments . . . We showed you that we are your equals in all of your arts and science. Nonetheless you despised, avoided and excluded us where you could do without our help. Would it be strange if we desired retribution? It is our status as an old people that determines that we refuse revenge, but settle up as is appropriate: in that we continue to be giving.[279]

His sense of solitude certainly points to his traumatic expulsion from Nazi Germany, yet he did not see himself as an exile from Germany. Such statements as "Palestine is our land. There we belong. There we must manage to get to," and his singling out of Jerusalem as the place where he "would so much like to live," reveal that Schoenberg identified with the existential longing of Jews in the Diaspora to return to the Promised Land, even though he occasionally described America with Zionist images like the Promised Land and paradise.[280] In 1951 he noted: "For more than four decades it has been a most cherished wish of mine to see erected an independent Israeli state. And more than that: to become a citizen residing in this state."[281]

The theme of loneliness also surfaced in Schoenberg's reflections about his sense of belonging to Jewry and his acceptance among Jews. Although he interacted with many Jews and Jewish organizations in America, Schoenberg was a supreme individualist and joined only a few Jewish musical and political groups; never did he belong to a religious community. His nonidentification with a religious community, however, was not unusual in America, where "group membership was considered strictly a private matter" and nonmembership did not entail "communal penalty or public sanction."[282] Yet Schoenberg was very concerned about his status as a composer and his acceptance among Jews. Already in the 1920s he felt that anti-Semitism harmed his music's Jewish reception, complaining to Albert Einstein that "in their hatred of me, the Jews and the Swastika bearers are of one mind."[283] In America, he continued to single out the Jews' supposed lack of interest in his music: "According to my experience, Jews look at me rather from a racial standpoint than from an artistic. They accordingly give me a lower rating than they give to their Aryan idols."[284] He also stated: "It is curious that Jews are always the last ones to accept my achievements, whether in Israel or in the rest of the world. They perform everything: Debussy, Ravel, Hindemith, Stravinsky, Shostakovich, Bartók etc.—but not me! In spite of my contributions, they are my greatest enemies!"[285] Even though such statements do not reflect the fact that Schoenberg had many Jewish supporters, they do reveal his uncertainty about belonging. By and large he perceived himself as an outsider from the Jewish community, despite his desire to become fully accepted by this group.[286]

Schoenberg tirelessly worked toward that goal. However, he was unable to gauge his music's reception and blind to its successes, and became ever more vulnerable to criticism and increasingly worried about his legacy. He progressively identified himself more with the role of a martyr. "Trained in martyrdom," he stated, "the Jew is a ready martyr on every mental front."[287] He also believed that "martyrdom is a specifically Jewish profession."[288] In his last years he felt that he had to struggle against a host of enemies and thieves of his music and thus confided to God in his Psalm No. 3: "I will never understand these criminals, who steal from me and rob me, lead a comfortable life in need and care. Is this just?"[289] The image of him as a martyr emerges most vividly in his 1947 address to the National Institute of Arts and Letters (often dubbed the "Boiling-Water Speech"): "Personally I had the feeling as if I had fallen into an ocean of boiling water, and not knowing how to swim or to get out in another manner, I tried with my legs and arms as best I could. I did not know what saved me; why I was not drowned or cooked alive . . . I have perhaps only one merit; I never gave up."[290]

Just as Jacob in his struggle with the angel endured pain and injury to be blessed (Genesis 32:28–29), Schoenberg was determined to persevere in his struggle for the survival of his art. Motivated by historical consciousness and a belief in history as a progressive process within which he saw himself as a major player, he hoped for belated success.[291] In his open letter to his well-wishers on his seventy-fifth birthday, he asked: "Is it readily understandable, that one does not give up, though facing the opposition of a whole world?" He expected "to become recognized only after his death" and joked that "the second half of this century will spoil by overestimation, all the good of me that the first half, by underestimation, has left intact."[292]

His discussion of his health and finances was also a part of his lachrymose rhetoric. He addressed his aches and illnesses time and again, while such contemporaries as Stravinsky (who suffered from just as many if not more illnesses) avoided this topic.[293] Throughout his American career Schoenberg felt that he did poorly financially, yet that feeling of hardship applies only to the time after his retirement in 1944.[294]

Schoenberg's lachrymose perspective was his way of coping with the major moments in modern German-Jewish history he lived through: the deceptive promises of the emancipation, assimilation, and secularization, the Jewish (and his own artistic) participation in modernity, the escalation of anti-Semitism, the annihilation of millions of European Jews in the Holocaust, the act of *teshuva*, emigration, and life in the Diaspora.[295] His outlook, however, should not be interpreted as an expression of complete pessimism. On the contrary, it was an inspiring force that fueled his fighting spirit, productivity, and creativity, and was accompanied by an unfailing ethical idealism and hope for events, some of which came true during his lifetime. The Jewish philosopher André Neher summed up Schoenberg's Jewish experience in America as follows: "Far from estranging him, America, on the contrary, drew him closer to the two contradictory phases of Jewish history which took place in Europe and Asia, and which Schönberg witnessed: the Shoa and the creation of the State of Israel . . . Moses did not enter the Promised Land but his people entered it . . . Thus, Schönberg saw events come full circle."[296]

POLITICAL ACTIVISM

Determined to focus on political activism after Hitler's rise to power, Schoenberg quickly chose, upon receiving a job offer from the Malkin Conservatory, to come to America because he considered it the best place both for the Jews and for the realization of his political projects. He explained:

> I had contacted prominent Jewish people intending to move them to start the right action. Among them were many Americans whom I considered the most useful, because America was and is in many respects the promised land, especially in what concerns the hopes of Jewry. It was my desire to come to America and start here that movement which in my belief offers the only way out of our problems. Therefore, when suddenly I was offered a position, although it was neither financially nor artistically commensurate with my reputation, I accepted at once, sacrificed my European chances and went over to do what I considered my duty as a Jew.[297]

Upon his arrival in America, Schoenberg fervently dedicated himself to the Jewish national cause, which he thought to be even "more important than [his] art."[298] He wrote: "I have decided to give up all my former activities as a composer, writer, music theorist and so forth, and to do from now on only one thing: to work for the salvation of the Jews."[299]

Schoenberg, interested in Zionism since the early 1920s, intended to lead a new and powerful Zionist movement in America with the goal of rescuing his fellow European Jews and offering them an independent state. Although critical of some of the foremost Zionists and never bound to any specific Zionist tendencies, in the 1920s he was close to Theodor Herzl's idea of a provisional Jewish state outside of Palestine, a fact reflected in his activist drama *Der biblische Weg* (1927).[300] With Vladimir Jabotinsky, the Revisionist Zionist and leader of the Jewish militant organization Irgun, he shared a belief in the urgency of a Jewish state and the use of arms to reach this goal. With Zionist writer Jakob Klatzkin, he had a common desire that the land of Israel be taken back to terminate the long historic Jewish diasporic existence. However, Schoenberg believed that boycotts against Germany and denouncements of anti-Semitism were ineffective and would jeopardize the remaining Jews in Europe. He also thought that anti-Semitism could not be successfully battled, for it resulted from the non-Jewish people's envy for Jewry's profusion of extraordinary talent and unique status as God's chosen people. To reach his Zionist goal he called for the replacement of Jewish self-hatred (caused by assimilationist urges) with Jewish self-esteem. Criticizing the disunion of Jews and the multiplicity of Zionist directions as inhibiting factors in the establishment of a Jewish homeland, he suggested in the 1930s the foundation of a new Jewish Unity Party. Under his leadership and with authoritarian means, this party would pursue the unification of the Jewish people and the creation of a free independent Jewish state. An opponent of pacifism, Schoenberg envisioned the militant destruction of Jewry's enemies.

Throughout the 1930s and less frequently in the 1940s, Schoenberg passionately promoted these ideas, producing numerous speeches, aphorisms, letters, and extended texts on Jewish matters. His "Four-Point Program for Jewry," completed shortly before *Kristallnacht*, was in Alexander Ringer's words his "political magnum opus" and an "all-encompassing last-minute call to action."[301] In this document Schoenberg detailed and systematized his previous plans for a Jewish Unity Party and an independent Jewish state in order to provide a practical program for action. He addressed four main themes: (1) "The Fight against Anti-Semitism Must Be Stopped"; (2) "A United Jewish Party Must Be Created"; (3) "Unanimity in Jewry Must Be Enforced with All Means"; and (4) "Ways Must Be Prepared to Obtain a Place to Erect an Independent Jewish State [in Palestine]." With great foresight, he warned that millions of European Jews were in danger and asked in the opening paragraph: "Is there room in the world for almost 7,000,000 people? Are they condemned to doom? Will they become extinct? Famished? Butchered?" He concluded by stressing that "the time of words is over and if action does not start at once, it may be too late."[302] However, Schoenberg was unable to publish this document, although he contacted editors of periodicals and such leading writers as Thomas Mann to help him find a publishing venue.[303] But Mann, like others, understandably took exception to the text's "violent" and "polemic" tone and the content's affinity with fascist principles.[304]

Besides specific rescue efforts for family members and friends, Schoenberg tirelessly wrote letters to important figures who represented Jewish interests in different ways, to draw attention to the urgency of the Jewish situation. He discussed the problem with the Boston-based rabbis Joseph S. Shubow and Samuel J. Abrams.[305] He resumed contact with the influential rabbi Stephen S. Wise, a presidential adviser and Zionist leader, who founded the Free Synagogue of New York (1907) and the Jewish Institute of Religion (1922). The two had met in Paris in 1933.[306] In the spring of 1934 Wise helped arrange an opportunity for Schoenberg to deliver one of his political speeches.[307] Wise had at first appeared to be very helpful to the Schoenbergs, but Schoenberg's skepticism toward internationalism, pacifism, democracy, and assimilation, along with his determination to become the uniter and leader of the Jewish people, may have prevented further contact between them.[308] As a Reform rabbi who represented assimilationist Jews, Wise would have had reservations concerning Schoenberg's anti-assimilationism. Reluctant to promote radical measures against the Nazis in the 1930s, Wise would also have questioned the urgency of Schoenberg's rescue mission. A harsh opponent of the Committee for a Jewish Army, he would have disapproved of Schoenberg's militant solution.[309] Such hurdles notwithstanding, Schoenberg continued to discuss the state of Jewry with other Los Angeles–based religious teachers, such as the prominent American Reform rabbi Edgar Magnin and Silesia-born independent liberal rabbi Jacob Sonderling.

Schoenberg also interacted with such institutions as the Jewish Philanthropic Societies, the Zionist Organization of America, the Jewish Club of 1933, the *Jewish Daily Bulletin*, the American Jewish Congress, the Jewish Agency for Palestine, the Hebrew Sheltering and Immigrant Aid Society, the American Committee for Relief of the Yemenite Jews, and American Friends of the Hebrew University. Underscoring his belief in a militant solution of the Jewish situation, Schoenberg enthusiastically lent his support to the controversial "Committee for a Jewish Army of Stateless and Palestinian Jews," founded in 1941 by Peter Bergson (Hillel Kook) to battle the Nazis and secure Palestine. In a letter to this organization's national chairman, Pierre van Paassen, Schoenberg expressed his regret that he could not serve as a soldier: "Twenty years ago, when I first pronounced this idea, I was still capable of active participation, of becoming a soldier, a fighter myself. This is my only regret, that [at] 68 I am not any more in the state of more than to help with [*sic*] my being a sponsor of such aims."[310] By joining this group Schoenberg became somewhat more visible in the public debate about Zionism. His name appeared as one of many signatories on full-page advertisements in the *New York Times* in 1942 and 1943. J. Edgar Hoover condemned the group as "thoroughly disreputable Communist Zionists."[311]

These political reasons compelled Schoenberg to contact European-born Jewish musicians, writers, and directors. For instance, he informed composer Ernst Toch and cellist Joachim Stutschewsky of his ideas on Jewish politics.[312] Convinced that his Zionist play *Der biblische Weg* would have a "propagandistic effect on the Jewish audience," he tried to get Werfel, Max Reinhardt, and Klatzkin interested in its performance and publication.[313] Yet Reinhardt showed no interest in it, and even

Klatzkin, a radical Swiss-based Zionist philosopher and anti-assimilationist, who thrashed out Jewish matters with Schoenberg from 1930 until his death in 1948, was unable to win over his circle for the play.[314]

Along with his letter-writing campaign, Schoenberg gave speeches on Jewish matters in New York and Los Angeles. One of his first speeches and extended writings in English was titled "Forward to a Jewish Unity Party," which he presented on April 29, 1934, in New York.[315] Organized by Wise and Abraham W. Binder, the Free Synagogue's music director, the event was hosted by the American-Palestine Institute of Musical Sciences (Mailamm).[316] Mailamm was founded in 1931 to advance Jewish music culture in America and Palestine, and included such prominent members as Joseph Achron, Ernst Bloch, Ossip Gabrilowitsch, George Gershwin, Louis Gruenberg, Lazare Saminsky, and Joseph Yasser.[317] Even though Schoenberg spoke to a large musical audience at this event, he argued for unanimity among Jews and for the foundation of a Jewish Unity Party and Jewish state, and addressed music only briefly. His speech was apparently met with warmth and surprise. The event's attendees included Achron, Binder, Mischa Elman, Gabrilowitsch, Gruenberg, and Saminsky; Cantor Gershon Ephros recalled that Schoenberg took "a revised Jabotinsky activist position."[318]

In January 1934 Schoenberg was slated to conduct an orchestra concert at Madison Square Garden in New York to crown the 1933 Campaign of the Jewish Philanthropic Societies, but the event was canceled.[319] Later in spring, however, Schoenberg made an appearance at a Carnegie Hall concert under the auspices of the Council of Jewish Organizations for the Settlement of German-Jewish Children in Palestine and the New York Zionist Region. Although the concert, arranged by Leopold Godowsky, was given in honor of Albert Einstein, Schoenberg too received acknowledgment in that the Kroll Sextet performed *Verklärte Nacht* (Figure 3.13). The event thus showcased two prominent fighters for the Jewish cause who had met (perhaps for the first time) a month earlier in Princeton, when Schoenberg delivered a lecture on twelve-tone composition.[320] Einstein and Schoenberg, however, viewed the Jewish situation very differently. Einstein believed in a spiritual form of Zionism, Jewish internationalism, and pacifism, and favored public denunciations of anti-Semitism. Confronted with Schoenberg's Zionist views in a letter of 1925, Einstein implicitly rejected them by not replying. Schoenberg disagreed with the physicist in an unpublished text, "Einstein's Mistaken Politics," a year before their meeting in the United States.[321] In 1936, however, Schoenberg was named in the *New York Times* as one of the ten greatest Jews, along with Einstein, Louis Brandeis, Martin Buber, Chaim Weizmann, and Wise, among others.[322] In 1942 Schoenberg joined Aaron Copland, Walter Damrosch, Josef Lhevinne, Fritz Mahler, and songwriter Earl Robinson in sponsoring a "Century of the Common Man" dinner at the Hotel Astor, organized by the Joint Anti-Fascist Refugee Committee.[323]

Most of Schoenberg's political activism, however, did not attract encouraging responses. His extreme and provocative ideas failed to resonate with the many American Jews or Zionists who viewed immigration to the British Territory of Palestine in the early 1930s as a viable option for European Jews. When the British limited immigration after Arab revolts in the mid-1930s and subsequently jeopardized the establishment of a Jewish state, American Zionists tended to turn away from European Jewry's plight. They hoped to continue their pursuit of a future Jewish homeland in Palestine, but feared a loss of British support for a Jewish state and an upsurge of anti-Semitism in America.[324]

FIGURE 3.13.
Leopold Godowsky, Albert Einstein, and Schoenberg. Courtesy Arnold Schönberg Center.

Although interested in Jewish politics since World War I, Schoenberg had no practical political experience, something he indirectly admitted in 1938 when referring to his function as the head ("a kind of dictator") of his Society for Private Musical Performances, his only leadership experience.[325] Schoenberg would neither dance to somebody's tune nor play second fiddle; instead he would always "see himself in a 'conductor's role,'" which effectively ruled out collaborations with other major American Zionist leaders or revisions of his politics.[326] Moreover, he did not "feel justified in interfering in American matters, only in Jewish ones."[327] In 1938 he reasoned: "In New York I talked to many prominent Jews against it [the idea of a boycott against Germany] and had always the satisfaction that my argument was never refuted. However, American Jewry was hypnotized by the boycott, and I found no opportunity to express my views in a magazine or newspaper."[328] Schoenberg even explored the idea of publishing his materials by founding his own newspaper in multiple languages, German, French or English, Yiddish, and Hebrew. He also had plans to broadcast his political speeches on his own radio station, to record and disseminate his speeches on disk and film, and to rent an airplane and trailer to bring his message to the most remote areas, but these ideas were never realized either.[329]

By the early 1940s, Schoenberg recognized that his engagement in American Jewish politics had failed. But his vision of himself as a leader and rescuer of the Jewish people—similar to the protagonists Max Aruns of *Der biblische Weg* and Moses of *Moses und Aron* (1932)—found its way into yet another illusory plan in 1946. He envisioned that on

the nth day of the month of (N) there will be a message broadcast (and re-broadcast at an adequate time) to all countries where Jews are living. I will speak to you, saying:

> Here I am, Arn[old] Sch[oenberg]; the President of the Gov[ernment] in Exile of the Jewish Nation. We are on a ship which I received through the generosity of Pr[esident] Tr[uman], the Am[erican] Government and the Am[erican] People . . . The Government in Exile of the Jewish Nation has thus far been recognized by all great powers and by most of the smaller nations . . . The establishment of a Jewish State will not interfere with our awe and longing for our Palestine.[330]

Needless to say, this idea, too, fell on deaf ears.[331] By that time hundreds of thousands of Jews had settled in Palestine and the foundation of the state of Israel was imminent.

Marked by conservatism and authoritarianism, Schoenberg's ideas for a Jewish state and politics could not succeed because they had an unfortunate affinity with the nondemocratic tendencies in European politics prior to 1945. They not only mirrored aspects of monarchism, but, as Alexander Ringer put it, "dangerously paralleled the reasoning of the enemy, and if there was a tragic flaw in Schoenberg's political activities on behalf of the Jewish people, it was precisely his tendency to castigate both the Nazis' bent on genocide and their stunned victims with figures of speech adopted from the totalitarian idiom."[332] After 1946 Schoenberg retreated from Jewish political activism, but continued to deal with Jewry in other forms.

HIS FAITH

Schoenberg's preoccupation with his Jewish identity was not limited to a political and ethical dimension, and his official return to Judaism (an act of *teshuva*) was not a mere political act devoid of spiritual significance. Long before the Nazis' rise to power, he had embraced important principles of the biblically grounded Jewish faith, in particular the belief in the one, eternal, unimaginable, and invisible God, and the idea of the chosenness of the Jewish people. His conversion to Protestantism in 1898 may have been less an effort to "quench his spiritual thirst" than an "act of purely social significance, an entry-ticket to bourgeois society."[333] Just a year after his reconversion to Judaism in 1933, Schoenberg stated, "I have never been convinced by Protestantism; but I had, like most of the artists in my time, a Catholic period."[334] He recalled how, since childhood, he had felt pressured to assimilate into German society "through clothing and adaptation of facial expression, through observation of language use, through a change of religion," and through "extraordinary achievements." He also remembered that by the early 1910s he had realized that despite some social advantages, assimilation did not prevent anti-Semitism. Then he began to wrestle with questions of faith and became aware that

> the religiosity of the Jews had subsided to such a deplorable level that not even the rabbis could provide the drive and the enthusiasm that may have won over the young people to their indigenous religion. The inner, emotional distancing from Judaism was the consequence of non-belief. Jewry is based on its faith. It is nothing without this faith . . . But when they [the Jews] stop to believe, they dig their own graves. For if we are not chosen to preserve the idea, there is no longer any reason why we should continue to exist . . . often it was not godlessness when we adopted their religion, although we henceforth ceased to honor the Only, Eternal One.[335]

Beside privately nurturing a strong personal relationship with God, Schoenberg reflected his Jewish faith in his music and writings, including *Jakobsleiter*; "Du sollst nicht, Du musst," from Four Pieces for mixed choir, op. 27 (1925); *Der biblische Weg*; and *Moses und Aron* (1932). Except for the Four Pieces, these works remained incomplete or unperformed during his lifetime and thus publicly unknown.

Considering his long engagement with Judaism, the question arises whether Schoenberg's official return to Judaism in 1933 was a "return" at all. Neher pointed out that "Jewish religious law does not recognize 'desertion': A Jew, even if converted to another religion, remains Jewish, and there is no need for a special ceremony to mark the return of the renegade to the Jewish fold."[336] The ceremony, however, was conducted upon Schoenberg's insistence, perhaps because, as Neher suggested, "there existed within him, in his life and in his work, an adventure, a drama of *teshuva*."[337] But even if one accepts the idea of Schoenberg's reconversion, one may ask to what Judaism he returned.[338] He never joined Hasidic, Reform, or Liberal Judaism, and was never associated with any specific Zionist group in America, making it difficult to specify his faith. Schoenberg himself seemed to be ambiguous about it, as he stated in 1933: "Now for the last week I have returned to the Jewish religious community, although it is not the religion, which separates me from them (as my *Moses und Aaron* [*sic*] will show) but my view of the necessity of the adaptability of the Church to the demands of modern life."[339] He resisted participation in Jewish communal life and rites, and even turned down individual invitations to attend services, as for instance at the Temple Ohabei Shalom in Brookline. In his reply to that temple's rabbi, he explained: "I would have used the occasion to come in the Temple at the occasion of a divine service. But there is a difficulty: I don't understand enough English . . . and also not Hebrew."[340]

After 1933 Schoenberg's idiosyncratic approach to the Jewish faith remained central to his Jewish identity. Not thoroughly steeped in the Hebrew language and traditional Judaic teachings, he was interested in a modern, unorthodox interpretation of the God-Idea (Gottesgedanke) and in various (musical) forms of prayer. The Bible provided him with spiritual nourishment throughout his life. Having touched on Christian themes in some of his early European works, he only rarely referred to Christianity in America in his art.[341] His late *Modern Psalm No. 9* is one of the few instances of his addressing Jesus in the context of Judaism. He practiced his faith apart from family life, and formal religion was of little significance in the American Schoenberg household.[342] The family celebrated Christian rather than Jewish holidays. Schoenberg's wife had descended from a Jewish family but converted to Catholicism, and did not follow in her husband's footsteps. Schoenberg's children, Nuria, Ronald, and Lawrence, were baptized Catholic, and the boys attended Catholic schools. In a letter to Stokowski in 1950 Schoenberg asked him to be Ronald's sponsor on the occasion of his Catholic confirmation, telling Stokowski: "I am Jewish. But Mrs. Schoenberg is katholic [*sic*], and as she is about a quarter of a century younger than I, I assumed, she will be longer together with my children than I. So I allowed them to be also katholic." Stokowski declined Schoenberg's request on the grounds that he was "not a good practicing Catholic" and disagreed with the Catholic Church's "fixed dogma."[343] Like his family life, Schoenberg's funeral featured a juxtaposition of Jewish and Christian elements. Rabbi Magnin, his longtime friend, held the service at the nonsectarian Wayside Chapel in West Los Angeles.[344] Rejecting as inappropriate the proposal of Schoenberg's colleagues to have excerpts from Mozart's Requiem performed, Magnin instead allowed the performance of Protestant organ music—Schoenberg's favorite Bach chorale preludes—played by his former UCLA colleague Alexander Schreiner, who was the organist of the Salt Lake City Tabernacle and a member of the Mormon Church.[345] Marked by his experience as a secular Jew, Schoenberg's idiosyncratic approach to the Jewish faith, family life, and funeral can be interpreted as examples of dissimilation.

Schoenberg's faith was intertwined with his political activism. He saw religion as the "only indisputable basis of Jewish claims for its existence as a people."[346] Religion was the basis for his Zionist politics and specifically for his idea to unify the Jewish people. He saw the escalating anti-Semitism in Europe as God's challenge.[347] In his text "A New Political Realism," he wrote: "God has dispersed us and put us in danger to become absorbed by our persecutors, but he has also repeatedly banished our persecutors and let us fend for ourselves. But we are his chosen people and he wants to protect us for the sake of the idea of an only, eternal, almighty, omnipresent, invisible and unimaginable God."[348] Schoenberg, a supreme individualist, never intended to combine his "political realism" with any kind of religious dogmatism, and his projected Jewish Unity Party would not have been a religious party.

Schoenberg's Interactions with Jewish Musician Friends

Through his political activism, Schoenberg made numerous new friends and met new colleagues. He seemed particularly to appreciate contact with members of the Mailamm Society—Joseph Achron, Abraham W. Binder, Ernest Bloch, Mario Castelnuovo-Tedesco, Paul Dessau, Darius Milhaud, Ernst Toch, and Eric Zeisl, among others—who were concerned with Jewish difference and who all worked toward the advancement of Jewish music culture. Schoenberg called them his "*confrères of art*, whose manner of feeling, their world impressions, are homogeneous with mine."[349] In 1939 he became Mailamm's honorary national president. Schoenberg's creation of Jewish-oriented works in America may to a certain degree have been indebted to the ideas and activities of this new peer group.

Schoenberg was particularly close to the Polish-born composer-violinist Joseph Achron, one of the founding members of the Mailamm Society in New York City and Los Angeles (Figure 3.14). Upon settling in the United States in 1925, Achron first taught at Westchester Conservatory in New York and from 1934 on worked in Hollywood as composer and violinist in the Twentieth Century-Fox studio orchestra. As a former member of the Society for Jewish Folk Music in St. Petersburg (founded in 1908), Achron wrote such Jewish-inspired works as *Hebrew Melody* (1911), a Hasidic-themed piece made famous by Jascha Heifetz, and *Golem Suite* and *Evening Service of the Sabbath* (both 1932). Schoenberg met Achron when he gave his New York Mailamm speech in 1934. Achron introduced him to the audience and conversed with him at length after his presentation.[350] He arranged for Schoenberg's next Mailamm speech at the Ebell Club in Los Angeles in 1935. That event featured greetings by Rabbi Magnin, Hugo Riesenfeld, and music theater impresario Lynden E. Behymer, as well as performances of Schoenberg's Third String Quartet and excerpts from *Das Buch der hängenden Gärten*. Walter Rubsamen, Schoenberg's colleague at UCLA, recalled that the relationship between the two men was marked by "genuine cordiality and affection, something like that of an elder for a younger brother." Yet he also noted that Schoenberg could barely tolerate Achron's habit of telling "somewhat bawdy jokes."[351] Achron's singer-composer wife Marie became one of Schoenberg's students. The Achrons and Schoenbergs regularly socialized and saw each other at concerts, including the "All Schoenberg" recital in Peter Yates's and Frances

FIGURE 3.14.
Joseph Achron. Courtesy Arnold Schönberg Center.

Mullen's "Evenings on the Roof" series in January 1940, the student concert at Schoenberg's home in February 1940, and an event featuring selections from Schoenberg's Five Orchestral Pieces under the composer's baton at Fairfax High School in 1941.[352] Schoenberg, who in the 1930s worked on a multi-movement program symphony on Jewish themes and a *Kol nidre,* may very well have discussed these projects with Achron. When on Yom Kippur 1938 Schoenberg conducted the world premiere of *Kol nidre* with a group of Fox Studio players, Achron served as his concertmaster.

Schoenberg thought highly of Joseph Achron's compositions, which are marked by atonality and polytonality.[353] In a 1937 interview with KFI radio host José Rodriguez he mentioned that Achron wrote "important works" before studying composition.[354] And in a 1939 letter to composer and acting chairman of the League of Composers Douglas Moore, he recommended Achron as a composer who writes "good new American music."[355] When Achron passed away in 1943, Schoenberg stated in his eulogy: "Joseph Achron is one of the most underestimated of modern composers, but the originality and profound elaboration of his ideas guarantee that his works will last."[356] He even informed his publisher Carl Engel that, along with Eisler, Gruenberg, Toch, and Weiss, he had founded a committee to publish and disseminate Achron's work, since he considered "the recently deceased Joseph Achron an original and great composer."[357]

A U.S. resident since 1916, the Swiss-born Ernest Bloch was another important member of the Mailamm Society, who attracted international attention with the "Israel" Symphony, *Three Jewish Poems,* and *Schelomo* (1912–16) of his "Jewish Cycle." In these works Bloch intended to intuitively express a "Jewish spirit" and "raise his head proudly as a Jew."[358] A few months before Schoenberg arrived in America, Bloch had completed one of the first symphonic settings of Jewish liturgical music, the *Avodah Hakodesh* (Sacred Service). Bloch, an advisory committee member of Malkin Conservatory who presumably had some input in the decision to hire Schoenberg, was apparently very sympathetic toward him. In a letter to his mistress Winifred Howe he exclaimed, "The poor man! They destroyed him!"[359] Bloch wrote him a touching welcome letter in November 1933:

> If my life had not been so terribly "hectic"—I am working 16 hours a day!—I certainly would have been at the pier, for your arrival—I thought I might have to sail to Europe any day but have been postponing my departure, greatly because I want to meet you and welcome you here on the 11 of November . . . Thus I am glad to send you through these clumsy words—I do not dare inflicting upon you my bad and forgotten German!—a very *hearty* and *sincere welcome* to America, to you, to your wife, to your child. May the people be *a little* respectful and . . . reserved . . . and not kill you through curiosity, snobbishness, and even . . . exaggerated kindness!! They mean well—only they do not *know* that a real artist needs help—and . . . silence! . . . I hope that you and your family may find here, Peace, Stimulation and Happiness.[360]

Bloch expressed his admiration for Schoenberg's *Harmonielehre* (which he read in 1916 and used as a teaching tool), his *Verklärte Nacht,* first two String Quartets, his First Chamber Symphony, and Piano Pieces. And he introduced Schoenberg to his publisher Clarence Birchard in Boston.[361] Bloch and Schoenberg met at the League of Composers welcome concert and reception for Schoenberg on November 11 in New York City. Soon thereafter they had dinner, after which Bloch confided to his mistress that Schoenberg was "a good man," but that "even though some of his music might be good," he himself "did not like it."[362] In that sense, his praise of Schoenberg's works in his welcome letter was more diplomatic than honest. Bloch was unable to attend Schoenberg's Mailamm speech in April 1934, but sent a greeting to be read on his behalf. Nothing is known about further encounters of the two men. They did not meet at the 1942 Festival of the International Society of Contemporary Music in Berkeley, at which both Bloch and Schoenberg were honored.[363]

Bloch seems to have felt increasingly antagonistic toward Schoenberg's music. Hearing a radio performance of his tonal Suite in G in 1936, he concluded that Schoenberg was an "impostor," "a skillful musician" who "had nothing to say."[364] Two years later he accused him of increasingly disseminating "his childish and sophisticated theories" in California.[365] Bloch's perhaps harshest remarks date from 1947 when he used anti-Semitic jargon to criticize the twelve-tone row as an "imposture" and a "degeneracy of our time," and counted Schoenberg among the Jews who "after poisoning Europe . . . have now come here, to this country, and poison it!"[366] This statement, however, may reflect Bloch's bitterness and fear that Schoenberg attracted attention at his expense. Even though Schoenberg was not a true supporter of Bloch's music, there is no evidence that he pronounced such a severe judgment. Although Schoenberg did not know much of his music, he may have studied his *Sacred Service,* whose score was sitting on his piano and was seen by a student during a lesson in his home.[367] He also owned the score of Bloch's *Helvetia* and heard a performance of *America.* While he found Bloch's music "technically not bad," he did not care for *America,* feeling that writing "Jewish, French, English, American, all nationalities . . . is not the right thing."[368] However, Schoenberg seemed to respect him enough to include him with Mahler, Zemlinsky, and Busoni in one of the categories he established in his "Notes for an Autobiography [1944–45]."[369]

Stranded in Northern California after France's fall in 1940, Milhaud also belonged to Schoenberg's friends and colleagues interested in musical explorations of their Jewish heritage and involved in Mailamm.[370] Having written such works as *Poèmes juifs* (1916), *Israël est vivant,* and *Hymne de Sion* (both 1925)—scores Schoenberg owned—back in Europe, Milhaud focused even more on works related to Jewish culture in the United States. In 1947 he set the entire Sabbath morning service, displaying elements of his Carpentras tradition.[371] While Milhaud and Schoenberg's friendship dated to the 1920s, it became stronger in the 1940s as they saw each other more often than they had in Europe.[372] Milhaud's wife Madeleine recounted that they frequently came down from their residence in Oakland to visit the Schoenbergs in Hollywood.[373] Milhaud even stated that they never went to Los Angeles without stopping by the Schoenbergs'. In December 1950 he saw Schoenberg for the last time.[374] The Schoenbergs also traveled north, though less often. When Schoenberg conducted *Pillar of Fire,* Antony Tudor's choreographed version of *Verklärte Nacht,* on February 8, 1945, in San Francisco, he set aside a whole day to spend with the Milhauds in Oakland. For health reasons, however, he had to turn down an invitation from the Milhauds and a guest lecture at the nearby Dominican College in San Rafael on February 24, 1949. The two composers also corresponded. After hearing Mitropoulos's performance of *Le Bœuf sur le toit* (1920) on the radio in 1945, Schoenberg spontaneously conveyed his enjoyment of the work in a note to Milhaud.[375] Milhaud kept him informed about his impressions of performances of the Second Chamber Symphony under Monteux and Variations on a Recitative for organ in San Francisco.[376] Since Milhaud commuted between America and Europe after the war, he was able to report to Schoenberg positive news about his music's reception in Europe.[377] Both composers also had reservations about each other's music. Schoenberg thought little of such works as Milhaud's *Suite Provençale,* and after listening to it on the radio, he even wondered: "How can such a nice man write music like that?"[378] Milhaud was skeptical about Schoenberg's dodecaphony, yet it did not keep him from honoring Schoenberg with articles in the 1934 Schoenberg festschrift, *Musical Quarterly* (1944), *Austro-American Tribune* (1944), and *Canon* (1949).

Milhaud and Schoenberg also collaborated professionally in America. In 1948 Milhaud and Schoenberg were joined by Roy Harris as colleagues at the newly founded Music Academy of the West in Carpinteria near Santa Barbara, where they taught summer courses in composition for three weeks (July18 through August 21).[379] Both composers contributed music to the *Genesis* Suite, an unusual collective composition featuring settings of texts from the First Book of Moses. Schoenberg supplied the Prelude and Milhaud the movement "Cain and Abel." Commissioned by conductor, composer, and Schoenberg student Nathaniel Shilkret in 1945, this seven-part work also involved the participation of Stravinsky, Mario Castelnuovo-Tedesco, Alexandre Tansman, Ernst Toch, and Shilkret.The last four named also socialized with Schoenberg in New York and Los Angeles.[380]

Castelnuovo-Tedesco, who set "The Flood" for *Genesis,* among many other works with Jewish connotations, got to know Schoenberg only about a year before Schoenberg's death. Similarly Tansman, who contributed the "Adam and Eve" movement to *Genesis,* in addition to other music expressing his Jewish identity, did not spend much time with Schoenberg, as he lived in Hollywood only from 1941 to 1946. In 1944, however, both composers served on the committee of the Los Angeles Philharmonic Young Artists' Competition.[381] Their correspondence suggests a friendly relationship.[382]

Schoenberg was better acquainted with the Viennese-born Ernst Toch, who composed the sixth movement of *Genesis,* "The Covenant (The Rainbow)," although it seems that Toch felt less compulsion than Bloch, Milhaud, Castelnuovo-Tedesco, or Schoenberg to express his Jewish identity in music. He pronounced himself against the creation of a Jewish Community Center in Santa Monica in 1945 and even suggested the "abolition of Religions."[383] Nevertheless, he conceived the *Cantata of the Bitter Herbs* for voices and orchestra, inspired by the Passover Haggadah (recalling the Jews' Exodus from Egypt) and based on a libretto by Rabbi Sonderling; two settings for Hans Nathan's *Folk Songs of the New Palestine* (both 1938); and the *Rhapsodic Poem "Jephta"* (1962). Schoenberg and Toch knew each other in Berlin, encountered each other in Paris in 1933, and met again in Los Angeles, where Toch settled in 1936. Yet despite their respect for each other, they repeatedly squabbled. Their strongest disagreement was probably on Jewish matters. At a political meeting in Paris in 1933, Schoenberg insisted that the Jews needed to be as nationalistic as the fascists were and "act as such in order to meet the situation," whereupon Toch skeptically asked: "Why should the Nazis have to tell me that I am a Jew and must be a Jew? I am who I am."[384] Unsurprisingly, he rejected Schoenberg's Jewish Unity Party project. Quickly forgiving the clash, Schoenberg recommended Toch for a job at the New School for Social Research in New York.[385] He considered him "a serious composer who works hard and has studied long."[386] In turn, Toch backed the doubling of Schoenberg's ASCAP royalties to supplement his small pension after 1944.[387] But in 1948 Schoenberg disappointed Toch when he refused to write a blurb for Toch's forthcoming music-theory treatise *The Shaping Forces of Music*.[388] Perhaps he was upset about the sparse reference to his ideas; perhaps he knew that Toch, in addition to Adorno, had discussed musical matters with Thomas Mann for *Doctor Faustus*. Whatever the case may have been, in January 1948 Mann tellingly inscribed Toch's copy of the novel: "Ernst Toch, der den Teufel nicht nötig hat [To Ernst Toch who does not need the devil]."[389]

Though not involved in the *Genesis* project, Paul Dessau was another friend of Schoenberg, whose exile also propelled him to write works reflecting his Jewish identity. As a refugee in Paris, Dessau began composing such Jewish-themed works as the oratorio *Haggadah* (1936). Upon his move to New York, he wrote more sacred vocal works, especially for the Temple Emanu-El and Park Avenue Synagogue.[390] He also worked for the music school of the Young Men's Hebrew Association and became co-editor of *Jewish Music Forum*, the journal of the Mailamm Society (renamed Jewish Music Forum in 1939). Having met Schoenberg just once, at Schoenberg's *Pierrot* performance in New York in 1940, Dessau turned to him a year later when he was preparing a lecture on Schoenberg's *Kol nidre* and an arrangement of this work for voices and three-manual organ or piano four hands. In December 1942 Dessau directed a performance of *Kol nidre* with an ad hoc chorus, pianist Bruno Eisner, cantor Moshe Rudinow, and composer Isadore Freed, and the pianists Erich Itor Kahn and Claude Frank. Dessau preceded it with a lecture on the work at the Jewish Music Forum in New York.[391]

When Dessau settled in Los Angeles in 1943 to collaborate more closely with Brecht and compose music for films, he saw Schoenberg almost on a weekly basis. Despite their irreconcilable beliefs—Dessau was an atheist and communist—they had common interests and became close friends.[392] Besides writing Jewish-themed music, the two composers were preoccupied with dodecaphony. Inspired by Schoenberg and under René Leibowitz's tutelage, Dessau had begun to explore the twelve-tone technique in the mid-1930s in France.[393] Dessau acquainted Schoenberg with Leibowitz, who had passionately promoted his work since the 1930s in France and from the late 1940s in America.[394] In the late 1940s Leibowitz conducted a performance of Schoenberg's *Ode to Napoleon*, with Dessau as narrator, at Schoenberg's home.[395] He also informed him about other Schoenberg champions nurtured by

Leibowitz, such as the New York-based composer-pianist Erich Itor Kahn. Dessau attended Schoenberg's Sunday music-analysis classes. He arranged to have some of Schoenberg's lectures typed on a typewriter with oversized letters at Warner Brothers after finding out about Schoenberg's poor eyesight; as a token of thanks he received a piano reduction of *Die glückliche Hand* that Schoenberg inscribed: "This is my lucky handwriting in gratitude for your lucky handwriting, which finally made my lectures legible for me." Schoenberg also gave him one of his birthday canons. In 1946 Dessau purchased a photocopy of the String Trio for $10 (about $110 in 2009).[396] After a thorough study of the score he pointed out numerous mistakes to Schoenberg, which he, however, refused to acknowledge.[397] Despite Schoenberg's interest in seeing some of his music, Dessau declined to show him any of his works, feeling that Schoenberg's "eyes should be spared that."[398]

In 1945 Schoenberg met Mailamm member Eric Zeisl, a forty-year-old composer, who had fled his native Vienna in 1938 and moved to Hollywood to work for the film industry in 1941. Schoenberg had heard Zeisl's musical commemoration of the Holocaust, the *Requiem Ebraico* (1945), on the radio—one of several works reflecting Zeisl's Jewish identity and today his most performed composition—and apparently liked it very much.[399] Little did he know that in 1965 his son Ronald would marry Zeisl's daughter Barbara.

Schoenberg's numerous relationships with American Jews who explored their Jewish roots allowed him to come to terms with his Jewish identity, ethnically, politically, religiously, and last but not least, musically.

Schoenberg and the Idea of Jewish Music

Having composed several Jewish-themed works before 1933, in deliberate defiance of rising anti-Semitism, Schoenberg became, in the face of the Holocaust, even more concerned with the musical expression of his Jewish identity in America. His new homeland offered him a more open cultural environment than Europe had, as well as a circle of like-minded composers who explored the idea of Jewish art music in manifold ways.

Jewish art music as a national and cultural concept is a complex subject open to ideological exploitation. As in the case of German music, it is hard to pin down objective and universally applicable musical criteria. What is more, Jewish art music, often defined as music "made by Jews, for Jews, as Jews," displays great diversity due to its creation in the Diaspora, which challenged the unity of Jewish artists on virtually every level—geographic, ethnic, linguistic, cultural, and religious.[400]

Schoenberg had wrestled with the concept of Jewish music since the 1920s. His early thoughts on this matter manifest pride in his Jewish roots and thus qualify his idea of German music and his self-identification as a German composer. In 1925 he wrote to Albert Einstein:

> To my knowledge there is no Jewish music—art music—at this time, though, as I believe, all western music points to Jews and even perhaps owes the development of its basic principles to the Jewish essence and spirit. The art of the Netherlanders on the one hand, is reminiscent in many ways of that which one knows from the Talmud and Kabbala, and on the other hand, in gypsy music, which has been partially influenced by Jews, can be seen an opposing tendency to cerebral art, based on scientific and occult knowledge. Apart from that (for these are hypotheses which do not lend themselves to be proved easily), there is only German, Italian, French music, which is written by Jews

and which, therefore, certainly contains Jewish traits. Were one to reclaim this as Jewish music, one would thereby lessen the above-explained influence of the Jewish spirit on western music, on the one hand, while, on the other, take away the value of their having been acknowledged within the artistic life of a people, who have regarded them as belonging to their national music.[401]

Schoenberg's belief that Jews influenced the national music of their adopted country and that Jewish art music was nonexistent typifies that of many assimilated German-Jewish artists who strove for a German-Jewish synthesis. But this view was a step in a gradual process. Believing "in *Deutschtum*, in Teutonism"—from lack of self-esteem—even self-loathingly swallowing Wagner's anti-Semitic diatribes in the 1890s, Schoenberg ultimately gravitated away from being "a true Wagnerian" when he realized in the 1920s that "it was not our destiny to disappear, to meld and assimilate with Germans or any other people."[402]

In the 1930s he went further. When composer Lehman Engel asked him in 1933 whether "race-traits are felt in music" and whether his music "presents definite Hebraic characteristics," he replied: "I hope, but I don't know. As a Jew, I show a measure of thinking certainly Jewish."[403] In the same year, Schoenberg planned to contribute to the "establishment of a national Hebrew music institute to disseminate and advance Hebrew music culture."[404] A year later he told the Mailamm members in New York: "to create a national Jewish music is a holy task, and especially interesting for Jews—who in great numbers in former times, as well as in our day, have helped Aryan music to become as perfect as it is today—for we can prove our superiority in spiritual matters in creating this new Jewish music."[405] In 1935 he praised the Mailamm movement and its support for the building of a music department for Hebrew University and its contribution to the restoration of Jewish artists' self-esteem.[406] Schoenberg, however, never emerged as a leader in the American Jewish art music movement, perhaps because he believed that "Jewish national music exists where a Jewish genius works."[407]

Jewish art-music composers are often classified into two main categories established by the pioneer of Jewish music research, Abraham Idelsohn. One group, comprising such composers as Joel Engel and Joseph Achron, primarily draws on Jewish folk and liturgical music in their works; the other, including figures like Mendelssohn and Meyerbeer, focuses on music devoid of "Jewish features."[408] Yet Schoenberg remains difficult to pigeonhole. He does not seem to fit the former category. Believing that traditional and classical music "mix as poorly as oil and water," he was quite skeptical about the notion of unchangeable traditions.[409] He stated: "What happens to a sentence, if along a line of men it is passed on only by whispering to one's neighbor, illustrates what tradition can have done to its originals." He also doubted consistency in the performance practice and arrangement of traditional Jewish music and asked: "If only elements of biblical cantillation should be used, why not also exclude all modern musical instruments and use only those of Bible-times?"[410] However he successfully used Jewish liturgical motives in his settings of *Kol nidre* and Psalm 130. By the same token, although Schoenberg may, at first glance, correspond to Idelsohn's category of Jewish composers who avoid "Jewish features" in their music, ultimately he resists this classification as well.

Schoenberg believed that classical music was the result of the evolution of traditional music and that contemporary art music must be organically rooted in the classical tradition, but he also felt that his music manifested Jewish thought. Although he himself never elaborated on this claim, several scholars have pointed out Jewish perspectives in his musical thought and ethical stance. While the array of interpretations is intriguing, their subjective and speculative nature defies the singling out of one definitive position. According to Steven Beller, Schoenberg's modernist musical critique of the beauty- and style-worshipping Viennese culture was an ethical and spiritual position aimed at the expression of truth and the musical idea, and can be directly related to the Jewish tradition of ethical stoicism. Beller pointed out that in this tradition, "Jews were concluding that 'God is conscience,'" an idea based on "the concept of man as made in God's image." Beller explained that "faith in God as conscience could further be secularized into a simple faith in 'the Good in man, in every person, also in oneself.'"[411] Even if Schoenberg had little self-awareness as a Jew in his early career, the influence of his critical Jewish peers would have drawn him to this tradition at the time. Beller stressed that "what emerged as the secularized form of Jewish stoicism was a great emphasis on the ethical mission of the individual, which based itself on what can only be called an areligious faith—whether it be in God or conscience, within Judaism or outside it."[412] Beller stated that such mottos as "music should not decorate, it should be true" are "criteria of the ethical stoic" used in the realm of aesthetics.[413] Similarly, Leon Botstein stated that, with his "radical epistemological and aesthetic critique of traditional views," Schoenberg "may have expressed secularized Judaic echoes, even unwittingly, of traditions and values derived from earlier incarnations of Jewish life and thought before emancipation and assimilation." Botstein interprets Schoenberg's approach to musical modernism as a "latter-day effort to render the essence of Judaism universal."[414]

Schoenberg's concern with one overriding musical idea and the use of one twelve-tone row underpinning an entire musical work has also been viewed as a reflection of the concept of "ethical monotheism." To Michael Meyer, ethical monotheism had replaced "Jewish ritual in its totality" by 1871 and had "become the foundation of their [the German Jews'] Jewishness."[415] Beller's point that Jewish stoicism's "idea of man as created in God's image, as the individual struggling to make sense of, to articulate the creation, as giving unity to the world," likewise refers to Schoenberg's endeavor to dodecaphonically unify musical space—even though Schoenberg himself compared these efforts to the Christian mystic Emanuel von Swedenborg's concept of heaven as portrayed in Balzac's *Séraphîta*.[416] Similarly Juan Allende-Blin observed a connection between the kabbalistic concept of monism (derived from monotheism) and Schoenberg's belief that one musical idea should be presented in a melodically and harmonically unified space and characterize a piece's totality.[417] Steven Schwarzschild suggested that the principle of serial transformations corresponds to the "variations of the alphabetic acrostic in the Biblical book of *Lamentations* and indeed, the kabbalistic uses of this practice."[418] Neher saw a (perhaps far-fetched) Jewish association in the pitch number of Schoenbergian tone rows, in that they correspond to the number of tribes of Israel or the sons of Jacob.[419]

Schoenberg composed a number of works in America that emphasize his Jewish identity more than his German musical heritage or the imprints of American culture.

Kol Nidre, op. 39

Composed in 1938, *Kol nidre* for speaker, mixed chorus, and orchestra was Schoenberg's first completed Jewish-themed composition in America and his first and only Jewish liturgical work. Rabbi Jacob Sonderling, founder of the progressive Society for Jewish Culture (also known as Fairfax Temple) had met Schoenberg through

Joseph Achron and commissioned the work. Keen on collaborating with such "great musical minds" as Schoenberg, Sonderling provided his own arrangement of the *Kol nidre* text.[420] Schoenberg, however, wrote *Kol nidre* not just for artistic reasons, but for political and financial reasons as well. In lieu of a commission fee, Sonderling was to supply "three to four affidavits" for his relatives and friends. Ultimately, however, he was unable to find the necessary sponsors.[421]

Opening the evening service on Yom Kippur, the Day of Atonement, *Kol nidre* (All Vows) functions as a quasi-legal procedure to invalidate vows and oaths made to God and to repent aberrations. The ritual may have held special significance for Schoenberg because it touched on his own "reconversion" or Jewish *teshuva*.[422] Yet Schoenberg, like many other German Jews, objected to one of its principles.[423] "Nobody could understand why Jews should be allowed to make oaths and vows and promises which they could consider as null and void," he noted. However, he strongly related to one of its other ideas: "Whenever under pressure of persecution a Jew was forced to make oaths, vows, and promises counter to his inherited belief in our religious principles, he was allowed to repent them and to declare them null and void. Thus he was allowed to pray with the community as a Jew among Jews."[424] In consideration of Schoenberg's views and the needs of his synagogue's American and émigré members, Sonderling created a new text for Schoenberg's composition. Drawing on core elements and structural principles found in other traditional Ashkenazic textual *Kol nidre* versions, he extended "the scope of the text's historical and thematic connections."[425] He added a novel reference to the Psalm verse "Light is sown for the sinner," which links the *teshuva* with the Creation, and the subject of "sacred task," pointing to a vital principle of German Reform Jewry.[426] Moreover, Sonderling chose English as the main language and presented, upon Schoenberg's request, one verse in Hebrew: "Bishivo Shel Malo Uvishivo Shel Mato [By the authority of the Heavenly Court above and of this court on earth]," prompting Schoenberg to set Hebrew text for the first time. Other textual changes include the stripping of the preamble's pictorial descriptions of God, the addition of lines to *Kol nidre*'s preamble and "All vows" section and the reorganization of the text to illuminate ideas central to Schoenberg's faith, as discussed earlier.[427]

Schoenberg used existing liturgical musical elements from different *Kol nidre* melodies compiled by such European and American cantors as Leon Kornitzer, N'ginoth Baruch Schorr, Reuben Rinder, Joseph Heller, and Hirsch Weintraub.[428] A key element is the "very striking" opening of the chant, marked by a three-note motif (G–F-sharp–D), its retrograde, and a G minor cadential phrase with pitches revolving mostly stepwise around the tonic G minor.[429] Corresponding to the musical material's mode, Schoenberg centered his setting's tonality on G and G minor. He also followed the chant's tradition in repeating the "All vows" phrase thrice and presenting each reiteration louder, at a higher pitch, and more elaborately. The first rabbinic presentation of the text (m. 58) on G is followed by the presentation through choir and winds (m. 94) on A flat and another choral presentation on C (m. 146).[430]

Schoenberg's *Kol nidre* setting, however, also reflects his German musical heritage.[431] He stated that he was "most satisfied" that he "could use traditional motifs without destroying his own style," indebted to Mozart, Beethoven, and Brahms.[432] He shaped the loose "structural appearance of the melody" into a tightly knit eleven-measure unit, beginning with the characteristic descending and ascending motives, climaxing on B-flat and D in the middle and ending with the G minor cadential figure (mm. 58–69) (Figure 3.15). He used sophisticated variations of the opening three-note motif (G–F-sharp–D), the work's main building block, to

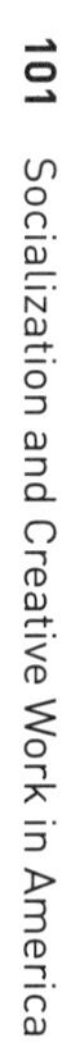

FIGURE 3.15.

Kol nidre, mm. 58–68 (reduction based on Leonard Stein's arrangement of *Kol nidre* for speaker, organ, and percussion ad lib.). Courtesy Belmont Music Publishers.

provide diversity, coherence, and unity throughout. He even used such serial procedures as inverted ascending forms and transposed descending forms of the motive.[433] In addition, Schoenberg created a new "light" motive that is related to the main "repentance" motive and its variants, and which illustrates, thanks to its chromaticism, the text's subject of light. He embedded the traditional monophonic chant in colorfully orchestrated melodrama, polyphonic, and homophonic textures. Opposing the too sentimental expression found in Max Bruch's *Kol nidre* setting for cello and orchestra (1880), he aimed at "vitriolising out the cello-sentimentality of the Bruchs, etc. and giving this decree the dignity of a law, of an edict."[434]

Schoenberg's *Kol nidre* setting displays his adjustment to his new environment. He chose *Kol nidre* knowing that many American Jews considered it one of the most significant communal rites. In order to provide a modern communal and cultural experience in the face of the worst crisis in the history of Jewry, Schoenberg and Sonderling softened the text content of the tribunal section by addressing transgressors who had been unfaithful because of fear and weakness, not because of their defiance of communal rites. Steven Cahn observed: "Sonderling's tone is therefore purposefully unaccusing in order to foster the ingathering of a refugee cultural community in order to help it remake itself in Los Angeles as both a cultural and religious community."[435] The choice of English instead of Hebrew as the work's primary language targeted such former apostates as Schoenberg who had little knowledge of Hebrew. The *Kol nidre* was Schoenberg's first vocal work completed in America and his first completed work based on an original English text. The music's accessibility, due to its tonal orientation and generous display of tone painting, reveals that he wanted to cater to as many listeners as possible. Its extroverted and dramatic character and use of melodrama have suggested to some "a film scene rather than a religious act."[436]

The circumstances of the work's world premiere refer to Hollywood as well. Most of the musicians who participated in this performance—the chorus and orchestra members including Achron as concertmaster—were employed in movie studios. Schoenberg himself conducted the work, and Sonderling, coached by Schoenberg's student Leonard Stein, served as reciter. Film composer Serge Hovey, a Schoenberg student, recorded the performance.[437] It was given in October 1938 shortly before the tragic *Kristallnacht* during the atonement service, which had to be held in the Coconut Grove nightclub at the Ambassador Hotel in Los Angeles because both the chapel and the social hall of the Fairfax Temple were too small to hold the numerous musicians and congregation. Not much is known about the reception of the work's first performance. Klemperer was present but did not comment on it. Schoenberg himself felt that its "effect was great," although he found the space acoustically unsatisfactory.[438]

Schoenberg's *Kol nidre* did not receive many further performances, even though it reflects an increased interest in art music based on Jewish liturgy in America in the 1930s and 1940s. Its opulent scoring and difficult execution, invoking such other unorthodox sacred works as Beethoven's *Missa solemnis*, certainly diminished its performability in synagogues. Schoenberg's suggestion to reduce the large forces was taken up, during his lifetime, only by Dessau who arranged and performed it in 1942.[439] Another hurdle was the work's hybrid character (the sacred scores of Bloch, Castelnuovo-Tedesco, Milhaud, and others were amalgams as well). Conceived as a universalistic work that would "be tremendously effective both in the synagogue and the concert hall," Schoenberg's *Kol nidre* appeared as a rather individualistic interpretation of previous textual and musical *Kol nidre* sources.[440] Composer Lazare Saminsky, who was music director of Temple Emanu-El in New York and had positioned himself as an authority on Jewish music, found the text "troublesome" and "too far from the standard version of even the Reform synagogue." He predicted that "the Rabbis will raise Cain about this," and not only refrained from performing the work, but also clandestinely advised Schoenberg's publisher against issuing it.[441] However, he may well have made up his mind about Schoenberg by the 1920s, when he declared him a "hysterical neurotic" Jew who "assimilates and accentuates ideas" and is unable to produce the type of Jewish art music that Saminsky and his former companions from the Russian Society for Jewish Folk Music had envisioned.[442]

Nonetheless, several other professional musicians—among them Kurt List, Joseph Yasser, Dessau, and David Putterman—approved of Schoenberg's *Kol nidre* setting.[443] Putterman, cantor of New York's Park Avenue synagogue, had heard Dessau's performance of this work at the Jewish Music Forum in 1942, and he invited Schoenberg several times to write "a composition for cantor, choir and organ . . . based on some portion of the Sabbath Eve liturgy." He felt that a work by him "would greatly enhance and enrich Jewish liturgy."[444] Putterman hoped that Schoenberg would use his English translations of Psalms 95–99 and "Who is like unto Thee" ("Mi kamoka," Exodus 15:11). Instead Schoenberg compiled his own biblical verses to produce a shorter text that was "closer to our present day's feelings," and which referred to European Jewry's current situation: "Who is like to thee, o Lord? [Exodus 15:11] Nations rose up, and were angry. [Exodus 15:14] Thou stretchest forth thy hand and the earth swallowed them. [Exodus: 15:12] Lord, Almighty [Exodus 15:3] thou hast become salvation to thy people [Exodus 15:2], thou wilt not make our enemies rejoice over us. [Psalm 29:2] Deliver thy people, o Lord, from all his [*sic*] tribulations. [Psalm 24:22]."[445] Putterman considered Schoenberg's text an "ideal" and "original addition" to liturgy and even planned to use it instead of the *Mi kamoka*. However, Schoenberg abandoned the project, hoping that Putterman would consider a performance of his *Kol nidre*.[446] Schoenberg also abandoned sketches for another liturgical work: a setting of the Yom Kippur hymn *Yaaleh* ["May it rise"].

Prelude to Genesis

Schoenberg's next religious work, his Prelude for wordless chorus and orchestra (1945), was among his most lucrative and unusual commissions. He was paid $1,500 (about $17,700 in 2009) for this six-minute, 83-measure-long work.[447] His Prelude opens the seven-part collective suite *Genesis* for narrator, chorus, and orchestra, and is followed by the movements "Creation" by Shilkret, "Adam and Eve" by Tansman, "Cain and Abel" by Milhaud, "The Flood" by Castelnuovo-Tedesco, "The Covenant" by Toch, and "Babel" by Stravinsky. Shilkret, *Genesis*'s initiator, was at the time music director at MGM, and this eclectic project was one of his long cherished wishes: "to put the Bible on records" and "to strike the sympathetic musical pulse of all people—the highbrows, sentimentalists, dreamers and jazzers alike."[448]

At the close of World War II, when the depth of the Nazis' atrocities began to come to light, Shilkret's *Genesis* emphasized the Bible's Jewish roots. Preceding the melodramatic presentations of selected Genesis episodes, Schoenberg's Prelude illustrates the beginning of God's Creation pictorially and abstractly. He evokes the fragmented state of space before the creation in the work's 24-measure-long introduction, using isolated sonic particles that rise from the depth and gradually form more extended melodic contours and textures of greater density. He depicts the act of creation itself in the following fugue. The use of the human voice at the end of the work symbolizes the impending creation of humankind and the absence of words signifies this pre-linguistic state. Schoenberg's utilization of the twelve-tone technique in the Prelude can stand for the unitary God-idea and his "Law, the one and only valid law."[449]

Stressing his affiliation with the Austro-German music tradition, Schoenberg invoked at least two of his chosen musical ancestors: Haydn and Bach. The fragmented texture at the Prelude's beginning and its ending on a unison C both recall the first movement of Haydn's *Creation*. Thematic contours point to antecedent-consequent structures similar to those employed in tonal works of the eighteenth and nineteenth centuries (see the fugue subject, mm. 25–30). The motivic-thematic work and developing variation, as evident in the introduction (mm. 1–24) and second half of the work (fugue episode, mm. 48–55; fugal section, mm. 56–65; conclusion, mm. 76–83), also allude to such composers as Brahms. The fugue (mm. 25–76), sometimes classified as a double fugue due to the tone row's distribution over two parts, recalls Bach and perhaps more specifically the fugue of his Passacaglia in C minor, BWV 582. The Prelude tries to achieve a synthesis of dynamic evolutionary techniques and static counterpoint.

Besides accentuating Schoenberg's Jewish and German identities, the Prelude, embedded in a work of mostly "cinematographically" conceived movements, conveys, intentionally or not, associations with Hollywood films.[450] The wordless mixed chorus enters at measure 66 as part of the fugue's concluding stretto and brings to mind the popularity of this device in many film scores of the time, including those for *Wuthering Heights* (1939) and *The Song of Bernadette* (1943) by Schoenberg's friend Alfred Newman. Ironically, Schoenberg critiqued the so-called "Newman" string sound, when he noted in the Prelude manuscript (m. 12): "Always without Hollywood style of vibrato and portamento; even larger intervals must not be connected by gliding but, if necessary, but streching [*sic*]. This gliding is of detestable sentimentality."[451] Like many of Schoenberg's American twelve-tone works, the Prelude is abundant in tonal connotations, using a basic twelve-tone set that has related forms containing many thirds and sixths. A generous amount of orchestrational octave doublings enhances the piece's tonal feel as well. The Prelude's final unison sound on C has even been called an "MGM ending."[452] In this sense the work adapts to its mostly tonal succeeding movements and their larger cultural contexts, while retaining many of Schoenberg's unshakable principles.

Werner Janssen, who gave the American premiere of Schoenberg's Handel arrangement, gave the first performance of the *Genesis* Suite, with the Janssen Orchestra and movie actor Edward Arnold as narrator, in November 1945 at the Wilshire Ebell Theater in Los Angeles. Shortly thereafter he recorded it for Victor Red Seal Records to be issued on five 78-rpm discs.[453] According to Los Angeles–based music critic Lawrence Morton, Schoenberg's Prelude "was the most successful piece, partly because it alone did not have to compete with the narrator, whose insistent and amplified voice constantly fought the music."[454] Yet Schoenberg's piece, effectively performable as an autonomous work, did not receive repeat performances until after his death. Shilkret, to whom he had sold the work for a lump sum on the condition that he would publish and record it, failed to issue the score and parts before 1951.[455] The Prelude's brevity, coupled with its requirement of a large orchestra and chorus, also had a negative effect on the frequency of performances.

A Survivor from Warsaw

Composed between August 11 and 23, 1947, *A Survivor from Warsaw* is Schoenberg's most prominent "Jewish" work—a cantata for narrator, men's choir, and orchestra that is unique in his oeuvre in its conflation of political, historical, and religious implications with emotional directness (Figure 3.16).

The idea for *Survivor* came from the Russian-born dancer-choreographer Corinne Chochem. In spring 1947, on Toch's advice, she approached Schoenberg about arranging a Jewish resistance hymn written by poet Hirsh Glick in the Vilna Ghetto and proposed a specific scenario in which the hymn could be embedded.[456] Soon Schoenberg replied to Chochem: "I plan to make it this scene—which you described—in the Warsaw Ghetto, how the doomed Jews started singing, before going to die." He also mentioned further specifics: it would be a "composition of 6–9 minutes for small orchestra and chorus, perhaps also one or more soloists, on the melody you gave me."[457] Schoenberg's fee of $1,000 [about $9,500 in 2009] was too high for Chochem, but the Koussevitzky Music Foundation offered him this very sum for a new work in the summer of 1947. He accepted the offer and decided to work out the idea that he had developed with Chochem.[458]

The seven-minute-long composition presents an imagined dramatic scene as it could have taken place during the Holocaust. It is "based partly on reports" that he "received directly or indirectly."[459] Despite the references to Warsaw in the work's text and title, the place of the scene is an anonymous concentration camp. Schoenberg symbolically alludes to two major events in the Warsaw Ghetto: the "Great Liquidation" of 1942 and the Jewish uprising in April and May 1943, when many Jews escaped through the sewers of Warsaw.[460] The mini-drama involves a survivor telling how a sergeant and his subordinates dehumanize Jewish internees through roll call, shouting, beating, and forcing them to count off to be delivered to the gas chamber.

FIGURE 3.16.

A Survivor from Warsaw, autograph, mm. 67–74. Courtesy Belmont Music Publishers.

The internees oppose the Nazi cruelties with dignity and face their death by collectively chanting the *Sh'ma Yisrael*. Glick's partisan hymn was not used.

Schoenberg's identification with Judaism is apparent in *Survivor*'s framework, which starkly contrasts the dignity of the Jews with the cruelty of the Nazis. Yet his use of the *Sh'ma Yisrael* [Hear, Israel], the most important expression of Jewish faith, is perhaps the most powerful symbol of his Jewish identity as well. Schoenberg may have learned this three-part prayer as a child, neglected it in his early adulthood and then re-embraced it as his creed. The *Sh'ma Yisrael* draws on Deuteronomy and Numbers and emphasizes the love of the one and only God.[461] It is recited in morning and evening prayer services and in times of joy and sorrow, as well as before death. Schoenberg placed it at the moment of the ghetto inmates' death, referring to the act of *Kiddush hashem* (sanctification of the name of God) in the Jewish tradition and denoting martyrdom, "spiritual courage and self-sacrifice for the sake of religion."[462] For dramatic reasons, however, he employed only the verses Deuteronomy 6:4–7 (instead of 6:4–9 and 11:13–21). The prayer's hopeful image "when you rise" is abruptly cut off by musical motifs, signaling the Nazis' continuation of their mindless extermination of Jewish lives.[463] Although Schoenberg did not know Hebrew, he presented the *Sh'ma* in Hebrew to create an extreme dichotomy between the narrator's text, cast in English, and the sergeant's brutal commands in German. Sonderling helped Schoenberg prepare a literal English translation and phonetic translation of the Hebrew prayer.[464]

Schoenberg also contrasted the settings of the sung and spoken texts to elevate the Jewish representation. The *Sh'ma* is sung in continuous memorable melodic lines, while the narrator's and sergeant's parts are cast in a jagged *Sprechstimme*. Furthermore, Schoenberg used a prayer melody that is rhythmically and melodically indebted to the traditional Jewish *Sh'ma Yisrael* melodies of the cantors Abraham Baer and Samuel Naumbourg.[465] This strictly dodecaphonic work, which is based on one twelve-tone set, draws the pitches of the prayer melody from the prime row and from two transpositions and some of their combinatorial inversions. Significantly, the prayer melody's dodecaphonic pitch material features a symmetrical augmented triad C–A-flat–E. Prominently used as a linear and chordal motif throughout the work, it suggests a special meaning and has been interpreted as representing the "Jews' inner connectedness with God," the "perfection and immutability of the Jewish God-idea," and the "God motif."[466] Apart from this abstract sonic symbol, Schoenberg refrained from using musical pictorialism in his *Sh'ma* setting for fear of undermining the notion of the invisible God. The prayer melody, sung by a men's choir in unison, stresses monotheism, the collective identity of the Jewish ghetto inmates, and the unifying power of faith. It also reflects Schoenberg's political hopes for a unification of Jewry through the Jewish faith. Nevertheless, despite the suggestion of hope in the chanting of the *Sh'ma*, which has often been read as an expression of transfiguration and triumph of Judaism over barbarism, the end of *Survivor* conveys a sense of ongoing terror. In the last three measures Schoenberg creates "excruciating tension between the text, which declares faith as it invokes rising, and the music which indicates oppression and extermination."[467] The return of the dreadful military motifs and use of the basic set hark back to the work's opening and describe a closed vicious circle (Figure 3.17).

Survivor also includes insinuations about Schoenberg's own German identity. Even though most of the text is spoken, it alludes to Bach's cantatas, not least because of its chorale-like last section.[468] David Schiller noted, "Like the chorale at the end of a Lutheran church cantata by Johann Sebastian Bach, the Sh'ma Yisrael implicitly

FIGURE 3.17.
A Survivor from Warsaw, mm. 97–99 (piano reduction by Kurt Frederick). Courtesy Belmont Music Publishers.

invites Jewish members of the audience to pray along, to remember that they are Jews."[469] Many other references to Germany, however, are negative. *Survivor*'s Germans are the oppressors and murderers of millions of Jews, and because German is the language of the tormentors, it is never sung. Using German with a Prussian dialect, Schoenberg exposes the roots of German militarism. The music that illustrates the Germans' horrific deeds in the first part and last three measures has sharp melodic contours, rugged rhythms, and brash timbres. The montage-like textures are permeated by leitmotifs, including ominous trumpet fanfares, tremolos and trills in high woodwinds to underscore the militaristic character of the actions, and abrasive oscillating figures to stress the counting-off of the victims. Other motifs depict through sighing minor seconds and pitch repetitions the fear and suffering of the Jews.

Survivor can also be seen as a reflection of Schoenberg's American identity and environment. It was his third completed work featuring the English language and his first composition using his own English prose. The English-speaking survivor-narrator may stand for the many émigré Jews who, after experiencing various levels of bigotry in Europe, found refuge in America. *Survivor* also evokes Hollywood, whether intentionally or not. Marked by a concise and dramatic style with short sentences in the past tense, its text is spoken over a vivid pictorial music that brims with leitmotifs and tone painting—a technique that recalls the underscoring practices in film and radio in the 1930s and 1940s.[470] *Survivor*'s underscoring is for the most part nondiegetic (background music). In one instance, however, the trumpet motifs become diegetic sounds (source music) when the narrator mentions the sound of the trumpets (mm. 32–34). The singing of the *Sh'ma* can be understood as diegetic music as well. Whether or not Schoenberg was influenced by Hollywood film scoring, the cinematic feel of this work has not gone unnoticed. His treatment of the Nazi sergeant's "clipped Prussian accent" was considered "out of Hollywood," and even dismissed as a "B-movie cliché," evoking "the Erich von Stroheim Nazi barking 'Achtung.'"[471] *Survivor* was also more positively called a "cinéma vérité creation."[472]

The circumstances of *Survivor*'s premiere were unusual. Serge Koussevitzky, whose foundation had commissioned the work, was not interested in giving its first performance.[473] Instead, the premiere fell to Kurt Frederick, the Austrian-born conductor and former member of the Kolisch Quartet, who was preparing for a *Pierrot* performance in Albuquerque when he learned about the possibility of premiering *Survivor* and readily seized the opportunity. He successfully presented *Survivor* on a program with Stokowski's arrangement of Bach's *Komm, süßer Tod* (Come, Sweet Death), Jaromir Weinberger's Concerto for Timpani, and Beethoven's Eighth Symphony at the University of New Mexico in Albuquerque in November 1948. Frederick conducted the 115 musicians of the Albuquerque Civic Symphony, an organization of amateur performers founded in 1932, along with the narrator Sherman Smith and male singers from the Albuquerque Choral Association and the University A Cappella Chorus.[474] An additional fourteen men from the Community Chorus in Estancia, New Mexico, who were mostly cowboys and ranchers, joined the chorus, driving "the sixty mountain miles to Albuquerque for rehearsals and the concert."[475] Some 1,800 concertgoers received the work with great enthusiasm and even demanded a repeat performance. The local press published positive reviews.[476] Dimitri Mitropoulos's New York premiere of *Survivor* in March 1950, however, prompted mixed reactions. Henry Cowell, who attended the performance, reported that "in spite of typically extreme dissonance and tonal fragmentation, the regular audience of the Philharmonic-Symphony Orchestra gave the work a vociferous ovation. The decision of Mitropoulos to repeat was in response to a real demand."[477] But Olin Downes, one of the early critics of this work, dismissed *Survivor* as "poor and empty music, even though it be couched in the most learned Schoenbergian formulas and craftsmanship." Downes also disliked—here agreeing with Schoenberg—Mitropoulos's theatrical enhancement of the performance, with the singers successively rising before they sang the *Sh'ma*.[478] The widespread but questionable view of *Survivor* as a universalist work (like Beethoven's Ninth Symphony), with a redeeming triumphant and heroic finale, fueled criticisms that condemned the work as inappropriate, unseemly, and trivial.[479]

Along with Kahn's *Nenia judais had aetate perierunt* (1943), Zeisl's *Requiem Ebraico* (1945), and Lazar Weiner's *Songs of the Concentration Camps* (1947), *Survivor* is one of the earliest musical responses to the Holocaust in American music. As a work with a political subject for speaker (with chorus) and orchestra, *Survivor* also relates to such 1940s compositions as Copland's *Lincoln Portrait*, Becker's Symphony No. 6 "Out of Bondage," and Blitzstein's Airborne Symphony.

His Last Works

Although Schoenberg worked on a variety of compositional projects in the last two years of his life, he concentrated—surely inspired by the recent foundation of the state of Israel—on the musical expression of his political ideas and faith. He worked on four short choral works (*Dreimal tausend Jahre* [Thrice a Thousand Years], *Israel Exists Again*, Psalm 130, and *Modern Psalm*), as well as on fifteen "Psalm" texts for a projected large-scale cycle of vocal music. But he completed only two of the choral works. Featuring three languages, English, Hebrew, and German, as well as dodecaphony, these scores are very personal and even confessional. Except for Psalm 130, none of them was a commission.

Composed in April 1949, the short a cappella chorus *Dreimal tausend Jahre* for four voices is based on Dagobert Runes's nostalgic German poem *Gottes Wiederkehr* (God's Return). Schoenberg discovered the poem in Runes's collection *Jordan Lieder: Frühe Gedichte* (1948), which Runes, president of the Philosophical Library, sent him when his firm was preparing Schoenberg's volume *Style and Idea* (1950) for publication.[480] Schoenberg, who at the time dreamed of a visit and move to the new state of Israel, was attracted to the poem's content because it addresses Israel's fate: the Temple's destruction, the exiled Jews' desire to return to their homeland, and their hope for God's return to the Promised Land.[481]

To emphasize the idea of God's return at the end of the poem, Schoenberg slightly modified its form and wording, especially in the third and last stanza.[482] He also highlighted God's return musically, casting the three stanzas in a through-composed, but tripartite form, with each section gaining in length. Furthermore, he abstractly expressed the idea of return through musical palindromes: hexachords followed by their respective retrogrades in the first and last section of the setting (mm. 1–4 and 13–16). Schoenberg's hope for unity among Jews through their—and God's—return to Israel is reflected in the interaction of the voices, which develops from rhythmic-melodic independence to close integration. Interestingly, he decided to leave the text in German and let the Swedish new-music journal *Prisma* publish it in a special issue honoring his seventy-fifth birthday.[483] The Lila Chamber Choir under Eric Ericson gave the work's world premiere in Stockholm in 1949. Although it seems unlikely that Schoenberg had an American audience in mind when he spontaneously composed this setting, the piece is nonetheless accessible. It musically illustrates the text, and the inversionally combinatorial twelve-tone set on which the setting is based contains such tonal suggestions as thirds and a perfect fifth, which Schoenberg exploited throughout the setting.

While working on *Dreimal tausend Jahre*, Schoenberg had also planned to write "music to greet the new state of Israel."[484] He hoped to obtain a poetic text for the project from Friedrich Torberg, a Viennese-born writer and fellow émigré, as the two were friends in Los Angeles and had pondered collaborations before.[485] Instead, Schoenberg began to outline his own text for the hymn. Fearing that the new state of Israel might turn to Christianity, Schoenberg felt the need to stress the "foundation of Judaism," and "the idea that Jehovah overthrew Hitler, that Jehovah overthrew Bevin and that he will overthrow all our enemies."[486] Schoenberg showed Torberg his lyrics and received his advice, only to reject it. He disliked Torberg's suggestion of a substantial expansion of the text to include verses mentioning Haman, Pharaoh, Titus, and Hitler—political enemies of Jewry.[487] The final version joyously opens with "Israel exists again. It has always existed though invisibly," and does not mention the names of Jewry's enemies. Instead Schoenberg names the biblical figures Adam, Noah, Abraham, Jacob, and Moses, and emphasizes that it was Moses who "saw He was our God and we His elected people: elected to testify that there is only one eternal God."[488]

Conceived for chorus and orchestra, *Israel Exists Again* is based on an inversionally combinatorial twelve-tone set, as was *Dreimal tausend Jahre*. The earliest sketches for this work reveal that Schoenberg first wrote the melodic contour of the opening words and then drew the tone row with its tonal implications from that setting. He also composed a festive and fanfare-like opening that evokes C major. Unfortunately, he abandoned his ambitious and large-scale "national hymn" for Israel in July 1949, leaving a total of 55 measures: an orchestral introduction and setting of only three (out of eighteen) verses, perhaps amounting to about a fifth of the whole work. It would have resulted in another hybrid work, reflecting his three identities in idiosyncratic ways. The text reflects not only his Jewish, but also his American identity. Schoenberg's choice of English for the lyrics suggests that he was presenting himself in the role of an American Jew. The music, similarly to his other works written after 1933, would have evoked both his Jewish roots and German musical heritage. *Israel Exists Again* has been performed, although infrequently, and received its world premiere in Hamburg, Germany in 1958.

Composed between June 20 and July 2, 1950, Psalm 130 for mixed chorus was Schoenberg's last completed score and his only commissioned late sacred work. The Polish-born conductor, composer, and ethnomusicologist Chemjo Vinaver from the Jewish Agency for Palestine was joined by Bernard Halpern in inviting Schoenberg to contribute to the *Anthology of Jewish Music* a setting of Psalm 130 ("Out of the Depths I have called to Thee, O Lord") in Hebrew.[489] Vinaver provided Schoenberg with the Hebrew text, a pronunciation guide, two English translations, a Hasidic melody of this psalm, an "old liturgical motif" extracted from it, and information about the psalm's cantillation practice.[490] Schoenberg must have been particularly attracted to this psalm of lament, which mirrored his "lachrymose" view of himself.[491] Moreover, its conclusion, in which Israel is urged to wait until God redeems her from her sins, underlines Schoenberg's belief in the Jews as God's chosen people.

Although Vinaver had hoped that Schoenberg would make use of the Hasidic melody he sent him, Schoenberg confessed to him that he "profited from the liturgical motif" he got from him, "writing approximately a similar expression."[492] Yet he used a sophisticated dodecaphonic structure with tonal implications, which roughly followed the Hasidic melody's pitch configurations. Schoenberg also adapted the chant's eight-part structure to mark the end of a musical unit with respective rests for all six voices, and had considered Vinaver's Hebrew text and transliteration. Conceived for a six-part a cappella chorus, this five-minute work features a wide range of vocal expression, including a combination of singing and spoken recitation, which aims at a "dramatic character" and also recalls the Orthodox tradition of rendering psalms in sung and spoken form.[493] Schoenberg stated that he "imagined the spoken parts to sound like a monotonous prayer murmured in a medium to low register."[494] Starting with the second soprano alone, which articulates the musical initials of Schoenberg's name (E-flat and A), the textural development moves toward a dense homogeneous rhythmic and serial structure, and concludes with the dramatic exclamation of the word "Israel." Because of the chorus's difficult execution, Schoenberg allowed the use of woodwinds to support the singers.

In the summer of 1950 Schoenberg grouped Psalm 130 with *Dreimal tausend Jahre* and his last unfinished work, *Modern Psalm No. 1*, and assigned them the opus number 50. Although he told Vinaver that he planned "to make this [Psalm 130], together with two other pieces, a donation to Israel," he did not supply a dedication for the opus 50 manuscripts.[495] Psalm 130, which earned Schoenberg $100 (about $880 in 2009), was first published by Israeli Music Publications in 1953 and shortly thereafter in Vinaver's *Anthology* (E. B. Marks, 1953).[496] It is arguably the most unusual and complex contribution to the *Anthology*, which comprises mostly traditional Jewish melodies in conservative settings. Bernhard Zimmermann gave the Psalm setting its world premiere in Cologne in 1954.[497] Two years later, Roger Wagner and his UCLA a cappella choir performed it at the dedication ceremony of Arnold Schoenberg Hall at UCLA.

Although his fascination with "modern man learning to pray" dates back to at least 1912, it was Schoenberg's preoccupation with the intense penitential prayer text of Psalm 130 that led him to explore, in greater depth and on a much larger scale, the idea of prayer as a modern-day conversation with God.[498] He explained: "I am of the opinion that we should try to revive our ancient religion again. But I believe that the forms of the ancient Biblical language are no more convincing in our present use of the language. One has to talk to the people of our time in our own style and of our own problems."[499] From September 1950 until shortly before his death in July 1951, he worked on sixteen prose texts, which he planned to set to music and include in a cycle of fifty or more pieces. Some of the texts relate to the biblical psalms and prayers, in that they often directly address and praise God, and comprise confessions, laments, pleas, and expressions of hope (Psalms 1, 3–5, 8, and 14).[500] Other texts, however, are "Conversations" or meditations about a wide variety of themes. He took an idiosyncratic approach to his search for God and prayer, addressing the Mosaic notion of God's invisibility, the Jews as God's chosen people, his identification with Israel, the Ten Commandments as a moral basis for most people, the pros and cons of Jewish orthodoxy, liberal Judaism as a problem, the position of Jesus in Judaism, the question of theodicy, superstition, the belief in miracles, childlike faith and ethical questions. The texts are hybrid: Although they are in German, they contain some English words and anglicisms.

Schoenberg initially called the texts "Modern Psalms," and even assigned them numbers starting with 151 to continue the Old Testament numbering of the Psalms. Yet he soon decided that "the title *Modern Psalms* has to be deleted everywhere," and removed the bold numbering, substituting the preliminary title "Psalms, Prayers and Conversations with and about God."[501] However, when these mostly "half finished" private texts were posthumously published, the editor Rudolf Kolisch entitled them *Modern Psalms* (Schott, 1956).[502] Schoenberg's unfinished setting of the first text for mixed six-voice chorus, speaker and orchestra, was published as *Modern Psalm No.1*.

In his *Modern Psalm No. 1* (1950), Schoenberg focuses on the meaning of prayer to the "omnipotent, omniscient and unimaginable" God, and uses ambitious dodecaphonic procedures based on a so-called "miracle set." This inversionally combinatorial set, whose second hexachord mirrors the intervallic contour of the first hexachord in contrary order, permits numerous palindromic melodic configurations, hexachords directly followed by their retrograde.[503] The set's sophisticated structural makeup provoked speculations as to its inherent meanings. Alexander Ringer saw in it a reflection of the kabbalistic *Tiferet*, the "principle of cosmic harmony or beauty."[504] Thanks to the basic set's inclusion of two tonal triads, A-flat major and F-sharp major, as well as two additional major thirds, the piece displays a distinct tonal flavor, alluding to A-flat major and E minor at the beginning. After the phrase "Und trotzdem bete ich" (And yet I pray to thee) at measure 86, *Modern Psalm No. 1* breaks off with a C minor sonority in the soprano. Other devices ensuring accessibility include text painting. The opening of the piece involves all the forces to underscore the words "alle Völker preisen Dich [all people praise You]." Thereafter the choir is reduced to a four-voice texture and alternates with the speaker.

Despite its fragmented character, *Modern Psalm No. 1* has received some performances, although not very many. Its world premiere in Cologne in 1956 was soon followed by American performances, including a rendition by the Juilliard Chorus and Orchestra in New York in August 1957.

The final large-scale psalm project stands as yet another item in a group of ambitious religious works—*Jakobsleiter, Der biblische Weg, Moses und Aron,* and a Symphony on Jewish themes—that Schoenberg left unfinished. Rather than blame his living and working conditions in America for his inability to complete these works, one should consider Schoenberg's shifting priorities, and above all his faith-based concerns. Dika Newlin wondered if

> Schoenberg might have come to believe that the Supreme Commander would not grant him the completion of his greatest artistic testament—or for that matter, of *Die*

> *Jakobsleiter* or of the *Modern Psalms*. As he says of Mahler, he himself 'was allowed to reveal just so much of the future; when he wanted to say more, he was called away.' Yes, even a Schoenberg dared not approach too near in his conversations with God: '. . . let not God speak with us, lest we die!'[505]

Similarly Ringer speculated whether the "ostensible unfinishedness of Schoenberg's religious-philosophical triptych [*Jakobsleiter, Moses* and the Psalms] corresponds to the kabbalistic notion of *En sof*, the infinite God, literally the One Without End."[506] And Mark Risinger noted the conflict between Schoenberg's preoccupation with the idea of the "unimaginable and unrepresentable God" and the fact that works of art are representational, which might also have prevented him from finishing such works as his *Modern Psalm No. 1*.[507]

SCHOENBERG'S AMERICAN IDENTITY

Living in America for eighteen years, Schoenberg gradually developed a recognizable American identity. Despite his advanced age and the political, economic, and cultural challenges that arose, he adapted to his new homeland more smoothly, conscientiously, and graciously than did such fellow émigrés as Adorno, Brecht, Alfred Döblin, and the Mann brothers. He was grateful to be in a country where, as he acknowledged, "I am allowed to go on my own feet, where my head can be erect, where kindness and cheerfulness is dominating, and where to live is a joy and to be an expatriate of another country is the grace of God."[508] To Alma Mahler-Werfel, he wrote in 1939: "We are very happy to be here."[509] Schoenberg was proud of his U.S. citizenship, which he attained in 1941, and he identified as an American in many ways. Yet he refrained from overly emphasizing his affiliation with his new home country. His failed assimilationist ambitions in Europe, his expulsion from Germany, the fact that many native-born Americans treated him the same way that they treated other first-generation immigrants, as an outsider, were all factors in making him more cautious. It comes as no surprise that most Schoenberg commentators have represented him as one of the émigrés who most resisted Americanization. European champions of Schoenberg who have denied his Americanization have made a show of their solidarity with their idol, and portrayed him as a nonconformist European of strong character—an argument that also protects themselves from the common anti-Semitic accusation of the Jews' alleged facility for adapting to any given environment.

To survive as well as Schoenberg did, in a country that was then in the grip of the Great Depression, required great adaptability. Schoenberg found well-paid employment, at a time when unemployment hovered between 25 percent and 35 percent, and when thousands of university faculty positions had been cut, and the jobs of innumerable American musicians eliminated with the spread of sound film, radio, phonographs, and jukeboxes.[510] He was able to pursue his art and build a network of American friends despite the relentless influx of political refugees—seen as both competitors for jobs and challengers in the realm of art—which added to the existential anxieties among Americans and increased both xenophobia and anti-Semitism.[511] Schoenberg also showed nimbleness in the face of tax increases, rationing, and price controls imposed on the American population during the war years, and he understood how to stay out of political trouble during the anticommunist witch-hunts after the war.[512]

Thanks to his adaptability, he was able to build a vibrant social life in Los Angeles, undaunted by its spaciousness, the decentralization of its cultural sites, or the lack of such European urban staples as public places, sidewalk cafés, and a historical atmosphere—all of which had suggested "lifelessness," "disconnection," and "counterfeit urbanity" to many émigrés.[513] Declaring California "the most beautiful point on the earth," Schoenberg embraced the sprawling city of Los Angeles, whose population grew from 1.2 million to nearly 2 million during his years there, and whose cityscape during the 1930s and 1940s was marked by exotic single-family homes, apartment buildings, a few lively boulevards, lush palms, and oil-drilling rigs.[514] Besides his contact with Americans, he surely appreciated living in one of the city's luxurious homes, breathing its then clean air and having a lower cost of living than that of Bostonians and New Yorkers.

Language and Lifestyle

Schoenberg, who felt "speechless" and "language-less" upon his departure from Europe, quickly realized that the key to his successful acculturation to America was the mastery of English, of which he had only rudimentary knowledge.[515] In the summer of 1933, he anglicized his last name, replacing the umlaut with *oe*, gave up his gothic handwriting, and began to learn and use English.[516] On November 11, 1933, at the League of Composers all-Schoenberg concert and reception, he delivered one of his first speeches in English. A week later, he had his first English interview with NBC.[517] By early December 1933 he had started working on one of his first comprehensive essays in English, "Forward to a Jewish Unity Party."[518] From the very beginning, he taught his classes in English. To make himself better understood, he initially relied on the assistance of an interpreter and invited his students or assistants to correct his English. He soon became quite fluent and used English as his primary language. In the summer of 1935 he attended a Shakespeare festival. In 1939 his student Dika Newlin confirmed his eagerness to master colloquial English, when she observed that Schoenberg "loved to work in a bit of the latest slang whenever he could."[519] Schoenberg used English to communicate with Americans and Europeans. To his former disciple Erwin Stein, who immigrated to England, he wrote in 1942: "I doubt that we two will ever take advantage of the 'Du,' because when we meet we will probably both speak English."[520] More than half of the letters from Schoenberg's American years are in English.[521] Moreover, Schoenberg urged vocal performers in America to use English translations of German texts in his early vocal works.[522]

Schoenberg was never able to perfect his English, which remained colored by Germanisms and retained a strong Austrian accent. While communicating with his children in English, he continued to speak his heritage language with his wife, although he used German less and less in a pure way.[523] In corresponding with German-speaking Americans, he employed his mother tongue irregularly or mixed it with English words and grammar. Writing to Austrian-born Kurt List, for instance, he used German influenced by English grammar: "Für diese habe ich *in 1932* einen Gesamtbetrag von $150.00 bekommen."[524] In a letter to Universal Edition, he slipped in and out of German: "Vor ungefähr zwei Wochen ersuchte ich Sie... [long text in German] . . . *I will send you a letter, which will explain my opinion about Mr. Winter. A letter from my lawyer*. Oh, jetzt hab ich englisch geschrieben: ich wiederhole . . ."[525]

This type of linguistic dissimilation is also apparent in his theoretical writings, especially his 1950 essay collection *Style and Idea,* which includes translations of older German texts and revisions of newer English articles. Schoenberg did not want to conceal that he was "not born in this language" or "to parade adorned by the stylistic merits of another person."[526] After struggling with editors and translators, who overstepped the boundaries of what his "Americanized conscience can permit," he found his ideal collaborator, his student Dika Newlin, who spoke and wrote fluent German.[527] She was able to conform to Schoenberg's peculiar linguistic ideas and "adhered as literally to the original style as English usage."[528] Yet he was often frustrated by the differences between the German and English languages and sometimes even felt that "the English language is really a plain business language which continually fails in metaphysical matters."[529] Overall, however, Schoenberg customized *Style and Idea* to American audiences. While he addressed cultural life in America in his shorter and newer articles, he purged the articles he had conceived in Europe of "most of the polemics which were right in Germany but not here."[530]

As Schoenberg enhanced his understanding of American English, he began adopting American ways of communication. This is especially evident in his correspondence with Americans, which is often speckled with such polite gestures as "I am very sorry, dear Mr. Smith," or "I gladly agree."[531] Schoenberg keenly observed American habits, often trying to wed them to his own. He enjoyed American foods, which he described to his son-in-law Felix Greissle in 1938 as follows: "Americans have coffee, bread with butter and cereal for breakfast. For lunch also cereal . . . or crackers in milk or if there are leftover meats or vegetables from the previous day, they have a sandwich. People frequently eat salads, cheese, vegetables and cereals. This is very nutritious and filling and I, for instance, like it very much."[532] He took pleasure in fixing his children peanut butter and jelly sandwiches, often cutting them into animal shapes. He loved American ice cream and discovered a taste for whiskey.[533] The Schoenbergs regularly observed American holidays in traditionally American ways, celebrating Thanksgiving with a turkey dinner.[534]

Schoenberg enjoyed going to the movies, even though he criticized the frequently low intellectual level of Hollywood films. He favored gangster, spy, and western films and movies featuring Chaplin, the Marx Brothers, and Harold Lloyd.[535] He liked Charlie Chaplin's last silent film *Modern Times* (1936), although he carped at its music.[536] In the spring of 1939 Schoenberg "stood in front of the class debating with himself as to whether or not he ought to dismiss" the students to yield to "his desire to go and see the afternoon showing of *La Grande Illusion*," Jean Renoir's 1937 antiwar movie starring Erich von Stroheim.[537] In the late 1940s, when he no longer frequented cinemas, he became engrossed with radio and TV shows, such as *The Lone Ranger* and *Hopalong Cassidy*. Schoenberg also followed UCLA football games on the radio and was fond of such radio shows as *Professor Quiz* and *Information Please!* The latter was launched in 1938 and featured his student Oscar Levant as a regular panelist. Newlin reported that Schoenberg once sacrificed ten minutes of a class "to figure out in the midst of the most uproarious hilarity, questions to send in to Mr. Levant for *Information Please!*"[538]

Schoenberg even embraced American clothing styles. He felt that in America "one does not need to wear expensive clothes, but they have to be clean, well-ironed suits, a perfectly clean shirt and a tie, gleaming shoes, always, at all hours of the day."[539] Newlin recalled her teacher's Hollywoodesque outfit when he taught a class in 1939: "It consisted of a peach-colored shirt, a green tie with white polka-dots, a knit belt of the most vivid purple with a large and ostentatious gold buckle, and an unbelievably loud gray suit with lots of black and brown stripes."[540] In 1944 Brecht was struck by Schoenberg's unusual appearance: clad in a "blue Californian silk jacket," he looked "astonishingly lively" and "Gandhi-like."[541] Charlie Chaplin, however, remembered seeing him at the tennis court "in bleachers wearing a white cap and a T-shirt."[542]

Schoenberg's Responses to American Politics

Schoenberg's acculturation is also manifest in his political thinking. Contrary to the self-created myth that he was an apolitical artist, Schoenberg was not only preoccupied with Jewish politics, as already discussed, but also an eager follower of American politics. American politics even influenced some of his musical works and writings.

Unlike many other émigrés, he was skeptical about democracy. Being a member of ethnic and cultural minorities, Schoenberg approached culture individualistically and aristocratically. He distrusted the notion of majority rule that is such a bedrock principle of democracy and insisted, "Democracy has always meant one thing for me: that in it I will *never* succeed even so much as to make my will known, let alone to have it prevail." He also felt that the will of the majority is "accidental" and that it "comes about only through compromises" and "corruption of the individual's will."[543] Distancing himself from egalitarian sentiments, he explained in 1939: "I am not a leftist. Namely, inasmuch as I would in no way grant to everyone the right of freedom of expression, only to those who actually possessed an opinion worthy of expressing. I would also not call myself a rightist, since I do not believe in the equalizing value of stultification. Perhaps I am a progressive conservative, who would like to develop and advance things worthy of preserving."[544] Having experienced the failure of the Weimar Republic democracy, he was doubtful about this system's merits:

> I know to value the worth of democracy, although I am not in a position to overlook its weakest points: included in the orthodox exaggeration of its principles is the possibility of overthrowing it. The free expression of opinion allows anyone to make propaganda for a change in the form of government, and as a result democracy everywhere has proven itself unable to deal with opposition. And I in no way overlook the evil of fascism, since the power that is bestowed through it can scarcely do other than to fall into the wrong hands.[545]

Pondering the consequences of a war between the United States and Nazi Germany in March 1939, Schoenberg worried that anti-Semitic propaganda would prompt President Roosevelt to let Americans democratically decide about the fate of German and Jewish residents in America. He feared that émigrés could be interned. Yet Schoenberg, who held Roosevelt in high regard, still hoped that this president would "find a way to protect faultless Germans (Jews or liberals)."[546] He wished that Roosevelt would "let them, based on declarations of suretyship by American citizens, attain American citizenship, or to enable them to perform patriotic activities, so that they won't have to leave the country."[547] Such worries probably sped up his application for U.S. citizenship, and he took the oath on April 11, 1941, just before the United States entered World War II.[548] Feeling "blessed to be an American citizen," he was deeply affected by the bombing of Pearl Harbor, Roosevelt's declaration of war on Japan after the "Date of Infamy" speech, and the ensuing patriotic fervor.[549] In 1942 he paid tribute to Roosevelt with his *Ode to Napoleon*, in which a text by Lord Byron serves to allude to the political alignments at the time.[550] Schoenberg even hoped that Roosevelt's administration would use this piece for wartime propaganda purposes! He also took pride in his two grandsons, Arnold and Hermann Greissle, when they joined the U.S. military to fight in World War II, and was gratified when one of them captured a German.[551]

After the war, however, Schoenberg began to portray himself as apolitical and declared that artists meddling in politics should, due to their naïveté, be "treated like immature children."[552] When America came under the spell of the "Second Red Scare," he witnessed the blacklisting and investigations of many friends, including his former student Hanns Eisler, before the House Un-American Activities Committee. Although he had always been an opponent of communism, in 1943 Schoenberg was classified as a "thoroughly disreputable Communist Zionist" by J. Edgar Hoover because of his support of the Jewish Army of Stateless and Palestinian Jews. He vigorously distanced himself from Eisler, who was questioned in 1947 and extradited.[553] No FBI file was made on Schoenberg, but he was cross-referenced thirteen times in Eisler's FBI file, which prompted the FBI to search his home.[554] The FBI agents thought they had found suspicious books in Schoenberg's library: Adolf Bernhard Marx's four-volume *Die Lehre von der musikalischen Komposition* (Leipzig, 1887) and *Anleitung zum Vortrag Beethovenscher Werke* (Regensburg, 1912). Fortunately Schoenberg was able to clarify that these were music books and that Adolph Bernhard (1795–1866) was not related to Karl.

As a retired professor of the University of California, Schoenberg was also affected by the controversy surrounding that institution's requirement of a loyalty oath (1949–51), forcing faculty to renounce any communist affiliations. While Schoenberg found the university's requirement "tactless," he wrote: "I was ready to furnish the oath, I was never a communist . . . I swear that I will be a reliable citizen and will live strictly as a law abiding citizen."[555] As a consequence Schoenberg seriously reflected about all his relationships with leftist and communist acquaintances, including the German conductor Hermann Scherchen.[556] Schoenberg's 1950 essay "My Attitude Toward Politics," in which he denied any interest and involvement in politics, can be read as a reaction to these political events.[557] The same is true of Schoenberg's much-quoted letter to his former student Josef Rufer, wherein he proclaims: "We who live in *music* have no place in politics and must regard them as something essentially alien to us. We are a-political and the most we can do is endeavor to stay quietly in the background."[558]

In the process of depoliticizing his image, Schoenberg prohibited the use of his works to advance political dogma. When José Limón in 1950 asked him for permission to choreograph his Second Chamber Symphony, Schoenberg authorized the use of his music on two conditions: "no reference to any political creed" and "no sexual vulgarities."[559] The latter stipulation can be interpreted as Schoenberg's adjustment to the so-called "Production" or "Hays Code" (1934–68), whose censorship guidelines for the production of films defined what was morally acceptable and unacceptable film content for the American public.

Schoenberg's Interactions with Hollywood Celebrities

As a resident of Hollywood and later Westwood, Schoenberg was more than ever confronted with the world of entertainment. The child actress Shirley Temple and the songwriter Cole Porter lived on the same street as Schoenberg, North Rockingham Drive.[560] Never immune to popular entertainment and hedonism, Schoenberg mingled with many American-born actors, screenwriters, and directors, including Harpo Marx, Clifford Odets, and Orson Welles, as well as composers, arrangers, songwriters, and lyricists, such as Irving Berlin, David Buttolph, George Gershwin, Werner Janssen, Albert Sendrey, and Herbert Stothart.[561] Notable talents such as Hugo Friedhofer, Skitch Henderson, Serge Hovey, Oscar Levant, Alfred Newman, Eddie Powell, Ralph Rainger, David Raksin, Leo Robin, and Nathaniel Shilkret also took lessons with Schoenberg, privately or at USC and UCLA, but they were more than just students. Besides the generous remuneration for their lessons, they offered Schoenberg insight into Hollywood, played tennis and ping-pong with him, and helped him with his everyday problems.

A legendary comedian and performer of Gershwin's music, Levant was one of the students with whom Schoenberg liked to spend time beyond their lessons (Figure 3.18). Schoenberg loved listening to Levant's radio appearances and no doubt must have found Levant an entertaining person with whom to discuss music and musicians in Hollywood. Levant occasionally drove Schoenberg around in an old Ford, and introduced him to Gershwin, Harpo Marx, Beatrice Lillie, and Fanny Brice.[562] In October 1935 he even arranged an introduction to Charlie Chaplin, whom Schoenberg admired greatly (Figure 3.19). Levant helped Schoenberg to become a member of the American Society of Composers, Authors, and Publishers (ASCAP), and engaged him to write a piano work that developed into his Piano Concerto, op. 42. However, the vague negotiations concerning this commission eventually strained the relationship between the two men. Levant had apparently requested a small piano piece, but backed out of the project when Schoenberg's piece grew into a large-scale work. Levant also felt unable to meet Schoenberg's increasing monetary demands.[563]

Music director at United Artists until 1939 and thereafter head of the music department at Twentieth Century-Fox, Alfred Newman was another student (1936–38) who was also a friend of Schoenberg. Newman played tennis with him, often at Newman's court in Beverly Hills, and invited Schoenberg and his wife to his parties, where they encountered the theater and film director Rouben Mamoulian and opera baritone Lawrence Tibbett, as well as the Friedhofers and Powells.[564]

FIGURE 3.18.
Oscar Levant. Bettmann Archive.

FIGURE 3.19.
Charlie Chaplin, Gertrud and Arnold Schoenberg, and David Raksin. Courtesy Arnold Schönberg Center.

Schoenberg followed Newman's musical activities with interest and attended concerts conducted by Newman at the Hollywood Bowl.[565] One of Schoenberg's most important contacts in the film industry, Newman not only helped his friends and students find work in Hollywood, but also initiated the first (private) recording of Schoenberg's four string quartets by the Kolisch Quartet (1936–37).[566] He convinced his boss, producer Samuel Goldwyn, to make the United Artists recording studio (Stage 7) available for this project and pay for the studio costs, which were at that time around $85 an hour (about $1,300 in 2009).[567] In 1938 Newman prided himself on having "had a chance to do something for music that the art for art's sake boys couldn't or wouldn't do, and we took it. Once in a while, you see, we can be unfaithful to the great god Profits."[568] That same year, he engaged Schoenberg to present the Academy Award for the best film score of 1937. Unfortunately, Schoenberg had to cancel his speech and his participation at the ceremonial banquet of the Academy of Motion Picture Arts and Sciences due to illness. Universal Pictures and its music director, Charles Previn (André Previn's second cousin), received the award for the score of *A Hundred Men and a Girl*, and some brief remarks of Schoenberg's were read. The film starred Deanna Durbin and Schoenberg champion Leopold Stokowski, and alluded to the programs of the Federal Music Project for improving the situation of unemployed musicians. In his Oscar speech, Schoenberg welcomed the honoring of excellence as a means to stimulate progress in the field of film scoring and endorsed the effort of the movie industry to make moviegoers more "music conscious."[569]

Rainger, Powell, and Raksin sponsored the first recording of Schoenberg's quartets by purchasing the four albums, at a total cost of over $70 (about $1,035 in 2009) for the twenty-three 12-inch disks. Both Rainger and Raksin studied with Schoenberg in 1936 and 1937. Rainger, the composer of Bob Hope's signature song "Thanks for the Memory" from *The Big Broadcast of 1938*, paid for his lessons a year in advance ($600, about $9,200 in 2009), enabling Schoenberg to finance the shipment of his furniture from Paris to Los Angeles.[570] Shortly before his premature death in 1942, Rainger tried to help Schoenberg with affidavits for his relatives. Introduced to Schoenberg by Levant, Raksin, the composer for Otto Preminger's film *Laura* (1944), took credit for proposing that Alec Compinsky, head of the record label ALCO, commercially reissue the recordings of Schoenberg's quartets, which ALCO did in 1950.[571] Shilkret had taken lessons with Schoenberg in New York and was music director of the Victor Talking Machine Company and, from the mid-1930s, music director of RKO and MGM. He arranged for Schoenberg to conduct the Cadillac Symphony in a 1934 radio concert, and offered him jobs for his son and a student.[572] Shilkret also commissioned him in 1945 to write the Prelude to *Genesis* for a generous sum of money, but failed to publish and rerecord it as quickly as he had promised.

Gershwin, who in the summer of 1936 had moved to Beverly Hills to work for the movies, also became one of Schoenberg's friends and supporters.[573] He even contemplated the possibility of studying with Schoenberg—his previous teacher Joseph Schillinger had suggested that he should "work with Schoenberg on four-part fugues"—but the idea came to naught.[574] Schoenberg and Gershwin played tennis weekly at Gershwin's Beverly Hills court, and, according to Levant, Schoenberg did not even miss the game on the day his son Ronald was born.[575] Hollywood composer Albert Sendrey once witnessed and described an episode of their game: "He, Gershwin, expresses linear counterpoint in his strokes, whereas Schoenberg concentrates on mere harmony, the safe return of the ball, the more than physical aspect of reaching a well-placed drive in the far corner of his side; he no longer places his returns, while George is more careful than ever to achieve clarity of his intentions."[576] At Gershwin's tennis court, Schoenberg, who often showed up "with an entourage of string quartet players, conductors and disciples," also met Gershwin's associates: his brother Ira, Harold Arlen, Jerome Kern, and Yip Harburg.[577]

Besides tennis, Schoenberg and Gershwin shared another passion: painting. Yet while Schoenberg focused on this art early in his career, Gershwin took it up in the last years of his life (1929–37). He commissioned the photographer Edward Weston to take pictures of Schoenberg so that he could use one of them as a model for his oil portrait of his friend. Completed in December 1936, this portrait was his last oil of over a hundred paintings (Figure 3.20).[578]

Schoenberg and Gershwin followed each other's music. Familiar with Schoenberg's music since the 1910s, Gershwin owned several Schoenberg scores and heard the American *Pierrot* premiere in 1923. He even studied the twelve-tone technique with his teacher Schillinger.[579] In Los Angeles, he attended the Kolisch Quartet's 1937 performances of all four Schoenberg string quartets, which "deeply" impressed him, and a Federal Music Project concert featuring *Pelleas*.[580] Gershwin supported Schoenberg and his music in various ways. Together with the Filene department-store owners in Boston, he contributed money to bring Schoenberg to the United States and to a scholarship fund enabling Malkin Conservatory students in Boston to study with Schoenberg.[581] On the occasion of Schoenberg's Mailamm lecture in New York in 1934, he prepared a welcome address that was read on his behalf.

FIGURE 3.20.
Gershwin and his portrait of Schoenberg. Courtesy Ira and Leonore Gershwin Trust and Henry Botkin Papers, 1917–1979, Archives of American Art, Smithsonian Institution.

Gershwin also supported the first recording of Schoenberg's String Quartets through the acquisition of a set of records, and even planned to commission a work from him, although that idea did not reach fruition.

Schoenberg, too, was supportive and fond of Gershwin's music. In February 1937 he attended a Los Angeles Philharmonic concert featuring the *Rhapsody in Blue*, Concerto in F, *An American in Paris*, and excerpts from *Porgy and Bess*, with Gershwin as soloist and Alexander Smallens as conductor.[582] Schoenberg tried, though unsuccessfully, to induce Klemperer to perform some of Gershwin's works with the Los Angeles Philharmonic. Yet only after Gershwin's death did Klemperer program David Broekman's orchestral arrangement of the Prelude in C sharp for a Gershwin memorial concert at the Hollywood Bowl.[583] Although Schoenberg loved Gershwin's music, he vacillated, like most commentators, in his categorization of his oeuvre, classifying it sometimes as serious and sometimes as popular music. In a 1934 letter he wrote to his European friends: "I am commonly appreciated here as one of the most important modern composers with Stravinsky, Tansman, Sessions, Sibelius, Gershwin, Copland, etc."[584] In a 1937 Gershwin memorial broadcast, he not only deplored the loss of a dear friend, but also called Gershwin a "great composer" who contributed to a "national American music" and "the music of the whole world."[585] And in his sketch for an orchestration treatise of the late 1940s, he listed

Gershwin with Barber, Copland, Carter, Cowell, Griffes, Sessions, and others, and not with Johann Strauss, Offenbach, and Lehár, representing popular music.[586] But in other statements, Schoenberg grouped Gershwin with Offenbach and Strauss, composers who do not "descend from their heights" to cater to the masses, but "whose feelings actually coincide with those of the 'average man in the street.'"[587] What impressed Schoenberg perhaps most was the organic and natural character of Gershwin's music, a quality Schoenberg wanted to achieve in his own music and which he often described with biological and botanical metaphors. In an essay on Gershwin, Schoenberg stated:

> An artist is to me like an apple tree: When his time comes, whether he wants it or not, he bursts into bloom and starts to produce apples. And as an apple tree neither knows nor asks about the value experts of the market will attribute to its product, so a real composer does not ask whether his products will please the experts of serious arts . . . Gershwin was an innovator. What he has done with rhythm, harmony and melody is not merely style. His melodies are not products of a combination, nor of a mechanical union, but they are units and could therefore not be taken to pieces . . . [He] expressed musical ideas; and they were new—as is the way in which he expressed them.[588]

Beyond Schoenberg's social involvement with Hollywood celebrities, he was, as he had expected, invited to contribute music to several films: MGM's *The Good Earth* (directed by Sidney Franklin, 1937), a projected Warner Brothers film about Beethoven, and Paramount's *Souls at Sea* (directed by Henry Hathaway, 1937).[589] Although none of these scoring prospects materialized, Schoenberg had considered *The Good Earth* project seriously. After analyzing Pearl S. Buck's best-selling novel, he filled two small books with musical sketches. Schoenberg's negotiations with this film's celebrated producer Irving Thalberg foundered in 1935 when Schoenberg insisted on full control of the soundtrack (including dialogue) and demanded a fee of $50,000 (about $773,500 in 2009).[590] No Hollywood studio would have accepted Schoenberg's rejection of the division of labor, and Schoenberg, while tempted by the creative challenge and the opportunity to earn a large fee, was not ready to risk his reputation as a prophet of high art.[591] In 1940 Schoenberg published the critical essay "Art and the Moving Pictures," in which he deplored the vulgar and sentimental character, simplistic plots, "realistic backdrops," and lack of classical music of many motion pictures, and pleaded for a high-quality cinematic art.[592] Yet this act did not signal his withdrawal from the film world. In 1941 he became a member of the honorary advisory group of the Hollywood Theater Alliance Music Council, an organization of directors, actors, composers, and performers working in movie studios.[593] In the 1940s Schoenberg planned the foundation of a "School for Soundmen" to educate a new generation of music professionals working in film and radio, and even contemplated taking lessons with a Hollywood arranger (but was discouraged by his son-in-law).[594] In 1948 he stated in an interview, "There are a number of talented musicians among radio and movie composers, but music will never be distinguished until the producers stop using their own taste as a yardstick." He also thought that there should be two filmic categories and explained: "You go to an opera twenty times and to most operettas only once. In the same way some pictures should be made to be seen over and over, and others simply for light amusement."[595] Perhaps he was thinking of John and James Whitney, two independent experimental filmmakers in California whom Schoenberg knew. John Whitney, a composer, studied twelve-tone technique with Schoenberg's admirer René Leibowitz during his stay in Paris before the war. Schoenberg's dodecaphonic music inspired some of the Whitney brothers' abstract animation films, most notably the *Twenty-Four Variations* (1940).[596]

Schoenberg's American family also dabbled in film. His wife Gertrud, trained in theater arts at the Max Reinhardt Seminar in Vienna, wrote several screenplays, which she submitted to various studios for consideration, to no avail.[597] But his children Nuria and Ronald actively participated in *Prelude to War* (1943), the first documentary feature in Frank Capra's *Why We Fight* patriotic wartime film series. They acted the roles of German schoolchildren who sang songs hailing Hitler.

Schoenberg was acquainted with several jazz musicians. He knew Artie Shaw, whom he had met through Eisler and Salka Viertel, and from whom he received advice on royalty matters.[598] His student George Tremblay was a very gifted improviser in the Los Angeles jazz scene. In a 1942 concert he improvised on a three-bar fugue subject provided by Schoenberg, turning it into a veritable jazz piece. The press felt that Tremblay "used a Schoenberg theme to make 'boogie-woogie.'"[599] In 1942 Dave Brubeck and Schoenberg had a brief encounter, as Brubeck considered taking lessons with Schoenberg. But nothing came out of it since the young Brubeck disliked his teaching style.[600]

Schoenberg may have known many more jazz (and popular-music) composers through his affiliation with ASCAP, a performing-rights society that then catered mainly to composers of jazz and popular music. He was appreciative of being accepted into this group of commercially successful artists, even though their manners were much more easy-going than his. One ASCAP songwriter apparently told him at a meeting: "You know, Arnold, I don't know your stuff, but you must be O.K. or you wouldn't be here."[601] Upon his election to ASCAP membership in 1939, he happily wrote to ASCAP's president: "I am much honored by belonging to a society, to which those American composers belong, who have been of the greatest importance to the development of American music."[602] He was actually fond of American jazz and popular music, and lent his support to composers of this music when needed. For instance, he financially supported songwriter L. Gilbert Wolfe and helped to get works of Albert Sendrey, an arranger of musicals at MGM, performed. He wrote to the manager of the Hollywood Bowl: "This serves to introduce Mr. Albert Sendrey, a very skillful young American-born composer, who wants to win your favour [*sic*] for his 'Jazz Symphony.' May [I] add, that I can recommend him very warmly because he does not compose in a 'Schoenbergian' style, but in a much more pleasant one."[603] Schoenberg even felt that this group of composers gained from some of his "new harmonies" and "effects of [his] orchestration." While this may have been possible—according to Schoenberg, Duke Ellington "laughingly stated that occasionally he might borrow from [him]"—he was wrong in expecting to be given credit for introducing the trombone glissando in 1901.[604]

Schoenberg had hoped for a "profitable" membership, and he greatly benefited from his association with ASCAP, being paid substantial fees "more as a tribute to his importance in the musical world than as an accurate measure."[605] Initially he received a yearly sum of $740 (about $11,300 in 2009), which in 1944 was raised to $1,100 (about $13,300 in 2009). In addition, he obtained, upon his request in 1942, a royalty advance of $500 (about $6,500 in 2009). From 1949 on, he obtained, in addition to royalty payments, an annual stipend of $1,500 (about $13,400 in 2009).

His mingling with artists from the entertainment scene may have contributed to the celebrity coverage he received from time to time in the *Los Angeles Times*. In 1935 the screenwriter Anita Loos placed him among the top ten "Gentlemen in

Hollywood";[606] in 1941 the famous heavyweight-boxing champion Joe Louis wanted to enlist Schoenberg's support for his charity to promote better race relations.[607]

Schoenberg's Interactions with American Classical Composers

Schoenberg's relationship with the American classical music scene was much more complex. His inclination to identify himself as an American composer was limited, perhaps because he could not completely sever himself from his European roots and because he thought that American classical music was still in its infancy. He never portrayed himself straightforwardly as an American composer. However, when Claire Reis approached him for biographical information for the third edition of her book *Composers in America* (Macmillan, 1938), he wrote: "May I first congratulate you on the splendid idea of compiling a book on American composers and including also such ones who did not come with the Mayflower!"[608] He approached the American Composers Alliance, which he joined when it was founded in 1938: "May I ask you whether I am considered now an American composer (as regards to the programs of the world fair)[?]"[609] A fervent supporter of performances of American music ever since his arrival in America, Schoenberg felt "that on all the programs given in this country at least half of the compositions should be required to be American."[610] Of course, he hoped that in such a case, he and his music would qualify as American. Nevertheless, throughout his American career Schoenberg worried that he would once again become the victim of nationalism.[611]

Many American composers and music-related organizations were of two minds about Schoenberg's presence in America, and generally identified him as a foreign composer. On the one hand, he was accepted as a member or honorary member of such organizations as the League of Composers, the American Composers Alliance's Advisory Council, the Los Angeles–based Pro Musica Society, and the Crescendo Club. On the other, he was treated like a foreigner or "other." On the occasion of the 1939–40 New York World's Fair, Schoenberg's name was inscribed on a "Wall of Fame" dedicated to "six hundred American citizens of foreign birth and American Indians and Negroes who have made outstanding contributions to our [America's] culture."[612] The National Institute of Arts and Letters honored him in 1947 with a $1,000 Award of Merit for Distinguished Achievement, given annually to an "eminent foreign artist living in America," instead of offering him full membership as an American composer in their organization. Furthermore, the American press typically spelled his last name with an umlaut, ignoring his preference for the anglicized version of his name.

American composers' acceptance or nonacceptance of Schoenberg as a fellow composer in the 1930s and 1940s was sometimes determined by their aesthetic direction, or how they defined themselves in relation to musical tendencies in Europe. Henry Cowell, Charles Ives, Wallingford Riegger, Roger Sessions, and other modernists welcomed his presence in America; numerous neo-classically inclined and politically engaged composers nurtured by the teachings of Nadia Boulanger seemed ambivalent: Paul Bowles, Aaron Copland, and Elie Siegmeister. Conservative figures, including Daniel Gregory Mason, William Schuman, and Deems Taylor, tended to be somewhat antagonistic toward Schoenberg. Yet aesthetic differences did not always thwart friendships between composers of these groups and Schoenberg. The main source of tension between many American composers and Schoenberg was that they felt that he (along with other émigrés) could stand in the way of their creation of a national American music. Many American composers saw

Schoenberg's compositional approach as either Teutonic or internationalist, and thus incompatible with their vision of musical Americanism.

As increasing numbers of refugee composers from Nazi Europe inundated the United States during rather lean years, American composers felt that they were losing both their struggle for visibility and opportunities for income from their art. American composer Mark Brunswick observed that, due to a lack of widespread European-style performance venues, "America was not ripe for a sudden musical renaissance through this immediate contact with a more intense and in that sense higher musical culture of Europe."[613] This situation led to xenophobia, anti-Semitism, and regional prejudice, and to the foundation of organizations rebelling against the dominion of foreign-born composers. One such group was the New York–based Composers-Authors Society (founded in 1946), which, oddly enough, invited Schoenberg to link up with it. He declined: "I would certainly have joined your group, were it not that you fight for native Americans, which means exclusion of Europeans. You have my sympathy for your fight for recognition but you cannot expect that I myself vote against me and against my colleagues from other European countries. Would you not find me a hypocrite, if I did?"[614] A similar organization reflecting resentment of foreign-born musicians was the Los Angeles–based Society of Native American Composers (SNAC, 1938–44), a continuation of the California Society of Composers (1936–38), formed by the local composers Charles Wakefield Cadman, Homer Grunn, Mary Carr Moore, and Richard Drake Saunders.[615] Schoenberg had only limited dealings with the group.

Several of Schoenberg's friendships with American composers dated to his European years. Adolph Weiss, who had studied with Schoenberg in Europe and promoted his work in America before 1933, was a member of Schoenberg's American circle from the beginning (Figure 3.21). He assisted him in both professional and private matters when Schoenberg first settled on the East Coast.[616] During Schoenberg's tenure at the Malkin Conservatory, Weiss served as his teaching assistant.[617] A bassoonist in the Chautauqua Symphony, Weiss convinced him to recover from his stressful first teaching year in beautifully located Chautauqua. The Schoenberg and Weiss families socialized there in the summer of 1934. Schoenberg reported to Berg that "we had a good time together, played a lot of tennis and my wife won the 'World Championship of Chautauqua' (a joke) in ping-pong, whereas in tennis we were both thrown out in the first round."[618] Weiss stayed in touch with Schoenberg as he joined the San Francisco Symphony (1936) and RKO and MGM Studio Orchestras in Los Angeles (1938–41). He frequently attended Schoenberg's parties, including birthday celebrations, and they played tennis together. They also supported each other professionally. Weiss temporarily worked on a translation of *Harmonielehre* to make it available as a textbook. He attended and organized Schoenberg concerts, performed his music, and wrote and lectured about it.[619] Schoenberg, who regarded Weiss highly, recommended his music, invited him to speak to his classes and wrote glowing recommendations to help Weiss find a publisher for his works and a teaching job—all to no avail.[620] Schoenberg, however, did successfully recommend Weiss for a Guggenheim fellowship in 1931.

Yet their friendship was not without tension. Weiss never found an academic appointment, and often had to accept positions in second-rank orchestras; he increasingly felt neglected as a composer, too. Blaming the influx of Jewish émigrés, he made no secret of his anti-Semitism when he complained about this situation to his composer-friend Otto Luening: "The Jews are sitting pretty with all the jobs in

FIGURE 3.21.
Schoenberg and Adolph Weiss, c. 1936. Courtesy Arnold Schönberg Center.

their pockets and we Aryan fools invite even more to come over here to take our jobs if we have any. Too bad that we have to draw the racial line, that the Jews are defining that line as time goes on."[621] In 1941 Weiss joined SNAC, perhaps as a result of his frustration.[622] In the meantime Schoenberg discovered Weiss's anti-Semitic inclinations and embarrassed him at a party hosted by UCLA psychology professor Caroline Fisher in 1939:[623] "Are you a Nazi?" he asked Weiss there. In a reconciliatory letter to Weiss, Schoenberg regretted his question's imprecision: "I should have asked you whether you are an anti-Semite," he wrote and explained his understandable sensitivity in this matter.[624] Yet the issue was not settled for good. In 1943 Weiss, then executive director of SNAC, falsely suspected Schoenberg of having secretly informed Ives about SNAC's anti-Semitic and pro-fascist tendencies. Ives, a SNAC sponsor from 1942 to 1944 and concerned about its ideology, threatened to resign. Yet defiantly, Weiss complained to Edgar Varèse:

I do not see Schoenberg at all. His anti-Semitic suspicions are recurring again. If these ardent Semites would only realize that we are no more anti-Semitic than they are anti-Aryan we might get along better. But they want the exclusive right of being anti-Aryan with impunity. For in every Jew there is a touch of anti-Aryanism just because Aryan is different from Semitic. We get along beautifully until this difference creeps into consciousness.[625]

In 1948 Weiss confided to Varèse: "We have not seen the Schoenbergs for months . . . The stars of friendship and love seem to be askew this past year."[626] Weiss was unable to understand the cause for Schoenberg's distancing himself. Yet despite such tensions, Schoenberg and Weiss surprisingly reconciled again before his death.

Henry Cowell's friendship with Schoenberg began in Europe as well. He met him through Weiss in 1932 in Berlin. When he learned about Schoenberg's move to the United States he raved:

America has benefited by the exile of many of Germany's leading musicians whose ancestry was 'impure.' Schreker is in Vienna, Toch is in England, Fitelberg is in Paris, but the greatest of them all, came to America under the auspices of the newly formed Malkin Conservatory of Boston, where he is teaching composition. His first appearances in America were huge successes . . . and the same critics who 10 years ago called him an unimportant juggler with discord and ugliness wrote that his coming was the most important event of the season.[627]

Unlike Weiss, Cowell fully recognized foreign-born artists as fellow American citizens contributing to America's culture (Figure 3.22). In an article "On Programming American Music," he emphasized:

Last, but not least, let us not exclude those men who choose America as their country. Many of us are Americans through accident of birth. How proud we should be that the opportunities and principles of America have attracted many of the world's greatest composers to become citizens! All too often they are forgotten in American programs; yet they ARE Americans, and have no other country. And they represent every sort of music.[628]

Cowell tried to promote Schoenberg in various ways. When Schoenberg quit his Malkin Conservatory job, Cowell contemplated a scenario where Schoenberg "might work shoulder to shoulder with him" at the New School for Social Research.[629] Until 1936 he lectured on and promoted performances of Schoenberg's music through his New Music Workshops (directed by Gerald Strang) and New Music Society of California.

In 1936 when Cowell's career was suddenly interrupted by his imprisonment on a charge of a homosexual relation with an adolescent, Schoenberg in return lent Cowell his support. To help get him out of prison, he wrote a strong petition, in which he called Cowell "the most distinguished, noble-minded, idealistic character" and "a composer of greatest originality." He admitted that he was distraught when he heard about the charges, but said that "when I realized it was true, I understood what the great interpreter of the human soul and passions, William Shakespeare, said: 'There are more things in heaven and earth than are dreamt of in your philosophy.'"[630] Unlike Ives, he never severed his relations with Cowell because of this episode, but more or less remained in regular contact with him. Weiss and Schoenberg's assistant Gerald Strang, who served as interim director of Cowell's New Music Quarterly publishing venture, regularly updated Schoenberg on Cowell's situation.

FIGURE 3.22.
Henry Cowell, 1935. Courtesy David and Sylvia Teitelbaum Fund, Inc.

After Cowell was released from prison in 1940, he saw little of Schoenberg. Cowell visited him once before moving to the East Coast that year and again, in 1945 and 1950, when he traveled to California. But they stayed in touch by letter, and Cowell regularly informed Schoenberg about important New York concerts of his music. On the occasion of Mitropoulos's 1948 performance of the Five Orchestral Pieces, Cowell wrote: "Dear Friend: I was completely enthralled by the score, of course but the performance was magnificent, and the work itself is marvelous! We sat with John Cage, who was in raptures, and spoke afterwards to Schnabel, who was terribly pleased too."[631] Schoenberg thanked Cowell "especially cordially" for sending him reports and clippings immediately after the concert.[632] Furthermore, Cowell regularly wrote favorable reviews of Schoenberg performances in the *Musical Quarterly* and gave lectures on Schoenberg at the New School for Social Research. Cowell's endorsement of Schoenberg's music is testimony to his musical openmindedness and interest in experimental techniques. Yet Cowell never "adopted any of his [Schoenberg's] techniques."[633] Conversely, Schoenberg had a very limited understanding of an area of interest to Cowell: non-Western music, which he thought incompatible with Western ideas, though he was openminded toward most other innovative compositional directions.[634] Although Schoenberg and Cowell diverged in their compositional viewpoints, they felt and expressed respect for each other. Schoenberg remarked to Greissle: "Of course there are differences between him [Cowell] and me, differences of approach, of style, and even of opinion. But most important, he has always an aim . . . It places him on my side."[635]

Like Cowell, Sessions met Schoenberg in Berlin shortly before Schoenberg's departure.[636] Back in America, he soon discovered that he would become his colleague at the Malkin Conservatory: "Boston promises to be interesting," he wrote to Copland. "What do you think of my having Schönberg for a colleague? I am quite excited about it."[637] However, when Schoenberg moved to California, the two composers temporarily lost sight of each other and communicated only occasionally, through their mutual friends, Edward Steuermann, Rudolf Kolisch, Felix Greissle, and Heinrich Jalowetz.[638] Sessions and Schoenberg eventually met again in Los Angeles in 1941 at one of Caroline Fisher's parties, and in 1944 they resumed contact by letter. That year Sessions was inspired by the extraordinary festival at Black Mountain College celebrating Schoenberg's seventieth birthday. Upon returning from North Carolina, he wrote the lengthy article "Schoenberg in the United States" for *Tempo* and sent it to Schoenberg with belated "very warm and affectionate birthday wishes."[639] Very pleased about this essay, Schoenberg gave him as a sign of friendship autographed copies of the first page of *Jakobsleiter* and his two Birthday Canons for Carl Engel.[640] Thereafter their friendship intensified when Sessions, a professor at the University of California, Berkeley, from 1945, was able to visit Schoenberg in Los Angeles several times. Their camaraderie even brought together Schoenberg's and Sessions's sons, Ronald and John, who both learned a string instrument and were passionate about tennis.

On a professional level they discussed general musical ideas, the pros and cons of Heinrich Schenker's theories, Mann's *Doctor Faustus*, and teaching approaches; they also exchanged such students as Richard Cumming, Earl Kim, Leon Kirchner, Newlin, Roger Nixon, and Leonard Rosenman. Sessions had lectured on Schoenberg's music at least since 1933, when he introduced the Five Piano Pieces, op. 23 to students at the New School for Social Research.[641] Having initially been quite skeptical about dodecaphony, he gradually warmed to it and in 1947 gave two analysis courses where he explored with his students in greater detail Schoenberg's Fourth String Quartet and Piano Concerto. Sessions felt compelled to tell Schoenberg: "What a deep joy it has been to *me* to study your work again; how it grows constantly greater for me as I know it better. It is truly a source of deep comfort and faith to know that such music can be written in one's own time, and it gives one immensely renewed faith in the relevance of one's own efforts, as well as renewed courage to go on making them."[642] In his own music, Sessions steadily gravitated toward twelve-tone music, which he used for the first time in 1953 in his Sonata for Violin Solo and in many other works thereafter. Theoretical works such as his treatise *Harmonic Practice* (1951) are equally indebted to Schoenberg.[643] In addition, he discussed Schoenberg's ideas in many articles and interviews.

Schoenberg, too, showed his appreciation for Sessions's compositions. When he was asked in 1933 about his views on American music, he admitted: "I am not familiar with much American music," but added, "I of course know Roger Sessions's work which greatly pleases me."[644] Perhaps he overstated his knowledge of Sessions's music, for it is unlikely that he heard the European performances of such works as Sessions's First Symphony in Geneva in 1929 or First Piano Sonata in Bad Homburg in 1931. Yet in America, he listened to several works of Sessions on the radio and heard an acetate tape of his Second Piano Sonata (1946) with the score, which Kirchner had brought to him in 1948. Schoenberg wrote to Sessions about this work: "I was very pleased that I could follow your thoughts almost throughout the whole piece and it is that, why I said: 'This is a language' I mean, it conveys a message and in this respect it seems to me one of the greatest achievements a composer could arrive at [*sic*]" (Figure 3.23).[645] Kirchner recalled that Schoenberg said: "Now I know how Schumann must have felt when he first heard the music of Brahms."[646] Roger Nixon recalled Schoenberg's admiration for Sessions's music, too, especially its "freedom of the dissonance without the twelve-tone technique."[647] In 1950 Sessions sent Schoenberg the score of his Second Symphony (Schirmer 1949), which he inscribed: "To Arnold Schoenberg with homage, admiration and affection—most warmly New York, January 16, 1950 Roger Sessions." In June 1951 Schoenberg sent him a copy of his newly published *Style and Idea*, perhaps to show his gratitude for Sessions's score.

Mark Brunswick, who like Sessions was keenly aware of the dark side of political nationalism in Europe and was suspicious of nationalistic tendencies in music, had met Schoenberg at the 1924 festival of the International Society for Contemporary Music in Prague, where he heard the premiere of *Erwartung*. He lived in Vienna from 1924 to 1937, where his wife Ruth Mack, a psychoanalyst, studied and collaborated with Freud. Brunswick initially planned to study with Schoenberg, but was unable to accept his "stringent stipulations" and opted to study with Boulanger; he also befriended Webern.[648] Back in America, as founder and chairman of the National Committee for Refugee Musicians (1938–46), Brunswick helped several of Schoenberg's friends. He visited the Schoenbergs in California in October and December 1938 and again in August 1940. As a member of the East Coast Schoenberg circle, he furthered performances of Schoenberg's works, including *Das Buch der hängenden Gärten* and the Suite, op. 29, in concerts of the Contemporary and Classical Chamber Music Society in New York (1939 and 1940), and at City College, where he chaired the music department (1946–67). In the summer of 1944, he was among the guest faculty at Black Mountain College on the occasion of the Schoenberg festival. In 1946 Schoenberg briefly considered Brunswick as a translator for *Style and Idea*. While Schoenberg appreciated Brunswick's loyalty, he never expressed his opinion about his music in writing. It seems, however, that Brunswick was compositionally obliged to Schoenberg, although he never embraced dodecaphony. His small oeuvre reveals emotional intensity, abundant dissonance, and economy of means.

Louis Gruenberg was another American composer whom Schoenberg knew in Europe and met again in the United States. Having taught at the Chicago Musical College from 1933 to 1936, in February 1937 Gruenberg moved to Beverly Hills, where he resumed his acquaintance with Schoenberg. Their friendly relationship, however, sometimes suffered from their incompatible musical tastes and other differences of opinion. In 1935 Gruenberg displeased Schoenberg with his review of a performance of Schoenberg's Orchestral Variations at the ISCM festival in Prague.

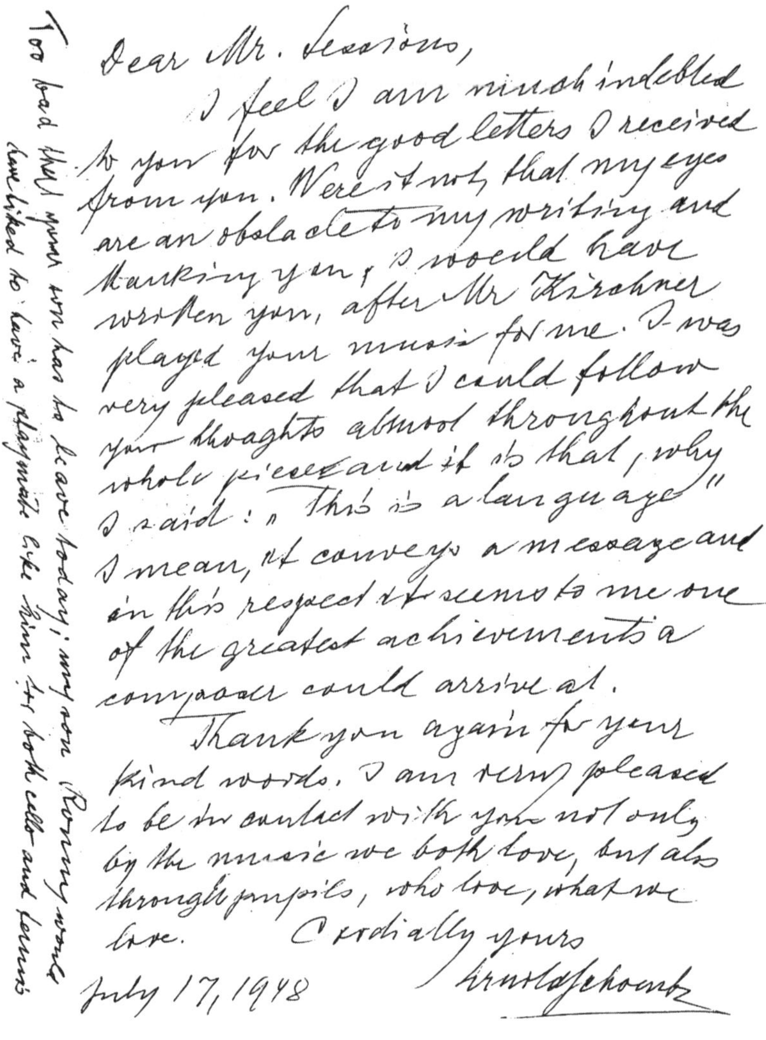

Dear Mr. Sessions,

I feel I am much indebted to you for the good letters I received from you. Were it not, that my eyes are an obstacle to my writing and thanking you, I would have written you, after Mr Kirchner played your music for me. I was very pleased that I could follow your thoughts almost throughout the whole pieces and if it is that, why I said: "This is a language" I mean, it conveys a message and in this respect it seems to me one of the greatest achievements a composer could arrive at.

Thank you again for your kind words. I am very pleased to be in contact with you not only by the music we both love, but also through pupils, who love, what we love.

Cordially yours

Arnold Schoenberg

July 17, 1948

Too bad that your son has to leave today; my son Ronny would have liked to have a playmate like him for both cello and tennis

FIGURE 3.23.
Facsimile of a letter from Arnold Schoenberg to Roger Sessions, 17 July 1948. Courtesy Arnold Schönberg Center.

Unable to hear a theme and its variations, he described the work as "mathematical," "non-spontaneous, unhappy and long."[649] Schoenberg in turn did not care for Gruenberg's trademark fusion of folk, jazz, and classical elements. Yet he seemed to have turned a blind eye on these issues when he assisted Gruenberg in his 1937 application for an Alchin professorship at USC, writing: "I know that Gruenberg is one of the best teachers of composition. A friend and pupil of Busoni, he stayed for many years in Europe and had the ability to learn their [*sic*] the best one can, but did not forget to be an American composer and accordingly understood to use his knowledge including what he learned in Europe in a very singular and doubtless American way."[650] As nothing came of it, Gruenberg began to compose for the films to make a living. In 1937 Gruenberg invited Schoenberg to join his planned Composers Society of America, which would have published the music of its members and fought for more performances of contemporary music and higher ASCAP ratings for composers of serious music. Its membership would have included such naturalized and native American composers as Joseph Achron, George Antheil, Copland, Howard Hanson, Ernst Toch, and Kurt Weill. Yet when Schoenberg realized that he was supposed to serve as the group's director, he backed out of the project.[651] In 1940 Schoenberg disagreed with the programming of Gruenberg's League Broadcast and asked that his music not be played by Gruenberg.[652] Yet the Schoenbergs and Gruenbergs kept seeing each other at parties, and in July 1946 Schoenberg gave Gruenberg an autographed copy of the short score of his Prelude to the *Genesis Suite,* which he inscribed: "To Louis Gruenberg in friendship Arnold Schoenberg."[653]

Supportive of Schoenberg despite his own affiliation with Boulanger, Virgil Thomson returned to the United States in 1940 after a fifteen-year stay in Europe. He had encountered Schoenberg in Paris in 1933, joining him on walks and escorting the Schoenberg family to the steamer S. S. *Ile-de-France,* which took them to New York in October of that year. When Thomson gave two papers at a Los Angeles music criticism conference in 1946, Schoenberg attended it so he could greet him in person.[654] Regardless of his francophile penchant as a composer and critic of the *New York Herald Tribune,* Thomson regularly invoked Schoenberg in his columns. He discussed his musical ideas, wrote birthday tributes, and lucidly reviewed performances of such works as *Verklärte Nacht,* Five Orchestral Pieces, *Pierrot,* Third Quartet, Organ Variations, and the Piano Concerto.[655] Additionally, Thomson gave him a platform in printing and discussing some of his speeches. When he published Schoenberg's 1947 address to the National Institute of Arts and Letters, Thomson dismissed this organization's classification of Schoenberg as a foreign artist as "discourtesy," noting that, as an American citizen, he would have been "eligible to full membership." Schoenberg's address to the National Institute, in which he compared his situation to that of a man in an ocean of boiling water who is forced to swim against the tide, struck Thomson as "a sort of Gettysburg Address, coming from the conqueror at the end of a long esthetic civil war."[656] In 1949 Thomson printed Schoenberg's birthday radio address in which he accused critic Olin Downes, conductors in America, and Copland of hampering the dissemination of his music. While he backed Schoenberg's criticism of the conductors, he deemed the attack on the incorrigibly conservative Downes "weak," and on (his friend) Copland "unjustified."[657] Taking on the role of mediator, Thomson helped to resolve the dispute between Schoenberg and Copland.[658]

In 1944 Schoenberg thanked Thomson for his engagement on his behalf: "I wanted already long time ago to write you that I am very pleased with the manner in which you write about my works. It raises hope that one day in the future there will be an understanding of my music. Thank you!"[659] Schoenberg always considered Thomson a loyal acquaintance and confided to Cowell: "Virgil Thompson [*sic*] always writes well of me."[660] Schoenberg once singled out Thomson's Stabat Mater (1931) as one of the pieces he liked, and acknowledged him as a composer in his draft for an orchestration treatise.[661]

Schoenberg was also friends with Nicolas Slonimsky, a Russian-born naturalized U.S. citizen, who was one of the most important figures in American music (Figure 3.24).[662] They met for the first time in Boston in 1933. He regarded Slonimsky highly for his performance of his dodecaphonic *Begleitmusik* in Los Angeles a few months before Schoenberg's arrival in the United States. As both lived in Boston and taught at the Malkin Conservatory, Slonimsky and Schoenberg spent much time together, laying the groundwork for a lifelong friendship. Thanks to his open personality, Slonimsky had many musical contacts on the East (and West) Coast, and he introduced Schoenberg to music circles in Boston, New York, and at the

FIGURE 3.24.
Nicolas Slonimsky. Courtesy Electra Slonimsky Yourke.

New School for Social Research in New York. When Slonimsky introduced him to American music politics and the composers he endorsed—Charles Ives, Carl Ruggles, Cowell, Edgar Varèse, Amadeo Roldán—Schoenberg remarked: "Now, in Amerika [*sic*], I can better understand the tendencies of your composers and I can say: I find them interesting."[663] He also relayed to Schoenberg his assessment of Koussevitzky's musical and conducting preferences. However, Slonimsky's own equivocal attitude toward Koussevitzky (who had once fired him) kept him from praising the conductor to Schoenberg. Slonimsky and Schoenberg met only sporadically from the late 1930s on, but they continued to correspond regularly with each other. Working on his first important reference work, *Music since 1900* (1937), Slonimsky approached Schoenberg with questions about dodecaphony's origin and prompted some of the most detailed answers from him.[664] Slonimsky also informed him about his arrangement for violin and piano and performance of the Woodwind Quintet, op. 26, and the South American and Soviet reception of Schoenberg's music. Schoenberg in turn praised Slonimsky's "Schoenberg Chronology," an offshoot of *Music since 1900* for Merle Armitage's Schoenberg monograph, as an "extremely original contribution" and followed his exploration of musical scales with interest.[665] Unhappy with Weiss's translation of *Harmonielehre*, Schoenberg in 1939 officially enlisted Slonimsky as translator, having already put the suggestion to him in 1934.[666] Yet this collaboration soon failed. Since Slonimsky, busy with editions of music encyclopedias, did not seem fully committed to this project, Schoenberg decided—after a meeting with him in Los Angeles in September 1940—to release him from the task.[667]

Although disappointing for both, this unsuccessful collaboration apparently did not affect their friendship. Slonimsky still supported Schoenberg's music in lectures and writings in such venues as the *Christian Science Monitor*, *Saturday Review of Literature*, and *Etude*.[668] He also offered special tributes for Schoenberg's seventieth and seventy-fifth birthdays. In 1944 he composed a four-part canon based on motives of Schoenberg's *Ode to Napoleon*, which Schoenberg found to be an "ingenious idea."[669] In 1949 he wrote a clever poem expressing his unwavering admiration for Schoenberg:

> People talk glibly of the 12-tone system:
> "Take all 12 notes, shake them well, and then list 'em."
> But Arnold Schoenberg, the originator,
> Called it a method; the system came later...
> The 12-tone melody, not bound to any key,
> Strode in wide intervals, magnificently free.
> Then, by a deft maneuver of tergiversation,
> It rolled off in reverse, in true reciprocation.
> Melodic intervals then pointed in an opposite direction,
> High notes becoming low, in mirror-like reflection...
> "Excruciatingly cacophonous," the old-guard critics cried.
> "Say, this stuff's hep," opined the younger side...
> From California, where Schoenberg lives, this method spread around,
> Like some new form of radiant energy transmuted into sound...
> And on the musical horizon, not too far,
> The Schoenberg star shines blazingly, a dodecuple star![670]

The poem documents Slonimsky's fascination with twelve-tone rows, which he systematically explored in the process of compiling his *Thesaurus of Scales and Melodic Patterns* (1947). In this collection he even included a symmetrical eleven-interval series comprising all twelve chromatic tones, which he whimsically dubbed the "grandmother chord."[671] Upon receipt of a copy of *Thesaurus*, Schoenberg wrote to Slonimsky that he "was very interested to find that you might [have] in all probability organized every possible succession of tones" and called it "an admirable feast of mental gymnastics." Yet Schoenberg added: "As a composer, I must believe in inspiration rather than in mechanics."[672] In the 1960s and 1970s Slonimsky used a kind of "tonal dodecaphony" in such conceptual pieces as *Möbius Strip Tease* (1965) and *51 Minitudes* (1971–77), which are based on four mutually exclusive triads (C major, D minor, F-sharp major, and G-sharp minor) and a linear succession of all twelve chromatic pitches.

Another important acquaintance of Schoenberg throughout his American years was Edgar Varèse (a naturalized U.S. citizen since 1927). Having corresponded with each other about the American *Pierrot* premiere in 1923, Varèse and Schoenberg met at the League of Composers Schoenberg reception in New York in November 1933, and frequently socialized when Varèse lived in Los Angeles (1938–40). In 1939 Varèse invited Schoenberg to join his projected California-based new music society "The Ten," modeled on his former International Composers Guild (1921–27). Other members would have included Achron, Dane Rudhyar, and Weiss. Yet nothing came of it. Schoenberg withdrew from this venture just ten days after the group's first meeting, explaining that he did not want to interfere with the destiny of his work, which in his estimation would be recognized no sooner than in the 1960s.[673] In 1942 Varèse asked Schoenberg to serve on the advisory committee of his newly founded Greater New York Chorus, which he gladly agreed to do, and even planned to perform some of his choral music.[674] While the performance came to naught, due to a persistent shortage of male voices, Varèse followed through with his plan to give a lecture on Schoenberg as part of his lecture series "Twentieth-Century Tendencies in Music" at Columbia University in 1948. Varèse may have already discussed Schoenberg's music in the context of his lecture series at the Pius X School of Liturgical Music at Manhattanville College in Purchase in 1943–44, for which he asked Schoenberg for materials in 1943. Schoenberg was delighted: "I am very pleased that you are giving a lecture about me, especially because I am sure you are one of the few musicians of today, who by his own writings is in the position to understand aims like mine."[675] He even shared with him his paper on composition with twelve tones. In his Columbia lecture, Varèse described Schoenberg as a "curious mixture of German professor, Talmudic dialectician, aesthete and innovator" and discussed dodecaphony. While he had dismissed the twelve-tone idea in 1934 as "a fallacy of thought" and a "system" that was unlikely to "leave its impress on the future," he revealed a greater appreciation of the technique in the 1940s.[676] He deemed dodecaphony as important as cubism in the visual arts and the experimental work of Stéphane Mallarmé and e. e. cummings in poetry. Furthermore, he found that the most "outstanding achievement in twelve-tone music was the amalgamation of harmony and counterpoint to one unit, which yet preserves each as separate entities." Ever skeptical of artistic systems, Varèse pointed out that Schoenberg "produced works of equal excellence outside this system" and often created great works in spite of the twelve-tone technique.[677]

Schoenberg's relationship with Aaron Copland, one of the most prominent American composers of the time, was not as close and warm as his associations with most of the composers discussed so far. The two composers met for the first time at the League of Composers Schoenberg reception in November 1933, and they saw each other again at a meeting of the American Composers Alliance in Los Angeles in December 1939. Four years later they met at a celebration of Schoenberg's sixty-ninth birthday.[678] Copland intended to have a further encounter with Schoenberg after attending a show of Schoenberg's paintings and a performance of his String Trio and First Quartet at the Modern Institute of Art in Beverly Hills in November 1948. But since Schoenberg had canceled his pre-concert talk for that event due to illness, Copland felt disheartened "to make an attempt to renew our slight acquaintanceship."[679] Copland was not entirely hostile toward Schoenberg's music. He lectured on it at the New School for Social Research, supported performances of it, and backed both the League of Composers sponsorship of the first *Pierrot* recording and the commissioning of *Ode to Napoleon*.[680] Neither was Schoenberg completely unreceptive to Copland's music. He praised his Piano Sonata, which the Hungarian pianist Andor Foldes played for him at his home around 1949. He wrote to Copland: "I appreciated your music without any restriction."[681] And he planned to include examples from Copland's orchestral works in his orchestration treatise.

Yet both men had strong reservations about each other's influence and certain aspects of each other's works. Copland protested Schoenberg's impact on Americans in 1935 when he proclaimed that young composers should "say to themselves once and for all, 'No more Schoenberg.'"[682] In a 1937 review of Schoenberg's Suite in G, he critically asked "whether the artistic sum total of the *Suite* is commensurate with the amount of ingenuity and complexity involved."[683] In 1941 Copland found that "atonal music resembles itself too much" and that "it creates a certain monotony."[684] While he considered the twelve-tone idea important, he disliked the "old German weltschmerzy kind of expression" of dodecaphonic music.[685] For that reason he also dismissed Berg's *Wozzeck, Lulu*, Violin Concerto, and *Lyric Suite* as "music without a future."[686] Moreover, he objected to Schoenberg's suggestion that dodecaphony represents the only logical continuation of the classical musical tradition.[687] In turn Schoenberg was typically prejudiced against Boulanger students—and Copland was no exception. Always extremely sensitive to criticism and receptive to his disciples' negative musico-political gossip, he was no doubt aware of Copland's disapproving views toward his music.

Schoenberg's famous attack on Copland on the air and in the *New York Herald Tribune* on his seventy-fifth birthday was prompted by his chagrin over the perceived poor reception of his dodecaphonic music and small number of performances of his orchestral works in America. For this situation he blamed Downes, European-born conductors, and startlingly, Copland, whom he portrayed as a musical dictator comparable to Stalin:

It should be discouraging to my suppressors to recognize the failure of their attempts. You cannot change the natural evolution of the arts by a command; you may make a New Year's resolution to write only what everybody likes; but you cannot force real artists to descend to the lowest possible standards to give up morals, character, and sincerity, to avoid presentation of new ideas. Even Stalin cannot succeed and Aaron Copland even less.[688]

Needless to say, Copland was shocked about these public accusations and, in view of the McCarthyist witch-hunt of left-wing musicians and his own leftist sympathies, very concerned about having been paired with Stalin.[689] Puzzled about Schoenberg's reason for this comparison, Copland wondered: "Mr. Schoenberg must have seen my picture in the papers in company with Shostakovich on the occasion of his brief visit here last spring. In America it is still possible (I hope) to share a forum platform with a man whose musical and political ideas are not one's own without being judged guilty by association."[690] In an effort to control damage, Schoenberg publicly clarified: "If my words could be understood as an attempt to involve Mr. Copland in a political affair, I am ready to apologize—This was not my intention."[691]

Schoenberg's blast was in all likelihood caused by an analysis of the 1947–48 repertoire of twenty-four American orchestras in *Musical America*. In the compilations of American works, foreign established repertoire, and foreign modern works, Copland made the top of the American list with twenty-two performances of seven different works, while Schoenberg was omitted.[692] Crucially, however, Schoenberg's friend and publisher Kurt List in the spring of 1949 planted the idea in Schoenberg's mind that certain American musicians had set out to suppress his music. List declared that there were American composers who

always say how great your music is, but then avail themselves of schemes to hinder performances and publications. I don't think that there is *one* person, but several cliques of which the one surrounding Koussevitzky, with Copland as its leader, and the one at the Juilliard School with William Schuman are the most powerful . . . I believe that these two cliques are the most dangerous ones, not only because they have power, but also because they present themselves as very "modern" and reject your music as "reactionary."[693]

Processing this information, Schoenberg must have concluded that Copland had the power to hinder his music's dissemination. Thus the Stalin comparison, as Jennifer DeLapp rightly pointed out, "was more a rhetorical device than anything like a substantive issue in Schoenberg's mind."[694]

In February 1950 Schoenberg and Copland ended their squabble. Copland clarified his musical standpoints, and Schoenberg offered his willingness "to live in peace."[695] Curiously, it was at this time, perhaps as a result of his dispute with Schoenberg, that Copland began the composition of his Piano Quartet, the first of four obviously serial works. Copland may have wished to acknowledge Schoenberg's musical significance. In resorting to an abstract compositional technique, Copland may also have wanted to demonstrate the disparity between his freedom to make compositional choices and the obligation of Soviet artists to bow to their regime in aesthetic matters.[696]

Many other American composers knew Schoenberg personally, yet often only for a short period of time. Lehman Engel, a young progressive composer from Jackson, Mississippi, who later made a name as musical director for shows on Broadway, welcomed him on his arrival in October 1933 and shortly thereafter conducted one of the first American interviews with him.[697] Marion Bauer, a conservative, but open-minded, New York–based composer, got to know Schoenberg in New York and Chautauqua in the early 1930s. Having featured him in her newly published book *Twentieth-Century Music* (1933), she was delighted to meet him and give him an inscribed copy soon after his arrival in New York.[698] Bauer interviewed him in Chautauqua in 1934 and described him as a "sincere, direct person," who "can be generous to those who are sincere whether they are for or against his musical point of view." Schoenberg confided to Bauer that the Chautauqua community gave him "an entirely new impression of America." He found it hard to define his new homeland and say, "This or that is America." He could not classify Americans since "they are all different."[699] During his trip to Chicago in 1934, Schoenberg also had short and pleasant interactions with John Alden Carpenter, no devotee of his music. Carpenter arranged a performance of Schoenberg's Chamber Symphony and a dinner reception in his honor at the Chicago Arts Club, which Schoenberg apparently treasured as a "wonderful" experience.[700] In 1944 David Diamond, a prolific tonal composer, introduced himself to Schoenberg with a birthday letter and visited him during his stay in California in June 1949. Since he planned to go to Austria later that summer, he offered to retrieve autographs of Schoenberg's works still in the hands of Universal Edition. But he was also quick to ask a reciprocal favor of him. Diamond desired one of Edward Weston's 1936 Schoenberg photographs, which he wanted to have inscribed with the opening theme of the Largo from Schoenberg's Fourth Quartet. Diamond flatteringly explained that he liked to be surrounded "by the faces of those kindred spirits who keep shake [*sic*] the world, and make me conscious more and more of the great creative power and fertility resident in our time." While Diamond did receive the photo, he was unable to obtain any of the autographs, which were, except for the *Harmonielehre* manuscript, still owned by Universal Edition.[701]

Besides these acquaintances Schoenberg was in touch with other American composers mostly by letter, among them Anis Fuleihan, Roy Harris, Harrison Kerr, Otto Luening, Douglas Moore, and Deems Taylor. His dealings with these figures concerned for the most part professional matters: membership in various musical organizations, publication questions, assessment of musical talent, and various types of advice. While Schoenberg's exchanges with these composers were friendly, he came to dislike Taylor, director of ASCAP and radio commentator, whose CBS broadcasts he had generally enjoyed and whom he had described as a "good musician" in 1943.[702] But in the late 1940s Schoenberg bore him a grudge for belittling the successful world premiere of *Survivor* on the radio and for attacking him in his book *Music to My Ears* (Simon and Schuster, 1949).[703]

In California Schoenberg met with many lesser known conservative local composers, including Pauline Alderman, Louis Danz, Wesley LaViolette, Mary Carr Moore, Gertrude Ross, Richard Drake Saunders, and Elinor Remick Warren. He encountered them early on at events of such institutions as the Crescendo Club, the Los Angeles Chapter of the Pro Musica Society, Schubert-Wa Wan Club, American Composers Alliance, and various salons. While some of these composers, such as

Moore, Warren, and other members of SNAC, were skeptical toward Schoenberg, others accepted his presence. For instance, Ross, president of Pro Musica's Los Angeles branch, pledged in 1935 to "extend the definition of American music to include that of all composers living in America—Ernest Bloch, Joseph Achron, Arnold Schoenberg, Ruth Crawford and others."[704] Similarly Saunders, his SNAC membership notwithstanding, was friends with Schoenberg throughout Schoenberg's California years. Saunders and Schoenberg were both members of the Crescendo Club, which counted many local composers among its membership.[705] Saunders, a prolific writer, often lent Schoenberg visibility in his local and national publications, especially in the *Musical Courier*. Schoenberg, too, supported Saunders's Bureau of Musical Research publications with essay contributions and served as a chairman of the Honorary Editorial Advisory Board (from 1950). For Christmas 1939 both exchanged musical gifts. Saunders gave Schoenberg a setting of a Yuletide greeting song, and Schoenberg composed for Saunders a four-part infinite canon with the text: "Mister Saunders, I owe you thanks for at least four years. Let me do it in four voices so that ev'ry one of them counts for one year. Merry Christmas four times, listen how they sing it! Also Merry Christmas to Missis [*sic*] Saunders."[706]

Last but not least, Schoenberg was good friends with Alderman, a music professor at USC. Alderman organized Schoenberg's first two private classes in Los Angeles and helped secure his first academic position at her institution. Together with some colleagues, she reserved a tennis court in the summer of 1935 so that Schoenberg could round off his daily classes by playing tennis with his students. Alderman shared her office with him and arranged picnics out in the country and at the beach. She also took the Schoenbergs to the movies and in 1936 assisted them with house hunting. Yet she never showed Schoenberg any of her operas or songs, fearing that he might not like her works. Eventually they lost touch after Schoenberg accepted a teaching position at UCLA and Alderman traveled to Europe to prepare for a doctorate in musicology.[707]

Schoenberg and the Idea of American Music

Although he never fully came to terms with the fact of being an American composer, practically speaking Schoenberg *was* an American composer. Although he remained true to his European roots and self-aware as a Jew, he was also an American citizen with a real commitment to advancing American music. He followed American music on the radio, in live performances, and as a reader of *Musical America*. He participated in American music organizations, nurtured young American composers, and fought for an adequate representation of American music on concert programs. Most significantly, he composed works reflecting his American identity and America's influence: works initiated by Americans, which used the English language, concerned American political and musical and trends, and were intended for American performers and audiences.

A believer in musical nationalism, who was once determined to fight for the supremacy of "German music" and thereafter resolved to create a national Jewish music, Schoenberg also strove for the superiority of a national American music, which he thought to be in its formative stages. In 1934 he was optimistic about this goal: "I find there is in America so much talent for music and so much love for it, that America will certainly in a short time be the first as regards to musical culture."[708] He also claimed: "I seem to hear an American national character speaking very clearly in what I know of American music." And he wondered "whether this comes from the landscape, the climate, from the spiritual or physical mentality." He stressed that "a sensitive organism, a musical seismograph, registers the fact that the disturbances caused by American music are different, even when not much is visible in the externals, in the style."[709] To achieve the preeminence of American music, he pledged: "I intend to pass a portion of my life in this land—if I am wanted—and I shall not grow false to my old habits there: *I shall go on giving*, as before." He also added: "I should like here to pass on to you some of my experiences from almost forty years in the battle of art."[710]

Schoenberg's attitude toward American music, however, was complex. He loved American popular music and jazz, and valued it as an important part of America's musical culture. He stated: "When I speak of American music, I cannot pass over American light music. Who can doubt that it adds up to something American?" He compared his own love of American popular music to Brahms's appreciation of light music and ability to value "its purely musical substance." Schoenberg also stressed that "light music could not entertain me unless something interested me about its musical substance and its working-out. And I do not see why, when other people are entertained, I too should not sometimes be entertained . . . and enjoy light music."[711] Schoenberg was also fond of jazz. When asked whether "modern jazz music might have any permanent place in musical literature," he replied: "Maybe. Some of it is really good. And some is, I would rather say much of it is, very amusing and I like to listen to it . . . It's often full of a very peculiar spirit, you know, yes, which I like very much."[712] He, however, did not believe in a fusion of jazz and classical music. "In the long run," he said, "they [swing music and jazz] do not fit in [as part of modernism] very much at all. Swing music is a result of life during a short period of time. Sometimes it may possibly influence the higher—or long time—art in one way or another, but it of itself is temporary."[713]

Schoenberg was much more ambiguous in his assessments of American classical music. He owned scores of Charles Ives and was apparently "terribly excited" about his *Concord Sonata*.[714] He famously praised Ives's artistic independence: "There is a great Man living in this Country—a composer. He has solved the problem how to preserve one's self-esteem and to learn. He responds to negligence by contempt. He is not forced to accept praise or blame. His name is Ives."[715] In his sketches for an orchestration treatise, he intended to include 150 examples from such American composers as Samuel Barber, Nikolai Berezowski, Charles Cadman, Carpenter, Copland, Cowell, Gershwin, Morton Gould, Howard Hanson, Harris, Moore, Walter Piston, Schuman, Sessions, William Grant Still, Thomson, and Weiss.[716] When asked to name ten representatives of classical American music, Schoenberg singled out more: Copland, Cowell, Diamond, Fuleihan, Gruenberg, Harris, Lou Harrison, Newlin, Piston, Schuman, Sessions, Gerald Strang, and Weiss. Yet he stated: "In all these persons' compositions I have found talent and originality, though I could not deny that in many cases the technical performance was not on the same level as the talent."[717]

Schoenberg blamed American composers' alleged lack of technique on their faulty approach to learning the craft of composition. "They learn more from theories and from lectures than from master models," he observed, and regretted that "they all suffer from a lack of education." "We in Europe," he explained, "had to study at least one year of harmony, two years of counterpoint, at least three years of a thorough formal study—if not longer. Here, they believe they can do it in three years, which is untrue."[718] He also felt that many American composers tended to adhere to the "wrong" compositional philosophy. These would have been the ones, who—propelled by the teachings of Boulanger and the popularity of American folksong—had embraced neo-classicism and often imitated or incorporated folk elements in classical contexts, especially in the late 1930s and 1940s.[719] Believing that a "simple idea must not use the language of profundity," and that "the discrepancy between the requirements of larger forms and the simple construction of folk tunes cannot be solved," he rejected such folksong-based efforts to create a national art-music as Harris's *When Johnny Comes Marching Home: An American Overture* (1934).[720] Furthermore Schoenberg took exception to American composers who were indebted to "mass-production" and "produced music on the 'running band' [conveyor belt]."[721]

Nearing the end of his life, he felt that American music had not yet achieved superiority, despite his own creative efforts and encouragement of such young composers as Lester Trimble, who in his opinion "aimed for a contemporary American style" and whom he advised "to create a style of [his] own."[722] His wish that Boulanger's "influence might be broken and the real talents of the Americans be allowed to develop freely," had, in his opinion, not yet come true, even though he had the impression that "America now thinks her time has come to achieve hegemony in music." To him, at least two factors could contribute to this goal: the adoption of dodecaphony to ensure "coherence in a piece of music," and the birth of musical geniuses.[723] He reasoned: "It seems that nations which have not yet acquired a place in the sun will have to wait until it pleases the Almighty to plant a musical genius in their midst. As long as this does not occur, music will remain the expression of those nations to whom composing is not merely an attempt to conquer a market, but an emotional necessity of the soul."[724]

His reservations against the music and attitudes of some of his American colleagues notwithstanding, he drew nearer to some of their stances in the process of acculturating to America. He aimed at the widest possible dissemination of his music and audience appreciation, features of mass culture. In 1947 he proclaimed: "There is nothing I long for more intensely (if for anything) than to be taken for a better sort of Tchaikovsky—for heaven's sake: a bit better, but really that's all. Or if anything more, then that people should know my tunes and whistle them."[725] In October 1949 he grew impatient about a release of a disc with his piano music and Violin Phantasy, which he wanted to be "ready for the Christmas market."[726] While his concern to reach out to broad audiences dated to the late 1920s, it gained more weight in America, where, during the Depression, many other artists rethought their relationship to society and made their art more accessible.[727] Like his American colleagues, Schoenberg used tonality. When writing dodecaphonic works, he laced them with tonal elements. He wrote pieces based on folksong, and he explored the concepts of functional and politically engaged music, which were very topical among American composers in the 1930s and 1940s.

Schoenberg's modification of his compositional approach in America points to multiple motivations. He may have wanted to fit into the artistically more conservative new society and offer something acceptable—an obvious step for any migrant artist. He sought to revise his image as "a modern dissonant twelve-tone experimenter" (something that is also reflected in his initial conservative repertoire choices as a conductor).[728] He intended to familiarize audiences with his tonal styles first and incrementally prepare them for his dodecaphonic works. He developed a new perspective marked by a distance from Europe and its music history, and alternating freely and flexibly between different forms of artistic expression.[729] He probably hoped to facilitate and experience more recognition, if not fame, before the end of his life. Finally he expected, like his American colleagues, to increase his income through his art. Monetary considerations often influenced his choices of genre, instrumentation, and style and are also documented by such statements as "I wish to receive informations [*sic*] about the market value of my products, by dealing directly with the customer."[730]

This is not to say that Schoenberg sacrificed his modernistic perspective. Despite his modification of artistic decisions, he retained modernist elements, complexity, and intense expressiveness, which lent his works a dissimilative quality. What unified his late compositions (and entire oeuvre) was not style, but an underlying musical idea and the sophisticated treatment of musical materials. His late works remained as technically demanding to performers as they were challenging to audiences, despite his increased concern with greater accessibility.

The remainder of this chapter investigates those works in which Schoenberg stressed his American identity more than his Jewish and German musical roots.

Suite in G For String Orchestra

Begun in Chautauqua in September 1934 and finished in Hollywood three months later, the Suite in G (originally titled *Suite in Olden Style*) for string orchestra was Schoenberg's first completed work in America. It was also, after more than twenty-five years, his first completed lengthy original work with a key signature.[731] Martin Bernstein, a New York University music professor and double bassist in the Chautauqua Symphony, prepared the way for this composition when he met Schoenberg in Chautauqua in 1934. Bernstein's interest in finding adequate and technically feasible contemporary literature for his student string orchestra and Schoenberg's belief that a piece tailored to Bernstein's group "might have a widespread reception among other American school and college orchestras," inspired him to explore the concept of functional music.[732] He felt that "a new spiritual and intellectual basis can be created for art; here young people can be given the opportunity of learning about the new fields of expression and the means suitable for these."[733] Moreover, he felt motivated to fight against what he called "infamous conservatism."[734] "Today," he proclaimed, "so many call themselves 'conservative' who have nothing to conserve because they possess nothing that is worth conserving or maintaining."[735]

In conceiving the Suite, Schoenberg reached out to American students in several ways. He opted for a convenient suite layout in five short movements, including an introductory "Ouverture," an "Adagio," and three dance movements, "Menuet and Trio," "Gavotte" and "Giga." Determined to spare young Americans "a premature dose of 'Atonality Poison,'" he emphatically embraced tonality.[736] The work has a key signature, and its movements follow a conventional key pattern, with the first, third, and fifth movements in G, and the second and fourth movements in the keys of E minor and B-flat.

Although the Suite seems at first glance no less conservative than the works of his contemporaries, Schoenberg made it clear that his choice of classical elements and harmony "represented *no repudiation*" of his modernistic direction. He aimed at building a bridge between the music of the past and "his present style of composition."[737] He used triadic harmony, and freely and boldly juxtaposed chords, whose succession is no longer controlled by traditional rules of tonality, but rather by motivic-thematic work. This approach to tonality, which he discussed in his 1934 essay "Problems of Harmony," would lead students to "modern feelings" and a "better understanding of modern music" and serve "composers who hate 'atonality'" as a "model for the advances that are possible within tonality."[738] Schoenberg combined "ancient style" features—slow dotted rhythms and fast fugatos in the Ouverture, drone basses, and fluid 12/8 meter in the Giga—with techniques evoking his German ancestors Bach, Mozart, and Brahms: intricate counterpoint, asymmetrical melodic structures, developing variation, and complex rhythms. Yet Schoenberg instilled the Suite also with novel complexity and reinterpreted the Ouverture's binary form by alternating between four largo and three fugal allegro sections, and by gradually shortening the slow and lengthening the fast segments. While the Ouverture's slow sections, initially marked by homophony and developing variation, receive increasingly contrapuntal treatment, the fugal segments are progressively penetrated by motivic-thematic work. Compared to Stravinsky, Hindemith, or Weill, Schoenberg's approach to "olden style" is more sophisticated and experimental and devoid of parody.

Despite Schoenberg's intent to offer young musicians a performable piece, the Suite turned out to be a technically difficult work with intricate phrasing, fingering, bowing, and intonation. For this reason Bernstein's group may have lost the privilege of premiering the Suite. Yet even the members of the Los Angeles Philharmonic, who gave its first performance under Klemperer in May 1935, seemed to have struggled with its technical intricacies. Schoenberg tellingly scribbled on the Suite's manuscript: "The spots are drops of Klemperer's sweat."

The Suite surprised and confused American audiences, especially composers and critics. Critical of Schoenberg's atonal music, composer Israel Citkowitz praised the Suite's "rigorous logic, contrapuntal mastery, subtle variations of tone-color," and "logical progress of the *grande ligne*" and opined that the Suite "has given us more of the essence of Schönberg than there is in all of his 'Schönbergian' atonalities."[739] Yet Copland, who granted that the work was a "perfect demonstration of Schönberg's complete mastery of his musical materials," felt that "mastery does not necessarily result in masterworks."[740] Charles Seeger (alias Carl Sands) mercilessly accused Schoenberg of putting "old spoiled wine in old spoiled bottles" and making his music "safe for 'bourgeocracy.'" Charging him with using "more tricks of the trade than the average pedagogue could think up in his whole life," he concluded that "one page of Aaron Copland can blow the whole Schoenberg suite away like the dust it is."[741] West and East Coast critics were divided. While West Coast reviewers praised the work as an example of "profound music without forsaking the beautiful," eastern critics, who heard the work in the fall of 1935, ridiculed it.[742] Olin Downes mocked the work's alleged Hollywood influence and claimed to "now expect atonal fugues by Shirley Temple."[743] And Winthrop Sargeant wondered: "Has the much advertised Californian sunshine thawed out the gloomy apostle of the twelve-tone Grundgestalt and left him singing roundelays among the poppies?"[744] These critics certainly overlooked the work's pedagogical purpose and perhaps felt offended that Schoenberg had not deemed Americans ready for a stylistically more advanced work.

The Suite became neither a staple of college orchestra repertoires, nor a favorite of professional orchestras, although it was revived and recorded in the 1960s. The reason for that may lie in its dissimilative character. On the one hand, Schoenberg reached out to American musicians and audiences with more euphonious sounds and classical musical structures. On the other, he preserved the highest European standards by refraining from structurally and technically simplifying his music. Schoenberg's acculturation indeed led to a kind of utopian "music for the people."

My Horses Ain't Hungry and *Fanfare for a Bowl Concert on Motifs of Die Gurrelieder*

Like many American composers in the mid-1930s, Schoenberg tried his hand at American folk music, setting in 1935 the Appalachian ballad *My Horses Ain't Hungry*.[745] Schoenberg's publisher Carl Engel, president of G. Schirmer, encouraged this arrangement, feeling that "interest here in such a work would likely be very keen."[746] Having accepted his Concertos after Monn and Handel (1932–33) for publication and approaching the final advance payment, Engel invited him to release his new Suite in G to Schirmer and to add a new short choral work. Engel suggested that he set a poem from Whitman's *Leaves of Grass*. But Schoenberg opted for a small a cappella "Fantasy" on an English chorale or madrigal and asked Engel to send him hymnals or songbooks.[747] Engel mailed him *Songs of the Hill-Folk: Twelve Ballads from Kentucky, Virginia, and North Carolina* (1934), collected and arranged for voice and piano by the Kentucky balladeer John Jacob Niles, and Schoenberg chose from that collection the tenth song.

In the five stanzas of Niles's *Horses* version, Johnnie is bidding farewell to Polly, but after a dialogue in which Johnnie and Polly trade verses back and forth, Polly decides to go with him. Schoenberg was perhaps intrigued by the dialogue concept, for in his five-part a cappella choral setting, he allotted the tune of Johnnie's first and third stanzas to the tenors and of Polly's second, fourth, and fifth verses to the sopranos. He was possibly attracted to this simply structured tune due to its contrapuntal potential. Its beginning can be combined with its own augmentation, the melody can be presented canonically at the octave, and the tune's third phrase is its own retrograde. Schoenberg's sketches reveal five- and six-part imitative contrapuntal treatments of the tune, and his setting displays much contrapuntal elaboration. He modified Niles's arrangement by inserting a half-measure extension between the second and third melodic phrases, by subjecting the tune to multiple melodic variations, and by presenting it, within the framework of A major, in the keys of C-sharp minor, C, and E major, while avoiding dense chromaticism.

The *Horses* setting exemplifies how Schoenberg negotiated his American and German identities by combining American folksong with techniques of his European musical heritage. His rapprochement with American folk music seems remarkable, if one considers how often he questioned the purpose of fusing folk and art elements and claimed that they were incompatible.[748] As already mentioned, he opposed artificial expansions of folksongs in large-scale classical works, believing that folksongs are already perfect units and do not pose compositional problems. But he felt that straightforward arrangements of folk tunes "in the form of variation or in rondo-like structure" were artistically legitimate."[749]

Unfortunately, he never finished his *Horses* setting. He completed the texture of the first stanza and left sketches for all of the song's verses and an incomplete continuity draft indicating the arrangement's overall layout. One can only speculate about why the setting remained incomplete. He often found it hard to complete a composition after having suspended work on it for a week or more.[750] Or he may have wished to work on other projects: the revision of his First Chamber Symphony, the libretto for *Moses und Aron*, and the Violin Concerto. Severine Neff discovered the setting in 2004 and Allen Anderson reconstructed it. The University of North Carolina Chamber Singers under Susan Klebanow premiered the piece in Chapel Hill in April 2006.

In 1945 Schoenberg embarked on another small and unusual project, the composition of a fanfare for three trumpets, four horns, three trombones, tuba, and percussion. Fanfares had become very popular in America during World War II. Copland wrote his *Fanfare for the Common Man* in 1942, which was one of eighteen fanfares Eugene Goossens commissioned "as stirring and significant contributions to the war effort."[751] Similarly, Stokowski invited fifty-six composers from Los Angeles, including Schoenberg, to write an opening fanfare for one of his Hollywood Bowl concerts in the summer season of 1945. After some hesitation and the consideration of fanfare motifs from *Moses und Aron*'s "Dance Around the Golden Calf," Schoenberg decided to base it on three motifs from part three of *Gurrelieder*, Waldemar's "Summons to his Vassals," "Night Ride," and the concluding "Sunrise" motif in C major.[752] Schoenberg repackaged for Hollywood audiences materials from a European work that Stokowski had introduced in America in 1932 and dedicated the piece to the conductor as a token of his friendship. Yet, as in the case of the *Horses* setting, Schoenberg interrupted work on this project and never managed to add the finishing touches, even though he had completed "two thirds of the score and the whole in sketch."[753] In August 1945 he sent the incomplete thirty-one-measure-long condensed score (just short of the concluding fourteen bars) with an apology to Stokowski. Leonard Stein completed the work and initiated its premiere at the opening of the Arnold Schoenberg Institute in Los Angeles in February 1977.

Fourth String Quartet, Opus 37

Written between April and July 1936, the Fourth String Quartet was Schoenberg's first completed American twelve-tone work. During this period, in which he taught summer courses at USC and moved to his house in Brentwood Park, he also worked on his dodecaphonic Violin Concerto (begun in 1934 or 1935 and finished in September 1936). The Fourth Quartet was Schoenberg's first commission in America, although in 1927 the work's sponsor, American music patroness Elizabeth Sprague Coolidge, had already commissioned his Third Quartet. She not only paid Schoenberg the generous fee of $1,000 (about $15,300 in 2009), but also subsidized the new quartet's premiere, which was played by the Kolisch Quartet in a series of four concerts at UCLA's Royce Hall in January 1937, featuring all of Schoenberg's numbered string quartets paired with Beethoven's late quartets. In gratitude Schoenberg dedicated the new piece to Coolidge and the Kolisch Quartet.

With the Fourth Quartet, Schoenberg intended to provide another accessible work for American audiences, and confidently related to Coolidge that he believed that "it will be much more pleasant than the third [quartet]."[754] Yet, unlike his Suite, his new quartet reveals Schoenberg's goal to create a substantial and at the same time very palatable twelve-tone work. He achieved this aim through various strategies. As in other dodecaphonic works, he freely built on familiar forms (sonata form, scherzo, lyrical slow movement, and rondo), and utilized textures and syntax from the previous two centuries (which also served to pay homage to his German musical ancestors). He achieved greater comprehensibility through memorable themes marked by pitch repetition, tonal reposes, and emphases on the twelve-tone set's consonant intervals, as well as through frequent reprises of themes within a movement and the cyclical use of themes.[755] The first movement, for instance, has a dominant energetic main theme (mm. 1–6), a contrasting lyrical second theme (mm. 66–71) in the exposition, and two other clearly delineated recurring thematic ideas, which are introduced in mm. 27–28 and mm. 116–21, respectively, and serve as guides for the listener.[756] The third movement (largo), however, features what is arguably the work's most memorable theme. Prominently presented at the movement's opening (mm. 614–18) and again toward the end (mm. 664–68), this main theme is cast as a rhapsodic recitative played in unison by all four strings. Because of its chant-like character, its pitch repetitions, and quasi-improvisatory rhythm recalling Hebrew cantillation, this theme can be interpreted as an expression of Schoenberg's Jewish identity. The intervallic contour of the theme's first three notes (a descending minor second and major third), marking the first movement's main theme too, has suggested to some commentators an affinity to the opening of the *Kol nidre* (Figure 3.25).[757] Schoenberg also attained greater euphony through subtle tonal undercurrents in the vertical distribution of his twelve-tone rows and limited the use of linear row statements in favor of partitioned statements, aggregates, and polyphonic combinations of inversionally related hexachords. The opening of the Quartet's first movement, for instance, alludes to D minor with the first violin articulating the root, leading tone, and fifth and the cello the third of D minor (Figure 3.26). Schoenberg indeed believed that the difference between tonality and atonality was only "a *gradual* one" and hoped that "in a few decades audiences will recognize the *tonality* of this music today called *atonal*."[758]

Prior to its world premiere, the Fourth Quartet was played at Schoenberg's house for a private audience, including Achron, Buhlig, Cage, Caroline Fisher, Klemperer, Edward Steuermann, and Strang.[759] Despite little publicity, the work's premiere attracted an audience of about 1,500.[760] Although the premiere felt to Schoenberg like "a perfectly commonplace affair" without "special excitement," he "was very content with the attitude of the public," which "listened with respect and sincerity to the strange sounds with which they were faced."[761] Bruno Ussher, a Los Angeles critic, detected in the new quartet "fewer intervallic experimentations" and "more extensive and sustained themes" than in the previous two quartets. He found that it was, despite the "at times coldly gray harmonization," "more spontaneous, uncalculated."[762] The Kolisch Quartet broadcast and recorded the work and also played it in other American cities, including Denver and New York. Other ensembles, among them the Pro Arte, California, and Juilliard String Quartets, took the work up as well during Schoenberg's lifetime.

String quartet writing was popular among American composers in the 1930s. Barber, Becker, Cowell, Diamond, Ross Lee Finney, Piston, Riegger, Schuman, and Sessions, among others, contributed to this genre. The second movement from Barber's First Quartet (1936)—transcribed as the famous Adagio for Strings—was certainly performed much more often than Schoenberg's Fourth Quartet. Yet the Largo from Schoenberg's quartet soon became a compositional model for many young American composers. Schoenberg started work on another quartet in four movements in 1949, but left it unfinished.

Ode to Napoleon Buonaparte, op. 41

The League of Composers, on the occasion of its twentieth anniversary, invited Schoenberg to write a chamber work in January 1942, a politically eventful time. The previous month, Japan bombed Pearl Harbor and the United States declared war on Japan. Hitler then declared war on the United States, and Reinhard

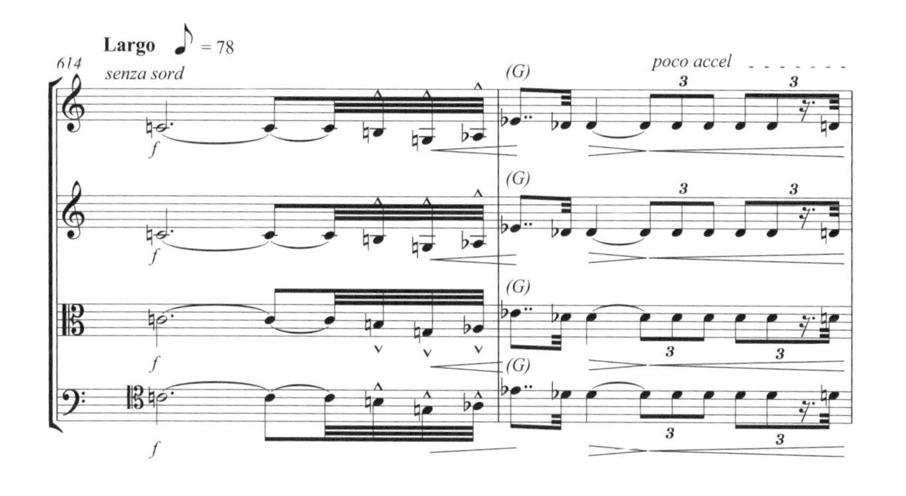

FIGURE 3.25.

Fourth String Quartet, opening of movement 3, mm. 614–18. Courtesy G. Schirmer.

FIGURE 3.26.

Fourth String Quartet, opening of movement 1, mm. 1–2. Courtesy G. Schirmer.

Heydrich announced the Jewish genocide, the "Final Solution to the Jewish Question." Schoenberg, having just become a U.S. citizen, followed these events with great empathy, and according to his student Leonard Stein, he "conceived the idea of what was to be his first musical statement on the war."[763] Schoenberg himself recalled: "I had at once the idea that this piece must not ignore the agitation aroused in mankind against the crimes that provoke this war. I remembered Mozart's *Marriage of Figaro,* supporting repeal of the *jus primae noctis,* Schiller's *Wilhelm Tell,* Goethe's *Egmont,* Beethoven's *Eroica,* and *Wellington's Victory,* and I knew it was the moral duty of the intelligentsia to take a stand against tyranny."[764] As the basis for his new work, Schoenberg selected the *Ode to Napoleon Buonaparte* from a volume of Byron's poetry, which he had recently bought at a Westwood bookstore. His choice of a Byron poem may have been motivated by America's increased interest in Byron in the 1930s and 1940s. Honored with articles on the occasion of his sesquicentennial in 1938, the poet received renewed appreciation as a freedom fighter and "poet laureate of liberty" in view of Europe's deteriorating political situation.[765]

In the *Ode,* a lengthy poem in nineteen rhymed stanzas of nine lines each, Byron fervently expresses his disdain about Napoleon's abdication in 1814.[766] One of the reasons Schoenberg was drawn to this specific text was that he saw a parallel between Napoleon and Hitler. Although very problematic, this comparison was a "much (ab) used trope" in America since the beginning of the war.[767] Schoenberg related to his daughter: "The text is full of allusions to Hitler and today's events." He was surprised by the poem's end, "an homage to Washington" as a symbol of freedom.[768] To conductor Hermann Scherchen, he confided at the end of the war that the poem "deals with Napoléon like we would have dealt with Hitler if we had caught him alive."[769] With its many allusions to biblical, historical, and mythological themes and ethical implications, the poem strongly resonated with Schoenberg's three identities. Through the filter of Byron's condemnation of Napoleon as a tyrant, Schoenberg as a Jew could take a stance against Hitler and his crimes against Jewry. Byron's references to the Old Testament books of Daniel and Isaiah, predicting the end of Israel's Babylonian exile and her return to Zion, also echo Schoenberg's Jewish heritage. The text references Schoenberg's previous homeland as well, in an allusion to Napoleon's second wife, Marie-Louise of Habsburg, as "Austria's mournful flower." Napoleon had married her to expand his power, and thus the Austrian princess, like Austria after the *Anschluss,* had to share a "long despair."[770] Finally, in the last stanza, Byron points to the new world, glorifying George Washington as the "Cincinnatus of the West," a hero in early Roman history. Byron's positive image of Washington mirrors Schoenberg's hopes for the leadership of Roosevelt.

Schoenberg set the Byron poem for speaker, string quartet, and piano, and finished this work—his first completed composition entirely based on an English text—between March and June 1942 (Figure 3.27). He cast Byron's passionate rhetoric in *Sprechstimme,* paying much attention to idiomatic prosody and declamation, and giving the narrator in terms of pitch contour more leeway than in *Pierrot,* thanks to a single stave-line as reference. While Winston Churchill's skills as orator may have served Schoenberg as an inspiration for the text's declamation, Orson Welles's voice could have been on his mind as well. Welles would have been his first choice as performer of the narrator's part.[771] He confided to Welles: "I have heard you over the radio, and I was deeply impressed by your reading; by the great number of characters and shades your voice is capable to produce; by the very artistic and unconventional manner of structural composition; by the sincerity and by the purity of your expression. When the problem came about, who could take the part of the recitation I suggested—primo loco—your name."[772]

The *Ode*'s music is through-composed and descriptive, and captures "the 170 different shades of irony, contempt, sarcasm, parody, hatred and indignation with which Byron treats his victim."[773] To illustrate lines like "The triumph, and the vanity, the rapture of the strife, the earthquake voice of victory, to thee the breath of life," Schoenberg quotes the opening of the *Marseillaise* and the opening motif from Beethoven's Fifth Symphony (mm. 59–64) (Figure 3.28), which not only evoke Napoleon, the French Revolution, and Beethoven as a one-time admirer of Napoleon, but also have political significance as symbols for antifascist resistance in

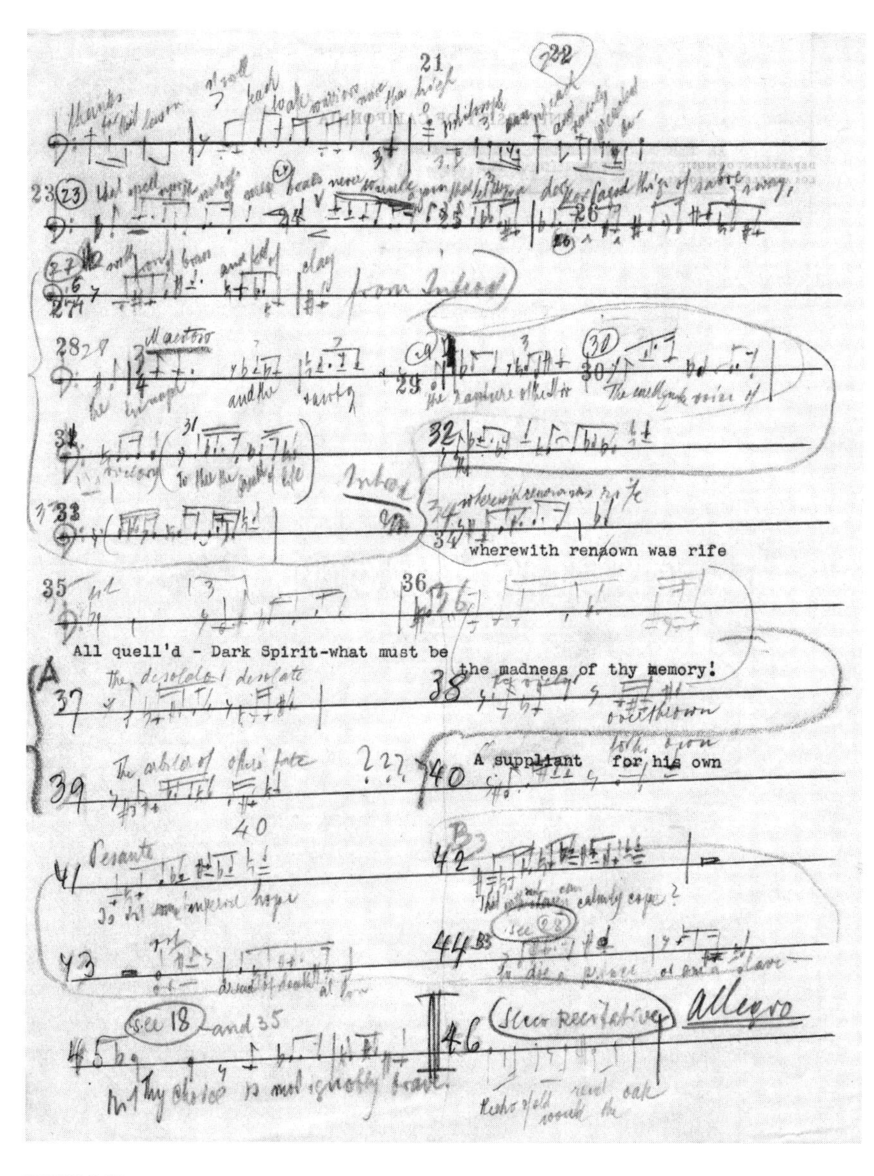

FIGURE 3.27.
Ode to Napoleon, sketch, mm. 19–46. Courtesy Belmont Music Publishers.

America in the 1940s. During that time the Beethoven motif, suggesting the Morse code "v" for victory, became known as the "Victory" motif.[774]

The *Ode* is Schoenberg's third and most unusual American twelve-tone work. Unlike most of his other dodecaphonic compositions, which are built on a single ordering of twelve pitches, the *Ode* is based on a symmetrical source hexachord (C, C-sharp, E, F, G-sharp, A) with only three other possible transpositions.[775] Through reordering of their pitches Schoenberg gained a variety of major, minor, and augmented triads of which he made as much use as of octave doublings. The *Ode* concludes with E-flat major to underscore Byron's glorification of an American president and to recall another "great 'Napoleonic' work, the *Eroica* Symphony."[776] Yet the *Ode*, despite the occurrence of chord successions and its tonal ending, is not a tonal work. Chord successions (in contrast to chord progressions) used in "descriptive music" are, in his words, usually "aimless" and "functionless, neither expressing an unmistakable tonality nor requiring a definite continuation."[777] When asked about the reason for the *Ode*'s tonal ending, Schoenberg replied evasively: "It is true that the *Ode* at the end sounds like E-flat. I don't know why I did it. Maybe I was wrong, but at present you cannot make me feel this."[778]

With his *Ode*, Schoenberg catered to the American public in manifold ways. He made a political and patriotic musical statement at a time when American soldiers began to risk their lives in the fight against Nazism. He selected a work by an English-language poet who was popular in America and built on the topical Napoleon-Hitler comparison. He chose to center his music on a straightforward declamation that

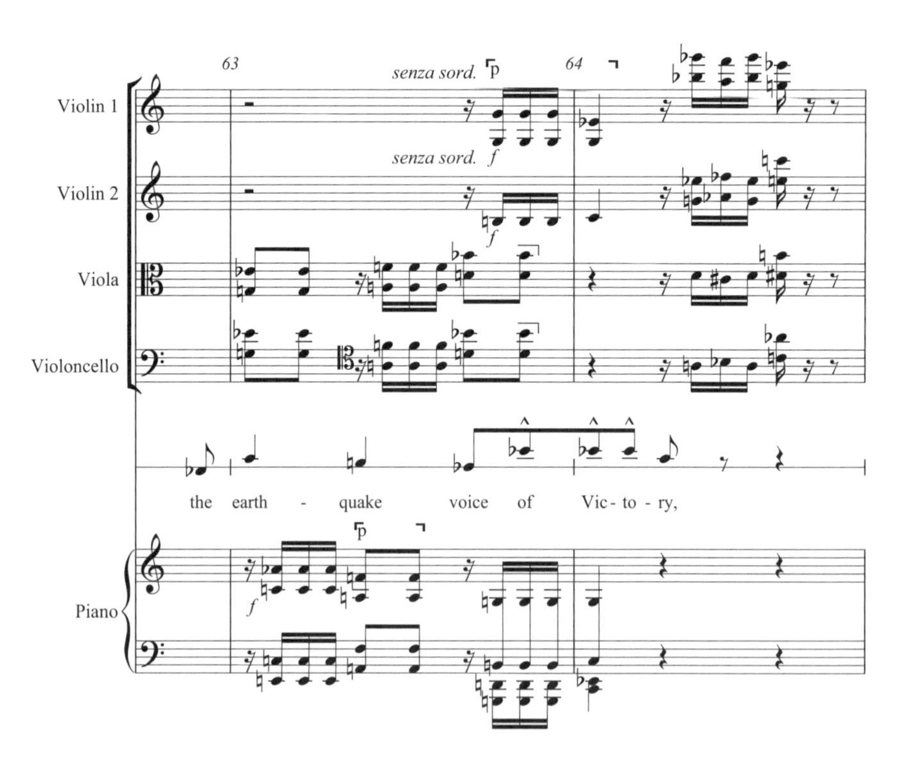

FIGURE 3.28.
Ode to Napoleon, quotation of *Marseillaise* and "Victory" motif from Beethoven's Fifth Symphony, mm. 63–64. Courtesy Belmont Music Publishers.

could facilitate the perception of the harder-to-digest instrumental sounds. He used existing motifs, allusions to past genres, and tonal elements as varying means of guiding audiences, and softened his image as an "atonalist." He also simplified the performance directions for the *Sprechstimme* part, hoping to attract not only singers, but also such famous American actors as Welles, Basil Rathbone, Paul Robeson, and Alan Hale.[779] Yet this is not to say that Schoenberg's efforts resulted in an easily accessible work. The *Ode* is a structurally dense work with montage-like juxtapositions of motifs and many texture and tempo changes. Despite his awareness that the complexity of his style would hinder the appreciation of his music perhaps more than atonality and dissonance, he was unwilling to sacrifice it.[780]

Although the composition of the *Ode* was not unusual in the context of American music in the early 1940s—his compatriots, including Becker, Copland, Gould, and Harris, wrote works honoring Lincoln, and Blitzstein had paid tribute to the Army Air Force in his *Airborne Symphony* (1943–46)—it is a remarkable work within Schoenberg's oeuvre at that time.[781] It was his first major completed work with overt political connotations. Most important, the *Ode* contradicted Schoenberg's rhetoric and his attempts to portray himself as an apolitical artist. In the 1920s he had dismissed Eisler's music for compromising artistic standards to speak to the masses, insisting that "the arts cannot influence political happenings."[782] Feeling that political messages can "divert one's attention from the ideas that lie far below," in 1928 he had attested that works like Mozart's *Nozze di Figaro* and *Zauberflöte* and Beethoven's *Fidelio* had "greatness," but not "immortality."[783] Yet in 1949, when he admitted that he himself had "written some pieces which are undeniably political," he reasoned: "In my inspiration I did not feel that I deviated from any artistic principle in this case."[784] The *Ode* may indeed be understood as an autonomous, politically and historically ambiguous piece of music, since it can relate to many different times and figures.

The *Ode* received its world premiere in New York City on November 23, 1944, not in its chamber version, but in an arrangement for speaker, string orchestra, and piano. The baritone Mack Harrell from the New York Metropolitan Opera, pianist Edward Steuermann, and the New York Philharmonic string players under Artur Rodzinski performed the work as a celebration of Schoenberg's seventieth birthday. The audience response was favorable. The critical response, however, was mixed. Some remarked positively on its timely political connotations and greater accessibility. Thomson spoke of the "constantly delicious sounds" and called the *Ode* "the best music, take it round, anybody is writing today."[785] Even Downes found the work acceptable, because it "was homeopathically delivered, and the dose went down with little resistance."[786] The *Ode*'s melodrama element and musical pictorialism, however, prompted both Thomson and Downes to comment on its affinity with Hollywood film music, and both criticized the poem as one of Byron's lesser works. Other critics were less complimentary. Oscar Thompson felt that "it was not great music, in the sense of being momentous, as is, for instance, the Beethoven Fifth Symphony," and Robert Bagar thought it was "good Schoenberg," but "far from being either good music or good drama or both."[787] Nevertheless the *Ode* was subsequently broadcast repeatedly and presented live in Boston, Chicago, Madison, Los Angeles, San Francisco, New York, and Berkeley as a chamber or orchestra work.[788] However, the *Ode* never became the hit Schoenberg had thought it could be. Schoenberg's hope that this piece could be used by the U.S. government, the Office of War Information (OWI), for propaganda purposes and might be performed in military camps did not materialize, even though the OWI apparently made a recording of the work.[789]

Theme and Variations for Wind Band, Opus 43a

Completed in August 1943, Theme and Variations for Wind Band is another work with which Schoenberg paid tribute to America. Thanks to the academic band movement in the nineteenth and early twentieth centuries, wind bands were among the most prevalent and popular musical institutions in this country. Schoenberg became aware of this phenomenon soon after his arrival in America, when the famous bandmaster and composer Edwin Franko Goldman informed him about the existence of "one hundred thousand or more school bands, not to mention the professional bands," discussed his efforts to elevate the band's status and artistic standards, and invited him to compose a piece for band.[790] Although Schoenberg was not prepared to accept Goldman's invitation at that time, he eagerly contributed a brief statement to his book *Band Betterment* (1934).[791] Less than ten years later, Schoenberg wrote his first work for band, at the request of his publishers Carl Engel and Felix Greissle.

In an effort to tailor it effectively for American music groups before he began writing the work, Schoenberg asked his publishers questions regarding the number of "good, average and weak bands" in America and the performers' technical abilities (keys, pitch range, intonation, rhythm, phrasing, dynamics). He was curious about the general aptitude of first players as soloists, second players, and the other band members, and pondered the inclusion of "ad libitum" passages and alternative solutions for smaller bands.[792] Greissle soon provided feedback, classifying the Goldman Band (mostly consisting of Metropolitan Opera orchestra members) as a prime example within the American band world, followed by some very good university bands. Yet he urged Schoenberg to consider university bands as part of the class of twenty thousand lower-level school bands. Greissle provided him with instrument lists and instrumental ranges, suggesting that Schoenberg orchestrate chiefly for a "torso" of reliable band instruments and treat the other parts as "addition or doubling." Greissle advised him to write the most sophisticated parts for first players, but not "to trust second and third players," and to write only "filling-in parts" for saxophonists, as these were often third-rank clarinetists. He encouraged him to write short soloistic passages for first players, but not for the first oboist, because the oboe is usually the "worst-played instrument" in the band. He also warned him against writing a difficult part for the clarinet in E-flat, since it is often played by a weak musician and seldom doubled. He recommended the avoidance of sustained notes as they expose bad intonation, advocating instead "music of a flowing character."[793] Greissle sent Schoenberg several band scores for study, including Percy Grainger's band version of *The Immovable Do* (1939).

In view of these issues, Schoenberg decided to deviate from his "ordinary manner of writing" and approach the composition from a pedagogical standpoint. He also found that the "imbalance inherent in the combination of instruments" could easily lead to a "poor, unclear and trivial sound."[794] Hence he adopted many of Greissle's suggestions, including the core instruments of Goldman's Band, the standard instrumentation used by other band composers at the time. In general, Schoenberg aimed at a rich symphonic sound with a focus on the clarinet family. He frequently juxtaposed distinct sonorities through texture and timbre variation, and unusual instrumental mixtures. Instead of conceiving technically challenging long soloistic lines, he assigned small segments of a melody to different instruments or instrument groups, using short solos sparingly. He favored fluid rhythms and steered clear of long notes. Yet he could not deny himself the use of such demanding chamber music traits as extreme pitch ranges (mainly in woodwinds and low brass), extended techniques, and very individual and distinct treatments of such instruments as the cornet, trumpet, flugelhorn, euphonium, baritone horn, bass, and tuba. Such choices ultimately reduced this work's playability. Oddly, though, Schoenberg believed that "by skillfully using cues and adding a part for Hammond Organ, it could be accessible also to weaker bands, which might also omit some of the more difficult variations."[795]

Other factors shaped this work as well. Schoenberg revisited tonality to spare young Americans the experience of intense atonality. The Band Variations have the key signature of G minor and articulate this key at important formal points, although they display, instead of traditional chord progressions, unusual successions of chords connected through linear chromatic processes. Schoenberg concluded the piece in tongue-in-cheek fashion on G major colored with blue notes—perhaps a bow to Gershwin (Figure 3.29).[796] In casting the work in variation form, he complied with "the desire of band authorities" and his publisher's demand to write a composition with "as many different characters and moods in one piece as possible."[797] The work thus features a twenty-one-measure theme in a solemn march-like character, seven contrasting variations, a summarizing finale, and a coda. Yet this concept also allowed him to point to his German musical roots and to instill the work with complexity. The chamber music imprint of the Variations is reminiscent of Brahms's economical symphonic orchestrations. The theme's treatment throughout its seven variations and finale feature "developing variation," and its irregular phrase structures refer to Brahms as well. Schoenberg's predilection for counterpoint, canon (Variation V), fugue (Variation VI), and chorale prelude (Variation VII) evokes Bach.

After several postponements due to World War II, the Goldman Band finally premiered the work in June 1946 in Brooklyn's Prospect Park—playing it again the next day in Manhattan's Central Park—and prompted very positive press reactions. Noel Straus described the work as "eloquent" and "impressive," and Lou Harrison was delighted to hear "swings and swells through a series of 'blues harmonies'" in the work's finale.[798] Yet Schoenberg, who heard and generally liked the recording of the performance, was disappointed about the omission of three variations, which he called "pure murder."[799] After the premiere, the University of Oregon's band performed the work in 1947 in Eugene, and the Eastman School's band played it in Rochester in 1949, when the score had finally become commercially available. Despite being tuneful, light, and more accessible, this hybrid work (another case of utopian functional music) did not receive the thousands of performances and yield the monetary profit that Schoenberg and his publisher had hoped for. Like most of Schoenberg's other American works, it reflects his multiple identities and dissimilation. Had he written it without complexities, it might have qualified as an example of complete assimilation; had he written a dissonant twelve-tone work, it could have exemplified his resistance to adaptation.

Nonetheless, Schoenberg was proud of the composition, and gave it an opus number, stressing that he wrote it "with great pleasure." He defended it as "one of those compositions which one writes in order to enjoy one's own virtuosity and, on the other hand, to give a certain group of music lovers—here it is the bands—something better to play."[800] The American band world felt quite honored. Edwin Franko Goldman raved: "Your name on a band work is going to mean much to the bands of the world." His son Richard called it "a landmark in the history of band music."[801] Indeed, Theme and Variations became, along with works by Paul Creston,

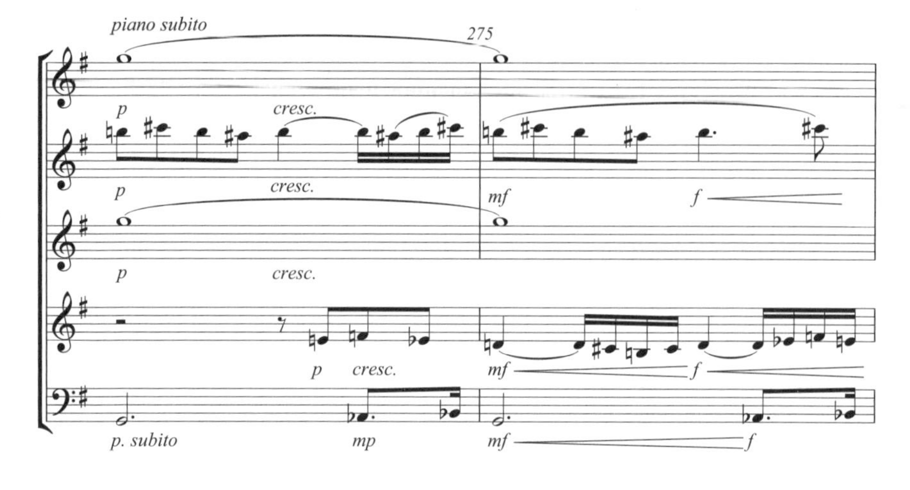

FIGURE 3.29.

Theme and Variations for Wind Band, mm. 274–78 (reduction). Courtesy Belmont Music Publishers.

Morton Gould, Grainger, Milhaud, Piston, Riegger and others, an important contribution to the band repertoire. It is one of the earliest substantive band works written by an internationally recognized composer, and it is one of few compositions in the band repertoire that was first conceived for band and thereafter arranged for other forces.[802]

On Greissle's advice, Schoenberg arranged the Band Variations for symphony orchestra to increase the number of performances.[803] The premiere of Theme and Variations, op. 43b, given by the Boston Symphony under Koussevitzky, actually took place in October 1944, two years before the premiere of the band version. Despite the mixed reviews of Koussevitzky's performance, the orchestral version was quickly embraced by such conductors as Victor Alessandro, Karl Krueger,

Pierre Monteux, Eugene Ormandy, Fritz Reiner, and George Szell, who performed it many times during Schoenberg's lifetime.

Schoenberg paid tribute to his three identities in manifold ways, while thoroughly engaging with his new home country. Like many of his new compatriots, he had roots in different countries, and thus shared with them such feelings as a nostalgic look at his former homeland from a geographical and historical distance, and the confidence that it is possible to begin anew. In common with many Americans, he also had an individualistic spirit, a pragmatic attitude, idealism, hope, and dreams. Although Schoenberg often argued from a purist standpoint, it would be misleading to assess his life and work in America from a purist or narrow point of view. He was neither an elitist who stubbornly refused to adapt to his new environment, nor an opportunist who accommodated to America in a facile manner. Instead, he negotiated his German, Jewish, and American identities through acculturation and dissimilation. The hybrid nature of his life and work, resulting from retention, transformation, and fusion of diverse social, intellectual, and cultural elements, should not be viewed as detrimental to his biographical and artistic integrity. Rather, his life and work gained in significance, humanity, and universality through this experience.

4 Schoenberg Performance in America

Schoenberg is well known for such elitist statements as "If it is art, it is not for the masses. If it is for the masses, it is not art," which suggests that he had little concern about the widespread dissemination of his music. Yet in reality, he hoped that his music would eventually achieve mass appeal.[1] Approaching the twilight of his life, Schoenberg increasingly felt that America was unable to satisfy his hunger for performances of his music, nurturing the now common view that in America his music remained "practically not performed."[2]

For Schoenberg, like so many other émigré musicians, settling in the United States meant coming to terms with a musical infrastructure and classical performance tradition that were very different from what had existed in Western Europe. American classical performances were generally presented in less hierarchical ways and featured a conservative and accessible repertoire where the boundaries between "cultivated" and "vernacular" music were often blurred. Performances largely depended on private patronage and box-office receipts, and so catered to wider audiences that were less discriminating and less immersed in classical traditions.[3] Among the relatively few prestigious performing institutions concentrated on the East Coast, the focus was on glamorous conductors and performers, not composers, and that fact was not lost on Schoenberg (who in his home surrounded himself with busts and paintings of himself) (Figure 4.1).[4] The majority of performing venues were small, inconspicuous private and academic settings for music making, which lay outside the visible and illustrious highbrow concert world and therefore were not taken seriously by most European-born musicians. Schoenberg's assessment of America's orchestra scene is symptomatic. He regretted in 1939 that "there exist perhaps ten good orchestras and a few second- and third-rate ones," when the United States at that time had sixteen major orchestras (with budgets from $125,000

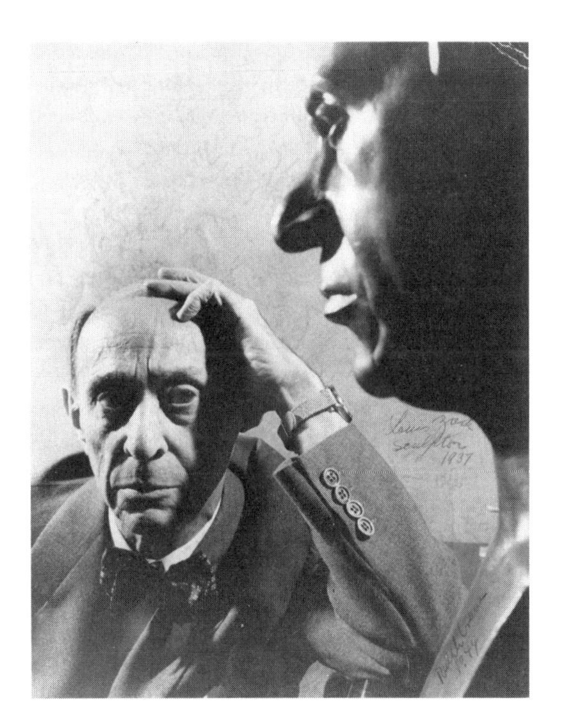

FIGURE 4.1.
Schoenberg with Schoenberg bust. Courtesy Arnold Schönberg Center.

to $750,000), more than 250 lesser orchestras, and an estimated 300,000 amateur orchestras.[5]

The music scene in Los Angeles in the early twentieth century can be considered a case in point. Despite a rich tradition of music making and the presence of many musicians and music institutions at that time, the city was considered a "musical vacuum," as Catherine Parsons Smith pointed out.[6] Besides its celebrated Philharmonic Orchestra and several large venues (Philharmonic Auditorium, Hollywood Bowl, Shrine Auditorium, Wilshire Ebell Theater, USC's Bovard Auditorium), Los Angeles featured many inconspicuous institutions that were often led and supported by women. These included a prosperous club culture, salons, music conservatories, orchestras (Women's Orchestra, and community, school, church, theater, movie, and industrial orchestras), chamber ensembles (Los Angeles Chamber Music Society, and the Vertchamp, Noack, and Bartlett-Frankel Quartets), and societies dedicated to the performance of old and new classical music.[7] Perhaps due to these venues' lack of highbrow ideals and representation in the national press, émigré musicians arriving in Los Angeles after 1933 took little note of or completely ignored their existence and past and present achievements. Hindemith lamented, "Apart from the movies, one can hardly speak of a musical life in this huge city. There is not even a real music school . . . There is not any musically educated society . . . if one does not consider the usual crowd of fat old women, the Board of Trustees or something like that."[8] In 1934 Schoenberg complained to the Philharmonic manager Lynden Ellsworth Behymer that his music had not been performed on the West Coast in the past twenty-five years. Yet between 1915 and 1933 there were at least thirty performances of his works, including the Five Orchestral Pieces, *Pierrot*, the dodecaphonic *Begleitmusik* (American premiere), and Woodwind Quintet.[9]

Determined to replicate a European-style musical infrastructure, Schoenberg and his many fellow émigrés faced numerous challenges. The Great Depression forced music institutions to cut back financially, putting thousands of performers out of work. New developments in sound-recording technology, for talking film, radio broadcasts, and phonograph records, also added to the jobs lost in the 1930s. According to the American Federation of Musicians, the advent of sound film rendered jobless approximately 18,000 out of some 22,000 musicians active in cinemas in the 1920s. The spread of radio and phonograph records further reduced the number of performance opportunities, even though it led to the foundation of such groups as the NBC Symphony Orchestra in 1937 and introduced new and diverse mass audiences far from cultural centers to classical music.[10] President Roosevelt's Federal Music Project (FMP) of the Works Progress Administration (1935–41), which provided occupation for about 16,000 musicians and subsidized opera and orchestra performances, among other initiatives, encouraged the education of broad audiences, fostered traditionalist and populist repertoire, and avoided a highbrow-lowbrow division of music making. During these lean years, American-born composers, their music having long been eclipsed by European repertoire, expected to receive a greater share of the FMP concerts and other musical events than their newly arrived contenders.

The émigrés from Nazi Europe did in fact alter the homegrown expression of democratic and eclectic types of music making, as their presence led to the creation of many new institutions embracing highbrow ideals and modernist repertoire, from which Schoenberg greatly benefited. The 1930s and 1940s saw the emergence of such Los Angeles ventures as Arthur Leslie Jacob's Festival of Modern Music, the New Music Forum of the American Society of Music Arrangers (1938), Peter Yates's Evenings on the Roof chamber music series (1939), Bronislav Gimpel's Hollywood Youth Orchestra (1940–42), Werner Janssen's Janssen Symphony and Concerts (1940–52), John Bauer's Ojai Music Festival (1947), Franz Waxman's Los Angeles Music Festival (1947), Harold Byrns's (formerly Hans Bernstein) Los Angeles Chamber Symphony (1948), and Peter Jona Korn's New Orchestra of Los Angeles (1948).

SCHOENBERG'S CHANGING VIEWS ON PERFORMANCE AND SCHOENBERG'S PERFORMANCES

To promote performances of his music, Schoenberg adapted to his new musical environment in several ways. He advocated the programming of his tonal works to revise his image as a musical bogeyman and to familiarize Americans first with his most accessible works before confronting them with his nontonal oeuvre. Although his programming choices pleasantly surprised audiences, they puzzled critics. Upon hearing Schoenberg conduct his *Pelleas* in Boston, an eastern critic wondered: "Why a work thus unrepresentative should have been selected by Schönberg (he himself and no other made the selection) remains a riddle as unsolvable as that of the sphinx itself."[11] Despite such reactions and Schoenberg's anticipation of a gradual acceptance of his progressive music into the orchestral repertoire, performances of his tonal orchestral works prevailed throughout his American years. His initial push for his tonal music turned, especially in the realm of orchestral music, into a situation comparable to that of Goethe's *Sorcerer's Apprentice*: "Spirits that I've cited my commands ignore." Significantly, during his entire American conducting career (1934–45), Schoenberg never chose to direct any of his twelve-tone works.

In the realm of chamber music, however, hearings of his nontonal works increased, thanks to the growth of chamber music activities and the emergence of contemporary music groups in America. Yet these events, often presented at small venues, if noted in the press, were not reviewed. Thus their immediate impact was subtle.

Schoenberg also changed his views on the role of the performer, and on performance practice and aesthetics with respect to his music.[12] Although he consistently adhered to the idea that a performer needs to be an "advocate of the work and its author" and should communicate a work's musical idea in a manner comprehensible to the audience, he took a more democratic stance toward performers, regarding them at a higher status than he did in his European years.[13] Before his emigration he had stressed the importance of a performer's fidelity to the score and opposed interpretative deviations from it; in America he admitted that musical notation had multiple meanings and that "music cannot exist without interpretation," because "musical notation is still so imperfect that, as every composer knows, many important details remain undefined or even untold."[14] Having previously argued that the score alone embodies a composer's musical idea, Schoenberg came to emphasize that the act of performance is "also a part of the task of presenting an idea."[15] Underscoring the performer's creativity, he stated that music was "the expression of the soul or character of the performer or of such persons of whom the player acts like an impersonator."[16] As a result Schoenberg allowed performers in America more freedom in their execution of his scores (with respect to articulation, playing the correct notes, and so forth). He no longer insisted on an unusually high number of rehearsals and took greater liberties (regarding tempi, execution of *Pierrot*'s *Sprechstimme* notation, for instance) when conducting his own music.[17]

This elevation of the role of the performer is a departure from Schoenberg's former, aristocratically based performance ideals and can be seen as his adjustment to a new, performer-oriented musical environment that was less hierarchical and more democratic.[18] His emphasis on a performer's creative expressivity, however, seems to have been a reaction to the strong focus on technical brilliance among certain musicians in America. Schoenberg rejected mechanical performance styles that were influenced by popular dance music, exemplified for him by such conductors as Toscanini and Koussevitzky, whom he classified as inflexible time-beaters.[19] Believing in "art music's inclination toward metrical freedom," he warned against practicing through mechanical repetition.[20] Yet he also rejected exaggerated expressivity marked by an overuse of vibrato and portamento-legato and a "goat-like bleating used by many instrumentalists to curry favour [*sic*] with the public."[21] He advised performers to silently read a score, imagine it as an organic whole, and feel the "center of gravity" of each phrase before playing it.[22]

Interestingly, Schoenberg also promoted the performance of chamber instead of orchestral music among amateurs to build a foundation for the performance and reception of his own music. He hoped to awaken music lovers' enthusiasm for active music making at a time when the recording and radio industries initiated a trend toward passive music listeners.[23]

Schoenberg advanced performances of his music as a conductor. In spite of a heavy teaching schedule, he successfully directed several leading American orchestras in performances of *Verklärte Nacht*, *Pelleas*, the First Chamber Symphony, Op. 9b (for full orchestra), *Gurrelieder*'s "Song of the Wood Dove," *Five Orchestral Pieces*, Suite in G, and his Bach and Brahms arrangements. Among the orchestras were the Chicago Symphony (February 1934), Boston Symphony (March 1934), Cadillac Symphony in Washington D.C. (April 1934), Los Angeles Philharmonic (March and December 1935), and San Francisco Symphony (February 1945). He also worked with less prestigious groups, including the FMP Symphony Orchestra of Los Angeles (February and April 1937), Bay Region Federal Symphony in San Francisco and Oakland (September 1937), San Diego Symphony Orchestra (July 1938), members of the Fox Studio Orchestra (1938), and the Rehearsal Orchestra in Los Angeles; according to Schoenberg, the last of these, the Rehearsal Orchestra, was "an excellent group of movie musicians" gathering on Sunday mornings to perform classical music (December 1940 and May 1941) (Figure 4.2).[24] With these orchestras he performed his *Pelleas*, Six Songs, op. 8, Five Orchestral Pieces, *Kol nidre*, and the Second Chamber Symphony. In addition, he conducted *Pierrot* performances in San Francisco, Los Angeles, and New York, as well as this work's premier recording (between 1935 and 1940). Some of Schoenberg's conducting activities nicely supplemented his income. For instance, he received $500 (about $7,928 in 2009) for his Chicago engagement, $400 (about $6,340 in 2009) for conducting in Boston, probably $500 (about $7,735 in 2009) for each of the two engagements in Los Angeles, and $185 (about $2,790 in 2009) for his concert in San Diego. For his conducting of the San Francisco Symphony in a performance of Antony Tudor's ballet *The Pillar of Fire* [*Verklärte Nacht*], Schoenberg again earned $500.[25]

As one might expect, Schoenberg was a capable and meticulous conductor, even though he spent much less time in rehearsal than he had in Europe.[26] For the 1935 performance of *Pierrot* and the First Chamber Symphony in San Francisco, he asked for six to eight rehearsals, stipulating that the musicians would arrive prepared. He intended to "rehearse twice a day" and work with "each man alone for two or three hours."[27] Schoenberg's assistant Gerald Strang, who witnessed the rehearsals, recalled his "tremendous concern with every little detail": "Every grade of dynamic had to be worked out and every attack, every phrasing in every instrument, whether it was conspicuous or not, was the subject of endless attention and care."[28] Dissatis-

FIGURE 4.2.
Schoenberg conducting the Los Angeles FMP Symphony in a dress rehearsal, April 14, 1937, at Trinity Auditorium in Los Angeles. Courtesy Arnold Schönberg Center.

fied with the outcome of his rehearsals, he decided at the last minute to conduct only seven numbers from *Pierrot* and to present the First Chamber Symphony twice. Schoenberg also had stressful experiences with the Cadillac Symphony and the Los Angeles Philharmonic due to uncooperative orchestra members.[29] He was more pleased with the rehearsals and results of his other conducting engagements. He praised his experience in Chicago and commended the Boston Symphony as a "very fine orchestra," adding, "I had no trouble getting just what I wanted."[30] His assistant Leonard Stein remembered that he "tremendously enjoyed" conducting the FMP Symphony and the Rehearsal Orchestra, with whom he "hit it off very well."[31] His performances in Chicago, Boston, Washington, Los Angeles, and San Diego attracted large and predominantly sympathetic audiences, and some of these performances were broadcast repeatedly. Even the atonal Five Orchestral Pieces "found their admirers."[32] Yet the overall critical response to his appearances as a conductor was mixed. A Chicago critic raved that "he [Schoenberg] came, he conducted, and he conquered," and that there was "not even a single hiss—from the audience, much tapping of bows and at the end a great fanfare from the orchestra."[33] After his first Boston and first radio appearance, he was praised as a "baton leader of superior quality." Critics in other cities, however, decried his retrospective programming. They disliked the lengthiness of *Pelleas*, the orchestration of his transcriptions, and his conducting, especially his slow tempo in *Verklärte Nacht*.[34]

CONDUCTORS AND ORCHESTRAS

Besides his conducting engagements, Schoenberg tirelessly networked with many performers, building an ever growing circle of émigré, immigrant, and American-born musicians, who championed his music in the United States. As performances of orchestral music provided the greatest visibility within the American concert world, Schoenberg was especially keen on establishing and maintaining relationships with as many conductors as possible. He interacted with such European-born conductors as Harold Byrns, Ingolf Dahl (formerly Walther Ingolf Marcus), Frederick Dorian (formerly Friedrich Deutsch), Kurt Frederick, Walter Herbert (formerly Walter Herbert Seligmann), Jascha Horenstein, Fritz Jahoda, Heinrich Jalowetz, Hans Kindler, Otto Klemperer, Fritz Mahler, William Steinberg (formerly Hans Wilhelm), Fritz Stiedry, Bruno Walter, and Fritz Zweig, most of whom had already been associated with him in Europe.[35] Dorian, Herbert, Jalowetz, Mahler, and Zweig were his students. Kindler was the cellist in *Pierrot*'s world premiere. Jalowetz gave *Gurrelieder*'s Berlin premiere (1923). Klemperer premiered *Begleitmusik*; Steinberg, *Von heute auf morgen* (1930); and Stiedry, *Die glückliche Hand* (1913). The majority of these conductors programmed Schoenberg's music in the 1930s and 1940s, but preferred to offer his tonal works—surely in an effort to adjust to the prevailing populist leanings during the Depression era and ensuing war years.

Schoenberg fostered a turbulent, yet warm, relationship with Otto Klemperer, director of the Los Angeles Philharmonic (1933–39) and the most prominent conductor in Los Angeles (Figure 4.3). Their egos—Schoenberg's sensitivity to neglect and Klemperer's ambivalent attitude toward Schoenberg's music—stood in the way of a sturdy friendship.[36] Klemperer's struggle with manic depression may have affected his acquaintance with Schoenberg (and others), too. Apart from *Pierrot*, *Begleitmusik*, the Violin Concerto, and String Trio, Klemperer disliked most of Schoenberg's nontonal works. He also had an aversion to such tonal compositions as *Pelleas*, *Gurrelieder*, and the two Chamber Symphonies—a fact that

FIGURE 4.3.
Schoenberg at Klemperer's party in 1935. *From left:* José Iturbi, Otto Klemperer, Richard Lert, Henry Svedrofsky, Pietro Cimini, Bernadino Molinari, Arnold Schoenberg, Pierre Monteux, William van den Burg. Courtesy Arnold Schönberg Center.

had not escaped Schoenberg. To make matters worse, Klemperer thoughtlessly told Schoenberg that "his works had become alien to him."[37] Hence Schoenberg distrusted Klemperer, even though he managed to program his music more frequently than any other West Coast conductor during Schoenberg's lifetime, despite substantial hurdles.[38] Klemperer had to bow to the dictates of the Southern California Symphony Association that controlled the financially struggling orchestra in 1934, which meant limited rehearsal time and accommodating the conservative audience tastes. He focused on *Verklärte Nacht*, the Suite in G, *Gurrelieder*'s "Song of the Wood Dove," and many of Schoenberg's transcriptions, and gave the world premieres of the Suite in G (1935) and the Brahms Piano Quartet arrangement (1938, one of Klemperer's favorites). He also presented the American premiere of Schoenberg's Monn arrangement with cellist Emanuel Feuermann (1936) and the West Coast premiere of his Handel transcription with the Kolisch Quartet as soloists (1938).[39] Klemperer invited Schoenberg to conduct his orchestra and presented most of the just-named works on the East Coast, where he had conducting engagements with the New York Philharmonic. West Coast audiences and critics applauded Klemperer's Schoenberg performances, yet in the East Klemperer's programming was largely dismissed. Schoenberg, although appreciative of Klemperer's high-quality performances, accused Klemperer of failing to "represent the sense of his historical task" and of portraying him instead as an "average arranger" in Hollywood.[40]

After his difficult recovery from a brain tumor, which cost him his conducting post in Los Angeles, Klemperer made futile attempts at premiering Schoenberg's Violin Concerto and conducting *Pierrot* in New York.[41] Leopold Stokowski had already scheduled the Violin Concerto's premiere, and Schoenberg wanted to conduct *Pierrot* himself. Disappointed over these missed opportunities, Klemperer was also infuriated when he was inadvertently excluded from a 1940 reception given in Schoenberg's honor by his publisher in New York.[42] However, Klemperer got over these disappointments and, in honor of Schoenberg's seventieth birthday, guest-conducted the Los Angeles Philharmonic in a 1945 performance of the Second

Chamber Symphony. It was the last time he presented a Schoenberg work in America. His interpretation generated positive reviews, yet Klemperer disliked the work, whose second part remained particularly "alien" to him.[43]

If Schoenberg distrusted Klemperer's attitude toward his music, he admired his performances of Beethoven's Seventh Symphony, Brahms's Second Symphony, Mahler's Second Symphony, and *Das Lied von der Erde*, and he loved to discuss this music with him. The two also interacted on other levels. In the summer of 1935 Klemperer attended Schoenberg's lectures at USC, and in 1936 Schoenberg gave him free private lessons, which Klemperer described as being "among the greatest experiences of my life as a musician."[44] Schoenberg thought highly enough of Klemperer at that time to recommend him as a composer for the music of a Beethoven film (although he later revealed that Klemperer had been "unable to harmonize a chorale and to become acquainted with music without playing it on the piano").[45] Schoenberg taught Klemperer's daughter Lotte, for whom he seems to have had a soft spot.[46] Grateful for Klemperer's help in getting his professorship at UCLA, Schoenberg tried to convince UCLA President Sproul to hire Klemperer as instructor for the newly established opera division, praising him as "one of the most outstanding men in the field."[47] Due to Klemperer's mental volatility, however, he was not appointed. Beyond their professional dealings, Schoenberg and Klemperer regularly socialized at birthday parties, dinners, and formal receptions. Schoenberg's and Klemperer's irritations often vanished as quickly as they emerged.

Compared to Klemperer, the Viennese-born Fritz Stiedry, conductor at the Berlin Municipal Opera (1929–33) and of the Leningrad Philharmonic (1934–37) before his immigration to the United States in 1938, had an uncomplicated relationship with Schoenberg (Figure 4.4).[48] Although Stiedry conducted fewer American performances of his music than Klemperer had, Schoenberg fully trusted his musical taste and skills, perhaps because Stiedry never expressed any doubts about his works. Stiedry became involved with the New Friends of Music, a Manhattan-based chamber music institution, and convinced them to add an orchestra, of which he

FIGURE 4.4.
Erika Wagner-Stiedry, Arnold Schoenberg, and Fritz Stiedry. Courtesy Arnold Schönberg Center.

became the first music director. Eager to present new works with this group, Stiedry asked Schoenberg to complete his Second Chamber Symphony (begun in 1906) and negotiated for Schoenberg a fee of $600 (about $9,080 in 2009) for the right of the work's first performance, even though the New Friends were not in a financial position to commission works.[49] Stiedry premiered this work at Carnegie Hall in 1940. The well-attended event was broadcast live, allowing Schoenberg to listen to it at his home, and was extensively covered in the press. The reviews were mixed.[50] Stiedry also conducted performances of *Pierrot* with his wife Erika Stiedry-Wagner as vocalist and arranged for Schoenberg to conduct *Pierrot* in New York as part of the New Friends of Music concert series. Despite his active performance schedule—Stiedry conducted at the Chicago Civic Opera and Metropolitan Opera in the 1940s—he and his wife visited the Schoenbergs in Los Angeles several times. On one of his last visits in 1949 he taught Schoenberg a new card game, "Napoléon-Patience," which Schoenberg often played thereafter.[51]

Austrian-born opera conductor Heinrich Jalowetz was not only one of Schoenberg's earliest and most talented students, but also among his closest musician friends to settle in America. Jalowetz arrived in 1939, and with Schoenberg's recommendation became a professor (1939–46) at the unconventional Black Mountain College in North Carolina. Although Jalowetz could no longer conduct operas, he became a highly regarded and versatile teacher, and applied the leadership and economic principles he learned from Schoenberg's Society for Private Musical Performances. The college lacked a library of music scores and orchestra parts, and Jalowetz made, in the fashion of Schoenberg's society, arrangements of Schoenberg's and other composers' orchestral music for performance with students and faculty in Saturday-evening concerts.[52] He also mounted a highly influential Schoenberg Festival on the occasion of the composer's seventieth birthday in 1944. The presence and creative interaction of Mark Brunswick, Marcel Dick, Hugo Kauder, Rudolf Kolisch, Ernst Krenek, Roger Sessions, and Edward Steuermann, mostly Schoenbergians, gave Schoenberg's reception in America a great boost, even if its impact was not immediate and widely felt.[53] Until his untimely death in 1946, Jalowetz, as a performer, teacher, and writer, tirelessly contributed to the dissemination of Schoenberg's music and advanced musical modernism in America.[54] Jalowetz and Schoenberg regularly shared private and professional matters by letter, but never saw each other in America, although Jalowetz had planned to visit Schoenberg in California.[55]

As Jalowetz was a Schoenberg satellite in America's Southeast, Kurt Frederick, another Austrian-born conductor, served as a Schoenberg advocate in the Southwest. A violinist and violist, Frederick had performed Schoenberg's music in the 1920s. After his emigration in 1939 he joined Stiedry's New Friends Orchestra and the Kolisch Quartet as a violist (until 1942). In 1944 he moved to Albuquerque, serving from 1945 to 1950 as conductor of the Albuquerque Civic Symphony Orchestra (now the New Mexico Symphony). With this amateur group, Frederick gave the world premiere of *Survivor* in 1948. While planning a *Pierrot* performance and discovering that Schoenberg had just completed *Survivor*, Frederick quickly offered to premiere *Survivor*, and Schoenberg entrusted this task to him without hesitation. He considered Frederick "a real Viennese musician of the best tradition, but simultaneously with modernistic spirit," and in this case did not object to the involvement of nonprofessionals and sacrifice of a substantial performance fee.[56] In lieu of money, Frederick actually copied out the parts and handed them to Schoenberg after the concert. With over one hundred amateur musicians in the orchestra and chorus, Frederick produced a moving event attended by nearly two thousand listeners.[57] Frederick's performance received positive reviews in the local and national press, and Schoenberg exclaimed that Frederick had "produced a miracle, about which not only Albuquerque, but probably the whole of Amerika [*sic*] 'Kopfstehen wird' [to be in a state of excitement]."[58] Through the *Survivor* premiere, among many other achievements, Frederick attained the status of a legendary figure in New Mexico's musical life.

Schoenberg also communicated with immigrant conductors of major orchestras: Richard Burgin (Boston), Eugene Goossens (Cincinnati), Dimitri Mitropoulos (Minneapolis, New York), Pierre Monteux (San Francisco), Eugene Ormandy (Philadelphia, Minneapolis), Fritz Reiner (Pittsburgh), Arthur Rodzinski (New York), Frederick Stock (Chicago), and Leopold Stokowski (Philadelphia, New York), to name only a few of them. And most of them, in particular Burgin, Goossens, Monteux, Ormandy, Reiner, Rodzinski, and Stock, regularly programmed his orchestral works with a focus on his old and new tonal music and the arrangements. Burgin, Rodzinski, and Stock occasionally presented some of his progressive works, and Stokowski and Mitropoulos consistently championed Schoenberg's most uncompromising works.

Schoenberg had a friendly and tension-free relationship with the German-born Stock, leader of the Chicago Symphony since 1905, who gave the American premiere of Five Orchestral Pieces in 1913 and introduced Chicagoans to *Pierrot* in 1926. Stock initiated Schoenberg's guest-conducting of the Chicago Symphony in a 1934 concert featuring *Verklärte Nacht*, Five Orchestral Pieces, and his arrangement of Bach's Prelude and Fugue ("St. Anne's"), which was one of the highlights of Schoenberg's early American years. Moved by this experience, he wrote to the orchestra:

> My dear colleagues, it is a great pleasure to remind [*sic*] the wonderful hours of the rehearsals and of the performances I had the privilege to enjoy. Your marvelous technic [*sic*], your spontaneous understanding of my intentions, the capacity to realize immediately the most difficult tasks asked by the problems of my music—all that fills me with admiration. You will believe me, that my thanks for all that is as sincere, as it is cordial, and that I envy your Mr. Stock as much to have you, as I envy you, to have him. Auf Wiedersehn![59]

Schoenberg also admired Stock's performance of his First Chamber Symphony at the Chicago Arts Club during the same trip. The work was played twice: after the first rendition, the local composer-critic Felix Borowski explained the composition and Stock invited the audience to sing its themes, whereupon the work was played again.[60] On this occasion Stock may have suggested that Schoenberg arrange the First Chamber Symphony for full orchestra. Upon completing the new orchestration, Schoenberg thanked Stock and revealed that "this arrangement is a perfectly new one . . . done now in a very independent way" and that he was "very content with the sound."[61] In the late 1930s, on Schoenberg's advice, Stock programmed his Handel and Brahms transcriptions. When Stock died in 1942, Schoenberg lost one of his important supporters in America's orchestral world.

Schoenberg also had a close relationship with London-born Stokowski, dating back to the 1920s. Schoenberg appreciated Stokowski's reputation as one of his most important advocates in the United States, who led the American premieres of the First Chamber Symphony (1915), Orchestral Variations (1929), and *Die glück-*

liche Hand (1930). Schoenberg welcomed the fact that Stokowski's performances never failed to attract great attention, thanks to his prestige, stage persona, showmanship, bold programming, and collaboration with major East Coast orchestras. He seems to have liked Stokowski's expressive conducting style, his use of ritardandos, and choice of certain soloists. After hearing him conduct "Song of the Wood Dove" with Rose Bampton as vocalist, he raved: "Bampton's voice is a miracle and how marvelous the sound of the orchestra was and how convincing the moods and architecture and the 'Steigerung' [intensification] was: everybody must have felt it." He also endorsed some of Stokowski's orchestrations: "May I also congratulate you to the orchestration for Debussy's 'Clair de lune.' Frankly—and this seems to me better than a compliment—I thought it was an original of Debussy."[62]

However, at Schoenberg's arrival in America, the relationship between the two was strained. Stokowski's American premier of *Gurrelieder* in 1932 disappointed Schoenberg, who had reserved the right to give it himself. Stokowski's neglect of Schoenberg's Monn and Handel arrangements hurt Schoenberg as well. (Stokowski preferred his own highly successful transcriptions.) Yet Stokowski pleased Schoenberg with the world premieres of two major dodecaphonic works: the Violin Concerto with Russian-born violinist Louis Krasner (who commissioned and premiered Berg's Violin Concerto) and the Philadelphia Orchestra and the Piano Concerto with Polish-born pianist Edward Steuermann and the NBC Symphony.

The Violin Concerto premiere was part of Stokowski's last set of concerts with the Philadelphia Orchestra in 1940, and it posed unusual challenges for him. The orchestra's board of directors tried to get around its performance by refusing to pay for the work's performance rights and the soloist. Yet Stokowski rebelliously proceeded with his plan and paid these expenses out of his own pocket, even insisting that Krasner, who offered to play the concert for free, must accept a check from him.[63] Stokowski also experienced resistance from some orchestra members, although Krasner testified that most of them "worked seriously and attentively, prodded on perhaps by a handful of colleagues who were personally involved in composition and avant-garde music." Benar Heifetz, the orchestra's principal cellist and former member of the Kolisch Quartet, hosted a preview performance of the work at his home to "engage the musicians in extended discussions of the structure, musical content, and melodic outline of the work."[64] Despite these efforts, the premiere triggered antagonism among audiences and critics, and Stokowski lectured the concert attendees on tolerance. About a dozen people walked out, some tittered during the performance, and others hissed at the end of the piece. Critics called the concerto a "30-minute-long chaos of caterwauling" and "the most cacophonous world premiere ever heard."[65] Schoenberg, who could not hear the concert for lack of a broadcast, expressed his gratitude to both Stokowski and Krasner, praising Stokowski's "brave stand toward my work and against illiterate snobs" and commending Krasner for performing the work "so shortly after it has been called unplayable."[66]

In 1944, toward the end of his short tenure as conductor of the NBC Symphony (a post he shared with Toscanini), Stokowski programmed Schoenberg's Piano Concerto. He began preparations for this event in 1943, inviting Steuermann to come to Los Angeles and play the work together with Leonard Stein in an arrangement for two pianos so that Stokowski could "fit the piano part and the orchestral part in his thoughts."[67] In New York he continued to study the concerto this way, thanks to Steuermann's teaming up with Austrian-born pianist-conductor Fritz Jahoda. The two played the concerto's two-piano version for Stokowski nine times before the orchestra rehearsals started.[68] Although Schoenberg's son-in-law Felix

Greissle, present at all the orchestra rehearsals, felt that Stokowski spent too much time going through the entire work without interruption and comments, the concerto's premiere was a success.[69] Schoenberg, who was among millions of people hearing the performance over the radio, found it "excellent" and praised its "great spirit." He believed that the performance reflected Stokowski's love for the piece.[70] The critics were split in their assessment of the work. Downes deemed it "disagreeable and unconvincing," and Oscar Thompson considered it "a very ugly affair."[71] Virgil Thomson, however, applauded Stokowski for programming this work with its "poetical and reflective" character, and "lyrical, intimate, thoughtful, sweet and sometimes witty inspiration and communication."[72] Stokowski once again had to pay a high price for his championing of modernist compositions. Soon after this performance, which Toscanini wanted to prevent, he was fired.[73] That same year Stokowski founded a new orchestra, the New York City Symphony, with which he performed Schoenberg's Second Chamber Symphony.

Schoenberg and Stokowski became good friends and regularly saw each other, especially when Stokowski resided in Hollywood. Stokowski, who had financially backed Schoenberg when he lived in Europe, gave him $1,000 (about $10,870 in 2009) in 1946, after discovering that he had fallen sick and faced high medical bills. As a token of his friendship Schoenberg gave Stokowski one of his self-portraits from c. 1911 and wrote for him the *Fanfare on Motifs of Die Gurrelieder* (1945).[74]

In September 1949 Schoenberg wrote to Stokowski: "You are the only conductor in America who remains somehow in step with my production."[75] At that moment he may not have thought of another great supporter of his music: the eminent Greek-born Mitropoulos. After settling in the United States in 1936, he developed into a staunch Schoenberg advocate as principal conductor of the Minneapolis Symphony (1937–49) and leader of the New York Philharmonic (1949–58). Besides frequent performances of *Verklärte Nacht* in the early 1940s, Mitropoulos programmed in 1945 Schoenberg's arrangement of his Second Quartet for soprano and string orchestra (1929) with noted soprano Astrid Varnay, and his Violin Concerto with Krasner as soloist. Schoenberg and Mitropoulos corresponded cordially, although their attempts to meet failed. Mitropoulos invited Schoenberg to come to Minneapolis (November 25 through December 2, 1945) to hear him conduct the Violin Concerto and lecture at two different universities. Ready to leave and with plane tickets in hand, the Schoenbergs discovered that the U.S. military had unexpectedly canceled all air travel on November 25. As there was no broadcast of the concert, Schoenberg could not hear the performance, which was received much more politely than the work's premiere had been.[76] Schoenberg tried to arrange a meeting with Mitropoulos in spring 1946, when Schoenberg was a visiting professor at the University of Chicago. Yet this time Mitropoulos had conducting engagements in New York and Europe.

Between 1948 and Schoenberg's death, Mitropoulos conducted several influential Schoenberg performances in New York. His 1948 rendition of the Five Pieces met with very positive responses from both audiences and critics, including Downes.[77] The critics even regretted that the work was "denied the radio and a nationwide audience on Sunday's broadcast" due to CBS's restriction on the broadcasting of modernist works.[78] Delighted about the reviews and enthusiastic reports from such friends as Henry Cowell, Schoenberg wrote to Mitropoulos: "Let me thank you most cordially for the great success you procured to [*sic*] my work. I realize that what I wrote in 1908 can not be called 'obsolete' inspite [*sic*] of the wishes of my enemies."[79] In 1949 Mitropoulos conducted the Serenade and the first New York performance of the *Ode*'s chamber version. In 1950 he gave the New York premiere of *Survivor*, which was a moving experience for most Philharmonic patrons and critics, but once again not broadcast. This performance, however, led to a disagreement between Schoenberg and Mitropoulos. From Downes's negative review Schoenberg gathered that Mitropoulos had asked the chorus to remove their robes and rise in shirtsleeves one by one in order to dramatize the beginning of their singing and the moment before their extermination. Schoenberg protested: "You should have seen that I did not compose such an action, not only because of higher taste, but also because the concert stage is not a theatre."[80] Mitropoulos defended himself: "I must confess that your last letter hurt me more than anything ever hurt me in my life. I want you to know that whatever I did beyond your indications in the score was done purely on an over-devotion basis to make the work as effective as possible, and believe me, I don't think that I harmed your spirit." Mitropoulos also begged: "Please, I beseech you, be more tolerant, especially when you write letters of complaint. To me, that has no importance, because I am devoted enough to your works to bow myself to your will, but, believe it or not, some of your complaints have made you so antipathetic that it makes even my personal effort to propagate your music in this country a very hard one."[81] Without hesitation Schoenberg offered peace: "Believe me, it was not my intention to hurt you. I appreciate your friendship toward me too highly to do this." He remorsefully added: "You are right, in my age I should not be anymore as temperamental as I was—very much to my disadvantage—during my whole life. True, I lost many friends and won only their respect. Thus nothing has been left to me than to hope that people who understand me will continue to perform my music, even if they dislike my behaviour [*sic*]."[82] In another letter Schoenberg offered Mitropoulos his friendship: "Dear Friend: It is with pride that I address you 'dear friend,' because I am proud of my anticipation to tell you that it is no risk to write you straight forwardly, even if one disagrees . . . I shake your hand, dear friend, real cordially."[83]

All in all Schoenberg heard three of his works under Mitropoulos's direction: a radio broadcast of his 1945 performance of the Second Quartet for voice and string orchestra, a noncommercial recording of the 1950 New York Philharmonic performance of the Orchestral Variations, and a 1949 commercial recording of the Serenade. Schoenberg "deeply appreciated" his interpretation of the Second Quartet, was "very satisfied" about the Variations performance, and called the Serenade recording "one of the very best performances of my works . . . made under a 'happy star' because also the record's sonority is unusually beautiful."[84]

Schoenberg also developed good relations with Artur Rodzinski, the renowned Polish-born conductor and former student of Schoenberg's friend Franz Schreker. Rodzinski had repeatedly performed the Bach transcriptions with the Los Angeles Philharmonic in 1930 and 1931, and presented the Brahms arrangement with the Cleveland Orchestra during that orchestra's 1938–39 season and in ten further performances on a midwestern concert tour and with the New York Philharmonic and the NBC Symphony in the late 1930s and early 1940s.[85] Despite these efforts, however, Schoenberg was initially not sure if Rodzinski would be capable of premiering the *Ode*'s arrangement for voice, string orchestra and piano (1944). "I am a little afraid of his 'interpretation' as I heard a few weeks ago one of his concerts," he confided to Steuermann.[86] But Steuermann and Greissle, whose idea it had been to create the arrangement and recruit Rodzinski for this task, convinced him of his suitability. Nonetheless Schoenberg felt it necessary to urge Rodzinski to "ask the leaders of every instrument to write in the parts' fingerings because it could be players would not be able to find the best ones."[87] According to Steuermann,

Rodzinski worked more intensively with the orchestra than Stokowski, and successfully premiered the work in fall 1944.[88] Opera singer Mack Harrell performed the vocal part, and Steuermann was the pianist. The last of a set of three performances was broadcast live and repeatedly featured on radio programs in the following years.[89] Schoenberg heard it over the radio and was pleased with Rodzinski's achievement, agreeing with his friend Kurt List's positive evaluations of the work's execution.[90] Yet as was so often the case, the press reactions to this performance varied. Virgil Thomson endorsed the work and its performance, while Downes, Oscar Thompson, and Robert Bagar from the *Washington Times* predictably rejected the piece, although they praised its performers.[91] Rodzinski often visited Schoenberg on his trips to Los Angeles, and Schoenberg expressed his friendship toward Rodzinski in a four-part infinite canon written in celebration of the birth of Rodzinski's son Richard (dated March 12, 1945). The canon whose text "Sleep, Richard, sleep! Dein Vater hat Dich lieb! [Your father loves you]" is modeled on the German lullaby "Schlaf, Kindlein, schlaf!" and is inscribed: "To Artur Rodzinski's son, Richard, wishing his career may continue as successful as it began."

American-born conductors also embraced Schoenberg's music and fostered a friendly relationship with him. Werner Janssen, who in 1934 made his American conducting debut with the New York Philharmonic and became its first American-born conductor, gave the American premiere of Schoenberg's Handel arrangement with members of the Philharmonic as soloists in New York in 1935. In 1939 he moved to Los Angeles, where he composed music for films and founded the Janssen Symphony (1940–52), an orchestra that brought together the members of the London String Quartet and musicians from the Hollywood studios. It was dedicated to the performance of contemporary music and competed with the Los Angeles Philharmonic. Schoenberg got to know Janssen personally and lent his name in support of this new institution.[92] With his group, Janssen did more than perform some of Schoenberg's early tonal works: he premiered and recorded the Prelude to *Genesis* in 1945 in Los Angeles. In 1951 Columbia released a recording of Janssen conducting his orchestra and the Manuel Compinsky Quartet in a performance of Schoenberg's Handel transcription. Janssen also performed Schoenberg's music with other orchestras, such as the Portland Symphony.

Schoenberg interacted with the celebrated American bandmasters Edwin Franko Goldman and his son Richard. In 1934 Edwin, excited about Schoenberg's move to America, sought his help in stressing the significance of the band in the music world and the fact that it is "a satisfactory means of expression."[93] Schoenberg gladly contributed a statement to his book *Band Betterment* of that year.[94] Goldman also invited him to compose a work for band, but it took Schoenberg a decade to embrace this idea. Having completed Theme and Variations, op. 43 for this medium in 1943, he showed Edwin an excerpt of the score to assess its feasibility and offered the Goldman Band the world premiere. Edwin did not think that the score was difficult for his band, but indicated that for school and college bands the piece might be too hard.[95] Although both Goldmans had underestimated the work's complexity—at the premiere three variations were skipped due to limited rehearsal time—they loved the music's "imagination" and the "unusual timbres of the instrumental combinations" and declared the work "a landmark in the history of band music."[96] Schoenberg, who heard a recording of the performance, liked it, but deemed the omission of three variations objectionable for structural reasons.[97]

Toward the end of his life Schoenberg also enjoyed contact with young American conductors who had taken an interest in his music, such as Bernard Herrmann and

Thor Johnson. Herrmann, who was primarily a composer, now best remembered for his scores for Orson Welles's *Citizen Kane* and several of Alfred Hitchcock's films, championed works by Schoenberg and Ives when he was music director of the CBS Symphony (1942–59). Herrmann and Schoenberg came into contact when Herrmann conducted his Second Chamber Symphony on the air in June 1949. Schoenberg informed Herrmann about the broadcast's poor transmission, whereupon Herrmann sent him a recording of that performance. Schoenberg was overjoyed: "Let me tell you I find now that your performance was very good, very convincing and expressive." He also expressed his desire to meet him: "I hope to see you should you once visit California."[98] Johnson, the first American-born music director of the Cincinnati Symphony (1947–58), wrote Schoenberg in the course of preparing *Gurrelieder* for performances in February 1951, having previously presented *Verklärte Nacht*. Schoenberg replied that he was delighted "to realize that you seem to like my music—at least my music of this period—and you like to do this performance. I appreciate this very much."[99] Detailing the pros and cons of Stokowski's *Gurrelieder* recording, Schoenberg made many helpful suggestions. On his advice, Johnson hired Erika Stiedry-Wagner, although he ignored his proposal to perform the work in English. Schoenberg was most thrilled to see that Johnson had scheduled twenty rehearsals and predicted that this vision would make him a "leader among American artists, creating an American school of conductors."[100] Given twice and broadcast, Johnson's *Gurrelieder* rendition earned the praise of the national press. Yet Schoenberg did not have a chance to hear it.

Perhaps the youngest and most ambitious American conductor to communicate with Schoenberg in his final years was the twenty-seven-year-old Robert Craft, Stravinsky's close associate and conductor of some of the Evenings on the Roof concerts in Los Angeles. Beginning in the summer of 1950, Craft regularly informed Schoenberg about his plans to conduct *Pierrot*, the Suite, op. 29, the choral works, opp. 27 and 28, Woodwind Quintet, Serenade, and *Begleitmusik* on both coasts. Open about his enthusiasm for Schoenberg's music, he even flatteringly called the Three Satires, op. 28 "a kind of 20th-century *Musikalisches Opfer*."[101] Craft asked Schoenberg to autograph scores he had recently purchased, and he borrowed from him scores and recordings of works he could not obtain. He also impressed Schoenberg with his meticulous analysis and critique of Mitropoulos's noncommercial recording of the Orchestral Variations.[102] Schoenberg was so taken by Craft that when Stiedry-Wagner, the vocalist in Craft's 1950 *Pierrot* performance expressed reservations about him, Schoenberg came to his defense: "Mrs. Stiedry . . . You should not discourage such young friends of mine as Mr. Craft. He slowly gets used to my music by performing it often and he will eventually succeed. I would like for you to encourage all of my friends, such young people as Craft and the young hornist Gunther Schuller or the Juilliard Quartet. I hear rumors about an 'old know-all Schoenberg clique.' They are of course true."[103]

Despite the programming efforts of these and other conductors, Schoenberg resented that he was ignored by the so-called "Big Three," Toscanini, Walter, and Koussevitzky, who enjoyed a great reputation as leaders of the most prestigious orchestras, and by Alfred Wallenstein, the first American-born conductor of the Los Angeles Philharmonic (1943–56).[104] While Toscanini and Walter's musical tastes were hopelessly conservative, Koussevitzky and Wallenstein favored contemporary works indebted to Stravinsky and Boulanger's teachings. Toscanini performed Schoenberg's transcription of Bach's Prelude and Fugue in E-flat, BWV 552 only once in 1932. Walter conducted only *Verklärte Nacht*, in 1924 and 1944.

Koussevitzky programmed Schoenberg's Bach arrangements and *Verklärte Nacht* in 1934 and 1937, and premiered Theme and Variations, op. 43b in 1944. Wallenstein performed *Verklärte Nacht* in New York in 1941 and *Gurrelieder*'s "Song of the Wood Dove" in Los Angeles in 1949. Although assistants and guest conductors of the Boston Symphony and Los Angeles Philharmonic (Burgin, Eleazar de Carvalho, Charles Munch, Byrns, Craft, Dahl, Janssen, and Klemperer) often performed Schoenberg's music in lieu of Koussevitzky and Wallenstein, Schoenberg still felt that it was the musical directors' duty to advocate his music (even though he had a low opinion of their conducting skills). Their endorsement of his works might have drawn more attention to his achievements. In the 1930s Schoenberg had believed: "There must come soon a time when all the American orchestras will have to perform my works as regularly as they perform today already Debussy, Sibelius and Ravel. I am the next to whom the younger generation will turn, as soon as they get the places now occupied by older uncles and aunts. All depends on the right propaganda."[105] By the late 1940s, however, he had grown impatient. Ignoring the rise in performances of his orchestral music, he publicly declared: "Thanks to the attitude of most American conductors and under the leadership of Toscanini, Koussevitzky and of Walter, suppression of my works soon began with the effect that the number of my performances sank to an extremely low point."[106] Taken at face value, this inaccurate statement, among other similar remarks, served to underscore the idea that Schoenberg's music was neglected in America.

PERFORMERS OF SCHOENBERG'S CHAMBER, VOCAL, AND KEYBOARD MUSIC

Schoenberg was also well connected with numerous European- and American-born chamber musicians who propagated his music all over the United States, although he could by no means have known all the performers of his music or been aware of all their performances, which often took place in inconspicuous settings, received little publicity, and did not yield performance fees. In the 1930s and 1940s the number of chamber musicians performing his music exceeded by far that of orchestras.

Among the ensembles featuring members from Europe, which regularly programmed his chamber music with strings, were the Kolisch, Pro Arte, Budapest, Mischakoff, Manhattan, and Roth Quartets and the Albeneri Trio. Predominantly American groups such as the Abas, California, Fine Arts, Hollywood, Juilliard, Kaufman, Kroll, Vertchamp, and Walden Quartets included his works in their repertoire as well. The New School Chamber Orchestra, Boston Sinfonietta, Contemporary Music Group in Cleveland, and Barati Chamber Orchestra in San Francisco, among others, scheduled his chamber music for mixed ensembles.

Schoenberg had the closest relationship with the Kolisch and Pro Arte Quartets, of which Rudolf Kolisch, his brother-in-law and former student, was the leader. Founded in 1922 in Vienna and famous for their performances from memory, the Kolisch Quartet (whose other long-term members included Felix Khuner, Eugene Lehner, and Benar Heifetz) settled in the United States in 1936 and successfully premiered Schoenberg's Fourth Quartet in 1937 in Los Angeles (Figure 4.5). They recorded all of his numbered quartets at the United Artists Studio (1936–37) and regularly presented them (often paired with Beethoven's late quartets) as a cycle in West and East Coast cities and in the Midwest in live performances as well as radio broadcasts.[107] After the original group disbanded in 1939, Kolisch championed

FIGURE 4.5.
Schoenberg and the Kolisch Quartet. Courtesy Arnold Schönberg Center.

Schoenberg's music in various other capacities: with reorganized quartet formations (including Stefan Auber, Marcel Dick, Daniel Guilet, Frederick, Khuner, and Jascha Veissi), as a teacher at the New School for Social Research, and as participant in New York performances of the First Chamber Symphony, the Suite, op. 29, and *Pierrot*, including the latter work's premier recording under Schoenberg.[108] In 1944 he became the leader of the Pro Arte Quartet, which frequently performed Schoenberg's four quartets, *Verklärte Nacht*, *Ode*, and Trio at the University of Wisconsin, where the group was in residence, and in cities all over America.

Schoenberg considered the members of the Kolisch Quartet "marvelous players" and the "best string quartet I ever heard." "Everything seems so simple," he raved, "so self-evident in their performance, that one would think it is easy. Their virtuosity, their sonority, their understanding, their style, are admirable."[109] During their last years of existence the group spent much time with Schoenberg in Los Angeles, rehearsing with him Beethoven's and his own quartets in preparation for concerts and recordings. Lehner vividly remembered the rehearsals of the Fourth Quartet: "Pencil in hand, Schoenberg interrupted us countless times to ask about our approaches and conceptions. With time, there would be less and less pencil tapping, fewer stops, until finally we played an entire movement without interruption. There was a long pause, and then he spoke, 'Tell me, do you understand this music? Do you like it? Why don't you play Mozart?'"[110] According to Lehner, Schoenberg emphasized "clarity," "transparency," and the "human element."[111] Khuner recalled that "liveliness" and "the musical intensity of the performance counted for much more than the polish," although in America "the polish of the performance is more important than the musical content."[112] As late as 1950 Schoenberg warned Kolisch against "stiff perfection," which he thought to be typical of many American performances.[113] During their visits in Los Angeles, the Kolisch Quartet also enjoyed parties, tennis matches, and card and chess games with Schoenberg. When Kolisch, Lehner, Khuner, Dick, and Frederick later assumed teaching positions, they conveyed their individual understanding of Schoenberg's performance ideals to several generations of young musicians. Curiously, however, between 1939 and 1950 Schoenberg hoped that Kolisch would trade his various teaching jobs for employment at a Hollywood studio.[114]

Kolisch was among Schoenberg's most dedicated performers. In 1934 he relayed to Schoenberg that he wanted to use his performing abilities for the best possible performances of his music, considering himself Schoenberg's disciple and messenger.[115] Schoenberg in turn identified Kolisch as one of his "ideal interpreters."[116] Schoenberg often addressed Kolisch affectionately as "Liebster Rudi [Dearest Rudi]" and advised him like a father in many different matters, including health, travel, instrument choice, quartet crises, job search, and his ideas on the performance of Beethoven's music.[117] He trusted Kolisch as he did no other musician and was always anxious to get Kolisch's critical feedback on his newest works.[118] Suggesting that Kolisch program the first two rather than the latter quartets, he explained: "You know, I am always a little afraid of the two later string quartets."[119] Schoenberg also consulted him about his Trio: "I would like to know if the double stops and harmonics are not too hard in the fast tempo. If necessary I plan to rework it into a string quintet."[120] In 1949 Schoenberg shared with Kolisch his unfounded fear of a widespread boycott of his music.[121]

Schoenberg also enjoyed close contact with the West Coast–based Vertchamp, Abas, and Hollywood Quartets, and in his final years with the Juilliard Quartet. The Vertchamp Quartet, led by Albert Vertchamp, was the first chamber ensemble to welcome him in California with a performance of his Second Quartet with soprano Margaret Coleman, hosted by the Los Angeles Chamber Music Society at the Hollywood Women's Club in December 1934. Schoenberg, who supervised the group's rehearsals, befriended Vertchamp, who became one of his many tennis partners. The Abas Quartet, headed by Nathan Abas, soon followed Vertchamp, playing Schoenberg's first three quartets at local concerts and at Schoenberg's USC lectures in 1935 and 1936.[122] The Abas musicians also socialized with Schoenberg and his students. The California Quartet (1946–50), headed by Khuner, and the Hollywood Quartet, formed in 1939 and led by Felix Slatkin, played for Schoenberg at his home.[123] The former group included Schoenberg's Fourth Quartet in its repertoire, and the latter distinguished itself with a recording of *Verklärte Nacht* for Capitol Records (1950).

Schoenberg, however, was perhaps most pleased with the highly visible, New York–based Juilliard Quartet and its exceptional devotion to his music. The group featured at the time first violinist Robert Mann, violinist Robert Koff, violist Raphael Hillyer, and cellist Arthur Winograd. Soon after its formation in 1946 this ensemble, nurtured by Steuermann and Lehner, mastered all of Schoenberg's four quartets and presented them at such prestigious venues as the New Friends of Music, Ojai Festival, Tanglewood, and ISCM concerts. Having been introduced to Schoenberg by Steuermann as "undoubtedly very talented," the members of the Juilliard Quartet visited Schoenberg in May 1949 to study the quartets with him.[124] Although their very polished performance style differed considerably from that of Kolisch's groups, Schoenberg greatly enjoyed working with them and considered them to be his friends. To his delight they presented in New York in 1950 a widely acclaimed four-concert cycle featuring his four quartets and his *Ode*, for which he had eagerly provided the program notes.

Other string players who interacted with Schoenberg included Jascha Heifetz, Sol Babitz, Helen Swaby, and Adolf Koldofsky. With Heifetz, the most illustrious violinist in Los Angeles, Schoenberg was at loggerheads. Schoenberg hoped Heifetz would perform his Violin Concerto, from which he had sent him excerpts. "Have you played it? Have you got any kind of impression of it? Do you intend to play it? Or, even, are you no more interested in this work?" he queried after waiting six weeks for Heifetz's response.[125] Only at second hand did he learn that Heifetz deemed the work unplayable. After this experience Heifetz was unable to win Schoenberg's favor even though he purchased and praised the premiere recordings of Schoenberg's quartets and wished for his daughter to study with the composer. Schoenberg did not reject his latter request, but established unacceptable conditions by asking for $1,500 (about $16,305 in 2009) for six months worth of lessons.[126] In contrast, Babitz, a violinist in the Los Angeles Philharmonic and studio orchestras, showed much interest in the Violin Concerto, and even introduced Schoenberg in 1940 to his "new system of 'back-handed' fingering (playing with the fourth finger underneath the third, for example) which makes the hardest spots in the Concerto much easier."[127] Yet in the end he did not perform it, preferring to play baroque violin and Stravinsky's music. A young local violinist, Helen Swaby, however, mastered the concerto's first two movements in 1940, played them for Schoenberg, and even won his approval for a public performance with piano accompaniment before the concerto's official premiere later that year. Swaby also performed an excerpt of the concerto's slow movement for Schoenberg's NBC broadcast in February 1940.[128] Schoenberg's relationship with the Canadian-born violinist Koldofsky, who settled in Los Angeles in 1945 and joined the RKO Orchestra, was even more rewarding (Figure 4.6). Koldofsky presented the West Coast premiere of the Trio (1948) and made its premiere recording (1950). In 1949 he commissioned Schoenberg to write the *Phantasy*, which Schoenberg dedicated to Koldofsky because his performance of the Trio had pleased him so much. Koldofsky premiered the *Phantasy* with Leonard Stein at a concert of the Los Angeles ISCM chapter on Schoenberg's seventy-fifth birthday and, together with Steuermann, made the work's premiere recording (1951). Koldofsky became one of Schoenberg's trusted musician friends in whose performances he detected "deep understanding and

FIGURE 4.6.
Adolf Koldofsky and Arnold Schoenberg. Courtesy Arnold Schönberg Center.

feeling of the meaning and expressions of my music."[129] His death at age forty-six, preceding Schoenberg's own by a few months, was a great blow to Schoenberg.

Innumerable singers, including such nationally renowned vocalists as Rose Bampton, Eva Gauthier, Mack Harrell, Belva Kibler, Alice Mock, Astrid Varnay, and Reinald Werrenrath, performed Schoenberg's vocal works. Yet only a fraction of them were in touch with Schoenberg. Among the European-born singers who endorsed Schoenberg's music and knew him personally in America were Johanna Klemperer, Erika Stiedry-Wagner, Irene Hanna (Hanna Schwarz), and Astrid Varnay. Schoenberg was also acquainted with several American-born vocalists, including Nancy Ness, Nell Tangeman, and the California-based Clemence Gifford, Radiana Pazmor, and Calista Rogers. He had a long and friendly association with Metropolitan Opera soprano Bampton (Figure 4.7). Having sung the role of the Wood Dove in *Gurrelieder*'s American premiere and the premiere recording in 1932, she performed "Song of the Wood Dove" with Schoenberg conducting the Cadillac Symphony in Washington, D.C., for a 1934 General Motors broadcast and thereafter with various other orchestras. She also sang *Das Buch der hängenden Gärten*, whose first performance in 1949 Schoenberg supervised. He lavished praise after hearing her recording: "It makes great pleasure to hear you. Your musicianship, your capacity of presentation, your poetic feeling and your wonderful voice." In 1950 he invited her back: "When will you come again to Los Angeles? Then you must have more time for us, for a longer meeting."[130] Yet he died before they could meet again.

During his American years, Schoenberg's choral works received few performances, while the operatic oeuvre remained unperformed. Margarethe Dessoff, the Austrian-born founder of the New York–based Dessoff Choirs; Frederick Dorian in Pittsburgh; Jacob Avshalomov in New York; and the Los Angeles–based choral directors Robert Craft, Arthur Leslie Jacob, Allen Lannom, and Roger Wagner were among the conductors who embraced Schoenberg's choral music. *Friede auf Erden* and his folksong settings were performed most often, although the score and parts of some of the pre-1933 compositions were difficult to obtain. Dorian, for instance, seemed to be unable to get the scores for *Friede*, and had to ask Schoenberg to provide photostat copies of his own materials.[131] As is typical of Schoenberg's former

FIGURE 4.7.
Schoenberg and Rose Bampton. Courtesy Arnold Schönberg Center.

students, Dorian faithfully promoted his teacher in his capacity as a faculty member at the Carnegie Institute of Technology (later Carnegie-Mellon University), teaching and performing Schoenberg's music. The *Friede* performance with his large Carnegie Institute choir in April 1942 was apparently a big success—perhaps because Dorian followed Schoenberg's advice to sing the work in English and to place one or two clarinets between the soprano and alto sections and one or two bassoons between the tenors and basses.[132] Dorian reported that his students were very enthusiastic and that many of them had memorized their part. He also emphasized the audience's great applause.[133] As head of the Pittsburgh ISCM chapter, Dorian conducted and organized further Schoenberg performances.[134] Moreover, Dorian, whose parents' Vienna apartment had served as the headquarters of Schoenberg's Society for Private Musical Performances, dedicated a chapter to the interpretation of Schoenberg's music in his 1942 book *History of Music in Performance*.[135] Dorian visited Schoenberg in California in the 1930s and in 1948, and made two unsuccessful attempts to invite Schoenberg to lecture in Pittsburgh. The first time Schoenberg was too busy; the second time he was not well enough to travel.

Schoenberg cultivated fruitful relationships with numerous pianists, who participated in performances of his chamber music and played his works in their solo recitals all over the country. As might be expected, he benefited from the presence of a substantial number of European-born pianists in America. Yet a growing group of American pianists, including many of his American students and pupils of his friends and colleagues, embraced his music as well.

Of the pianists of European origin who performed Schoenberg's music in America—Gerhard Albersheim, Robert Goldsand, Lydia Hoffmann-Behrendt, Fritz Jahoda, Gunnar Johansen, Erich Kahn, Rudolph Reuter, and Grete Sultan, among others–Edward Steuermann stands out. He was arguably the most actively devoted performer of Schoenberg's oeuvre and one of the most enduring members of his circle. A student of Schoenberg (1912–14), he had participated in most world premieres of his chamber works with piano, including *Pierrot*, and was the leading pianist of the Society for Private Musical Performances (1918–21). After his emigration in 1936 and a brief sojourn in Los Angeles, Steuermann established himself as one of Schoenberg's most important exponents, his "ambassador of the piano" on the East Coast.[136]

Steuermann served as soloist in the world premiere of Schoenberg's Piano Concerto (1944), and as pianist in both the *Ode*'s first performance (1944) and *Pierrot*'s premiere recording (1940). He regularly performed Schoenberg's piano works, as well as the Second Chamber Symphony and Piano Concerto arranged for two pianos.[137] During Schoenberg's lifetime, he recorded the Six Little Piano Pieces, the Five Piano Pieces, and the *Phantasy* with Koldofsky. Moreover, he was a mediator between Schoenberg and the East Coast music scene. He confided to Schoenberg his impressions of conductors, marveling at Stokowski's reliance on "playing through" a piece in rehearsals and Burgin's fervent musicianship, in spite of his "lack" of conducting skills.[138] Steuermann collaborated with such musicians as Brunswick, Jahoda, Kahn, Kolisch, and Schoenberg's publishers Felix Greissle and Kurt List to mount performances of his works. In his function as a teacher, mentor, and lecturer at Juilliard, the Philadelphia Conservatory, Black Mountain College, and the New School for Social Research, he broadened the Schoenberg circle, introducing Schoenberg's work to up-and-coming American musicians such as the members of the Juilliard Quartet, hornist-composer Gunther Schuller, and pianists Simon Sadoff and Russell Sherman.[139]

Schoenberg and Steuermann were also very close friends. Despite their geographical separation, they managed to see each other during Schoenberg's 1940 trip to New York and Steuermann's multiple travels to Los Angeles. Schoenberg shared personal matters with Steuermann, and entrusted his pupil and teaching assistant Clara Silvers to him in 1944 for advanced piano studies, remarking, "I believe it will give you joy to instruct her." Little did he know that he had acted as a matchmaker.[140] Five years later Silvers became Steuermann's second wife.[141]

American-born pianists performed Schoenberg's music as well—among them Martin Boykan, Delia Calapai, Johana Harris, Katherine Ruth Heyman, Wesley Kuhnle, William Masselos, Hortense Monath, Frances Mullen, Harrison Potter, Simon Sadoff, Maxim Shapiro, Russell Sherman, David Tudor, and Beveridge Webster. Most of these pianists did not know Schoenberg personally. The noted Chicago-born pianist Richard Buhlig, acquainted with Schoenberg since the early 1910s, however, can be counted among Schoenberg's most faithful performers and friends. Schoenberg considered him "the most cultivated pianist."[142] Buhlig regularly included Schoenberg's piano pieces, opp. 11 and 19 in his transcontinental lecture recitals until a crippling accident in 1946 ended his concert career. Based in Los Angeles since the early 1920s, he resumed his friendship with the Schoenbergs when they settled there and was a frequent guest at their parties. A trailblazer for Schoenberg in California as both a performer and teacher, Buhlig prepared several students, including John Cage, Stein, and Leon Kirchner, for studies with Schoenberg. Significantly, Buhlig's pupils Kuhnle, Stein, and Mullen, who pursued careers as professional pianists, became dedicated performers of Schoenberg's piano and chamber works.

In America Schoenberg taught numerous students who became concert and/or chamber pianists of note, including John Crown, Emil Danenberg, Hugh Hodgson, Warren Langlie, Oscar Levant, Natalie Limonick, Dika Newlin, Béla Rósza, Leonard Stein, and James Sykes. All were committed to the performance of his music. Sykes and Stein, however, stand out in terms of the frequency of their Schoenberg performances and breadth of repertoire. Sykes studied only briefly with Schoenberg at USC in 1936 and soon thereafter enjoyed an international career as concert pianist. Celebrated for his refined technique and advocacy of contemporary music, Sykes showcased Schoenberg's Piano Suite, op. 25, presenting it at many different venues. Schoenberg must have been pleased to read Sykes's 1951 update of his activities and plans. Since 1937 Sykes had played the Suite in about thirty recitals and wanted to record the piece. He felt that his audiences received Schoenberg's music with increasing understanding.[143]

One of Schoenberg's long-term and most loyal students (1935–42), Leonard Stein served as his teaching assistant (1939–42), co-editor of his books, and performer and teacher of his music. He played his piano works and chamber music with piano as well as arrangements for piano (sometimes authored by Stein himself). Stein collaborated, to Schoenberg's delight, with such other openminded pianists as Danenberg and Mullen and contralto Pazmor in an all-Schoenberg concert at Evenings on the Roof in 1940. In 1945 Stein organized a Schoenberg festival at UCLA featuring organist Lawrence Petran, Schoenberg's former colleague at UCLA, and singer Irene Hanna. He gave the world premieres of the *Phantasy* with Koldofsky and the Three Songs, op. 48 with baritone Peter Page in 1950. Stein gave numerous performances of the four-hand versions of the First and Second Chamber Symphonies with Langlie, Limonick, Newlin, Petran, and Silvers Steuermann..

Having completed *Variations on a Recitative,* his first and only organ work, Schoenberg attracted the attention of several organists in America. He hoped that

German-born Alexander Schreiner, who was his colleague at UCLA before becoming organist at the Mormon Tabernacle in Salt Lake City, could give the work's first performance. But Schreiner offended Schoenberg with his criticism of the piece's length and difficulty. Consequently, Carl Weinrich, a renowned American-born organist at the Princeton University Chapel, was recruited by Steuermann and other Schoenberg advocates to premiere it at the Church of St. Mary the Virgin in New York in 1944.[144] His performance was, in Steuermann's words, "very good technically and musically, although perhaps the total comprehension was not always at his disposal."[145] Although Schoenberg never heard the performance, he invited Weinrich to edit the work for H. W. Gray.[146] Schoenberg was not happy with Weinrich's 1947 edition, yet remained on friendly terms with him, hoping to hear him perform the work and make his acquaintance.[147] Beginning in 1945, his former colleague Petran gave several West Coast performances of *Variations*, although Schoenberg may have missed them. Marilyn Mason, the twenty-four-year-old American organist, had repeatedly performed his *Variations* in public before coming to Los Angeles in 1949 to receive Schoenberg's feedback on the work. Only then was he able to hear it for the first time. Mason visited him once more in 1950, promoting the work nationwide and making, on his advice, its premiere recording.

SPONSORS OF SCHOENBERG PERFORMANCES

Beyond his numerous contacts with performers, Schoenberg maintained relationships with music patrons, concert managers and organizers, dancers, and radio and record producers, who advanced performances of his music in many different settings.

Elizabeth Sprague Coolidge, an internationally recognized patroness of contemporary chamber music, deserves special mention. A backer of Schoenberg's chamber music before 1933, she commissioned his Fourth Quartet in 1936 and subsidized performances by such ensembles as the Kolisch, Pro Arte, Kroll, and Budapest Quartets after Schoenberg's emigration.[148] Memorable events given under her aegis include an all-Schoenberg welcome concert and reception at the Library of Congress in 1933 with the Pro Arte Quartet, Kroll Sextet, and vocalist Olga Averino; welcome concerts and receptions at Yale and Harvard; the Kolisch Quartet's presentation of Schoenberg's first three numbered Quartets at the Coleman Chamber Music Concerts in Pasadena in June 1936; and the celebrated 1937 UCLA cycle of four concerts, at which the Kolisch Quartet with Clemence Gifford performed Schoenberg's four quartets, including the Fourth Quartet's world premiere.[149] The last-named series attracted large audiences, up to 1,500 concertgoers per event, and positive responses in the national press.[150] Although unwilling to back a performance of Schoenberg's Violin Concerto with Kolisch and the Los Angeles Philharmonic under Klemperer, she funded Klemperer's 1938 performance of his Handel arrangement, because it featured the Kolisch Quartet as soloists.[151] Grateful for her support, Schoenberg called Coolidge the "ideal patron of chamber music" and remained in friendly contact with her throughout his American years.[152] Occasionally, as in 1941 when Coolidge was in town, he invited her to his home for a reception.[153]

Claire Reis, executive director of the League of Composers from 1923 to 1948, also supported performances of Schoenberg's music. Like Coolidge, she had cosponsored such pre-1933 performances of his works as the American *Pierrot* premiere.[154] She organized the League's all-Schoenberg welcome concert and reception in November 1933 in New York with the Pro Arte Quartet, singers Ruth Rodgers and Rita Sebastian, and pianists Nadia Reisenberg and Edna Sheppard. Hosting a pre-concert dinner party for Schoenberg and inviting them as guests in her box, Reis sensed that Schoenberg was a warm person, amazed at the response to his music. "May I tell you that for me this was a truly great joy. I had the feeling during the evening that there are a great many people here who are not altogether without an understanding of my work," he relayed to Reis after this event.[155] Later he applauded her decision to include naturalized American composers (like himself) in her 1947 book *Composers in America.*[156] Reis supported the selection of *Pierrot* (with Schoenberg conducting hand-picked musicians) as the League's first sponsored recording, released in 1940. Under her leadership, the League commissioned Schoenberg's *Ode* to celebrate its twentieth anniversary. Although grateful for these privileges, Schoenberg objected to the recording's omission of a complete English translation of the *Pierrot* texts and the League's plan to engage the Budapest Quartet for the *Ode*'s first performance.[157] Doubtful of the Budapest group's competence and loyal to Kolisch's struggling quartet, Schoenberg renounced a League-sponsored *Ode* premiere.[158]

Ira Hirschmann, vice president of Bloomingdale's department store, and his pianist-wife Hortense Monath can be considered important sponsors of Schoenberg's music as well. In 1936 Hirschmann and Monath, students of Artur Schnabel and advocates of new music, founded the influential nonprofit New Friends of Music to present high-quality chamber music concerts in New York. Significantly, the Hirschmanns invited Schoenberg in 1940 to conduct *Pierrot* with some of his favorite performers—an event eliciting many favorable reviews. They also sponsored the composition and world premiere of the Second Chamber Symphony under the direction of Stiedry and agreed to pay Schoenberg $600 (about $9,080 in 2009) and cover the copying of the parts, returning the materials to Schoenberg at no cost.[159] In the 1940s the New Friends hosted the Kolisch, Pro Arte, Juilliard, Budapest, and Fine Arts Quartets, Bampton, Louise Bernhardt, Kahn, and Newlin, all presenting Schoenberg's works in concerts that were often broadcast and always reviewed. Schoenberg had a friendly relationship with the Hirschmanns, whom he had met personally in the 1930s and in 1940 on his trip to New York. He praised their institution as a "model to all places of culture" whose mission was "to create culture, to promote the arts [and] to increase the values of life."[160] Schoenberg was also complimentary about Monath's achievements as a performer.[161] Monath had publicly performed the Suite, op. 25 in the early 1930s.

Schoenberg had many sponsors in California. Gertrude Ross, composer-pianist and president of the Los Angeles Pro Musica chapter; Mrs. Thomasset, who chaired the Los Angeles Chamber Music Society; Alice Coleman-Batchelder, founder of the Coleman Chamber Music Concerts in Pasadena; Henry Cowell and Gerald Strang of the New Music Society of California; and various Women's Clubs were among the first to welcome him and to host Schoenberg performances by the Vertchamp, Abas, Kolisch, and Kaufman Quartets, singer Rudolphine Radil, and pianist Douglas Thompson.

Los Angeles-based Peter Yates and his pianist-wife Frances Mullen initiated Evenings on the Roof in 1939. This nonprofit chamber concert series proved influential, promoting musical modernism, above all the chamber and choral music of Schoenberg. During the existence of the series (1939–54), the Yateses presented nine all-Schoenberg concerts, of which two celebrated his seventieth and seventy-fifth birthdays with performances of *Pierrot.* They also mounted the West Coast premieres of *Herzgewächse*, the Serenade, three of the Four Pieces for Mixed Choir, the

Trio, and *Dreimal tausend Jahre.*[162] For these and other Schoenberg performances, Yates recruited the vocalists Sara Carter, Kibler, Mock, Marni Nixon, and Pazmor; the string players Koldofsky, Kurt Reher, and Swaby; the pianists Buhlig, Danenberg, Kuhnle, Mullen, and Stein; the New Music Quintet (later called the Los Angeles Woodwinds); and the conductors Craft, Ernest Gold, Jacob, and Dahl. Their low-budget concerts, largely dependent on the performers' good will, attracted larger and larger audiences over the years—although Schoenberg himself was rarely present—and received further exposure through local radio broadcasts and coverage in local newspapers.[163] The Roof Concerts' promotion of Schoenberg's music even gained national recognition, thanks to Yates's reports on his efforts in *Arts and Architecture* and the *New York Times.*[164]

The Yateses, who met Schoenberg through Buhlig, fostered friendly relations with him through regular meetings and correspondence. Yates consulted him about Roof programs and invited him to coach such performers as Mullen, Pazmor, and Swaby. Although Schoenberg sometimes expressed concern about the number of rehearsals for such works as *Pierrot,* he was touched by Yates's tireless advocacy for his music, as both impresario and writer. He must also have been pleased to learn from him that Ives had contributed $50 (about $600 in 2007) toward facilitating performances of Schoenberg's music—a fact Ives wanted to keep secret.[165] As a token of gratitude, Schoenberg gave Yates a facsimile of one of his letters. The Yateses shared with Schoenberg a fascination with Busoni's music and followed each other's family matters with great interest.

Schoenberg was honored with several festivals during his American years. In October 1937 the Denver Art Museum presented the Cooke-Daniels Memorial Lectures in the form of a Schoenberg festival at which the Kolisch Quartet, Gifford, and Sykes performed his four Quartets, *Verklärte Nacht,* and Songs, op. 6. Schoenberg himself gave the lecture "How One Becomes Lonely." On the occasion of his seventieth and seventy-fifth birthdays in 1944 and 1949 many celebratory events took place in the United States, some of which deserve special mention. In 1944 Jalowetz mounted, as mentioned earlier, a highly influential Schoenberg festival at Black Mountain College, well known for its promotion of modernism in the arts. The festivities comprised two all-Schoenberg programs; public rehearsals of the First Quartet with screen projections of the score, presented by Kolisch and Dick; a piano workshop offered by Steuermann; and a lecture on Schoenberg delivered by Krenek. The creative exchange of these and other Schoenbergians gave his reception in America a considerable boost.[166] In the spring of 1945 Stein organized a belated seventieth-birthday tribute to Schoenberg at UCLA, consisting of three all-Schoenberg concerts and the West Coast premiere of the Organ Variations, given by Petran. Newlin and Kolisch arranged festivals honoring Schoenberg's seventy-fifth birthday at Syracuse University in December 1949 and at the University of Wisconsin in the spring of 1950 respectively. Newlin presented an evening with a lecture and performances of Schoenberg's piano works and Kolisch five concerts dedicated to Schoenberg's music for strings, voice, and piano.

Schoenberg's Dancers

Although Schoenberg did not build close relationships with dancers in America, a number of them—in particular representatives of the modern-dance movement that flourished in the 1930s and 1940s—were attracted to his music and choreographed it. Having been opposed to combinations of his music with dance in

Europe, Schoenberg now welcomed dancers to use his music. "I have changed this viewpoint," he explained to dancer Minsa Craig, "because it seemed to me that today's dancers have a different approach to music and a deeper understanding of the problems of style."[167]

In the 1930s the modern dancer and choreographer Sophia Delza used his Piano Piece, op. 11, no. 3 for her *Dance of Frenzy* (early 1930s). Martha Graham, one of the most influential modern dancers and choreographers, based her *Phantasy* (1934) on "Prelude," "Musette," and "Gavotte" from his Piano Suite. A Graham protégée, Elna Lillback, presented *Femina* to unspecified music by Schoenberg in the 1930s as well. In the 1940s dancer-choreographer Valerie Bettis created *Five Abstractions in Space* to Schoenberg's Five Piano Pieces, op. 23. No communication between Schoenberg and these dancers is extant, and it is unclear whether he was even aware of their work, which was repeatedly presented in a variety of modern dance venues and received positive press.[168]

Choreographer and dancer Eleanor King, who conceived the film *Moon Dances* using the 1940 Columbia recording of *Pierrot*, informed Schoenberg about her work, and he was pleased to let her use his music for this educational film. The British-born Antony Tudor and the Mexican-born José Limón, both major figures in the American dance world, were in touch with Schoenberg as well, and created highly successful dances to his music. Based on *Verklärte Nacht*, Tudor's *The Pillar of Fire* was premiered in 1942 at the Metropolitan Opera House in New York, with Antal Dorati conducting the Metropolitan Opera Orchestra. *Pillar* became one of Tudor's most highly acclaimed dances in America, performed frequently nationwide. When the production came to San Francisco in 1945, Schoenberg conducted the San Francisco Symphony. He benefited from the extensive publicity and also from substantial royalty payments—a welcome source of income after his retirement from UCLA.[169] *Pillar*'s success even tempted him to arrange *Pelleas* as a multi-movement dance suite for Tudor, who would have been interested in such a project, but the idea did not reach fruition. In 1950 Limón premiered his influential dance *The Exiles* to Schoenberg's Second Chamber Symphony at the American Dance Festival in New London, Connecticut. Pianists Simon Sadoff and Russell Sherman, both students of Steuermann, performed the work in its arrangement for two pianos. When Schoenberg was introduced to the dance plot (about two exiles expelled from paradise), he found it "pleasant and satisfactory."[170] Schoenberg, however, did not live to see a performance of this enduring choreography.

Schoenberg's Radio and Record Producers

An avid listener to radio broadcasts and phonograph records, Schoenberg saw these technologies as ideal tools to facilitate his music's propagation and to reach large audiences outside conventional concert spaces; he even used these means for his teaching.[171] However, he often regretted the restrictive policies with regard to the broadcasting of modernist music that certain radio stations implemented in the 1940s. Seeing royalties from recordings as an attractive source of income, Schoenberg also lamented that more of his mature works were not recorded sooner and with his approval.[172] Yet due to radio's immense popularity and the public's reduced buying power in the 1930s, record sales plunged. When record sales rose again in the late 1930s, the recording industry gradually added more concert music, including Schoenberg's works, to their catalogs.

Schoenberg established ties with several radio producers, usually contacting them (or prompting his adherents to contact them) only when he disagreed with their programming—as with CBS's decision not to broadcast his Five Orchestral Pieces, *Pierrot*, and *Survivor*, or the snide remarks of Deems Taylor as commentator for the New York Philharmonic broadcasts.[173] His progressive works, however, were not absent from radio programs. Such stations as NBC, CBS, WJZ, WEAF, WABT, KECA, KFWB, and KMPC featured (if not as regularly as his tonal works) the Five Orchestral Pieces, *Pierrot*, Serenade, Woodwind Quintet, Orchestral Variations, the piano works, opp. 11 through 33b, the four Quartets, the *Ode*, Piano Concerto, and Trio. Schoenberg was invited to comment on his own music by several national and local radio stations including NBC, WQXR, KFAC, KFWB, and KNX (University Explorer program).[174]

Schoenberg interacted with such radio representatives as Walter Koons (NBC), Lisa Sergio (WQXR), Alan Pratt of RCVD, Raoul Gripenwaldt (KOWL), and Hale Sparks (KNX). He was friends with the California-based radio host José Rodriguez from KFI Radio (part of NBC), and Maurice Zam and Julius Toldi from KFWB. In Toldi, Schoenberg found perhaps one of his greatest radio allies. The Hungarian-born composer-violist was his former student and owed his job in the Fox studio orchestra to Schoenberg's friendship with Alfred Newman. Toldi featured Schoenberg's music on his California radio program *Music of Today*, initiated in 1948 and dedicated to the advancement of modernist music.[175] Along with Schoenberg's own comments, Toldi offered live broadcasts of *Pierrot*, *Herzgewächse*, and the Trio, performed in Yates's Roof concerts. Honoring Schoenberg's seventy-fifth birthday in 1949, Toldi created a cycle of four broadcasts featuring his Five Orchestral Pieces, Second Quartet, and *Pierrot*. Although this cycle could be heard only over KFWB in Los Angeles, it nevertheless caught national attention because it opened with Schoenberg's controversial speech accusing Toscanini, Koussevitzky, Walter, and Copland of suppressing his music.[176]

Although regretting these remarks, he thanked Toldi for granting him so much exposure: "Dear Friend: Through your four broadcasts devoted to my works you have rendered me a service the value of which I deeply appreciate. I am convinced that should my work still be appreciated later on, this deed will never be forgotten."[177]

In America Schoenberg was also involved in several major recording projects of his music.[178] Three of them were realized, in spite of the challenges of the Great Depression and World War II when record producers faced restrictions on materials, limited manpower, and the American Federation of Musicians' proscription of recording.

The 1937 landmark recording of Schoenberg's four Quartets with the Kolisch Quartet and Gifford was initiated by Alfred Newman, United Artists (UA) music director, who convinced his supervisor Samuel Goldwyn to make available for free the UA recording studio, despite the expensive studio hours. Schoenberg, who provided spoken commentary and liner notes, persuaded the musicians to perform gratis. Only twenty-five copies of the set (comprising twenty-three 12-inch discs) were made and sold at about $70 to Hugo Friedhofer, George Gershwin, Heifetz, Newman, and David Raksin, among others. The performers did not receive copies.[179] Until their commercial release in 1950, Schoenberg duplicated these recordings for friends.[180] Schoenberg's Prelude with Janssen's Symphony was also privately recorded at RCA in Los Angeles in 1945, thanks to Nathaniel Shilkret; a limited edition of sets of five 78-rpm discs was released before its commercial reissue in 1951. Having sold the piece and all rights to Shilkret, Schoenberg was little involved in this venture, although he became concerned with this work's availability later in his life.

Perhaps the most prestigious project in the 1940s was the commercial recording of *Pierrot* for Columbia, initiated, as mentioned earlier, by the League of Composers. As Schoenberg conducted the work, he could influence musical decisions and choose the musicians and takes. However, he was unable to convince Columbia's director Moses Smith and his assistant Goddard Lieberson to record the work in English. He also regretted that—perhaps due to "wartime copyright problems" and additional costs—the German texts and their English translation by Dika Newlin were replaced with English text summaries by Nicolas Slonimsky.[181] Otherwise, Schoenberg was pleased to have *Pierrot* on four 78-rpm discs, selling more than two thousand copies in one year.[182] Although Schoenberg challenged the CBS royalty statements, the firm retained in its catalog until 1951 recordings of *Verklärte Nacht* with the Philadelphia Orchestra under Ormandy, "Song of the Wood Dove" with Martha Lipton and the New York Philharmonic under Stokowski, and the Handel arrangement with Janssen's Symphony and the Compinsky Quartet.

After the war many new, small record labels emerged, and some of them, including ALCO, Dial, and Esoteric, showed an interest in Schoenberg's music. Alco, founded by Alec Compinsky, cellist of the Los Angeles–based Compinsky Trio, specialized in early and contemporary music. On Raksin's suggestion and with Schoenberg's approval, Compinsky issued commercially in 1950 the private recordings of the four Quartets in a four-LP set with liner notes by Yates. Yet this release, with a pressing of between three hundred and five hundred sets, was not without challenges. Schoenberg was impatient about the production process, and the former members of the Kolisch Quartet, doubtful about the recordings' musical and technical quality, hesitated to give their approval. Ross Russell, director of the competing Dial Records, was also interested in releasing this Kolisch recording or a new recording of the Quartets, and he attempted to block the release. Knowing that the Kolisch Quartet had made the recording gratis, he hoped that a commercial issue might be considered illegal and alerted the musicians' union, the American Federation of Musicians. In the end the Kolisch Quartet members, unwilling to thwart Schoenberg's plans, signed an agreement to transfer to Schoenberg "any and all compensations and royalties" for these recordings.[183] After the release of the LPs, Compinsky paid directly to Schoenberg—in compliance with Schoenberg's wishes and circumventing his publisher's contractual stipulations—the royalties for the nearly twelve hundred copies sold during the first six months.[184]

Of all record producers Russell was perhaps the most passionate about releasing Schoenberg's works on discs. At first devoted solely to progressive jazz, Russell discovered Schoenberg's music through such Schoenberg admirers as musicologist Lou Gottlieb and Schuller. When in 1949 the French Blue Star Records offered to trade a master tape of the First Chamber Symphony (Orchestre Pasdeloup under Pierre Dervaux) for Dial jazz masters, Russell accepted the recording into his Library of Contemporary Classics. Happy to hear from Russell that some American classical composers had "insisted that he [Russell] should proceed with [Schoenberg's music] rather than record even one of their own works just now," Schoenberg expressed his "admiration for the unselfishness of the six composers: René Leibowitz, Lou Harrison, Ben Weber, John Cage, Edgar Varèse and David Diamond who have the noblesse to act against their own interest in favor of mine."[185] Between 1950 and 1951 Russell issued nine Schoenberg works—including premier recordings of the First Chamber Symphony, Woodwind Quintet, *Ode*, Trio, and Phantasy—on six long-playing records.

Following Schoenberg's wish, Russell engaged some of his favorite performers—the Pro Arte Quartet, Steuermann, Koldofsky, and Schuller. He also respected his desire to have his music on all-Schoenberg LPs, as Schoenberg explained: "I do not want to depend on the attractiveness of other people's music, nor suffer from their failure to be attractive." He was unwilling to even "give up half an inch from the space which can serve my music to [be]come known."[186] Russell may have considered Schoenberg's curious advice to avoid too many retakes in recording sessions. Schoenberg thought it pointless "to aim for a perfection which is not human."[187] Yet Russell disregarded his reservations against releasing the First Chamber Symphony's poor recording, for which Schoenberg was to write liner notes for free. Russell also ignored Schoenberg's disapproval of Leibowitz's *Ode* performance featuring a female instead of a male narrator.[188] Russell crushed Schoenberg's unrealistic expectations of earning royalties from these recordings as a composer, conductor (in the sense of a coach), and author of liner notes, and receiving direct payments from his company without the interference of his publishers,[189] once Russell discovered that Schoenberg's publishers "owned and controlled all world rights to his music, its mechanical licensing and all matters."[190] While the disappointed Schoenberg suspected the existence of "American pirate laws, making him to lose returns," the frustrated Russell was no longer inclined to invest any more energy and money into Schoenberg records, ending his relationship with Schoenberg in 1951 on a sour note.[191]

In 1950 Schoenberg also did business with Jerry Newman, who ran the small Esoteric Records label, specializing in jazz and contemporary classical music. Newman issued two premiere recordings of Schoenberg's works: the Serenade conducted by Mitropoulos in 1949 and the Organ Variations performed by Mason in 1951. Schoenberg's friendly communication with Newman focused on the Serenade recording, which he highly praised (despite the singer's intonation problems). "I have never heard a record of any of my works approximating the merits of this," he raved. "The performance is of high order: great beauty of tone quality, precision, clarity, expression is real first class."[192] Newman sold 1,479 copies of this recording in less than two months.[193]

Finally, Schoenberg dealt with Richard Jones, the director of Capitol Records in Hollywood, a major popular music label founded by Johnny Mercer in 1942. When Capitol began to release a few classical albums in the late 1940s, Jones quickly included Schoenberg's music, issuing the premiere recording of *Pelleas* with the Radio Symphony Orchestra Frankfurt under Winfried Zillig (1949), and recordings of *Verklärte Nacht* with the Hollywood Quartet (1950) and the Prelude with Janssen's orchestra (1951).[194] For a fee of $100 (about $880 in 2009) Schoenberg wrote the liner notes for *Verklärte Nacht*. He seemed happy and cooperative, perhaps because he received royalty statements soon after *Pelleas*'s release. After learning that due to illness Schoenberg had to stay in his bedroom upstairs, Jones gave him an attachment for his record player downstairs, enabling him to listen to records in bed. As a token of thanks, Schoenberg gave Jones an autographed score of *Pelleas*.

Considering Schoenberg's interactions with so many promoters of performances of his music, the myth that he was isolated and that his music was neglected in America pales. Schoenberg faced many challenges—economically strained times, a different musical infrastructure, conservative musicians and audiences, limited availability of scores and parts for some of his works—and sometimes he hindered performances of his music. But along with several longtime disciples, he indefatigably created an impressive network of performers. According to my findings, American musicians gave over seven hundred performances of tonal and nontonal works during his American years; they also conveyed Schoenberg's ideas of performance practice and aesthetics to young musicians. Although he was always in need of recognition and impatiently waiting for the big breakthrough, Schoenberg could monitor only a fraction of performances of his music due to the geographic diversity of America's new music scene, insufficient press coverage, and elusive royalty statements. Nevertheless he scored innumerable successes on many different levels and laid the groundwork for the future reception of his work.

5 Schoenberg's American Publishers

The publication and dissemination of scores, essential for musical performances, was among Schoenberg's greatest concerns when settling in the United States. With the Nazis' disruption of the publication and performance of music by Jewish composers in Europe, Schoenberg's royalty-based income and the availability of his scores in and outside Nazi Europe were greatly reduced. His European publishers were often unable to collect royalties for the declining performances of Schoenberg's music due to a loss of control and because they had failed to take out a copyright or renew the copyright for certain works. Schoenberg's main European publisher, Universal Edition (UE), experienced serious financial trouble, especially after Austria's *Anschluss*, and its American distributor, Associated Music Publishers (AMP), could not reliably supply American performers with all of Schoenberg's UE works. Other publishers of Schoenberg's music, such as C. F. Peters and Breitkopf & Härtel did have American distributors, but Tischer & Jagenberg and Drei Lilien Verlag, among others, did not even have a representative in the United States.

To cope with this situation Schoenberg revised earlier works and secured their copyright protection, effectively assuming a music publisher's duties: renting his own materials or making duplicates of scores at cost for performers in America and Mexico. But most important, although he was ever distrustful of publishers, Schoenberg lost no time in his search for a new one in America after his attempts to publish in France and England had foundered in the summer of 1933.[1] Music publishing in America, however, was very different from its European counterparts, and tended more toward specialization in genres: classical, sacred, choral, band, instrumental, popular music, or songs. The major publishing houses dedicated to classical music, including Gustave Schirmer, Carl Fischer, Edwin Kalmus (solely devoted to reprints), and Theodore Presser, favored a conservative repertoire. For this reason most progressive composers tended to turn to small nonprofit organizations, such as Henry Cowell's New Music Edition or Alma Wertheim's Cos-Cob Press (from 1938, Arrow Music Press). The New Music Edition had published Schoenberg's Piano Piece, op. 33b prior to his emigration. In the 1930s American music publishers felt the hardships of the Great Depression, and during the war they faced such problems as reduced manpower and paper shortages. Not until 1948, with the founding of C. F. Peters New York and Boelke-Bomart (headed respectively by the German émigrés Walter Hinrichsen and Margot and Walter Boelke) were there commercial publishing houses devoted to modernist music.

In view of these hurdles—not to mention Schoenberg's controversial reputation—it is remarkable that he saw most of his works published and was compensated for them, unlike many of his fellow composers, both émigré and American-born. Thanks to his indefatigable networking and the fruitful, if sometimes tense relationships with such staunch supporters of his music as Carl Engel, Felix Greissle, Kurt List, Walter Hinrichsen, and Dagobert Runes, Schoenberg saw eight American publishing firms—Schirmer, E. B. Marks, H. W. Gray, Boelke-Bomart, Peters, Edition Shilkret, Associated Music Publishers, and the Philosophical Library—issue twenty-one of his scores, both original compositions and arrangements of his own and other composers' works, in the years from 1934 to 1951. Three books were published as well.

G. SCHIRMER AND E. B. MARKS

Schoenberg's first and most important American publisher was G. Schirmer in New York, a very prestigious firm established in 1866. Schirmer's most prominent and best selling contemporary composers of the time, aside from authors of sheet music, were Samuel Barber, John Alden Carpenter, Roy Harris, Gian Carlo Menotti, and William Schuman—all conservative musical figures. Yet between 1935 and 1944, Schirmer added the majority of works Schoenberg composed and arranged in America and provided the engraving or autography of eleven orchestral and three chamber scores.

Original Compositions and Arrangements of His Own Works

- Suite in G for string orchestra (1934; first printing: 1935)
- First Chamber Symphony for large orchestra, op. 9b (1935; first printing: 1935 facsimile of score; first engraved study score: 1963)
- Violin Concerto, op. 36 (1934–36; first printing: 1939; Greissle piano reduction: 1939?)
- Fourth String Quartet, op. 37 (1936; first printing: 1939)
- Second Chamber Symphony for orchestra, op. 38a (1906–39; first printing: 1952)
- Second Chamber Symphony for two pianos, op. 38b (1942)
- *Ode to Napoleon Buonaparte* for narrator, piano, and string quartet, op. 41a (1942; first printing: 1945)
- *Ode to Napoleon Buonaparte* for narrator, piano, and string orchestra, op. 41b (1942; first printing: 1944)
- Piano Concerto, op. 42 (1942; first printing: c. 1946; piano reduction: 1944)
- Theme and Variations for band, op. 43a (1943; first printing: 1949)
- Theme and Variations for orchestra, op. 43b (1943; first printing: 1944)

Arrangements of Other Composers' Works

- Cello Concerto after G. M. Monn (1932–33; first printing: 1935 or 1936?; piano reduction: 1936 and 1944)
- String Quartet Concerto after G. F. Handel (1933; first printing of study score: 1968)
- Johannes Brahms's Piano Quartet no. 1 in G minor for orchestra (1937; first printing: 1937)

In addition, Schirmer published Schoenberg's textbook *Models for Beginners in Composition* (1942) and the monograph *Schoenberg*, edited by Merle Armitage (1937), with two essays by Schoenberg.

Schoenberg had adapted to Schirmer's conservative publishing trend, offering them first his Monn and Handel transcriptions, and new arrangements of the tried and tested First Chamber Symphony, along with the newly composed tonal Suite in G and Band Variations, catering to young performers and conservative audiences. Only four of his Schirmer compositions—the Violin and Piano Concertos, the Fourth Quartet, and *Ode*—are twelve-tone works.

The publication of these works would not have been possible without the support of one of Schoenberg's most reliable friends in the American music-publishing world, Carl Engel (Figure 5.1). A composer-musicologist of German descent, Engel came to the United States in 1905 and served as head of the Library of Congress music division and as president of Schirmer from 1929 until his death in 1944.[2] Schoenberg met Engel in the fall of 1933 through Elizabeth Coolidge, and soon thereafter Engel accepted Schoenberg's works for publication. While Engel flattered Schoenberg that it would be "a cause of gratification if your name should be added to the Schirmer catalog," he also warned him against high demands: "Schirmers are still rather hampered in bringing out large scores. We are working on a very slim margin, and that has to be reinvested in publications of more or less immediate commercial possibilities."[3] Engel offered him contracts granting a 10–15 percent royalty on sales and 50 percent of the rental and performing fees. He paid Schoenberg unusually

FIGURE 5.1.
Carl Engel. Courtesy G. Schirmer.

large royalty advances and also bought some of his works outright. For the publication of the Monn and Handel arrangements, Schoenberg received an advance of $1,500 (about $23,780 in 2009) on royalties and performing fees, to be paid in five monthly installments of $300.[4] In 1935 Engel granted him another royalty advance of $1,500 for the Suite in G, Fourth Quartet, and Violin Concerto. Schoenberg had hoped to get this amount for the Suite in G alone, but because of Schirmer's straitened finances that was not possible.[5] Engel also accepted a revised version of Schoenberg's First Chamber Symphony for orchestra, paying, for the complete score and parts on onionskin, a royalty advance of $250 (about $3,870 in 2009). Schoenberg made this new revision for standard orchestra because UE had failed to copyright his first orchestral arrangement of 1922, which he now deemed too large for small halls and too small for large spaces.[6] In 1939 Engel bought the Brahms Piano Quartet arrangement for $1,000, paying an additional $400 for the extraction of the orchestral parts by Schoenberg's children, and $200 for *Fundamentals of Musical Composition*, although it was never published by Schirmer (the total amount of $1,600 corresponds to about $24,450 in 2009).[7] In 1942 Engel accepted the textbook *Models for Beginners in Composition* for a royalty advance of $1,000 (about $13,020 in 2009). In 1943 he bought the Second Chamber Symphony, Piano Concerto, and *Ode* for narrator, string quartet, and piano for $7,200 (about $88,350 in 2009), payable over three years. For the Band Variations, op. 43a and 43b Schoenberg was paid a bonus (not an advance) of $500 (about $6,140 in 2009). This money nicely supplemented his income from other publications, commissions, ASCAP royalties, conducting engagements, public lectures, and private and university teaching. The large sum of $7,200 helped Schoenberg pay off the mortgage on his house in less than ten years, before his retirement from UCLA in 1944.[8]

Engel also guided Schoenberg's creativity, suggesting in 1935 that Schoenberg compose an a cappella choral work with an English text.[9] Although Schoenberg disregarded Engel's suggestion of setting a text from Walt Whitman's *Leaves of Grass*, he began a setting of the Appalachian folksong "My Horses Ain't Hungry," based on John Jacob Niles's 1934 Schirmer edition in *Songs of the Hill-Folk*, which Engel had sent Schoenberg. Although this project was unfortunately left incomplete, he did compose at Engel's encouragement Theme and Variations for Wind Band. Engel publicized Schoenberg's works through leaflets and announcements, and commissioned Merle Armitage's essay collection *Schoenberg*, featuring contributions from Schoenberg himself and an international group of Schoenberg advocates.[10] Thanks to Engel, Schirmer hosted a reception with performances of Schoenberg's music on the occasion of Schoenberg's New York visit in November 1940, and secured such important performances of his music as Koussevitzky's premiere of Theme and Variations, op. 43b in October 1944. Beyond his duties as Schoenberg's publisher, Engel arranged lecture engagements at American universities, though with moderate success. He tried to get the composer a position at Juilliard, and helped him sell a manuscript page from *Moses und Aron* for $100 (about $1,585 in 2009).[11] Engel also gave Schoenberg's impecunious children Georg and Gertrud and his son-in-law Felix Greissle in Austria music-copying work.[12] When the Greissles immigrated to America in 1938, Engel hired Felix as music editor on the recommendation of Schoenberg. Shortly before his death, Engel fought for the establishment of an endowed Schoenberg Chair at UCLA to supplement Schoenberg's retirement. This idea did not reach fruition.[13]

Nonetheless, tensions arose from time to time. Schoenberg was disappointed when in the early 1940s Engel rejected his 1929 German folksong arrangements for republication, arguing that "even if Mr. Hitler should descend upon our shores, arrangements of such songs made by Mr. Schoenberg are not likely to meet with official favor."[14] He also disapproved of Engel's assessment of his *Kol nidre* as unsuitable for Orthodox or "free" services, and was rankled by Schirmer's begrudging acceptance of it into the publisher's rental catalogue in 1943.[15] Schoenberg deplored Schirmer's limited publicity efforts and sluggish production of his scores, which hindered the dissemination of his music and affected his income.[16] He even glorified his European publishers by comparison, forgetting that he had accused them of the same shortcomings.[17] Yet the slow progress was not Engel's fault. Often copyists, including Schoenberg's own unreliable son Georg, and engravers delivered their jobs late and/or with too many errors in the proofs, and Schoenberg took a long time to sign his contracts.[18] America's entrance into the war and the ensuing military draft caused Schirmer to lose engravers, among other professionals. It also led to paper shortage, mail-delivery problems, and a "serious drop in record and radio business," for which "not even a slightly increased sale in copies of *The Star Spangled Banner* could make up."[19] In the early 1940s Engel had to lecture Schoenberg about his own limits. Even though he did "not own the Schirmer business," he "had not only exercised [his] so-called 'power' with regard to A.S., but intentionally overstepped it"—implying that his royalty advances had been unrealistically generous and could not be expected to be earned back any time soon.[20]

Despite these disagreements, Engel remained one of Schoenberg's closest friends. In 1940 the two even switched to the familiar "du" when they communicated in German, and they greatly enjoyed each other's company.[21] When Schoenberg visited New York in 1940, he stayed with the Engels; when Engel came to California, he was Schoenberg's guest. Schoenberg frequently revealed his deep appreciation for Engel's assistance and friendship in such statements as: "Lieber, alter Freund, sei herzlichst gegrüsst von einem old friend of new music [Dear, old friend, cordial greetings from an old friend of new music]."[22] In 1943 he honored Engel's sixtieth birthday by furnishing new, humorous English texts for two canons he had composed in 1933. In these lyrics Schoenberg disclosed, "I, too, was not better off, but I have rapidly consoled myself and enjoyed the dignity of wisdom, that, at forty, I should have possessed," and assured Engel, "Life begins at sixty" (Figure 5.2).[23]

Another important contact person at Schirmer, especially after Engel's death in 1944, was Schoenberg's son-in-law, former student, and rehearsal coach of his Society for Private Musical Performances, Felix Greissle (Figure 5.3). Thanks to Schoenberg, he had already received work from Schirmer before his emigration in 1938; he was one of the copyists of Schoenberg's Fourth Quartet, Violin Concerto (for which he also prepared an arrangement for violin and piano), and Brahms arrangement. In 1938 he officially joined Schirmer, where he worked as a music editor until the end of 1946. Although Greissle's influence on Schirmer's publishing politics was much more limited than Engel's had been, he was a tireless Schoenberg advocate who directed Schoenberg's compositional projects toward greater accessibility and performability. Greissle suggested the orchestration of the *Ode* and Band Variations. When Schoenberg pondered a band arrangement of Schubert's four-hand piano music, he convinced him to write an original band work and instructed him in how to write for American bands. Greissle successfully recruited Stokowski, Rodzinski, and Goldman for the world premieres of the Piano Concerto, *Ode*, and Band Variations; he also persuaded Monteux, Ormandy, and Reiner to perform the orchestral version of the Band Variations, and coached rehearsals for the first performances of the Piano Concerto and Band Variations.

Birthday Canons

BIRTHDAY CANONS

By ARNOLD SCHOENBERG

To Carl Engel

My dear friend:

Jedem geht es so; keiner bleibt bei zwanzig ewig steh'n. Auf einmal ist man sechzig, und ist erstaunt und ist bestürtzt, und fragt sich: Was ist plötzlich mit mir los? Was hab' ich denn getan, dass ich nicht mehr hüpfen kann wie früher?

No man can escape; no man yet remained forever twenty. Suddenly one is sixty, and is surprised, and is perplexed, and asks oneself, "What is the matter now? Did I do something wrong? Why can I not dance and jump as formerly?

Selbst die Noten sind zu schnell; ich bin ausser Atem! Soll ich die langsam're Stimme nicht lieber singen?

"Even the music is too fast. I am really out of breath! Should I now sing perhaps only slower voices?"

Mir auch ist es so ergangen, doch ich hab' mich rasch getröstet, und hab' geschwelgt im Hochgenuss der Weisheit, die mit vierzig ich schon sollt' besitzen, die sich jetzt aber ganz allmählich einstellt, jetzt, wo ich nichts mehr davon hab'!

I, too, was not better off, but I have rapidly consoled myself, and enjoyed the dignity of wisdom, which at forty I should have possessed, but which drops slowly and gradually down upon me, now, when its benefits come too late!

Glaub's nicht! das ist alles Schwindel. Nur die immer alt gewesen sind, niemals Jugendstreiche wagten, prahlen jetzt mit Weisheit; doch wir ander'n wagen stets noch uns zu blamieren, denn wir glauben fest: *Life begins at sixty.*

Nonsense! that is silly trash! and only those who never have been young or have risked a foolish blunder boast now of their wisdom. We who are of different stuff dare still to expose our faults, because we know: Life begins at sixty.

FIGURE 5.2.
Birthday Canon for Carl Engel. Courtesy Belmont Music Publishers.

Greissle served as Schoenberg's mediator with both Engel and Engel's successor, the firm's owner Gustave Schirmer, whenever Schoenberg's moments of frustration had alienated his business partners. In 1942 Greissle prevented Schoenberg from accusing Engel of neglecting contemporary composers, reminding him of Engel's accountability to Schirmer and Schirmer's view of Schoenberg's music as "expensive window-dressing."[24] When in 1944 Schoenberg condemned the slowed-down production of his scores, Greissle disclosed to him that the cause was—apart from the dismal wartime conditions—Schirmer's prioritization of commercially successful music at the expense of "'prestige' music," and that for this reason Schoenberg's contracts did not specify publication dates.[25] Hence the first printed scores of the *Ode*'s original chamber version, the Band Variations, Piano Concerto, and Second Chamber Symphony appeared between 1945 and 1952.

Because Greissle's influence at Schirmer dwindled, in 1947 he joined the New York–based music-publishing house E. B. Marks. Although the firm specialized in American and Latin American popular music, it was then in the process of developing a serious-music division, and Greissle became its head. Concealing from Schoenberg his department's smallness, he boasted that he now had "sweeping powers" and even more authority than Engel had at Schirmer (due to the absence of a board of directors) and that Marks was more progressive than Schirmer.[26] But when Schoenberg offered Greissle his *Kol nidre*, Organ Variations, Trio, *Survivor*, and *Structural Functions of Harmony* for publication, he declined the works, citing financial reasons. Thereafter, Schoenberg rejected Greissle's suggestion of publishing a set of yet-to-be-composed clarinet études and an English translation of *Harmonielehre*. Schoenberg explained that an "etude-like treatment would require repetitions and sequences which are not easy to apply to my style," and that he had already allowed the Philosophical Library to publish his *Harmonielehre*.[27] Another project for 1947, about which both Schoenberg and Greissle were enthusiastic, did not materialize: this was the publication of an arrangement of *Pelleas* as a suite of four or five short and accessible movements for standard orchestra to be used in ballet and pantomime performances

FIGURE 5.3.
Felix Greissle. Courtesy Arnold Schönberg Center.

(preferably by dancer-choreographer Anthony Tudor). Greissle, however, was unable to reach an agreement with UE, the owner of the rights to *Pelleas*, and the Alien Property Custodian, an American agency mediating with "enemy firms." (In 1947 there was still no peace agreement between the United States and Austria.)[28]

At Marks, Greissle only once successfully initiated and published a new work by Schoenberg: the Three Folksongs, op. 49 of 1948. Having intended to republish his 1929 German folksong settings for choir, originally issued by Peters, Schoenberg was forced to rework them, because of copyright problems. Following Greissle's advice, he limited the pitch range of these settings to make them suitable for high-school choirs.[29] Happy about the relatively swift production process, Schoenberg found the proofs "very fine and nicely engraved and printed."[30] Although he was also satisfied with the royalty advance of $300 (about $2,640 in 2009) and Greissle's active promotion of this work, he was (as always) disappointed about the early sales, some three thousand copies in the first year. There was also another problem. Marks was a member of BMI, since 1940 the rival of ASCAP as performing rights society, which controlled performances of Schoenberg's music. Therefore, Schoenberg was entitled only to an annual flat sum from ASCAP for performances of these choruses. Schoenberg undoubtedly noted that Greissle, the "powerful executive," was favoring works by Schnabel, Sessions, and others over his own music. In 1950 he tartly inquired: "How are you, how is your business? Satisfactory? Have you published many new works? I suppose only American ones."[31]

Schoenberg and Greissle's relationship, however, remained cordial. Schoenberg appreciated Greissle's advice and loyalty, and even though Greissle had failed to publish more of his music, he did serve Schoenberg in other ways. He recruited for him such well-paying pupils as Serge Frank, transcribed some of his works, and propagated Schoenbergian thought as a theory and composition teacher at Columbia University, the Philadelphia Academy of Music, Princeton, Yale, Rutgers, and the Juilliard School.[32] The two men considered themselves relatives even after the untimely death of Greissle's wife in 1947. Greissle kept addressing Schoenberg as "Papa," and Schoenberg continued to care about Greissle's well-being after he founded a new family.

In the meantime, Schoenberg's business relations with Schirmer deteriorated further. Schirmer's negative opinion of Schoenberg's music was reinforced by such new employees as William Schuman and Hans Heinsheimer. An influential conservative composer, Schuman was chief adviser of publications and focused on promoting his own works and those of like-minded figures at Schirmer.[33] Heinsheimer, whom Schoenberg knew as head of UE's opera department before 1933, had become the director of Schirmer's symphonic and operatic repertoire department in 1947. A supreme opportunist, Heinsheimer lampooned Schoenberg in his 1947 book *Menagerie in F Sharp* as a "man who belongs to Hollywood like a battleship belongs in the lake of Central Park," and he disliked both Schoenberg's personality and his music.[34] Needless to say, neither Schuman nor Heinsheimer was interested in promoting Schoenberg's music, nor did they seriously consider for publication his *Violin Phantasy*, a "cello sonata" version of his Monn transcription, or *Structural Functions*. They hardly expected that any of Schoenberg's scores would pay off Schirmer's investments. Little did they know that by 1970 the study score of the Fourth Quartet would "outsell all the other Schirmer study scores combined."[35]

Schoenberg justifiably distrusted their words, actions, and royalty statements, and suspected Schirmer of not reprinting and disseminating his scores.[36] Knowing that performers had difficulties obtaining Schirmer scores of his works, he discovered in 1949 that his Suite in G was omitted from the Schirmer catalog.[37] Schoenberg also detected inconsistencies in Schirmer's royalty statements, which Heinsheimer sheepishly explained as "clerical errors."[38] In the last five years of his life, Schoenberg's relations with Schirmer, Schuman, and Heinsheimer remained largely unpleasant. The frustrated Schoenberg occasionally felt entitled to violate his Schirmer contracts. In his negotiations with record producers, for instance, he often tried to work out royalty deals that excluded his publishers. When José Limón choreographed his Second Chamber Symphony in 1950, Schoenberg circumvented Schirmer by charging him ten dollars per performance "as long as the profits of your company do not exceed $1,000 per performance. In this case I would demand a minimum of 2–3% of the box office takings . . . P.S. I forgot: these royalties have to be paid directly to me."[39]

H. W. GRAY AND NATHANIEL SHILKRET MUSIC COMPANY

In the early 1940s Schoenberg began relations with two music publishers that commissioned works from him. The first commission, *Variations on a Recitative* for organ, op. 40, came in 1941 from H. W. Gray, a firm devoted to organ and choral music. The second commission, Prelude to *Genesis*, op. 44 for orchestra and choir, came in 1945 from Nathaniel Shilkret, the Schoenberg student who ran a publishing enterprise on Long Island.

Schoenberg probably accepted Gray's commission for creative reasons. Having received an invitation to contribute a piece to Gray's "Contemporary Organ Series," he immediately sketched a twelve-tone Organ Sonata. When he discovered that Gray expected him to write "'Variations for Organ' of not too great length nor of excessive difficulty," he quickly adjusted and completed the work within a few months in October 1941. Although Schoenberg unrealistically demanded a royalty advance of $3,000 (about $43,240 in 2009) for a sixteen-minute work, he accepted Gray's offer of only "200 dollars [about $2,880 in 2009] advanced royalty on 10 percent of the list price and 50% of all performing and recording fees."[40] Unfortunately, the work's production took six years, and both Schoenberg and his editors were to blame. Schoenberg turned in a manuscript that needed heavy editing; Gray's editor, William Strickland, was a professional organist and conductor who intended to premiere, record, and edit the work, but he also held up its production due to his service in the army. After Strickland dropped out in 1943, Carl Weinrich took over; he premiered the Variations the following year, and published the score in 1947. Schoenberg seemed happy with the result at first and offered Gray his *Kol nidre*, Prelude, *Survivor*, Trio, and an arrangement of the Organ Variations for two pianos. But only the last proposal materialized, and by 1948 Schoenberg's business relations with Gray turned sour.[41] Because of Weinrich's notational changes and his specialized registration, Schoenberg abruptly rejected the edition, expecting Gray to publish a new one.[42] Schoenberg also expressed frustration about the modest sales figures and eventually alienated the firm's owner, Donald Gray, to the point that he offered to sell Schoenberg the copyright and entire stock, which Schoenberg, of course, could not afford to accept. Hence the work remained in Gray's hands until Belmont Music Publishers included it in the firm's catalog in 1975.

Unlike the case of the Organ Variations, Schoenberg's acceptance of Shilkret's commission was financially motivated. He received $1,500 (about $17,700 in 2009) for this six-minute orchestral work. As part of the seven-part collective Suite *Genesis*, the Prelude was repeatedly performed and recorded. The production of the score and parts, however, proceeded so slowly that Schoenberg joked in 1950: "Nathaniel Shilkret (RCA Building, N.Y.) has bought all the rights, but he sits on it like Fafner: 'Hier lieg' ich und besitz' [Here I lie and here I hold].'"[43] One of the main reasons for the delay was Shilkret's goal to publish the Suite as a whole, which involved negotiations with five other composers. Concerned about the availability of this score toward the end of his life, Schoenberg suggested that Shilkret offer the piece to either Peters or the Ars Viva Verlag, owned by Swiss conductor Hermann Scherchen.[44] Perhaps because of Shilkret's repeated gestures of generosity, Schoenberg remained friendly with him. Although Shilkret's son Arthur informed Schoenberg in 1951 that he had in hand the printed materials of the Prelude, Schoenberg did not live to see the score, which was eventually transferred to Belmont Music Pubishers.[45]

BOELKE-BOMART

In 1948 Schoenberg began negotiating with the small publishing firm Boelke-Bomart, founded that same year by German immigrant Walter Boelke and his wife Margot Tietz. Before establishing his own company, Boelke was the head of Schirmer's engraving department and had met Schoenberg in 1934 when he toured Schirmer's engravers' room on Long Island. Boelke admired Schoenberg and seemed ideally suited to publish his works.[46] He was altruistically committed to modernist music, and dedicated to first-class engraving on high-quality paper. He hired Schoenberg disciple Kurt List as editor who had been associated with such Schoenberg friends as Steuermann, Dessau, and Krenek. Yet another connection was Boelke-Bomart's affiliation with ASCAP. "Bomart's whole essence is an Hommage [*sic*] to Schoenberg's music," raved List when he invited Schoenberg to submit his works for publication.[47] But Boelke-Bomart was a small and unknown firm, lacking the experience, capital, facilities, and prestige of such publishing houses as Schirmer—a reality Schoenberg was soon to discover.

His main contacts at Boelke-Bomart were List, chairman of the editorial board, and Tietz, the business manager. An Austrian-born musicologist-composer and a member of Schoenberg's circle of friends, List had already wanted to publish Schoenberg's music in 1946, when he was on New Music Edition's editorial board.[48] But Schoenberg declined his offer because he did not want to entrust his works to a nonprofit enterprise. At Bomart, List convinced Schoenberg to let this young firm publish *Survivor,* the *Kol nidre,* Trio, and Three Songs, op. 48 and he arranged for Schoenberg to receive for the four works a flat fee of $3,000 (about $26,450 in 2009) to be paid within two years—in addition to a 10 percent royalty and rental fees. Soon thereafter, however, List lost his influence at Bomart; although he did not quit his job immediately, he could no longer help Schoenberg deal with problems as they arose.[49]

And problems arose quickly. Although Bomart's financial deal was better than most previous offers, Schoenberg was disenchanted and argued that "with respect to the present devaluation of the dollar, I must mention that this is less than I have ever received for any of my works."[50] Struggling to make the payment of $3,000, a huge sum for the small firm, Bomart sent its last installment four months late. There were also problems with the pace of the production. Committed to the expensive and time-consuming production of engraved scores (instead of cheaper copied and autographed scores), Bomart had to postpone work on the *Kol nidre.* The many errors in Schoenberg's manuscripts, however, also slowed down the production process. Hence Bomart was able to publish only *Survivor* (1949) and the Trio (1950) during Schoenberg's lifetime; *Kol nidre* and Three Songs were issued posthumously. Financial reasons prevented the firm from accepting other Schoenberg works, such as the *Phantasy.*[51]

Nonetheless Boelke-Bomart followed through in the fall of 1949 with its goal to make *Survivor* its premiere publication—including a limited, hand-bound deluxe edition on special paper with an original photo of Schoenberg—in honor of his seventy-fifth birthday. The firm overcame many hurdles. Missing phrases in the work's Hebrew text required Schoenberg to make musical changes. The available parts, extracted in lieu of a fee for the first performance in Albuquerque, were unusable and had to be newly autographed.[52] The proofreading was slowed down by Schoenberg's eye trouble and the busy schedules of the other proofreaders. Yet when Boelke and Tietz proudly presented Schoenberg with copies of their *Survivor* edition, including one with "Birthday Greetings to the greatest and most controversial composer of our time!" they were not prepared for his initial negative reaction. He resented Bomart's omission of his preferred notational format: subdividing groups of instruments by brackets throughout and printing certain words and symbols in a large-letter type. He also dismissed the inclusion of a German translation of the English and Hebrew texts, which neither he nor List had seen and approved. He disapproved of the omission of printing the price on each copy and suspected that Bomart lacked promotional strategies.[53] However, after this fury, he apologized and admitted, "it looks very fine what you have done."[54]

Tensions arose again in 1950. Despite Bomart's dedication to his music, the firm was minimally staffed and still establishing its business and catalog. Expecting too much too soon, Schoenberg was disappointed with the early sales figures and accused Bomart of neglecting his works' promotion.[55] Tietz, too, was upset when she discovered that Schoenberg had erroneously told Dial Records that he owned the mechanical rights for the Trio.[56]

Despite his diminishing influence at Bomart, List tried to win such conductors as Ernest Ansermet, René Leibowitz, Carl Weinrich, Dimitri Mitropoulos, and Chemjo Vinaver for *Kol nidre* and *Survivor* performances. His promotional efforts on behalf of Schoenberg's music were most effective in intellectual circles. List was connected with editors of major literary and intellectual journals, and he wrote influential essays about *Kol nidre* and *Survivor* in such venues as *Commentary*, a monthly magazine dedicated to Jewish-American politics and culture; he also invited Leibowitz to contribute a highly polarizing article on Schoenberg and Stravinsky to the *Partisan Review*.[57] List discussed East Coast performances and publishing politics with Schoenberg. He alarmed Schoenberg by hinting at the existence of anti-Schoenberg cliques around Koussevitzky, Copland, and Schuman, and assured him of a growing Schoenberg camp among performers and budding twelve-tone composers. List, however, thought little of the young dodecaphonists, whose works he saw as editor at Bomart: "the most stupid diatonic or chromatic music based on rows."[58] It remains unclear whether this verdict should be contributed to his growing frustrations at Bomart. He himself may have deemed some of these works worthy of publication.

C. F. PETERS CORPORATION NEW YORK

After a long hiatus, Schoenberg revived his relationship with Peters in 1948. Headed by Henri Hinrichsen, the company had been based in Leipzig and had published Schoenberg's Five Orchestral Pieces in 1912, its revised edition in 1922, and seven settings of German folksongs in 1929. But Schoenberg lost contact with Peters when the Nazis came to power. The Nazis confiscated Peters in 1938 for the sake of "Aryanization" and murdered Hinrichsen in Auschwitz in 1942. His son Walter Hinrichsen, however, had traveled to Chicago in 1936 to work for Peters's American representative, Clayton F. Summy. He served in the U.S. Army, and after the war reclaimed his father's company in Leipzig and in 1948 founded a Peters branch in New York. Schoenberg's communication with Walter Hinrichsen began with inquiries about the availability and copyright status of his Five Orchestral Pieces and resulted in two more tension-producing publishing ventures: a new version of the Five Pieces for standard orchestra and the *Violin Phantasy*.

Assuming that performing materials for the Five Pieces were unavailable in America, Schoenberg revealed to Hinrichsen that he had repeatedly rented out his own full score and set of parts of this work to such conductors as Carlos Chavez, and was offering them to Mitropoulos for his performance in October 1948.[59] Although Schoenberg had breached his contract with Peters and caused the firm to lose money, Hinrichsen was on the defensive because both he and Schoenberg suspected that Peters had failed to renew the copyright for the 1912 Five Pieces edition in 1940. Feeling victimized, Schoenberg expected Hinrichsen to offer a publishing deal and monetary compensation.[60] While unwilling to pay reparations, Hinrichsen agreed to publish a new, third version of Five Pieces when he learned that Schoenberg had improved the 1912 edition with revised dynamics and expressive markings to achieve more structural clarity and with a reduced orchestration to facilitate performances.[61]

Hinrichsen offered Schoenberg an advance of $500 (about $4,450 in 2009) on a 50 percent royalty on all rental and performance fees (but with a 50 percent share in the production expenses) and $50 for his editorial assistant Richard Hoffmann.[62] Although Schoenberg completed his revision in just a few days in September 1949, the production process dragged on for over three years. While Hinrichsen tried to resolve disagreements about the production methods and struggled to get the engraving done with a shortage of proofreaders, he discovered that, miraculously, Peters Leipzig had renewed the copyright of the 1912 version in 1940 in Schoenberg's name and that it would have been Schoenberg's duty to assign the publisher the right to renew the copyright.[63] Dedicated "To the Memory of Henri Hinrichsen, the Great Gentleman Publisher," the score of the new version appeared posthumously in February 1953.

Schoenberg also offered Hinrichsen his *Phantasy*, for which Schirmer had made a half-hearted offer and Bomart had had no funds to bid.[64] Hinrichsen immediately accepted it, offering an advance of $250 (about $2,200 in 2009) on 10 percent royalties of the retail price.[65] Although this was the same deal Schirmer had offered him, Schoenberg was happy, disclosing to Hinrichsen: "I am proud about my reappearance in the Peters Edition."[66] He treasured his association with a firm whose prestige and worldwide reputation were built on the long tradition of publishing works of Bach, Mozart, and Beethoven. The production of the *Phantasy*, however, was no less excruciating than that of the Five Pieces because the manuscript contained many errors and Schoenberg continued to make changes while the piece was being engraved in England. The involvement of Hoffmann, musicologist Richard S. Hill and violinists Watson Forbes and Adolf Koldofsky, who all disagreed on the changes, further complicated the production. The day before Schoenberg's death Hinrichsen related to his brother Max in London that "the whole thing is a complete mess" and that a second engraving was necessary.[67] After "back orders in his office [had been] piling up quite high" for more than a year, this "most outstanding modern work by any composer," in Hinrichsen's view, finally appeared in July 1952.[68] The edition, printed on special 80-pound paper, included an inscribed photo of Schoenberg, which Hinrichsen had requested in lieu of the *Phantasy* manuscript. Its inscription records Schoenberg's esteem for both Walter and Henri Hinrichsen: "Meinem lieben Freund, Walter Hinrichsen, der offenbar Peters Editions Verleger so sein wird, wie es sein verehrter Vater war: ein Freund des Künstlers [To my dear friend Walter Hinrichsen, who evidently will be Peters Edition's publisher in the same way as his esteemed father was: as a friend of the artist] Arnold Schoenberg, September 1950" (Figure 5.4). Schoenberg had planned to arrange the *Phantasy* for violin and orchestra, an arrangement that Hinrichsen would have happily published, but unfortunately Schoenberg did not live to do so.[69]

Schoenberg often described Hinrichsen as a "wonderful man" and as his preferred publisher.[70] But this affection did not preclude occasional conflicts, which arose when Hinrichsen gently declined some of Schoenberg's unrealistic publishing proposals. Hinrichsen was unwilling (and financially unable) to take over Schoenberg's thirty-odd works published by UE and his First Chamber Symphony for full orchestra published by Schirmer.[71] He showed little interest in Schoenberg's textbooks and choral works, opp. 50a and 50b, especially after learning that one chorus had already appeared in the journal *Prisma* in 1949 and the other was written for Chemjo Vinaver's *Anthology of Jewish Music*. Schoenberg's reactions to these decisions ranged from frustration to the acceptance of a "bitter pill from my friend Walter Hinrichsen."[72]

FIGURE 5.4.
Schoenberg portrait with dedication to Walter Hinrichsen. Courtesy Christian Hinrichsen.

Once, however, Schoenberg almost cut his ties with Hinrichsen due to a fundamental misunderstanding. Prompted by an improbable rumor, he asked Hinrichsen in 1950 if he had played a role in the "Aryanization" of UE. Schoenberg, who should have known better, pressed him: "Where have you been during the Nazi regime? Was your father a Jew, a half-Jew or an Aryan? You understand that I must be clear about this."[73] Hinrichsen felt so insulted that he vowed not to correspond with him anymore.[74] Gradually, however, their friendship recovered from this unfortunate clash.

ASSOCIATED MUSIC PUBLISHERS, UNIVERSAL EDITION, BOOSEY & HAWKES, AND EDWIN F. KALMUS

Schoenberg had to interact with Associated Music Publishers (AMP) in New York, the American agency of his former publisher UE. Distributing some thirty of his works (published between 1909 and 1928), AMP along with UE arguably caused him the most difficulties.

AMP undoubtedly failed to stock enough of the UE scores before the start of World War II, and its staff may indeed have been as disorganized and as untrustworthy as Schoenberg viewed them, but UE was clearly at the root of AMP's problems.[75] Founded as a joint-stock company with many Jewish stockholders, UE was operated mostly by Jews and featured numerous Jewish composers in its catalog. Beginning in 1933, performances of UE's composers drastically declined, and the firm experienced severe financial difficulties. Although UE assisted Schoenberg with his flight to France and America, he was no less disappointed than Kurt Weill by UE's payment cuts in the summer of 1933.[76] Exacerbating Schoenberg's frustration was his discovery that UE had never copyrighted his successful First Chamber Symphony and *Verklärte Nacht* for string orchestra.[77] The *Anschluss* and ensuing war halted the printing of his scores and effective dissemination of his music with UE under the management of such "Aryanizers" as Ernst Geutebrück, Johannes Petschull, and Alfred Schlee.[78] This is why AMP could no longer reliably order, stock, and sell his UE works. Viewing UE's deeds as a breach of contract, he decided to divorce himself from this firm: "I consider the former contract between myself and Universal Edition as broken by U.E. and accordingly it is not any longer binding to me. Universal Edition has eliminated my name from all their catalogues. They have neglected to reprint sold-out editions and have accordingly failed to fulfill the obligations of a publisher toward a composer."[79]

From 1934 until the end of his life, Schoenberg tried to transfer UE's rights for his works to such publishers as AMP, Boosey & Hawkes, Peters, and Associated Musicians Inc. (AMI).[80] Yet UE was unwilling to release him from his contracts. Boosey's New York branch, founded in 1930, briefly considered taking over his works. In 1941 Ralph Hawkes, the head of Boosey, even visited Schoenberg in Los Angeles to discuss these plans.[81] Yet because of the war nothing came of these negotiations. During and after the war, the Custodian of Alien Property, a government trust initiated by Roosevelt to control enemy property, would have restricted the transfer of these rights to an American publisher. Yet Schoenberg was not deterred and increasingly deluded himself that he could simply terminate his contract with UE, informing various institutions, including record companies, that he had "canceled" his UE contract and that royalty payments had to be sent directly to him.[82]

In addition to the UE-induced problems, Schoenberg had to challenge AMP and the Custodian of Alien Property about the payment of royalties for performances and radio broadcasts of his orchestral music in the United States.[83] As UE (and not AMP) was officially in charge of the royalty payments, Nazi foreign-exchange laws had to be followed. UE apparently tried, but unfortunately did not reach a royalty payment agreement for its "non-Aryan" composers.[84] Hence the Custodian of Alien Property controlled the rights and royalties of Schoenberg's music as distributed by AMP, and his money was regularly impounded.[85] The Alien Property Custodian's confiscations unfortunately continued after the war, until the agency was shut down in 1966.

Schoenberg did achieve one satisfactory deal with AMP. Although founded in 1927 primarily to serve as sole representative of such major European publishers as Breitkopf & Härtel, Doblinger, Schott, and UE, AMP also published works on its own, including music by Henry Cowell, Roy Harris, Walter Piston, and Wallingford Riegger.[86] Schoenberg communicated with AMP's vice president Hugo Winter, whom he knew as one of UE's directors (1932–38), yet never trusted. Although Winter repeatedly declined Schoenberg's requests to take over his UE scores and publish some of his new works—perhaps due to AMP's affiliation with BMI—he did accept in 1943 Schoenberg's second string-orchestra version of *Verklärte Nacht*, first arranged in 1917.[87] Schoenberg initially negotiated with Edwin Kalmus, the Austrian-born owner of a profitable New York–based music-reprint company, who had threatened back in 1934 to reprint the unaltered 1917 version and pay Schoenberg voluntarily a 10 percent royalty.[88] Kalmus's modest proposal for his new version precluded a royalty advance, so Schoenberg accepted Winter's offer of an advance of $350 (about $4,300 in 2009) against royalties of 10 percent of the retail price, 15 percent of the rental fees, and 50 percent of performance fees.[89] To Schoenberg, this publication may have signified Winter's only positive deed. Winter seemed unwilling to support a new *Pelleas* arrangement or to monitor seriously the many performances of Schoenberg's UE works in America.[90] In view of the numerous unreported performances, lost fees, flawed royalty statements, and impounded funds, Schoenberg often felt trapped and helpless in the bureaucratic conglomerate of UE, AMP, and the Custodian of Alien Property.

BELMONT MUSIC PUBLISHERS

Publishers often considered Schoenberg's music incompatible with their commercial ideas, and Schoenberg never fully trusted any of them. None met his high demands: generous fees, fast production, broad accessibility of performing materials, and extensive publicity, as well as regular and accurate royalty statements. Tired of dealing with many different firms, Schoenberg increasingly toyed with the idea of concentrating his works in one music-publishing house, even though the plan seemed far-fetched. He asked Ralph Hawkes in 1940: "Would it not be useful—for the publisher, for the author and for our customers—if all my works were in one hand?"[91] In 1948 he discussed with List the idea of a "Schoenberg Verlag," based on shares and the participation of all his publishers, arguing that costs would be reduced because "all the propaganda would be unified" and "one single place of delivery could deliver all the works."[92] In 1951, he proposed to Emil Hilb, a Los Angeles–based composer and founder of Associated Musicians, Inc., an "independent Schoenberg Publication within the frame of AMI and UE."[93]

Schoenberg's idea of a "Schoenberg Verlag" came to fruition only after his death, when his widow Gertrud and son Lawrence founded Belmont Music Publishers. The word "Belmont" is a French translation of "schön[er] Berg" (beautiful mountain). Initially this Los Angeles–based firm served as an agency for Schoenberg's European publishers in the United States, including UE, which after 1965 was no longer represented by AMP. Besides selling and renting music, Belmont began to reprint out-of-print scores and issue such unpublished works as *Nachtwandler*, Three Pieces for Chamber Orchestra, and Scherzo for String Quartet. When B. Schott's Söhne in Mainz published *Moses und Aron*, Belmont retained the work's American rights to effectively market its scores in the United States. Belmont retrieved the rights of many of Schoenberg's works when their previous copyright term expired, thus making them more readily available internationally.[94] Since its foundation, Belmont has acquired from Schoenberg's American publishers the Second Chamber Symphony's two-piano version, both versions of the *Ode*, the Piano Concerto, both versions of the Band Variations, the Organ Variations, Prelude, Trio, *Survivor*, Three Folksongs, op. 49, and the choral works, op. 50a and 50b. Freeing these rights from the former publishers, Belmont has been successful in establishing a unified catalog of Schoenberg's oeuvre, which also includes theoretical writings.

PHILOSOPHICAL LIBRARY

Schoenberg had been able to place only one of his books, *Models for Beginners in Composition*, with a music publisher (Schirmer, 1942), but intended to publish all his literary and theoretical writings in several volumes. Hence he fostered relationships with several American book publishers. Negotiations with Gottfried Beermann-Fischer, the Curtis Publishing Company, Doubleday, Doran & Company, Norton, Prentice-Hall, Simon & Schuster, and University Press (the predecessor of the University of California Press) did not bear fruit, but Schoenberg did conduct profitable, if complicated, business relations with the New York–based Philosophical Library. Founded by the Romanian-born philosopher Dagobert Runes in 1941, this small publishing house featured books by such émigrés as Albert Einstein, Max Graf, and Franz Werfel. Schoenberg's business relations with the Philosophical Library began in 1941 when Runes invited him to contribute an article on "Theory of Performance" to his 1946 *Encyclopedia of the Arts* and join his editorial board.[95] Although Schoenberg did not write this dictionary entry, he was invited in

1943—probably thanks to Runes's editor Max Graf, a Viennese-born Schoenberg advocate— to publish some of his music-theory essays in the form of a book.[96] The outcome, after a seven-year struggle, was the 1950 volume *Style and Idea,* preceded by the 1948 publication of *Theory of Harmony,* an abridged English version of *Harmonielehre.*[97]

Although the Philosophical Library produced it in less time than *Style and Idea,* the publishing history of *Theory of Harmony* dates to 1921, when Schoenberg and UE began looking for English translators. Initial translation attempts by Carl Engel, Bernard van Dieren, Cort van der Linden, Adolph Weiss, Dika Newlin, Nicolas Slonimsky, and Gustave Arlt failed, as did negotiations with the Boston Music Company and University Press. Finally Robert D. W. Adams, a pupil in Schoenberg's 1935 summer classes at USC, successfully completed the English translation of *Harmonielehre* in 1946.[98] Following Schoenberg's advice, he omitted *Harmonielehre*'s "mere esthetic, theoretical and polemical parts."[99] Yet he excluded Schoenberg from the translation process to speed up the completion of his task. Reviewing the galley proofs in 1947, Schoenberg was nonetheless "very satisfied" with the translation, deemed it "fluent, elegant and natural," and suggested only a few amendments.[100] He was also satisfied with the Philosophical Library's offer of an advance of $750 (about $8,150 in 2009) on a 10 percent royalty for the first 2,000 copies of the book, and a lump sum for Adams. As with all his scores, he was frustrated by the book's early sales figures (1,200 copies in the first six months). His questioning of the royalty statements' accuracy, however, may have undermined the publication of a translation of the unabridged *Harmonielehre* after the sale of 5,000 copies, as stipulated in the contract.[101] Although Schoenberg had deemed the availability of two versions necessary—"the condensed [being] for the musician, the full for cultured people"—it took another thirty years until Roy E. Carter and the University of California Press fulfilled this wish.[102]

Style and Idea was a much more problematic publishing venture, slowed down by many delays. First came disagreements about the book's content. While the Philosophical Library envisioned a one-volume essay collection, Schoenberg imagined an encompassing multi-volume set and explained: "This book should be the first volume of a more or less 'complete edition' of my literary works, which might comprise at least 5 to 6 volumes and should contain: theory, esthetics, criticism, poetry and many other subjects."[103] Hampered by a war-induced paper shortage, the Philosophical Library eventually insisted on a single volume with fifteen articles.[104] Some of the selected articles were in German, and an acceptable translator had to be found. Dissatisfied with several samples produced by the Philosophical Library's three translators ("a distinguished local musicologist," Alvin Bauman, and Helga Nagy), Schoenberg suggested the involvement of his own people.[105] Gradually, however, it became clear that even his chosen associates, Greissle, List, Brunswick, and his former student Frank, proved unreliable.[106] Finally, in 1948 he turned to Dika Newlin, who successfully translated and edited the texts. Possessing a keen understanding of Schoenberg's personality and goals, Newlin tried as a translator to "adhere as literally to the original style as English usage" would permit.[107] As to her editorial task, Newlin remembered, "We were back to our old tricks again . . . I'd correct his Germanic English; he'd respond bristling with offended pride; I'd apologize abjectly; we'd start all over again."[108] Other minor stumbling blocks were lost music examples and disagreements about the book's title and the contract, according to which Schoenberg in the end received an advance of $375 (about $4,420 in 2009) on a 10 percent royalty for the first 5,000 copies, but was to pay $200 for Newlin's work out of his own pocket.

Despite these difficult interactions, in 1949 the Philosophical Library published on Schoenberg's recommendation Leibowitz's book *Schoenberg and His School*, which Newlin had translated from French in only two weeks.[109] Conversely, Schoenberg honored Runes by setting a poem from his poetry collection *Jordan Lieder* (Philosophical Library, 1948) and publishing it as *Dreimal tausend Jahre* in the Swedish magazine *Prisma* in 1949.[110] Their cordial relationship, however, turned sour when Schoenberg, dissatisfied with the reviews of *Style and Idea*, expected the Philosophical Library to defend him.[111] When Schoenberg accused him of holding back royalties for *Style and Idea* and *Theory of Harmony* and threatened to launch a public protest against his firm, Runes broke off his dealings with Schoenberg.[112] In his last letter to Schoenberg, Runes charged him with "German insolence and arrogance" and demanded that he should stop making "wild accusations" without considering the facts.[113] Needless to say, Philosophical Library refrained from publishing Schoenberg's *Structural Functions of Harmony* and a projected volume with his program notes.[114] Little did they know that both books would become publishing successes. In 2010 the Philosophical Library reprinted the first edition of *Style and Idea* and the University of California issued a hundredth-anniversary edition of *Theory of Harmony* (translated by Roy E. Carter in 1978) and a sixtieth-anniversary edition of *Style and Idea* (edited and expanded by Leonard Stein in 1975).

Considering the many complex relationships Schoenberg entertained with his American publishers and the ways he sometimes worked against his own business interests, it is surprising that he was able to place most of his finished mature works (except *Von heute auf morgen* and the textbooks *Structural Functions*, *Fundamentals of Musical Composition*, and *Preliminary Exercises in Counterpoint*) in the hands of a publisher before his death—an achievement no doubt due to his yearning for the breakthrough of his music and his determination to make it available to performers and audiences. Although Schoenberg had similar problems with his European publishers (and was in this respect by no means an isolated case), his irritability and impatience increased in the last few years of his life when he sensed that he was running out of time. Although it was unfortunate that many of his publications were delayed, Schoenberg often had to share the blame with his publishers and the political and economic circumstances of the 1930s and 1940s. The limited availability of his scores surely foiled some performances of his music, although Schoenberg and his disciples found ways to furnish performers with scores, even if it meant a breach of publishing contracts. A timelier publication of *Theory of Harmony* would have undeniably benefited Schoenberg's teaching, and an earlier edition of *Style and Idea* would have facilitated the reception of his ideas. Yet before 1950 Schoenberg regularly published articles in the American press, and some essays in *Style and Idea* had already appeared in such venues as the *New York Times*, *Musical America*, *Modern Music*, *Proceedings of the Music Teachers National Association*, and Robert B. Heywood's book *The Works of the Mind* (University of Chicago Press, 1947), widening Schoenberg's exposure in musical and intellectual circles. For Schoenberg, publication delays had financial consequences. His push for release dates before Christmas and his unrealistic expectations of sales of his works bespeak not only his yearning for fame and recognition, but also his considerations of the market and a longing for financial success.[115] As he confided to the head of E. B. Marks: "It would be hypocrisy, would I deny, that I like also profitable dealings."[116] All things considered, Schoenberg did remarkably well in the field of publishing.

6 Schoenberg's American Teaching Career

Schoenberg may well have had his greatest impact on American music as a teacher. Although he often complained about having to teach for a living—and under worse conditions than he had known in Europe—he in fact thrived as a teacher and developed a well-deserved reputation as a pedagogue. In his own estimation, Schoenberg taught more than a thousand students in America.[1] His unique gifts for music education are reflected in numerous writings and confirmed by the successful careers of his pupils. This chapter examines Schoenberg's teaching activities and his impact on students and music education in America. It debunks the Eurocentric myth that Schoenberg as a teacher in America was not well compensated, that his teaching was unappreciated, and that of his "hundreds of pupils, only Berg and Webern succeeded."[2] The Anglocentric supposition that his "reactionary" teaching impeded the development of an "emerging American musical language" for his students is challenged as well.[3]

SCHOENBERG'S TEACHING POSITIONS AND STUDENTS

Malkin Conservatory and Chautauqua

As a teacher in America, Schoenberg initially faced major challenges. He had to develop a nuanced English vocabulary for conveying technical information about music, which would satisfy his own high standards of exactitude. He also had to adjust to an educational system very different from that of Europe. Yet another hurdle was his adaptation to the cultural backgrounds and expectations of American students; he had to deal with very heterogeneous bodies of students and their varying levels of commitment to musical studies.

Schoenberg's first teaching position in America was at the Malkin Conservatory of Music in Boston, a small music school housed in an old mansion on 299 Beacon Street, which was founded in 1933 by the Russian-born cellist Joseph Malkin.[4] Malkin had known Schoenberg since Schoenberg's early Berlin years and was aware of his dismissal from the Prussian Academy of the Arts. He invited him to join his faculty, which included Malkin's brothers Manfred (piano) and Jacques (violin), Anton Witek (violin), first-chair wind players from the Boston Symphony, Eva Gauthier (voice), Arthur Fiedler (conducting), Suzanne Bloch (harmony, solfeggio, and ear training), Renée Longy-Miquelle (Dalcroze eurythmics), Nicolas Slonimsky (music theory), and Roger Sessions (composition). Initially the conservatory had only five or six classrooms, lacked an orchestra, and did not offer any degrees, but it would prosper before being shut down in 1943 due to the war.

Schoenberg received a guaranteed annual salary of $4,800 (about $78,700 in 2009) for twelve students and 50 percent of the annual tuition for each additional student. The annual student fee was $400 (about $6,550 in 2009) and the cost for single lessons was $25 (about $410 in 2009). He was also allowed to teach private students at home at a minimum charge of $30 per hour. The conservatory students had to be taught a minimum of sixty-four hours over the course of two semesters (each comprising sixteen weeks) and could be combined in groups meeting for an hour twice a week. The teaching load for Schoenberg was low and his salary was very high: higher than his Berlin annual income of 18,000 Reichsmark, equaling about $4,500 at that time and more than four times the average full-time American wage of $1,050 in 1933 and 1934. Nevertheless Schoenberg complained about his remuneration.[5] He oddly expected Malkin to compensate him for the loss of his two-year Berlin contract and to pay for his and his family's travel expenses (about $500 [approximately $8,200 in 2009]), but Malkin was unable to secure more funds because of the Great Depression. The drawback of Schoenberg's job was that Malkin had recruited students in both Boston and New York, and he expected Schoenberg to travel by train to New York once a week to teach there for six or seven hours.[6] In the spring, however, Malkin arranged for him to stay in New York and made the Boston students take the boat to New York every other weekend for lessons with Schoenberg. Furthermore, Malkin generously agreed to shorten Schoenberg's teaching period, which he began a month late and finished a month early.

Schoenberg wrote Webern in February 1934 that he had a total of seven students in Boston and nine in New York.[7] A "Schoenberg Scholarship Fund" with gifts from Boston-based philanthropist Therese Filene, George Gershwin, Stokowski, Steinway & Sons, Knabe Pianos, Ernest Dane, and others enabled less well-off but gifted students to study with Schoenberg. From thirty-five scholarship applicants Schoenberg selected Annabel Comfort, Lovina Knight, Lois Lautner, and Béla Rósza. Comfort was a composer-pianist who had studied with Adolf Weidig, Rosario Scalero, and Boulanger; her music had been featured in a radio concert sponsored by the Pan American Association of Composers in spring 1933.[8] Knight had studied music theory with Sessions and Herbert Elwell, and as a music major at Vassar College, she had composed a movement for string quartet in 1931 under Paul Henry Lang's tutelage. Lautner had studied composition with Percy Goetschius at what later became the Juilliard School; she became a college teacher and author of several books, including *Two-Part 16th Century Counterpoint: A First Year Course* (Homeyer, 1948) and works of Western fiction.[9] Rósza, a composer-pianist and chess champion, performed Three Piano Pieces, op. 11 in November 1933 for Schoenberg's first American radio interview and was later hailed by Schoenberg as an "extremely brilliant composer and pianist" of "enchanting vitality."[10] Rósza became an admired professor of music theory and keyboard at the University of Tulsa (1945–74). Schoenberg's Boston class also included Lowndes Maury, who had studied piano and composition in Chicago and was later active as a composer, arranger, and pianist in Hollywood, where he met Schoenberg again in 1948. Privately Schoenberg taught Frank Glazer, a recognized American concert pianist.[11] Among his New York students, Thomas Griselle and Nathaniel Shilkret were, like the students already mentioned, hardly beginners either. Both Griselle and Shilkret had developed a reputation as composers of popular music. Griselle was well known for his symphonic jazz, and Shilkret, director of the Victor Talking Machine Company and Victor Salon Orchestra, had earned fame with such songs as "The Lonesome Road."[12]

Although Schoenberg was contractually required to instruct his students in harmony and composition, he taught them a mix of analysis, harmony, counterpoint, and composition (what he would later call "Form and Analysis"), tailoring his instruction to the needs of individual students whose backgrounds differed widely. He even engaged Adolph Weiss as his unofficial teaching assistant to coach some of his New York students in harmony and to occasionally serve as an interpreter in his classes.[13] At the end of his stint at Malkin, Schoenberg admitted that he "enjoyed the actual teaching."[14] He even acknowledged that there were "many talented people (whether significant masters I do not know, but in any case: good students!)."[15] To his European friends, however, he reported that with the exception of "two really talented students and a few with some talent," they were "complete beginners" and that "even the more mature pupils had covered the ground-work very inadequately."[16]

Some accounts of Schoenberg's students confirm his assessments. Knight, who knew the pupils in both the Boston and New York classes, observed that "compositions written in both classes were few." Knight wrote a choral work, and Lautner, who received individual lessons from Schoenberg in the first semester, completed an invention, a fugue, and a three-movement string quartet.[17] Maury felt he did not write anything of value because his creativity seemed hampered.[18] Four students reworked earlier pieces and started new ones, yet "completed no big work. The rest were working on basics." While most students felt they were "unprepared for Schoenberg" and lacked a "firm grasp of the principles of harmony and counterpoint," they declared that the "sum of intangible accomplishment was, of course, incalculable." These students learned to set higher standards for their own work and gained new appreciation for traditional forms.[19]

Schoenberg could have kept his Malkin position—he was offered a three-year contract—but after vacationing in Chautauqua in the summer of 1934, he decided to move to California. He had unrealistically expected to draw larger crowds as a result of Malkin's 1933 advertising campaign and failed to take into account the conservatory's costly tuition at an economically dismal time. Schoenberg suspected that the conservatory "was caught in a cross-fire of intrigues stemming from poverty and philistinism."[20] He disliked the building's poorly soundproofed classrooms. Significantly, however, he wanted to escape the severe East Coast climate, which had aggravated his asthma—the reason he also turned down job offers from Juilliard and the Chicago Musical College, with annual salaries between $4,000 and $5,000. Schoenberg always remained grateful to Malkin for letting him "discover America," and in 1938, he joined his conservatory's Honorary Board.[21]

During his sojourn in Chautauqua from mid-July through mid-September 1934, Schoenberg's main goal was to relax and regain his health. Yet soon after his arrival he announced in the *Daily Chautauquan* (July 27) that he would accept students.

Although he was not an official faculty member of the Chautauqua Summer Schools, he was allowed to instruct students at this institution's music school, which at that time was the summer home of the Juilliard Graduate School of Music. His pupils were Elizabeth Merz Butterfield and Dorothea Bestor Kelley, each of whom received individual lessons. Kelley, whom Schoenberg once described as "a very fine musician," recalled that he "taught in a shingled studio in the Chautauqua woods, seated at the piano, with a large pipe organ as inert background." She also remembered that his wife served as a translator since at that point her knowledge of English was more advanced than his.[22] Although neither of these two students became professional composers, they both pursued remarkable creative careers. Butterfield authored several books for children, including *The Goop Song Book* (Willis Music Company, 1941) with music she had composed. Kelley, a composition student at Juilliard and violinist in the New Haven Symphony when she studied with Schoenberg, became a violist of the Buffalo Philharmonic, Chautauqua Symphony, and Dallas Symphony; in 1955 she founded the Dallas Chamber Music Society and was its artistic director for over fifty years.

Private Teaching in Los Angeles, USC, and UCLA

Although Schoenberg arrived in Los Angeles with no job offers in hand, he soon benefited from his contact with two USC faculty members who were enthusiastic about contemporary music and his presence in their city:[23] Pauline Alderman, who was an assistant professor of music theory and a composer of operas and operettas, and Julia Howell, the head of the music-theory division. Alderman had wanted to study with Schoenberg but could not afford his very high fee, so on his advice she organized a small class in the fall of 1934 to share the costs with others. Alderman, Howell, and the high-school music teachers Ina Davids and Marjorie Eischen met over the course of three months at Schoenberg's home on Canyon Cove to analyze such works as Beethoven's Piano Variations in C minor and Brahms's Fourth Symphony.[24] For spring 1935 Alderman and Howell arranged another private class dedicated to music from Bach to Schoenberg for a flat fee of $600 (about $9,300 in 2009) to be divided among the twenty-five to forty participating students.[25]

Besides Alderman, the class included other young composers, such as John Cage, Hugo Friedhofer, and Elinor Remick Warren. Prepared by Buhlig, Cowell, and Weiss for these lessons, Cage arrived in Los Angeles in December 1934 and worked for his father's company to afford his share of this class (Figure 6.1).[26] Friedhofer was an orchestrator for Max Steiner and Erich Korngold, who had also been composing uncredited film scores at Fox since 1930. Warren was a well-known, Los Angeles–based composer of tonal music, who attended the classes because Schoenberg was then "the man of the hour" and she wanted "to see what he had to say."[27] The class also comprised concert pianists Bernice Abrams (who later married Karl Geiringer, a Haydn and Brahms scholar), John Crown (later a faculty member at USC), and Olga Steeb, who had her own highly respected private conservatory in Los Angeles and performed the music examples for Schoenberg's lectures.[28] Other attendees were such college teachers as Leslie Clausen and Edmund Cykler, the former a music teacher and the latter a violist and chair of the music department at Los Angeles City College.[29] Alderman, Cage, and Friedhofer remembered the depth of Schoenberg's analyses of Bach's *Art of the Fugue* and excerpts from his *Well-Tempered Clavier*, Schubert's *Winterreise*, Strauss's *Blue Danube* Waltz, Brahms's Third and Fourth Symphonies, and Schoenberg's Third String Quartet.[30] Cage wrote to

FIGURE 6.1.
John Cage (c. 1935). Courtesy John Cage Trust.

Weiss: "I manage to keep my ears open and absorb what I can."[31] Friedhofer testified that he learned much and found Schoenberg "brilliant."[32] Warren, however, found that Schoenberg was "a little edgy" when he talked about his own music.[33] One of the course's highlights was, as Alderman recounted, live performances by the Abas Quartet in some class meetings to illustrate Schoenberg's lecture on his Third String Quartet. The Abas Quartet gave a complete rendition of this work at the class's end-of-semester picnic at Cykler's ranch in the San Fernando Valley.[34]

Additionally, in spring 1935 Schoenberg taught a small private class on counterpoint at his home. This course continued throughout the summer and included Abrams, George Tremblay, and Cage, who joined the class late after a meeting with Schoenberg on May 1. According to Cage, Schoenberg suggested that he could, with the help of Tremblay, become conversant with what he missed because the class had already started.[35] Catching up quickly, Cage wrote to Pauline Schindler that "my work seems to please Schoenberg" and that it was "proceeding excellently."[36] Abrams remembered Cage as a talented student who had "one of the clearest minds."[37] She also recalled that he had a friendly relationship with his teacher. Cage was invited to Schoenberg's home for dinner and concerts, and occasionally borrowed his mother's car to take Schoenberg to the university and home or to rehearsals and concerts.[38]

As the summer of 1935 neared, Alderman and Howell provided Schoenberg with teaching opportunities at USC. Advisory members of the Alchin Chair committee, which selects a visiting professor to teach at USC during the six-week-long summer session, convinced USC's president Rufus Von KleinSmid, "the world's most stubborn musical conservative," along with USC's unadventurous composition department, headed by Charles E. Pemberton, to offer Schoenberg this position for the summers of 1935 and 1936. Alderman and Howell also secured a part-time teaching position (two classes taught once a week) for Schoenberg for the academic year of 1935–36. Schoenberg was once again paid very well, despite

USC's Depression-induced financial problems. The university's School of Music was downsized to a division within the College of Letters, Arts and Sciences; employees were dismissed; and Alderman's own full-time position was reduced to half-time with a 60 percent salary cut.[39] Schoenberg received $1,000 for each summer session (about $15,300 in 2009) and $2,000 for the half-time position, drawn from the Alchin funds.[40] In addition, Schoenberg was offered up to $1,000 for extracurricular lectures.[41] Money was also provided for Gerald Strang's teaching assistantships (1935–36) from the Alchin funds and Samuel Goldwyn. Schoenberg was better paid for the summer appointments than his predecessors Howard Hanson and Arne Oldberg had been, and he benefited from the lower cost of living in California, but in letters to his European friends he downplayed his earnings as not being "princely."[42] Compared to the average annual full-time American wage of $1,146 in 1936, Schoenberg, however, did very well.[43]

During his tenure at USC, Schoenberg taught eight classes in which Strang, who had been trained in composition by Edward Stricklen and Charles Koechlin, served as his teaching assistant. Initially he sat at a desk near Schoenberg "to supply the necessary word or expression when he ran out of English," and later helped him write his theory books.[44] Beyond his manifold duties as teaching assistant, Strang, whom Schoenberg soon affectionately called "Gerry," even served as his chauffeur and as Santa Claus for his children and became a friend of his family. Despite attending all of Schoenberg's classes as teaching assistant until 1938 and making free use of dodecaphony in his music, Strang never viewed himself as a Schoenberg student and only sporadically showed him some of his own music. In 1948 under Toch's tutelage he received a doctorate in music from USC.

In the 1935 summer session, which required teaching for six weeks with a two-hour day and five-days-a-week schedule, Schoenberg offered "Composition I" for students with little background and focused on in-depth analysis of Beethoven piano sonatas. He also taught a small class called "Composition II" in which advanced students wrote a string quartet. The first summer session culminated in Schoenberg's public lecture on "Composition with Twelve Tones," presented in collaboration with the Abas Quartet at USC's Faculty Club in Bovard. Schoenberg would generally wear informal tennis clothes because after most classes he played tennis with his students on a court reserved for him.[45] Sometimes he went with his students or colleagues to early shows of films or picnics at Howell's cabin in the Arroyo Secco and at the public beach near Malibu. The 1936 summer session also featured "Composition I" and "Advanced Composition," but there were no special events (perhaps due to Alderman's absence from campus), and Schoenberg held most of his classes in his new and spacious Brentwood home.

The first summer session's "Composition I" attracted between forty and sixty students and "Composition II" about fifteen, who always gathered around the grand piano in USC's Mudd Hall of Philosophy. Among the talented and well-known students in these classes were Robert D. W. Adams, Wayne Barlow, Cage, Leonard Stein, and Alan Wells.[46] Adams became the chair of the University of Kansas City's music department and translated Schoenberg's *Harmonielehre* into English (Philosophical Library, 1948). Barlow became a noted conservative composer and a professor at Eastman and was the first recipient in America of a Ph.D. degree in composition (Eastman School, 1937). Stein enrolled in these courses on the advice of his piano teacher Buhlig. Serving as pianist, he performed all of Schoenberg's music examples and gradually developed into one of Schoenberg's most energetic and articulate champions.[47] Wells became a California-based musician, teacher, and composer. Schoenberg's 1935 summer offerings also attracted occasional visitors, including Alderman, Howell, Buhlig, Schoenberg's wife, pianist Alice Coleman Batchelder, Klemperer, and Tremblay.[48] The 1936 summer session was again a magnet for a large crowd including such mature students as James Sykes and Leroy Robertson. Sykes, who held a B.A. from Princeton and an M.A. from the Eastman School (1933), was at that time chair of Colorado College's music department and later became internationally known as a pianist of Schoenberg's works and other contemporary music.[49] Robertson had studied composition with George Chadwick, Bloch, and Toch (in Berlin); he earned a master's degree from the University of Utah in 1932 and became one of Utah's most noted composers, with some of his mostly tonal music based on the *Book of Mormon*.[50] A composer and professor of music, first at Brigham Young University and later at the University of Utah, Robertson remained friends with Schoenberg, whom he visited at his home when he was in Los Angeles and with whom he hoped to carry out a collaborative Beethoven-analysis book project. Following Robertson's invitation, Schoenberg hoped to give a guest lecture at his university in the summer of 1951.[51]

In the academic year of 1935–36, Schoenberg taught two regular classes: "The Art of Contrapuntal Composition" (advanced counterpoint) and "The Construction of Themes." These classes were small because they did not count toward the degree requirements and attracted few students beyond Cage, Stein, Strang and a few others. Cage recalled that the USC counterpoint class never comprised more than four students.[52] Schoenberg also gave two series of eighteen evening lectures open to "teachers, students and music lovers," entitled "The Evaluation of Musical Works: A School of Criticism" and "The Elements of Musical Forms as Discovered by Analysis," in which Schoenberg intended to instruct his audience how to "describe, compare, evaluate, criticize and judge music."[53] Although attendance was not as large as he had expected (fifty to sixty people), he was gratified that among the most frequent attendees were "very enthusiastic" USC and UCLA professors from such disciplines as philosophy.[54] To enhance the academic year, Alderman and Howell hired the Abas Quartet to play Schoenberg's three quartets (the fourth had not been written) in a series of campus concerts. The Phi Mu Alpha student members, offering Schoenberg honorary membership in their organization, hosted a performance of *Verklärte Nacht* with the Los Angeles Philharmonic under Schoenberg at Bovard Auditorium.

In his first California broadcast in the fall of 1935, Schoenberg commended his students' "youthful ardor," "eagerness to learn," and "remarkable" intelligence, confessing that "I feel young with them, when I feel the touch of their power."[55] Yet he was challenged. Although experienced in teaching large classes that included fledgling teachers and performers (his 1918–19 "Seminar for Composition" at the Schwarzwald School had an enrollment of fifty-five students), he struggled with his large classes containing mostly middle-aged public-school or college teachers and performers, with very few aspiring composers.[56] He also regretted his students' limited knowledge of musical repertoire, which he compared to "Swiss cheese—almost more holes than cheese."[57] "Even the less admirable types of musicians in Germany and Austria had," according to him, "a better grounding, a basis on which one could build."[58] He also deplored that American students could not listen to live performances of classical music more frequently and afford their own miniature scores of these works, as was standard in Europe.[59] Schoenberg wrestled with American academic bureaucracy, including the grading system and evaluation of each student. When Schoenberg was about to give everybody an F, due to his students' knowledge gaps, Strang had to convince him that he and Stein deserved at least a B and that he should make use of other grades as well.[60] Schoenberg never liked grading his students. He reluctantly gave As and resorted to the passing grade of C for most students.[61] With such limitations on his mind, he laconically related to his European friends that his instruction would be "as much a waste of time as if Einstein were having to teach mathematics at a secondary school."[62] Ten years later, however, he admitted that "class teaching is more stimulating to me than single teaching."[63]

Besides his private and USC classes, Schoenberg gave individual lessons to several affluent or very talented students, charging between $25 and $50 (about $390–$780 in 2009) per single lesson.[64] In the summer of 1936 Schoenberg taught about ten private lessons each week, yielding several thousand dollars of additional income.[65] According to Schoenberg's date books, Tremblay was one of his first private pupils in Los Angeles. A gifted improviser who had already experimented with dodecaphony, Tremblay studied with Schoenberg from October 1934 and apparently wrote under his tutelage one of his first major works, the dodecaphonic First String Quartet (1936). Tremblay expanded and propagated dodecaphony throughout his career and remained friendly with Schoenberg.[66] In the spring and summer of 1936, Schoenberg also taught the esteemed pianist-composer Hugh Hodgson, founder and chair of the University of Georgia music department. Hodgson paid fifty dollars per lesson and composed under Schoenberg, among other works, the highly chromatic piano piece *Polka Dots (A Study in Black and White)*. After his return to Georgia, he championed Schoenberg's music as a performer and teacher, and retained cordial ties with him.[67] For a brief period of time, and free of charge, Schoenberg also taught Klemperer.

As previously mentioned, Schoenberg attracted many film composers, whom he may have had in mind as students when he decided to settle in Los Angeles. These composers could easily afford his high prices and often felt that "this was a chance for them to make a [financial] contribution" to Schoenberg.[68] Most were seriously interested in deepening and broadening their techniques and strove for recognition on the concert stage as well. They were surely eager to explore with Schoenberg new uses of dissonance, always needed in suspense sequences, and in horror, thriller, and science fiction genres. However, due to fluctuations within the movie business, these composers could quickly run short of money, forcing them to end their studies with Schoenberg.

Starting in April 1935 Oscar Levant was among the first Hollywood composers to take private lessons with Schoenberg.[69] Thereafter, Alfred Newman, music director at Twentieth Century-Fox, orchestrator Edward Powell (both May 1936), songwriter Ralph Rainger (June 1936), composer David Raksin (December 1936), and lyricist Leo Robin (January 1937) followed his example. Under Schoenberg's guidance, Levant composed a Piano Concerto (1936), a String Quartet (1937), and a *Nocturne* for orchestra that was premiered in a 1937 Federal Music Project concert with Schoenberg's *Pelleas*.[70] Levant made ample use of dissonance in all three works. He later recalled that Schoenberg taught him "that modernism is not merely a matter of hitting the keys with your elbow and seeing what happens," but that "it is logical, and formed with an orderly, if unconventional, development."[71] Schoenberg enjoyed tutoring Levant not only because of his wit, but also because of his compositional gift. He praised him as a "very talented young American composer" in letters to his daughter, Adolph Weiss, and Elizabeth Coolidge. He even envisioned Levant as his teaching assistant.[72]

When UCLA had to replace its recently deceased composition professor Theodore Stearns in spring 1936, Klemperer immediately urged its president Robert Sproul to hire Schoenberg, calling him "undoubtedly the most important among contemporary musicians."[73] Vern Knudsen was crucial in UCLA's hiring of Schoenberg. Dean of graduate studies and a member of the search committee, he was interviewing candidates for the post on the East Coast, and upon learning of Schoenberg's presence in Los Angeles from pianist Maurice Zam, he immediately initiated job negotiations with him.[74] Soon UCLA offered Schoenberg a full-time professorship with tenure and retirement benefits at an annual salary of $4,800 (about $73,500 in 2009). Schoenberg accepted, although he had unrealistically expected to get more than twice as much. His salary later increased to $5,100 in 1939 and to $5,400 in 1942. USC also hoped to hire him with Alchin funds at an annual salary of $3,000 (about $46,000 in 2009) for part-time teaching in the following academic year. But USC at that time did not offer tenure and retirement benefits to its music faculty, which Schoenberg deemed important.[75]

While UCLA, a state university, seemed to be in slightly better financial shape than the private USC, its music division was academically weaker than that of USC.[76] Its music faculty, for instance, did not include a musicologist until 1938, when Robert Nelson and Walter Rubsamen were hired.[77] The Master of Arts degree was established in 1940. The UCLA music library was set up in 1942, two years before Schoenberg retired. A Ph.D. degree was first granted in 1949. The department chair during Schoenberg's tenure was Leroy Allen, a trumpet player and band director, who hoped Schoenberg would bring prestige to the department.[78] Yet he asked him to teach courses offering students of all college levels the required credits toward Bachelor's and Master's degrees.[79] Non–music majors from other departments sometimes registered for his classes as well. Teaching students with widely varying levels of ability, Schoenberg was also assuming a workload much higher than that of USC: between four and seven classes per semester, most of them to be taught two hours a week. The classes were much larger, too.[80] Therefore, Schoenberg divided his classes in counterpoint, harmony, form and analysis, and composition into elementary and advanced sections and recruited some of his strongest students as assistants to instruct the weaker ones. In later years he taught only upper-division courses: "Harmonic Construction" (or "Structural Functions of Harmony"), "Double Counterpoint, Canon and Fugue," "Form and Analysis," "Special Studies," "Orchestration," and "Advanced Composition."

His first teaching assistants at UCLA were Strang (1936–38) and Stein (1939–42), the latter of whom earned Bachelor of Arts and Master of Music degrees at UCLA. Dika Newlin and Harold Halma served as Schoenberg's unofficial personal assistants in the early 1940s. A child prodigy, Newlin was fifteen when she enrolled in his classes in 1938, probably his youngest composition student.[81] Under his guidance, she set poems by A. E. Housman, Hsu Hun, Sara Teasdale and Franz Werfel, and composed a sonata, a serenade, a piano quintet, and a string quartet. In 1941 she completed her master's degree in composition under Schoenberg and only four years later her Ph.D. in musicology at Columbia University with the dissertation "Bruckner, Mahler, Schoenberg" under Paul Henry Lang (Figure 6.2).[82] This study was the first of Newlin's many publications on Schoenberg's life and work. In 1945 she began her teaching career as a professor at Western Maryland College, championing Schoenberg's music and ideas as a composer and performer. Strang, Stein, and Newlin were among Schoenberg's most talented students and also served as his editors.[83] Halma was an excellent student in Schoenberg's 1941–42 classes and

FIGURE 6.2.
Newlin and her book *Bruckner, Mahler, Schoenberg* (1947). From *Schoenberg Remembered* by Dika Newlin (New York: Pendragon, 1980). Used by permission.

became one of his unofficial assistants in the following year to prepare for an official assistantship (Figure 6.3).[84] During Schoenberg's leave of absence from December 21, 1942, to January 4, 1943, Halma taught his eighty-two students in "Form and Analysis," "Advanced Counterpoint," and "Composition and Special Studies.".[85] But in the summer of 1943 he left for New York City and turned to professional photography. Having made beautiful photographs of Schoenberg, he became most famous for his 1947 picture of Truman Capote *en odalisque*.[86] Clara Silvers served as one of Schoenberg's last assistants from 1943 to 1944, the year she received her master's degree in music theory.[87] On Schoenberg's advice she studied piano with Edward Steuermann, whom she married in 1949. Silvers Steuermann advocated Schoenberg's music as a pianist, editor, and festival organizer, and was archivist of the Arnold Schoenberg Institute from 1975 until her untimely death in 1982.

Several other Schoenberg students at UCLA also developed remarkable careers and deserve special mention. Having taken one private and three USC classes with Schoenberg, Cage enrolled in Schoenberg's courses in harmony and counterpoint at UCLA in the fall of 1936.[88] But Schoenberg's harmony class, in which more than fifty mostly freshmen students were expected to write "choral-school-forms" and use the German *Harmonielehre*, prompted Cage to stop studying with him. Interested in exploring unconventional pitch relationships and encouraged by Cowell to become active in "his chosen field of creation," Cage soon provocatively claimed that he had "no feeling for harmony."[89] Cage turned to all-percussion music and, from 1950 on, to chance-based composition, but he held Schoenberg, who had critiqued and commended his class work, in high regard. Shortly before Cage died, he even returned to Schoenberg's *Harmonielehre*, which arguably influenced harmonic aspects of his last works.[90] Much has been made of Schoenberg's alleged description of Cage as "an inventor of genius—not a composer" (related to Cage by Peter Yates

FIGURE 6.3.
Arnold Schoenberg and Harold Halma. Courtesy Belmont Music Publishers.

in 1953), raising the question whether Schoenberg recognized Cage as a composer. Yet in 1950, when Schoenberg expressed his appreciation for six "unselfish" and "noble" composers granting priority to his recording projects, he listed Cage among them.[91]

Another unusual artist, who followed his music studies at Columbia Teachers College with Schoenberg's UCLA classes in the fall of 1939, was Cage's friend and pioneer of percussion music William Russell (Russell William Wagner). Russell recalled how Schoenberg, after looking at his Fugue for 8 Percussion Instruments (1932), published in *New Music Edition* in 1933, "had a few kind words to say about it."[92] Russell came to Schoenberg to satisfy his appetite for thorough musical training. After studying analysis, counterpoint, and harmony with him, he soon decided to give up composition and devote himself to jazz scholarship and performance in New Orleans.[93] As a token of gratitude, however, Russell published a memoir about his experience in Schoenberg's classes in *Tempo* (1940), in which he praised Schoenberg as "the world's greatest teacher of musical theory and composition."[94]

Following the example of his friends Cage, Halma, and Russell, Lou Harrison went to study with Schoenberg in spring 1943 (Figure 6.4). Harrison had heard Schoenberg conduct his own music at the 1935 New Music Society concert and the

FIGURE 6.4.
Lou Harrison. Courtesy Lou Harrison Estate.

1937 FMP Orchestra concert in San Francisco, and he devoured Schoenberg scores at San Francisco's Public Library.[95] During his studies with Cowell in the mid-1930s, Harrison had not only analyzed Schoenberg's Woodwind Quintet but also experimented with dodecaphony.[96] Thanks to Halma's intervention and Schoenberg's approval of samples from Harrison's prolific early work, he was able to enroll in a small weekly UCLA composition seminar with three or four students.[97] Harrison greatly benefited from Schoenberg's lessons and proudly remembered when he brought his published Saraband and Prelude for Grandpiano (*New Music Quarterly*, 1938) to class, and Schoenberg asked the others: "Why do you not bring me such music?"[98] Having moved to Los Angeles in August 1942 to work for Lester Horton's dance company, Harrison decided to follow the group when they relocated to New York in 1943. When he bade Schoenberg farewell after only six months, Schoenberg advised him: "You are going for fame and fortune. Good luck. And, do not study anymore—only Mozart."[99] Soon thereafter Schoenberg gave Harrison an inscribed copy of Birthday Canons and singled him out as one of the most promising young American composers.[100] Harrison confided in a 1944 letter to Schoenberg: "No person has given me so much confidence in myself and I have had much need since then, in the face of fads and fashions, of just that intense and real belief in the importance of honesty towards oneself and honesty towards the art which I profess that you seemed to give me."[101]

Earl Kim and Leon Kirchner were also among Schoenberg's UCLA students and developed remarkable careers as composers and teachers. Both had attended Los Angeles City College before taking Schoenberg's 1940–41 music theory classes, and thereafter both studied with Sessions at Berkeley and joined Harvard's music faculty.[102] Enrolled in "Structural Functions of Harmony," Kim remembered that this class had about forty students. Although he never attended any of Schoenberg's composition classes, he showed him some of his music on one of his visits in the 1940s. He also had an in-depth discussion of Schoenberg's Piano Concerto, which Kim had to introduce in one of Sessions's classes.[103] Shortly before Schoenberg's death, Kim and the violinist Nathan Rubin performed the *Phantasy* at Schoenberg's home, receiving valuable feedback from Schoenberg.[104] Kirchner had discovered Schoenberg through his piano teachers Buhlig and Crown and through Strang's *Pierrot* guest lecture at Los Angeles City College. Like Kim, Kirchner fondly recalled Schoenberg's classes, especially "Structural Functions of Harmony," admiring the depth of his harmonic analyses and his exacting language.[105] Kirchner stayed in touch with Schoenberg after his brief studies at UCLA and always declared that Schoenberg had made the strongest impact on his development as a composer. Resisting fashionable musical trends, Kirchner followed his artistic belief in a self-expression attuned to the continuity of musical tradition.

Thanks to Stein's intervention, the fledgling Berlin-born composer Peter Jona Korn, who had taken lessons from Stefan Wolpe in Palestine and come to America in 1940, was allowed to take classes with Schoenberg in 1941–42. Refusing Schoenberg's prescribed and in his view unreasonable five-year regimen of strict counterpoint studies, Korn continued his training with Toch, Eisler, and Miklos Rózsa.[106] Later Korn, a conservative composer, turned vehemently, if unconvincingly, against Schoenberg, modernism, and avant-garde music in his 1975 book *Musikalische Umweltverschmutzung* (Musical Pollution).

At UCLA Schoenberg also tutored such noted pianists as Emil Danenberg, Nathalie Limonick, and Warren Langlie, who promoted and performed his music widely. Danenberg took several classes with Schoenberg when earning a B.A. (1942) and M.A. (1944) at UCLA. While embarking on an international career as concert pianist, in 1944 he joined the music faculty of Oberlin College, where he later became the Conservatory's dean (1971–74) and the college's president (1975–81). Limonick enrolled in one of Schoenberg's last UCLA classes in 1944 and, after his retirement, in his small private seminars at his home. Limonick has been described as one of Schoenberg's most talented and engaged students.[107] Chair of the opera departments at UCLA and USC, she was a sought-after accompanist of such singers as Elly Ameling and Marni Nixon and one of the first women to coach singers at Wagner Festivals in Bayreuth in the 1950s. Langlie was one of Schoenberg's most faithful American students (although initially trained by Boulanger). He studied with Schoenberg from 1940 through 1950, both at UCLA and privately. Langlie also conducted lengthy interviews with Schoenberg and even made wire-recordings of some of his seminars as well as a piano reduction of excerpts from *Gurrelieder* for Erika Stiedry-Wagner.[108] In 1960 he completed a Ph.D. dissertation at UCLA on "Schoenberg as a Teacher." He further distinguished himself as a fine pianist in California.

Noted musicologists and theorists, such as Leonard Ratner and Patricia Carpenter, were also fostered by Schoenberg at UCLA, even though he tended not to hold musicologists in high esteem. Ratner was initially active as both a composer and musicologist and briefly studied with Schoenberg in the late 1930s. Inspired by Schoenberg, he explored new ways of analyzing the role of harmony and periodicity in late eighteenth-century and early nineteenth-century music. Under the guidance of Manfred Bukofzer, Ratner earned the first Ph.D. degree in music at Berkeley in

1949. He led a distinguished career as scholar and teacher at Stanford University. Carpenter studied with Schoenberg on the advice of her piano teacher Ruth Slenczynska and was among the few American Schoenberg students who, like his European pupils Berg and Webern, worked with Schoenberg over a long period of time.[109] She enrolled in all his UCLA courses in analysis, counterpoint, harmony, orchestration, and composition (1942–44), and also took individual lessons and attended private classes until 1949. In 1944 Carpenter gave, along with university organist Lawrence Petran, one of the earliest performances of Schoenberg's Piano Concerto in a version for two pianos. In that year she earned a master's degree under Schoenberg and in 1971 a Ph.D. in musicology at Columbia University. The first woman to give a keynote address to the Society for Music Theory, Carpenter was a highly respected scholar and passionate teacher of music theory at Barnard College and Columbia University (1961–89). She handed down Schoenberg's teaching to several generations of music theorists, many of whom have devoted themselves to Schoenberg research.[110]

Other students of Schoenberg's at UCLA entered folk and popular music. Lou Gottlieb studied with Schoenberg in the early 1940s.[111] After completing a dissertation on the Cyclic Masses of Trent Codex 89 at Berkeley in 1958, he co-founded the folk music group The Limeliters and became a highly successful "new comedy" performer. Skitch Henderson and John Scott Trotter both frequented Schoenberg's UCLA classes. A celebrated radio and television entertainer, Henderson led the "Tonight Show" band on TV in the 1950s and 1960s, and founded and directed the New York Pops in 1983. Trotter worked as musical director for Bing Crosby and the Charlie Brown cartoon specials.

During his eight-year tenure at UCLA Schoenberg continued to teach private students. There were strikes in Hollywood studios in 1937, and he instructed fewer film composers from 1938 on, according to his date books. As a result his supplementary income substantially decreased.[112] Vocal-music composer Serge Hovey, who researched, arranged, and recorded the extensive folk-song collection of Robert Burns, sought instruction from Schoenberg in 1937. From 1938 through 1939 Schoenberg taught Francis Burkley, a composer whom he held in high esteem, recommending him to Alfred Newman for a position in the film studios.[113] A faculty member of Juilliard in the 1930s, Burkley later became a Catholic priest and served as music director of the Old St. Patrick's Church in New Orleans in the 1950s and 1960s.[114] In the summer of 1942 Canadian composer Jean Coulthard, a former student of Vaughan Williams, took lessons with Schoenberg. Impressed by her music, he even recommended some of her works for publication at Schirmer.[115] In 1943 Serge Frank became his private student and later assisted him as a translator and editor.[116] There were also several students from Schoenberg's UCLA classes, including Simon Carfagno, Don Estep, Langlie, and Newlin, who took individual lessons with him in the late 1930s and 1940s.[117]

Schoenberg's individual lessons were expensive. In the late 1930s and early 1940s he charged a fee of $70 (about $1,000 in 2008) for four lessons per month, or $120–$130 for eight lessons per month.[118] After his retirement in 1944 Schoenberg had teaching appointments as visiting professor at the University of Chicago in May 1946 and at the Academy of the West in Carpinteria near Santa Barbara in the summer of 1948, earning $1,200 (about $10,600 in 2009). But he relied more than ever on private teaching. Having worked at UCLA for only eight years, he received the small monthly pension of $28.50 (about $345 in 2009), which increased to $40.38 in March 1945 (about $480 in 2009). Schoenberg, who had expected to obtain his full salary in retirement and had generously supported relatives and friends from Europe, had not set aside funds for a time of need.[119] For this reason he decided to sell manuscripts of his music and to charge, from 1944 on, $50 (about $600 in 2009) per lesson. His prices, however, fluctuated. In 1946 he charged $50 (about $550 in 2009) for a preliminary interview and $250 for two lessons weekly.[120] Yet as Carpenter remembered, he gave the financially underprivileged young professionals a discount or offered them a job at his house. When in the late 1940s Carpenter told Schoenberg that she had to discontinue her lessons for lack of money, he asked her: "'Miss Carpenter, you are one of my oldest students. What can you do? Can you type?'" Replying "Yes, I can type," she soon found herself at his home typing his letters, but also discovered that another penniless student was "washing the dog, and somebody was washing the car, and somebody was helping Mrs. Schoenberg peel tomatoes."[121]

Schoenberg's students after 1944 included Carpenter, the noted photographer and composer Alfred Carlson, Langlie, Limonick, and Stein, who had already taken instruction from him at UCLA. He also attracted such new pupils as H. Endicott Hanson; José Vélez; Richard Hoffmann; the renowned pianists Jacob Lateiner and Rosalyn Tureck; Schoenberg's former UCLA colleague, musicologist Robert U. Nelson; and the composers Roger Nixon and Leonard Rosenman.[122] Hoffmann, a distant relative of Schoenberg from New Zealand, joined the Schoenberg household in 1947 and became one of his last private composition students, serving as his teaching assistant and secretary.[123]

Langlie, Nixon, and Tureck may have been among Schoenberg's most affluent later students. Langlie took private lessons from c. 1941. According to Carpenter, he may have paid the lion's share of the later seminars.[124] Nixon, a talented pupil of Sessions and Bloch, later became noted for his band compositions. He took individual lessons with Schoenberg from July through mid-September 1948, paying a monthly fee of $150 (about $1,320 in 2009) for two one-hour lessons a week. The lessons, however, always lasted twice as long.[125] Although Nixon did not officially enroll at the Music Academy of the West, he attended all of Schoenberg's lectures (many of which were published in *Style and Idea*) and continued his private lessons with him there. He also helped Schoenberg market the latest recordings of his works.[126] Vélez took instruction in 1947 for a monthly fee of $250 (about $2,375 in 2009) for two lessons per week.[127] Tureck had lessons from Schoenberg in August and September 1949, for which she paid between $100 and $200 [(about $890 and $1,780 in 2009).[128] Manus Sasonkin, a composer, pianist, and harpist who later taught at the University of Alberta, however, paid only $25 (about $220 in 2009) per lesson in 1950.[129] How much pianist Jacob Lateiner paid for his lessons is unknown. But in 1950, when he went to Los Angeles from New York to fulfill his "life-long dream" to study with Schoenberg, he indicated that he struggled to pay his fees.[130]

Besides individual lessons, Schoenberg taught small analysis classes with around ten students, which were organized by Carpenter and Limonick and took place at his home. For the ten two- to three-hour meetings on Sunday mornings, Schoenberg charged a flat fee of $500 (about $4,750 in 2009), to be divided among the participants. When Limonick set up the first seminar for the summer of 1947, Schoenberg raved that her group "reminds me with pleasure of a number of my best pupils in UCLA whose talent and devotion to our subjects made teaching worthwhile to me."[131] The first Sunday class included Carpenter, Langlie, Limonick, Hanson, and Rosenman. The last-named would later gain fame for scoring two James

FIGURE 6.5.
Arnold Schoenberg teaching private classes. *Front row, from left:* Natalie Limonick, H. Endicott Hanson, and Alfred Carlson. Photo by Richard Fish. Courtesy Arnold Schönberg Center.

Dean films, *East of Eden* and *Rebel Without a Cause*. When the seminar ended, another one was organized: "We all liked it so well that another one seemed in order," recalled Limonick, "The class kept going that way; as soon as one seminar was completed, we'd start another." She remembered that Schoenberg focused on musical form and analysis, and "tried out his well-known counterpoint text and others he was working on, on us."[132]

Schoenberg's last such seminar took place on eleven Sunday mornings between October 24, 1948, and January 9, 1949. Against his usual custom, he focused on theme-and-variation forms in his own works. Hoffmann served as Schoenberg's assistant and played a recording when asked. When needed, Limonick and Stein performed musical excerpts at the piano. Other attendees included Carlson, Carpenter, Hanson, Langlie, and Nelson; both Carpenter and Nelson captured details of this class in interviews and articles.[133] A famous photograph by Richard Fish provides a snapshot of this class, showing Schoenberg seated next to a big easel with large sheets of self-made music paper (Figure 6.5).

Schoenberg's Teaching Philosophy, Subjects, and Methods

Schoenberg's teaching philosophy was based on his lofty vision of an artist. He believed that artists and teachers of the arts had a moral responsibility to serve as role models and show integrity and the utmost devotion to their art.[134] According to Schoenberg, true artists displayed craftsmanship steeped in the classical masterpieces, conceived evolutionary musical ideas (*musikalische Gedanken*) through inspiration, and worked them out organically and logically. True artists distinguished themselves, in his view, from composers of neo-classical and cheap popular music, which he perceived to be put together mechanically and superficially "in the manner a cook would deliver recipes."[135] Hence one of Schoenberg's main motivations as a teacher was "to break" the strong Franco-Russian neo-classicist influence on American music so that "the real talents of the Americans be allowed to develop freely."[136]

Schoenberg's most important point of reference in his teaching was an admittedly limited body of works by such Austro-German composers as Bach, Mozart, Beethoven, Schubert, Brahms, Wagner, Bruckner, and Mahler—in his view the "loftiest models that have been granted to us."[137] Competing with the music of other nations, this canon legitimized his compositional genealogy and development, and served as a moral reference for critical judgment of his American students. Schoenberg introduced them to what he considered timeless hidden laws and evolutionary tendencies in this repertoire. In understanding and mastering these "universal" compositional techniques, his students would, like Schoenberg himself, ideally be able to create sophisticated music rooted in the past and connected to the present. He taught his students, according to Kim, greatly to respect "something that has been created which is a masterpiece."[138] The core works of Schoenberg's canon included Bach's *Art of the Fugue*; Haydn's and Mozart's string quartets (especially Mozart's "Haydn Quartets"), symphonies, and piano works; Beethoven's Symphonies Nos. 2, 3, 4 and 9, string quartets (above all op. 18), piano sonatas, and the thirty-two Piano Variations in C minor; Schubert's piano trios and quintets; and Brahms's Symphonies Nos. 1, 3 and 4, and chamber music for strings and piano. Occasionally Schoenberg discussed music examples by Mendelssohn, Wagner, Liszt, Bruckner, Mahler, and Richard Strauss, and touched on such "non-German" composers as Berlioz, Verdi, Debussy, Ravel, and Sibelius. While categorizing Verdi as a "great composer," and "admiring" Ravel, however, he oddly lumped Mendelssohn, Berlioz, Liszt, and Sibelius together as second-rank composers.[139] He planned a class on modern counterpoint involving examples by Wagner, Brahms, Mahler, Debussy, Reger, and himself, but nothing came of it.[140]

Schoenberg discussed some of his own compositions in class as well, although he most often focused on his nondodecaphonic works.[141] In his Boston classes he spoke about *Pelleas* (as it was performed there in March 1934), the Two Ballads, op. 12, Five Orchestral Pieces, and his Handel arrangement. He thoroughly analyzed his First Quartet, showing the students his sketches for this work. Knight reported him saying that "it was perhaps the tenth he had written, but the first he considered worth publishing."[142] Newlin, too, testified that her "Special Studies" class in spring 1939 covered this quartet and that Schoenberg enjoyed pointing out its subtleties.[143] Harrison remembered how in 1943 Schoenberg showed his class "how easy it was to write" the First Quartet.[144] Occasionally Schoenberg also illuminated his didactic Suite in G, especially when it was premiered in Los Angeles in May 1935. Cage raved: "There is nothing old about it. Although it begins with an Overture (Prelude and Fugue) the whole 'idea' is basically a new concept of fugue."[145] Schoenberg analyzed the Suite in a 1939 "Special Studies" course, prompting Newlin to praise the work's first movement: "It is a remarkable piece of constructive contrapuntal technique, of the greatest strictness and yet far from lacking interest aside from that of a mathematical problem."[146] Newlin also observed that Schoenberg assigned one student to arrange his Suite's "Minuet" for two pianos, and that Stein created a four-hand version of its Overture with Schoenberg's approval.[147] At UCLA and in private lessons Schoenberg used his Eight Songs, op. 6, First Chamber Symphony, Second Quartet, *Pierrot*, and his Bach and Handel arrangements to explain orchestration issues.[148]

From time to time, Schoenberg gave in to his students' petitions for a taste of the "forbidden fruit," introducing them to his dodecaphonic works. Upon the request of his private class in spring 1935, he illuminated his Third Quartet, for which occasion all the students had purchased the score. Alderman recalled that the class "lived and breathed the third quartet for several weeks—until we could sing the 'row' and the themes by heart."[149] Cage had a similar experience, writing to a friend: "I had another unusual dream. I heard the entire III String Quartet in my sleep."[150] At UCLA Schoenberg guest-lectured on dodecaphony in his colleagues' classes, and in some courses touched on his Serenade, Suite, op. 29, and *Three Satires*.[151] Sometimes he even chose twelve-tone works to clarify aspects of variation and counterpoint. In his very last private seminar (October 1948 to January 1949), he focused on his own twelve-tone and non–twelve-tone variation-based works: the Orchestral Variations, Organ Variations, Band Variations, and variation movements of his Second Quartet, Serenade, and Suite, op. 29.[152]

Schoenberg rarely discussed other contemporary music, and if Hindemith's, Stravinsky's, or Krenek's names were mentioned, he generally disassociated himself from them. He criticized Hindemith's and Stravinsky's "use of old-fashioned pseudo-contrapuntal rhythmic figures with 'modernistic' intervals" and, according to Newlin, "thought little" of Stravinsky's Piano Sonata, after Stein had performed it in class, "except for the second theme of the Adagietto."[153] Schoenberg also disapproved of Krenek's provision of rules of thumb for dodecaphonic composition in his 1940 manual *Studies in Counterpoint*.[154]

As Schoenberg considered himself first and foremost a composer and teacher of the craft of composition, and only secondarily a theorist, he taught form and analysis, harmony, counterpoint, and orchestration based on his personal canon as necessary tools for composition and not as self-sufficient theoretical disciplines. Indeed, he taught all of his students—regardless of their level, creative talent, and specialization—compositional skills and thinking in music. He even suggested that it was possible to instruct the most mediocre students in composition and that his pragmatic approach would make them "understand the game" and its "fine points" better than music-appreciation or basic ear-training classes could:

> One often hears the question, "Why teach composition to people who will never try it again after their student days are over, people who have neither creative ability nor creative impulse, for whom it is a nightmare to have to express something in an idiom quite foreign to their minds?" The answer is this: just as almost anyone can be trained to draw, paint, write an essay or deliver a lecture, it must also be possible to make people with even less than mediocre gifts use the means of musical composition in a sensitive manner.[155]

Recognizing "an extraordinarily large amount of talent, inventive ability and originality" among many of his students, Schoenberg felt that America needed "not so much new methods of music, as men of character" equipped with the "courage to express what they feel and think," despite the temptations of materialism and commercialism.[156] Determined to "fortify the morale of his students," Schoenberg was "unrelenting in his demands upon the students." He exposed them to rigorous criticism and taught them to use critical judgment and self-criticism.[157] Schoenberg held all his American students to the highest standards. Determined to prevent the promotion of "superficially instructed" parvenus with "commonplace talents" that lessen compositional standards, he felt that one of his "greatest merits" was the way he discouraged most of his pupils from becoming professional composers.[158] Students like Cage were astonished to hear their teacher say: "My purpose in teaching you is to make it impossible for you to write music."[159] Yet Schoenberg argued: "I find such who need encouragement must be discouraged, because only such should compose to whom creation is a 'must,' a necessity, a passion, such as would not stop composing if they were discouraged a 1000 times."[160] Both Cage and Newlin have remarked on Schoenberg's rigorous teaching style. Cage recalled: "In all the time I studied with Schoenberg, he never once led me to believe that my work was distinguished in any way."[161] Elsewhere he recounted: "If I followed the rules too strictly he would say, 'Why don't you take a little more liberty?' and then when I would break the rules, he'd say, 'Why do you break the rules?'"[162] Similarly, Newlin remembered: "He picked on the Andante of my Serenade; didn't like the theme; these sixths did not liquidate, but only annoyed; that chunk of Brahms had no excuse for cropping up; these syncopations were cheap."[163]

Form and Analysis

Musical analysis was a part of Schoenberg's holistic approach to teaching; he often combined analysis, harmony, counterpoint, and orchestration. In America he taught classes with a focus on the analysis of selected works, and he included in his harmony, counterpoint, orchestration, and composition courses analysis to show how the masters solved certain compositional "problems."[164] "Analyze," Schoenberg urged his students in Boston: "It is the only reason most composers are so helpless, because they know only what they hear, and not also the fundamental construction which you can know only by studying the works themselves."[165]

Through analysis Schoenberg conveyed his views about ideal structures of musical works, representing a unified organic whole marked by unity, variety, contrast, and a concisely and logically presented, all-pervading evolutionary musical idea (*musikalischer Gedanke*). "[Musical] Logic is an important thing with the Austrian composer," noted Bestor Kelley, "the lack of logic—of the power to bring out and develop all the potentialities of a simple musical idea—is to Schoenberg the greatest fault of young composers today."[166] In his early American years Schoenberg worked on a treatise on this subject, *The Musical Idea, and the Logic, Technique and Art of Its Presentation,* which was later co-edited and published by his long-term student Carpenter and her student Severine Neff.[167] Other universally valid concepts Schoenberg covered included basic shape (*Grundgestalt*), developing variation, and liquidation. A *basic shape* can be defined as a fundamental, recurring, and unifying musical unit often embracing more than one motive.[168] It is closely connected to the principle of developing variation in that it is subjected to variation. *Developing variation* transcends the merely ornamental variety by gradually weaving in new ideas: "introducing as much new material as possible, material which, though new, has subtly grown out of the material preceding it, related to the idea as a whole," as Knight described it.[169] *Liquidation* denotes a special variation technique, the "gradual elimination of characteristic features [of a motif or theme], until only uncharacteristic ones remain, which no longer demand a continuation."[170] Such a process allows for organically rounding off a theme or section.

Schoenberg provided a novel analytical understanding of such traditional melodic components as "period" and "sentence" and of sonata form. He suggested that, unlike the period's closed antecedent-consequent structure, the sentence was a "higher form of construction than the period," arguing: "It not only makes a statement of an idea, but at once starts a kind of development."[171] As to sonata form, he believed that "the development starts in the first or second measures immediately," and hence proposed to consider the exposition part of the "development." As Newlin recounted, "There is where the themes are really developed!!"[172] For the commonly called "development" section, he suggested the term "elaboration," as "little development (in the sense of growth, maturation, evolution) takes place in the material used."[173]

Many students remembered how meticulously Schoenberg examined classical works. His analysis of Beethoven sonatas, said Cage, "was so detailed and revealing that we never got very far along in even the one Sonata [No. 31 in A-flat, op. 110]."[174] To Wells, Schoenberg's Beethoven analyses were like a "treasure hunt to discover all the ramifications of motive force in thematic, rhythmic, and harmonic structure."[175] Yet his analyses were not at all pedantic, as Alderman noted, because he always stayed focused on the main point of his rationale.[176]

When Schoenberg taught advanced students, he allowed them to study pieces of their own choice. Nixon once brought in Bartók's *Petite Suite* for piano (1936), and Schoenberg let him analyze the first movement's motivic structure (variation, extension, development, phrase formations, contrapuntal relations), adding to Nixon's sightings until every note in the piece was accounted for. To Nixon, such lessons were marked by a "sense of mutual discovery." Schoenberg, who had been unfamiliar with the Suite, concluded at the end of that lesson: "Bartók was a real master."[177]

Harmony

Although Schoenberg had been asked to teach harmony in Boston, he offered his first American course on this subject in his first semester at UCLA. Before that, he had integrated harmony into his form and analysis, counterpoint, and composition classes, even though he did not believe in "teaching harmony and composition concurrently." Newlin cited Schoenberg's reasons: "The compositions you'd write while just learning would be Czerny exercises harmonically, and what would be the meaning of that?"[178] Schoenberg's first American harmony class, however, was frustrating for himself and many of his fifty-six, mostly first-year students who were supposed to use *Harmonielehre* as a textbook, but who could neither read German nor, at $28 (about $430 in 2009) per copy, afford to buy it.[179] Thanks to Strang's assistance, Schoenberg was able to provide music examples on handouts, and corrected the many practical exercises required for this class in a timely fashion.

Cage studied in this class and seemed disappointed with the use of "choral-school-forms," but Schoenberg built on his *Harmonielehre* in which he challenged old methods in several ways.[180] Instead of harmonizing a figured bass line or existing chorale melody, he required his students to conceive harmonic progressions from scratch, because he felt "harmonizing given melodies is in contradiction to the process of composition" as "a composer invents melody and harmony simultaneously."[181] In this and subsequent advanced harmony classes, Schoenberg taught fundamental harmonic principles based on Simon Sechter's degree method, unique concepts discussed in his *Harmonielehre* (1911), and additional new ideas. One important concept was "monotonality." Connected to the idea of organic relatedness, monotonality implies that one single tonality is seen as the center of a piece and that digressions from there to other scale degrees are regarded as movements to so-called "regions" (subordinate to the tonal center). Through the concept of monotonality, Schoenberg was able to explain harmony in terms of its *structural functions* within a piece and to present uses of extended tonality as unified wholes. He explained: "Every digression from the tonic is considered to be still within the tonality, whether directly or indirectly, closely or remotely related."[182]

At UCLA Schoenberg developed a new advanced course called "Structural Functions of Harmony," which he, assisted by Stein, offered for the first time in fall 1939.[183] Focusing on constructive functions of harmony, Schoenberg used both his own examples and excerpts from his classical canon to "illustrate and clarify every problem."[184] The course involved analysis and practical exercises. Kim attended this class in spring 1941 and marveled at Schoenberg's ability to "slap an entire Brahms quartet all over the board from memory, zip zap, the way you'd dash off a shopping list," and then ask the class "'Now, dell me about the superdonic.'" According to Kim, Schoenberg spent six weeks explaining the harmonic functions of the supertonic.[185] Carpenter recalled: "We started out with modulations and then there would be problems that had to do with the harmonic structure of formal functions, such as write the harmony for a contrasting middle section, or the harmony for a modulatory transition or for a Scherzo and middle section."[186]

While slowly working toward an English translation of *Harmonielehre* for use in his classes, Schoenberg clarified previously developed ideas based on his experience of teaching American students, eventually leading to a new book, titled after his course, *Structural Functions of Harmony*.[187] Planned in the early 1940s and, with the help of Stein, completed in 1948, this volume was published posthumously in 1954 and is Schoenberg's last comprehensive reflection on tonal harmony. Although *Structural Functions* draws from *Harmonielehre*, it differs in including a refinement of such ideas as monotonality and regions (illustrated by a "Chart of Regions"), and contains analytical remarks on examples from classical-music literature.[188] *Structural Functions* is also devoid of the speculative, philosophical, and polemical comments found throughout *Harmonielehre*, and is thus a more concise and pragmatic tool for fledgling composers.

As mentioned earlier, a translation of *Harmonielehre*'s abbreviated version was prepared and published by Schoenberg's student Adams in 1948. Although it was too late for Schoenberg to use this text in his lessons, he was convinced that "Americans need to learn harmony and write it," and that "this book is what Americans need."[189] It took another thirty years until Roy E. Carter's English translation of the unabridged version of *Harmonielehre* appeared for the first time in print.[190]

Counterpoint

Schoenberg's Chautauqua student Bestor Kelley testified that counterpoint was, "next to logic, the object of Schoenberg's strongest emphasis" and that he regarded American students as "not as thoroughly grounded in counterpoint as they are in Europe." Yet Schoenberg never taught counterpoint systematically in Boston, New York, or Chautauqua.[191] In spring 1935 he privately offered his first explicit counterpoint course and continued to teach this subject at USC and UCLA on a regular basis at both elementary and advanced levels. This focus on teaching the craft of "true" counterpoint seems to have been in part Schoenberg's ethical and aesthetic reaction against what he perceived as the promotion of "quasi-counterpoint" by Hugo Riemann and others; it also opposed the widespread use of what he jokingly termed "Rhabarber counterpoint" in neo-classical works of Boulanger-trained composers. This type of "quasi-counterpoint" is based on a preconceived harmonic progression, and the movements of the parts are manipulated to suggest the effect of counterpoint (whereas for Schoenberg, "harmony is achieved through the intelligent motion of independent parts").[192] According to Newlin and Raksin, Schoenberg derived the term "Rhabarber counterpoint" from "the German theatre where extras would yell 'Rhabarber' (rhubarb) over and over again to give the effect of a large crowd."[193]

Schoenberg viewed counterpoint not as a theory, but as a method of training composers in "thinking systematically," "developing a sense of rhythm and melodic balance," in the disciplines of listening to, and thinking of, several lines simultaneously, and in the fluency of part writing.[194] Determined to introduce students to "very artistic and compositional principles," he devised his own rules "as concisely as possible, in the positive, not in the negative," because he felt that "advice given to a student in the negative tends to nullify his creative ability."[195] Russell recalled that Schoenberg often questioned rules and believed they "can never express all that is right." "Only the ear," he declared, "can be the final guide."[196] Schoenberg's counterpoint classes involved practical exercises, application of counterpoint to free composition, and analysis.[197]

In his introductory counterpoint class Schoenberg taught species counterpoint in two, three, and four voices. Cage attended his first counterpoint course and provided glimpses into Schoenberg's workshop. After the class completed the "five species of 2-part writing and working on mixed species," he wrote, it proceeded to "3-part counterpoint, first species, second species (a) with one moving voice and (b) with two moving voices, and third species (syncopation—which, by the way, is fourth species in most textbooks) with one voice only in syncopes."[198] Elsewhere Cage noted that Schoenberg preferred a specific cantus firmus (C, D, F, E, D, C).[199] According to Langlie, Schoenberg required students to write all their (generally short) exercises in always differing combinations of old clefs to prepare them for reading early music and transposing instruments.[200] Langlie, Russell, and Stein commented on Schoenberg's emphasis on dissonance treatment and its allowed types, the passing note, accented passing note, cambiata (and its inversions), and suspension (and its interrupted resolution), which Schoenberg termed "conventionalized formulas," believing that they originated in ornamentation.[201] Teaching species counterpoint only in the major and minor modes, he used the concept of "neutralization" in the minor mode to avoid cross-relations and an arbitrary use of accidentals as well as the principles of monotonality and tonal regions.[202] He also conceived exercises without cantus firmus, featuring instead cadences, modulations, imitations, and canons to direct students toward a compositional application of the learned subject matter.

Schoenberg's experience of teaching counterpoint to American students led to his textbook *Preliminary Exercises in Counterpoint*, which he began with the aid of Strang in 1936 and continued, in collaboration with Stein, in 1942–46 and 1948–50, when he prepared most of the materials for the volume.[203] Stein completed and edited the book for posthumous publication in 1963. Intended as a method rather than a theory for future composers, the volume falls into three parts, covering counterpoint in two through four voices, and presents many more contrapuntal problems and solutions than previous manuals. Each problem is illustrated by Schoenberg's own examples and enhanced by critical commentaries to guide students toward critical thinking. Schoenberg conceived *Preliminary Exercises* as the first of three counterpoint volumes, which he unfortunately could not finish. The second volume, entitled *Contrapuntal Composition*, which he began in 1943, would have drawn on his advanced counterpoint classes at UCLA, covering multiple counterpoint and fugue. *Counterpoint in Homophonic Music,* the third planned volume, would have been based on a new "class in modern counterpoint: the counterpoint of Wagner, Brahms, Mahler, Debussy, Reger and Schoenberg," which Schoenberg began to develop in the 1940s, but never taught.[204]

From the fall of 1936 Schoenberg regularly offered classes in advanced counterpoint, covering double counterpoint, canon, and fugue to enable his students to freely use these techniques in their own compositions.[205] According to Carpenter, Schoenberg made his students "write voices above and below which would cadence on the first or second note of the new phrase of the chorale. And the point to that was not only the contrapuntal writing but especially to practice cadences of all sorts because that note would change all along."[206] Thereafter he introduced exercises in invertible (or, as he called it, "multiple") counterpoint at the octave, the tenth, and the twelfth. First his students wrote invertible counterpoint against canti firmi, then turned to invertible canons, and finally applied their acquired contrapuntal skills to fugue writing.[207]

In the advanced counterpoint class Schoenberg analyzed only works by Bach, who in his opinion was "the last real contrapuntal composer" and "always thought in terms of multiple counterpoint."[208] Often students were to examine the subjects, harmonic patterns, and contrapuntal combinations in Bach fugues to obtain ideas for their own work.[209] As in homophonic composition, Schoenberg stressed the principles of unity and variety in fugue writing and urged students to avoid monotony by using unusual harmonic patterns, "derivatives of the basic subject," and by "exploiting the numerous possibilities of contrapuntal combination."[210] Unlike many other teachers, Schoenberg advised his students to employ church modes so that they would not always use the first and fifth degrees for dux and comes and arrive at a richer harmony. He also asked them "to write themes with all kinds of beginnings" and analyze them in terms of lower and upper hexachords. Carpenter remembered that he asked students to experiment with all sorts of basic combinations in their fugue expositions: "We would take the subject and write the countersubject in whatever double counterpoint we could above and whatever double counterpoint below and shifted canonically, too. So, we would end up with a large sheet of many possibilities of contrapuntal combinations."[211] Students also wrote entire fugues: first tripartite, featuring various types of stretto and pedal point in the last exposition; later fugues with multiple counterpoint in the second and third expositions and augmentation, diminution, inversion in contrary motion and retrograde; finally, fugues with two or three subjects and increasingly more freedom.[212]

Orchestration

From time to time Schoenberg offered orchestration classes at UCLA, although he also discussed this subject in his analysis, harmony, and composition courses. As orchestration was part of his holistic concept of the "musical idea," he expected his students to imagine motives, themes, or whole pieces in their sonic entirety and capture the details in a shorthand score. "A real artist," Schoenberg noted, "thinks in his material" and "a true composer for orchestral music hears in his imagination the whole music in a manner and sonority, as if it were presently played by the orchestra."[213] Hence he criticized composers who conceived chamber and orchestra works as piano pieces to be orchestrated later. He joked: "If you wanted to write a piece for piano—a sonata, a suite, an intermezzo etc., would you perhaps write it at first for string quartet or wood-winds and afterwards arrange it for piano?"[214] In his orchestration classes, he used extracts of orchestral works "which already function in an orchestration" and "serve better than piano pieces" for the purpose of re-orchestration.[215] He also suggested, as Knight and Newlin recalled, that students "follow a piano score at an orchestra concert" and "try to reconstruct the orchestration from the piano score." He advocated the use of c-scores (with all parts notated at sounding pitch).[216]

Schoenberg emphasized the structural function of orchestration and the depend ence of orchestrational choices on the given homophonic, semi-contrapuntal, or contrapuntal texture. As orchestration had to elucidate the musical structure and render it comprehensible and transparent, he advocated soloistic, differentiated, and economical uses of instruments rather than superficial timbral effects and volumes of sound. He discussed "the relative weights of the instrumental groups and the importance of a pianissimo in every orchestral instrument."[217] He advised his students, as Maury recalled, to "write what is possible for instruments, not what is probable."[218] Levant reported that Schoenberg detected that he lacked "personal knowledge of strings. Schönberg set me to studying the quartets of Mozart and Brahms, to learn not the language of music but that of strings in their own realm . . . One of the first things a composer must learn is the language of the medium for which he writes."[219] Knight and Langlie pointed out that Schoenberg expected them to "sit in instrumental classes to learn the capacities of each instrument" or to study the specific instrumental techniques in private lessons.[220]

Schoenberg asked his students to orchestrate for string orchestra, ten woodwinds, or string orchestra with added woodwinds, such works as C. P. E. Bach sinfonias, Schubert songs, and Beethoven's violin sonatas and piano trios. He analyzed with them the orchestration of works by Beethoven, Brahms, Mahler, Richard Strauss, Debussy, Ravel, Berg, and himself.[221] When he discussed the piano writing in his Two Ballads, op. 12, he revealed that "the two hands working together play one part" and that the "principal voice is the piano."[222] He made no secret of his dislike of the sustaining pedal, comparing it to the "muddy, brown tone in pictures."[223] Yet he only rarely touched on his most innovative orchestration concept: *Klangfarbenmelodie* (sound-color melody), a succession of sound colors viewed as melody.[224]

Schoenberg planned to document his orchestrational ideas in a textbook, begun in the late 1940s, but never finished. It would have focused on musical textures, styles, instrumental combinations, forms, genres, character, mood, and illustration. Interestingly, the sketches for this book show a substantial broadening of his canon, including in the section on forms and genres examples of "popular dance music of several nations." The volume was to have featured music by British, French, Italian, Scandinavian, Central European, and American composers, and presented forty examples by Debussy versus thirty-six examples each by himself and Stravinsky.[225] One hundred fifty examples would have featured such American composers as Barber, Carpenter, Copland, Cowell, Gershwin, Harris, Piston, Schuman, Sessions, and Thomson.[226]

Composition

Although Schoenberg considered analysis, harmony, counterpoint, and orchestration as integral parts of the craft and technique of composition, he explicitly offered classes and individual lessons in composition. Based on principles of the classical style, students learned how to coordinate melody and accompaniment, and to write themes in sentence and period forms, small ternary forms, minuets, scherzos, rondos, theme and variations, and sonata forms. Advanced students composed under his guidance such larger works as string quartets, piano quintets, and piano concertos.

Never offering a "foolproof 'recipe' for composition," Schoenberg naturally propagated his own organicist philosophy and aesthetic values.[227] He advised his students to write music without a piano, to hear a musical idea (*musikalischer Gedanke*) in their minds and write it down as fast as possible. He advocated a creative process that was "half instinctive and half deliberate," involving spontaneity and "conscious application of technical knowledge."[228] Schoenberg urged his students to conceive an evolutionary multi-movement work at once and to work out the movements in their corresponding order. When one of his students planned to write her string quartet's finale before the slow middle movement, he asked her whether she "would put on her shoe before she put on her stocking."[229]

As Schoenberg expected his students to compose "logically constructed" pieces, he attached the greatest importance to variation techniques, feeling that variation was the "most important tool for producing logic in spite of variety." He also found that variation stimulated invention and creative fluency.[230] Schoenberg advised Knight, for instance, to instinctively write down up to fifteen themes "which have a connection, then to construct a piece on the variations of a single idea."[231] Opposing such "poor habits" as "talkativeness, superficiality, and bombast," Schoenberg suggested that students strive for a resourceful use of musical material and organic connectedness in their musical structures.[232] Often he described the development of musical ideas with such biological metaphors as "to wax, to grow like a tree, and bear blossoms, leaves and fruit."[233]

Schoenberg urged his students to "try to express something" and "never write mere dry notes," even in the smallest exercises.[234] Believing that musical expression could be most easily achieved in the classical idiom, he emphasized: "The student should never fail to keep in mind a special character. A poem, a story, a play or a moving picture may provide the stimulus to express definite moods."[235] According to Knight, Schoenberg once described a good theme as follows: "Now, a good theme is made up of many ideas. For example, 'the man puts on his coat, he gets into his auto, he goes to the theater' . . . These three ideas work into a story. There are many possible combinations of the ideas man, coat, auto. The coat may not be warm enough, the auto may run into another auto! So with a musical theme—it must contain the seeds of a story."[236]

Schoenberg's American composition classes prompted him to conceive, with the assistance of both Strang and Stein, two important textbooks: *Models for Beginners in Composition* and *Fundamentals of Musical Composition*. Strang felt that, with these two volumes, Schoenberg made a virtue out of necessity. Most American students could not afford a library of scores, and useful textbooks were unavailable.[237] Published in 1942, *Models* originated from a six-week-long UCLA summer course for beginners in composition.[238] A small and highly pragmatic manual, *Models* falls into two parts, a "Syllabus and Glossary" with condensed instructions, and a section with nearly 300 music examples, ranging from one-measure units to a complete minuet and scherzo. The manual systematically teaches students how to compose small forms in the classical style. The examples, composed by Schoenberg himself, reveal in manifold ways how musical problems can be solved and how musical materials can be transformed.

Schoenberg simultaneously conceived *Fundamentals of Musical Composition*, which was incomplete at the time of his death, but was prepared by Strang and Stein for posthumous publication in 1967.[239] Like *Models, Fundamentals* is a practice-oriented guide that conveys the compositional craft, gradually proceeding from small to large musical units, but it also expands upon *Models,* targeting both beginning and advanced composition students. It is more detailed and broader in scope, including theme and variations and such larger forms as rondos and sonatas. In the summer of 1939, Schoenberg proudly introduced Webern to this volume's unique concept:

I believe from an aesthetic, theoretical, intellectual and . . . moral viewpoint it will be very good. But especially looking at it from a pedagogical standpoint . . . The examples conceived by myself have in part almost the value of compositions (if this is possible without thematic originality) and are principally based on the idea to show how many solutions or respective continuations can result from one specific case. Thus one motive, produced from a broken chord, goes through the whole book. From this motive I derived hundreds of phrases, antecedents, consequents, periods and movements of various characters and with different types of piano setting.[240]

In the final version of *Fundamentals,* Schoenberg replaced many of his own examples with excerpts from Beethoven (especially his piano sonatas), Mozart, Brahms, and other composers, intending to add methods for the analysis of classical works.[241] Although mostly focusing on "technical matters in a very fundamental way," he fleshed them out with interesting commentary, including an entire chapter on self-criticism. Some Schoenberg commentators have regretted the primarily didactic nature of this textbook and blamed the "modest level of knowledge" of American students for whom it was written. However, *Fundamentals* allowed Schoenberg to rethink and clarify important theoretical and terminological problems in a new and more accessible way.[242] *Fundamentals* has become Schoenberg's most popular American textbook and is still in print and used in analysis and composition classes at American universities to this day.

Schoenberg advised many students who had already mastered the writing of large forms in the classical idiom and allowed them to work in their chosen styles. Although he judged such works from his own aesthetic standpoint (involving "clarity of statement, contrast, repetition, balance, variation, elaboration, proportion, connection, transition"), he refrained from prescribing specific styles:[243] "I do not ask my pupils to write in my style," he told Bestor Kelley, "all I ask is that they write logically."[244] Schoenberg often predicted: "Each of you will find your own way, I have found mine."[245]

Yet unlike Krenek, Schoenberg did not teach any modernist techniques, believing that modernist expression "might come in a natural way, by itself to him who proceeds gradually by absorbing the cultural achievements of his predecessors."[246] However, he willingly gave his advanced and talented students feedback when they brought in twelve-tone pieces, explaining:

I don't want to bar talented composers from employing this method. But I want to warn beginners, who believe that the mere use of a row is already music. He who has not studied harmony and counterpoint thoroughly and long enough and who has not worked his way through all the forms created by the masters of our art and obtained a certain sense for proportion and shape, should not make his compositional process harder through the requirements of this difficult technique. For the composer who is able enough, it is an impediment; it is more difficult than requiring good counterpoint from an amateur.[247]

Schoenberg feared that his students might easily confuse his "method" with a "system": "Curiously and wrongly most people speak of the system of the chromatic scale. Mine is no system but only a method, which means a modus of applying regularly a preconceived formula. A method can, but need not be of the consequences of a system."[248] He felt that American students were "extremely good at getting hold of principles," and that "they want to apply them too much 'on principle.'"[249]

Many Schoenberg students, however, explored dodecaphony independently, "counted the notes" in dodecaphonic scores, and wrote twelve-tone works on their own.[250] Cage, Coulthard, and Harrison did the latter. But because Cage at that point had neither completed his counterpoint studies nor mastered the classical sonata form, Schoenberg refused to look at his serial Allemande for clarinet or answer questions about dodecaphony.[251] Coulthard, one of Schoenberg's advanced students, confessed to him that she composed dodecaphonic music, but was dissatisfied with the results and refused to show it to him. Schoenberg advised her to follow her own voice.[252] Curious about the twelve-tone technique, Newlin was told to embrace it at a more mature stage in her career. She thus waited until 1949 to show him one of her twelve-tone works, a Piano Trio, which Schoenberg apparently liked.[253] Harrison, another advanced student, wrote a twelve-tone Piano Suite when he took Schoenberg's Advanced Composition seminar. Written for and dedicated to his pianist-friend Frances Mullen, who had played Schoenberg's Piano Suite, Harrison's lyrical five-movement work was modeled on Schoenberg's Suite and built on a row with great intervallic variety and three transformations.[254] Harrison had completed much of the piece, but "had written himself into a corner in III, the Conductus." Asking Schoenberg for assistance, he played for him the suite's first two movements, which he quickly identified as being twelve-tone and approved. Schoenberg seemed especially delighted by the second movement's "very wide, soft spacing." "By the time I had played to the point of my blockage in Movement III," Harrison noted, "he plunged directly in, already aware of my structure, and with splendid illuminating instructions, permanently disposed of for me not only that particular difficulty but also any of the kind that I might ever encounter."[255] Schoenberg advised him to focus on "the essentials, not the complications."[256] The Suite became one of Harrison's lengthiest and technically most challenging works for piano solo. Although Harrison never consistently or dogmatically adhered to serial techniques, he used them occasionally in such later works as *Schoenbergiana* (1945), Symphony on G (1948), *Rapunzel* (1954), *Pacifika Rondo* (1963) and *The Clays' Quintet* (1987). Harrison also included a chapter on dodecaphony in his *Music Primer* (1966).

Schoenberg gave feedback to composers of neo-classical works, symphonic jazz, and film scores. Harrison reported that "the first piece I took him was a neo-classic piece. He didn't bat an eye."[257] Griselle and Shilkret would have shown Schoenberg their works in symphonic jazz or ballad style.[258] Similarly, Levant and Raksin had a popular music and jazz background, which marked their works written under Schoenberg. Levant's tripartite one-movement Piano Concerto is a good example, featuring atonality, blues-inspired harmonies, Gershwinesque driving rhythms, and bits of jazzy orchestration. Using such devices, Levant may have actually followed Schoenberg's advice to lighten his "relentlessly serious music" and incorporate "a little of his humor" in it.[259] But Levant later sardonically devalued his concerto: "I wanted to make it palatable to popular taste so I inserted a boogie-woogie strain in the middle of it. It spoiled the whole thing."[260] Raksin testified that Schoenberg gave him advice on his film scores: "Since I was almost always busy with film scores, I would bring him bits and pieces as the work progressed . . . we would spend our time together analyzing scores that seemed pertinent to the subject of the moment. Schoenberg would bring from his library an example of someone's solution of a problem with which we were occupied, and if I could not elucidate both problem and solution he would either guide me toward them or explain the significance of the passage himself."[261] When Raksin was scoring *Wings over Honolulu* (1937) and stood in need of descriptive music for aviators and planes, Schoenberg suggested that he study classical examples evoking bees. Raksin also worked with Schoenberg on an orchestral piece whose opening idea became the main theme in his score for *Force of Evil* (1948).[262]

In 1948, looking back on having taught so many and so diverse students, Schoenberg reasoned: "All my pupils differ from one another extremely and though perhaps the majority composes twelve-tone music, one could not speak of a school. They all had to find their way alone, for themselves. And this is exactly what they did; everyone has his own manner of obeying rules derived from the treatment of twelve tones."[263]

Teaching Personality and Style

Schoenberg made a strong impression on many of his American students. Equipped with an awe-inspiring command of the Austro-German classical repertoire, Schoenberg was a passionate and charismatic teacher. Approaching him from varying agendas and levels of ability, his American students experienced his complex personality in different ways. For Cage, he "was a god, not a mere human being."[264] Cage remembered: "He could be generous, aggressive, witty, sardonic, profound, courageous, charming, sympathetic and suspicious." In his view, "each student trembled, knowing Schoenberg's wit might at any moment hit in his direction."[265] Yet others described Schoenberg as a thoughtful and perceptive mentor, who, despite a kind of strictness, cared deeply about his students.

He sensed when a student was insecure or had private difficulties and tried to find encouraging words, as was the case with Abrams. She found him to be a very understanding teacher, recalling how he once said to her: "Miss Abrams, you're not made of glass."[266] Strang remembered that Schoenberg was believed to be very difficult to get along with when he arrived in California, yet he never experienced him as a domineering teacher. Strang recalled that Schoenberg showed "a great sensitivity" to obtuse pupils who were sincere and serious. He could be "so sweet to a music student who asked a stupid question, but really wanted to know."[267] According to Strang, Schoenberg showed "an incredible warmth of interest in the people around him" and was "always concerned about his students" and "would do anything for them."[268]

In class situations, he tended to favor such extroverted students as Cage, Newlin, Stein, and Langlie, "whom he could count on to respond."[269] Schoenberg was also generous with his time. He often went overtime when teaching single lessons and generously hosted student concerts and receptions at his home (Figure 6.6). Popular with his many female students, he served as faculty adviser for the chapter of the international music fraternity for women, Sigma Alpha Iota.[270] He wrote recommendations for many students to help them find jobs and music publishers.[271] Maury testified that Schoenberg never forgot his students' names. When, after a hiatus of fourteen years, he saw Schoenberg again, Schoenberg addressed him without hesitation as "Mr. Maury."[272] Such pupils as Alderman, Cage, Carlson,

FIGURE 6.6.
Student party at Schoenberg's home,1939. Courtesy Arnold Schönberg Center.

Carpenter, Cycler, Halma, Langlie, Levant, Scott Merrick, Newlin, Newman, Silvers, Stein, and Strang developed an association with Schoenberg going beyond a mere professional student-teacher relationship. They assisted him with musical and everyday matters, and spent leisure time with him. Newlin and Stein wanted to found a Schoenberg Society as early as 1940.[273] None of his American students imitated Berg and Webern in their Schoenberg personality cult; then again, few could afford to study with him for six to ten years, as many of his European pupils did. Yet many became his loyal supporters, performing or promoting his works in manifold ways.[274]

A number of his students might have agreed with Levant's characterization of Schoenberg's educational accomplishments: "To my mind Schönberg is the greatest teacher in the world. The very contact with such a person either brings out something that is in you, or lets you see that there is nothing to be brought out. Either way, it is helpful to know where you stand. Schönberg not only permits each of his pupils to be completely himself, he insists on it."[275] Schoenberg often used the Socratic method and encouraged class interaction to inspire independent thinking among students.[276] Russell pointed out, "Schoenberg's frequent questioning is not to draw out parrot-like answers, but to develop a searching attitude and to stimulate self-criticism . . . The class room becomes a laboratory in which master and pupils are co-adventurers in attacking problems."[277] Students were supposed to make discoveries and learn how to find solutions.[278] As Schoenberg publicly stated in 1948: "I hope that my pupils will be seekers! For they will learn that we seek only in seeking further and finding which to be sure is the goal, may easily be but an end to striving."[279] Moreover, he encouraged his students "to help one another, to correct their own mistakes and thus gain self-dependence."[280] As a result Kim, Kirchner, Newlin, and Stein, among others, founded the UCLA Composers' Workshop.[281] In composition classes, Schoenberg "seldom spoke first or gave an opinion" after the presentation of a student piece and instead invited students to offer their honest criticism. "Sometimes," Knight observed, "he would immediately disagree with a criticism, at other times find it to the point and support it."[282] When students ran into compositional problems, he wrote various solutions on the blackboard or pointed to solutions in the classical-music literature.

Even though Schoenberg had an overall plan and goal for his lessons, he often proceeded freely and unsystematically, and frequently changed his methods, adapting to the individual needs of each student.[283] He usually prepared only a limited amount of material, allowing for unplanned discussions and for the need to improvise music examples on the blackboard in response to compositional questions that unpredictably arose. Students marveled at his spontaneity, great adaptability, and pragmatism in classroom situations.[284] Schoenberg readily used current technology (records, projectors, and radio), and prepared individualized exercises, questionnaires for listening reports of radio broadcasts, and exams for each of his students.[285]

In his teaching, Schoenberg often behaved in a theatrical manner and displayed a quirky sense of humor. For his private classes he used large sheets of butcher paper, on which he drew staves with a self-constructed device: a staff-liner fitted with crayons. He disliked blackboards and chalk.[286] Students remarked on his unusual clothing. Earl Kim felt that Schoenberg enhanced his small stature by "dressing beautifully, almost foppishly." He remembered that "he would always come through the back door of the two doors to the classroom, so that he might wave to the class as he entered, as if he were, at the very least a concert pianist, if not a conductor. He would wave to the class, saying, 'How do you do? How do you do?' with his eyes sparkling, and the class would all dutifully say, 'How do you do, Mr. Schoenberg?' And that's how every class began."[287] Both Kim and Newlin recalled how he visually dramatized a harmonic problem in a class about minor scales and alterations. He sharpened a yellow pencil with his pocketknife and then "deliberately broke it against the side of the piano." When he asked the puzzled class what it meant and could not get an answer, he posed the question: "Why should I take such trouble to sharpen, if immediately I flatten?" Thereafter students avoided this error in exercises with altered tones.[288] He was easily distracted by outside noises and mystified and irritated by airplanes flying over the building. In such moments he interrupted his lecture to rush to the window, commenting on the air traffic.[289]

BEYOND SCHOENBERG'S ACADEMIC APPOINTMENTS

During his American teaching career Schoenberg developed many innovative educational ideas which never materialized. He devised plans for unusual music and composition schools. In "Proposal for the Foundation of a Contemporary Music Education Institute," drafted in Chautauqua, he suggested new and creative ways to train superior performers and teachers, and the dissemination of the highest possible forms of music culture.[290] Dismissing mechanical types of practicing, he stressed creative imagination and artistic integrity and, perhaps influenced by Chautauqua's peacefulness, proposed to set up his institute far from big and noisy cities. In California he envisioned an independent "Arnold Schoenberg School of Composition," directed by himself with the support of Eisler, Strang, Stein, and Estep, which would offer individual lessons and classes to beginners and advanced students.[291] In his "School for Soundmen" (1940), he planned to provide musical and studio technical training for sound engineers, composers, arrangers, and orchestrators working in the film, radio, and recording industry. The curriculum included introductory science and music courses, as well as instruction tailored to each student's projected professional specialization. Some of these ideas found their way into another outline for the music department at the University of Chicago and are now implemented in music programs of numerous universities throughout the United States.[292]

Schoenberg formulated numerous novel ideas for various music departments. In 1933 he proposed to Malkin special analysis courses in which "students gradually discover by themselves (through thinking and observation)" the fundamental elements of form. He suggested a course entitled "Sprechstunde," in which students would discuss aesthetic questions under his guidance.[293] In 1935 he devised analysis classes on "New Music (1900–1934)" and "Bad Music," involving pseudo-modern, mannered, and conservative examples from different eras to convey merits and demerits of music.[294]

In 1936 he envisioned for UCLA's music department a "school of composition" to offer gifted composition students "the highest degree of training" and a doctorate.[295] In July 1937 he pondered the establishment of a music department within the College of Letters and Science, aimed at instructing only students in composition, conducting, musicology, and music education, and not instrumentalists and vocalists. Unusually, he expected this department's faculty above all to promote respect for the arts and their strict, morally based laws. They would demonstrate utmost devotion to music and "idealism to help balance materialism," and teach students to become "models for ordinary every day citizens and to behave accordingly."[296] He suggested the establishment of a so-called "Music Club" with divisions for orchestra and choir, and "schools" for conducting, orchestration, and copyists. He imagined that the Music Club's divisions and students would make extensive use of recordings and would interact with local music institutions and artists.[297] Moreover, he proposed a "Curriculum for Composers" (c. 1940–41), consisting of seven undergraduate and two graduate courses in harmony, counterpoint, analysis, and composition. The last few classes dedicated to composition would have required the "consent of the instructor."[298] Schoenberg would have recruited all his own best students as readers and assistants.[299] He also pondered a "contest for students for recognizing music played on records. He would have prizes totaling, say, a hundred dollars, with a fifty-dollar first prize, and the rest distributed proportionally."[300] He worked to make scores more accessible to students. In 1937 he begged UCLA president Sproul in vain to provide $150 or $200 "to build a library for the classes in analysis and composition."[301] He also unsuccessfully proposed to Schirmer the publication of inexpensive pocket scores of the most important classical works.[302]

Beginning in 1939 he planned a music lending library operated by a student library foundation financed by students paying a membership fee of a nickel per week.[303]

On the university level, Schoenberg suggested in 1940 a visionary interdepartmental and interdisciplinary project, the "Forum of the Arts and Esthetics" to promote cross-fertilization among the arts and sciences. He invited UCLA colleagues from the humanities and sciences to exchange ideas and discuss the influence of changes in technology, sociology, and economics on the arts, envisioning far-reaching conferences on aesthetics.[304] Even though this project never came to fruition, Schoenberg treasured his interactions with such colleagues as psychologist Caroline Fisher and physicist Vern Knudsen, whose acoustics expertise influenced Schoenberg's "School for Soundmen," and stimulated his interest in microtonality.[305]

Some of these projects foundered due to Schoenberg's complex relationship with UCLA. He experienced a "relatively happy period of teaching at UCLA" and "very nice educational successes," financial security, and friendly bonds with such colleagues as Alexander Schreiner, George McManus, Lawrence Petran, Robert

Nelson, and Walter Rubsamen.[306] In 1941 UCLA's library hosted an exhibit of his works, and he was named the "Seventeenth Faculty Research Lecturer" and invited to present his lecture "The Composition with Twelve Tones," which was "the first and the only instance in which a professor in any of the fine arts at UCLA has been so honored."[307] In 1944 Albert Elkus, chair of the music department at the University of California, Berkeley, tried unsuccessfully to establish an Arnold Schoenberg Chair, the endowment of which would have provided Schoenberg with an additional income during his retirement, and after his death would have financed a professorship in composition.[308] In 1945 UCLA offered Schoenberg an honorary doctorate, which he declined.[309] In 1949 UCLA invited him to deliver the talk "My Evolution" in a lecture series and to hold a seminar for its composition students.[310] But UCLA was also slow in overcoming its status as a teachers' college. Having joined the faculty with high expectations, Schoenberg struggled with a high teaching load and a lack of funds for teaching materials and assistants. He was never granted much influence, and his proposals to appoint other qualified refugees were ignored; he was also never offered the opportunity to chair the department.[311] Schoenberg, however, made his suggestions without much discernment and diplomacy. By the same token, UCLA administrators may not have been immune to xenophobia and a certain "competitive fear."[312] Stein remembered that Schoenberg was considered "a rare one that they had to tolerate."[313] Predictably, Schoenberg often criticized UCLA and the head of its music department. To Weiss and Webern he confided that he was dissatisfied with his position because he had to teach beginners and that UCLA did not keep its promises.[314] To Stiedry he wrote: "Our music department is more inclined to get rid of capable musicians than to engage new ones. There is a man in power [Leroy Allen], the chairman of the department, a band man, one of the poorest men dealing with music, I ever met. And this man decides about everything in the music department."[315] Schoenberg's relationship with UCLA deteriorated further when he could not push back his mandatory retirement (which had already been postponed by five years). He argued to no avail that, at age seventy, he did not feel like an old person, and that he was still refining his teaching methods despite his exceptional teaching record and "long list of excellent pupils." He even suggested that due to the war, "only men over 64 will be available for teaching," and that there were teachers at other institutions who at age eighty or older were still teaching.[316] When it became official that he had to retire on October 31, 1944, he felt betrayed by UCLA's president, who had once described his appointment as a "life position."[317]

Schoenberg's influence on American music education, however, exceeded UCLA's boundaries. He advised administrators at Columbia University, the St. Louis Institute of Music, and the Universities of Chicago and Idaho, and established ties to many colleges and universities through his students.[318] Schoenberg also supported music education as an active member of the Phi Mu Alpha Sinfonia Fraternity of America at USC and UCLA, and through his involvement in the Music Teachers National Association (MTNA), Music Educators National Conference (MENC), the National Educational Alliance, Music Teachers' Association of California, and California-Western Music Educators Conference, at which he regularly presented papers.[319] Engaging his colleagues in a dialogue about new music, he spoke about "Education for Contemporary Music" at a December 1934 luncheon of the State Music Educators at USC.[320] In 1939 he was very prominently featured at the annual MTNA convention in Kansas City with two papers, "Ear Training Through Composing" and "How a Music Student Can Make a Living." In 1940 he delivered a paper entitled "Learning Through Teaching" at the MENC in Los Angeles.[321] In

1943 he spoke about "Composers in War Time," and in 1944 on "Some Problems for the Educator" at MTNA meetings in Los Angeles. He published some of these and other articles on music education in conference proceedings, journals, and newspapers.[322]

Schoenberg left an immeasurable mark on American music instruction at the local and national levels. Although he based his teaching on much the same materials, music literature, and music examples he had used in Europe, he skillfully tailored these materials to the needs of his American students and to the requirements of the American educational system.[323] He complemented these materials with new examples and developed into a more pragmatic and straightforward teacher, with less use of polemics and philosophical speculation. The heritage of his American teaching is documented in many provocative articles and several textbooks filling gaps in the available literature, which Schoenberg considered "pompous and affected" (Marx and Schenker) or "fossilized aesthetics" (English and American theory books).[324] After his death his textbooks, especially *Structural Functions* and *Fundamentals of Musical Composition*, became widely used teaching tools in music theory and composition, and contributed to the rise of music analysis as a major discipline within music theory.

Schoenberg's teaching legacy is also reflected in the many well-prepared and intelligent students he attracted, who developed remarkable careers as composers, musicologists, performers, and educators. Virgil Thomson observed in 1950: "Los Angeles where Arnold Schoenberg lives, the founding father of it all, is a sort of Mount Athos to which pilgrimages are made."[325] It is, however, misleading to view his American pupils (in contrast to his European students) as "beginners" who wasted his time. Except perhaps for his small group of handpicked students at the Prussian Academy, Schoenberg taught many "beginners" in Europe, including Alban Berg and Anton Webern, and was critical of teaching German music students.[326] His complaints about teaching "beginners" and his definition of them, however, often show that he did not recognize his students' previous training under such teachers as Boulanger, Cowell, Hanson, Sessions, Weiss, or Wolpe as being compatible with his teaching approach and aesthetics.[327] Moreover, he expected his pupils to study with him (as Berg and Webern did) for at least five, but ideally up to eight years—too expensive a prospect for most Americans, and irreconcilable with UCLA's curricula. Schoenberg nonetheless benefited from his contact with the many fledgling American musicians, regardless of their knowledge and talent levels. He stated at the end of his life: "I must confess that I was a passionate teacher, and the satisfaction of giving to beginners as much as possible of my own knowledge was probably a greater reward than the actual fee I received."[328] Schoenberg's many affluent students helped him afford a very comfortable living before his retirement, and provided him with a substantial income after 1944.[329] He could also propagate his aesthetic views and guide his students toward a greater understanding of his own music, often winning them as champions of his music and ideas.

In 1933 when Marc Blitzstein learned that his former teacher was to settle and teach in the United States, he wrote:

> Arnold Schönberg is an extremely good thing for America. In particular his almost fanatical academism is an unfamiliar and needed quality among us. We are very used to a dry musty brand of academism . . . That Schönberg should ardently advocate a rigid, inflexible course of study (strict counterpoint, exhaustive analyses of Bach, Beethoven, Mozart) may strike the superficial observer as strange. It is not strange, nor is it worth-

while any longer to reiterate the fact that his music (its "madness") is produced with a dogmatic adherence to method and minutiae.

Blitzstein also wondered about the "effect Schönberg will have upon his pupils (and through them upon the music of the country at large)." He felt that "a danger for them lies in his insistence on genius, on perfection, in his ruthlessness with the near-perfect: the danger of paralysis and despair." Blitzstein argued: "A good thing, perhaps: the world will be cluttered up with less bad music; and a bad thing: since a cultural epoch is made up not only of the perfect work of geniuses, but also of the combined efforts of lesser talents, a whole geological formation of them. With them wiped out, the genius exists without subsoil, becomes isolated, ingrown, 'eccentric.'"[330] While it is true that Schoenberg discouraged many of his American students from becoming composers, Blitzstein misunderstood Schoenberg's goal as providing music lovers and practicing musicians with a solid music education to create the conditions for the emergence of future "geniuses."[331] As Blitzstein foresaw, Schoenberg contributed to the growth and transformation of music education in America, singled out by French-born composer Jacques-Louis Monod as "the only country where music education has brought itself up to date," putting more emphasis on the study of twentieth-century and contemporary music.[332] Predicting that "the time will come when the ability to draw thematic material from a basic set of twelve tones will be an unconditional prerequisite for obtaining admission to the composition class of a conservatory," Schoenberg prepared the rise of serialism and the emergence in the 1950s of the much-maligned "university composer" dedicated to serialism and complexity.[333]

Numerous American composers who trained under Schoenberg did join academia and convey his ideas to their students, but they did not necessarily fit the category of "university composer." The majority wrote tonal and atonal music, with only a small minority employing the twelve-tone technique consistently. Other Schoenberg-educated composers, often outside academia, used dodecaphony temporarily and freely in such new contexts as film and jazz; some also experimented with it.[334] The American Schoenberg students who decided not to become composers generously paid tribute to their teacher's music and ideas with their writings and performances inside and outside academia. Many of them helped lay the groundwork for the flourishing reception of his work in the three decades following his death.

7 The American Reception of Schoenberg's Music after 1945

Schoenberg's presence in the United States prompted many responses to his music in performance, scholarship, and composition. Far from living in an ivory tower, he showed himself to be persevering and versatile, accommodating his knowledge, expertise, and creativity to his adopted homeland. He was also certainly not neglected, winning strong support from fellow émigrés, his American students, and Americans outside his circle, who became important torchbearers after his death.

Once considered peculiar, Schoenberg's ideas began to gain momentum after 1945, thanks to many favorable circumstances. Postwar America's renewed faith in progress, science, and technology led to a revaluation of his ideas, especially in the light of his reputation as the "Einstein of music."[1] Recognizing that the war was won in part because of advanced science and atomic power—with Albert Einstein in the background—America soon attached more importance to science, making Einstein into a popular icon and showing a greater interest in science-inspired art. In this spirit Schoenberg's champions eagerly emphasized the progressive and quasi-scientific aspects of his music, while neo-classicism, very popular in the 1930s and 1940s, lost ground, seeming old-fashioned and even contradictory to a sense of progress. Neo-classicism's most prominent representative, Stravinsky, discarded it in favor of serialism just after Schoenberg's death.

The reputation of Schoenberg's music profited from Cold War politics as well. Contending with Europe's nonrepresentational and abstract art, the U.S. government began to sponsor abstract visual and musical art as culturally on a par with its competitors, changing the image of a country mainly dedicated to commercial entertainment and materialism. Schoenberg's dodecaphony became not only a politically correct compositional approach, but also a symbol of creative freedom in both America and Europe, epitomizing resistance against the repressive cultural politics

FIGURE 7.1.
Arnold Schoenberg Institute at USC. Photo by Allan Dean Walker. Courtesy Arnold Schönberg Center.

of both fascist and communist regimes.[2] The demand for music conveying socialist and patriotic messages declined with the end of the war, and McCarthyism arguably propelled left-wing artists (including Copland) to abandon their politically engaged art in favor of the "safe" territory of abstract expression.[3] Dodecaphonic music attained new prestige, and in 1948 and 1949 twelve-tone works such as Wallingford Riegger's Third Symphony and Milton Babbitt's *Composition for Four Instruments* began to receive major awards.[4]

Schoenberg's music and ideas profited also from the immense growth of college education, prompted by such measures as the GI bill and a tendency toward teaching specialized rather than general knowledge. In 1956 UCLA honored Schoenberg with the dedication of Schoenberg Hall, a concert space in the university's new music building seating over 500, and with performances of his music, speeches, and the unveiling of Anna Mahler's Schoenberg bust.[5] In 1974, Schoenberg's centenary and the peak of his popularity in academia, USC, California State University at Los Angeles, UCLA, and the California Institute of the Arts together honored his legacy with the foundation of the Arnold Schoenberg Institute, a research and performance center on the USC campus housing the 60,000 pieces of Schoenberg's estate, including scores, manuscripts, paintings, letters, and his library, among other items, which Schoenberg's children had generously donated to USC (Figure 7.1). It was a milestone that prompted the Los Angeles City Bureau of Music to propose the celebration of September 13, his birthday, as "Arnold Schoenberg Day."[6]

PERFORMANCE

Thanks to their newly earned prestige, Schoenberg's atonal and dodecaphonic works enjoyed more performances by a growing number of renowned musicians.

The foundation of new symphony orchestras, music centers (Chandler Pavilion in Los Angeles, New York's Lincoln Center, and the Kennedy Center in Washington, D.C.), and music festivals (Aspen, Cabrillo, Marlboro, and Ojai), as well as the growth of radio stations and the recording industry, enabled Schoenberg's music to reach new and more receptive ears. While many of these venues had to consider marketplace rules and audience expectations, musical academia offered its own subsidized performance structure and professionally trained performers. Academic musicians were able to emulate Schoenberg's Society for Private Musical Performances and European models of publicly sponsored music making and to facilitate performances of Schoenberg's and other new music.

Although traditional orchestral and opera venues catered to their audience's large appetite for standard classical repertoire and assigned small program slots for new music, in the 1950s and 1960s such adventurous orchestra and opera conductors as Dimitri Mitropoulos, Robert Craft, Zubin Mehta, William Steinberg, Seiji Ozawa, Irwin Hoffman, Osbourne McConathy, and Robert Baustian gave highly acclaimed performances of Schoenberg's stylistically progressive works. With vocalist Dorothy Dow, Mitropoulos gave the American premiere of *Erwartung* (concert performance) in 1951 and recorded this work, as well as the Piano Concerto with the twenty-five-year-old pianist Glenn Gould and the Violin Concerto with Louis Krasner.[7] Craft gave Los Angeles premieres of *Die glückliche Hand* and Four Songs, op. 22 at Franz Waxman's Los Angeles Music Festival in 1961. He also conducted numerous performances of most of Schoenberg's orchestral, choral, and ensemble works nationwide and recorded them for a seminal Schoenberg record series issued by Columbia. The series featured premiere recordings of Schoenberg's Songs, opp. 8 and 22, choral works, opp. 27, 28, and 50c, Orchestral Variations, and many compositions without opus numbers. Craft recorded a pathbreaking, four-LP set of Webern's music, triggering a Webern vogue in the mid-1950s. Nurtured by Schoenberg student Josef Polnauer, Mehta presented numerous works of Schoenberg with the Los Angeles Philharmonic (1962–78), among them Los Angeles premieres of the Piano Concerto with Alfred Brendel in 1965 and Orchestral Variations in 1966. As conductor of the Pittsburgh Symphony, Steinberg programmed in major American cities Five Orchestral Pieces, Four Songs, op. 22, *Ode*, and *Survivor*, among other works. Rather than offering Schoenberg's music in a "quid pro quo" fashion, he boldly presented an all-Schoenberg concert, including the New York premiere of Four Songs at Carnegie Hall in 1965.[8] Ozawa, director of the Ravinia Festival, and Hoffman conducted the Chicago Symphony in Schoenberg performances. Ozawa presented the Piano Concerto with soloist William Masselos in 1967, and Hoffman conducted the Violin and Piano Concertos and *Erwartung* in 1967 and 1968. The 1960s also saw the American premieres of Schoenberg's stage works. In 1966 Sarah Caldwell's Boston Opera Company featured *Moses und Aron*, sung in English, under the musical direction of McConathy. In 1968 the Santa Fe Opera offered *Jakobsleiter* under Baustian—seven years after the work's world premiere in Vienna.

In the 1970s orchestral performances of Schoenberg's music peaked. Directing the New York Philharmonic (1971–77), Pierre Boulez performed much Schoenberg, including an informal all-Schoenberg-Berg-Webern program and an all-Schoenberg "rug" concert.[9] Boulez, Mehta, Ozawa, Gerhard Samuel, Stanislaw Skrowaczewski, and Gregg Smith, among others, offered musical tributes to Schoenberg in his centenary year, 1974. Lawrence Foster, conductor of the Houston Symphony, James Levine at the Ravinia Festival and as guest conductor of the New York Philharmonic and Los Angeles Philharmonic, and Georg Solti, director of the Chicago Symphony, also championed his music before and after the centenary. Solti offered Chicago and New York concert-version premieres of *Moses* in 1971. In addition to Boulez and Mehta, such conductors as Michael Gielen in Cincinnati, Sergiu Commissiona and Christoph von Dohnányi in Cleveland, Levine in New York, Michael Tilson Thomas in Los Angeles, and Edo de Waart in Minneapolis promoted Schoenberg in American orchestra halls in the 1980s and 1990s. Schoenberg's orchestral music even found its niche in programs of less prominent groups, from the Kalamazoo Symphony to the Westchester Philharmonic. Although most of his orchestral oeuvre has remained in the repertoire, *Verklärte Nacht* and Five Pieces for both large and standard orchestra have ranked among his most performed works.

Performances of Schoenberg's chamber music surpassed renditions of his orchestral music, particularly in the first postwar decades. This was due to the greater flexibility and independence of chamber musicians and the increase of new ensembles and chamber venues featuring Schoenberg's work. The League of Composers and ISCM, which merged in 1954 under the latter name, became an important forum for Schoenberg performances. Furthermore, many of his academically affiliated émigré friends, along with his American students and colleagues, created new-music environments at their universities, which often granted chamber groups residence status.[10] Such university-based ensembles as the Pro Arte, Juilliard, Walden, Galimir, and LaSalle Quartets frequently performed his quartet oeuvre. The Juilliard and LaSalle Quartets recorded all five quartets.[11] Unaffiliated quartets, including the California-based Amati, California, Hollywood, Los Angeles, and Sequoia Quartets, also performed Schoenberg's chamber music for strings, if less consistently than the groups already named. Among these, the Los Angeles Quartet played all the numbered quartets in a series at the Monday Evening Concerts in Los Angeles in 1970, and the Sequoia Quartet (founded in 1972) recorded and presented many performances of the Second Quartet with the famous soprano Bethany Beardslee. In the 1960s and 1970s the Second Quartet became Schoenberg's most performed quartet, often showcasing such extraordinary sopranos as Beardslee, Jan DeGaetani, and Benita Valente. Since the 1970s new groups, including the Emerson, Orion, and Brentano Quartets, nurtured by the previous generations of quartet players, have emerged and continue to feature Schoenberg's quartets in their repertoire.

Different mixed ensembles gave numerous performances of Schoenberg's other chamber music, including the University of Chicago's Contemporary Chamber Players (formed in 1954), directed by Ralph Shapey; Columbia's Contemporary Chamber Ensemble (founded in 1960) under Arthur Weisberg; and the Aeolian Chamber Players, initiated in 1960 at Sarah Lawrence College. There was a special focus on *Pierrot*, and from the 1950s through the 1970s in America, it became one of the most played of Schoenberg's atonal works. Many other mixed ensembles—the Da Capo Chamber Players, Light Fantasticks, New York New Music Ensemble, Speculum Musicae, and Voices of Change, among others—modeled their instrumental combination after *Pierrot* and showcased this work on their programs. Since the late 1970s further *Pierrot* ensembles, including the California EAR Unit, the Pierrot Consort, and Eighth Blackbird, have emerged. *Pierrot* has intrigued many American vocalists. Noteworthy among the generation following Erika Stiedry-Wagner are Beardslee, Cathy Berberian, DeGaetani, and Alice Howland; they were succeeded by such eminent singers as Judith Bettina, Phyllis Bryn-Julson, Lucy Shelton, and Susan Narucki.

Schoenberg's piano music was another beneficiary of the numerous technically accomplished and openminded postwar pianists in and outside academia, many of whom had studied with him.[12] Edward Steuermann and Leonard Stein promoted Schoenberg's cause most actively with all-Schoenberg recitals and recordings. In 1957 Steuermann made the first recording of Schoenberg's complete piano works for Columbia (Figure 7.2). Stein participated as accompanist in premiere recordings of *Herzgewächse*, Three Satires, and Three Songs, op. 48 (all for Columbia); and *Brettllieder*, among other songs without opus number, featuring the famous soprano Marni Nixon (for RCA Red Seal) (Figure 7.3). Robert Goldsand, Fritz Jahoda, Gunnar Johansen, Erich Kahn, Grete Sultan, and other émigré pianists who had performed Schoenberg's music in the late 1940s and 1950s were gradually superseded by young American artists, such as Easley Blackwood, David Burge, Richard Goode, Robert Helps, Paul Jacobs, William Masselos, Charles Rosen, Russell Sherman, and David Tudor. Jacobs gained recognition at age twenty-six when he presented all of Schoenberg's piano works in a 1956 concert series in Paris and recorded them two years later for the British label Ducretet Thomson. Rosen, like Jacobs a Juilliard graduate then in his mid-twenties, also drew the attention of the public with his discriminating Schoenberg interpretations. Throughout his long career, Rosen not only performed Schoenberg and recorded the Suite, op. 25 and the Piano Pieces, op. 33, but also lectured and wrote the seminal monograph *Arnold Schoenberg* (University of Chicago Press, 1975).

The sensational and eccentric Canadian pianist Glenn Gould, an untiring devotée of Schoenberg's music, was perhaps the most prominent Schoenberg pianist in the United States in the 1950s and 1960s. Performing Schoenberg's Piano Concerto

FIGURE 7.2.
Clara and Edward Steuermann, late 1940s or early 1950s. From *The Not Quite Innocent Bystander: Writings of Edward Steuermann*, ed. Clara Steuermann, David Porter, and Gunther Schuller. ©1989 University of Nebraska Press. Used by permission.

FIGURE 7.3.
Leonard Stein and Pierre Boulez outside the Arnold Schoenberg Institute. Photo by Allan Dean Walker. Courtesy Arnold Schönberg Center.

with the New York Philharmonic under Mitropoulos in 1958, he often programmed the Piano Pieces, opp. 11, 19, and 23, and the Suite, which he considered unmatched among piano works of the first quarter of the twentieth century. Having signed an exclusive contract with Columbia Records in 1955, Gould also granted Schoenberg visibility in the record market with his recordings of Schoenberg's entire piano oeuvre, *Pierrot*, *Ode*, the *Phantasy* (with Israel Baker and again with Yehudi Menuhin), and Piano Concerto.[13]

Peter Serkin also created a stir in the 1970s when, long-haired and dressed in Indian tunics, he gave provocative recitals focusing on Schoenberg, Berg, Webern, and Messiaen. Serkin has remained a sought-after soloist for performances of Schoenberg's Piano Concerto, which he recorded multiple times; in 2006 he recorded Schoenberg's entire oeuvre for piano solo for Arcana. Other highly visible American pianists who developed reputations as Schoenberg advocates are Ursula Oppens, Emanuel Ax, who once described himself as a "total fanatic for Schoenberg," and in recent years, Marilyn Nonken and Thomas Schultz.[14]

After World War II, Schoenberg's music lived on in the American dance world, thanks to a number of distinguished choreographers. Both Antony Tudor's acclaimed 1942 *Pillar of Fire* to *Verklärte Nacht*, and José Limón's much-admired 1950 dance *The Exiles* to the Second Chamber Symphony have remained in the contemporary-dance repertoire. In 1952 Limón choreographed Three Piano Pieces, op. 11, resulting in the dance *The Visitation*. George Balanchine created *Opus 34* (1954) to *Begleitmusik* and *Brahms-Schönberg Quartet* (1966) to Schoenberg's arrangement of Brahms's Piano Quartet in G minor. The latter dance has remained in the New York City Ballet's active repertory. Herbert Ross based *Ovid Metamorphosis* (1958) on Five Orchestral Pieces, for the American Ballet Theatre. Roland Petit and Gray Veredon choreographed *Pelleas* in 1969 and 1978 respectively. Mark Morris set his dance *Wonderland* to *Begleitmusik* in 1989, Paul Taylor based *Spindrift* in 1993 on Schoenberg's Handel arrangement, and Richard Tanner of the New York City Ballet set *Schoenberg Variations* (1996) to the Orchestral Variations, op. 31, arranged for two pianos by Charles Wuorinen. *Pierrot* was embraced by such choreographers as Robert Joffrey (1955), Glen Tetley (1962), and Don Redlich (1982).

Tetley's version, famously danced by Nureyev in the 1970s, has been performed most widely.

Press responses to these performances were many and appeared in all the major American daily newspapers and weeklies across the country, as well as in many music periodicals. Yet as Schoenberg has remained a divisive figure in the American music world, reactions were mixed, depending on whether or not a critic was kindly disposed toward new music and/or toward Schoenberg himself. Schoenberg's music has had many adversaries, among them Martin Bernheimer, Harold Blumenfeld, Olin Downes, Donal Henahan, Bernard Holland, Joan Peyser, John Rockwell, Edward Rothstein, David Schiff, Harold Schonberg, and Richard Taruskin. Yet he also had numerous wellwishing commentators, including Arthur Berger, Claudia Cassidy, Edward Downes (Olin's son), Albert Goldberg, Paul Griffiths, Carter Harman, Harriett Johnson, Leighton Kerner, Allan Kozinn, Lawrence Morton, Tim Page, Andrew Porter, John von Rhein, Alex Ross, Eric Salzman, Anthony Tommasini, and Thomas Willis, as well as staunch apologists such as René Leibowitz, Kurt List, Dika Newlin, Nicolas Slonimsky, Konrad Wolff, and Peter Yates.

One of the most popular targets of Schoenberg's opponents was his twelve-tone music, which they attacked using a variety of negative tropes many of them showing an affinity with those used in early reviews of Schoenberg's music. Its detractors deplored the method's artificiality, "cerebral frigidity," and dogmatism.[15] They condemned it as being aristocratic, authoritarian, and even totalitarian.[16] They denounced it as being pathogenic, causing such physical discomforts as "a queasy stomach," "nausea," and "disorientation," and deemed the works themselves pathological: "morbid," "arteriosclerotic," "varicose-veined," an "alien growth in the garden of music."[17] Schoenberg was declared a box-office killer, "shrinking the public for serious music to the size and importance of a masochistic cult."[18] His music was pronounced dead many times throughout the twentieth century.[19] Some critics, however, asserted that he deserved some degree of merit as the catalyst who borrowed the twelve-tone idea from "amateur composer" Josef Matthias Hauer and conveyed it to Berg and Webern, who both used it more successfully than their teacher had. Schoenberg was merely trying "to steal the show."[20] Yet his dissemination of the twelve-tone idea was also seen as a poisonous influence on "Germanophile" American composers, who "lined up behind the somber academicism of Serialism" and tried to establish a serial "oligarchy."[21]

But Schoenberg also had a veritable defense team in the early postwar years, which countered some of these accusations. They praised his music's emotion, validity, and prestige, and promoted dodecaphony's flexibility, "new freedom," compatibility with other compositional approaches, quasi-scientific implications, and historical inevitability.[22] Besides applauding specific aspects of Schoenberg's atonal and twelve-tone works, these commentators commended his technique's originality, rootedness in the great European tradition, and its wide-reaching influence, even affecting jazz composers and minimalists.[23] They hailed impresarios' and performers' programming of Schoenberg as an act of bravery and encouraged the public to be open-minded and patient in the face of a new musical language.[24]

SCHOENBERG'S IMPACT ON COMPOSITION IN AMERICA

In the postwar era, more and more American composers adopted features of Schoenberg's music: atonality, structural complexity, the instrumentation of *Pierrot*, and above all, dodecaphony. Schoenberg and his associates had laid the groundwork for this development in the 1930s and early 1940s, and thanks to the political and cultural changes after World War II, it quickly grew into an important compositional trend that marked American music for several decades. Far from accepting Schoenberg's application of the technique as a yardstick, American composers took advantage of dodecaphony's malleability. In tailoring it to their specific needs, they greatly contributed to an ever-growing variety of serial approaches.

Early American twelve-tone composers, including Adolph Weiss and Wallingford Riegger, were joined in the 1930s and early 1940s by such émigrés as Schoenberg, Paul Dessau, Hanns Eisler, Erich Kahn, Ernst Krenek, Paul Pisk, Steuermann, and Stefan Wolpe, who together disseminated twelve-tone techniques as composers, performers, teachers, and writers in and outside of academia. To most of them, the embrace of dodecaphony signified an anti-fascist gesture and/or an accentuation of their Jewish identity, as it was considered a Jew's invention. All of them chose approaches that differed from Schoenberg's mature twelve-tone technique in which the basic set is treated as a referential background. Weiss and Riegger focused on the linear-thematic and contrapuntal possibilities of dodecaphony. Eisler combined dodecaphony with triadic elements, avoiding Schoenbergian self-expression and contrapuntal complexity. Wolpe, a formerly left-wing activist composer, used a personalized serial technique, often alternating between diatonicism, octatonicism, and twelve-tone ideas. He employed pitch cells within completely chromatic settings and fused serial ideas with traditional harmonic devices. Later Wolpe refrained from the constant exhaustion of the chromatic palette, giving fewer notes greater weight and exploring pitch sets with fewer or more than twelve pitches.[25] Krenek was perhaps most instrumental in using and promoting polyphonic and modal approaches to dodecaphony, thanks to his widely read treatise *Studies in Counterpoint Based on the Twelve-Tone Technique* (1940) and his seminal composition *Lamentatio Jeremiae Prophetae* (1942). In the latter, he used modal counterpoint and applied the principle of rotation to the row, dividing it into two hexachords and systematically alternating the pitches within these hexachords. Thematic and modal treatments of the row became popular in the 1940s and early 1950s with American-born composers such as Aaron Copland, Roger Sessions, and Ben Weber.

John Cage and Lou Harrison, among other American Schoenberg students, also used serialism in their works from the 1930s through the 1950s. But because they engaged extensively in experimentalism, they tend to be overlooked as heirs of the Schoenberg legacy, even though Schoenberg remained a lifelong inspiration to them. Cage explored various unorthodox forms of serialism in the mid-1930s, using a twelve-tone row and its classical transformations in his Sonata for Clarinet (1933); unordered rows of twenty-five pitches based on the principle of nonrepetition in Sonata for Two Voices (1933); and rows as collections of small motives subjected to various serial transformations in *Metamorphosis* (1938). Harrison, for much of his career, alternated twelve-tone or quasi-serial composition with a huge array of different techniques. Modeled after Schoenberg's Suite, op. 25 and written under Schoenberg, Harrison's dodecaphonic Piano Suite (1943) is based on a thematically treated, seven-interval set. Later Harrison used various serial approaches, involving very lyrical tone rows with tonal implications or with fewer than twelve notes, as well as permutation principles. This approach found expression in such compositions as *Schoenbergiana* (1945), Symphony on G (1948–65), and *Rapunzel* (1954).

George Perle and Milton Babbitt, both Schoenberg scholars since the 1930s, emerged in the 1940s as perhaps the most dedicated and influential twelve-tone composers, who took dodecaphony to new levels of sophistication. Perle developed his own twelve-tone modal system in the late 1930s.[26] Rather than using the row as a source for motives and themes, he employed it as a scalar abstraction. He conceived twelve-tone sets with ascending and descending circles of fifths, which determined the vertical dimension of the work. Next Perle refined this tone-centered approach, now calling it twelve-tone tonality and basing it on cyclic sets, twelve-tone sets consisting of symmetrical cells that are combined in pairs to form symmetrically interrelated arrays of chords. Only marginally related to the work of Schoenberg, whose dodecaphonic approaches Perle critiqued, twelve-tone tonality became the focus of many of Perle's compositions after the 1940s.

Equipped with a strong background in mathematics, Babbitt seized on dodecaphony's quasi-scientific potential and transformed it into an intricate system of structurally interrelated sonic textures articulated by pitch, rhythm, timbre, dynamics, and register (Figure 7.4). In his *Three Compositions for Piano* of 1947 he pioneered new types of combinatoriality and invariance, and developed, earlier than his colleagues in Europe, integral serialism by serializing duration and dynamics. Further, in what he called partitioning, Babbitt expanded Schoenberg's approach by constructing trichordal rows whose four forms could be superimposed and could unfold horizontally and vertically at the same time. These so-called arrays would then lead to more complex types of textures, such as all-partition arrays (involving all possible partitionings of a set) and superarrays (arrays of arrays). Babbitt's exploration of serial rhythm led to so-called "time-point sets," based on the division of a measure into twelve points of attack or time units. While Schoenberg believed in stylistic progress as Babbitt does, Schoenberg emphasized emotion and intuition, while Babbitt stresses quasi-scientific and technical qualities in his music. Although he greatly illuminated Schoenberg's dodecaphonic procedures, Babbitt, with his penchant for logical positivism and academicism, reinforced the cliché of Schoen-

FIGURE 7.4.
Milton Babbitt. Courtesy C. F. Peters.

berg's music as cerebral. A charismatic teacher at Princeton and Juilliard, Babbitt drew a host of young composers to serialism, among them Benjamin Boretz, Mario Davidovsky, Donald Martino, and Peter Westergaard, and convinced his institutions to endorse serial composition through scholarships, grants, performances, and employment. Princeton soon became a stronghold of serialism.

Thanks to such Babbitt followers as Davidovsky, Harvey Sollberger, and Charles Wuorinen, Columbia University developed into a center for twelve-tone music as well. In 1959 Princeton and Columbia composers, spearheaded by Babbitt, Otto Luening, and Vladimir Ussachevsky, together established the Columbia-Princeton Electronic Music Center to explore electro-acoustic music, a medium that seemed well suited for the application of serial concepts. Babbitt and Wuorinen soon created strictly serial works for synthesized sound. In 1970 Wuorinen became the first composer to win a Pulitzer Prize for a purely electronic serial work, *Time's Encomium* (1969). One of the most outspoken American advocates of dodecaphony, Wuorinen began using twelve-tone principles in the late 1950s with such works as his Third Symphony (1959). Generalizing and expanding Schoenbergian principles, he punctuated sets with additional tones, used pitch rotation, and serialized intervals, duration, register, and texture. He also produced a treatise on this subject, *Simple Composition* (1979). In recent years, he has focused on pitch centricity in atonal contexts and fused dodecaphony with tonal elements. Having gained sufficient visibility and power, Wuorinen and other members of the so-called "Columbia-Princeton School" or "University Avant-garde" organized themselves in 1966 as the American Society of University Composers (ASUC).[27]

By then numerous older and long-established figures had turned to dodecaphony. Roger Sessions embraced twelve-tone principles for the first time in his Second String Quartet (1951) and Sonata for Violin (1953), influenced by his student Babbitt as well as by Schoenberg and the Italian twelve-tone composer Luigi Dallapiccola. Unlike many of his younger colleagues, however, Sessions tended to use basic sets thematically and freely in his emotionally charged and contrapuntally dense music. Like Schoenberg, he insisted that the work should come out of musical inspiration. Ross Lee Finney, another highly influential composer and teacher, overcame his initial skepticism and adopted dodecaphony in 1950. A student of Berg and Sessions, Finney generally embedded serialism in tonal contexts. His first twelve-tone work was his String Quartet No. 6 in E (1950). Never believing in the equality of all twelve tones, Finney developed the concept of "complementarity," whereby tonality controls large-scale forms, and twelve-tone procedures govern chromatic pitch integration. Although Finney often conceived his rows as singable themes, he also explored rows built from two symmetrical hexachords ("mirror-image hexachords") and serialized non-pitch elements. Finney guided his students George Crumb and Roger Reynolds toward serialism.

Outside academia, Copland and Stravinsky, two of the most powerful figures in contemporary American music in the early 1950s, "converted" to serialism. Initially dismissive of dodecaphony, Copland began to consider it seriously in his Piano Quartet (1950), which featured a thematically treated eleven-note row, embedded in tonal and atonal textures derived from row segments.[28] Beyond the development of his own musical language and search for new challenges and techniques, this turn to serial techniques by Copland can also be seen as motivated by the serialist fad in Europe, his discovery of Webern's and Boulez's emotionally detached serial works, and by Cold War pressures as well. Deflecting attention from his own leftist leanings, Copland stated in 1952 that composers wrote twelve-tone music "*against* a vocal and militant [communist] opposition."[29] He also recognized that, while allowing the retention of his style and aesthetic, dodecaphony "freshened up" his compositional approach, making him hear chords he "wouldn't have heard otherwise."[30] Copland, however, only used serialism occasionally in such works as *Piano Fantasy* (1957), *Connotations* (1962), and *Inscape* (1967).

When the septuagenarian Stravinsky embraced serialism in the early 1950s, it seemed as if he had intentionally waited for Schoenberg to die, thereby denying him the pleasure of witnessing dodecaphony's triumph. Yet Stravinsky's decision resulted less from a long hidden love for this method than from his own artistic crisis brought about by the lukewarm reception of *The Rake's Progress* at its 1951 premiere and by the rejection of *Oedipus Rex* at a Paris concert the following year, where Stravinsky's oratorio was booed and Schoenberg's *Erwartung* was enthusiastically applauded.[31] Guided by his assistant Robert Craft, Stravinsky gradually proceeded from non–twelve tone serialism in his Cantata (1952), Septet (1953), *Three Songs from William Shakespeare* (1953), and *In memoriam Dylan Thomas* (1954), to works with complete twelve-tone sets and more serial stringency, such as *Canticum sacrum* (1955) and *Threni* (1958). Beginning with *Movements* (1960), Stravinsky adapted Krenek's device of cyclic permutation.[32] In such later works as Variations (1964), he extracted pitches from columns in hexachord arrays to produce chords (or "verticals"). Focusing on textural transparency and discipline, Stravinsky's serial approaches owe much to Webern and composers of the Renaissance, while retaining features of his own earlier works such as diatonicism, octatonicsm, and tonal centers. With his serial works, Stravinsky, too, conformed to Cold War ideologies of cultural freedom, publicized at the 1948 International Congress of Composers and Music Critics in Prague. His serial works were also initiated to some degree by his friend Nicolas Nabokov and the CIA-sponsored Congress for Cultural Freedom, an organization to restore postwar cultural life in Western Europe.[33] Stravinsky's turn to serialism had a substantial impact on the American contemporary music scene, blurring the dichotomy of the Stravinsky and Schoenberg camps. Following Stravinsky, Arthur Berger, Irving Fine, Louise Talma, and a host of other composers previously dedicated to neo-classicism began to use serial techniques and often fused them with Stravinsky-like rhythms.

In the mid-1960s musicologist Gilbert Chase observed: "Today the tone-row—and by extension the whole principle of serialization—is no longer the symbol of a particular group or movement, but rather a compositional device that musicians of many persuasions have found useful."[34] Serial principles were even used in experimental, jazz, and film contexts. Dedicated to experimental approaches, Ben Johnston combined serialism with just intonation, microtonality, and indeterminacy in his first two string quartets (1959 and 1964) and *Quintet for Groups* (1966). Lejaren Hiller used twenty-four-note rows for his serially organized String Quartet No. 5 (1962), tuned in quarter-tones. Lukas Foss's *Echoi* (1961) combined serial procedures with performance freedoms. Earle Brown, an associate of Cage, integrated serialism into his open-form works. William Duckworth used the twelve-tone row conceptually in his *Pitch City* (1969), which asks four performers to move via individual routes through a twelve-tone matrix. Classical composers with a jazz background, including Larry Austin, Meyer Kupferman, Gunther Schuller, and Hale Smith, blended serial principles with jazz and improvisation; in 1957 Schuller coined the term "third stream" for such approaches. His 1959 *Conversations*, merging serially conceived textures with jazz improvisation, required the collaboration of a classically trained string quartet and the Modern Jazz Quartet. Smith, who arranged jazz and composed scores for Dizzy Gillespie and Eric Dolphy, featured in his dodecaphonic piano work *Evocations* (1961) rows whose descending consecutive fourths are compatible with the quartal and modal harmony found in bop and post-bop styles. Genuine jazz composers toyed with twelve-tone elements as well. Leonard Feather based the melody of his 1959 *Twelve-Tone Blues* on a twelve-tone row and its standard transformations, harmonizing it with ninth and whole-tone chords. Dolphy combined a row and its retrograde with the Dorian mode on B in *Red Planet*. Bill Evans incorporated three statements of a twelve-tone set in the thematic section of his *T.T.T.* (Twelve Tone Tune, 1971), which he fleshed out with traditional and chromatically altered harmonies. Composers scoring features, cartoons, and experimental films turned to dodecaphony as well. Eisler inserted a twelve-tone passage in the 1943 feature *Hangmen Also Die* (directed by Fritz Lang). Scott Bradley used serial elements in such cartoon scores as the *Tom and Jerry* vehicle "Puttin' on the Dog" (1944), directed by William Hanna and Joseph Barbera, and Tex Avery's classic "The Cat That Hated People" (1948). Leonard Rosenman, Ernest Gold, Franz Waxman, and Miklos Rózsa used dodecaphony in *The Cobweb* (1955), *On the Beach* (1959), *The Nun's Story* (1959), and *King of Kings* (1961), respectively, invariably to suggest negativity. John Whitney, Sr., who studied dodecaphony with Leibowitz in Paris, pioneered new forms of visual-aural fusion with techniques borrowed from musical serialism in such abstract films as *Catalog* (1961) and *Arabesque* (1975).

As serialism peaked in the late 1960s, more and more of its proponents, both in and out of the academy, began to develop reservations about it. The use or nonuse of twelve-tone ideas became an increasingly divisive issue, especially when such powerful proponents as Babbitt and Wuorinen suggested that serialism was the only legitimate compositional approach and expressed little concern about the disconnect between themselves and mainstream audiences.[35] Some composers felt that serialism was no longer innovative enough and left it for new and experimental musical systems that were indebted to science and non-Western cultures. Spearheaded by the one-time serialist Cage and his composer-friends Brown, Morton Feldman, David Tudor, and Christian Wolff, a countercultural "downtown" Manhattan movement emerged with artists who were mostly unaffiliated with academia, countering the uptown serial center at Columbia University.[36] Squabbles about which group continued Schoenberg's heritage and was the "real" avant-garde emerged as well. Viewing themselves as Schoenberg's true heirs, "uptown" composers dismissed downtown music as "theatrico-musical expressions" and "Cagean amateurism" and questioned Cage's studies with Schoenberg.[37] Conversely, downtown composers poked fun at the "university" avant-garde and its "anti-experimental Einstein[s]."[38]

Another group of composers who were once thoroughly immersed in twelve-tone composition challenged university-based serialists in a different way. Yearning for self-expression and audience appeal, they questioned serialism's premise of musical progress, as well as its intellectualism and prestige value, and instead emphatically embraced tonality, and the styles, forms, and genres of the past. Although initially panned as renegades, these "neo-Romantic" composers—among them Jacob Druckman, Lukas Foss, Roger Hannay, George Rochberg, and David Del Tredici—wound up retracing some of Schoenberg's compositional steps in America. Perhaps the most famous "deserter" was Rochberg, who turned from a staunch Schoenberg apologist and prolific twelve-tone composer in the 1950s into a Schoenberg adversary in the 1960s, resenting the "abstraction and rationalization" of serialism and dismissing the belief that it represented the "necessary extension of the past."[39] Yet while Rochberg rejected serialism in favor of eclectic explorations of past styles, he admitted that he "didn't throw over the expressionistic aspects of atonality."[40]

As the neo-Romantic movement gained momentum, new tonal works were welcomed by impresarios, audiences, and critics in the 1970s, and serialism began to lose steam. Having long suffered from a bad reputation in the concert world, serial composers became underdogs. John Corigliano poked fun at them in his tonal cabaret song of 1997 "Dodecaphonia (or they call her Twelve-Tone Rose)," about a serial criminal seductress. But despite the widely accepted claim of serialism's alleged death, American composers, old and young, still use twelve-tone principles in their music, though they do so in a more subtle and flexible fashion than that of the early postwar decades. And they use them with the audience in mind.[41] However, to avoid the prejudices of audiences and critics, composers now tend not to discuss openly the technical aspects of their music, and refrain from using serial terminology in program and CD liner notes.[42]

Numerous American composers have paid tribute to Schoenberg without adopting dodecaphonic methods themselves. Elliott Carter and Ralph Shapey, though interested in Schoenberg's work, shunned serial methods. Carter's structuring of chromatic pitch materials concentrated on specific timbrally fixed intervals and harmonies in such works as his Second String Quartet (1959), Piano Concerto (1965), and *Night Fantasies* (1980). Shapey's contrapuntally dense music used dissonant harmonic aggregates altered by sophisticated variation techniques. Yet both reveal an affinity to twelve-tone music. Mark Brunswick, Leon Kirchner, and Seymour Shifrin also responded to and built upon Schoenberg's expressivity, nonserial use of chromaticicism, and contrapuntal complexity. Even such jazz composers as Anthony Braxton, Charles Mingus, and Cecil Taylor professed their debt to Schoenberg's advocacy of dissonance.

A broad range of American composers with widely differing aesthetic persuasions paid homage to Schoenberg through specific choices of genre and instrumentation and through parody during the later twentieth century. Apart from writing chamber symphonies and string quartets with a soprano part, composers from Babbitt to Joan Tower and Pauline Oliveros wrote works based on the instrumentation of *Pierrot*, reinterpreting its unique instrumentation (voice, eight instruments and five players), vocal treatment, musical structure, and theatricality.[43] Both John Adams, with his 1985 *Harmonielehre* and 1992 Chamber Symphony, and Dika Newlin, who was once called the "foremost American woman dodecaphonist," with her punk rock songs "Alien Baby" and "Rockingham," furnished tongue-in-cheek responses to Schoenberg's life and work.[44]

SCHOLARLY RESPONSES TO SCHOENBERG'S MUSIC

Although Schoenberg considered himself only secondarily a music theorist, he made a great impact on American musicology. Lending itself to theorization and science-inspired thinking, his music was extensively studied and taught at many American universities, and inspired American scholars to develop highly influential theories and analyses of dodecaphonic and atonal music. Thanks to his lectures and published writings on tonal music, Schoenberg also instigated new analyses of classical works, spurring the rise of music theory as an autonomous academic discipline and a sea change in musical thought and practice in America.

Schoenberg had been vague about dodecaphony's theoretical implications, producing only one talk, "Composing with Twelve-Tones," which he delivered several times between 1934 and 1946 and included in *Style and Idea* in 1950.[45] American musicologists and composers began to fill this void in the 1930s and early 1940s. To Schoenberg's amazement, Richard Hill published an in-depth study of Schoenberg's twelve-tone works in the January 1936 *Musical Quarterly*, identifying his thematic and nonlinear row treatments, superimpositions of rows, and a device later to be termed "combinatoriality" (a set whose second hexachord forms, together with the first hexachord of one of its transformations, a twelve-tone aggregate).[46] Krenek issued several studies of twelve-tone techniques between 1939 and 1944, including *Here and Now* (1939) and *Studies in Counterpoint Based on the Twelve-Tone Technique* (1940), in which he explained nonthematic, thematic, and polyphonic uses of tone rows.[47] Concurrently, Perle published his first essays on his twelve-tone modal system and twelve-tone tonality combining dodecaphonic ideas with hierarchic relations among pitch classes and chords comparable to those existing in tonal practice.[48] With these systems, however, Perle intended to replace what he saw as accidental harmonic relationships in Schoenberg's dodecaphonic music.

After 1945 the study of dodecaphony rapidly and radically advanced. In 1949 René Leibowitz, a Polish-born French composer and passionate Schoenberg promoter on both sides of the Atlantic, for the first time provided broad coverage of music by Schoenberg, Berg, and Webern in his landmark study *Schoenberg and His School* (Philosophical Library, 1947).[49] While widely read and appreciated, the book was also severely criticized by Copland, Babbitt, and Perle for its "dogmatic" and "fanatical tone," shallow musical discussions, and allegedly deceptive analogies between tonal and dodecaphonic music.[50] With his scathing 1950 review of Leibowitz's volume, Babbitt publicly revealed for the first time his sophisticated insights into dodecaphony and set the stage for many detailed studies of this subject in the years to come.[51] In 1946 he had completed his Ph.D. dissertation at Princeton University, "The Function of the Set Structure in the Twelve-Tone System"—which, due to a lack of competent readers on the faculty, was not accepted until 1992. Nevertheless it became a widely read and authoritative manuscript on dodecaphony in America. Drawing on set theory rather than on Schoenberg's metaphysical and organicist remarks on dodecaphony, Babbitt rationalized and extended the theoretical foundation of twelve-tone music. He coined a soon commonly used mathematicized terminology—"pitch class," "set," "aggregate," "combinatoriality"—to describe manifold serial concepts, and developed positivistic methodologies to analyze twelve-tone music. Babbitt published his research in three seminal articles: "Some Aspects of Twelve-Tone Composition" (1955), "Twelve-Tone Invariants as Compositional Determinants," and "Set Structure as Compositional Determinant" (both 1961).

Although other scholars—among them Krenek, Perle, and Rochberg—also published twelve-tone studies in the 1950s and 1960s, Babbitt was by far the most influential theorist, turning Princeton into a major center of serial theory. In 1961 he initiated a Ph.D. program in musical composition, which emphasized the theoretical side of composition and granted composition the weight of scientific research. While his Ph.D. program was imitated by numerous other American universities, Babbitt conferred doctorates and master's degrees on many composer-theorists, including Benjamin Boretz, David Lewin, Donald Martino, Peter Westergaard, and Godfrey Winham. Their twelve-tone research built on Babbitt's and was published in such newly founded music-theory journals as the Princeton-based *Perspectives of New Music*, a veritable mouthpiece for twelve-tone theorists for many years, and the Yale-based *Journal of Music Theory*.[52] From the 1970s on, such theorists as Ethan

Haimo, Lewin, Robert Morris, Bruce Samet, and Charles Wuorinen have contributed important book-length studies to the ever growing theoretical and analytical literature on dodecaphony. Lewin illuminated twelve-tone syntax through the use of mathematical group theory in his 1987 *Generalized Musical Intervals and Transformations*. Wuorinen and Morris conceived in their respective treatises, *Simple Composition* (1979) and *Composition with Pitch Classes* (1987), new extensions of existing twelve-tone practices. Samet addressed perceptive issues of twelve-tone music in his 1987 *Hearing Aggregates*, and Haimo, drawing on Babbitt's theories, provided detailed analyses of Schoenberg's works from 1914 to 1928 in *Schoenberg's Serial Odyssey: The Evolution of His Twleve-Tone Method* (1990).

Musicologists such as Adele Katz, Paul Henry Lang, Richard Taruskin, and William Thomson, however, questioned the structural value, alleged historical inevitability, and compositional and theoretical legacy of dodecaphonic music. Thomson, a USC-based music theorist, dedicated an entire (albeit flawed) book, *Schoenberg's Error*, to denigrating the music and theories of Schoenberg and his followers.[53] Other critics, including composer-theorist Fred Lerdahl, raised concerns about the "cognitive constraints" of twelve-tone music.[54] Such scholars as Edward Cone, Joseph Kerman, and Leo Treitler, along with composers Krenek, Perle, and Rochberg—all of whom had once contributed to the literature on twelve-tone techniques—attacked Babbitt-influenced analytical and theoretical approaches to twelve-tone music because of their affirmative tone, quasi-scientific language, formalism and their failure to address a composition's audible aspects or to communicate between the composer and the audience.[55] Treitler, a music historian, also deplored the split between music history and theory caused by music theory's quasi-scientific direction, which forced readers to choose between narrowly focused and normative analyses, and historical, aesthetic, and critical examinations of musical works.[56]

In the early 1960s American theorists began considering Schoenberg's nonserial atonal oeuvre, which had been commonly viewed as a mere pre-serial experiment. Once again, most scholars favored formalist approaches, drawing on Babbitt's serial theories, rather than Schoenberg's own preliminary analysis of his atonal Four Orchestral Songs, op. 22, in which he focused on motivic and thematic relationships as they are also found in music of the past.[57] Perle and Lewin were among the first to analyze seriously the horizontally and vertically occurring small groups of intervals and their intervallic connections in Schoenberg's atonal works, and to publish their findings.[58] Expanding on Babbitt's serial theory and Perle's and Lewin's studies, the eminent Yale-based music theorist Allen Forte wrote his seminal 1973 book *The Structure of Atonal Music*. He formulated for the first time a general theory and tools for a systematic analysis of atonal music, the so-called pitch-class set theory, in which he defined the interrelations of recurring vertical and linear note groups (or "unordered pitch-class sets") in terms of intervallic equivalency (related by transposition and inversion) and similarity (meaning nonequivalency or complementarity). As Forte and his disciples soon refined and expanded his theory and added to the growing formalist music-theory literature, critics such as Haimo, Perle, and Taruskin raised concerns about the usefulness of Forte's theory as an analytical device. They noted that it failed to illuminate Schoenberg's compositional thought processes or the contextual meaning and perceptible qualities of Schoenberg's atonal works.[59]

Several American Schoenberg scholars, however, refused to conform to the formalist mainstream. Never relying on Babbitt's or Forte's theories, Dika Newlin was one of the few who published many articles on Schoenberg's nontonal works from the late 1940s through the 1970s, focusing on his music's perceptive aspects (audibility of form and syntax), historical-cultural contexts, and performance questions. Her Ph.D. dissertation "Bruckner, Mahler, Schoenberg," completed in 1945 at Columbia University and published as a book in 1947, was not only one of the first dissertations on Schoenberg in English, but also a pioneering musical-cultural study foreshadowing the so-called "new musicology" of the 1980s. She eschewed historical determinism and evolutionary concepts, and examined musical issues along with the literary, artistic, and political background, as well as the personal relationships of the three composers, in order to gauge the "interplay and contrast of convention and revolt" in Schoenberg's work.[60] Although she was long treated as an outsider, such scholars as Joseph Auner, Elizabeth Keathley, and Bryan Simms have in a sense followed her model in steering clear of a dogmatic use of quasi-scientific theories.[61]

Although many American theorists were infatuated with Schoenberg's nontonal works, especially in the first three postwar decades, several scholars investigated his early tonal works, tools for the analysis of tonal works, and general compositional philosophy. Walter Frisch cogently analyzed and contextualized Schoenberg's early tonal music in his book *The Early Works of Arnold Schoenberg, 1893–1908* (1993). In his 2006 volume *Schoenberg's Transformation of Musical Language*, Haimo traced the subtle and gradual changes of Schoenberg's harmonic idiom, which led him to atonality. Having been initially overshadowed by Heinrich Schenker's tonal theories, Schoenberg's ideas about tonal music began to attract greater attention after the publication of his *Fundamentals of Musical Composition* in 1967.[62] Significantly, scholars explained and applied in analysis such Schoenbergian concepts as the "musical idea," "basic shape [*Grundgestalt*]," and "developing variation," through which Schoenberg elucidated connections between the music of the past and his own oeuvre. Patricia Carpenter, Charlotte Cross, and Severine Neff discussed Schoenberg's notion of the musical idea, a crucial category in his musical thought, which denoted a small musical entity such as a motive, the "totality of a piece," and a method that turns musical imbalance into balance.[63] Carpenter and Neff published the first annotated edition of Schoenberg's compositional treatise on this topic, *The Musical Idea, and the Logic, Technique, and Art of Its Presentation* (1995). Neff and Cross edited and translated seminal writings by Schoenberg in a book entitled *Coherence, Counterpoint, Instrumentation, and Instruction in Form* (1993). Carpenter and David Epstein, among others, explicated, reinterpreted, and analytically employed "basic shape," another significant concept with a unifying referential function.[64] However, the principle of "developing variation," transcending repetitive and ornamental variation, has received most attention and was freely interpreted and applied to repertoire from the late nineteenth century to the present. Among the many scholars intrigued by this concept, Frisch effectively adapted it to illuminate the sophisticated motivic development of Brahms's later variation techniques in his 1984 book *Brahms and the Principle of Developing Variation*.

Against all odds Schoenberg had successfully adapted to American culture and was able to plant seeds that continue to bear rich fruit, in performance, composition, and scholarship, in the United States. He inspired many esteemed performers to champion his works, despite a largely conservative music environment, not only during his lifetime but also after his death. Although he was sometimes dubbed "the greatest unperformed composer," his music retained its niche in American concert programs and fared well in the recording industry, even as performance institutions and record labels struggled in the last three decades of the twentieth century, facing such economic challenges as inflation and the nonregulated business culture unleashed by Ronald Reagan. In defiance of the shrinkage or disappearance of some performance venues, American Schoenberg aficionados have found new outlets, such as the Internet, to present performances of his music to international audiences. Schoenberg's twelve-tone ideas have also fallen on fertile ground. Schoenberg and other composers were able to compose twelve-tone works and, as teachers, prepare young composers for the adoption of this technique, during a time when serial music was largely banned in Nazi Europe. The diverse compositional interpretations of the twelve-tone idea filled the gap that Schoenberg had created with his relative silence on this subject. They also generated very pluralistic consequences that he might not have anticipated.

Although he cherished being associated in the popular mind with Einstein, Schoenberg regarded his art as standing in opposition to science, and would have been surprised by the serial vogue and quasi-scientific creative interpretations of his ideas fueled by postwar American academia.[65] Neither could he have foreseen the experimental, jazz, and film composers' reactions to his twelve-tone concepts, although he pointed to the viability of tonality ("On revient toujours") and the integration of twelve-tone and tonal ideas in his own American oeuvre. To this day numerous American composers still build on his compositional ideas, although Princeton and Columbia, among other universities, are no longer hotbeds of serial research, and the relocation of USC's Arnold Schoenberg Institute to Vienna has made Schoenberg scholarship more difficult for scholars based in North America.[66] But his music and ideas continue to fascinate American scholars, many of whom have earned an international reputation in the field of Schoenberg research. His music greatly enriched twentieth-century American music and found its secure place in today's culture. Schoenberg's works and ideas are very much alive and here to stay.

List of Abbreviations

ARCHIVES

ASC	Arnold Schönberg Center, Vienna
LC	Library of Congress, Washington, D.C.
NYPL	New York Public Library
WB	Wienbibliothek (formerly Wiener Stadt- und Landesbibliothek), Vienna,

PERIODICALS

AfMw	*Archiv für Musikwissenschaft*
CSM	*Christian Science Monitor*
JAMS	*Journal of the American Musicological Society*
JASC	*Journal of the Arnold Schönberg Center*
JASI	*Journal of the Arnold Schoenberg Institute*
JMT	*Journal of Music Theory*
LAT	*Los Angeles Times*
MA	*Musical America*
MC	*Musical Courier*
ML	*Musical Leader*
MM	*Modern Music*
MQ	*Musical Quarterly*
NYT	*New York Times*
PNM	*Perspectives of New Music*

BOOKS

ASGA	*Arnold Schönberg Gedenkausstellung 1974*. Ed. Ernst Hilmar. Vienna: Universal Edition, 1974.
ASL	*Arnold Schoenberg Letters*. Ed. Erwin Stein, trans. Eithne Wilkins and Ernst Kaiser. London: Faber, 1964.
ASLIB	*Arnold Schönberg, 1874–1951. Lebensgeschichte in Begegnungen*. Ed.Nuria Nono-Schoenberg. Klagenfurt, Austria: Ritter, 1998.
ASR	*A Schoenberg Reader: Documents of a Life*. Ed. Joseph Auner. New Haven: Yale University Press, 2003.
ASSG	*Arnold Schönberg. Stile herrschen, Gedanken siegen. Ausgewählte Schriften*. Ed. Anna Maria Morazzoni. Mainz: Schott, 2007.
ASSP	*Arnold Schoenberg Self-Portrait: A Collection of Articles, Program Notes and Letters by the Composer about His Own Work*. Ed. Nuria Schoenberg Nono. Pacific Palisades: Belmont Music Publishers, 1988.
ASSW	*Arnold Schönberg Sämtliche Werke*. Ed. Josef Rufer et al. Vienna, 1966–.
BSC	*The Berg-Schoenberg Correspondence: Selected Letters*. Ed. Juliane Brand,

	Christopher Hailey, and Donald Harris. New York: Norton, 1987.
DIP	*Driven into Paradise: The Musical Migration from Nazi Germany to the United States*. Ed. Reinhold Brinkmann and Christoph Wolff. Berkeley:University of California Press, 1999.
HHS	H. H. Stuckenschmidt. *Arnold Schoenberg: His Life, World and Work*. Trans. Humphrey Searle.New York: Schirmer, 1977.
MI	*The Musical Idea and the Logic, Technique, and Art of Its Presentation*. Ed. Patricia Carpenter and Severine Neff. New York: Columbia University Press, 1995.
SI	*Style and Idea: Selected Writings of Arnold Schoenberg*. Ed. Leonard Stein, trans. Leo Black. Berkeley: University of California Press, 1984.
SR	Dika Newlin. *Schoenberg Remembered: Diaries and Recollections, 1938–1976*. New York: Pendragon, 1980.
SW	*Schoenberg and His World*. Ed. Walter Frisch. Princeton: Princeton University Press, 1999.
TASC	*The Arnold Schoenberg Companion*. Ed. Walter Bailey. Westport, CT: Greenwood, 1998.

Notes

CHAPTER 1

1. See Egon Wellesz, *Arnold Schönberg*, trans. William Kerridge (London: Dent, 1925); René Leibowitz, *Schoenberg et son école* (Paris: Janin, 1947) and *Schoenberg* (Paris: Editions du Seuil, 1969).
2. See, for instance, Malcolm Gillies, "Bartók in America," in *The Cambridge Companion to Béla Bartók*, ed. Amanda Bayley (Cambridge: Cambridge University Press, 2001), 190–201; and Stephen Hinton, "Kurt Weill: Life, Work, and Posterity," in *Amerikanismus, Americanism, Weill – Die Suche nach kultureller Identität in der Moderne*, ed. Hermann Danuser and Hermann Gottschewski (Schliengen: Argus, 2003), 209–20.
3. Jan Meyerowitz, *Arnold Schönberg* (Berlin: Colloquium, 1967), 30. See also Michael Mäckelmann, *Arnold Schönberg und das Judentum. Der Komponist und sein religiöses, nationales und politisches Selbstverständnis nach 1921* (Hamburg: Musikalienhandlung K. D. Wagner, 1984), 257; and Hartmut Krones, *Arnold Schönberg. Werk und Leben* (Vienna: Steinbauer, 2005), 114.
4. See Jost Hermand, "A Survivor from Germany. Schönberg im Exil," in *Exil. Literatur und Künste nach 1933*, ed. Alexander Stephan (Bonn: Bouvier, 1990), 108; and "Ein Überlebender aus Deutschland. Zur Radikalität von Arnold Schönbergs zionistischer Wende," in *Judentum und deutsche Kultur. Beispiele einer schmerzhaften Symbiose*, ed. Jost Hermand (Cologne: Böhlau, 1996), 177.
5. See David Schiff, "Schoenberg's Cool Eye for the Erotic," *NYT*, 8 August 1999, 30; and Anthony Heilbut, *Exiled in Paradise: German Refugee Artists and Intellectuals in America, from the 1930s to the Present* (New York: Viking, 1983), 135–36.
6. Kevin Starr, *The Dream Endures: California Enters the 1940s* (New York: Oxford University Press, 1997), 382–83, 363.
7. Malcolm MacDonald, *Schoenberg* (London: Dent, 1976), 49–50. Compare MacDonald's revised *Schoenberg* (New York: Oxford University Press, 2008), 73–76; and Eberhard Freitag, *Schönberg* (Reinbek: Rowohlt, 1973), 136–37.
8. See *HHS*, 476–78, 483. Reich's two short chapters on Schoenberg's American years consist mostly of quotations. Willi Reich, *Schoenberg: A Critical Biography*, trans. Leo Black (Edinburgh: Longman, 1971), 189–235.
9. See *ASL*, 197–301. Thousands of letters Schoenberg wrote during his American years have remained unpublished and have not been considered by most of Schoenberg's recent biographers.
10. See Wilhelm Sinkovicz, *Mehr als zwölf Töne. Arnold Schönberg* (Vienna: Paul Zsolnay, 1998); and Manuel Gervink, *Arnold Schönberg und seine Zeit* (Laaber: Laaber, 2000). Sinkovicz titled the chapter on Schoenberg's American years "Isolation – der Komponist im amerikanischen Exil," and called America Schoenberg's "Gastland" (host land) (249–313). See also Dominique Jameux, *L'école de Vienne* (Paris: Fayard, 2002), 595–641.

11. Walter Rubsamen, "Schoenberg in America," *MQ* 37, no. 4 (October 1951): 469–89.
12. Dika Newlin, "Schönberg in America, 1933–1948," *Music Survey* 1, nos. 5–6 (1949): 128–31, 185–89; and *SR*.
13. *SR*, 337–38.
14. Newlin conveyed that Rubsamen's essay "drew the wrath of some Schoenberg friends for its stress on the composer's superstition." See *SR*, 90. German musicologist Michael Mäckelmann criticized Newlin's "Schoenberg in America" articles as "transfigured descriptions." See Mäckelmann, *Arnold Schönberg*, 256.
15. Matthias Henke, *Arnold Schönberg* (Hamburg: Deutscher Taschenbuch Verlag, 2001); and Allen Shawn, *Arnold Schoenberg's Journey* (New York: Farrar, Straus and Giroux, 2002), 248–49, 264.
16. Richard Taruskin, "The Poietic Fallacy: Review of *Arnold Schoenberg's Journey*, by Allen Shawn," *Musical Times* 145, no. 1886 (Spring 2004): 13.
17. Laura Fermi, *Illustrious Immigrants: The Intellectual Migration from Europe, 1930–41* (Chicago: University of Chicago Press, 1968), 223.
18. MacDonald, *Schoenberg* (1976 ed.), 44.
19. Alexander Ringer, *Arnold Schönberg. Das Leben im Werk* (Stuttgart: Metzler, 2002), 287.
20. Gillies, "Bartók in America," 194.
21. See Oliver Neighbour and H. Wiley Hitchcock, "Arnold Schoenberg," in *The New Grove Dictionary of American Music*, ed. H. Wiley Hitchcock and Stanley Sadie (London: Macmillan, 1986), 158–59; see Reich, *Schoenberg*, 227; and Sinkovicz, *Mehr als zwölf Töne*, 304.
22. Meyerowitz, *Arnold Schönberg*, 5.
23. Sinkovicz, *Mehr als zwölf Töne*, 286.
24. Ibid., 285. The pension was initially $28.50 (about $340 in 2009) and rose to $40.38 per month by 1945 (about $475 in 2009). These and the following figures were obtained from S. Morgan Friedman's inflation calculator at http://www.westegg.com/inflation/infl.cgi
25. *HHS*, 469. Edgar Varèse's several applications for a Guggenheim were also rejected.
26. Alma Mahler-Werfel, *Mein Leben* (Frankfurt am Main: Fischer, 1960), 278. See also Alma Mahler quoted in Freitag, *Schönberg*, 151; and Hermand, "A Survivor," 112.
27. Michael Kater believes that UCLA authorities exploited Schoenberg, but fails to mention that his salary was well above the average annual full-time American wage of $1,146 (1936) and $2,292 (1944) (about $17,550 and $27,650 respectively in 2009). See Michael Kater, *Composers of the Nazi Era: Eight Portraits* (New York: Oxford University Press, 2000), 187; *The Value of a Dollar, 1860–2004*, ed. Scott Derks (Lakeville, CT: Greyhouse Publishing, 2004), 206–54; and *National Income and Product Accounts of the United States, 1929–2000*, electronic resource (Washington, D.C.: U.S. Department of Commerce, Economics and Statistics Administration Bureau of Economic Analysis, 2001).
28. See Arnold Schoenberg to Georg Schönberg, 21 August 1950, LC; Arnold Schoenberg to the American Committee for the Relief of Yemenite Jews, Israel, 26 September 1950, LC.
29. This success is mentioned by Rubsamen, Reich, and Ringer. See Rubsamen, "Schoenberg," 480; Reich, *Schoenberg*, 214; and Ringer, *Arnold Schönberg*, 59. Yet Stuckenschmidt touches only briefly on two performances of *Pillar of Fire*, one of which was conducted by Schoenberg himself on 8 February 1945. *HHS*, 453, 470.
30. Schoenberg had been a member of ASCAP since 1939. Rubsamen stated in 1951: "As it turned out, the royalties from ASCAP, subsequently increased in most generous fashion, were a boon to the composer during the last years of his life." Rubsamen, "Schoenberg," 471.

31. Sinkovicz, who omitted discussions of Schoenberg's occupation with Jewish matters in his monograph, also belongs in this list of names.
32. *HHS*, 367–70.
33. MacDonald, *Schoenberg* (1976 ed.), 56.
34. See Mäckelmann's above quoted monograph; and Alexander Ringer, *Arnold Schoenberg: The Composer as Jew* (New York: Oxford University Press, 1990). See, for instance, Hermand's above quoted two essays; Charlotte Cross and Russell Berman, eds., *Political and Religious Ideas in the Works of Arnold Schoenberg* (New York: Garland Publishing, 2000); William Kangas, "The Ethics and Aesthetics of (Self)Representation: Arnold Schoenberg and Jewish Identity," *Leo Baeck Institute Yearbook* 45 (2000): 135–69; Steven Cahn, "Dépasser l'universalisme: Une écoute particulariste d'*Un survivant de Varsovie*, op. 46 et du *Kol nidre* op. 39 de Schoenberg," *Ostinato rigore. Revue internationale d'études musicales* 17, no. 1 (2001): 221–34; "'Kol nidre' in America," *JASC* 4 (2002): 203–18; David Schiller, *Bloch, Schoenberg, Bernstein: Assimilating Jewish Music* (New York: Oxford University Press, 2003); and Klára Móricz, *Jewish Identities: Nationalism, Racism, and Utopianism in Twentieth-Century Music* (Berkeley: University of California Press, 2008).
35. Gervink, *Arnold Schönberg*, 290–91, 302–6; Ringer, *Arnold Schönberg*, 252ff., 271–73, 288; Shawn, *Arnold Schoenberg's Journey*, 237–41; and Hartmut Krones, *Arnold Schönberg. Werk und Leben* (Vienna: Steinbauer, 2005), 228–39. Schoenberg's Jewishness has recently been challenged since he neither practiced his Jewish faith at home nor attended the temple. Camille Crittenden, "Texts and Contexts of *A Survivor from Warsaw*, op. 46," in Cross and Berman, *Political and Religious Ideas*, 246; and Móricz, *Jewish Identities*.
36. See Richard Taruskin, "The Dark Side of Modern Music: The Sins of Toscanini, Stravinsky, Schoenberg: Review of *Music in Fascist Italy*, by Harvey Sachs," *New Republic* 199, no. 10 (5 September 1988), 33–34. Bluma Goldstein, "Schoenberg's *Moses und Aron*: A Vanishing Biblical Nation," in Cross and Berman, *Political and Religious Ideas*, 187–89; and Móricz, *Jewish Identities*, 214–16.
37. See, for instance, Stuckenschmidt's, Reich's and Freitag's monographs. Schoenberg's political views, his residency in America, and musical individualism hindered his reception in the former DDR for many years. Yet from the mid-1970s on, musicologists approached the topic of Schoenberg in America by focusing on his antifascist engagement. Frank Schneider, "Versuch einer musikgeschichtlichen Positionsbestimmung," *Beiträge zur Musikwissenschaft* 16, no. 2 (1974): 75–95, 277–96; and "Schönberg und die 'politische Musik'," *Beiträge der Musikwissenschaft* 20, no. 1 (1978): 23–27; and Mathias Hansen, "*Ode to Napoleon* – Zum antifaschistischen Engagement Arnold Schönbergs," in *Arbeitsheft 24. Forum: Musik in der DDR. Arnold Schönberg 1874–1951. Zum 25. Todestag des Komponisten*, ed. Mathias Hansen and Christa Müller (Berlin: Akademie der Künste der DDR, 1976), 79–88. See also Hanns-Werner Heister, "Zum politischen Engagement des Unpolitischen," in *Herausforderung Schönberg. Was die Musik des Jahrhunderts veränderte*, ed. Ulrich Dibelius (Munich: Hanser, 1974), 27–46; and "Musikalische Reaktion und politisches Engagement. Über drei Werke Arnold Schönbergs," *Beiträge zur Musikwissenschaft* 16, no. 4 (1974): 261–76; and Wes Blomster, "The Reception of Arnold Schoenberg in the German Democratic Republic," *PNM* 21, nos. 1–2 (Fall–Summer 1982/1983): 114–32.
38. Albrecht Dümling, "Zwischen Außenseiterstatus und Integration. Musiker-Exil an der amerikanischen Westküste," in *Musik im Exil. Folgen des Nazismus für die internationale Musikkultur*, ed. Hanns-Werner Heister, Claudia Maurer-Zenck, and Peter Petersen (Frankfurt am Main: Fischer, 1993), 315; Gervink, *Arnold Schönberg*, 309; and Ringer, *Arnold Schönberg*, 286–93.

39. See Gervink, *Arnold Schönberg*, 309–10; and Ringer, *Arnold Schönberg*, 286.
40. See Martin Jay, "The German Migration: Is There a Figure in the Carpet?" in *Exiles and Emigrés: The Flight of European Artists from Hitler*, ed. Stephanie Barron and Sabine Eckmann (Los Angeles: Harry Abrams, 1997), 331.
41. Theodor W. Adorno, "Einführung in die Zweite Kammersymphonie von Schönberg (1954)," in *Theodor W. Adorno: Gesammelte Schriften*, ed. Rolf Tiedemann (Darmstadt: Wissenschaftliche Buchgesellschaft, 1998), vol. 18, 629.
42. Heilbut, *Exiled*, 74.
43. Albert Goldberg, "The Sounding Board: The Transplanted Composer," *LAT*, 14 May 1950.
44. Theodor W. Adorno, "Arnold Schoenberg, 1874–1951," in *Prisms*, trans. Samuel and Shierry Weber (London: Neville Spearman, 1967), 171; and Adorno, *Philosophy of Modern Music*, trans. Anne G. Mitchell and Wesley Bloomster (New York: Seabury Press, 1973), 119–20.
45. Adorno, *Prisms*, 168.
46. Pierre Boulez, "Arnold Schoenberg," in *Encyclopédie de la musique*, ed. François Michel (Paris: Fasquelle, 1961).
47. Pierre Boulez, "Schoenberg Is Dead (long version)," in *Notes of an Apprenticeship*, trans. Herbert Weinstock (New York: Knopf, 1968), 268–76.
48. Similarly, several works from Schoenberg's European years, including his folksong arrangements (1929,) the Six Pieces for Male Chorus, op. 35 (1930), and his Cello Concerto after Monn (1933), were neglected or deemphasized due to their heterogeneous tendencies.
49. Arnold Whittall, "Schoenberg since 1951: Overlapping Opposites," *Musical Times* 142, no. 1876 (Fall 2001): 18; and David Lieberman, "Schoenberg Rewrites His Will: *A Survivor from Warsaw*, op. 46," in Berman and Cross, *Political and Religious Ideas*, 212.
50. Joseph Auner, "Schoenberg's Handel Concerto and the Ruins of Tradition," *JAMS* 49, no. 2 (Summer 1996): 312. Dahlhaus pointed out in 1983 that "all the impulses that emerged in the last decade were already present (albeit under different historical conditions) in Schoenberg's late works." Carl Dahlhaus, "Schoenberg's Late Works," in Dahlhaus, *Schoenberg and the New Music*, trans. Derrick Puffet and Alfred Clayton (Cambridge: Cambridge University Press, 1987), 168.
51. Many works, from his Suite, op. 25 (1921) through his String Trio (1946), combine twelve-tone ideas and elements of the past. See also Auner, "Schoenberg's Handel," 312; and Whittall, "Schoenberg since 1951," 12–14.
52. Olin Downes, "New Suite by Arnold Schoenberg," *NYT*, 13 October 1935. See also Lawrence Gilman, "New Music by Schoenberg," *New York Herald Tribune*, 19 October 1935.
53. *SI*, 109.
54. Adorno, *Philosophy*, 120; and Pierre Barbaud, *Schoenberg* (Paris: Editions Main d'Oeuvre, 1997), 151.
55. Adorno, *Philosophy*, 121.
56. Ibid.
57. Eisler quoted in Heilbut, *Exiled*, 157. Unlike Schoenberg, Eisler successfully made concessions to the American market as a film composer in Hollywood from 1942 to 1948. Soon thereafter, back in the DDR, Eisler unsuccessfully attempted to rehabilitate Schoenberg's music, which had been branded as "decadent formalism."
58. See Goldberg, "The Sounding Board." See also Ernst Krenek, "America's Influence on its Emigré Composers," *PNM* 8, no. 2 (Spring–Summer 1970): 112–17; and see Boulez, "Schoenberg Is Dead," 273.

59. See Jay, "The German Migration," 328; and Gerald Abraham, "Arnold Schoenberg," in *Grove Dictionary of Music and Musicians*, ed. Henry Colles, 4th ed., suppl. vol. (London: Macmillan, 1940).
60. Albrecht Dümling, "Zwischen Außenseiterstatus und Integration. Musiker-Exil an der US-amerikanischen Westküste," in Heister and Maurer-Zenck, *Musik im Exil*, 331.
61. Jarrell Jackman, "Exiles in Paradise: German Emigrés in Southern California, 1933–1950," *Southern California Quarterly* 41, no. 2 (1979): 183. See also Lydia Goehr, "The Romantic Legacy of a Double Life," in *DIP*, 76–77.
62. Shawn, *Arnold Schoenberg's Journey*, 255.
63. Krenek, "America's Influence," 113.
64. Claudia Maurer-Zenck, "Challenges and Opportunities of Acculturation: Schoenberg, Krenek, and Stravinsky in Exile," in *DIP*, 182; see also Krenek, "America's Influence," 112; and Sinkovicz, *Mehr als zwölf Töne*, 263.
65. Alan Lessem, "The Emigré Experience: Schoenberg in America," in *Constructive Dissonance: Arnold Schoenberg and the Transformations of Twentieth-Century Culture*, ed. Juliane Brand and Christopher Hailey (Berkeley: University of California Press, 1997), 59.
66. Christian Schmidt, "Arnold Schönberg – Doyen der Wiener Schule in Amerika?" in *Innenleben. Ansichten aus dem Exil. Ein Berliner Symposium*, ed. Hermann Haarmann (Berlin: Fannei und Walz, 1995), 126; and Marc Kerling, "Kontinuität und Bruch. Leitlinien im Spätwerk – Verarbeitungsstrategien der Exilsituation," *JASC* 4 (2002): 42–43.
67. Crawford, "Arnold Schoenberg in Los Angeles," *MQ* 86, no. 1 (Spring 2002): 34; Hermand, "A Survivor," 108–10; and "Ein Überlebender," 177. See also the general discussion on opposing views of the émigrés' "deradicalization" and accommodation to American culture in Jay, "The German Migration," 332–33.
68. Freitag, *Schönberg*, 136.
69. Crawford, "Arnold Schoenberg in Los Angeles," 34.
70. Hermand, "A Survivor," 108–10.
71. See René Leibowitz, *Schoenberg and His School*, trans. Dika Newlin (New York: Philosophical Library, 1949), 118, 126; and *HHS*, 389–90.
72. Quoted in Heister, "Zum politischen Engagement," 37.
73. Adorno, *Prisms*, 171–72.
74. See Hermann Danuser, "Composers in Exile: The Question of Musical Identity," in *DIP*, 162; and Friedrich Zehentreiter, "'Guilty Glory.' Zum Verhältnis von ästhetischer Autonomie und biographischer Krise am Beispiel der *Ode to Napoleon Buonaparte* op. 41 (1942) von Arnold Schönberg," in *Exilmusik. Komponisten während der NS-Zeit*, ed. Friedrich Geiger und Thomas Schäfer (Hamburg: von Bockel, 1999), 141–62.
75. See *HHS*, 486; see also Heister, "Zum politischen Engagement," 37; and Dirk Buhrmann, "Arnold Schönbergs *Ode to Napoleon Buonaparte* op. 41," *JASC* 4 (2002): 68. See also Meyerowitz, *Arnold Schönberg*, 82.
76. Michael Strasser, "*A Survivor from Warsaw* as Personal Parable," *Music and Letters* 76, no. 1 (February 1995): 52; Reinhold Brinkmann, *Arnold Schönberg und der Engel der Geschichte* (Vienna: Picus Verlag, 2001), 53–54, 60; and Christian Schmidt, "Schönbergs Kantate *Ein Überlebender aus Warschau*," *AfMw* 33, no. 4 (Winter 1976): 277.
77. David Lieberman, "Schoenberg Rewrites His Will: *A Survivor from Warsaw*, op. 46," in Berman and Cross, *Political and Religious Ideas*, 212; and Crittenden, "Texts and Contexts," 247.
78. Theodor W. Adorno, "Engagement," in *Noten zur Literatur, Gesammelte Schriften*, ed. Rolf Tiedemann (Darmstadt: Wissenschaftliche Buchgesellschaft, 1998), vol. 11, 423; Harold Schonberg, "Records: 'Survivor,'" *NYT*, 2 August 1952; Richard Taruskin, "A

Sturdy Musical Bridge of the 21st Century," *NYT*, 24 August 1997; Móricz, *Jewish Identities*, 255–99.

79. Meyerowitz, *Arnold Schönberg*, 29; *HHS*, 469; MacDonald, *Schoenberg*, 48; Sinkovicz, *Mehr als zwölf Töne*, 286; and Shawn, *Arnold Schoenberg's Journey*, 272. Yet Adorno's supposition that Schoenberg did not finish the large-scale oratorio and opera because "the urge to bring a work to a conclusion was totally alien to him" is equally outlandish. See Adorno, *Philosophy*, 120–21.
80. Krenek, "America's Influence," 117.
81. "Die USA waren nicht der Platz, an dem Schönbergs Ideen auf fruchtbaren Boden fallen konnten." Sinkovicz, *Mehr als zwölf Töne*, 254–55.
82. Lessem, "The Emigré Experience," 59.
83. Henke, *Arnold Schönberg*, 7–21; and Shawn, *Arnold Schoenberg's Journey*, 247–52.
84. See Goldberg, "The Sounding Board"; and Raoul Gripenwaldt, "KOWL Radio Interview with Schoenberg, 7 July 1948," unpublished manuscript, ASC.
85. *ASL*, 198.
86. *ASL*, 210.
87. *HHS*, 373–80; and Freitag, *Schönberg*, 137.
88. Lessem, "The Emigré Experience," 65.
89. Meyerowitz, *Arnold Schönberg*, 29–30; Freitag, *Schönberg*, 143; Sinkovicz, *Mehr als zwölf Töne*, 264–65; and Gervink, *Arnold Schönberg*, 294.
90. *HHS*, 112; Reich, *Schoenberg*, 200–201; MacDonald, *Schoenberg*, 46; Lessem, "The Emigré Experience," 62–63; and Kater, *Composers*, 191.
91. Oscar Levant, *A Smattering of Ignorance* (New York: Doubleday, 1940), 125–26.
92. For more detail see Sabine Feisst, "Arnold Schoenberg and the Cinematic Art," *MQ* 38, no. 1 (Spring 1999): 93–113.
93. Freitag, *Schönberg*, 149; *HHS*, 409, 412, 455–57.
94. Rubsamen, "Schoenberg in America," 473. From Rubsamen's list Simon Carfagno and Don Estep sank into obscurity.
95. *SI*, 386; and Meyerowitz, *Arnold Schoenberg*, 30.
96. Henke, *Arnold Schönberg*, 131, 135, 143; Ringer, *Arnold Schönberg*, 287; and Crawford, "Arnold Schoenberg in Los Angeles," 15–28.
97. See the articles by Murray Dineen, Robert Pascall, and Colleen Conlon in *JASC* 4 (2002).
98. These include Michael Hicks, "John Cage's Studies with Schoenberg," *American Music* 8, no. 2, (Summer 1990): 125–40; David Bernstein, "John Cage, Arnold Schoenberg and the Musical Idea," in *John Cage: Music, Philosophy, and Intention, 1933–50*, ed. David Patterson (New York: Routledge, 2002), 15–45; and Elizabeth L. Keathley, "'Dick, Dika, Dickest.' Dika Newlin's 'Thick Description' of Schönberg in America," *JASC* 4 (2002): 309–24.
99. Sinkovicz, *Mehr als zwölf Töne*, 254–55, 279; and Leibowitz, *Schoenberg*, 141.
100. Krenek, "America's Influence," 117.
101. *HHS*, 483–84, 505–6; and Jameux, *L'école*, 643.
102. André Riotte, Preface to Pierre Barbaud, *Schoenberg*, 9.

CHAPTER 2

1. William Blumenschein, "Munich Music," *MC* 61, no. 9 (31 August 1910): 18; Caroline Kerr, "Music in Europe," *ML* 21, no. 16 (19 October 1911): 5; and *ML* 21, no. 20 (18 May 1911): 19.
2. M. Marvin Grodzinsky, "Vienna," *MC* 54, no. 12 (20 March 1907): 40.

3. Der Wanderer, "What Is Arnold Schönberg?" *MA* 17, no. 2 (16 November 1912): 21.
4. Schoenberg's aims, however, were quite different from futurist artists in that he embraced subjectivity and the expression of feelings.
5. See "Russia's Schoenberg, Latest of Modernists: Stravinsky, Another Striking 'Ultra' Figure in the Compositional World," *ML* 26, no. 7 (14 August 1913): 190.
6. Antony Stern, "Schönberg in Advance of His Day," *MA* 16, no. 20 (21 September 1912): 4.
7. Ethel Smyth, "Schönberg's *Gurrelieder*," *MC* 67, no. 11 (10 September 1913): 19; and Addie Funk, "Cheers and Jeers for Schönberg," *MA* 17, no. 20 (22 March 1913): 40.
8. Karleton Hackett, "About Schoenberg and His Remarkable Works," *ML* 24, no. 20 (14 November 1912): 31.
9. Philip Clapp, "Schoenberg: Futurist in Music," *ML* 25, no. 7 (13 February 1913): 240; and Ernest Newman, "The First Futurist Composer: Schoenberg's Strange Music," *Boston Evening Transcript*, 28 September 1912.
10. James Huneker, "Schoenberg, Musical Anarchist, Who Has Upset Europe," *NYT*, 19 January 1913. This article's illustrations stem from the 1912 Schoenberg festschrift.
11. Karleton Hackett, "Chicago Is to Hear Schoenberg in Fall," *ML* 26, no. 1 (3 July 1913): 13.
12. Glenn Dillard Gunn, "Concerts for the Week," *Chicago Tribune*, 2 November 1913; Eric Delamarter, "This Schoenberg Music," *Chicago Inter-Ocean*, 1 November 1913; and Maurice Rosenfeld, "Hisses for Schönberg in Chicago," *MA* 19, no. 1 (8 November 1913): 36.
13. Delamarter, "This Schoenberg Music."
14. Karleton Hackett, "Symphony 'Bomb' Proves a Fizzle," *Chicago Post*, 1 November 1913; Delamarter, "This Schoenberg Music"; S. F. Newhall, "Is There to Be a Schoenberg Period?" *Chicago Examiner*, 5 November 1913; Eric Delamarter, "Our Sunburst of Schoenberg," *Chicago Inter-Ocean*, 2 November 1913; and E. C. Moore, "Symphony Orchestra Introduces Arnold Schoenberg," *Chicago Journal*, 1 November 1913.
15. Maurice Rosenfeld, "Hisses for Schoenberg"; Isabel Lowden, "Orchestra's Third Concert," *Chicago Daily News*, 1 November 1913; and Eric Delamarter, "This Schoenberg Music."
16. Philip Hale, "Miss Hinkle Shows Skill as Soloist," *Boston Herald*, 19 December 1914; and Henry Taylor Parker, "The Symphony Concert: Schoenberg's Notorious Pieces Played," *Boston Evening Transcript*, 19 December 1914.
17. "Schoenberg Would Restate Architectural Rules of Music in His 'Five Pieces'," *CSM*, 28 November 1914; Philip Clapp, "Schoenberg's Music Stoutly Championed: The Five Pieces for the Next Symphony Concerts in Clear and Warm Survey," *Boston Evening Transcript*, 16 December 1914; and Arthur Eaglefield-Hull, "Schönberg Explained," *Monthly Musical Record* 44 (2 March–1 July 1914): 59–61, 87–89, 116–18, 145–46, 176–77.
18. Hale, "Miss Hinkle"; and Henry Taylor Parker, "The Symphony Concert," *Boston Evening Transcript*, 19 December 1914.
19. Ibid.
20. John Burk, "Schönberg's Five Little Pieces," *Harvard Musical Review* 3, no. 3 (November 1914): 16.
21. S. Foster Damon, "Schönberg, Strindberg and Sibelius," *Harvard Musical Review* 3, no. 9 (June 1915): 9–11.
22. "Flonzaley Quartet," *Philadelphia Inquirer*, 7 April 1914; and "Flonzaley Quartet," *Philadelphia Record*, 7 April 1914.

23. "Schoenberg's 'Kammer Symphonie,'" *Philadelphia Evening Telegraph*, 6 November 1915.
24. Harold Quicksall, "Schoenberg's Discords Fail to Disturb Philadelphia," *MC* 71, no. 19 (11 November 1915): 56; and "Nothing Amazing in 'Kammer-Symphonie,'" *MA* 23, no. 2 (13 November 1915): 20.
25. "Musicians Wage War of Sounds," *New York Tribune*, 28 February 1916.
26. "Stransky Presents Schoenberg and Destinn," *ML* 30, no. 22 (4 November 1915): 622; and "Musical Frightfulness," *New York Evening Post*, 20 November 1915.
27. "Schoenberg's 'Pelléas et Mélisande,' Played Last Week by the Philharmonic," *NYT*, 21 November 1915; and Herbert Peyser, "Schönberg Poem in First Hearing," *MA* 23, no. 3 (27 November 1915): 21.
28. "Reinald Werrenrath Gives an Evening of Distinctive Singing," *New York Journal*, 24 October 1913.
29. "Novel Programme by Mr. Werrenrath," *NYT*, 24 October 1913; and "Werrenrath's Novel Songs," *MC* 67, no. 18 (29 October 1913): 40.
30. Kurt Schindler, *Arnold Schönberg's Quartet in D Minor Op. 7* (New York: Schirmer, 1914).
31. "Flonzaleys Give Schoenberg Quartet Private Hearing," *MA* 19, no. 9 (3 January 1914): 23.
32. "Little Harmony in Schoenberg's Latest Music," *New York Herald*, 27 January 1914; and Henry Krehbiel, "Schoenberg's String Quartet," *New York Tribune*, 27 January 1914.
33. "Schoenberg Music Has First Hearing," *New York Sun*, 27 January 1914; Richard Aldrich, "Schoenberg's Quartet," *NYT*, 27 January 1914; and "Flonzaleys Play Schoenberg," *New York Post*, 27 January 1914.
34. Olin Downes, "First Hearing of Quartet," *Boston Post*, 30 January 1914; and "Schönberg Work No Bugaboo to Boston," *MA* 19, no. 14 (7 February 1914): 46.
35. Maurice Rosenfeld, "Schönberg Novelty Played in Chicago," *MA* 21, no. 14 (6 February 1915): 43; and "The Kneisel Quartet in New York," *ML* 29, no. 8 (25 February 1915): 224.
36. Griffes, eminent American composer and pianist, played (though never publicly) Schoenberg's Six Little Piano Pieces, op. 19, which he called "strange nothings, very easy to play." Griffes's last completed compositions, the Three Preludes of 1919, seem to be a tribute to Schoenberg's Six Little Pieces, evoking them in their conciseness and texture. Edward Maisel, *Charles T. Griffes: The Life of an American Composer* (New York: Da Capo Press, 1972), 147; and Donna K. Anderson, *Charles T. Griffes: A Life in Music* (Washington, D.C.: Smithsonian Institution Press, 1993), 193.
37. "Society," *Grand Rapids Herald*, 2 May 1914.
38. A. Walter Kramer, "Ornstein Plays His Own Music," *MA* 21, no. 13 (30 January 1915): 43; and "Very Modern Music," *MC* 70, no. 5 (3 February 1915): 23.
39. "Leo Ornstein, Futurist," *New York Post*, 27 January 1915; James Huneker, "The Seven Arts," *Puck*, 17 April 1915, 11; and Herbert Peyser, "Ornstein Presents His *Dwarf Suite*," *MA* 21, no. 15 (13 February 1915): 26.
40. Frederick Martens, *Leo Ornstein: The Man – His Ideas, His Work* (New York: Breitkopf & Härtel, 1918), 47.
41. Margaret Anderson, "Leo Ornstein," *Little Review* 3, no. 3 (May 1916): 15.
42. Schmitz quoted in Leonard Liebling, "Variations: Shall We Have German Music?" *MC* 79, no. 1 (17 July 1919): 22.
43. Pitts Sanborn, "The War and Music in America: The Metropolitan Opera House Frees Itself from German Musical Frightfulness," *Vanity Fair* 9, no. 5 (January 1918): 88.
44. The orchestral songs, opp. 8 and 22 (1904 and 1916), and the operas *Erwartung* (1909) and *Von heute auf morgen* (1929) did not receive performances before 1933.
45. Paul Rosenfeld, "Musical Chronicle," *Dial* 74 (April 1923): 220.

46. Oscar Thompson, "Bach à la Schönberg," *MA* 37, no. 8 (16 December 1922): 36.
47. Leonard Liebling, "Variations," *MC* 99, no. 18 (2 November 1929): 31.
48. Downes quoted in Marion Bauer, "Music in New York: Concerning the Latest Schoenberg," *ML* 57, no. 17 (24 October 1929): 6.
49. William J. Henderson, "Philadelphia Orchestra Concert," *New York Sun*, 23 October 1929; Oscar Thompson, "Novelty Hissed at Opening of Stokowski Series," *MA* 49, no. 20 (25 October 1929): 14; and Bauer, "Music in New York."
50. Bauer, "Music in New York."
51. Olin Downes, "Stokowski Gives Contrasting Music," *NYT*, 23 April 1930.
52. Greenville Vernon, "Modernism in Extremis," *Commonweal*, 14 May 1930.
53. Leopold Stokowski to Arnold Schoenberg, 15 March 1920, LC.
54. Stokowski quoted in "Arnold Schoenberg – *Gurrelieder*," *Chord and Dischord* 1, no. 2 (November 1932): 17. Before 1932, however, the famous *Gurrelieder* excerpt "Song of the Wood Dove" was given at least twice. Eva Gauthier performed it in Berg's arrangement for voice and piano in 1923, and Johanna Klemperer (accompanied by her husband Otto) offered its orchestral version in 1927.
55. Ibid. See also "The Tonal Schönberg: *Gurrelieder*, a Brilliant Performance," *ML* 62, no. 17 (28 April 1932): 7.
56. Olin Downes, "Stokowski Gives New York Premiere of Schoenberg's 'Gurrelieder' at Metropolitan Opera House," *NYT*, 21 April 1932.
57. The recording was reissued on LP in 1954 and 1976 and on CD in 1990.
58. Arnold Schoenberg to Thor Johnson, 24 July 1950, in *ASL*, 281.
59. Arnold Schoenberg to Leopold Stokowski, 14 November 1933, LC. This letter gives a taste of Schoenberg's struggle with the English language shortly after arrival in the United States.
60. Isabel Jones, "What Is Test of Ability for an Orchestral Conductor?" *LAT*, 23 July 1933.
61. Arnold Schoenberg to Edgard Varèse, 23 October 1922, in *ASL*, 78–79.
62. Gershwin kept a program of this concert. Howard Pollack, *George Gershwin: His Life and Work* (Berkeley: University of California Press, 2006), 37. Charles Ives knew about the *Pierrot* premiere through his pianist friend Clifton Furness, but he did not witness the event. In 1931 he conveyed to Schmitz that he had never heard a note of Schoenberg. Clifton Furness to Charles Ives, 22 January 1923, Ives Collection, Yale University. Charles Ives to E. Robert Schmitz, 10 August 1931, in *Charles E. Ives Memos*, ed. John Kirkpatrick (New York: Norton, 1972), 27.
63. Henry Finck, "Dreary Musical Tomfooleries," *New York Evening Post*, 5 February 1923; and "What Happened at Futuristic Concert," *New York Evening Post*, 17 February 1923; Richard Aldrich, "Music," *NYT*, 5 February 1923; Henry Krehbiel, "Composers' Guild Heard," *New York Tribune*, 5 February 1923; and "The Curse of Affectation and Modernism in Music," *New York Tribune*, 11 February 1923.
64. Paul Rosenfeld, "Musical Chronicle," *Dial* 74 (April 1923): 426–32; "Schoenberg's Muse Snared and Searched," *Boston Evening Transcript*, 14 April 1923; Pitts Sanborn, "'Loony Pete' and Sublunary Matters Come to the Klaw," *Globe and Commercial Advertiser*, 5 February 1923; Emilie Bauer, "New York Debates Merits of 'Pierrot Lunaire'," *ML* 45, no. 6 (8 February 1923): 126; Katherine Spaeth, "Schoenberg's Novelty," *New York Evening Mail*, 5 February 1923; and "Composers' Guild Offers New Music," *Evening Telegram New York*, 5 February 1923. For a detailed discussion see David Metzer, "The Ascendancy of Musical Modernism in New York City, 1915–1929" (Ph.D. diss., Yale University, 1993) and "The New York Reception of *Pierrot lunaire*: The 1923 Premiere and Its Aftermath," *MQ* 78, no. 4 (Winter 1994): 669–99.

65. Lawrence Gilman, "Music," *New York Tribune*, 12 March 1923.
66. R. M. K., "International Guild Sponsors New Works," *MA* 39, no. 16 (9 February 1924): 2.
67. Olin Downes, "Samuel Dushkin, Violinist," *NYT*, 7 January 1924.
68. T. M. P., "Chamber Music in Berkshires," *New Haven Journal-Courier*, 24 September 1924.
69. Oscar Thompson, "Schönberg, Satie, Eichheim and Varèse Novelties on Program of Modern Music," *MA* 41, no. 20 (7 March 1925): 13; and Olin Downes, "Music: International Composers' Guild," *NYT*, 2 March 1925.
70. Claire Reis, *Composers, Conductors, and Critics* (New York: Oxford University Press, 1955), 53.
71. Paul Rosenfeld, "Musical Chronicle," *Dial* 80 (May 1926): 442.
72. Marion Bauer, "League of Composers Experiments," *ML* 51, no. 11 (18 March 1926): 3.
73. Coolidge also commissioned Schoenberg's Fourth String Quartet (1936).
74. "German Chamber Music: Schoenberg's Work Wins Praise at Mrs. E. S. Coolidge's Berlin Concert," *NYT*, 23 October 1927.
75. Ibid. Also Olin Downes, "European Concert Series Given by Mrs. E. S. Coolidge," *NYT*, 2 October 1927.
76. "New Schoenberg Quartet Has First Performance in America," *ML* 55, no. 13 (27 September 1928): 6; W. P. T., "Schönberg's Third Quartet," *CSM*, 27 September 1928; and Irwin Fisher, "Gordon Quartet Plays Schoenberg's Latest," *ML* 56, no. 13 (28 March 1929): 15.
77. Henry T. Parker, "Chamber Music," *Boston Evening Transcript*, 22 September 1928.
78. Aaron Copland and Vivian Perlis, *Copland 1900–1942* (New York: St. Martin's Press, 1984), 182.
79. This issue has been explored in depth in Metzer, "The Ascendancy of Musical Modernism," 14–34.
80. Henry Finck, "The Musical Messiah – or Satan?" *Nation*, 15 November 1915.
81. Arthur Foote, "Will the Music of Ultra-Modernists Survive?" *Etude* 34, no. 5 (May 1916): 331; and Henry Holden Huss, "The Anarchic Element in Some Ultra-Modern Futurist Music," *Art World* 2, no. 2 (May 1917): 139–41.
82. Frederick Corder, "On the Cult of Wrong Notes," *MQ* 1, no. 3 (July 1915): 381–86.
83. Carl Van Vechten, *Music and Bad Manners* (New York: Knopf, 1916), 213.
84. A. Walter Kramer, "This Man Schönberg! A Word of Warning to the Unwise," *Musical Observer* 12, no. 2 (February 1915): 109–10.
85. Marion Bauer, "As Others See Them – As Twentieth Century Musicians View Their Contemporaries," *ML* 33, no. 19 (10 May 1917): 610.
86. Edward Kilenyi, "Arnold Schönberg's 'Harmony'," *New Music Review* 14, no. 167 (October 1915): 324–28, 360–63.
87. Daniel Gregory Mason, "Schönberg's Harmony," *New Music Review* 14, no. 167 (October 1915): 364.
88. Susan Neimoyer, "Rhapsody in Blue: A Culmination of George Gershwin's Early Musical Education" (Ph.D. diss., University of Washington, 2003), 55–102.
89. Egon Wellesz, "Schönberg and Beyond," trans. Otto Kinkeldey, *MQ* 2, no. 1 (January 1916): 76–95.
90. Frederick Martens, *Schönberg* (New York: Breitkopf & Härtel, 1922); and Egon Wellesz, *Arnold Schönberg* (New York: Dutton, 1925).
91. Frank Patterson, "Arnold Schoenberg," *MC* 83, no. 1 (7 July 1921): 7; "Continental Composers Figure in New Books," *MA* 33, no. 22 (26 March 1921): 39; "Musical Evolution of Arnold Schönberg Traced in Biography by Egon Wellesz," *MA* 42, no. 19

(29 August 1925): 13, 22; "Schoenberg – The Traveler of New Paths," *ML* 50, no. 8 (20 August 1925): 176; and Stefan Freund, "Arnold Schoenberg," *Pro Musica Quarterly* 2, no. 4 (1924): 6–10.

92. Carl Engel, *Discords Mingled: Essays on Music* (New York: Knopf, 1931), 84–97; Hugo Leichtentritt, "Schönberg and Tonality," *MM* 5, no. 4 (May–June 1927): 3–10; Paul Stefan, "Schoenberg's Operas," *MM* 2, no. 1 (January 1925): 12–15; and *MM* 7, no. 1 (December–January 1929–30): 24–28.
93. Dane Rudhyar, "Looking Ahead into Paths Opened by the Three S's," *MA* 46, no. 11 (2 July 1927): 5, 11.
94. Darius Milhaud, "Polytonality and Atonality," *Pro-Musica Quarterly* 2, no. 4 (April 1924): 11–24; and Alfredo Casella, "Tone Problems of To-day," *MQ* 10, no. 2 (April 1924): 150–71.
95. Henry Cowell, "Who Is the Greatest Living Composer?" *Northwest Musical Herald* 5, no. 5 (1933): 7.
96. Cowell's overtone series theory, which implies that overtones progressing from consonant to dissonant intervals reflect Western composers' growing preference for dissonances over consonances, builds on ideas expounded in *Harmonielehre*. See Henry Cowell, "The Impasse of Modern Music," *Century Magazine* 114, no. 6 (October 1927): 671–77; and Arnold Schoenberg, *Harmonielehre* (Vienna: Universal Edition, 1911), 19.
97. Ada Hanfin, "Henry Cowell, Composer, Talks on Primitive Music and Modern Composers," *San Francisco Examiner*, 11 June 1933.
98. Joseph Yasser, "The Supra-Diatonic Scale as an Organic Basis for the Music of the Future," *Pro-Musica Quarterly* 7, nos. 3–4 (June 1929): 8–34.
99. Dane Rudhyar, "Schoenberg and Musical Anarchism," *The Arts* 3, no. 4 (1923): 268–69; and "Carl Ruggles, Pioneer: As Seen by a Fellow-Modernist," *MA* 46, no. 19 (27 August 1927): 3, 20.
100. Henry Cowell, "America Takes a Front Rank in Year's Modernist Output," *MA* 41, no. 23 (28 March 1925): 5.
101. Charles Seeger, "On Dissonant Counterpoint," *MM* 7, no. 4 (June–July 1930): 25–26.
102. Hauer's new "keyless" music was mentioned in *MC* in 1923, but the term "twelve-tone music" was not used. D. H. L., "The Ultra-Ultra," *MC* 86, no. 6 (8 February 1923): 23.
103. Cesar Saerchinger, "Schoenberg Serenade the Climax of Fourth Donaueschingen Festival," *MC* 89, no. 7 (14 August 1924): 6–7.
104. Cesar Saerchinger, "Schönberg and Stravinsky Present Own Works at International Festival at Venice," *MC* 91, no. 14 (1 October 1925): 18.
105. Louis Gruenberg, "Fourth Festival of Modern Music at Zurich," *ML* 51, no. 29 (27 March 1926): 6.
106. Marion Bauer, "League of Composers Experiments," *ML* 51, no. 11 (18 March 1926): 3; and W. H. Haddon Squire, "The Zurich Festival," *CSM*, 10 July 1926.
107. Hugo Leichtentritt, "Vienna Hears Schönberg's Twelve-Tone Scale Quintet and Two Strauss Pseudo Premieres," *MC* 89, no. 19 (6 November 1924): 7.
108. Paul Pisk, "The Tonal Era Draws to a Close," *MM* 3, no. 3 (March–April 1926): 6–7.
109. Erwin Stein, "Schönberg's Third String Quartet," *Dominant* 1, no. 5 (1928): 14–16; "Twelve-Tone Music," *CSM*, 16 February 1929; and "Schoenberg's New Structural Form," *MM* 7, no. 4 (June–July 1930): 4–10.
110. Stein, "Schoenberg's New Structural Form," 5.
111. *ASL*, 164–65.
112. Erwin Stein, "Schoenberg and the German Line," *MM* 3, no. 4 (May–June 1926): 22–27.
113. Hugo Leichtentritt, "German Music of the Last Decade," *MQ* 10, no. 2 (April 1924): 195.

114. Paul Rosenfeld, "The Music of Post-Straussian Germany," *Vanity Fair* 19, no. 3 (November 1922): 110.
115. Paul Rosenfeld, *Musical Portraits: Interpretations of Twenty Modern Composers* (New York: Harcourt, Brace and Howe, 1920), 241; and "A View of Modern Music," *Dial* 79 (November 1925): 390.
116. Lazare Saminsky, "Neurotic Composers and Hebrews in Music of Today," *MA* 37, no. 20 (10 March 1923): 9.
117. Caroline Smith, "London," *MC* 44, no. 7 (14 February 1912): 13; and Caroline Kerr, "Music in Europe: Adolphe Borchard and Richard Buhlig Recitals," *ML* 23, no. 11 (14 March 1912): 4–5.
118. Schoenberg, however, dismissed Gruenberg's performance. See Arnold Schoenberg, *Berliner Tagebuch. Mit einer Hommage à Schönberg*, ed. Josef Rufer (Frankfurt am Main: Propylän, 1974), 11.
119. Arnold Schoenberg to Alma Mahler, 20 September 1914, Otto Albrecht Music Library, University of Pennsylvania.
120. Emil Hertzka to Breitkopf and Härtel, 1 September 1916, ASC.
121. "Schönberg Intrenched," *MC* 70, no. 17 (24 February 1915): 25.
122. César Saerchinger, "Schönberg's *Pierrot Lunaire* Is Given a Truly Worthy Performance in Vienna," *MC* 82, no. 25 (23 June 1921): 27.
123. Arnold Schoenberg to Lucy Bogue, 17 November 1923, ASC; "Schoenberg Doesn't Want His 'Pierrot Lunaire' Played," *New York Herald*, 14 January 1923; and "Schönberg to Visit America This Year, Says Report," *MA* 37, no. 13 (20 January 1923): 4.
124. Arnold Schoenberg to Emil Hertzka, 4 April 1928, WB.
125. Arnold Schoenberg, "Interview mit mir selbst," in *Arnold Schönberg: Stil und Gedanke. Aufsätze zur Musik*, ed. Ivan Vojtěch (Frankfurt am Main: Fischer, 1976), 241.
126. Arnold Schoenberg to Adolph Weiss, 6 February 1932; and Adolph Weiss to Arnold Schoenberg, 28 February 1932, LC.
127. Arnold Schoenberg to Joseph Asch, 24 May 1932, in *ASLIB*, 287.
128. Arnold Schoenberg, "Fashion," in *ASR*, 211; and "Mein Stil," unpublished manuscript, ASC.
129. César Saerchinger, "Schönberg and Jazz," *MC* 84, no. 14 (3 April 1924): 6; and "Schoenberg on Modern Music," *NYT*, 8 February 1931.
130. Schoenberg, "Interview mit mir selbst," 242; and "Schoenberg on Modern Music."
131. Arnold Schoenberg, "Krise des Geschmacks [Crisis of Taste]," *Berliner Börsen-Zeitung*, 1 January 1931, in *SW*, 291–92.
132. Arnold Schoenberg, "Comment on Jazz," for the *Midwest Chicago Daily News* (n.d., c. 1925–32), in *SW*, 290–91.
133. *SI*, 167.
134. *SI*, 173.
135. Arnold Schoenberg, "Ich und die Hegemonie der Musik," unpublished manuscript, ASC.
136. "Adolph Weiss on Schoenberg," *MC* 93, no. 4 (22 July 1926): 30.
137. Adolph Weiss, "Autobiographical Notes," *Bulletin of the American Composers Alliance* 7, no. 3 (1958): 3.
138. William B. George, "Adolph Weiss" (Ph.D. diss., University of Iowa, 1971), 35–36.
139. Arnold Schoenberg, "Klavierstück," *New Music Quarterly* 5, no. 3 (1932).
140. Adolph Weiss, "The Lyceum of Schoenberg," *MM* 9, no. 3 (March–April 1932): 99–107.
141. Paul Rosenfeld, *An Hour with American Music* (Philadelphia: Lippincott, 1929), 92.
142. Ibid.

143. Quoted in Marion Bauer, "Whither Are We Wandering with Our New Music?" *ML* 52, no. 16 (21 April 1927): 10.
144. "I am not familiar with much American music. I of course know Roger Sessions' work which greatly pleases me, and some compositions by Marc Blitzstein which are excellent." "Arnold Schönberg, on First Visit, Receives the American Press," *MC* 107, no. 20 (11 November 1933): 7.
145. Marc Blitzstein, "Lecture at Brandeis University, 2 April 1962," quoted in Eric Gordon, *Mark the Music: The Life and Work of Marc Blitzstein* (New York: St. Martin's Press, 1989), 28; and "Four American Composers," *This Quarter* 2 (July–September 1929):163.
146. Marc Blitzstein, "Forecast and Review: Talk – Music – Dance," *MM* 11, no. 1 (November–December 1933): 34–40.
147. "Marc Blitzstein Announces Ten Lecture-Recitals on the Modern Movement in Music, 1928–29, Philadelphia–New York." Marc Blitzstein, Manuscripts of Lectures, Wisconsin Center for Theatre Research, University of Wisconsin Madison.
148. Ibid.
149. Gordon, *Mark the Music*, 28. See also Marc Blitzstein, "Toward a New Form," *MQ* 20, no. 2 (April 1934): 216.
150. Leonard Lehrman completed *Idiots First* in 1973. It was premiered in New York in 1978.
151. Leonard Liebling, "Variations," *MC* 106, no. 17 (29 April 1933): 17.
152. "Prussia Ousts Musicians," *NYT*, 31 May 1933.
153. John Becker to Evelyn Becker, November 1933, NYPL.

CHAPTER 3

1. Lydia Goehr, "Music and Musicians in Exile: The Romantic Legacy of a Double Life," in *DIP*, 72.
2. For more details see Tina Frühauf, *The Organ and Its Music in German-Jewish Culture* (New York: Oxford University Press, 2008), 5.
3. See Moshe Lazar, "Arnold Schoenberg and His Doubles: A Psychodramatic Journey to His Roots," *JASI* 17, nos. 1–2 (June–November 1994): 13.
4. Arnold Schoenberg, "Sketches for a Jewish Unity Party," unpublished manuscript, ASC.
5. Paul Mendes-Flohr, *German Jews: A Dual Identity* (New Haven: Yale University Press, 1999), 12–13. See also Steven Cahn, "Schoenberg, the Viennese-Jewish Experience and Its Aftermath," in *The Cambridge Companion to Schoenberg*, ed. Jennifer Shaw and Joseph Auner (Cambridge: Cambridge University Press, 2010), 191–206.
6. Thanks to E. Randol Schoenberg and Therese Muxeneder for information on this issue.
7. Schoenberg's grandson suggested that this statement, which his grandfather made to Rufer in 1921, has been misused to portray his grandfather as a "fanatical German supremacist, like Hitler," and to relate the twelve-tone technique to fascism. Yet this obsessive claim of German identity was a common reaction among *Deutschjuden* (German Jews) against anti-Semitism in Germany, and indicates Schoenberg's insecurity, rather than megalomania. See Josef Rufer, *The Works of Arnold Schoenberg: A Catalogue of His Compositions, Writings and Paintings* (Kassel: Bärenreiter, 1959), 26; and E. Randol Schoenberg, "The Most Famous Thing He Never Said," *JASC* 5 (2003): 27.
8. Rabbi Louis-Germain Lévy led the ritual at which the painter Marc Chagall and Dimitri (David) Marianoff, Albert Einstein's step-son-in-law, were present.
9. Bruno Nettl, *Theory and Method in Ethnomusicology* (London: Macmillan, 1964), 235; and David Sorkin, "Emancipation and Assimilation: Two Concepts and Their Application to German-Jewish History," *Leo Baeck Institute Yearbook* 35 (1990): 17–33.

10. For discussions of acculturation see Sorkin, "Emancipation," 19–27; and Zygmunt Bauman, "Modernity and Ambivalence," *Theory, Culture & Society* 7, no. 2 (June 1990): 143–69.
11. For information on dissimilation see Sorkin, "Emancipation," 28; Shulamit Volkov, "The Dynamics of Dissimilation: *Ostjuden* and German Jews," in *The Jewish Response to German Culture: From the Enlightenment to the Second World War*, ed. Jehuda Reinharz and Walter Schatzberg (Lebanon, NH: University Press of New England, 1991), 195–211; Jonathan Skolnik, "Dissimilation and the Historical Novel: Hermann Sinsheimer's *Maria Nunnez*," *Leo Baeck Institute Yearbook* 43 (1998): 228–30; and Frühauf, *The Organ*, 213–20.
12. Under very different terms, the Nazis forced dissimilation onto the Jewish people as the first step in their Final Solution's fatal Three-Point Plan. See Frühauf, *The Organ*, 216–17.
13. *ASL*, 286.
14. For a discussion of this issue see *DIP*, 5. The concept of "emigration" is equally controversial. Adorno preferred it to "immigration," because to him it connoted forced displacement. Brecht indicated in his poem "On the Name of Emigrants" (1937) that the term *emigration* was too neutral and that he felt the word *exile* expressed more powerfully the idea of involuntary expatriation. Both men had feelings toward America that were very different from those of Schoenberg. Theodor W. Adorno, "Fragen an die intellektuelle Emigration (1945)," in *Theodor W. Adorno Gesammelte Schriften*, ed. Rolf Tiedemann (Darmstadt: Wissenschaftliche Buchgesellschaft, 1998), vol. 20–1, 352–59; and see *Bertolt Brecht Poems*, ed. John Willett, Ralph Manheim, and Erich Fried (London: Eyre Methuen, 1979), 301.
15. Bruno Nettl, "Displaced Musics and Immigrant Musicologists: Ethnomusicological and Biographical Perspectives," in *DIP*, 63.
16. R. Wayne Shoaf, "The Schoenberg-Malkin Correspondence," *JASI* 13, no. 2 (November 1990): 198.
17. Arnold Schoenberg to Georg Schönberg, 10 June 1934, LC; and Arnold Schoenberg to Hanns Eisler, 20 August 1934, in *ASR*, 256–57. A few months later he wrote to Erika and Fritz Stiedry that he never wanted to go back to Europe again: "Ich habe nicht die Absicht, jemals wieder nach Europa zu gehen – wenn ich nicht muss" (Arnold Schoenberg to Erika Stiedry-Wagner, November 1934, LC).
18. For financial reasons Schoenberg briefly contemplated immigrating to New Zealand. See Arnold Schoenberg to Richard Hoffmann, Sr., 17 October 1944, in *ASL*, 220.
19. See, for instance, Jost Hermand, "Ein Überlebender aus Deutschland. Zur Radikalität von Arnold Schönbergs zionistischer Wende," in *Judentum und deutsche Kultur. Beispiele einer schmerzhaften Symbiose*, ed. Jost Hermand (Cologne: Böhlau, 1996), 180.
20. In the following discussion I will use the national category "German," even though Schoenberg was born in Vienna and spent more time in Austria than in Germany. Schoenberg generally saw Austria and Germany as one entity, a notion pointing to the two countries' former union in the Holy Roman Empire of the German Nation, the German Confederation under the presidency of Austria, and the temporary name given to Austria after World War I: Republic of German Austria.
21. Alban Berg to Anton Webern, 26 August 1933, in *Die Wiener Schule und das Hakenkreuz. Das Schicksal der Moderne im gesellschaftspolitischen Kontext des 20. Jahrhunderts*, Studien zur Wertungsforschung 22, ed. Otto Kolleritsch (Vienna: Universal Edition, 1990), 47–48.
22. Carl Engel, "Schoenberg and 'Sentiment,'" in *Schoenberg*, ed. Merle Armitage (New York: Schirmer, 1937), 157.

23. Goehr, "Music and Musicians," 66.
24. Jarrell Jackman, "Exiles in Paradise; German Emigrés in Southern California, 1933–1950," *Southern California Quarterly* 61, no. 2 (Spring 1979): 183.
25. Thomas Mann, *Briefe. 1948–1955* (Frankfurt am Main: Fischer, 1965), vol. 3, 73, 504; and Heinrich Mann, *Der Sinn dieser Emigration* (Paris: Europäischer Merkur, 1934), 12, 26, 33.
26. Goehr, "Music and Musicians," 68; and James Clifford, "Diasporas," *Cultural Anthropology* 9, no. 9 (August 1994): 302, 307–8.
27. Goehr, "Music and Musicians," 67–68.
28. Clifford, "Diasporas," 311.
29. Ibid., 311–19.
30. Arnold Schoenberg to Moritz Violin, 9 April 1940, LC.
31. Vivian Perlis, "Interview with Gerald Strang" (Oral History of American Music Archives, Yale University, March 1975).
32. Arnold Schoenberg to Felix Greissle, 7 June 1938, in *ASL*, 204.
33. Arnold Schoenberg to Moritz Violin, 9 April 1940, LC.
34. Arnold Schoenberg to David Bach, 13 March 1935, in *ASR*, 258.
35. *ASL*, 204.
36. *ASR*, 258.
37. Arnold Schoenberg to Moritz Violin, 9 April 1940, LC. "Goethe's Götz" refers to the title character of Goethe's 1773 play *Götz von Berlichingen*, a medieval German imperial knight, who in response to the occupation of his castle and a captain's demand for surrender uttered the ill-mannered phrase: "kiss my arse."
38. Arnold Schoenberg to Jacob Landau, 1 December 1933, LC; and see also *ASR*, 258–59.
39. Arnold Schoenberg to Oskar Kokoschka, 3 July 1946, in *ASL*, 242.
40. Arnold Schoenberg to Felix Greissle, 7 June 1938, LC.
41. Arnold and Gertrud Schoenberg to Mitzi Seligmann, 30 January 1936, in *ASLIB*, 350.
42. Arnold Schoenberg to Felix Greissle, 11 July 1938, LC.
43. Arnold Schoenberg to David Bach, 11 May 1934, LC.
44. Arnold Schoenberg to Adolf Rebner, 26 February 1940, in *DIP*, 3.
45. Arnold Schoenberg to Felix Greissle, 11 July 1938, LC.
46. *ASR*, 258.
47. Arnold Schoenberg to Anton Webern, 13 November 1934, WB.
48. *ASL*, 192; and *BSC*, 458.
49. Arnold Schoenberg to Alexander Zemlinsky, 9 February 1940, in *Zemlinskys Briefwechsel mit Schönberg, Webern, Berg und Schreker*, ed. Horst Weber (Darmstadt: Wissenschaftliche Buchgesellschaft, 1995), 278.
50. Lovina Knight, "Classes with Schoenberg January through June 1934," *JASI* 13, no. 2 (November 1990): 156.
51. The Schoenbergs initially had a two-year visitor's visa, but in order to stay, they needed immigration visas. The quota for Czechoslovakian immigrants for 1935 had already been filled when they discovered this problem, and they had to get immigration visas through the American consulate in Mexicali, Mexico. Pauline Alderman and Rufus von KleinSmid provided the affidavits. See *ASLIB*, 321.
52. Arnold Schoenberg to Hans Rosbaud, 15 February 1949, LC.
53. Clifford, "Diasporas," 302.
54. His family would have been even larger if Schoenberg's wife had not suffered several miscarriages.
55. *SR*, 153.

56. Thanks to Lawrence Schoenberg for this information.
57. Vivian Perlis, "Interview with Gerald Strang" (Oral History Archives, Yale University, March 1975).
58. This story is published in German: Arnold Schönberg, *Die Prinzessin*, ed. Matthias Henke, with an epilogue by Nuria Schoenberg Nono and illustrations by Peter Schössow (Munich: Hanser, 2006).
59. See Nuria Schoenberg Nono, "Mon père Schoenberg," *Schweizerische Musikzeitung* 116, no. 2 (1976): 78–79; and Arnold Schoenberg to Arnold, Hermann, and Felix Greissle, 15 October and 18 December 1943, LC.
60. Nuria Schoenberg Nono, "The Role of Extra-Musical Pursuits in Arnold Schoenberg's Creative Life," in *Arnold Schoenberg: Playing Cards*, ed. Nuria Schoenberg-Nono and Ernst Ragg (Vienna: Piatnik, 1981), 16–31; and Therese Muxeneder, "Schönberg-Werkstätte und – Patentrezepte," *JASC* 7 (2005): 55.
61. Katia Mann, *Unwritten Memoires*, ed. Elisabeth Plessen and Michael Mann, trans. Hunter and Hildegarde Hannum (London: André Deutsch, 1975), 124–25. See also Thomas Mann, *Tagebücher 1940–43*, ed. Peter de Mendelssohn (Frankfurt am Main: Fischer, 1982), 617.
62. See Mann, *Unwritten Memoires*, 125; and *Hanns Eisler: A Miscellany*, ed. David Blake (Edinburgh: Harwood, 1995), 414.
63. Alma Mahler-Werfel with E. B. Ashton, *And the Bridge Is Love* (New York: Harcourt, Brace, 1958), 280.
64. *Arnold Schönberg – Catalogue raisonné*, ed. Christian Meyer and Therese Muxeneder (Vienna: Arnold Schönberg Center, 2005), 46–55, 132–42, and 368.
65. The Greissles left before their affidavits from Schoenberg's student lyricist Leo Robin arrived. Lacking proper travel documents, they ran into legal problems, but luckily received a quota visa in 1941. See Arnold Schoenberg to Leo Robin, 14 July and 1 August 1938, LC.
66. See Arnold Schoenberg to Hugh Hodgson, 5 April 1939, LC; and Arnold Schoenberg to Joseph Malkin, 16 June 1938, LC.
67. Arnold Schoenberg to Alexander Zemlinsky, 9 February and 29 December 1940, in *Zemlinskys Briefwechsel*, 278–79.
68. Schoenberg even enlisted his cousin, opera tenor Hans Nachod, when traveling from Prague to London, to personally hand over immigration documents and money to Görgi. Görgi, however, steered clear of this meeting. *The Arnold Schoenberg-Hans Nachod Collection*, ed. John Kimmey, Jr. (Detroit: Information Coordinators, 1979), 49–54. For late efforts see Arnold Schoenberg to Kurt List, 11 December 1948, LC; and Felix Greissle to Arnold Schoenberg, 10 and 27 September 1948, LC.
69. Görgi copied music for Schirmer and Cowell's New Music Edition. See Arnold Schoenberg to Georg Schönberg, 10 December 1938, WB.
70. Arnold Schoenberg to Georg Schönberg, 21 August 1950, LC.
71. Schoenberg unsuccessfully provided affidavits for the three Nachods. See Kimmey, *The Arnold Schoenberg–Hans Nachod Collection*. Similarly, he provided in vain affidavits for Feder, Goldschmied, and Arthur Schönberg and his wife Eveline, who ended up staying in Europe. Schoenberg also got affidavits for such family friends as Karl Grünwald and family, the Paul Klugs, and Erna Lensberger. See Arnold Schoenberg to Lotta Loeb (Emergency Rescue Committee), 23 February 1941, LC; and Arnold Schoenberg to Heinrich Goldschmied, 16 January 1940, LC, and *ASLIB*, 343, 45, 381.
72. See *ASLIB*, 409.
73. Relatives receiving packages included Brigitte Schönberg, his sister Ottilie, and Susanne

Remus (née Blumauer), and Hans Nachod. See Bertel Ott Schönberg to Arnold Schoenberg, 9 June 1946, LC. Feder and Olga Nachod von Pascotini, another cousin of Schoenberg, died before 1945. See Arnold Schoenberg to Josef Polnauer, 21 October 1945, WB.

74. Arnold Schoenberg to Elizabeth Coolidge, 28 December 1933, LC.
75. Dolbin, Dorian, Eisler, Goehr, Herbert, Jalowetz, Mahler, Pisk, Serkin, Steuermann, Toldi, and Zweig were all former students of Schoenberg.
76. From 1941 this institution was called National Committee for Refugee Musicians.
77. Mark Brunswick to Arnold Schoenberg, 25 November 1940, LC.
78. Arnold Schoenberg to F. R. Mangold (Black Mountain College), 17 May 1939, LC; and see Arnold Schoenberg to Robert Hutchins (University of Chicago), 2 June 1946, in *ASL*, 240; and Arnold Schoenberg to Robert Stuart (St. Louis Institute of Music), 27 January 1940, in *ASR*, 284.
79. See Julius Schloss to Arnold Schoenberg, 17 December 1948, LC; and Arnold Schoenberg to Julius Schloss, 18 December 1948, LC; Karl Weigl to Arnold Schoenberg, 31 June 1938, LC; and Arnold Schoenberg to Karl Weigl, 16 June 1938, LC.
80. Arnold Schoenberg to Alfred Hertz, 2 May 1938, in *ASL*, 203–4.
81. Arnold Schoenberg to Rudolf Goehr, 5 May 1934 and 10 September 1940, LC. See Arnold Schoenberg to Adolf Rebner, 26 February 1940, LC; and Fritz Stiedry to Arnold Schoenberg, 8 December 1937 and 14 February 1938, LC.
82. *SR*, 137, 277.
83. *SR*, 147, 195.
84. Nono-Schoenberg, "Mon père," 79; *SR*, 72; and Arnold Schoenberg to Alfred Newman, 26 July 1941, LC.
85. Bertolt Brecht, *Journals*, ed. John Willet and trans. Hugh Rorrison (New York: Routledge, 1993), 251. This symphony lasts more than an hour.
86. Several of these parties were captured on film and have been made available on YouTube by the Arnold Schönberg Center.
87. Dorothea Kelley, "Arnold Schoenberg's Sixtieth Birthday in Chautauqua," *JASI* 11, no. 2 (November 1988): 157.
88. *SR*, 249.
89. See, for instance, *SR*, 183; and "String Quartet Plays at Composer's Party," *LAT*, 6 January 1937.
90. Kelley, "Arnold Schoenberg's Sixtieth," 157; *SR*, 183, 248–52; and David Raksin, "Schoenberg as Teacher, Part II," *Serial: Newsletter of the Arnold Schoenberg Institute/USC School of Music* 3, no. 1 (1989): 5.
91. Riesenfeld scored such films as DeMille's *The Ten Commandments* (1923) and *The King of Kings* (1927 and 1931), and Murnau's *Sunrise* (1927) and *Tabu* (1931).
92. Arnold Schoenberg to ASCAP, 30 July 1941, LC.
93. Leonard Stein to the author, 1 February 1999, Personal Archive; and Lawrence Schoenberg and Ellen Kravitz, "Catalogue of Arnold Schoenberg's Paintings, Drawings and Sketches," *JASI* 2, no. 3 (June 1978): 184.
94. In 1939 Dieterle, Liesl Frank, director Ernst Lubitsch, and film agent Paul Kohner initiated the European Film Fund to provide German exiles with one-year job contracts in the film industry. Hoping to get Bach a position in Hollywood, Schoenberg sent Dieterle and Lubitsch his book with three film scripts, scores, and theoretical reflections on film: *Der Kugelmensch. Die Filmfläche: Phantasien und Gedanken* (Leipzig: Anzengruber, 1938).
95. Arnold Schoenberg to Charlotte Dieterle, 30 July 1936, in *ASL*, 198.

96. Together with fellow film director Fritz Lang, Dieterle also sponsored the immigration of Bertolt Brecht and Kurt Weill.
97. *Arnold Schönberg, 30 Kanons,* ed. Josef Rufer (Kassel: Bärenreiter, 1963), 54–55.
98. See Arnold Schoenberg to Charlotte Dieterle, 2 March 1941, in *SR,* 301. Fascinated with anagrams of "Arnold," Schoenberg's son Ronald and his wife Barbara (née Zeisl) gave their children names derived from "Arnold:" Eric *Randol,* Marlena *Lorand,* Frederic *Roland* and Melanie *Raldon.*
99. Luzi Korngold, *Erich Wolfgang Korngold* (Vienna: Lafite, 1967), 69, 71.
100. Julius Korngold quoted in Brendan Carroll, *The Last Prodigy: A Biography of Erich Wolfgang Korngold* (Portland: Amadeus Press, 1997), 292.
101. Arnold Schoenberg to Franz Waxman, 1937, Syracuse University, Manuscript Collection.
102. *SR,* 220.
103. Arnold Schoenberg to Hanns Eisler, 20 August 1934, in *ASR,* 256.
104. The film-music project resulted in four experimental film scores and the book *Composing for the Films* (1947), co-written by Adorno.
105. Other "consultants" included Rudolf Kolisch and Bertolt Brecht. See Jürgen Schebera, *Hanns Eisler im USA-Exil 1938–1948* (Meisenheim: Anton Hain, 1978), 79.
106. Arnold Schoenberg to Gertrud and Felix Greissle, 18 December 1943, LC.
107. Arnold Schoenberg to Robert Hutchins, June 1946, in *ASL,* 240.
108. Ashley Pettis, "Eisler, Maker of Red Songs," *New Masses,* 26 February 1935, 272–73.
109. Hanns Eisler, *Gespräche mit Hans Bunge. Fragen Sie mehr über Brecht,* ed. Hans Bunge (Munich: Rogner and Bernhard, 1976), 19.
110. Arnold Schoenberg to Robert Stuart, 27 January 1940, in *ASR,* 285. Invited by film composer Alex North to join the Eisler Reception Committee, Schoenberg refused: "As a stranger in this country, I feel I have to keep out of the way of any participation in political matters. I myself should find it unsuitable otherwise. Nevertheless: I appreciate the musical talents of Mr. Hanns Eisler very much and if I should be in New York, I would not fail to come to see him and to bid him welcome." Arnold Schoenberg to Alex North, 23 January 1935, LC.
111. Gunther Schuller, "A Conversation with Steuermann," *PNM* 3, no. 1 (Fall–Winter 1964): 32.
112. Arnold Schoenberg to Josef Rufer, 18 December 1947, in *ASL,* 252.
113. Brecht's journal entries of 24 April and 9 May 1942, in Brecht, *Journals,* 224, 229. In other places Brecht described Schoenberg's music as "circular," "the movement isn't going anywhere, the logic only satisfies itself." See Brecht's journal entry of 22 October 1944, in Brecht, *Journals,* 331–32.
114. Brecht's journal entry of 27 April 1942, in Brecht, *Journals,* 224.
115. *Brecht: As They Knew Him,* ed. Hubert Witt and trans. John Peet (New York: International Publishers, 1974), 94.
116. Brecht's journal entry of 29 July 1942, in Brecht, *Journals,* 250–51.
117. Brecht's journal entry of 2 August 1945, in Brecht, *Journals,* 351.
118. See Eisler, *Gespräche,* 173–74; and *SR,* 234.
119. Both Alma Mahler and Schoenberg studied composition with Zemlinsky and were introduced to each other by Zemlinsky.
120. *SR,* 312.
121. Arnold Schoenberg to Franz Werfel, undated letter, written after 1933 and printed in Lazar, "Arnold Schoenberg," 111–13.
122. See Alma Mahler-Werfel, *Mein Leben* (Frankfurt am Main: Fischer, 1960), 283.

123. Franz Werfel, "No Title," in *Arnold Schönberg zum 60. Geburtstag, 13. September 1934* (Vienna: Universal Edition, 1934), 14; and "Tribute," in *Arnold Schönberg*, ed. Merle Armitage (New York: Schirmer, 1937), 205; and Alma Mahler-Werfel, "A Birthday Message," *Canon*, Arnold Schönberg Jubilee Issue, 3, no. 2 (September 1949): 85.
124. The celebration was organized by Meyer Krakowski at Los Angeles Community College. See *SR*, 270–95.
125. Arnold Schönberg, *30 Kanons*, 66–67.
126. Thomas Mann, *Tagebücher 1937–39*, ed. Peter de Mendelssohn (Frankfurt am Main: Fischer, 1980), 204, 211. Schoenberg and Mann corresponded with each other in 1930, 1938, and 1939 about supporting the architect Adolf Loos and about Jewish matters.
127. Thomas Mann, *Tagebücher 1940–43*, ed. Peter de Mendelssohn (Frankfurt am Main: Fischer, 1982), 152–53.
128. Mann, *Tagebücher 1940–43*, 618; and *Tagebücher 1944–46*, ed. Inge Jens (Frankfurt am Main: Fischer, 1986), 173–75, 226.
129. Mann inscribed his novel: "Arnold Schönberg, dem kühnen Meister, zum 13. September 1943 von Einem, der auch Musik zu bauen versucht" (To Arnold Schoenberg, the bold master, on the occasion of 13 September 1943, from one who also attempts to build music).
130. Thomas Mann, *Tagebücher 1944–46*, 100.
131. Arnold Schoenberg to Thomas Mann, 6 June 1945, in *Arnold Schoenberg – Thomas Mann. A propos du Docteur Faustus, Lettres 1930–1951*, ed. E. Randol Schoenberg and Bernhold Schmid (Lausanne: La Bibliothèque des Arts, 2002), 42–43.
132. Arnold Schoenberg to Thomas Mann, 3 October 1944, in Schoenberg and Schmid, *Arnold Schoenberg – Thomas Mann. A propos du Docteur Faustus*, 40–41, 44; Thomas Mann, *Tagebücher 1946–48*, ed. Inge Jens (Frankfurt am Main: Fischer, 1989), 40.
133. Salka Viertel, *The Kindness of Strangers* (New York: Holt, Rinehart and Winston, 1969), 259–60; Thomas Mann, *The Story of a Novel: The Genesis of Doctor Faustus*, trans. Richard and Clara Winston (New York: Knopf, 1961), 714–15; and Angelika Abel, *Musikästhetik der klassischen Moderne. Thomas Mann – Theodor W. Adorno – Arnold Schönberg* (Munich: Wilhelm Fink, 2003), 222–23.
134. Mann, *Unwritten Memoirs*, 124.
135. Mann, *The Story*, 29.
136. For more details see Abel, *Musikästhetik*, 87–94.
137. Thomas Mann, *Selbstkommentare: "Doktor Faustus" und die "Entstehung des Doktor Faustus,"* ed. Hans Wysling and Marianne Eich-Fischer (Frankfurt am Main: Fischer, 1992), 164.
138. Schoenberg gave Mann an autograph with notes and numbers illustrating old types of variation. Mann, *The Story*, 103–4; and *Tagebücher 1944–46*, 131–32.
139. Thomas Mann to Agnes Meyer, 27 August 1943, in *Thomas Mann – Agnes E. Meyer. Briefwechsel 1937–1955*, ed. Hans Vaget (Frankfurt am Main: Fischer, 1992), 510.
140. Leverkühn uses theme-and-variation form in his dodecaphonic *The Lamentation of Doctor Faustus*.
141. Mann, *The Story*, 152.
142. Paul von Klenau and Winfried Zillig, for example, composed dodecaphonic works in Nazi Europe.
143. Mann, *Tagebücher 1940–43*, 572–73.
144. Mann, *The Story*, 217.
145. Ibid., 103.
146. Arnold Schoenberg to Robert Stuart, 27 January 1940, in *ASR*, 285. Schoenberg kept calling Adorno by his Jewish father's last name "Wiesengrund," although in his exile Adorno had dropped it in favor of his mother's Italian last name.

147. Arnold Schoenberg, "Wiesengrund," in *ASR*, 336.
148. For critical views on the Mann-Adorno relationship see Hans Rudolf Vaget, "Thomas Mann: Pro and Contra Adorno," in *Sound Figures of Modernity: German Music and Philosophy*, ed. Jost Hermand and Gerhard Richter (Madison: University of Wisconsin Press, 2006), 201–31; see also Evelyn Cobley, "Avant-Garde Aesthetics and Fascist Politics: Thomas Mann's *Doctor Faustus* and Theodor W. Adorno's *Philosophy of Modern Music*," *New German Critique* 86 (2002): 43–70.
149. This 1945 essay exists in two versions, one of which is published in Theodor W. Adorno, *Gesammelte Schriften*, ed. Rolf Tiedemann (Darmstadt: Wissenschaftliche Buchgesellschaft, 1998), vol. 16, 413–32, while the other appeared in Theodor W. Adorno, *Essays on Music*, ed. Richard Leppert, trans. Susan Gillespie (Berkeley: University of California Press, 2002), 373–90.
150. *Alban Berg*, ed. Willi Reich (Vienna: Herbert Reichner, 1937). Mann also had access to Adorno's unpublished book on Wagner (published in 1952) and his essay on Beethoven's late style (1934).
151. Thomas Mann to Theodor W. Adorno, 30 December 1945, in Thomas Mann and Theodor W. Adorno, *Briefwechsel 1943–1955*, ed. Christoph Gödde and Thomas Sprecher (Frankfurt am Main: Suhrkamp, 2002), 18–22.
152. The novel appeared first in 1947 in Germany in a limited Swedish edition. In 1948 it was published by Fischer in German and by Knopf in an English translation by Helen T. Lowe Porter.
153. Mann and Adorno, *Briefwechsel 1943–1955*, 34–35. Mann's wife and daughter Erika, who disliked Adorno, prevented him from presenting all the details of Adorno's involvement in the novel's genesis. See Rolf Tiedemann, "'Mitdichtende Einfühlung.' Adornos Beiträge zum *Doktor Faustus* – noch einmal," *Frankfurter Adorno Blätter* 1 (1992): 10.
154. Arnold Schoenberg to Thomas Mann, 22 February 1948, in Schoenberg, *Arnold Schoenberg – Thomas Mann*, 53. *Faustus* was apparently one of György Ligeti's earliest sources of information on dodecaphony.
155. Arnold Schoenberg to René Leibowitz and Josef Rufer, 20 October 1948, in *ASR*, 324.
156. Mahler-Werfel gave herself and Katia Mann credit for Mann's accommodation: "I called again and again, always consulting Schönberg in between, and after dinner Katia Mann finally promised that 'Tommy' would insert an explanation in future editions and have it pasted into copies already in print." Mahler-Werfel and Ashton, *And the Bridge Is Love*, 301; and Thomas Mann, *Doctor Faustus: The Life of the German Composer Adrian Leverkühn as Told by a Friend*, trans. Helen T. Lowe-Porter (New York: Knopf, 1948), 512.
157. Arnold Schoenberg, "'Doctor Faustus' Schoenberg? Letter to the Editor," *Saturday Review of Literature*, 1 January 1949, 22.
158. Ibid.
159. Thomas Mann, "Letter to the Editor," *Saturday Review of Literature*, 1 January 1949, 23.
160. Walter Levin, "Adorno's Zwei Stücke für Streichquartett, Opus 2 (und Gedanken zum gestörten Verhältnis Schönberg/Adorno)," in *Theodor W. Adorno: Der Komponist*, ed. Heinz-Klaus Metzger and Rainer Riehn (Munich: Edition Text & Kritik, 1989), 79; *SI*, 386; and Schoenberg, "Letters to the Editor," 22.
161. Arnold Schoenberg, "Further to the Schoenberg-Mann Controversy," *Music Survey* 2, no. 2 (1949): 78.
162. *SR*, 337. According to Adorno, Schoenberg also shared this view with Mann: "Schoenberg asked Thomas Mann, why he did not turn directly to him for help in devising Leverkühn's fictional works; Schoenberg maintained that he could have told him about

countless methods of construction other than the twelve-note technique which he practised himself and which appears in *Doctor Faustus* as Leverkühn's own." Theodor W. Adorno, "Berg's Discoveries in Compositional Technique," in *Quasi una fantasia: Essays in Modern Music*, trans. Rodney Livingstone (London: Verso, 1992), 186.

163. Thomas Mann to Arnold Schoenberg, 19 December 1949; and Arnold Schoenberg to Thomas Mann, 2 January 1950, in Schoenberg and Schmid, *Arnold Schoenberg – Thomas Mann*, 84–85.
164. The English translation of *Philosophie der neuen Musik* by Anne Mitchell and Wesley Blomster was published by Seabury Press in 1973.
165. Arnold Schoenberg to Kurt List, 10 December 1949, in *ASR*, 335–36.
166. Arnold Schoenberg to Josef Rufer, 5 December 1949, in *HHS*, 508.
167. Arnold Schoenberg to Gertrud Schoenberg, letter and codicil to his two wills, 1 October 1950, in *HHS*, 513.
168. Holger Gumprecht, *"Neu Weimar" unter Palmen. Deutsche Schriftsteller im Exil in Los Angeles* (Berlin: Aufbau Taschenbuch Verlag, 1998), 74.
169. Steven Schwarzschild, "Adorno and Schoenberg as Jews Between Kant and Hegel," *Leo Baeck Institute Yearbook* 35 (1990): 451–452.
170. Lydia Goehr, "Music and Musicians," 66.
171. Schoenberg quoted in Olin Downes, "*Pierrot lunaire* – Schoenberg's Conception of His Score Brings Out Its True Merit," *NYT*, 24 November 1940.
172. For critical discussions of Germanness in music, see Alfred Einstein, *Nationale und Universale Musik. Neue Essays* (Zurich: Pan-Verlag, 1958), 232; Pamela Potter, *Most German of the Arts: Musicology and Society from the Weimar Republic to the End of Hitler's Reich* (New Haven: Yale University Press, 1998), 200–234; and Bernd Sponheuer, "Reconstructing Ideal Types of the 'German' in Music," in *Music and German National Identity*, ed. Celia Applegate and Pamela Potter (Chicago: University of Chicago Press, 2002), 36–58.
173. This ideology was promoted, for instance, by German nationalist Hans Joachim Moser's three-volume *Geschichte der deutschen Musik* (Berlin, 1922–24).
174. *SI*, 173.
175. *MI*, 88–89, 422. Schoenberg planned to include this text written on 17 August 1931 in his 1934 preface for *Der musikalische Gedanke und die Logik, Technik und Kunst seiner Darstellung* (The Musical Idea and the Logic, Technique, and Art of Its Presentation).
176. Hermann Danuser, "Arnold Schönberg und die Idee einer deutschen Musik," in *Zwischen Wissenschaft und Kunst. Festgabe für Richard Jacoby*, ed. Peter Becker, Arnfried Edler, and Beate Schneider (Mainz: Schott, 1995), 254.
177. Indebted to the nineteenth-century idea of organicism, Schoenberg conceived his works as "organic" creations or "living organisms," aiming at coherence, wholeness, and unity within variety and describing the relationship of a work's parts to the whole with biological and botanical metaphors. Schoenberg's concept of the musical idea (*Gedanke*) reflects both a unifying evolutionary small musical unit and the entirety of a piece. The idea of developing variation points to variation techniques involving the introduction of new ideas and their development. *MI*, 8.
178. Goehr, "Music and Musicians," 75–76.
179. Quoted in Albert Goldberg, "The Sounding Board: The Transplanted Composer," *LAT*, 14 May 1950.
180. *ASL*, 192.
181. Ernst Bloch, "Disrupted Language, Disrupted Culture," *Direction* 2, no. 8 (December 1939): 36.

182. Between 1929 and 1933 Schoenberg arranged German folksongs for mixed chorus, a keyboard concerto by Georg Matthias Monn for cello and orchestra, and the Concerto Grosso, op. 6, no. 7 by Handel for string quartet and orchestra. These works can be interpreted as his attempt to reach out to the public and as idiosyncratic responses to contemporary debates about neo-classicism and tonality. For more detail see Joseph Auner, "Schoenberg's Handel Concerto and the Ruins of Tradition," *JAMS* 49, no. 2 (Summer 1996): 222–36.
183. Arnold Schoenberg to Alfred Frankenstein, 18 March 1939, in *ASL*, 207–8.
184. Walter Frisch, *Brahms and the Principle of Developing Variation* (Berkeley: University of California Press, 1984), 76.
185. Schoenberg told his daughter that he arranged the work for financial reasons. Arnold Schoenberg to Gertrud Greissle, 11 November 1939, LC; and *Verteidigung des musikalischen Fortschritts. Brahms und Schönberg*, ed. Albrecht Dümling (Hamburg: Argument, 1990), 76.
186. Günter Berghaus, ed., *Theatre and Film in Exile: German Artists in Britain, 1933–1945* (Oxford: Berg, 1989), xvi.
187. *ASL*, 208.
188. Peter Gülke, "Über Schönbergs Brahms-Bearbeitung," in *Arnold Schönberg. Musik-Konzepte Sonderband*, ed. Heinz-Klaus Metzger and Rainer Riehn (Munich: Edition Text und Kritik, 1980), 240.
189. *ASL*, 207.
190. Dümling, *Verteidigung*, 75. Schoenberg's arrangement was published by Schirmer in 1937.
191. Lou Harrison, "Schoenberg in Several Ways," *National Centre for the Performing Arts Bombay Quarterly Journal* 4 (1975): 20.
192. "Soloists Appear with Chicago Symphony," *MA* 58, no. 20 (25 December 1938): 20; "An NBC Christmas Eve," *MA* 59, no. 1 (10 January 1939): 10; and Howard Taubman, "Rodzinski Directs Shostakovich 1st," *NYT*, 27 November 1942.
193. *Hanns Eisler: A Miscellany*, ed. David Blake (Luxembourg: Harwood, 1995), 175.
194. His plan to arrange *Pelleas* as a suite for ballet failed due to copyright problems. He declined Greissle's suggestion to publish his canons as choral works because he viewed them as "specimens of higher counterpoint . . . rather to be read and studied than to be sung." Arnold Schoenberg to Felix Greissle, 20 May 1948, LC.
195. C. F. Peters published these folksongs in the *Deutsche Volksliederbuch*. Upon receipt of an "unrestricted release" from the Nazi administrator at Peters in Leipzig, Schoenberg failed to publish these settings in America in the early 1930s because there was obviously no market for German folksongs at that time. See Arnold Schoenberg to Felix Greissle, 21 May 1948, LC.
196. Arnold Schoenberg to Felix Greissle, 5 June 1948, LC. "Es gingen zwei Gespielen gut" existed already as a version for solo voice and piano and as a choral piece.
197. Felix Greissle to Arnold Schoenberg, 8 July 1948, LC.
198. Arnold Schoenberg to Felix Greissle, 28 February 1948, LC.
199. Arnold Schoenberg to Felix Greissle, 26 June 1948, LC.
200. "I would suggest that the translator makes a more 'sad' poem for 'Der Mai tritt ein . . .' Because this Dorian is trister than a minor tonality." Ibid. The translators were Elizabeth A. Kulka (op. 49, no. 1) and Harold Heiberg (op. 49, nos. 2 and 3). The English text underlay was done by Eric Simon.
201. Arnold Schoenberg to Felix Greissle, 9 September 1948, LC.
202. Arnold Schoenberg to Felix Greissle, 26 June 1948, LC.

203. Cecil Smith, "Three Song Settings by Arnold Schönberg," *MA* 69, no. 3 (February 1949): 290.
204. Schoenberg received $600 (about $9,080 in 2009) for this commission. He had expected $1,000.
205. As a parallel, émigré writers often embraced the historic novel.
206. *SI*, 109.
207. *MI*, 15–18, 108–9.
208. Arnold Schoenberg to Fritz Stiedry, 1 December 1938, in *ASLIB*, 361.
209. Ibid.
210. Schoenberg even joked that in case the work grew "through a disease some cancroid reproductions, and one could call them musical ones, I would not deny my duty to give you the right on them—if you still want them." Arnold Schoenberg to Ira Hirschmann, 8 December 1940, LC.
211. Severine Neff, "Cadence after Thirty-Three Years: Schoenberg's Second Chamber Symphony, Opus 38," in *The Cambridge Companion to Schoenberg*, ed. Jennifer Shaw and Joseph Auner (Cambridge: Cambridge University Press, 2010), 209–25.
212. Ibid.
213. Arnold Schoenberg to Fritz Stiedry, 2 April 1940, LC.
214. Arnold Schoenberg to José Limón, 22 April 1950 LC.
215. Arnold Schoenberg to Fritz Stiedry, 27 September 1939, LC.
216. Virgil Thomson, "New Conducting," *New York Herald Tribune*, 16 December 1940.
217. Olin Downes, "New Friends Play Schoenberg Work," *NYT*, 16 December 1940.
218. *ASL*, 275–76.
219. Arnold Schoenberg to José Limón, 22 April 1950, LC. Schoenberg approved of Limón's plan: "The outline of the action of a dance to my Second Chamber Symphony seems to me pleasant and satisfactory."
220. *ASL*, 248.
221. Ibid.
222. Glenn Watkins, "Schoenberg and the Organ," *PNM* 4, no. 1 (Fall–Winter 1965): 125.
223. In the Orchestral Variations Schoenberg also evokes the passacaglia (specifically Bach's Passacaglia in C minor) and quotes the B-A-C-H motif. See Ethan Haimo, "Schoenberg, Bach, and B-A-C-H," *JASC* 7 (2005): 85–98.
224. Schoenberg had hoped that Alexander Schreiner, chief organist at the Mormon Tabernacle in Salt Lake City and his former colleague at UCLA, would perform it and help him with editorial issues. Arnold Schoenberg to Alexander Schreiner, 10 November 1941, quoted in Paul Hesselink, "*Variations on a Recitative for Organ, Op. 40*: Correspondence from the Schoenberg Legacy," *JASI* 7, no. 2 (November 1983): 149. Shortly before the work's world premiere Schoenberg explained to Mark Brunswick: "I have written this music in about the same manner as I write for orchestra, of course taking constantly in consideration the playability for a keyboard instrument and having always the fingering in mind. Of course it is an unusual manner of writing for organ. Especially the addition of one or more octaves is admissible in this piece. In perhaps every case I have definitely indicated the position which should sound. But there might still be problems about that and about the colors." Arnold Schoenberg to Mark Brunswick, 13 February 1944, LC.
225. Gray offered Schoenberg a royalty advance of $200 (about $2,880 in 2009) against "ten percent of list price and 50% of all performing and recording fees" of the piece. William Strickland to Schoenberg, telegram of 3 October 1941, Hesselink, "*Variations*," 144.
226. Virgil Thomson, "A Wealth of Dissonance," *New York Herald Tribune*, 11 April 1944.

227. Mason recorded the variations on the organ of Calvary Church, Gramercy Park, New York, for Esoteric Records (1951).
228. Arnold Schoenberg, *Variations on a Recitative*, arranged for two pianos by Celius Dougherty (New York: H. W. Gray, 1955). Dougherty, who had played Schoenberg's music since the early 1930s, performed it with his duo partner Vincenz Ruzicka. An unpublished version for two pianos by Schoenberg's student Serge Frank was performed by Wesley Kuhnle and Frances Mullen in Los Angeles in 1946.
229. Reconsidering his relationship with his public during the early 1930s, Schoenberg turned to the solo concerto genre. In 1933 he sketched though never finished a piano concerto in D major. He viewed the Monn and Handel solo concerto arrangements as studies for dodecaphonic solo concertos. *ASSW* VII, Series B, vol. 27, 2, p. xxi. See Auner, "Schoenberg's Handel Concerto," 264–313.
230. Hermann Danuser, "Identität oder Identitäten? Über Komposition im Exil," in *Exilmusik. Komposition während der NS-Zeit*, ed. Friedrich Geiger and Thomas Schäfer (Hamburg: Von Bockel, 1999), 91.
231. Such references can also be found in his European twelve-tone works, including his Piano Suite, op. 25, Third String Quartet, op. 30, and Variations for Orchestra, op. 31.
232. *German-Jewish History in Modern Times*, ed. Michael Meyer (New York: Columbia University Press, 1995), vol. 2, 351–52; and Steven Cahn, "On the Representation of Jewish Identity and Historical Consciousness in Schönberg's Religious Thought," *JASC* 5 (2003): 97.
233. These tonal qualities tempted such scholars as Dika Newlin and Jan Maegaard to uncover potentially hidden functional harmonies in the concerto's opening despite Schoenberg's statement, "I do not know where in the Piano Concerto a tonality is expressed." Dika Newlin, "Secret Tonality in Schoenberg's Piano Concerto," *PNM* 8, no. 1 (Fall–Winter 1974): 137–39; and Jan Maegaard, "Schoenberg's Late Tonal Works," in *TASC*, 198–200.
234. Marion Bauer, "Interview with Arnold Schoenberg," *Chautauquan Daily*, 17 August 1934.
235. Walter Bailey, *Programmatic Elements in the Works of Schoenberg* (Ann Arbor: UMI Research Press, 1984), 136–51.
236. For in-depth discussions of the concerto's possible programmatic implications, see Stefan Litwin, "Musik als Geschichte, Geschichte als Musik. Zu Arnold Schönbergs Klavierkonzert op. 42 (1942)," *Dissonanz* 59 (February 1999): 12–17; and Claudia Maurer-Zenck, "Arnold Schönbergs Klavierkonzert. Versuch, analytisch Exilforschung zu betreiben," in *Musik im Exil. Folgen des Nazismus für die internationale Musikkultur*, ed. Hanns-Werner Heister, Claudia Maurer-Zenck, and Peter Petersen (Frankfurt am Main: Fischer, 1993), 357–84.
237. Peter Petersen, "'A grave situation was created.' Schönbergs Klavierkonzert von 1942," in *Die Wiener Schule und das Hakenkreuz. Das Schicksal der Moderne im gesellschaftspolitischen Kontext des 20. Jahrhunderts*, Studien zur Wertungsforschung vol. 22, ed. Otto Kolleritsch (Vienna: Universal Edition, 1990), 79–81.
238. William Smith, "Work by Schönberg Receives Premiere," *MA* 60, no. 20 (25 December 1940): 27.
239. Georg Krieger, *Schönbergs Werke für Klavier* (Göttingen: Vandenhoeck und Ruprecht, 1968), 118–19; Richard Hauser, "Schönbergs Klavierkonzert – Musik im Exil," in *Arnold Schönberg, Musik-Konzepte, Sonderband*, ed. Heinz-Klaus Metzger and Rainer Riehn (Munich: Edition Text und Kritik, 1980), 243–72.
240. Alfred Brendel, "Herz, Kopf und Zahl. Kabbalistisches im Zeichen der Sechs. Zu Schönbergs Klavierkonzert Opus 42," *Frankfurter Allgemeine Zeitung*, 25 February 1995.

241. Arnold Schoenberg, "My Fatality," in *ASR*, 314. To his son Georg, Schoenberg mentioned that the commission fee and a monetary gift from Stokowski ($1,000, or about $10,870 in 2009) helped pay his medical bills. Arnold Schoenberg to Georg Schönberg, 1 March 1947, WB. See also Thomas Mann, *Tagebücher 28.5.1946–31.12.1948*, ed. Inge Jens (Frankfurt am Main: Fischer, 1989), 56.
242. Dahlhaus saw in the first part the exposition of the main theme, in the first episode the exposition of the second theme, in the second part a scherzo, in the second episode a development in contrapuntal fashion and in the last part the recapitulation and finale. Schoenberg only spoke of "three actions" and "two episodes." Carl Dahlhaus, "Schönberg und die Programmusik," in *Schönberg und andere. Gesammelte Aufsätze zur Neuen Musik* (Mainz: Schott, 1978), 133; and Arnold Schoenberg to A. Tillman Merrit, 15 June 1946, LC.
243. See Haimo's discussion in *TASC*, 168–75.
244. For more details see Theodor W. Adorno, "Phantasie für Geige mit Klavierbegleitung Op. 47," in *Der getreue Korrepetitor. Interpretationsanalysen neuer Musik*, ed. Rolf Tiedemann (Frankfurt am Main: Suhrkamp, 2003), 318; and Martin Boykan, "The Schoenberg Trio: Tradition at an Apocalyptic Moment," in *Music of the Future: The Schoenberg Quartets and Trio*, ed. Reinhold Brinkmann and Christoph Wolff (Cambridge, Mass.: Harvard University Press, 2000), 170–73. Glenn Gould claimed that "Schoenberg used an instrumental equivalent of Sprechgesang in much of his fiddle music" (see *The Glenn Gould Reader*, ed. Tim Page [Toronto: Key Porter, 1998], 123).
245. Walter Rubsamen, "Schoenberg in America," *MQ* 37, no. 4 (October 1951): 481; Michael Cherlin, "Memory and Trope in Arnold Schoenberg's String Trio, op. 45," *JAMS* 51, no. 3 (Fall 1998): 559–602; and Arnulf Mattes, "Reflected Colours and Reflective Forms: On the Interpretation of Arnold Schoenberg's Late Chamber Music Works" (Ph.D. diss., University of Oslo, 2006), 11ff. and 178ff.
246. Arnold Schoenberg to A. Tillman Merrit, 15 June 1946, LC.
247. Mattes, "Reflected Colours," 162–64.
248. John Cage to Dieter Schnebel, 11 December 1973, Northwestern University Library; and Eugene Lehner to Arnold Schoenberg, 9 June 1947, LC.
249. Roger Sabin, "Music Critics Gather at Harvard," *MA* 67, no. 7 (May 1947): 36; and Arthur Berger quoted in Daniel Gregory Mason, "Atonality on Trial," *Musical Digest* 29, no. 14 (October 1947): 15.
250. See Claus Raab, "Fantasia quasi una Sonata. Zu Schönbergs 'Phantasy for Violin and Piano Accompaniment' op. 47," *Melos/Neue Zeitschrift für Musik* 2, no. 3 (1976): 193.
251. Arnold Schoenberg to Josef Rufer, 5 February 1951, Preußischer Kulturbesitz Berlin.
252. Mattes, "Reflected Colours," 107–45.
253. *SI*, 91–92.
254. Arnold Schoenberg to Adolf Koldofsky, 17 September 1949, ASC.
255. See, for instance, Albert Goldberg, "Schoenberg's 75th Birthday Observed," *LAT*, 14 September 1949; and E. L., "Schoenberg Work Introduced Here," *NYT*, 28 December 1949.
256. I use the complex concept of Jewish identity in a broad sense, and consider religious, ethnic, and cultural facets. For detailed discussions of Jewish identity see the following: Steven Martin Cohen, *American Modernity and Jewish Identity* (New York: Tavistock, 1983), 39–75; *German-Jewish History in Modern Times: Integration and Dispute, 1780–1871*, ed. Michael A. Meyer (New York: Columbia University Press, 1997), vol. 3, 281–304; and Ernest Krausz and Gitta Tulea, *Jewish Survival: The Identity Problem at the Close of the Twentieth Century* (New Brunswick: Transaction, 1998), 90–100.

257. Arnold Schoenberg to Anton Webern, 4 August 1933, in *Die Wiener Schule und das Hakenkreuz. Das Schicksal der Moderne im gesellschaftspolitischen Kontext des 20. Jahrhunderts*, Studien zur Wertungsforschung 22, ed. Otto Kolleritsch (Vienna: Universal Edition, 1990), 45–47.
258. Arnold Schoenberg to Jakob Klatzkin, 13 June 1933, originally in German, English trans. Lazar in "Arnold Schoenberg," 105.
259. Shmuel Noah Eisenstadt, *Jewish Civilization: The Jewish Historical Experience in a Comparative Perspective* (Albany: SUNY Press, 1992), 120.
260. See Matthew Jacobson, *Whiteness of a Different Color: European Immigrants and the Alchemy of Race* (Cambridge, Mass.: Harvard University Press, 1998).
261. *SI*, 502.
262. Arthur Hertzberg, *The Jews in America: Four Centuries of an Uneasy Encounter: A History* (New York: Simon and Schuster, 1989), 13–14.
263. Arnold Schoenberg, "Classification of Jewry," *JASI* 3, no. 1 (March 1979): 2.
264. Some authors, however, incorrectly suggested that Schoenberg was only intermittently or superficially Jewish, and even criticized him for being too non-Jewish a Jew. See Irene Heskes, *Passport to Jewish Music: Its History, Traditions, and Culture* (Westport, CT: Greenwood Press, 1994), 276; Klára Móricz, "Jewish Nationalism in Twentieth-Century Art Music" (Ph.D. diss., University of California, Berkeley, 1999); Hermann Danuser, "Identität oder Identitäten? Über Komponisten im Exil," in *Exilmusik. Komponisten während der NS-Zeit*, ed. Friedrich Geiger and Thomas Schäfer (Hamburg: von Bokel, 1999), 90; and Camille Crittenden, "Texts and Contexts of *A Survivor from Warsaw*, Op. 46," in *Political and Religious Ideas in the Works of Arnold Schoenberg*, ed. Charlotte Cross and Russell Berman (New York: Garland, 2000), 231–58.
265. Jan Assmann, "Collective Memory and Cultural Identity," *New German Critique* 25 (Spring–Summer 1995): 131–32; see also Paul Mendes-Flohr, "Secular Forms of Jewishness," in *Blackwell Companion to Judaism*, ed. Jacob Neusner and Alan Avery-Peck (Oxford: Blackwell, 2000), 469.
266. The "lachrymose" concept has been used by such eminent Jewish historians as Salo Wittmayer Baron and Ismar Schorsch and was first applied to Schoenberg's biography by Steven Cahn.
267. Steven Cahn, "On the Representation of Jewish Identity and Historical Consciousness in Schönberg's Religious Thought," *JASC* 5 (2003): 101–2.
268. Lucy Dawidowicz, *The Jewish Presence: Essays on Identity and History* (New York: Holt, Rinehart and Winston, 1977), 23. See also Hannah Arendt, *The Jew as Pariah: Jewish Identity and Politics in the Modern Age*, ed. Ron H. Feldman (New York: Grove Press, 1978).
269. Schoenberg, "Jeder junge Jude [Every Young Jew]," *JASI* 17, nos. 1 and 2 (June–November 1994): 451. See Hannah Arendt, *Die verborgene Tradition* (Frankfurt am Main: Suhrkamp, 1976), 79; and Steven Beller, *Vienna and the Jews, 1867–1938: A Cultural History* (Cambridge: Cambridge University Press, 1989), 212–13, 217.
270. *ASR*, 242.
271. Arnold Eisen, "The Rhetoric of Chosenness and the Fabrication of American Jewish Identity," in *American Pluralism and the Jewish Community*, ed. Seymour M. Lipset (New Brunswick: Transaction, 1990), 54.
272. Schoenberg quoted in Ringer, *Arnold Schoenberg: The Composer as Jew* (New York: Oxford University Press, 1990), 134, 231.
273. Arnold Schoenberg, "The Jewish Government in Exile," unpublished manuscript, ASC.
274. Móricz, "Jewish Nationalism," 463.

275. Ringer, *Arnold Schoenberg*, 81.
276. Arnold Schoenberg, "How One Becomes Lonely," in *SI*, 41.
277. The German original reads: "Wien, Wien, nur Du allein, Du sollst von allen verachtet sein! Andern mag, wer's kann verzeih'n, Dich wird man nie von der Schuld befrei'n. Du sollst zugrunde geh'n, nur Deine Schande soll weiter besteh'n! Du bist gebrandmarkt in Ewigkeit für Falschheit und Scheinheiligkeit." Facsimile in *SW*, 303–5.
278. *SR*, 252.
279. Arnold Schoenberg, "Ihr, die uns verachtet," unpublished manuscript, ASC. Translation by author.
280. Facsimile in Alexander Ringer, *Arnold Schoenberg: The Composer as Jew* (New York: Oxford University Press, 1990), 243; and Schoenberg to Georg Wolfsohn, 20 April 1950, ASC. See also David Schiller, *Bloch, Schoenberg, Bernstein: Assimilating Jewish Music* (New York: Oxford University Press, 2003), 79–80.
281. Arnold Schoenberg to Ödön Partos, 26 April 1951, Partos Collection, Tel Aviv University.
282. Dawidowicz, *The Jewish Presence*, 62–63.
283. Arnold Schoenberg to Albert Einstein, 1 January 1925, in E. Randol Schoenberg, "Arnold Schoenberg and Albert Einstein: Their Relationship and Views on Zionism," *JASI* 10, no. 2 (November 1987): 155.
284. Arnold Schoenberg to the Editor of *The Jewish Year Book*, 28 March 1948, in *ASL*, 238. See also *SI*, 504.
285. Arnold Schoenberg, "Four Statements," in *ASR*, 340. See a similar statement in his letter to Ödön Partos, 15 June 1951, in *HHS*, 519.
286. Ernest Bloch was just as vulnerable as Schoenberg toward a poor Jewish reception of his music. See Schiller, *Bloch, Schoenberg, Bernstein*, 67–68.
287. Arnold Schoenberg, "A Four-Point Program for Jewry," in Ringer, *Arnold Schoenberg*, 232.
288. Arnold Schoenberg to Jakob Klatzkin, 16 December 1931, LC.
289. Quoted and translated by Dika Newlin. Compare Schoenberg's *Moderne Psalmen*, ed. Rudolf Kolisch (Mainz: Schott, 1956), n.p. Newlin compared this "Psalm" to Job 10:2–3: "I will say unto God, do not condemn me; show me wherefore thou contendest with me. Is it good unto thee that thou shouldst oppress, that thou shouldst despise the work of thine hands, and shine upon the counsel of the wicked?" Dika Newlin, "Self-Revelation and The Law," *Yuval* 1 (1968): 220.
290. Arnold Schoenberg to the National Institute of Arts and Letters, 22 May 1947, in *ASL*, 245.
291. Cahn pointed out that "the developmental view of history" and the idea of historical consciousness was adapted by Jewish thinkers from German philosophy for "the sake of preserving and revitalizing their religious ideals." Cahn, "On the Representation," 103.
292. Arnold Schoenberg, "Open Letter on His Seventy-Fifth Birthday," in *ASR*, 333.
293. Although Schoenberg's lachrymose rhetoric has been taken at face value by many of the commentators, who have portrayed him as a symbol of persecution and a victim of American cultural politics, it may be taken with a grain of salt. Far from being lonely, Schoenberg was always surrounded by family, friends, and disciples. He remained actively involved in the dissemination of his music until the end of his life, and his music scored successes. Although Schoenberg was plagued by several ailments, including asthma, his lifestyle in America did not differ much from that of a healthy person, except for his very last years. He followed a heavy work schedule, pursued sports (tennis until 1942, ping-pong, swimming), attended parties, and consumed cigarettes (until

1944), alcohol, and coffee. See Arnold Schoenberg, "Gentlemen: My Case Differs in Some Respects," in *ASR*, 347–48.

294. While his income cannot be compared to that of Stravinsky or composers in the film industry, he did much better than many of his other fellow émigrés.
295. *Teshuva* is a Hebrew word and literally means "return." In Judaism it refers to the act of repentance. *Baal teshuva* points to a Jew who, after neglecting Jewish religious practices, returns to Judaism.
296. André Neher, *They Made Their Souls Anew* (Albany: SUNY Press, 1990), 159–60. Schoenberg, however, did not literally witness the *Shoa*.
297. Schoenberg quoted in Ringer, *Arnold Schoenberg*, 231.
298. Arnold Schoenberg to Anton Webern, 4 August 1933.
299. Arnold Schoenberg, "Judenfrage," in *ASSG*, 294. Translation by author.
300. Ironically Schoenberg did not see himself as a Zionist. Arnold Schoenberg to Hans Nachod, 7 October 1933, in *The Arnold Schoenberg–Hans Nachod Collection*, ed. John Kimmey (Detroit: Harmonie Park, 1979), 36–37. In *Der biblische Weg*, Schoenberg modeled the protagonist on Herzl. He later regretted Herzl's failure to pursue the idea of creating a Jewish state in Uganda; it would have been "a land, a home, a place where refugees were safe." Ringer, *Arnold Schoenberg*, 234.
301. Ringer, *Arnold Schoenberg*, 140.
302. Schoenberg quoted in ibid., 230–44.
303. Arnold Schoenberg to Thomas Mann, 28 December 1938, in Schoenberg and Schmid, *Arnold Schoenberg – Thomas Mann*, 24–25.
304. Ibid., 26–28.
305. Arnold Schoenberg to Rabbi Joseph Shubow, 23 December 1933; and Arnold Schoenberg to Rabbi Samuel Abrams, 23 February 1934, LC.
306. Arnold Schoenberg to Stephen Wise, 12 May 1934, in Schoenberg, "Arnold Schoenberg and Albert Einstein," 162–68.
307. Heskes, *Passport*, 278–79. See also Arnold Schoenberg to David Bach, 11 May 1934, LC; and Gertrud Schoenberg to David Bach, 14 January 1935, ASC. In her letter to Bach, Gertrud wrote: "Dr. Rabbi Weiss in New York is a very helpful and nice man who knows of you already; and last year we talked a lot about you. If he can help you he will do it." Translation by author.
308. Arnold Schoenberg to Stephen Wise, 12 May 1934, in Schoenberg, "Arnold Schoenberg and Albert Einstein," 162–68.
309. Ringer saw a growing affinity between Schoenberg and Wise, arguing that "the rapid and ominous turn of events inevitably led composer and Rabbi to common ground." Ringer, *Arnold Schoenberg*, 151.
310. Arnold Schoenberg to Pierre van Paassen, 13 September 1942, LC.
311. "200,000 Stateless and Palestinian Jews Demand the Right to Fight," *LAT*, 10 November 1942; and *NYT*, 5 January 1942. See Yitshaq Ben-Ami, *Years of Wrath, Days of Glory* (New York: Robert Speller, 1982), 325.
312. The letter to both musicians is printed in *HHS*, 541–42.
313. Arnold Schoenberg to Max Reinhardt, 24 May 1933, and to Jakob Klatzkin, 26 May 1933. See *JASI* 17, nos. 1–2 (June–November 1994): 444–45, and LC. Reinhardt was not interested in this play, but staged Werfel's and Weill's *Eternal Road* in 1937. *Der biblische Weg* remained unperformed and unpublished during Schoenberg's lifetime. It was first published in an Italian translation in *Testi poetici e drammatici: editi e inediti*, ed. Luigi Rognoni and trans. Emilio Castellani (Milan: Feltrinelli, 1967). In 1994 Lazar published it in German and English in *JASI* 17, nos. 1–2 (June–November 1994): 162–443.

314. In 1932 Klatzkin sent Schoenberg the third edition of his book *Probleme des modernen Judentums*, in which he questioned the survival of modern Judaism in America (Berlin: Lambert Schneider, 1930), 52ff. Arnold Schoenberg to Jakob Klatzkin, 13 June 1933 and 21 April 1946, LC. The former letter is printed in *JASI* 17, nos. 1–2 (June–November 1994): 446–48.
315. This speech is also entitled "The Jewish Situation" and is printed in *ASR*, 251–56.
316. Mailamm, sometimes misspelled as Mailam, is an acronym of the organization's Hebrew name. The location of this event was the Jewish Club at 23 West 73rd Street. Heskes, *Passport*, 278; and Irene Heskes, "Shapers of American Jewish Music: *Mailamm* and the Jewish Music Forum, 1931–62," *American Music* 15, no. 3 (Fall 1997): 307.
317. Mailamm was reorganized and renamed Jewish Music Forum in 1939.
318. Heskes, *Passport*, 213, 278–79.
319. Boris Morros to Arnold Schoenberg, 27 December 1933, LC; Benjamin Buttenwieser to Arnold Schoenberg, 9 January 1934, LC.
320. Schoenberg's Princeton lecture took place on 6 March 1934. Einstein apparently told his secretary that he deemed the twelve-tone method "crazy." See Schoenberg, "Arnold Schoenberg and Albert Einstein," 186.
321. Arnold Schoenberg to Albert Einstein, 1 January 1925; and two drafts of "Einsteins falsche Politik," in Schoenberg, "Arnold Schoenberg and Albert Einstein," 153–55 and 175–82.
322. Ludwig Lewisohn, "Picks 10 'Greatest Jews,'" *NYT*, 28 March 1936.
323. "Sponsor Anti-Fascist Dinner," *NYT*, 21 October 1942.
324. Aaron Berman, *Nazism, the Jews and American Zionism: 1933–1948* (Detroit: Wayne State University Press, 1990), 36, 63–67, 89.
325. Ringer, *Arnold Schoenberg*, 235.
326. Lazar, "Arnold Schoenberg," 107–8.
327. Arnold Schoenberg to Stephen Wise, 12 May 1934, in Schoenberg, "Arnold Schoenberg and Albert Einstein," 167.
328. Ringer, *Arnold Schoenberg*, 231.
329. Arnold Schoenberg, to Hans Nachod, 7 October 1933, in Kimmey, *The Arnold Schoenberg–Hans Nachod Collection*, 36–37; and Arnold Schoenberg, "Ich beabsichtige in den Vereinigten Staaten," unpublished manuscript, ASC.
330. Arnold Schoenberg, "The Jewish Government in Exile," unpublished manuscript, ASC.
331. Jakob Klatzkin to Arnold Schoenberg, 3 May 1946, LC.
332. Ringer, *Arnold Schoenberg*, 131.
333. Ringer, *Arnold Schoenberg*, 7; Neher, *They Made Their Souls Anew*, 150.
334. Arnold Schoenberg to Peter Gradenwitz, 20 July 1934, in Lazar, "Arnold Schoenberg," 110.
335. Arnold Schoenberg, "Jeder junge Jude," *JASI* 17, nos. 1–2 (June–November 1994): 451, 453. Translation by author.
336. Neher, *They Made Their Souls Anew*, 13–14.
337. Ibid., 151.
338. One may also ask to what Judaism did Schoenberg belong before his conversion to Protestantism. His birth was registered in the Israelitische Cultusgemeinde in Vienna, yet little is known about his religious upbringing. His mother was a devout Orthodox Jew, but his father, was a freethinker. William Kangas, "The Ethics and Aesthetics of (Self)Representation: Arnold Schoenberg and Jewish Identity," *Leo Baeck Institute Yearbook* 45 (2000): 139–41, 167.
339. Arnold Schoenberg to Anton Webern, 4 August 1933, in *HHS*, 369–71.

340. Arnold Schoenberg to Rabbi Samuel Abrams, 23 February 1934, LC.
341. Schoenberg explored Leibniz's concept of the theodicy when composing his *Gurrelieder* (1900–1911) and based his chorus *Peace on Earth* (1907) on Conrad Ferdinand Meyer's Christian-inspired poem. Before 1910 and in 1919 Schoenberg painted two visions of Christ. *Arnold Schoenberg. Catalogue raisonné*, ed. Christian Meyer and Therese Muxeneder (Vienna: Arnold Schoenberg Center, 2005), 79, 80.
342. Crittenden, "Texts and Contexts," 246, 256.
343. Arnold Schoenberg to Leopold Stokowski, 16 April 1950, LC; and Leopold Stokowski to Arnold Schoenberg, 20 April 1950, LC.
344. Schoenberg and Rabbi Magnin met in 1935 through Pauline Alderman and remained close friends until Schoenberg's death. Pauline Alderman, "Schoenberg at USC," unpublished address given at the opening of the Arnold Schoenberg Institute in 1974, ASC.
345. Walter Rubsamen, "Schoenberg in America," *MQ* 37, no. 4 (October 1951): 489.
346. Arnold Schoenberg, "Forward to a Jewish Unity Party," in *ASR*, 253.
347. Arnold Schoenberg, "Jewish United Party," ASC. Excerpts in German translation published in Mäckelmann, *Arnold Schönberg und das Judentum. Der Komponist und sein religiöses, nationales und politisches Selbstverständnis nach 1921* (Hamburg: Verlag der Musikalienhandlung Karl Dieter Wagner, 1984), 305–6.
348. Arnold Schoenberg, "Eine neue Realpolitik," unpublished manuscript, ASC. Translation by author.
349. Arnold Schoenberg, "Forward to a Jewish Unity Party," in *ASR*, 252.
350. Heskes, *Passport*, 279.
351. Rubsamen, "Schoenberg in America," 476.
352. See Dorothy Crawford, *Evenings On and Off the Roof: Pioneering Concerts in Los Angeles, 1939–1971* (Berkeley: University of California Press, 1995), 115; and *SR*, 183, 318.
353. Schoenberg owned scores of Achron's *Statuettes* for piano (1931), Sextet for wind instruments, and Two Pieces for viola and piano (both 1942), the first and second of which were published in Cowell's New Music Edition. The Sextet's score is inscribed: "To the great master Arnold Schoenberg from his friend Joseph."
354. See *Schoenberg*, ed. Merle Armitage (New York: Schirmer, 1937), 151.
355. Arnold Schoenberg to Douglas Moore, 30 November 1939, in *ASLIB*, 358.
356. *ASLIB*, 389.
357. Arnold Schoenberg to Carl Engel, 19 October 1943, in *ASLIB*, 389.
358. Suzanne Bloch quoted in Robert Strassburg, *Ernest Bloch: Voice in the Wilderness: A Biographical Study* (Los Angeles: Trident Shop–California State University, 1977), 27.
359. Bloch was friends with the Malkin brothers. His daughter Suzanne and his student Roger Sessions, both teachers at the Malkin Conservatory, became Schoenberg's colleagues. "Je reste ici pour rencontre et accueillir Schönberg le 11 novembre – le pauvre homme! Ils l'ont détruit!" Ernest Bloch to Winifred Howe, 5 November 1933, in Joseph Lewinski and Emmanuelle Dijon, *Ernest Bloch (1880–1959). Sa vie, sa pensée suivi du catalogue d'œuvre* (Geneva: Slatkine, 2004), vol. 3, 297.
360. Ernest Bloch to Schoenberg, 5 November 1933, LC.
361. Ibid.
362. "J'ai vu Schönberg, j'ai diné avec lui. C'est un homme très bien. Cependant, bien qu'une partie soit bonne, je n'aime pas sa musique!" Ernest Bloch to Winifred Howe, 16 November 1933, in Lewinski and Dijon, *Ernest Bloch*, vol. 3, 305.
363. At this event (7 August 1942) Maxim Shapiro played Schoenberg's Six Little Piano Pieces, and Shapiro and Bernard Abramovich performed Bloch's *Poèmes de la mer* for piano and Piano Sonata.

364. "Samedi soir, nous avons pu entendre à la radio d'Angleterre, la nouvelle Suite pour cordes de Schönberg. Musicien habile, maître, mais sans rien à dire, pédant, assommant, cuistre de 1er ordre, un grand 'imposteur,' je pense de plus en plus." Ernest Bloch to Louise Hirsch, 3 February 1936, in Lewinski and Dijon, *Ernest Bloch*, vol. 3, 428.
365. Ernest Bloch to Winifred Howe, 30 October 1938, in Lewinski and Dijon, *Ernest Bloch*, vol. 3, 639.
366. Ernest Bloch to Albert Elkus, 26 January 1947, in Móricz, "Jewish Nationalism," 20–21.
367. Knight, "Classes with Schoenberg," *JASI* 13, no. 2 (November 1990): 154.
368. Warren Langlie, "Interview with Arnold Schoenberg," 29 December 1948 and 24 February 1949, unpublished transcript, ASC.
369. See *ASR*, 8.
370. Heskes, "Shapers," 309.
371. The *minhag* Carpentras is an ancient Jewish liturgical tradition of the French Provence.
372. Milhaud conducted the French *Pierrot* premiere in Paris in 1922.
373. Gertrud Schoenberg always asked the Milhauds if they would see the Stravinskys as well. Madeleine Milhaud, *Mon XXème siècle*, ed. Mildred Clary and Pascal Fardet (Paris: Bleu nuit, 2002), 64, 96.
374. Darius Milhaud and Claude Rostand, "Begegnungen mit Schönberg," *Melos* 22 (1955): 100.
375. Arnold Schoenberg to Darius Milhaud, 5 August 1945, LC.
376. Darius Milhaud to Arnold Schoenberg, 8 April 1945 and 1 May 1951, LC.
377. Having returned from one of his trips to France, Milhaud conveyed to Schoenberg that there was now a popular twelve-tone school using his serial methods, to which Schoenberg apparently replied, "Ach so! Und machen sie damit auch Musik?" (Oh really! But do they use it to make music?) Darius Milhaud and Claude Rostand, "Begegnungen," 101.
378. Rubsamen, "Schoenberg in America," 483.
379. Darius Milhaud, *Ma vie heureuse* (Montreal: Pierre Belfond, 1987), 244. This institution was initiated by singer Lotte Lehmann and Otto Klemperer in 1947 and is still in existence.
380. Schoenberg saw, but did not meet, Stravinsky, the project's only non-Jew, at the dress rehearsal of the *Genesis Suite*. The two composers decided "to remain on opposite sides of the hall." According to Leonard Stein, "not a word was exchanged. I left the hall with Schoenberg just at the completion of the Stravinsky piece. Only one sentence was forthcoming from Schoenberg when I asked him what he thought of the piece. 'It didn't end; it just stopped.'" Stravinsky and Schoenberg saw each other at least seven times: at Werfel's funeral, at the rehearsal and premiere of *Genesis Suite*, at a performance of *Firebird* conducted by Stravinsky in 1937 in Los Angeles, at a performance of *Pillar of Fire* conducted by Schoenberg in 1943 in San Francisco, at a dinner for Alma Mahler at the Beverly Hills Hotel in 1948, and at a concert on 23 October 1949, in Los Angeles celebrating the honor of freedom of the city of Vienna given to Schoenberg by an Austrian consul. On this occasion his First Chamber Symphony (original version) was performed, and Schoenberg gave a speech. Igor Stravinsky and Robert Craft, *Expositions and Developments* (London: Faber, 1962), 78; Leonard Stein, "Schoenberg and 'Kleine Modernsky,'" in *Confronting Stravinsky*, ed. Jann Pasler (Berkeley: University of California Press, 1986), 315; Igor Stravinsky and Robert Craft, *Dialogues and a Diary* (Garden City: Doubleday, 1963), 55; and Robert Craft, *Down a Path of Wonder: Memoirs of Stravinsky, Schoenberg and Other Cultural Figures* (Norfolk: Naxos Books, 2006), 6.
381. Arnold Schoenberg to Los Angeles Philharmonic Young Artists' Competition, 23 March 1944, LC.

382. Alexander Tansman to Arnold Schoenberg, 12 September 1944 and 10 March 1947, LC.
383. Ernst Toch to David Brimm, 4 March 1945, in *Quellen zur Geschichte emigrierter Musiker 1933–1950*, ed. Horst Weber and Manuela Schwartz (Munich: Saur, 2003), vol. 1, 276–78.
384. *Lilly Toch: The Orchestration of a Composer's Life*, interview conducted by Bernard Galm in 1978, Center for Oral History Research, Young Research Library, UCLA, transcript of audio recording, vol. 1, 318–22.
385. Arnold Schoenberg to Horace Kallen, 6 December 1933, Yivo Institute for Jewish Research. Toch taught seminars in music theory at the New School in 1934–35.
386. Warren Langlie, "Interview with Arnold Schoenberg," 9 June 1944, unpublished, ASC.
387. Franz Werfel to Ernst Toch, 11 August 1944, UCLA Library.
388. Ernst Toch to Arnold Schoenberg, 11 September 1949; and Arnold Schoenberg to Ernst Toch, 13 September 1949, LC.
389. See Toch Collection, UCLA Library.
390. Some of these works include *Havel Havalim* for chorus and keyboard (1939), *Yevarechecha Adonay* for voices and organ (1941), and *Song of Songs (Song of Solomon)* for women's choir (1942).
391. Dessau's lecture was published: "Arnold Schoenberg's *Kol nidre*," *Jewish Music Forum* 3, no. 1 (1942): 10–12. See also Heskes, "Shapers," 312–13. Dessau hoped to convince Binder to conduct another performance of *Kol nidre* and to recruit Wise as narrator. Paul Dessau to Arnold Schoenberg, 27 December 1941, LC.
392. Dessau joined the U.S. Communist Party in 1946. He returned to Europe in 1948 and was spared the public humiliation of the HUAC hearings. He joined the SED (Socialist Unity Party) in the DDR, while Eisler and Brecht declined the invitation to join this party. Frank Schneider, "Dessau und Schönberg im amerikanischen Exil," in *Paul Dessau: Von der Geschichte gezeichnet*, ed. Klaus Angermann (Hofheim: Wolke, 1994), 62.
393. Ibid., 62–63. Dessau's dodecaphonic works written in France and America include *Guernica* for piano (1938), *Les voix* for voice and orchestra (text by Paul Verlaine, 1939–43), and his Second and Third String Quartets (1943–46). In 1963 he paid tribute to Bach and Schoenberg, specifically in his Orchestral Variations, op. 31, with his large-scale dodecaphonic orchestral Bach-Variations.
394. In 1940 Dessau had asked Schoenberg to help liberate Leibowitz, who was interned in France, whereupon Schoenberg offered his assistance, even though at that time he did not know Leibowitz and his work. Arnold Schoenberg to Paul Dessau, 23 September 1940, LC.
395. Paul Dessau and Christa Müller, "Ein Gespräch über Arnold Schönberg," in *Arnold Schönberg 1874–1951. Zum 25. Todestag des Komponisten*, Forum: Musik in der DDR, Arbeitsheft 24, ed. Matthias Hansen and Christa Müller (Berlin: Akademie der Künste der DDR, 1976), 123.
396. Frank Schneider, "Dessau und Schönberg," 66–67.
397. Dessau and Müller, "Ein Gespräch," 125.
398. Paul Dessau, "Here Are a Few Remarks Schoenberg Made to Me," *PNM* 11, no. 2 (Spring–Summer 1973): 85.
399. Malcolm Cole, "Eric Zeisl: His Life and Music: Interview with Gertrude Zeisl" (Oral History Program, UCLA, 1978), 25, 358.
400. Curt Sachs's definition, as used in his lecture at the First International Congress of Jewish Music in Paris in 1957, quoted in Heidy Zimmermann, "Was heißt 'jüdische Musik'?" in *Jüdische Musik? Fremdbilder – Eigenbilder*, ed. Eckart John and Heidy Zimmermann (Cologne: Böhlau, 2004), 30.
401. Schoenberg, "Arnold Schoenberg and Albert Einstein," 155.

402. *SI*, 502–5.
403. A. Lehman Engel, *This Bright Day: An Autobiography* (New York: Macmillan, 1974), 60.
404. Arnold Schoenberg, Draft of a letter without address, 28 June 1933, ASC. Translation by author.
405. *ASR*, 252.
406. *SI*, 502–5.
407. Arnold Schoenberg to Hans Nathan, 11 February 1938, LC.
408. Abraham Idelsohn, *Jewish Music: Its Historical Development* (New York: Henry Holt, 1929), 471–77.
409. *SI*, 162.
410. *ASR*, 339. For this reason, he abandoned sketches he made for a setting of the Palestinian folksong "Holem Tsa'adi [My Step resounds]" in 1937. He also left incomplete sketches for a setting of the hymn *Jahlech* [or *Yaaleh*, "May it rise"] for the evening Yom Kippur service. For *Jahlech* see *ASSW* V, Series B, vol. 19, 35.
411. Beller, *Vienna*, 114.
412. Ibid., 119.
413. Ibid., 121.
414. Leon Botstein, "Arnold Schoenberg: Language, Modernism and Jewish Identity," in *Austrians and Jews in the Twentieth Century: From Franz Joseph to Waldheim*, ed. Robert Wistrich (New York: St. Martin's Press, 1992), 174.
415. *German-Jewish History in Modern Times*, ed. Michael Meyer (New York: Columbia University Press, 1995), vol. 2, 351–52.
416. Beller, *Vienna*, 115; and see *SI*, 223.
417. Juan Allende-Blin, "Arnold Schönberg und die Kabbala – Versuch einer Annäherung," in *Arnold Schönberg, Musik-Konzepte Sonderband*, ed. Heinz-Klaus Metzger and Rainer Riehn (Munich: Text und Kritik, 1980), 117–45.
418. Steven Schwarzschild, "Adorno and Schoenberg as Jews Between Kant and Hegel," *Leo Baeck Institute Yearbook* 35 (1990): 466.
419. Neher, *They Made Their Souls Anew*, 153.
420. Sonderling quoted in Steven Cahn, "*Kol nidre* in America," *JASC* 4 (2002): 206. Sonderling also supplied Korngold and Toch with texts for Jewish-themed works.
421. Arnold Schoenberg to Moritz Violin, 23 December 1938, ASC; Arnold Schoenberg to Jacob Sonderling, 1 December 1938; and Jacob Sonderling to Arnold Schoenberg, 3 January 1939, LC. See also Rubsamen, "Schoenberg in America," 476.
422. Neher called Schoenberg's *Kol nidre* his "Ode of Teshuva." Neher, *They Made Their Souls Anew*, 165.
423. Cahn, "*Kol nidre* in America," 203.
424. *ASR*, 282.
425. Cahn, "*Kol nidre* in America," 206.
426. Ibid., 207, 209.
427. *ASSW* V, Series A, vol. 19, 24. Schoenberg explained to Lazare Saminsky on 6 February 1941 (LC): "The traditional text has been changed (on my desire, by Rabbi Sonderling and according to my belief). I think my version of the text reconciles this idea with the moral ideas onto which we Jews belong no less than every other people. I believe that my version reinstates the original meaning of this prayer."
428. Arnold Schoenberg to Paul Dessau, 22 November 1941, in *ASSP*, 98.
429. *ASR*, 282.
430. For more details see Steven Cahn's "Kol Nidre op. 39," in *Arnold Schönberg. Interpretationen seiner Werke*, ed. Gerold Gruber (Laaber: Laaber, 2002), vol. 2, 49–66.

431. *ASR*, 282.
432. Warren Langlie, "Interview with Arnold Schoenberg," 24 September 1947, unpublished, ASC.
433. Cahn, "*Kol nidre* in America," 212–13.
434. *ASSP*, 98.
435. Steven Cahn, "Dépasser l'universalisme: une écoute particlariste d'*Un survivant de Varsovie* op. 46 et du *Kol nidre* op. 39 de Schoenberg," *Ostinato rigore. Revue internationale d'études musicales* 17, no. 1 (2001): 234. English translation by Steven Cahn.
436. Alexander Ringer, *Arnold Schönberg. Das Leben im Werk* (Stuttgart: Metzler, 2002), 283–84.
437. An excerpt of a rehearsal for this performance is available on CD: *Arnold Schönberg: Dear Miss Silvers. Originalaufnahmen 1931–1951* (Cologne: supposé, 2007).
438. Arnold Schoenberg to Edwin Kalmus, 14 February 1940, LC.
439. To Saminsky Schoenberg suggested a reduction for twenty-four players and twenty-four singers or a double quartet of vocalists and organ. Arnold Schoenberg to Lazare Saminsky, 16 January and 6 February 1941, LC.
440. Arnold Schoenberg to Paul Dessau, 22 November 1941, in *ASSP*, 98.
441. Lazare Saminsky to Arnold Schoenberg, 20 April 1941, LC. Schirmer accepted *Kol nidre* only on a rental basis. Schoenberg withdrew the work from Schirmer's rental catalog in 1946. See Carl Engel to Arnold Schoenberg, 3 March 1941, LC; and Nathan Broder to Arnold Schoenberg, 25 October 1946, LC.
442. Lazare Saminsky, "Hebrew Song Lives in Modern Music," *MA* 41, no. 4 (15 November 1924): 9.
443. Dessau, "Arnold Schoenberg's *Kol nidre*," 10–12; and Joseph Yasser, "Serious Jewish Art Music," *NYT*, 2 May 1943.
444. David Putterman to Arnold Schoenberg, 4 November 1943, LC.
445. Arnold Schoenberg to David Putterman, 15 December 1943, LC.
446. David Putterman to Arnold Schoenberg, 22 December 1943, LC; and Arnold Schoenberg to David Putterman, 13 February 1945, LC.
447. Nathaniel Shilkret, *Sixty Years in the Music Business*, ed. Niel Shell and Barbara Shilkret (Lanham: Scarecrow, 2005), 197.
448. Eric Salzman, "Arnold Schoenberg: Prelude to the *Genesis* Suite," program notes for Robert Craft's 1965 CBS recording of *The Music of Arnold Schoenberg*, vol. 2, M2S 694/M2L 294 (New York: CBS 1965); and James Westby, "Genesis Suite," CD liner notes for *Genesis Suite* (Franklin: Naxos, 2004).
449. Ringer, *Arnold Schoenberg*, 71.
450. Alexandre Tansman, *Igor Stravinsky: The Man and His Music*, trans. Therese and Charles Bleefield (New York: Putnam, 1949), 130.
451. Arnold Schoenberg, Prelude, op. 44, fair copy, 3, ASC.
452. Robert Craft, *Down a Path of Wonder*, 36.
453. The concert program also featured Beethoven's "Egmont" Overture and Sibelius's First Symphony. In 1951 Capitol Records reissued another recording of the Suite on a 33-rpm LP album.
454. Lawrence Morton, "Los Angeles Interprets Genesis," *MM* 23, no. 1 (1946): 59.
455. Arnold Schoenberg to Nathaniel Shilkret, 21 April 1951, LC; and Arthur Shilkret to Arnold Schoenberg, 4 May 1951, ASC.
456. Chochem had commissioned such composers as Toch, Milhaud, Eisler, and Leonard Bernstein to contribute music to her anthology *Jewish Holiday Dances* (1947). Therese Muxeneder, "*A Survivor from Warsaw* Op. 46," in *Arnold Schönberg. Interpretationen*

seiner Werke, ed. Gerold Gruber (Laaber: Laaber, 2002), vol. 2, 132–33.

457. Arnold Schoenberg to Corinne Chochem, 20 April 1947, in *ASLIB*, 410.
458. Unable to compose, as required, a new orchestra work, he had turned down a commission from the Koussevitzky Foundation three years earlier.
459. Arnold Schoenberg, particell of *A Survivor from Warsaw*, LC. *Survivor* may have been influenced by Friedrich Torberg's 1943 novel *Mein ist die Rache* about a concentration camp survivor. Schoenberg had read and liked the book. See also Therese Muxeneder, "Lebens(werk)geschichte in Begegnungen. Vorgespräche zu Arnold Schönbergs *A Survivor from Warsaw*, op. 46," in *Schoenberg & Nono*, ed. Anna Maria Morazzoni (Venice: Leo Olschki, 2002), 110–11.
460. "The title will be *A Survivor from Warsaw* because it was my inspiration and the geographical meaning includes the ghetto and all what happened there." Arnold Schoenberg to Bomart Music Publications, 18 February 1949, LC.
461. Arnold Schoenberg to Kurt List, 1 November 1948, LC.
462. Philip Friedman quoted in Yisrael Gutman, *The Jews of Warsaw, 1939–1943: Ghetto, Underground, Revolt*, trans. Ina Friedman (Bloomington: Indiana University Press, 1982), 225. Steven Cahn, however, argued that this moment points to *Kiddush hahayyim* ("sanctification of life"), as the body and not the soul was under attack. See Cahn, "Dépasser l'universalisme," 229–30; and see also Emil Fackenheim, *To Mend the World* (Indianapolis: Indiana University Press, 1994), 223.
463. Cahn, "Dépasser l'universalisme," 224–25.
464. Schoenberg accidentally omitted four words in the Hebrew text. The mistake was discovered when the score was prepared for publication, and the words were inserted and the melody changed in mm. 89–90 and m. 94. René Leibowitz, who prepared the full score based on Schoenberg's musical shorthand particell, made spelling mistakes in the Hebrew texts, which caused confusion at the rehearsals for the work's premiere. Richard Hoffmann to Kurt Frederick, 28 November 1948, copy at ASC.
465. Charles Heller, "Traditional Jewish Material in Schoenberg's *A Survivor from Warsaw*, Op. 46," *JASI* 3, no. 1 (March 1979): 68–74.
466. Mäckelmann, *Arnold Schönberg und das Judentum*, 488; Timothy Jackson, "'Your Songs Proclaim God's Return' – Arnold Schoenberg, the Composer and His Jewish Faith," *International Journal of Musicology* 6 (1997): 283; and Schiller, *Bloch, Schoenberg, Bernstein*, 103–4.
467. Cahn, "Dépasser l'universalisme," 224–25. See also Schiller's insightful discussion of the *Survivor*'s conclusion in Schiller, *Bloch, Schoenberg, Bernstein*, 114–15.
468. Schoenberg referred to *Survivor* as a cantata in letters: Arnold Schoenberg to H. Willard Gray, 7 February 1948, LC; and Arnold Schoenberg to Kurt List, 17 March1948, LC.
469. Schiller, *Bloch, Schoenberg, Bernstein*, 125.
470. Beat Föllmi identified the many narrative and cinematic musical elements of *Survivor* in "'I cannot remember ev'rything.' Eine narratologische Analyse von Arnold Schönbergs Kantate *A Survivor from Warsaw*," *AfMw* 55, no. 1 (1998): 28–56.
471. Kurt List, "Schoenberg's New Cantata," 469; and Richard Taruskin, "A Sturdy Musical Bridge to the 21st Century," *NYT*, 24 August 1997. Although Stroheim acted Field Marshal Rommel in Billy Wilder's 1943 film *Five Graves to Cairo*, he was not known for Nazi parts. He mainly played Prussian types in the context of World War I.
472. Allen Shawn, *Arnold Schoenberg's Journey* (New York: Farrar, Straus and Giroux, 2002), 262.
473. Between 1942 and 1947 all the other Koussevitzky orchestral commissions received premieres in Boston, except Burrill Phillips's overture *Tom Paine*. Moreover, the

Koussevitzky foundation neither confirmed the receipt of *Survivor*'s condensed autograph score nor paid the commission fee on time.

474. After immigrating to America in 1938 and settling in Albuquerque in 1944, Frederick became the director of that orchestra in 1945 and a champion of contemporary music in the American Southwest.
475. Isabel Grear to Arnold Schoenberg, 8 November 1948, LC.
476. Winifred Reiter, "Albuquerque Symphony First Playing of New Schoenberg Work," *Albuquerque Journal*, 5 November 1948, and *South Western Musician* 25, no. 9 (1949): 20.
477. Henry Cowell, "Current Chronicle," *MQ* 36, no. 3 (July 1950): 451.
478. Olin Downes, "Schoenberg Work Is Presented Here," *NYT*, 14 April 1950.
479. Theodor W. Adorno, "Engagement," in *Noten zur Literatur, Gesammelte Schriften,* ed. Rolf Tiedemann (Darmstadt: Wissenschaftliche Buchgesellschaft, 1998), vol. 11, 423; Richard Taruskin, "A Sturdy Musical Bridge;" and Móricz, "Jewish Nationalism," 413–18.
480. Arnold Schoenberg to Dagobert Runes, 5 February 1949, LC.
481. Arnold Schoenberg to Georg Wolfsohn, 20 April 1950, ASC.
482. Naomi André, "Returning to a Homeland: Religion and Political Context in Schoenberg's *Dreimal tausend Jahre*," in Cross and Berman, *Political and Religious Ideas*, 268–69.
483. Schoenberg suggested a publication fee for this work in retrospect and thus was offered only $50 (about $440 in 2009). See Schoenberg to Jane Lundblad, 16 May 1950, LC.
484. Friedrich Torberg to Arnold Schoenberg, 5 October 1943; and Arnold Schoenberg to Friedrich Torberg, 31 January 1949, LC.
485. In 1943 Torberg sent him his poem "Kaddish" (1943), expecting that Schoenberg would set it to music. Yet the project did not materialize.
486. The British Labour leader and foreign secretary in the British postwar government, Ernest Bevin (1881–1951), had opposed the creation of a Jewish state. Arnold Schoenberg to Friedrich Torberg, 29 March 1949, LC. Translation by author.
487. Friedrich Torberg to Arnold Schoenberg, 16 June 1949; and Arnold Schoenberg to Friedrich Torberg, 20 June 1949, LC.
488. *ASSW* V, Series B, vol. 19, 138.
489. Vinaver, who immigrated to America in 1938, had planned to arrange and perform *Survivor* for small forces, but the project did not reach fruition. Chemjo Vinaver to Arnold Schoenberg, 23 March 1948, LC.
490. Vinaver explained the cantillation practice as follows: "The Leader of the Prayer (Ba'al tefillah) used to exclaim each verse with mystic fervor. The congregation repeated it with the same power and profound emotion – but with minor changes and in a faster tempo. This congregational response shifted key-centers frequently, unconsciously creating an atmosphere of unbridled, almost primeval, religious fervor." Chemjo Vinaver to Arnold Schoenberg, 29 May 1950, LC.
491. Steven Cahn, "On the Representation of Jewish Identity and Historical Consciousness in Schönberg's Religious Thought," *JASC* 5 (2003): 101–3.
492. Arnold Schoenberg to Chemjo Vinaver, 24 June 1950, LC; and *Anthology of Jewish Music*, ed. Chemjo Vinaver (New York: E. B. Marks, 1953), 203.
493. Arnold Schoenberg to Chemjo Vinaver, 29 May 1951; and Ringer, *Arnold Schoenberg*, 204.
494. Peter Gradenwitz, Preface to the score (Tel Aviv: Israeli Music Publications, 1953).
495. Arnold Schoenberg to Chemjo Vinaver, 29 May 1951, LC; and Mäckelmann, *Arnold Schönberg und das Judentum*, 344.
496. There was apparently "no budget which allows payment to composers for their compositions." Chemjo Vinaver to Arnold Schoenberg, 29 June 1950, LC. The Israeli Music

Publications edition of Schoenberg's Psalm 130 setting was funded by the Koussevitzky Foundation and ironically dedicated to the memory of Serge Koussevitzky. For a review of the *Anthology* see Albert Weisser, "Anthology of Jewish Music, by Chemjo Vinaver," *Commentary* 21, no. 1 (January 1956): 95–96.

497. Gradenwitz, Preface.
498. Arnold Schoenberg to Richard Dehmel, 13 December 1912, in *ASL*, 35–36.
499. Arnold Schoenberg to Georg Wolfsohn, 20 April 1951, in Peter Gradenwitz, "The Religious Works of Arnold Schönberg," *Music Review* 21 (1960): 19.
500. For more details see Mäckelmann, *Arnold Schönberg und das Judentum*, 364–78.
501. Arnold Schoenberg to Oskar Adler, 3 March 1951, in *ASL*, 286; and Arnold Schoenberg to Georg Wolfsohn, 24 April 1951, in Gradenwitz, "The Religious Works," 26.
502. When Schoenberg sent the first ten Psalms to Wolfsohn, he described them as incomplete. Arnold Schoenberg to Georg Wolfsohn, 24 April 1951, LC.
503. For more details on this work see Mark Risinger, "Schoenberg's *Modern Psalm*, Op. 50c and the Unattainable Ending," in Cross and Berman, *Political and Religious Ideas*, 289–306.
504. Alexander Ringer, "Faith and Symbol—On Arnold Schoenberg's Last Musical Utterance," *JASI* 6, no. 1 (June 1982): 88.
505. Dika Newlin, "Self-Revelation and the Law: Arnold Schoenberg in His Religious Works," *Yuval* 1 (1968): 216.
506. Ringer, "Faith and Symbol," 91.
507. Risinger, "Schoenberg's *Modern Psalm*," 294–95. See also David Schiff, "Jewish and Musical Tradition in the Music of Mahler and Schoenberg," *JASI* 9, no. 2 (November 1986): 229–30.
508. *SI*, 502.
509. Arnold Schoenberg to Alma Mahler-Werfel, 9 August 1939, University of Pennsylvania, Otto Albrecht Music Library.
510. Claus-Dieter Krohn, *Intellectuals in Exile: Refugee Scholars and the New School for Social Research*, trans. Robert and Rita Kimber (Amherst: University of Massachusetts Press, 1993), 22; and Catherine Parsons Smith, *Making Music in Los Angeles: Transforming the Popular* (Berkeley: University of California Press, 2007).
511. About one hundred militant organizations supported anti-Semitism in America. In California German-language papers such as the *California Staatszeitung* and *California Weckruf* (mouthpiece of the national-socialist German-American Volksbund, 1935–38), the German Consulate in Los Angeles, and the American Nazi party in Los Angeles actively promoted Nazism. The German American Bund organized several big Nazi rallies in the 1930s and early 1940s. See Holger Gumprecht, *"New Weimar" unter Palmen: Deutsche Schriftsteller im Exil in Los Angeles* (Berlin: Aufbau Taschenbuch Verlag, 1998), 29; and Ehrhard Bahr, *Weimar on the Pacific: German Exile Culture in Los Angeles and the Crisis of Modernism* (Berkeley: University of California Press, 2007), 5.
512. Alexander Stephan, *"Communazis": FBI Surveillance of German Emigré Writers*, trans. Jan Heurck (New Haven: Yale University Press, 2000), x.
513. Mike Davis, *City of Quartz: Excavating the Future of Los Angeles* (New York: Vintage, 1992), 47, 50.
514. Arnold Schoenberg to Rudolf Kolisch, 8 December 1934, LC; and Bahr, *Weimar on the Pacific*, 3. Although different from many European cities, Los Angeles was by no means "a peculiarly infertile cultural soil"–a myth chiefly promoted by film noir and European émigrés. Davis, *City of Quartz*, 17.
515. *ASL*, 192.

516. Earliest examples can be found in his correspondence with Joseph Malkin starting in June 1933. R. Wayne Shoaf, "The Schoenberg-Malkin Correspondence," *JASI* 13, no. 2 (November 1990): 174–75.
517. *SW*, 292–96.
518. *ASR*, 251–56.
519. *SR*, 146.
520. Arnold Schoenberg to Erwin Stein, 2 October 1942, in *ASL*, 215.
521. Christopher Hailey, "Briefe Schönbergs," in *Arnold Schönberg. Interpretationen seiner Werke*, ed. Gerold Gruber (Laaber: Laaber, 2002), vol. 2, 485.
522. Schoenberg suggested to Erwin Stein in 1942 to record an English version of *Pierrot*, regretting that his recording was "unfortunately, in spite of my protest, in German." See *ASL*, 215.
523. Lawrence Schoenberg to the author, e-mail of 23 October 2005.
524. Arnold Schoenberg to Kurt List, 2 November 1946, LC.
525. Arnold Schoenberg to Alfred Schlee, 1 March 1947, LC.
526. Arnold Schoenberg to Philosophical Library, 10 November 1943, LC; and Arnold Schoenberg to Dika Newlin, 25 January 1949, in *ASLIB*, 424.
527. *ASL*, 251.
528. Dika Newlin, "Editor's Foreword," in *Style and Idea* (New York: Philosophical Library, 1950), v; and Arnold Schoenberg to Dika Newlin, 12 January 1948, LC.
529. Arnold Schoenberg to Edward Steuermann, 13 April 1949, LC.
530. Arnold Schoenberg to Felix Greissle, 21 November 1945, LC. To Universal Edition, he wrote: "Die kürzeren Artikel in diesem Buch sind zu eng mit dem amerikanischen Kulturleben verknüpft als dass sie in Wien verstanden werden können." Arnold Schoenberg to Alfred Schlee, December 1946, LC.
531. Arnold Schoenberg to Moses Smith, 18 October 1941, LC; Arnold Schoenberg to Claire Reis, 24 April 1939, LC.
532. Arnold Schoenberg to Felix Greissle, 7 June 1938, LC.
533. Martin Bernstein, "On the Genesis of Schoenberg's Suite for School Orchestra," *JASI* 11, no. 2 (November 1988): 160.
534. See Vivian Perlis, "Interview with Gerald Strang," March 1975 (Oral History of American Music Archives, Yale University); and Arnold Schoenberg to Rudolf Kolisch, 16 January 1941, Houghton Library, Harvard University.
535. Pauline Alderman, "I Remember Arnold Schoenberg," *Facets* (USC magazine) (1976): 53.
536. Charlie Chaplin, *My Autobiography* (New York: Simon and Schuster, 1964), 397. The music for *Modern Times* was arranged by two of Schoenberg's students: Eddie (Edward) Powell and David Raksin.
537. *SR*, 60.
538. *SR*, 146, 196. Schoenberg wrote to Levant: "I hear you sometimes on 'Information please' which amuses me very much." Arnold Schoenberg to Oscar Levant, 2 October 1939, LC.
539. Arnold Schoenberg to Felix Greissle, 7 June 1938, LC.
540. *SR*, 58.
541. Bertolt Brecht, *Journals*, 333.
542. Chaplin, *My Autobiography*, 397.
543. Arnold Schoenberg, "Democracy," in *ASR*, 245.
544. Arnold Schoenberg to Thomas Mann, 15 January 1939; see excerpt in *ASR*, 279.
545. Ibid. See excerpt in *ASR*, 232.

546. *SR*, 275.
547. Arnold Schoenberg to Gertrud Greissle, March 1939, LC. Translation by author.
548. Arnold Schoenberg to Gustave Reese, 11 November 1939, LC.
549. "Schoenberg Takes Out Final Citizenship Papers," *California Daily Bruin* (UCLA magazine), 14 April 1941.
550. Leonard Stein, "A Note on the Genesis of the *Ode to Napoleon*," *JASI* 2, no. 1 (March 1977): 52.
551. Arnold Schoenberg to Felix Greissle, 10 July 1944.
552. Arnold Schoenberg, "A Dangerous Game," *MM* 22, no. 2 (November–December 1944): 4 and 5.
553. Arnold Schoenberg to Josef Rufer, 18 December 1947, in *ASL*, 252.
554. Thanks to E. Randol Schoenberg for this information.
555. Arnold Schoenberg, "Subordination," unpublished manuscript, ASC.
556. Arnold Schoenberg to Milton Koblitz, 9 August 1950 quoted in *ASR*, 340.
557. *SI*, 505–6.
558. Arnold Schoenberg to Josef Rufer, 25 May 1948, in *ASL*, 255.
559. Arnold Schoenberg to José Limón, 22 April 1950, LC.
560. O. J. Simpson moved into the neighboring house several decades after Schoenberg's death.
561. Little is known about Schoenberg's contact with Berlin, although he wrote to his son that he had much hope that Berlin could help him find a job for him: "Ich will auch Irving Berlin ansprechen, sobald ich ihn sehe und verspreche mir einiges davon" (Schoenberg to Georg Schönberg, 5 November 1938). Schoenberg said about Berlin: "He thinks in music. He has a sense of form, and harmonized clearly. It is conventional. It is also not without a certain degree of originality. I will tell you they are not the rank of Johann Strauss or Gershwin. Gershwin is of a much higher quality." Warren Langlie, "Interview with Arnold Schoenberg," 17 March 1949, unpublished, ASC. Schoenberg's acquaintance with Buttolph, who scored such films as *My Darling Clementine* (1946) and *Kiss of Death* (1947), dates back to the early 1920s when Buttolph studied in Europe. See Arnold Schoenberg to David Buttolph, 26 October 1923, LC.
562. Sam Kashner and Nancy Schoenberger, *A Talent for Genius: The Life and Times of Oscar Levant* (New York: Villard, 1994), 153; Oscar Levant, *A Smattering of Ignorance* (New York: Doubleday, 1940), 65–66.
563. Henry Clay Shriver, a student of Schoenberg's former teaching assistant Gerald Strang, stepped in with a gift of $1,000 and became the work's dedicatee. See Walter Bailey, *Programmatic Elements in the Works of Schoenberg* (Ann Arbor: UMI Research Press, 1984), 136–51.
564. Irene Kahn Atkins, "Hugo Friedhofer," American Film Institute/Louis B. Mayer Foundation Oral History, 13 March–29 April 1974.
565. Arnold Schoenberg to Alfred Newman, 26 July 1941.
566. Arnold Schoenberg to Alfred Newman, 23 July 1939, 26 July and 5 November 1941, LC.
567. A limited number of sets was printed by RCA Victor and sold at cost. Fred Steiner, "A History of the First Complete Recording of Schoenberg's String Quartets," *JASI* 2, no. 2 (February 1978): 122–37.
568. "A Movie Studio Records Arnold Schönberg's Quartets—About Alfred Newman," *New York Sun*, 23 July 1938.
569. Arnold Schoenberg, "Oscar Speech," in *SW*, 302.
570. Leo Robin provided the lyrics for this song.
571. Steiner, "A History," 130–31.

572. Arnold Schoenberg to Rudolf Goehr, April and 5 May 1934, LC; Arnold Schoenberg to Georg Schönberg, 10 June 1934, LC.
573. Howard Pollack stated that Gershwin apparently visited Schoenberg in Berlin on his 1928 trip to Europe, bringing back a photograph of Schoenberg inscribed "April 1928." *George Gershwin: His Life and Work* (Berkeley: University of California Press, 2006), 132.
574. Schillinger wrote to Gershwin: "I think it would be a good idea to work with Schoenberg on four-part fugues and to let Toch supervise your prospective symphonic compositions." Pollack, *George Gershwin*, 133–34.
575. Levant, *A Smattering*, 187.
576. Albert Sendrey in *George Gershwin*, ed. Merle Armitage (New York: Longmans Green, 1938), 105.
577. Levant, *A Smattering*, 186–87.
578. Pollack, *George Gershwin*, 134; and Herbert Glass, "Gershwin on Canvas," *Performing Arts* 21, no. 2 (1987): 29.
579. Correspondence with Howard Pollack, e-mail of 30 May 2001.
580. Pollack, *George Gershwin*, 134.
581. Gershwin was on the Advisory Committee of the Malkin Conservatory of Music.
582. Schoenberg went to the first of two performances. At the second concert, while playing his Concerto in F, Gershwin experienced a memory lapse, one of the first signs of his fatal illness.
583. Peter Heyworth, *Otto Klemperer: His Life and Times*, vol. 2: *1933–1973* (Cambridge: Cambridge University Press, 1996), 79.
584. *ASL*, 192.
585. Arnold Schoenberg, "At George Gershwin's Funeral," unpublished document, ASC.
586. *ASR*, 293.
587. *SI*, 124, 154.
588. Arnold Schoenberg in Armitage, *George Gershwin*, 97.
589. He wrote to his former student: "But I really think, that here one will require from me a film some day, and then I want to endavour [*sic*] to ask for you as my 'assistant' as they call it here." Arnold Schoenberg to Rudolf Goehr, 16 November 1934, LC.
590. Herbert Stothart, renowned for his scoring of *The Wizard of Oz* (1939), composed the music for *The Good Earth*. Stothart and Schoenberg became friends.
591. To Alma Mahler he confided: "it would have been the end of me." Arnold Schoenberg to Alma Mahler, 23 January 1936, in *ASL*, 197. In a similar case, he explained: "My position in musical life would compel me to maintain a certain attitude even if I did not myself feel that way." Arnold Schoenberg to Charlotte Dieterle, 30 July 1936, in *ASL*, 199. See Sabine Feisst, "Arnold Schoenberg and the Cinematic Art," *MQ* 83, no. 1 (Spring 1999): 95–98. The news about Schoenberg's encounters with the Hollywood film industry soon reached Europe, and his daughter Trudi and son-in-law Felix hoped that their father would be able to support them with bigger amounts of money. Gertrud and Felix Greissle to Arnold Schoenberg, 23 August–8 October 1937, LC.
592. Arnold Schoenberg, "Art and the Moving Pictures," *Arts and Architecture* 57, no. 4 (April 1940): 40.
593. Isabel Jones, "Hollywood Council Backs Film Talent," *MA* 61, no. 1 (10 January 1941): 20.
594. Feisst, "Arnold Schoenberg and the Cinematic Art," 103–5; and Felix Greissle to Arnold Schoenberg, 10 September 1948, LC.
595. Ruth Rivkin, "Five More Tones Than Most," *Californian* (October 1948): 43, 65.

596. Maureen Furniss, *Art in Motion: Animation Aesthetics* (Eastleigh: John Libbey, 1998), 259.
597. Crittenden, "Texts and Contexts," 239–41. Under the pseudonym "Jolly Joker," Gertrud Schoenberg had already written screenplays in the 1920s.
598. Karin Kathrein, "Wir hatten nicht das Gefühl, dass unser Vater verbittert war," interview with Nuria Nono Schoenberg, *Bühne* (September 1991): 22.
599. Interview with Leonard Stein, 12 February 1999, New York City. See also Arnold Schoenberg to Arthur Leslie Jacobs ("Here is a theme for Mr. Tremblay's contrapuntal improvisation"), 5 March 1942, LC; and Isabel Jones, "'Ballad for Heroes' Given at Modern Music Festival," *LAT*, 25 May 1942.
600. Ilse Storb and Klaus-Gotthard Fischer, *Dave Brubeck: Improvisationen und Kompositionen. Die Idee der kulturellen Wechselbeziehungen* (Frankfurt am Main: Lang, 1991), 5–6; and John Salmon, "What Brubeck Got from Milhaud," *American Music Teacher* 41, no. 4 (May 1992): 26.
601. Quoted in Walter Rubsamen, "Schoenberg in America," *MQ* 37, no. 4 (October 1951): 471.
602. Arnold Schoenberg to Gene Buck, 23 October 1939, LC.
603. Arnold Schoenberg to Florence Irish, 22 June 1937, LC.
604. Arnold Schoenberg to ASCAP, 5 September 1941 and 25 June 1945. Rimsky-Korsakov already used trombone glissandi in his 1892 opera *Mlada*, and in America trombone glissandi probably emerged in the music of southern street bands in the 1890s, finding their way into pieces like Arthur Pryor's *Trombone Sneeze* for the Sousa Band (c. 1901).
605. Arnold Schoenberg to Gene Buck, 23 October 1939, LC; and Deems Taylor to Alma Mahler, 6 September 1944, copy at ASC. ASCAP did not collect royalties from performances in concert halls, but it did collect from broadcasts and performances in dancehalls, clubs, and cafés.
606. "Anita Loos Hits Back," *LAT*, 17 August 1935.
607. Joe Louis to Arnold Schoenberg, 27 September 1941, LC.
608. Arnold Schoenberg to Claire Reis, 20 June 1937, NYPL.
609. The American Composers Alliance was founded by Aaron Copland, Wallingford Riegger, and Virgil Thomson to further the interests of both native and foreign-born American composers. Arnold Schoenberg to Shirley Brandt, 22 December 1938, LC. Brandt replied: "since you are an American citizen [*sic*], we would consider you, technically speaking, an American composer." Shirley Brandt to Arnold Schoenberg, 13 January 1939, LC.
610. William Russell, "Schoenberg the Teacher," *Tempo* 8, no. 12 (1940): 13.
611. See, for instance, Arnold Schoenberg to K. Aram, November 1947, in *ASL*, 250.
612. Robert Kohn to Arnold Schoenberg, 12 September 1940, in *ASLIB*, 367.
613. Mark Brunswick, "Refugee Musicians in America," *Saturday Review of Literature*, 26 January 1946, 50–51.
614. Arnold Schoenberg to Composers-Authors Guild, 4 May 1947, LC. Schoenberg might have read Isadore Freed's article "The Composers-Authors Guild Fights for American Music," in *Volume of the Proceedings of the Music Teachers National Association*, ed. Theodore Finney (Pittsburgh: Music Teachers National Association, 1947), 50–52.
615. Catherine Parsons Smith, *Making Music in Los Angeles: Transforming the Popular* (Berkeley: University of California Press, 2007), 232–35.
616. Knight, "Classes with Schoenberg," 139.
617. William B. George, "Adolph Weiss" (Ph.D. diss., University of Iowa, 1971), 44.
618. Arnold Schoenberg to Alban Berg, 16 August 1934, in *BSC*, 452.

619. Weiss, for instance, attended the first all-Schoenberg concert in the Los Angeles "Evenings on the Roof" series in 1940. He performed Schoenberg's Woodwind Quintet on May 10, 1948. He sat in on Schoenberg's UCLA classes.
620. See, for example, Dorothea Bestor, "An Interview with Arnold Schoenberg," *Musical Review* 3, no. 7 (October 1934): 3; and Arnold Schoenberg to Douglas Moore, 30 November 1939, in *ASLIB*, 358.
621. Adolph Weiss to Otto Luening, 29 April 1938, Special Collections, Columbia University Library. Much of Weiss's rhetoric in correspondence with Schoenberg and others implies that he sympathized with Hitler's Germany.
622. In 1942 Weiss became the active director of the Los Angeles chapter of this organization. Ives, who was persuaded by Weiss to serve as honorary national president of the Society and support it financially, soon voiced second thoughts about its aims and threatened to withdraw his endorsement.
623. Caroline Fisher (1889–1985), who taught at UCLA in the 1940s and 1950s, belonged to Schoenberg's California circle of colleagues and friends.
624. Arnold Schoenberg to Adolph Weiss, 24 August 1939, LC.
625. Adolph Weiss to Edgar Varèse, 1 July 1943, Paul Sacher Foundation Basel.
626. Adolph Weiss to Edgar Varèse, 19 January 1948, Paul Sacher Foundation Basel.
627. Henry Cowell, "Music," in *The Americana Annual: An Encyclopedia of Current Events*, ed. Alexander McDannald (New York: Wise, 1934), 392.
628. Henry Cowell, "On Programming American Music," *Music Clubs Magazine* 31, no. 5 (1952): 23.
629. Henry Cowell to Adolph Weiss, 19 July 1934, in George, "Adolph Weiss," 305.
630. Quoted in Sabine Feisst, "Henry Cowell und Arnold Schönberg – eine unbekannte Freundschaft," *AfMw* 55, no. 1 (1998): 66.
631. Henry Cowell to Arnold Schoenberg, 22 October 1948, in ibid., 67.
632. Arnold Schoenberg to Henry Cowell, 6 November 1948, in *ASL*, 256.
633. Cowell quoted in Russell Kerr, "50 Years of Cowell at 65," *MC* 164, no. 4 (May 1962): 11.
634. *SI*, 162–63. And see Arnold Schoenberg to Roy Harris, 17 May 1945, in *ASL*, 234.
635. Schoenberg quoted in Oliver Daniel, "American Composer Henry Cowell," *Stereo Review* 33, no. 6 (December 1974): 78.
636. *HHS*, 351.
637. Roger Sessions to Aaron Copland, 23 September 1933, in *The Correspondence of Roger Sessions*, ed. Andrea Olmstead (Boston: Northeastern University Press, 1992), 210.
638. Greissle became Sessions's editor at E. B. Marks.
639. Roger Sessions to Arnold Schoenberg, 30 October 1944, in Andrea Olmstead, "The Correspondence Between Arnold Schoenberg and Roger Sessions," *JASI* 13, no. 1 (June 1990): 48. Sessions's 1944 article is reprinted in *SW*, 327–36. A revised text version appeared again in *Tempo* in 1972 (103: 8–17).
640. Arnold Schoenberg to Roger Sessions, 3 December 1944, in Olmstead, "The Correspondence," 49.
641. Sessions's New School course, entitled "The Roots of Contemporary Music," included a session on Schoenberg's opus 23.
642. Roger Sessions to Arnold Schoenberg, 30 October 1947, in Olmstead, "The Correspondence," 50.
643. Sessions thanked Schoenberg in his preface to *Harmonic Practice* (New York: Harcourt, Brace, 1951), xxiii: "I owe a debt of another kind, of course, to Arnold Schönberg, to whom the whole epoch which coincides with my own musical experience and career

owes so incalculably much. It becomes always clearer that the influence of this truly remarkable man is not limited to his most immediate or obvious followers, but has had a far-reaching effect on friend and foe alike."

644. Arnold Schoenberg in *MC* 107, no. 20 (11 November 1933): 7. Schoenberg singled out Sessions as an original composer in other venues, including a 1945 letter to Roy Harris in *ASL*, 234.
645. Arnold Schoenberg to Roger Sessions, 17 July 1948, in Olmstead, "The Correspondence," 52.
646. Ibid., 51.
647. Interview with Roger Nixon, 4 June 2008.
648. Gerald Warfield, "Interview with Mark Brunswick," *Contemporary Music Newsletter* 3, nos. 3–4 (1969): 1.
649. Louis Gruenberg, "Modern Youth at Prague, 1935," *MM* 13, no. 1 (November–December 1935): 39.
650. Arnold Schoenberg to Julia Howell, 26 July1937, LC.
651. Robert Nisbett, "Louis Gruenberg: His Life and Work" (Ph.D. diss., Ohio State University, 1979), 62–63.
652. Arnold Schoenberg to Louis Gruenberg, 26 February 1940, LC.
653. See Gruenberg Collection, NYPL.
654. Virgil Thomson, *Virgil Thomson* (New York: Knopf, 1966), 227.
655. Overall Thomson found Schoenberg's works "instrumentally delicious," "tonally the most exciting," but considered the "organization of their pulses, taps and quantities" naïve. Further, he thought that while the music "positively drips with emotivity," "emotions are examined rather than declared." Virgil Thomson, "Reflections," *Score* 6 (May 1952): 13–14.
656. Virgil Thomson, "Historic Remarks," *New York Herald Tribune*, 1 June 1947.
657. Virgil Thomson, "Music in Review: Schoenberg Celebrates Seventy-Fifth Birthday with Attack on Conductors," *New York Herald Tribune*, 11 September 1949.
658. Arnold Schoenberg to Virgil Thomson, 25 February 1950, LC.
659. Thomson, *Virgil Thomson*, 227. The draft of the letter reads: "I feel I must finally do, what I intended long ago to do: write to you, to tell you that I am glad there is at least *one man* in New York who – understands what I am doing – I mean among newspaper men. Excuse me for saying so, but there is no doubt, I have been treated in New York worse than at any place I can remember." Arnold Schoenberg to Virgil Thomson, 3 October 1944.
660. Arnold Schoenberg to Henry Cowell, 6 November 1948, *ASL*, 256.
661. Warren Langlie, "Interview with Arnold Schoenberg," 10 October 1950, unpublished, ASC.
662. Born in St. Petersburg in 1894, Slonimsky settled in America in 1923 and attained U.S. citizenship in 1931.
663. Arnold Schoenberg to Nicolas Slonimsky, 23 December 1933, LC.
664. Arnold Schoenberg to Nicolas Slonimsky, 3 June 1937, in Nicolas Slonimsky, *Music since 1900* (New York: Norton, 1937), 574–75.
665. Arnold Schoenberg to Nicolas Slonimsky, 2 January 1940, LC.
666. Arnold Schoenberg to Nicolas Slonimsky, 25 December 1939; see also Arnold Schoenberg to Adolph Weiss, 2 January 1939, LC.
667. Arnold Schoenberg to Nicolas Slonimsky, 18 March 1941; and Nicolas Slonimsky to Arnold Schoenberg, 23 March 1941, LC. At this point Schoenberg considered Gustave Arlt, German professor at UCLA, his student Dika Newlin, organist Alexander Schreiner, and pianist George McManus as possible translators. See *SR*, 244–45, 261–64, 301.

668. Schoenberg especially appreciated Slonimsky's article "Arnold Schoenberg's New World of Dodecaphonic Music," written under the anagrammatical pseudonym L. O. Symkins and published in *Etude* 68, no. 9 (September 1950): 12–14.
669. Arnold Schoenberg to Nicolas Slonimsky, 3 October 1944, LC.
670. Nicolas Slonimsky to Arnold Schoenberg, 13 September 1949, LC.
671. Nicolas Slonimsky, *Thesaurus of Scales and Melodic Patterns* (New York: Coleman-Ross, 1947), 185; and *Perfect Pitch: A Life Story* (New York: Oxford University Press, 1988), 173–80.
672. Arnold Schoenberg to Nicolas Slonimsky, 8 February 1949, LC.
673. Arnold Schoenberg to Edgar Varèse, 23 May 1939, *ASR*, 282–83.
674. Edgar Varèse to Arnold Schoenberg, 6 November 1943, LC.
675. Arnold Schoenberg to Edgar Varèse, 27 October 1943, *ASR*, 295.
676. Varèse quoted by Michael Sperling, "Varèse and Contemporary Music," *Trend* 2, no. 3 (May–June 1934): 127.
677. Edgar Varèse, Draft for lecture no. 24 of 5 August 1948 on Arnold Schoenberg, unpublished manuscript, Sacher Foundation Basel.
678. Aaron Copland to Arnold Schoenberg, 13 February 1950, in *The Selected Correspondence of Aaron Copland*, ed. Elizabeth Crist and Wayne Shirley (New York: Oxford University Press, 2006), 197–98.
679. Aaron Copland to Arnold Schoenberg, 13 February 1950, in Crist and Shirley, *The Selected Correspondence of Aaron Copland*, 197–98.
680. Aaron Copland to Virgil Thomson, 11 September 1949, in *Arnold Schoenberg Correspondence: A Collection of Translated and Annotated Letters Exchanged with Guido Adler, Pablo Casals, Emanuel Feuermann and Olin Downes*, ed. Egbert Ennulat (Metuchen, NJ: Scarecrow, 1991), 262–63.
681. Arnold Schoenberg to Aaron Copland, 21 February 1950, in Ennulat, *Arnold Schoenberg Correspondence*, 270–71.
682. "For it is obvious that those young people who just a few years ago were writing pieces filled with the *weltschmerz* of a Schoenberg now realize that they were merely picturing their own discontent and that the small audience which existed for Schoenberg's music could never be stretched to include their own. Let these young people say to themselves once and for all, 'No more Schoenberg. The music I write must have more pertinence than Schoenberg's had even to his own Vienna.'" Aaron Copland, "A Note On Young Composers," *Vanguard* 1, no. 1 (March–April 1935): 15.
683. Aaron Copland, "Scores and Records," *MM* 14, no. 2 (January–February 1937): 101.
684. Aaron Copland, *Our New Music: Leading Composers in Europe and America* (New York: McGraw-Hill, 1941), 56.
685. Vivian Perlis, "Interview with Aaron Copland," 23 December 1976 (Oral History of American Music Archives, Yale University).
686. Copland, *Our New Music*, 56–57.
687. Aaron Copland, "The World of A-Tonality," *NYT*, 27 November 1949.
688. Arnold Schoenberg, "Radio Address (1949)," broadcast as part of "Music of Today" on September 13, 1949, over KFWB in Los Angeles and printed in Virgil Thomson, "Music in Review: Schoenberg Celebrates Seventy-Fifth Birthday with Attack on Conductors," *New York Herald Tribune*, 11 September 1949, in Ennulat, *Arnold Schoenberg Correspondence*, 260–61.
689. See Jennifer DeLapp's detailed coverage of this quarrel in "Copland in the Fifties: Music and Ideology in the McCarthy Era" (Ph.D. diss., University of Michigan, 1997), 100–106; and "Aaron Copland and the Politics of Twelve-Tone Composition in the Early

Cold War United States," *Journal of Musicological Research* 27, no. 1 (January 2008): 31–62.

690. Aaron Copland to Virgil Thomson, 11 September 1949, in Ennulat, *Arnold Schoenberg Correspondence*, 263. Schoenberg had refused to sign a welcome greeting on the occasion of Shostakovich's attendance at the Cultural and Scientific Conference for World Peace in New York in March 1949, but on March 11, 1949, he provided his own idiosyncratic greeting: "Being a scapegoat of Russian restrictions on music I cannot sign. But I am ready to send the following: Disregarding problems of styles and politics, I gladly greet a real composer." Ennulat, *Arnold Schoenberg Correspondence*, 259.
691. Arnold Schoenberg to Aaron Copland, 23 December 1949, in Ennulat, *Arnold Schoenberg Correspondence*, 265.
692. Robert Sabin, "The Orchestral Repertoire in 1947–1948: Audiences Begin to Accept New Music," *MA* 68, no. 9 (September 1948): 4. Schoenberg annotated this article, jotting down the names of fourteen conductors whom he suspected of ignoring his music. However, some of them actually performed in this season his *Verklärte Nacht*, First Chamber Symphony, and "Tove's Song" from *Gurrelieder*. They include Fritz Reiner (Pittsburgh Symphony), Eleazar de Carvalho (Boston Symphony Orchestra), Vladimir Golschmann (Chicago Symphony Orchestra), and Fritz Mahler (Erie Philharmonic).
693. Kurt List to Arnold Schoenberg, 20 May 1949, LC. Translation by author. Besides Copland and Schuman, Schoenberg also suspected Boulanger, Howard Hanson, Everett Helm, and Douglas Moore to be part of this alleged plot. Arnold Schoenberg to Josef Rufer, 8 April, 13 and 25 July, and 10 August 1949, Preußischer Kulturbesitz, Berlin; and Arnold Schoenberg to Winfried Zillig, 15 July 1949, LC.
694. DeLapp, "Copland in the Fifties," 104.
695. Aaron Copland to Arnold Schoenberg, 13 February 1950; and Arnold Schoenberg to Aaron Copland, 21 February 1950, in Ennulat, *Arnold Schoenberg Correspondence*, 269–72.
696. DeLapp, "Copland in the Fifties," 104–5.
697. A. Lehman Engel, "'We Need Character – We Have Talent' – Schönberg," *MA* 53, no. 18 (25 November 1933): 5, 34.
698. Schoenberg carefully read and annotated the chapter. He seemed to approve of her discussion of opp. 11, 16, 17, and 21, complete with music examples, but found fault with her claim that he was influenced by Kandinsky; see Marion Bauer, *Twentieth Century Music: How It Developed, How to Listen to It* (New York: Putnam, 1933), ASC.
699. Marion Bauer, "Arnold Schoenberg Sees No Reason for World to Treat His Theories as Radical: Interview with Arnold Schoenberg," *Chautauquan Daily*, 17 August 1934, 5.
700. John Alden Carpenter to Arnold Schoenberg, 21 December 1933, in Howard Pollack, *Skyscraper Lullaby: The Life and Music of John Alden Carpenter* (Washington, D.C.: Smithsonian Institution Press, 1995), 385.
701. David Diamond to Arnold Schoenberg, 10 September 1944, 11 June 1949, and 25 August 1949, LC.
702. Arnold Schoenberg to Deems Taylor, 10 March 1941, LC; and Arnold Schoenberg to Edward Steuermann, 27 November 1943, LC.
703. Arnold Schoenberg to Clara Steuermann, 29 January 1949, LC; and Arnold Schoenberg to Standard Oil Company, 18 March1949, and to Kurt List, 20 May 1949, LC.
704. Crete Cage, "Contemporary American Music Receives Support of Schubert-Wa Wan Club," *LAT*, 11 January 1935.
705. Richard Drake Saunders to Arnold Schoenberg, 31 December 1940, LC. Among the members of the Crescendo Club were Achron, Ingolf Dahl, Gruenberg, Miklós Rózsa, Toch, Tremblay, Varèse, Weiss, and many performers.

706. Arnold Schönberg, *30 Kanons*, 60–61.
707. For more details see Pauline Alderman, *We Build a School of Music* (Los Angeles: Alderman Book Committee, 1989), 125–33; and Susan Pearl Finger, "The Los Angeles Heritage: Four Women Composers, 1918–1939" (Ph.D. diss., University of California, Los Angeles, 1986), 255–57.
708. *SW*, 300.
709. *SI*, 177.
710. Ibid., 176.
711. Ibid., 178.
712. John Campbell, "Interview with Arnold Schoenberg," 1950, unpublished, ASC.
713. Quoted in Louis Banks, "What Is 'Modern' Music?" *LAT*, 27 June 1937.
714. *Studies in the Schoenbergian Movement in Vienna and the United States: Essays in Honor of Marcel Dick*, ed. Anne Trenkamp and John G. Suess (Lewiston: Edwin Mellen Press, 1990), 103–4. Schoenberg and Ives never met. Yet, despite Harmony Ives's and Sidney Cowell's assurance of this fact, Peter Yates claimed that Schoenberg told him that he met him at the 1933 League of Composers' reception for Schoenberg and received a check from him. See Harmony Ives to Gertrud Schoenberg, 25 November (no year), ASC; and Adelaide Tusler, "Peter Yates – Evenings on the Roof, 1939–1954" (Los Angeles: University of California, Oral History Program, 1972), 87–88. See also Geoffrey Block and Peter Burkholder, *Charles Ives and the Classical Tradition* (New Haven: Yale University Press, 1996), 88. Schoenberg owned scores of the *Concord Sonata* (and *Essays Before a Sonata*), 114 Songs, "The Fourth of July" (from the *Holidays Symphony*) and *A Set of Pieces for Theater or Chamber Orchestra*. The latter score contains annotations regarding a rhythmic-metrical error ("Das brauch' ich nicht nach zu rechnen, das stimmt nicht!" See page 7 of the New Music Edition, ASC).
715. Quoted in Henry and Sidney Cowell, *Charles Ives and His Music* (New York: Oxford University Press, 1955), 114.
716. Printed in *ASR*, 293–94.
717. Arnold Schoenberg to Roy Harris, 17 May 1945, in *ASL*, 233–34. See also *SI*, 176; and Bestor, "Schoenberg Teaches," 3.
718. Arnold Schoenberg to G. F. Stegmann, 26 January 1949, in *ASL*, 267.
719. Barbara Zuck, *A History of Musical Americanism* (Ann Arbor: UMI Research Press, 180), 149.
720. *SI*, 163–66, 176. Schoenberg showed more appreciation for Harris's Third Symphony (1939), especially for its last part, containing "some genuine musical expression, even if overstylized." In *SR*, 198.
721. Arnold Schoenberg to G. F. Stegmann, 26 January 1949, in *ASL*, 266.
722. Arnold Schoenberg to Lester Trimble, 22 August 1944, in Lester Trimble, "Arnold Schoenberg and the American Composer," *Hifi/Stereo Review* 15, no. 4 (October 1965): 44.
723. Arnold Schoenberg to G. F. Stegmann, 26 January 1949, in *ASL*, 266–67; see also *SR*, 198.
724. *SI*, 166.
725. Arnold Schoenberg to Hans Rosbaud, 12 May 1947, in *ASL*, 243.
726. Arnold Schoenberg to Harry Robin, 30 October 1949, LC.
727. Joseph Auner, "Schoenberg and His Public in 1930: The Six Pieces for Male Chorus, Op. 35," in *SW*, 85–125.
728. Arnold Schoenberg to Hans Rosbaud, 12 May 1947, in *ASL*, 243; and "Protest on Trademark," in *SW*, 307–8.

729. *SI*, 109; see also Christian Schmidt, "Arnold Schönberg, der Doyen der Wiener Schule in Amerika?" in *Innenleben – Ansichten aus dem Exil. Ein Berliner Symposium*, ed. Hermann Haarmann (Berlin: Fannei und Walz, 1995), 125–27.
730. Arnold Schoenberg, "Broadcast," voice recording, unpublished, ASC; and Arnold Schoenberg to Ross Russell, 13 January 1950, Harry Ransom Center, University of Texas, Austin.
731. The last completed original work with a key signature was his Second String Quartet of 1908. Schoenberg made arrangements of tonal compositions in the 1920s and early 1930s, and sketched, among other tonal works, a piano concerto in D major (1933). Composed in 1929, the last chorus from Six Pieces for Male Choir, op. 35, "Verbundenheit," is also tonal.
732. Martin Bernstein, "On the Genesis of Schoenberg's Suite for School Orchestra," *JASI* 11, no. 2 (November 1988): 161.
733. Arnold Schoenberg, "Sketch of a Foreword to the Suite for String Orchestra," in *ASR*, 264.
734. Arnold Schoenberg to Alban Berg, 25 November1934, in *BSC*, 458.
735. Schoenberg, "Sketch of a Foreword," 264.
736. Arnold Schoenberg to Fritz Reiner, 24 April 1939, LC.
737. Ibid.
738. Arnold Schoenberg, "Sketch of a Foreword," and "Draft of a Letter to Olin Downes," in *ASR*, 264, 267. "Problems of Harmony" appeared in *Modern Music* in 1934. See *SI*, 268–87; also Arnold Schoenberg to Alban Berg, 25 November 1934, in *BSC*, 458.
739. Israel Citkowitz, "Schönberg's Suite for String Orchestra," *MM* 13, no. 1 (November–December 1935): 46.
740. Aaron Copland, "Scores and Records," *MM* 14, no. 2 (January–February 1937): 100.
741. Carl Sands, "Schoenberg's Latest Composition," *New York City Daily Worker*, 23 October 1935.
742. Richard Drake Saunders, "Los Angeles Reviews and Previews," *Pacific Coast Musician* 24, no. 13 (1 June 1935): 7.
743. Olin Downes, "New Suite by Arnold Schoenberg," *NYT*, 13 October 1935.
744. Winthrop Sargeant, "Arnold Schoenberg and the Atonal Style," *Brooklyn Daily Eagle*, 6 October 1935.
745. This fact has remained largely unknown since the work is omitted in catalogues of Schoenberg's works and the Complete Edition.
746. Carl Engel to Arnold Schoenberg, 14 January 1935, in Arnold Schoenberg, *My Horses Ain't Hungry: Traditional Appalachian Folksong Setting arranged for A Cappella Chorus*, reconstructed and completed by Allen Anderson, foreword by Severine Neff with Sabine Feisst (Pacific Palisades: Belmont Music Publishers, 2007), 1.
747. Arnold Schoenberg to Carl Engel, 20 January 1935; and Schoenberg, *My Horses*, 1.
748. *SI*, 162.
749. "Because a folksong can only be popular if it avoids such problems which are not resolved within their eight to sixteen measures – with other words: there are no problems [rich and daring in modulation, rich and colorful in the variety of orchestration, rich and superficial in semi contrapuntal addition, but poor in their musical idea], there is nothing which asks for continuation, nothing demanding consequences to be drawn from. One can use them in form of variation or in rondo-like structure." Arnold Schoenberg, "Folklorists (Sketch)," unpublished manuscript, ASC.
750. Rubsamen, "Schoenberg in America," 487.

751. Eugene Goossens quoted in Howard Pollack, *Aaron Copland: The Life and Work of an Uncommon Man* (New York: Henry Holt, 1999), 360.
752. Arnold Schoenberg to Leopold Stokowski, 2 July 1945, in Leonard Stein, "Stokowski and the *Gurrelieder Fanfare*: Further Correspondence," *JASI* 3, no. 2 (October 1979): 220.
753. Arnold Schoenberg to Leopold Stokowski, 18 July 1945, quoted in Stein, "Stokowski," 221.
754. Arnold Schoenberg to Elizabeth Coolidge, August 1936, in *ASL*, 200.
755. For a detailed discussion see Richard Kurth, "Moments of Closure: Thoughts on the Suspension of Tonality in Schoenberg's Fourth Quartet and Trio," in *Music of My Future: The Schoenberg Quartets and Trio*, ed. Reinhold Brinkmann and Christoph Wolff (Cambridge: Harvard University Press, 2000), 139–60.
756. *ASSP*, 87–88.
757. Peter Gradenwitz, "Beethoven Op. 131 – Schönberg Op. 37," in *Bericht über den internationalen musikwissenschaftlichen Kongreß Berlin 1974*, ed. Helmut Kühn and Peter Nitsche (Kassel: Bärenreiter, 1980), 370; and Alexander Ringer, *Arnold Schoenberg: The Composer as Jew* (New York: Oxford University Press, 1990), 76–77, 199; and *Arnold Schönberg. Das Leben im Werk* (Stuttgart: Metzler, 2002), 282.
758. Schoenberg, "Problems of Harmony," 284.
759. "String Quartet Plays at Composer's Party," *LAT*, 6 January 1937.
760. Arnold Schoenberg to Elizabeth Coolidge, 14 January 1937, in *ASLIB*, 334.
761. Arnold Schoenberg, "From the Prefaces to the Records of the Four String Quartets," in *ASR*, 281.
762. Bruno Ussher, "Schoenberg's New Quartet," *NYT*, 17 January 1937.
763. Leonard Stein, "A Note on the Genesis of the *Ode to Napoleon*," *JASI* 2, no. 2 (March 1977): 52–54.
764. Arnold Schoenberg, "How I Came to Compose the *Ode to Napoleon*," in *ASR*, 291.
765. P. W. Wilson, "Byron Still Flings a Challenge to Tyranny," *NYT*, 23 January1938; and Giuseppe Mazzini, "Byron – Poet of the United Nations," *Saturday Review of Literature*, 25 July 1942, 10. See also Dirk Buhrmann, "Arnold Schönbergs *Ode to Napoleon Buonaparte*, op. 41. Anmerkungen zur Textvorlage," *JASC* 4 (2002): 60–68.
766. This poem has a complex history. Byron's view of Napoleon was not as disdainful as the last three stanzas, written at the request of his publisher, suggest. See Buhrmann, "Arnold Schönbergs *Ode*," 60–68.
767. Steven Englund, "Napoleon and Hitler," *Journal of the Historical Society* 6, no. 1 (2006): 152. Some émigré writers from Germany pursued the Napoleon-Hitler comparison as well. See Bahr, *Weimar on the Pacific*, 278.
768. Arnold Schoenberg to Gertrud Greissle, 17 May 1942, in *ASLIB*, 384. Translation by author.
769. Arnold Schoenberg to Hermann Scherchen, 30 November 1945, LC.
770. Bahr, *Weimar on the Pacific*, 179.
771. Stein, "A Note on the Genesis," 52.
772. Arnold Schoenberg to Orson Welles, 19 September 1943, LC.
773. Ibid. Schoenberg and Welles knew each other, but Welles could not be engaged: "Welles is out: he goes to England." Arnold Schoenberg to Felix Greissle, 11 October 1943, LC.
774. Schoenberg named these motifs in a letter to his daughter: "Und auch in der Musik kann man an einer Stelle eine Andeutung auf die *Marseillaise* und sogar das 'Siegesmotiv' hören." Arnold Schoenberg to Gertrud Greissle, 17 May 1942, in *ASLIB*, 384.
775. Ethan Haimo, "The Late Twelve-Tone Compositions," in *TASC*, 160–61. See also Dirk Buhrmann, *Arnold Schönbergs "Ode to Napoleon Buonaparte," op. 41 (1942)*

(Hildesheim: Georg Olms, 2002), 144–82. George Tremblay claimed that the *Ode*'s unusual serial technique was inspired by his *Modes of Transportation* for string quartet (1940), which Schoenberg heard prior to composing the *Ode* and which uses three symmetrically constructed eight-tone rows and octave doublings. David Ewen, *American Composers: A Biographical Dictionary* (New York: Putnam's, 1982), 676.

776. Charles Rosen, *Arnold Schoenberg* (Chicago: University of Chicago Press, 1996), 93.
777. Arnold Schoenberg, *Structural Functions of Harmony*, rev. ed. (New York: Norton, 1969), 1. In a letter to Stuckenschmidt, Schoenberg described much of the *Ode*'s music as a background that constantly "underlines" and "illustrates." Arnold Schoenberg to Hans Heinz Stuckenschmidt, 15 January 1948, LC.
778. Arnold Schoenberg to René Leibowitz, 4 July 1947, in *ASL*, 248.
779. Rathbone, who studied it with Eisler, seriously considered the possibility of performing the *Ode*. Yet in the end, none of these actors was able to perform the *Ode*. Arnold Schoenberg to Gertrud Greissle, 18 December 1943, Arnold Schoenberg to Felix Greissle, 2 July 1943 and 27 October 1943, in *ASSW* VI, Series B, vol. 24, part 2, pp. 124, 129.
780. *SI*, 77–78.
781. Patriotic works by American composers include Becker's Sixth Symphony "Out of Bondage" (1942), Copland's *Lincoln Portrait* (1942), Gould's *A Lincoln Legend* (1942), and Harris's Sixth Symphony (1944), which refer to excerpts from Lincoln's "Gettysburg Address."
782. *SI*, 500–501.
783. Ibid., 500.
784. Arnold Schoenberg, "To the San Francisco Round-Table on Modern Art," in *ASR*, 330.
785. Virgil Thomson, "Beautiful String Work," *New York Herald Tribune*, 24 November 1944.
786. Olin Downes, "Rodzinski Offers *Ode to Napoleon*," *NYT*, 24 November 1944.
787. Oscar Thompson, "Rodzkinski Gives Schoenberg *Ode*," *New York Sun*, 24 November 1944; and Robert Bagar, "Schoenberg Premiere," *Washington Times*, 24 November 1944.
788. Bartók heard a performance of the *Ode*'s chamber version on November 29, 1944, and was apparently deeply impressed. Felix Greissle to Arnold Schoenberg, 11 January 1945, in *ASSW* VI, Series B, vol. 24, part 2, p. 139.
789. Arnold Schoenberg to Felix Greissle, 28 July 1943; and Felix Greissle to Arnold Schoenberg, 27 February 1945, in *ASSW* VI, Series B, vol. 24, part 2, pp. 125–26, 140.
790. Edwin Franko Goldman to Arnold Schoenberg, 5 January 1934, ASC.
791. Edwin Franko Goldman, *Band Betterment* (New York: Carl Fischer, 1934), 191.
792. Initially, however, Schoenberg wanted to arrange music by Schubert for piano four hands. Arnold Schoenberg to Carl Engel, 8 August 1942, LC.
793. Felix Greissle to Arnold Schoenberg, 21 August 1942 and 23 February 1943, LC. Greissle's information is based on a report of the School Music Committee to the American Composers Alliance.
794. Arnold Schoenberg, "About the Genesis of Theme and Variations for Wind Band, op. 43a," in *ASSW* IV, Series B, vol. 13, xxiv.
795. Arnold Schoenberg to Carl Engel, 6 October 1943, in *ASSW* IV, Series B, vol. 13, xxiv.
796. Rudolph Elie, Jr., stated that the work "sounds like something Gershwin might have written if he had studied with Richard Strauss and later with Schoenberg." "Music: Symphony Concert," *Boston Herald*, 21 October 1944. See also Ringer, *Arnold Schönberg*, 290.
797. Arnold Schoenberg to Fritz Reiner, 29 October 1944, in *ASL*, 221. Schoenberg decided to write variations in October 1942. See Arnold Schoenberg to Felix Greissle, 18 October 1942, LC.

798. Noel Straus, "New Composition Heard at Concert," *NYT*, 29 June 1946; and Lou Harrison, "Goldman Band: Schoenberg's Variations Has Manhattan Premiere," *New York Herald Tribune*, 29 June 1946.
799. Greissle attended the rehearsals, and without consulting Schoenberg he suggested the cuts due to the work's intricacies and the insufficient rehearsal time. Arnold Schoenberg to Felix Greissle, 9 July 1946, LC.
800. Arnold Schoenberg to Fritz Reiner, 29 October 1944, in *ASL*, 222.
801. Edwin Franko Goldman to Arnold Schoenberg, 30 July 1943; and Richard Franko Goldman to Arnold Schoenberg, 14 June 1946, LC.
802. Holst, Vaughan Williams, Grainger, Hindemith, Krenek, Respighi, Toch, and Prokofiev wrote pieces for band before Schoenberg, but Goldman considered these "minor efforts by well-known men." Richard Franko Goldman, "A New Day for Band Music," *MM* 23, no. 4 (Fall 1946): 262.
803. Felix Greissle to Arnold Schoenberg, 1 October 1942, ASC.

CHAPTER 4

1. Arnold Schoenberg to William Schlamm, 26 June 1945; Arnold Schoenberg to Hans Rosbaud, 12 May 1947, in *ASL*, 235, 243.
2. René Leibowitz, *Schoenberg* (Paris: Editions du Seuil, 1969), 141.
3. H. Wiley Hitchcock, *Music in the United States: A Historical Introduction* (Englewood Cliffs: Prentice Hall, 1988), x.
4. Joseph Horowitz, *Classical Music in America: A History of Its Rise and Fall* (New York: Norton, 2005), xiii–xv.
5. Margaret Grant and Herman Hettinger, *America's Symphony Orchestras and How They Are Supported* (New York: Norton, 1940), 13–20.
6. Catherine Parsons Smith, *Making Music in Los Angeles: Transforming the Popular* (Berkeley: University of California Press, 2007), xi.
7. Ibid. 187–94.
8. See Hindemith's entire inaccurate, arrogant, and sexist account of the Los Angeles musical scene: Paul Hindemith, *Briefe*, ed. Dieter Rexroth (Frankfurt: Fischer, 1982), 222. Translation by author. See also Ernst Krenek's negative assessment of musical life in America: *Musik im goldenen Westen* (Vienna: Hollinek, 1949).
9. Arnold Schoenberg to Lynden Behymer, 7 November 1934, LC. See also Arnold Schoenberg to Otto Klemperer, 8 November 1934, in *ASL*, 192–93. These are performances I discovered in my research. There may have been more.
10. Beginning in 1930 CBS broadcast weekly concerts by the New York Philharmonic. Other orchestras in Philadelphia, Boston, Detroit, and San Francisco soon established their own broadcast series. In 1931 the Metropolitan Opera began to broadcast its Saturday matinée performances. From the early 1930s such California stations as KFI-KECA, KHJ, and KNX broadcast live performances of classical music.
11. Alfred Meyer, "Schoenberg at Last Comes to Symphony Hall," *Boston Evening Transcript*, 17 March 1934.
12. Avior Byron explored this topic in depth in "Schoenberg as Performer: An Aesthetics in Practice" (Ph.D. diss., Royal Holloway College, University of London, 2007).
13. *SI*, 180; and see Severine Neff, "Two Unpublished Manuscripts: Excerpts from Arnold Schoenberg's Second Book on Harmony and His Text on Performance," *Gamut: Journal of the Georgia Association of Music Theorists* 8 (1998): 29.
14. Arnold Schoenberg, "Koussevitzki – Toscanini (c. August 1944)," in *ASR*, 307; and Neff, "Two Unpublished Manuscripts," 29.

15. *MI*, 292–93; and see Byron, "Schoenberg as Performer," 85–87, 93–96.
16. Arnold Schoenberg, "Expression [after 1933]," unpublished manuscript, ASC.
17. Louis Krasner, Leonard Stein, John Harbison, and Rosemary Harbison, "The Schoenberg Violin Concerto: A Panel Discussion I, Tanglewood [1992]," unpublished transcript, ASC; Byron, "Schoenberg as Performer," 50–55; and Arnold Schoenberg to Edward Steuermann, 3 October 1949, in *ASL*, 277. Schoenberg preferred to take slower tempi in performances of *Verklärte Nacht* and faster tempi in *Pierrot*. See Byron, "Schoenberg as Performer," 260–62.
18. Byron, "Schoenberg as Performer," 92–93.
19. Arnold Schoenberg, "Koussevitzki – Toscanini (c. August 1944)," in *ASR*, 305. See also *SI*, 320. Schoenberg's critique, however, has to be seen in the context of these conductors' neglect of his music.
20. Neff, "Two Unpublished Manuscripts," 27.
21. *SI*, 346.
22. See *ASSG*, 336; *ASLIB*, 364; and *SI*, 321
23. *ASSG*, 336; and Arnold Schoenberg to Edwin Franko Goldman, 17 January 1934, LC. Schoenberg underscored this grass-roots approach with three pedagogical works: Suite in G, Theme and Variations for Wind Band, and Three Folk Songs, op. 49.
24. See Arnold Schoenberg to Ira Hirschmann, 19 March 1941, LC; and Marjory Fisher, "Schönberg 'Pelleas' in San Francisco," *MA* 57, no. 15 (10 October 1937): 12.
25. Stravinsky was able to charge at least twice as much for a conducting engagement in America. See Claudia Maurer-Zenck, "Leben und Überleben als Komponist im Exil. Die ersten Jahre Strawinskys in den USA," in *Exilmusik. Komponisten während der NS-Zeit*, ed. Friedrich Geiger and Thomas Schäfer (Hamburg: Von Bockel, 1999), 69.
26. For more details, see Avior Byron, "Demystifying Schoenberg's Conducting," *Min-Ad: Israel Studies in Musicology Online* 1 (2006): 1–15.
27. Arnold Schoenberg to Henry Cowell, 3 February 1935, LC.
28. Strang quoted in Rita Mead, "Henry Cowell's New Music Society," *Journal of Musicology* 1, no. 4 (October 1982): 457.
29. When Schoenberg conducted "Song of the Wood Dove" and the second movement of Mahler's Second Symphony with the Cadillac Symphony, he had to "fight an unfriendly and sabotaging orchestra," although he found that "in spite of that we made a fine broadcast." It was featured on WBC, WJZ, and the NBC chain WMAL. Arnold Schoenberg to Rose Bampton, 4 October 1949, LC. Some members of the Los Angeles Philharmonic "deliberately sabotaged the music by playing wrong notes and horsed around" in Schoenberg's rehearsals for his concert in March 1935. Adelaide Tusler, "Evenings on the Roof, 1939–1954: Peter Yates Interviewed" (Oral History Program, University of California, Los Angeles, 1972), 66.
30. Lovina Knight, "Classes with Schoenberg, January through June 1934," *JASI* 13, no. 2 (November 1990): 148, 152.
31. Schoenberg wrote his friend that he had "many rehearsals and the performance was quite good," but that the musicians were "less enthusiastic" than the audience. Arnold Schoenberg to Adolph Weiss, 30 April 1937, in William B. George, "Adolph Weiss" (Ph.D. diss., University of Iowa, 1971), 327; Vivian Perlis, "Interview with Leonard Stein" (Oral History of American Music Archives, Yale University, 28 June 1975).
32. Margie McLeod, "Schönberg Leads Chicago Men in Presentations of His Music," *MA* 54, no. 4 (25 February 1934): 15. The Chicago Symphony played the Five Pieces under Frederick Stock and Walter Rothwell in 1913 and 1926.

33. Edward Moore, "Famed Music Rebel Appears with Orchestra," *Chicago Tribune*, 9 February 1934; see also M. S., "Schönberg Leads His Pelleas with Orchestra in Boston," *MC* 108, no. 12 (24 March 1934): 8; and R. K., "Schönberg, Elman and Bampton in Final Cadillac Concert," *MC* 108, no. 15 (14 March 1934): 21.
34. See, for instance, Glenn Dillard Gunn, "Orchestra Gives Fine Performance under Conductor," *Chicago Herald Examiner*, 9 February 1934.
35. Felix Greissle and Josef Schmid, students of Schoenberg and Berg, gave up their careers as conductors upon their immigration to the United States.
36. Peter Heyworth, *Otto Klemperer: His Life and Times*, vol. 2: *1933–1973* (Cambridge: Cambridge University Press, 1996), 84. Their difficult relationship, however, can be traced back to their Berlin years when the two intermittently quarreled.
37. Arnold Schoenberg to Otto Klemperer, 25 September 1940, in *ASL*, 211.
38. Schoenberg, however, downplayed this fact in numerous letters to his European friends.
39. Schoenberg was supposed to conduct his Suite's world premiere, but because of the many mistakes in the orchestral parts, Klemperer programmed it later in the season. Schoenberg deemed Klemperer's rendition of the Suite "very good." Heyworth, *Otto Klemperer*, 84. Klemperer initiated the Brahms transcription and paid Schoenberg out of his own pocket $200 (about $3,000 in 2009) for the copying of the manuscript. As it was not an official commission, Klemperer seemed to have wanted his money back in 1940. Arnold Schoenberg to Otto Klemperer, 28 November 1940, LC. Between 1938 and 1939 Schoenberg was able to earn $1,600 (about $24,500 in 2009) for performances of his Brahms transcription with an average charge of $75 (about $1,150 in 2009) per concert. Arnold Schoenberg to Fritz Stiedry, October 1939, LC.
40. Arnold Schoenberg to Fritz Stiedry, 2 April 1940, LC.
41. Klemperer had intended to conduct Schoenberg's Violin Concerto much earlier. In 1936 Klemperer contacted music patroness Elizabeth Sprague Coolidge about sponsoring an East Coast performance of this work, arguing that "the audience here is still not familiar with twelve-tone music." But Coolidge refused because she had confined herself to funding chamber music. A year later he unsuccessfully proposed to music patroness Claire Reis a program with Schoenberg's and Berg's Violin Concertos for a League of Composers concert. Heyworth, *Otto Klemperer*, 87, 89–90.
42. Heyworth, *Otto Klemperer*, 111–12.
43. Lawrence Morton praised the work's "full-bodied flavor of romanticism without the aftertaste of decadence." *MM* 22, no. 3 (March–April 1945): 187. See also Otto Klemperer to Lonny Epstein, 26 February 1945, in Heyworth, *Otto Klemperer*, 141.
44. Klemperer quoted in Heyworth, *Otto Klemperer*, 89.
45. Arnold Schoenberg to Charlotte Dieterle, 30 July 1936, in *ASL*, 199; Arnold Schoenberg, "Koussevitzki – Toscanini," 302.
46. *SR*, 268.
47. Otto Klemperer to Robert Sproul, 4 January 1936, UCLA Library Archives; and Arnold Schoenberg to Robert Sproul, 12 November 1943, LC.
48. In Leningrad, Stiedry conducted Schoenberg's Orchestral Variations, op. 31 and rehearsed Shostakovich's Fourth Symphony (1935–36) whose premiere, however, was suddenly canceled.
49. Fritz Stiedry to Arnold Schoenberg, 16 October 1939, LC.
50. Arnold Schoenberg to Fritz Stiedry, 15 December 1940, ASC. Virgil Thomson, "New Conducting," *New York Herald Tribune*, 16 December 1940; and Olin Downes, "New Friends Play Schoenberg Work," *NYT*, 16 December 1940.
51. Arnold Schoenberg to Fritz Stiedry, 17 April 1950, LC.

52. Anna Hines, "Music at Black Mountain College: A Study of Experimental Ideas in Music" (D.M.A. thesis, University of Missouri – Kansas City, 1973), 22–23.
53. See Jonathan Hiam, "Music at Black Mountain College: The European Years, 1939–1946," (Ph.D. diss. University of North Carolina, Chapel Hill, 2005); and Martin Brody, "The Scheme of the Whole: Black Mountain and the Course of American Modern Music," in *Black Mountain College: Experiment in Art*, ed. Vincent Katz (Cambridge: MIT Press, 2003), 239–67.
54. As to his writings, see, for instance, "On the Spontaneity of Schoenberg's Music," *MQ* 30, no. 4 (October 1944): 385–408. At the time of his death he was working on a Schoenberg biography.
55. Arnold Schoenberg to Heinrich Jalowetz, 19 August 1933, 5 April 1938, 8 September 1943, and 2 November 1945, LC. Schoenberg regarded Jalowetz as one of his "seven dead friends" (with Berg, Webern, Mahler, Franz Schreker, Adolf Loos, and Karl Kraus) whom he envisioned as dedicatees of *Style and Idea* (1950).
56. Arnold Schoenberg to Kurt Frederick, 12 November 1948, LC. Koussevitzky was not interested in *Survivor*'s first performance. Arnold Schoenberg to Serge Koussevitzky, 1 January 1948. Leibowitz, who had prepared *Survivor*'s full score from a short score with oversized staves during his Los Angeles sojourn in the winter of 1947–48, felt he had earned the right to give the work's world premiere. Yet Schoenberg apparently did not recall whether he granted him this privilege or not. Arnold Schoenberg to René Leibowitz, 12 November 1948, in *ASL*, 257. Leibowitz gave its European premiere in November 1949.
57. Isabel Grear to Arnold Schoenberg, 8 November 1948, LC.
58. Winifred Reiter, "Albuquerque Symphony First Playing of New Schoenberg Work," *Albuquerque Journal*, 5 November 1948, and *South Western Musician* 15, no. 9 (1949): 20; Ross Parmenter, "The World of Music: Schoenberg in Albuquerque," *NYT*, 31 October 1948; "Schönberg in Albuquerque," *Newsweek*, 15 November 1948; "Destiny and Digestion," *Time*, 15 November 1948; and Arnold Schoenberg to Kurt Frederick, 12 November 1948, LC.
59. Arnold Schoenberg to the Chicago Symphony Orchestra, 17 February 1934, LC.
60. M. M., "Schönberg Entertained by Chicago Club," *MA* 54, no. 5 (10 March 1934): 25.
61. Arnold Schoenberg to Frederick Stock, 6 March 1935, LC.
62. Arnold Schoenberg to Leopold Stokowski, 20 October 1939, LC.
63. Louis Krasner, "Schoenberg's Violin Concerto," *JASI* 2, no. 2 (February 1978): 89–90.
64. Ibid., 91.
65. "Not Hard Enough," *Time* 36, no. 25 (1940): 53–54; "Schoenberg 'Critics' Chided by Stokowski," *NYT*, 8 December 1940; and Edwin Schloss, "What's That Awful Din?" *Philadelphia Record*, 7 December 1940.
66. Arnold Schoenberg to Leopold Stokowski, 17 December 1940, LC; and Arnold Schoenberg to Louis Krasner, 17 December 1940, quoted in Krasner, "Schoenberg's Violin Concerto," 93.
67. Leopold Stokowski to Arnold Schoenberg, 7 June 1943, ASC.
68. Steuermann and Jahoda gave about one hundred performances of this version in the following years. Fritz Jahoda, interview with the author, 21 September 2000. A student of Steuermann and Josef Polnauer, Jahoda immigrated to America in 1939. He taught first at Converse College and then at City College in New York, championing Schoenberg as a pianist and conductor in many college concerts.
69. Oliver Daniel, *Stokowski: A Counterpoint of View* (New York: Dodd and Mead, 1982), 464–65. Greissle even takes credit for handing Stokowski a list with suggestions for the

last rehearsal. Many of Greissle's accounts, however, tend to be exaggerated. His criticism of Stokowski's (and Schoenberg's) conducting has to be seen in light of his own failed career as a conductor.

70. Arnold Schoenberg to Leopold Stokowski, 8 February 1944, in *ASLIB*, 391.
71. Olin Downes, "Stokowski Offers Schoenberg Work," *NYT*, 7 February 1944; and Oscar Thompson, "Stokowski Leads Schoenberg Work," *New York Sun*, 7 February1944.
72. Virgil Thomson, "Real Modern Music," *New York Herald Tribune*, 7 February 1944.
73. Daniel, *Stokowski*, 467–69.
74. Arnold Schoenberg to Leopold Stokowski, 2 and 18 July and 31 August 1945, and 2 September 1949, LC.
75. Arnold Schoenberg to Leopold Stokowski, 2 September 1949, LC.
76. Norman Houk, "Schoenberg Innovation Proves Rewarding," *Minneapolis Tribune*, 1 December 1945; see also William Trotter, *Priest of Music: The Life of Dimitri Mitropoulos* (Portland: Amadeus, 1995), 233–34.
77. Downes called the Five Pieces "a striking score." Olin Downes, "Szigeti Is Soloist for Philharmonic," *NYT*, 22 October 1948.
78. Irving Kolodin, "Schoenberg's 'Five Pieces' and Szigeti's First Piece," *New York Sun*, 22 October 1948.
79. Arnold Schoenberg to Dimitri Mitropoulos, 1 November 1948, LC.
80. Arnold Schoenberg to Dimitri Mitropoulos, 26 April 1950, LC.
81. Dimitri Mitropoulos to Arnold Schoenberg, 27 June 1950, LC.
82. Arnold Schoenberg to Dimitri Mitropoulos, 4 July 1950, LC.
83. Arnold Schoenberg to Dimitri Mitropoulos, 2 August 1950, LC.
84. Arnold Schoenberg to Dimitri Mitropoulos, November 1945, LC. In an exchange with Stiedry Schoenberg called Mitropoulos an "extraordinary musician," but expressed reservations about his conducting his scores from memory. Arnold Schoenberg to Fritz Stiedry, 2 January 1951, LC; Arnold Schoenberg to Dimitri Mitropoulos, 30 March 1950 and 2 June 1951, LC.
85. Rodzinski had hoped to premiere the Brahms transcription. See the correspondence between Schoenberg and the manager of the Cleveland Orchestra, Carl Vosburgh, LC. Schoenberg himself rented the materials, earning a total of $650 (about $9,800 in 2009). See Carl Vosburgh to Arnold Schoenberg, 26 November 1938, LC.
86. Arnold Schoenberg also urged Steuermann to "try to play it as often as possible for him, so he knows how fast or how slow he has to beat." Arnold Schoenberg to Edward Steuermann, 27 November 1943, LC.
87. Arnold Schoenberg to Artur Rodzinski, 30 January 1944, LC.
88. Edward Steuermann to Arnold Schoenberg, 9 November 1944, LC.
89. This is surprising in view of Halina Rodzinski's claim that radio audiences complained about the initial broadcast of the *Ode*. Halina Rodzinski, *Our Two Lives* (New York: Charles Scribner's Sons, 1976), 262. The performance was recorded and released on the Stradivarius label in 1990.
90. Kurt List, "*Ode to Napoleon*," *MM* 21, no. 3 (March–April, 1944): 139–45.
91. For details on the press reactions, see the discussion of the *Ode* in chapter 3.
92. Werner Janssen to Arnold Schoenberg, 12 December 1940, LC.
93. Edwin Franko Goldman to Arnold Schoenberg, 5 January 1934, ASC.
94. In his statement printed in German, Schoenberg emphasized the importance of genuine enthusiasm to foster the concert band movement. Edwin Franko Goldman, *Band Betterment* (New York: Carl Fischer, 1934), 191.
95. Edwin Franko Goldman to Arnold Schoenberg, 30 July 1943, LC.

96. Richard Franko Goldman to Arnold Schoenberg, 14 June 1946, LC.
97. Arnold Schoenberg to Felix Greissle, 9 July 1946, LC.
98. Arnold Schoenberg to Bernard Herrmann, 30 August 1949, in *ASL*, 275–76. Schoenberg, however, thought that the tempo of the first movement was too slow. Herrmann's performance was not reviewed.
99. Arnold Schoenberg to Thor Johnson, 24 July 1950, in *ASL*, 281–84.
100. Arnold Schoenberg to Thor Johnson, 20 February1951, LC.
101. Robert Craft to Arnold Schoenberg, 9 November 1950, LC. Schoenberg replied: "It is very flattering to me that through your comparison with the *Musikalisches Opfer* – though overestimating me – you put me in the neighbourhood of Bach." Arnold Schoenberg to Robert Craft, 11 November 1950, in *ASL*, 284.
102. Craft pointed out that "the 9/8 variation could have been much clearer, the trumpet left out the high E flat near the end, [and] in the 4/8 variation the viola is too prominent for the flute – how extraordinarily concertante the whole Opus 31 is. You hear everything, every mandoline note." Robert Craft to Arnold Schoenberg, 10 January 1951, LC.
103. Arnold Schoenberg to Fritz and Erika Stiedry, 2 January 1951, LC. Translation by author.
104. Virgil Thomson, "Schoenberg Celebrates Seventy-Fifth Birthday with Attack on Conductors," *New York Herald Tribune*, 11 September 1949.
105. Arnold Schoenberg to Ernst Voigt, 28 February 1939, LC.
106. Quoted in Virgil Thomson, "Schoenberg Celebrates Seventy-fifth Birthday."
107. The Kolisch Quartet also performed Schoenberg's Handel arrangement with the Chicago Symphony under Stock and the Los Angeles Philharmonic under Klemperer.
108. Unable to make a living from concertizing solely in the United States, three members of the Kolisch Quartet decided to join orchestras: In 1939 Heifetz became the Philadelphia Orchestra's principal cellist, and Lehner the principal violist of the Boston Symphony. In 1942 Khuner became a member of the San Francisco Symphony. For details see Rudolf Kolisch to Arnold Schoenberg, 12 January 1939, Harvard University, Houghton Library.
109. Arnold Schoenberg to Elizabeth Coolidge, 5 February 1937, in *ASL*, 201.
110. Ákos Pásztor, "Playing Schoenberg to Schoenberg: Jenö Lehner of the Kolisch String Quartet Remembers," *New Hungarian Quarterly* 33, no. 127 (1992): 173.
111. Ibid., 173–75.
112. Khuner confessed that the Kolisch Quartet sometimes decided to "rehearse for the 'American sound.' That means less scratches, better together, more homogeneity, better in sound, better in intonation." See Caroline Crawford, "A Violinist's Journey from Vienna's Kolisch Quartet to the San Francisco Symphony and Opera Orchestras: An Oral History Transcript: Felix Khuner," with introduction by Tom Heimberg (Bancroft Library, University of California, Berkeley, 4 February 1990).
113. Arnold Schoenberg to Rudolf Kolisch, 10 January 1950, Harvard University, Houghton Library.
114. Arnold Schoenberg to Rudolf Kolisch, 16 January 1939 and 2 June 1950, Harvard University, Houghton Library.
115. Rudolf Kolisch to Arnold Schoenberg, 2 September 1934, LC.
116. He used this phrase in the dedication of his Fourth String Quartet.
117. Arnold Schoenberg to Rudolf Kolisch, 31 May and 8 December 1934 and 16 January 1939, Harvard University, Houghton Library.
118. Arnold Schoenberg to Rudolf Kolisch, 13 March 1936, Harvard University, Houghton Library.
119. Arnold Schoenberg to Rudolf Kolisch, 23 October 1944, Harvard University, Houghton Library.

120. Arnold Schoenberg to Rudolf Kolisch, 30 September 1946, Harvard University, Houghton Library. Translation by author.
121. Arnold Schoenberg to Rudolf Kolisch, 9 March and 12 April 1949, in *ASL*, 270–71. Schoenberg feared the "great activity of American composers, the pupils of Boulanger, the imitators of Stravinsky, Hindemith and now Bartók," feeling that "William Schuman, Aaron Copland and Howard Hanson controlled the musical life in America," stifled "European influences," and promoted "nationalistic compositional methods following the model of Russia."
122. Founded in 1935, the quartet comprised Abas, Hubert Sorenson, Abraham Weiss, and Karl Rossner.
123. The California Quartet consisted of Khuner, David Schneider, Detlev Olshausen, and George Barati. The Hollywood Quartet featured Slatkin, Paul Shure, Paul Robyn, and Eleanor Aller. Schoenberg must have liked the latter group, as he wrote to Capitol: "I have not played the recording which they [Hollywood Quartet] made. But I am sure it is very good." Arnold Schoenberg to Richard Jones, 3 March 1950, LC.
124. Edward Steuermann to Arnold Schoenberg, 26 May 1949, LC.
125. Arnold Schoenberg to Jascha Heifetz, 6 December 1935, LC.
126. Alfred Newman to Arnold Schoenberg, 1938, LC; and Arnold Schoenberg to Jascha Heifetz, 30 September 1946, LC.
127. *SR*, 212.
128. Dorothy Crawford, "Peter Yates and the Performance of Schoenberg Chamber Music at 'Evenings on the Roof,'" *JASI* 22, no. 2 (November 1989): 191. On May 20, 1940, Schoenberg wrote to Gustave Arlt: "I want to mention, that she [Swaby] plays my Concerto for Violin (the 'unplayable') this Sunday in one of Mr. Yates' 'Concerts on the Roof.' I had a rehearsal today with her and can say, that I approve greatly with [*sic*] her playing."
129. Arnold Schoenberg to Adolf Koldofsky, 17 September 1949, ASC.
130. Arnold Schoenberg to Rose Bampton, 15 February 1950, LC.
131. Mildred Lawton to Arnold Schoenberg, 2 August 1941, LC.
132. Arnold Schoenberg to Frederick Dorian, 26 October 1941, LC.
133. Frederick Dorian to Arnold Schoenberg, 19 April 1941, LC.
134. Frederick Dorian to Arnold Schoenberg, 23 November 1940, LC.
135. Frederick Dorian, *The History of Music in Performance: The Art of Musical Interpretation from the Renaissance to our Day* (New York: Norton, 1942), 329–35.
136. Schoenberg and Steuermann's sister Salka Viertel, a Hollywood screenwriter since 1928, were unable to help him find a job on the West Coast. Arnold Schoenberg to Rose Bampton, 13 March 1950, LC.
137. Steuermann made a piano reduction of the *Ode* (unpublished) and a two-piano reduction of the Piano Concerto (Schirmer).
138. Edward Steuermann to Arnold Schoenberg, 31 January and 4 December 1944, LC.
139. Arnold Schoenberg to Clara Steuermann, 30 December 1950, LC. Steuermann also wrote about Schoenberg. See Edward Steuermann, "The Piano Music of Schoenberg," in *Schoenberg*, ed. Merle Armitage (New York: Schirmer, 1937), 125–33, and "A Great Mind and a Great Heart," *Canon* 3, no. 2 (September 1949): 111. Both essays were reprinted in *The Not Quite Innocent Bystander: Writings of Edward Steuermann*, ed. Clara Steuermann, David Porter, and Gunther Schuller (Lincoln: University of Nebraska Press, 1989), 42–44, 48–49.
140. Arnold Schoenberg to Edward Steuermann, 18 February 1944, LC. Clara's piano teacher in Los Angeles, Austrian-born Steuermann student Jakob Gimpel (1906–89), urged her to study with Steuermann as well.

141. Clara Steuermann became an important and lifelong Schoenberg ally. In 1974 she organized a Schoenberg festival at the Cleveland Institute of Music. From 1975 to 1982 she served as the first archivist of the Arnold Schoenberg Institute in Los Angeles.
142. Arnold Schoenberg to Carl Engel, 10 April 1944, LC.
143. James Sykes to Arnold Schoenberg, 14 June 1951, LC.
144. Paul Hesselink, "Variations on a Recitative for Organ Op. 40: Correspondence from the Schoenberg Legacy," *JASI* 7, no. 2 (November 1983): 146–50.
145. Edward Steuermann to Arnold Schoenberg, 12 April 1944, in Hesselink, "*Variations*," 157–58.
146. Arnold Schoenberg to Carl Weinrich, 16 March 1944, in Hesselink, "*Variations*," 161.
147. See Arnold Schoenberg to Felix Greissle, 1 and 28 October 1949, LC.
148. In 1927 she commissioned the Third Quartet and performances thereof, paying $1,000 for each of the two quartets.
149. The Kolisch Quartet received $2,400 (about $36,800 in 2009) for the four concerts.
150. Bruno Ussher, "Schoenberg's New Quartet," *NYT*, 17 January 1937.
151. Coolidge regretted the disbanding of the Kolisch Quartet, whose existence she could have saved by sponsoring a university residency. The residency of Kolisch's subsequent Pro Arte Quartet at the University of Wisconsin was underwritten by four alumni of that university. Daniel Harp, "Recalling the Kolisch String Quartet with Eugene Lehner," *Chamber Music* 5, no. 1 (Spring 1988): 44; and "Pro Arte Group Joins Wisconsin University," *MA* 60, no. 10 (July 1940): 33.
152. See Arnold Schoenberg to Elizabeth Coolidge, 3 August 1936 and 14 January1937, LC. He dedicated his Fourth Quartet: "To the ideal patron of chamber music Elizabeth Coolidge and to the ideal interpreters of it the Kolisch Quartet."
153. Elizabeth Coolidge to Arnold Schoenberg, 2 July 1941, LC.
154. See chapter 2.
155. Claire Reis, *Composers, Conductors and Critics* (New York: Oxford University Press, 1955), 199.
156. Ibid.
157. Arnold Schoenberg to Claire Reis, 24 August 1941, NYPL.
158. Arnold Schoenberg to Claire Reis, 12 March and 25 May 1942, NYPL.
159. Arnold Schoenberg to Ira Hirschmann, 29 October 1939, LC.
160. Arnold Schoenberg to Ira Hirschmann, 8 December 1940, LC.
161. When Schoenberg heard Monath play in a Philharmonic Concert broadcast, he exclaimed: "She was excellent!" Arnold Schoenberg to Ira Hirschmann, 19 March 1941, LC.
162. For more details see Dorothy Crawford, "Peter Yates," 175–201; and *Evenings On and Off the Roof: Pioneering Concerts in Los Angeles, 1939–1971* (Berkeley: University of California Press, 1995).
163. Schoenberg attended the all-Schoenberg Roof Concert on February 1, 1940.
164. Peter Yates, "Arnold Schoenberg," *Arts and Architecture* 61, no. 8 (1944): 27, 40; "Arnold Schoenberg: Apostle of Atonality," *NYT*, 11 September 1949.
165. Peter Yates to Arnold Schoenberg, 22 October 1944, LC. Schoenberg probably wrote in response to this information his famous note about Ives quoted in chapter 3.
166. For more details see Hiam, "Music at Black Mountain"; Martin Brody, "The Scheme," 239–67; and Roger Sessions, "Report on Black Mountain," *NYT*, 24 September 1944.
167. Arnold Schoenberg to Minsa Craig, 17 April 1950, in *ASL*, 279–80.
168. J. D. B., "Sophia Delza in Recital," *New York Herald Tribune*, 11 December 1933; John Martin, "Miss Graham Gives a Dance Recital," *NYT*, 19 February 1934; "Miss Graham

Dances Only to Modern Music," *LAT*, 16 February 1936; "Elna Lillback Presents Dance Group," *New York Herald Tribune*, 17 February1936; and John Martin, "The Dance: Current Events," *NYT*, 23 June 1946.

169. One reviewer wrote about *Pillar*'s premiere: "At the curtain, the audience cheered so long this reporter wearied of the applause (not of the ballet) and went out for a smoke. The acclaim did not die down until after he had finished two cigarettes." R. P. C., "Pillar of Fire," *Wall Street Journal*, 10 April 1942.
170. Arnold Schoenberg to José Limón, 22 April 1950, LC.
171. Schoenberg's interest in radio dated to the 1920s.
172. Crawford, "Peter Yates," 187.
173. "CBS excludes my music – as controversial from their broadcasts." Arnold Schoenberg to Gerald Strang, 28 April 1950, ASC. See also Roger Nixon's letter of 8 May 1950 to Board of Directors Philharmonic Symphony Society New York, copy at ASC.
174. Some of the radio interviews exist in published and unpublished transcripts. See "First American Radio Broadcast" and "First California Broadcast" in *SW*, 293–301; and the interview with Thomas Freeburn Smith: "Schönberg spricht. To the birthday of broadcasts of contemporary music," available online at the ASC website. See also Schoenberg's correspondence with Hale Sparks, LC.
175. To members of Music of Today, Toldi even sold scores and recordings at affordable prices. See *American Kaleidoscope* (New York: Philosophical Library, 1960), 361–69.
176. The speech caught the attention of various high-profile critics who published it and added their commentaries. Virgil Thomson, "Schoenberg Celebrates Seventy-Fifth Birthday with Attack on Conductors."
177. Toldi, *American Kaleidoscope*, 366.
178. Early recordings on American labels made without Schoenberg's involvement include *Gurrelieder* on RCA (Philadelphia Orchestra under Stokowski, 1932); *Verklärte Nacht* on RCA (Minneapolis Symphony under Ormandy, mid-1930s; and St. Louis Symphony under Vladimir Golschmann, mid-1940s); Three Piano Pieces, op. 11, no. 2 on Friends of Recorded Musik (Katherine Ruth Heyman, late 1930s); 5th and 12th songs from *Das Buch der hängenden Gärten* on Columbia (Erica Storm and Mosco Carner, late 1930s); and Six Little Pieces, op. 19 on RCA (Jesús Sanromá, late 1930s).
179. Fred Steiner, "A History of the First Complete Recording of the Schoenberg String Quartets," *JASI* 2, no. 2 (February 1978): 122–37.
180. See Frederick Dorian to Arnold Schoenberg, 10 May 1941, LC.
181. *SR*, 314, 322.
182. Arnold Schoenberg to Erwin Stein, 2 October 1942, in *ASL*, 215.
183. Copy of release drawn up by Thorner, sent to the Kolisch Quartet members on 23 May 1950, ASC. Fred Steiner incorrectly assumed that the musicians received royalties. See Steiner, "A History," 131–32.
184. Alec Compinsky to Arnold Schoenberg, 1 October 1950, LC.
185. Ross Russell to Arnold Schoenberg, 24 February 1950; and Arnold Schoenberg to Ross Russell, 3 March 1950, University of Texas, Harry Ransom Humanities Research Center.
186. Arnold Schoenberg to Ross Russell, 3 January 1950, quoted in David Smyth, "Schoenberg and Dial Records: The Composer's Correspondence with Ross Russell," *JASI* 12, no. 1 (June 1989): 76.
187. Arnold Schoenberg to Ross Russell, 16 January 1950, quoted in Smyth, "Schoenberg and Dial," 80.
188. This was another master tape from Blue Star Records received in lieu of money. Schoenberg found Leibowitz's recording "destructive," comparing the narration by Leibowitz's

wife Ellen Adler to "the nagging sound of a wife who is scolding." Schoenberg unsuccessfully offered to direct a new recording of the *Ode* to prevent this recording's release. See Smyth, "Schoenberg and Dial," 80–86.

189. Arnold Schoenberg to Edward Steuermann, 3, 21, and 29 October 1949, LC.
190. Smyth, "Schoenberg and Dial," 85.
191. Arnold Schoenberg to Edward Steuermann, 3 October 1949, LC.
192. Arnold Schoenberg to Jerry Newman, 2 and 15 February 1950, LC.
193. Jerry Newman to Arnold Schoenberg, 25 May and 22 August 1950, LC.
194. After initially planning to record a performance of *Pelleas* conducted by Schoenberg, Capitol asked the German Telefunken company to record the work in Frankfurt. See Arnold Schoenberg to Roger Nixon, 20 August 1949, LC.

CHAPTER 5

1. Schoenberg offered his Monn and Handel arrangements to Oxford University Press in London for a flat fee of £300. The negotiations, however, failed even after he asked for a £120 royalty advance. Arnold Schoenberg to Hubert Foss, 22 June, 3 and 10 August, and 1 September 1933, LC.
2. Engel had given the pre-concert lecture for the American *Pierrot* premiere in 1923.
3. Carl Engel to Arnold Schoenberg, 8 August 1934, ASC.
4. Schirmer to Arnold Schoenberg, 26 September1934; and Arnold Schoenberg to Carl Engel, 20 August 1934, LC.
5. Carl Engel to Arnold Schoenberg, 6 August 1935 and 6 January 1937, ASC.
6. Arnold Schoenberg to Carl Engel, 3 May and 2 October 1935, LC; and Carl Engel to Arnold Schoenberg, 14 October 1935, ASC.
7. This sum included $400 for the extracting of the orchestral parts of the orchestral score, to be done by Schoenberg's son and daughter in Austria. To his daughter Gertrud, Schoenberg confessed that the sum he received ($1,000) for the Brahms orchestration was two-fifths of the amount he expected, i.e., $2,500 (about $37,000 in 2009), and that he spent about $1,000 on the production of the performance materials. Arnold Schoenberg to Gertrud Greissle, 11 November 1939, LC.
8. Arnold Schoenberg to Carl Engel, 15 May 1943, LC.
9. Carl Engel to Schoenberg, 14 January 1935, in Arnold Schoenberg and Allen Anderson, *My Horses Ain't Hungry*, ed. Severine Neff with Sabine Feisst (Pacific Palisades: Belmont, 2007), 10.
10. The contributors were Armitage, Richard Buhlig, Louis Danz, Engel, Klemperer, Ernst Krenek, Paul Pisk, José Rodriguez, César Saerchinger, Boris de Schloezer, Roger Sessions, Nicolas Slonimsky, Paul Stefan, Erwin Stein, Edward Steuermann, Leopold Stokowski, Berthold Viertel, Adolph Weiss, and Franz Werfel.
11. Engel sent proposals to forty-seven universities and other institutions in the summer of 1934. Carl Engel to Arnold Schoenberg, 27 July 1934, ASC.
12. Carl Engel to Arnold Schoenberg, 31 July 1934, ASC.
13. Engel corresponded about this matter with Albert Elkus, chair of the music department at the University of California, Berkeley. See *Quellen zur Geschichte emigrierter Musiker 1933–1950*, ed. Horst Weber and Manuela Schwartz (Munich: Saur, 2003), vol. 1, 53.
14. Carl Engel to Arnold Schoenberg, 10 December 1940, LC.
15. Arnold Schoenberg to Carl Engel, 6 February 1941, LC; and Carl Engel to Arnold Schoenberg, 15 March 1941, LC. Carl Engel to Arnold Schoenberg, 3 March 1941 and 18 October 1943, LC: "We would like to attend to *Kol nidre* – and actually at the splendid conditions of 30% for Schirmer – if we can find faithful and non-faithful purchasers

for it." Schoenberg withdrew *Kol nidre* from Schirmer's rental catalogue in 1946. Nathan Broder to Arnold Schoenberg, 25 October 1946, LC.

16. See, for instance, Arnold Schoenberg to Gertrud Greissle, 17 May 1942, LC.
17. Ibid.
18. Schoenberg's children copied the Violin Concerto, Fourth Quartet, and the Brahms arrangement. Georg did not deliver the transparencies in a timely fashion. Gertrud and Felix struggled with the deadlines for the Violin Concerto and Brahms arrangement. See correspondence between Carl Engel and Arnold Schoenberg from 1 January 1937 to 1 March 1940, ASC. The Band Variations had many errors in the proofs.
19. Carl Engel to Arnold Schoenberg, 11 June 1942, LC; and see, for instance, Felix Greissle to Arnold Schoenberg, 1 October 1943 and 23 September 1944, LC.
20. Carl Engel to Arnold Schoenberg, 15 March 1941 and 26 May 1942, LC.
21. Arnold Schoenberg to Carl Engel, 19 October and 8 December 1934, LC.
22. Arnold Schoenberg to Carl Engel, 6 December 1940, LC.
23. "Two Canons for Carl Engel, 1943," in *ASR*, 295.
24. Felix Greissle to Arnold Schoenberg, 1942, LC.
25. Felix Greissle to Arnold Schoenberg, 23 September 1944, LC.
26. Felix Greissle to Arnold Schoenberg, 3 December 1946, LC.
27. Arnold Schoenberg to Felix Greissle, 23 September 1948, LC.
28. Felix Greissle to Arnold Schoenberg, 31 January 1947, LC. In 1950 Schoenberg unsuccessfully offered a new *Pelleas* version, "reducing the orchestration to normal size," to Southern Music Publishing Company (later Peer Music). Arnold Schoenberg to Wladimir Lakond, 8 January 1951, LC.
29. Felix Greissle to Arnold Schoenberg, 8 June 1948, LC.
30. Felix Greissle to Arnold Schoenberg, 5 March 1949, LC.
31. Arnold Schoenberg to Felix Greissle, 9 May 1950, LC.
32. For more details see Berthold Türcke, "Felix Greissle (1894–1982)," *JASI* 6, no. 1 (June 1982): 4–7.
33. Greissle quit Schirmer because of Schuman's peculiar publishing politics. See Philip Lambro, "The House of Schirmer (1960–1963)," unpublished manuscript, ASC.
34. Hans Heinsheimer, *Menagerie in F Sharp* (New York: Doubleday, 1947), 233.
35. Lambro, "The House," 5.
36. Arnold Schoenberg to Hans Heinsheimer, 3 February 1948, ASC.
37. Arnold Schoenberg to Hans Heinsheimer, 14 March 1949; and see also Lambro, "The House," 68.
38. Arnold Schoenberg to Hans Heinsheimer, 5 March and 7 November 1948, ASC; and Hans Heinsheimer to Arnold Schoenberg, 10 November 1948, LC. Although inaccuracies in royalty statements are common, Heinsheimer's practice of so-called "royalty filing" (omission of royalty payments), which may have affected Schoenberg along with several other composers, was illegal. Lambro, "The House," 56.
39. Arnold Schoenberg to José Limón, 22 April 1950, LC.
40. Arnold Schoenberg to William Strickland, 27 August 1941 and 7 October 1941; and William Strickland to Arnold Schoenberg, 22 August and 3 October 1941, in Paul Hesselink, "*Variations on a Recitative for Organ, Op. 40*: Correspondence from the Schoenberg Legacy," *JASI* 7, no. 2 (November 1983): 143–45.
41. Gray issued a two-piano version of the Organ Variations by Celius Dougherty. Schoenberg himself began such an arrangement, but never completed it.
42. Schoenberg received complaints about the registration from various European organists. See Hesselink, "*Variations*," 177–80.

43. Arnold Schoenberg to Kurt List, 17 November 1948, LC.
44. Arnold Schoenberg to Nathaniel Shilkret, 4 November 1950 and 21 April 1951, LC.
45. In the 1960s a fire at Shilkret's house destroyed the still unpublished scores and parts for the Suite, and only Schoenberg's and Stravinsky's scores survived.
46. George Sturm, "Encounters: Walter R. Boelke," *MadAminA!* 4, no. 1 (1983): 9.
47. Kurt List to Arnold Schoenberg, 24 October 1948, LC.
48. Schoenberg offered the New Music Edition his Organ Variations and *Kol nidre* for publication. This firm also wanted to publish his Trio. Arnold Schoenberg to Kurt List, 2 November1946; and Kurt List to Arnold Schoenberg, 8 December 1946, LC.
49. Kurt List to Arnold Schoenberg, 16 November 1949, LC.
50. Arnold Schoenberg to Margot Tietz, 15 September 1948, LC.
51. He offered Bomart his *Phantasy* for a $260 (about $2,320 in 2009) royalty advance payable in ten monthly installments only after Schirmer, which he had described to Bomart as a "powerful firm," proposed to accept it for a $250 royalty advance. Arnold Schoenberg to Margot Tietz, 13 April and 6 December 1949 and 24 February 1950, LC.
52. The autographer was the Berg student Julius Schloss, whose work pleased Schoenberg.
53. Arnold Schoenberg to Margot Tietz, 25 February and 22 October 1949, LC; and Margot Tietz to Arnold Schoenberg, 25 October 1949, LC.
54. Arnold Schoenberg to Margot Tietz, 31 October 1949, LC.
55. Arnold Schoenberg to Walter Boelke, 8 March 1951, LC.
56. Margot Tietz to Arnold Schoenberg, 13 February 1950, LC; see also David Smyth, "Schoenberg and Dial Records: The Composer's Correspondence with Ross Russell," *JASI* 12, no. 1 (June 1989): 68–90.
57. See, for instance, Kurt List, "The Renaissance of Jewish Music," *Commentary* 2, no. 12 (December 1947): 527–34; and "Schoenberg's New Cantata," *Commentary* 6, no. 5 (November 1948): 468–73; and René Leibowitz, "Music Chronicle: Two Composers: A Letter from Hollywood," *Partisan Review* 15, no. 3 (March 1948): 361–65.
58. Kurt List to Arnold Schoenberg, 20 May 1949, LC.
59. The materials, however, were available at the Fleisher Collection of the Free Library of Philadelphia. For his Five Pieces performance in 1948 Mitropoulos used materials from Philadelphia with permission from Summy, who had only one copy of the full score in stock, but no parts. Fleisher only provides materials if unavailable through a publisher. See Walter Hinrichsen to Arnold Schoenberg, 7 June 1951, ASC; and Clayton Summy to Arnold Schoenberg, 12 May 1945, LC.
60. Arnold Schoenberg to Walter Hinrichsen, 3 November 1948 and 31 August 1949, LC.
61. Arnold Schoenberg to Walter Hinrichsen, 3 November 1948, LC.
62. Walter Hinrichsen to Arnold Schoenberg, 6 and 16 December 1949, LC.
63. As Hoffmann was the only proofreader, this score contains more errors than other revised editions. See Pierre Boulez to Hans Swarsenski (Edition Peters, London), 26 December 1964, C. F. Peters New York Archives; and David Avshalomov, "Arnold Schönberg's Five Pieces for Orchestra, Op. 16: The Story of the Music and Its Editions, With a Critical Study of His 1949 Revision" (D.M.A. thesis, University of Washington, 1976), 102–4. See also Walter Hinrichsen to Arnold Schoenberg, 12 January 1950 and 23 February 1951, LC.
64. Arnold Schoenberg to Walter Hinrichsen, 12 July 1950, LC; Arnold Schoenberg to Hans Heinsheimer, 13 April 1949, LC.
65. Arnold Schoenberg to Walter Hinrichsen, 26 July 1950, LC. Schoenberg was dissatisfied with the 600 marks he received for the Five Pieces in 1912. In 1927 he declined Henri Hinrichsen's offer to publish his Third String Quartet for 3,000 marks. See *HHS*, 159, 317.

66. Arnold Schoenberg to Walter Hinrichsen, 25 April 1951, LC.
67. Walter Hinrichsen to Max Hinrichsen, 12 July 1951, C. F. Peters New York Archives.
68. Ibid.
69. Walter Hinrichsen to Schoenberg, 26 September 1950, LC.
70. Arnold Schoenberg to Nathaniel Shilkret, 4 November 1950, LC.
71. Arnold Schoenberg to Walter Hinrichsen, 12 and 26 July 1950, LC. Schoenberg offered the First Chamber Symphony, op. 9b to Southern Music. Arnold Schoenberg to Walter Lakond, 16 June 1951, LC.
72. Arnold Schoenberg to Walter Hinrichsen, 11 November 1950 and 12 June 1951, LC.
73. Arnold Schoenberg to Walter Hinrichsen, 25 November 1950, LC. Schoenberg quoted Gustave Beer, president of the American League of Authors and Composers, from Austria, as the source of the rumor: "Die U.E. ist mit Mr. Hendrichsen (!) [*sic*] in einem schweren Prozess . . . begriffen, da Mr. Hendrichsen, wie mir geschrieben wurde, der Ariseur der U.E. war . . . [The UE has instituted severe legal proceedings against Mr. Hendrichsen, since Mr. Hendrichsen, as I have been informed, was the "Aryanizer" of UE]." Arnold Schoenberg to Walter Hinrichsen, 5 December 1950, LC. The person who was among the chief "Aryanizers" of Peters and UE during the Nazi regime was Johannes Petschull.
74. Hinrichsen, however, replied: "Although you have already a detailed reply from me in previous correspondence in answer to your question of Nov. 25 concerning my father, may I *repeat* that he died in a Nazi concentration camp, as did also one of his sons, another of his sons was gased by the Nazis and his son-in-law and 2 of his grand sons were also gased by the Nazis in concentration camps. I am still unable to understand just *why* Arnold Schoenberg feels that he is in a position to request me to give continuously details of the tragedy to my family during the Nazi period." Walter Hinrichsen to Arnold Schoenberg, 30 November 1950, LC.
75. Hugo Winter to Arnold Schoenberg, 17 February 1950, LC.
76. Arnold Schoenberg to Universal Edition, 19 July 1933, LC.
77. Arnold Schoenberg to Walter Hinrichsen, 26 May 1951, LC.
78. Sophie Fetthauer, *Musikverlage im "Dritten Reich" und im Exil* (Hamburg: von Bockel, 2004), 184–214.
79. Arnold Schoenberg to Hugo Winter, 1944, LC.
80. See, for instance, Arnold Schoenberg to Alfred Kalmus, 8–10 March 1934, WB; Alfred Kalmus to Arnold Schoenberg, 9 June 1934, ASC; Arnold Schoenberg to Ernest Voigt, 28 February 1939, LC; Schoenberg to Hugo Winter, 1944, LC; Arnold Schoenberg to Ralph Hawkes, 19 July 1940, LC; and Schoenberg to Walter Hinrichsen, 12 July 1950, LC.
81. Erwin Stein to Arnold Schoenberg, 1 May 1941, LC.
82. Arnold Schoenberg to Alfred Schlee, 21 January and 1 March 1947; Alfred Schlee to Arnold Schoenberg, 5 June 1950; and Schoenberg to Merritt Tompkins, 20 November 1950. See also Arnold Schoenberg to Capitol Records, Dial Records, Esoteric Records, and RCA Victor, 23 May 1950, LC; and Arnold Schoenberg to Walter Hinrichsen, 12 July 1950, LC.
83. AMP could not collect fees for chamber music performances, as there were no arrangements made for such procedures. The collection of performance fees in the realm of chamber music would remain a problem. Alfred Kalmus to Arnold Schoenberg, 30 January 1935, ASC.
84. See, for instance, Alfred Schlee to Arnold Schoenberg, 7 March and 7 May 1951, LC; and Arnold Schoenberg to Ernest Voigt, 28 February 1943, LC.

85. Arnold Schoenberg to Ernest Voigt, 28 February 1939, LC.
86. In 1964 AMP became part of Schirmer.
87. Schoenberg made this version with changes in the double bass part, new dynamics, articulation, and tempo markings because UE had failed to copyright the 1917 version. *Verklärte Nacht*'s original sextet version published by Drei Lilien Verlag was not copyrighted either.
88. Alfred Kalmus to Arnold Schoenberg, 7 December 1934, ASC; and Edwin Kalmus to Arnold Schoenberg, 6 November 1939, LC.
89. Edwin Kalmus to Arnold Schoenberg, 14 March 1940, LC; Hugo Winter to Arnold Schoenberg, 13 January 1943; and Arnold Schoenberg to Hugo Winter, 9 February 1943, LC.
90. Greissle accused Winter of playing a double game. Felix Greissle to Arnold Schoenberg, 26 January 1947, LC.
91. Arnold Schoenberg to Ralph Hawkes, 19 July 1940, LC.
92. Arnold Schoenberg to Kurt List, 17 November 1948, LC.
93. Arnold Schoenberg to Emil Hilb, 27 June 1951, NYPL.
94. Anne Schoenberg, "Belmont Music," *Serial: Newsletter of the Arnold Schoenberg Institute* 1, no. 2 (Summer 1987): 1.
95. Dagobert Runes to Arnold Schoenberg, 8 November 1941, ASC; Theresa Gronich to Arnold Schoenberg, 3 and 20 October 1941, ASC; and Arnold Schoenberg to Theresa Gronich, 18 October1941, LC.
96. Graf discussed Schoenberg in two of his Philosophical Library publications: *Legend of a Musical City* (1945) and *Modern Music* (1946). See also Thomas McGeary, "The Publishing History of *Style and Idea*," *JASI* 9, no. 2 (November 1986): 181, 205.
97. *Harmonielehre*'s short version was made by Erwin Stein and published by UE in 1923 as *Praktischer Leitfaden zu Schönbergs Harmonielehre*.
98. For more details see Bryan Simms, "Arnold Schoenberg, *Theory of Harmony*. Translated by Roy E. Carter, Berkeley and Los Angeles: University of California Press, 1978 – Commentary," *Music Theory Spectrum* 4 (Spring 1982): 154–63. See also *SR*, 261–67, 274, 297, 314–15; 20 and Bernard van Dieren to Arnold Schoenberg, 20 January 1928; and Arnold Schoenberg to Bernard van Dieren, 11 June 1929, LC.
99. Arnold Schoenberg to Robert D. W. Adams, 27 June 1944, LC.
100. Arnold Schoenberg to Robert D. W. Adams, 26 January 1948, LC.
101. Arnold Schoenberg to Dagobert Runes, 31 January and 5 February 1949, LC.
102. Arnold Schoenberg to Rose Morse, 14 June 1946, LC.
103. Arnold Schoenberg to Reba Sparr, 1 July 1944, LC.
104. Rose Morse to Arnold Schoenberg, 24 April 1945, ASC; and Arnold Schoenberg to Philosophical Library, 4 May 1945, LC.
105. Reba Sparr to Arnold Schoenberg, 31 May 1944, ASC. See also McGeary, "The Publishing History," 190–97.
106. A Mr. Horan, Richard Hoffmann, and René Leibowitz also played a role in the translation process.
107. Dika Newlin, Foreword to Arnold Schoenberg, *Style and Idea* (New York: Philosophical Library, 1950), v.
108. *SR*, 336.
109. Dika Newlin, interview with the author, 26 May 2005.
110. Runes seemed pleased even though Schoenberg had failed to get his explicit permission for the setting and its publication, and *Prisma* had misspelled his name as "Runer." Arnold Schoenberg to Dagobert Runes, 31 August 1949 and 13 March 1950, LC.

111. Arnold Schoenberg to Dagobert Runes, 20 October 1950, LC.
112. Arnold Schoenberg to Dagobert Runes, 21 April 1951, LC.
113. Dagobert Runes to Arnold Schoenberg, 24 April 1951, ASC.
114. See Schoenberg's correspondence with the Philosophical Library 3 February–28 August 1947 and 19 January–20 October1950, LC; and Arnold Schoenberg to Dagobert Runes, 26 August 1950, LC.
115. Arnold Schoenberg to Philosophical Library, 22 November 1947; and Arnold Schoenberg to Dagobert Runes, 21 October 1949, LC.
116. Arnold Schoenberg to Herbert Marks, 25 January 1947, LC.

CHAPTER 6

1. *SI*, 388.
2. Ernst Krenek quoted in Joan Peyser, "Two Masters in Conflict: Music at Dartmouth," *NYT*, 8 September 1968.
3. Charles Hamm, *Music in the New World* (New York: Norton, 1983), 562.
4. R. Wayne Shoaf, "The Schoenberg-Malkin Correspondence," *JASI* 13, no. 2 (November 1990): 248.
5. "Malkin Conservatory offered me rather less than a quarter of what I had regarded as compensation for my Berlin salary, that is to say as a minimum." See *SI*, 25. See Scott Derks, *The Value of a Dollar, 1860–2004* (Millerton, NY: Greyhouse, 2004), 206; and *National Income and Product Accounts of the United States, 1929–2000*, electronic resource (Washington, D.C.: U.S. Department of Commerce, Economics and Statistics Administration Bureau of Economic Analysis, 2001). Bear in mind that during this year he also earned at least $1,400 from conducting engagements, made several hundred dollars for lectures in New York, Princeton, and Chicago, and received money from private students as well as some royalties, yielding at least an additional $2,000 (about $31,700 in 2009).
6. "The Letters of Webern and Schoenberg (to Roberto Gerhard)," *Score* 24 (1958): 40.
7. Ibid., 41; and *SI*, 26.
8. For more details on Comfort see "Two Schönberg Scholarships Awarded," *MC* 107, no. 27 (30 December 1933): 13. WEVD radio aired her Piano Sonatina (performed by Comfort), *Madrigal* for three sopranos and clarinet, *Nocturne*, *The Lonely Isle*, and *Wind in the Trees* for soprano on 21 May 1933. Dean Root, "The Pan American Association of Composers (1928–1934)," *Anuario Interamericano de Investigacion Musical* 8 (1972): 67. From the beginning Schoenberg taught many more women students in the United States than in Europe. In the 1930s women in America had better access to higher education than in Germany, where the percentage of women students in 1933 did not exceed 10 percent. Moreover, well-off young American women tended to study the arts and art education, while their male counterparts were inclined to study subjects promising financially prosperous careers.
9. Lautner and Knight documented their lessons with Schoenberg in memoirs: Lois Lautner, "Arnold Schoenberg in Kammern," *Michigan Quarterly Review* 16, no. 1 (Winter 1977): 21–27; and Lovina Knight, "Classes with Schoenberg January through June 1934," *JASI* 13, no. 2 (November 1990): 137–63.
10. Arnold Schoenberg to Robert Stuart, 27 January 1940, in *ASR*, 284.
11. Interview with Frank Glazer, 4 June 1999.
12. Other names of Schoenberg's students in Boston and New York are listed in Shoaf, "The Schoenberg-Malkin Correspondence," 249, 251–52.
13. Knight, "Classes with Schoenberg," 159, 161.
14. *SI*, 26.

15. Arnold Schoenberg, "Addendum [Unfinished Theoretical Works]," *JASI* 13, no. 2 (November 1990): 254.
16. *SI*, 26.
17. Knight, "Classes with Schoenberg," 160–61. See Schoenberg's laudatory recommendation for Lautner (n.d.), LC.
18. *HHS*, 376.
19. Knight, "Classes with Schoenberg," 160.
20. *SI*, 26.
21. Schoenberg gave Malkin an inscribed photo: "Herrn Joseph Malkin, mit dessen Hilfe ich Amerika entdecke mit freundlichen Neujahrswünschen 1934 Arnold Schoenberg [To Mr. Joseph Malkin, with whose help I am discovering America with kind wishes for the new year 1934 Arnold Schoenberg]." Shoaf, "The Schoenberg-Malkin Correspondence," 247.
22. Arnold Schoenberg to Minna Lederman, 7 March 1937, LC; and Dorothea Bestor, "Schoenberg Teaches: An Interview with Arnold Schoenberg," *Musical Review* 3 (October 1934): 3.
23. Schoenberg wrote to Malkin on November 12, 1934: "I came out here without anything certain, without any publicity, completely off-chance, simply for my health (which should tell you that it was primarily for that reason I couldn't accept your offer), and have by now as many students as in New York and continuous inquiries. Here, too people have no money and I had to be a bit cheaper. But at least they pay that." Shoaf, "The Schoenberg-Malkin Correspondence," 239.
24. Pauline Alderman, "Schoenberg at USC," *JASI* 5, no. 2 (November 1981): 204.
25. Arnold Schoenberg to Julia Howell, 12 February 1935, LC.
26. John Cage to Adolph Weiss, 30 March 1935, in William B. George, "Adolph Weiss" (Ph.D. diss., University of Iowa, 1971), 308–9.
27. Virginia Bortin, *Elinor Remick Warren: A Bio-Bibliography* (Westport: Greenwood, 1993), 50. Schoenberg felt that Warren's cantata *The Passing of King Arthur* (1939), though "partly not bad . . . lacked structure and form." See *SR*, 200.
28. Schoenberg was very fond of Steeb. See Warren Langlie's transcribed taped lessons with Schoenberg, 6 November 1950, ASC; Bernice Abrams Geiringer's class notes at the Davidson Library of the University of California, Santa Barbara; and unpublished interview conducted by Andrea Castillo-Herreshoff, 29 November 1993, ASC.
29. See Vivian Perlis, "Interview with John Cage" (Oral History of American Music Archives, Yale University, December 1975 and August 1976); and John Cage to Dieter Schnebel, 11 December 1973, Northwestern University Library. I would like to thank Kenneth Silverman for drawing my attention to this letter.
30. John Cage to Adolph Weiss, 30 March 1935, in George, "Adolph Weiss," 308–9; Alderman, *We Build a School of Music: The Commissioned History of Music at the University of Southern California* (Los Angeles: Alderman Book Committee, USC, 1989), 128; and "Arnold Schoenberg at USC," 206.
31. John Cage to Adolph Weiss, 30 March 1935, in George, "Adolph Weiss," 308–9. On December 11, 1934, Cage wrote to Pauline Schindler: "I will meet Schoenberg (whom you have already) by taking him presents from Mrs. Weiss who is not coming." On March 2, 1935, he wrote: "It is a certainty and miraculous Schoenberg asked me to come to see him. It will be some time next week. I hope many things will come of that. It will be my first really meeting him. I am completely nervous tingling and active in every direction." On March 19, 1935, he reported: "I took my first lesson in Schoenberg's class yesterday (Monday) evening. He is marvelous, indescribable, as a musician."

Maureen Mary, "Letters: The Brief Love of John Cage for Pauline Schindler 1934–35," *Ex Tempore* 8 (Summer 1996): 4, 15–18.

32. Irene Kahn Atkins, "Interview with Hugo Friedhofer" (American Film Institute/Louis B Mayer Foundation Oral History, March 1974).
33. Bortin, *Elinor Remick Warren*, 50.
34. Cycler remained friends with Schoenberg until he left Los Angeles in 1947 to join the School of Music of the University of Oregon in Eugene.
35. John Cage to Adolph Weiss, Spring 1935, in George, "Adolph Weiss," 314.
36. John Cage to Pauline Schindler, 24 May and 3 June 1935, in Mary, "Letters," 21–23.
37. Castillo-Herreshoff, "Interview with Bernice Abrams Geiringer."
38. See "String Quartet Plays at Composer's Party," *LAT*, 6 January 1937; and Cage to Schnebel, 11 December 1973.
39. Pauline Alderman, "Arnold Schoenberg at USC," *JASI* 5, no. 2 (November 1981): 205; and "Arnold Schoenberg at the USC School of Music," Address given on 13 September 1974, unpublished typescript, ASC. See also Rufus von KleinSmid to Arnold Schoenberg, 19 November 1934, LC.
40. Howell was the Alchin Chair committee's chairperson and Alderman its secretary. Ina Davids, who attended Schoenberg's private class in fall 1934, was also a committee member.
41. Rufus von KleinSmid to Arnold Schoenberg, 21 June 1935, LC.
42. *SI*, 28.
43. Adding to the more than $4,000 from USC (about 61,900 in 2009), he also received fees from private students, $3,000 in royalty advances from Schirmer (fall 1934–35), and $1,000 for conducting in 1935.
44. Vivian Perlis, "Interview with Gerald Strang" (Oral History of American Music Archives, Yale University, March 1975).
45. Alderman, *We Build*, 129.
46. Cage, Stein, and Wells were in the Beethoven analysis class. See Cage to Schnebel, 11 December 1973; Alan Wells, "Schoenberg's Class at USC," *JASI* 5, no. 2 (November 1981): 211–12; and Alderman, "Arnold Schoenberg at USC," 207. Few documents listing Schoenberg's USC and private students from this period have survived.
47. Stein's devotion to Schoenberg is reflected in his D.M.A. dissertation entitled "The Performance of Twelve-Tone and Serial Music for the Piano" (University of Southern California, 1965), his editions of Schoenberg's writings, his teaching activities, and directorship of the Schoenberg Institute.
48. Strang remembered that in one of the Beethoven analysis classes, Klemperer endeavored to comment on Beethoven's Ninth Symphony, whereupon Schoenberg replied "Falsch, Klemperer," "as though rebuking a little schoolboy." Peter Heyworth, *Otto Klemperer: His Life and Times*, vol. 2: *1933–1973* (Cambridge: Cambridge University Press, 1996), 86.
49. Gerald Strang to Arnold Schoenberg, 17 July 1937, LC.
50. Robertson's class notes are in the Leroy Robertson Collection at the University of Utah Library.
51. For his Ph.D. thesis defense at USC in 1954, Robertson listed Schoenberg's courses as part of his graduate studies. Thanks to Bruce Quaglia for this information. See also Rudolf Kolisch to Arnold Schoenberg, 19 May 1951; Arnold Schoenberg to Rudolf Kolisch, 25 May 1951, Harvard University, Houghton Library; and Arnold Schoenberg to Leroy Robertson, 26 May 1951, LC.
52. Cage to Schnebel, 11 December 1973.
53. The fee, according to a flyer, was $15 per lecture series (about $230 in 2009), $25 for

both series (about $390 in 2009), and $1.00 for single admission (about $16 in 2009). See Sointu Scharenberg, *Überwinden der Prinzipien. Betrachtungen zu Arnold Schönbergs unkonventioneller Lehrtätigkeit zwischen 1898 und 1951* (Saarbrücken: Pfau, 2002), 297.

54. Arnold Schoenberg to Bessie Fraenkel, 26 November 1935, LC.
55. Max van Leuwen Swarthout, "First California Broadcast: Interview with Arnold Schoenberg," in *SW*, 299; see also Arnold Schoenberg to Ernst Krenek, 1 December 1939, in *ASL*, 210.
56. It is often suggested that in Europe Schoenberg gave only small master classes and single lessons to highly gifted composition students, which contradicts his varied teaching activities at the Stern Conservatory in Berlin and at feminist Eugenie Schwarzwald's school in Vienna. Vivian Perlis, "Interview with Gerald Strang," 27; Jerry McBride, "Dem Lehrer Arnold Schönberg," *JASI* 8, no. 1 (June 1984): 33, 37–38.
57. *SI*, 376.
58. Arnold Schoenberg to Ernst Krenek, 1 December 1939, in *ASL*, 210.
59. Schoenberg suggested to his publisher the issuing of affordable miniature scores representing the classical music canon. See Arnold Schoenberg to Carl Engel, 12 December 1938, LC.
60. Perlis, "Interview with Gerald Strang," 27.
61. Perhaps this is what Schoenberg referred to when he groaned about "these terrible summer sessions at USC." Arnold Schoenberg to Elizabeth Coolidge, 3 August 1936, in *ASL*, 200. See also Arnold Schoenberg to USC's Registrar's Office, 31 January1947, ASC.
62. Arnold Schoenberg to Hermann Scherchen, 16 March 1936, in *ASL*, 198.
63. Arnold Schoenberg to Robert D. W. Adams, 27 June 1944, LC.
64. Perlis, "Interview with Gerald Strang," 40.
65. Arnold Schoenberg to Anton Webern, 27 August 1936, in *ASLIB*, 331.
66. Dispensing with inversion, retrograde inversion, and transposition, Tremblay created a cycle of 288 related twelve-tone rows on which he based many works and the book *The Definitive Cycle of the Twelve Tone Row* (New York: Criterion Music, 1974). Tremblay conveyed these ideas to many film composers.
67. Mozelle Young, "Atlanta Music Notes," *Atlanta Constitution*, 8 November 1936 and 20 March 1938. See also Schoenberg's 1936 diaries, ASC, and correspondence between Schoenberg and Hodgson, 1938–50, LC.
68. Perlis, "Interview with Gerald Strang," 40.
69. As Levant was active in Hollywood and New York, his lessons had to be scheduled accordingly. Between April and September 1935, Levant met with Schoenberg about twice a week, and from October 1936 to February 1938, between one and eight times per month.
70. The Piano Concerto was premiered by the NBC Symphony under Wallenstein with Levant as soloist in a live radio broadcast in 1942. The Kolisch Quartet premiered his String Quartet in 1938 in Denver.
71. Rose Heylbut, "The Odyssey of Oscar Levant," *Etude* 58, no. 5 (May 1940): 355.
72. Arnold Schoenberg to Elizabeth Coolidge, 19 May 1937, ASC. "Levant conducted his own piece which shows much talent." Arnold Schoenberg to Adolph Weiss, 30 April 1937, in George, "Adolph Weiss," 331; and Oscar Levant, *The Unimportance of Being Oscar* (New York: Putnam, 1968), 146.
73. Stearns joined UCLA in 1932 and died on 1 November 1935. Klemperer quoted in Heyworth, *Otto Klemperer*, 86.
74. A noted acoustician, Knudsen was a professor of physics (1922–58) and one of

Schoenberg's friends. He designed sound stages in the early Hollywood sound-film era and played a role in the acoustical design of the Los Angeles Music Center and Gammage Auditorium at Arizona State University.

75. Alderman, "Arnold Schoenberg at the USC School of Music," 8. See Rufus von KleinSmid to Arnold Schoenberg, 14 December 1935. Schoenberg's income pales when compared to Stravinsky's remuneration for his Charles Eliot Norton lectures at Harvard in 1939–40, for which he received $9,000 (about $137,560 in 2009. See Claudia Maurer-Zenck, "Leben und Überleben als Komponist im Exil. Die ersten Jahre Strawinskys in den USA," in *Exilmusik. Komponisten während der NS-Zeit*, ed. Friedrich Geiger and Thomas Schäfer (Hamburg: von Bockel, 1999), 57, 69.
76. Founded in 1919, UCLA was authorized to grant degrees in 1924. In 1934 a Graduate Division was added. In 1936 the first three Ph.D. programs (not in music) and a Center for the Performing Arts were established.
77. In the early 1930s few American universities employed musicologists. Rubsamen specialized in opera and film-music research and when he joined UCLA, he began to build a music library. He frequented Schoenberg's parties, but Schoenberg categorized him as a "Rascal" in his sketches for an autobiography and satirized him as the fictitious musicologist "Hugo Triebsamen" (derived from Hugo Riemann and Rubsamen), who in the third millennium attributes the origin of dodecaphony to Thomas Mann. See *ASR*, 9, 322–23.
78. Allen joined UCLA's music department in fall 1935 and became its chair when Stearns died.
79. Leroy Allen, "University of California at Los Angeles," in *Music and Dance in California*, ed. José Rodriguez (Hollywood: Bureau of Musical Research, 1940), 207–11.
80. "I teach at present ten hours a week, which is much more than a full professor is supposed to do." Arnold Schoenberg to Robert Sproul, 14 March 1939.
81. Newlin's *Cradle Song*, written at age eight, was premiered by the Cincinnati Symphony under Vladimir Bakaleinikoff in December 1935. She completed her B.A. in French when she was sixteen years old.
82. Her dissertation was published with the same title by King's Crown Press in 1947 (revised edition 1978) and in a German translation by the Viennese Bergland-Verlag in 1954.
83. Arnold Schoenberg to Roy Harris, 23 May 1945, in *ASL*, 234.
84. For Lou Harrison's recollections of Halma, see Neil Rutman, "The Solo Piano Works of Lou Harrison" (D.M.A. thesis, Peabody Conservatory of Music, 1983), 11. Schoenberg wrote about Halma: "I have a high regard for the ability and talent of Mr. Halma; this is best shown by the fact that I have given him the grade of 'A' in both courses which he took with me. But he is not yet well enough prepared in my system to teach students independently. If he audited one or two of these courses during the next year, he would [be] entirely competent at the end of that time." Arnold Schoenberg to Leroy Allen, 7 June 1942.
85. Arnold Schoenberg, Application for Special Leave of Absence, 12 December 1942, Correspondence with the University of California, ASC.
86. One of Halma's photos of Schoenberg walking toward UCLA's Kerkoff Hall (perhaps modeled on Schoenberg's self-portrait "South going north") is printed in *SR*, 246–47.
87. Silvers Steuermann began to study with Schoenberg in 1941. Clara Steuermann, David Porter, and Gunther Schuller, eds., *The Not Quite Innocent Bystander: Writings of Edward Steuermann* (Lincoln: University of Nebraska Press, 1989), 27.
88. Many commentators, including Roger Sessions, Ian Pepper, Matthias Schmidt, and Richard Taruskin, have cast doubt on Cage's study with Schoenberg. Cage's enrollment

in six Schoenberg classes over the course of two years, including the same counterpoint regimen that Berg had undergone, is documented in Cage's own correspondence; in accounts of such classmates as Alderman, Abrams, and Sykes; the class notes of Stein and Strang; and Cage's harmony and counterpoint exercises in the David Tudor Collection at the Getty Center in Los Angeles.

89. "I am sure that the value of study with Schoenberg is now past for you. It has a great value – I know the whole business well, having been in his Berlin class. He would never, never, permit you to create ever. Now is high time for you to do so. But of course, in your own chosen field of creation, principles of fine-wrought construction must also apply, and while not necessarily adopting those of S., the way of building up such things is shown through contact with him. I know how natural it is to react against the retrogrades, etc. of polyphonic form-devices; but the best is to remain balanced, not prejudiced against them because they were too vigorously crammed down your throat!" Henry Cowell to John Cage, 23 March 1937, Northwestern University Library. See also John Cage to Adolph Weiss, 1936, in George, "Adolph Weiss," 317; and John Cage, *Silence: Lectures and Writings* (Middletown: Wesleyan University Press, 1961), 261.
90. David Bernstein, "Themes and Variations: John Cage's Studies with Arnold Schönberg," *JASC* 4 (2002): 325.
91. Peter Yates to John Cage, 8 August 1953 quoted in Hicks, "John Cage's Studies," 134; Ross Russell to Arnold Schoenberg, 24 February 1950; and Arnold Schoenberg to Ross Russell, 3 March 1950, University of Texas, Harry Ransom Humanities Research Center.
92. Russell quoted in Don Gillespie, "William Russell: American Percussion Composer," *Southern Quarterly* 36, no. 2 (1998): 40.
93. Ibid., 49.
94. William Russell, "Schoenberg the Teacher," *Tempo* 8, no. 12 (April 1940): 6, 13.
95. Vivian Perlis, "Interview with Lou Harrison" (Oral History of American Music Archives, Yale University, March 1970).
96. Analyzing Schoenberg's Opus 26, Cowell and Harrison found errors in that score. Lou Harrison, Interview by author, 10 August 1997; and Perlis, "Interview with Lou Harrison."
97. See Lou Harrison to Arnold Schoenberg, 4 November 1944, LC; Lou Harrison, Interview by author, 10 August 1997; and Leta Miller and Fredric Lieberman, *Lou Harrison: Composing a World* (New York: Oxford University Press, 1998), 19–22.
98. Rutman, "The Solo Piano Works," 11.
99. Lou Harrison, Preface to his Piano Suite of 1943 (New York: C. F. Peters, 1964).
100. Arnold Schoenberg to Roy Harris, 23 May 1945, in *ASL*, 234.
101. Lou Harrison to Arnold Schoenberg, 4 November 1944, LC. For a detailed essay on the Schoenberg-Harrison relationship, see Severine Neff, "An Unlikely Synergy: Lou Harrison and Arnold Schoenberg," *Journal of the Society for American Music* 3, no. 2 (May 2009): 155–93.
102. The dates of Kirchner's studies with Schoenberg, as given in articles on Kirchner, vary and are often incompatible with the testimonies of Kirchner's classmates. Since Kirchner seems to have exaggerated the length of his study with Schoenberg, my dates are based on statements by Kim, Newlin, and Stein, and on Stein's class notes at ASC. Other students who shared Sessions, Bloch, and Schoenberg as teachers include Richard Cumming, Roger Nixon, and Leonard Rosenman. Violinist-composer Robert Gross took informal instruction from Sessions and Schoenberg.
103. Vincent Plush, "Interview with Earl Kim" (Oral History of American Music Archives, Yale University, 1983); and Kim quoted in Janet Tassel, "Golden Silences: The Flowering of Earl Kim," *Boston Globe Magazine*, 27 February 1983, 30.

104. Joel Lester, "Analysis and Performance in Schoenberg's Phantasy, Op. 47," in *Pianist, Scholar, Connoisseur: Essays in Honor of Jacob Lateiner*, ed. Bruce Brubaker and Jane Gottlieb (Stuyvesant: Pendragon, 2000), 152.
105. Mark Carrington, "Interview with Leon Kirchner" (Oral History Archives, Yale University, September 1981). Kirchner also took Schoenberg's class in composition for beginners, for which he wrote a brief minuet. See "UCLA Classroom Notes (1940–41)," Leonard Stein Satellite Collection, ASC.
106. Peter Korn, "Ernst Toch und seine Freunde – Die Österreichischen Komponisten im kalifornischen Exil," in *Österreichische Musiker im Exil*, Beiträge der Österreichischen Gesellschaft für Musik, ed. Monica Wildauer (Kassel: Bärenreiter, 1990), 136.
107. Scharenberg, *Überwinden*, 84.
108. Arnold Schoenberg to Warren Langlie and Fritz and Erika Stiedry, 2 January 1951, LC.
109. *SI*, 389.
110. Among her students are David Bernstein, Charlotte Cross, Murray Dineen, Severine Neff, and Jo-Ann Reif.
111. Michela Robbins, "A Schoenberg Seminar," *Counterpoint* 17, no. 2 (1952): 11.
112. Exceptions were Edward Powell, who studied with Schoenberg in 1941 and 1944, and Franz Waxman, who received individual instruction for only a short time in the summer of 1945.
113. Arnold Schoenberg to Alfred Newman, 5 November 1941, LC.
114. See Arnold Schoenberg to Francis Burkley, 10 and 23 June and 11 December 1938; and Francis Burkley to Schoenberg, 6 July 1950, LC.
115. In 1947 Coulthard joined the music faculty at the University of British Columbia. William Bruneau and David G. Duke, *Jean Coulthard: A Life in Music* (Vancouver: Ronsdale, 2005), 61.
116. Frank, who worked on a Schoenberg biography in the 1940s, was related to the writer and Holocaust martyr Anne Frank.
117. See Schoenberg to prospective student Leo Scheer, 7 October 1937, LC. Newlin reported that in fall 1939 she paid a flat fee of $60 a month (about $900 in 2009) for individual composition lessons. See *SR*, 110.
118. Arnold Schoenberg to Nancy Loncarie, 16 November 1941, LC. However, he made exceptions and gave Burkley, for instance, weekly lessons for $65 (about $980 in 2009) per month. Arnold Schoenberg to Francis Burkley, 23 June 1938, LC.
119. Vivian Perlis, "Interview with Leonard Stein," 28 June 1975 (Oral History of American Music Archives, Yale University), 17.
120. Arnold Schoenberg to Irving Beckman, 21 September 1946, LC.
121. Severine Neff, "Interview with Patricia Carpenter," Cincinnati, 24 February 1993, unpublished, ASC, 10.
122. Little is known about H. Endicott Hanson, who studied analysis with Schoenberg from 1947 to 1949.
123. Hoffmann became a respected composer and composition professor at Oberlin Conservatory of Music. See Walter Szmolyan, "Schönberg aus der Sicht seiner Schüler," *Österreichische Musikzeitschrift* 37, no. 10 (October 1982): 543–44.
124. Neff, "Interview with Patricia Carpenter," 10. See Langlie's classroom notes, unpublished, ASC.
125. Arnold Schoenberg to Roger Nixon, 3 June 1948, LC; Interview with Roger Nixon, 4 June 2008. See Arnold Schoenberg to José Vélez, 15 January 1947; and José Vélez to Arnold Schoenberg, 19 July 1947, LC.
126. Arnold Schoenberg to Roger Nixon, 1949, LC.

127. Arnold Schoenberg to José Vélez, 15 January 1947, LC.
128. See Schoenberg's handwritten note of the telegram by Langlie, 1 August 1949, LC. Tureck had planned to record Schoenberg's Piano Pieces, opp. 11 and 19 for the Allegro Recording Company. Yet it did not come to fruition. See Rosalyn Tureck to Arnold Schoenberg, 28 October 1949.
129. Arnold Schoenberg to Manus Sasonkin, 20 February 1950, LC.
130. Jacob Lateiner to Arnold Schoenberg, 10 April and 5 August 1950, LC.
131. Arnold Schoenberg to Natalie Limonick, 21 May 1947, LC.
132. Limonick quoted in Deena and Bernard Rosenberg, *The Music Makers* (New York: Columbia University Press, 1979), 332.
133. Neff, "Interview with Patricia Carpenter," 3–4; and Robert Nelson, "Schoenberg's Variation Seminar," *MQ* 50, no. 2 (April 1964): 141–64.
134. Arnold Schoenberg, "Plan for a Music Department, 1 July 1937," unpublished manuscript, ASC.
135. *SI*, 386.
136. Arnold Schoenberg to G. F. Stegmann, 26 January 1949, in *ASL*, 267.
137. *SI*, 173–74.
138. Plush, "Interview with Earl Kim."
139. *SR*, 137, 152–53; and see Perlis, "Interview with Gerald Strang," 32.
140. *SR*, 194.
141. Ibid., 154.
142. Knight, "Classes with Schoenberg," 145–46.
143. *SR*, 57–58, 61–62, 178, 193.
144. Rutman, "The Solo Piano Works," 11.
145. Cage continued his description of the movement: "There are, i.e., no two relationships of subject and answer identical. His feeling for the variation of idea did not allow of the opposite nor of another 'old' idea, – that of vagueness. So that the episodes (which are usually built of the latter) are here the development of the prelude. It is fascinating because the [prelude] is largo and is forever interrupting the fugue allegro. The work is convincing in every way and proves in a manner understandable to the most sluggish of ears the profundity and high seriousness of the composer." Mary, "Letters," 22.
146. *SR*, 17, 65, 203.
147. *SR*, 243, 309–10.
148. *SR*, 113–14, 136–38, 154–55, 192–93, 208.
149. Alderman, "Arnold Schoenberg at the USC School of Music,"
150. John Cage to Pauline Schindler, 15 April 1935, in Mary, "Letters," 20.
151. *SR*, 56, 106, 201, 226–27, 287.
152. For this class Schoenberg even prepared a motive list for his Variations on a Recitative. See *ASSW*, Series A, Vol. 5, xi, and Series B, Vol. 5, 71–73.
153. *SR*, 77–78.
154. *SR*, 37
155. *SI*, 379; and see Langlie, "Arnold Schoenberg as a Teacher," 117–18, 126.
156. *SI*, 176; William Lundell, "Interview with Arnold Schoenberg: First American Broadcast," in *SW*, 296.
157. Warren Langlie, "Arnold Schoenberg as a Teacher" (Ph.D. diss., University of California, Los Angeles, 1960), 117, 126.
158. *SI*, 383.
159. Jeff Goldberg, "John Cage Interviewed," *Transatlantic Review* 55–56 (May 1976): 104.

160. Note by Schoenberg attached to letter of 9 July 1945 from Alfred Leonard to Arnold Schoenberg, ASC.
161. Richard Kostelanetz, *Conversing with Cage* (New York: Limelight, 1988), 5.
162. Goldberg, "John Cage Interviewed," 104.
163. *SR*, 322.
164. See, for instance, *SR*, 43.
165. Knight, "Classes with Schoenberg," 161.
166. Bestor, "Schoenberg Teaches," 3. For other student remarks on this subject, see, for instance, Lautner, "Arnold Schoenberg in Kammern," 25; *SR*, 38; and Mary, "Letters," 22.
167. *MI*.
168. *MI*, 168–69.
169. Knight, "Classes with Schoenberg," 141.
170. Arnold Schoenberg, *Fundamentals of Musical Composition*, ed. Gerald Strang and Leonard Stein (London: Faber, 1967), 58.
171. Ibid., 58.
172. *SR*, 58.
173. Schoenberg, *Fundamentals*, 151.
174. Cage to Schnebel, 11 December 1973.
175. Wells, "Schoenberg's Class," 212.
176. Alderman, "Arnold Schoenberg at the USC School of Music," 3.
177. Telephone interview with Roger Nixon, 4 June 2008.
178. *SR*, 210.
179. *Alexander Schreiner Reminisces* (Salt Lake City: Publishers Press, 1984), 55–56.
180. John Cage to Adolph Weiss, n.d. [1936], in George, "Adolph Weiss," 317.
181. Arnold Schoenberg, *Structural Functions of Harmony*, ed. Leonard Stein (New York: Norton, 1954; rev. ed., 1969), xv; and Langlie, "Schoenberg as a Teacher," 98.
182 .Schoenberg, *Structural Functions*, 19.
183. *SR*, 89, 104.
184. Schoenberg, *Structural Functions*, vii.
185. Plush, "Interview with Earl Kim."
186. Neff, "Interview with Patricia Carpenter," 1.
187. *Harmonielehre* reflects Schoenberg's experience of teaching harmony to Berg, its music examples and their order of presentation coinciding with Berg's course of instruction and assignments. Rosemary Hilmar, "Alban Berg's Studies with Schoenberg," *JASI* 8, no. 1 (June 1984): 7–30.
188. Schoenberg, *Structural Functions*, 20, 30. Broadening his canon, Schoenberg considered such composers as Bizet, Debussy, and Tchaikovsky.
189. Arnold Schoenberg to Dagobert Runes, 5 February 1949, LC.
190. For more details see Bryan Simms, "Arnold Schoenberg, *Theory of Harmony* – Commentary," *Music Theory Spectrum* 4, no. 1 (April 1982): 158–62.
191. Bestor, "Schoenberg Teaches," 3, 6.
192. Arnold Schoenberg, *Preliminary Exercises in Counterpoint*, ed. Leonard Stein (London: Faber, 1963), 222.
193. *SR*, 56; and David Raksin, "Schoenberg as Teacher," *Serial: Newsletter of the Friends of the Arnold Schoenberg Institute* 2, no. 1 (1988): 5. See also Arnold Schoenberg, "Practical Counterpoint" and "Rhabarber Kontrapunkt" in Andreas Jacob, *Grundbegriffe der Musiktheorie Arnold Schönbergs* (Hildesheim: Olms, 2005), vol. 2, 922–23.
194. Langlie, "Arnold Schoenberg as Teacher," 55–57, 71, 84, 94; and "Arnold Schoenberg as an Educator," *ASGA*, 94.

195. Schoenberg, *Preliminary Exercises*, 222; and Langlie, "Arnold Schoenberg as an Educator," 94.
196. Russell, "Schoenberg, the Teacher," 5.
197. Langlie, "Arnold Schoenberg as Teacher," 84.
198. John Cage to Adolph Weiss, Spring 1935, in George, "Adolph Weiss," 314–15.
199. Cage to Schnebel, 11 December 1973.
200. Langlie, "Arnold Schoenberg as Teacher," 59.
201. Russell, "Schoenberg, the Teacher," 5; and Langlie, "Arnold Schoenberg as Teacher," 68–71; and Leonard Stein, Foreword to Schoenberg, *Preliminary Exercises*, xiii.
202. Neutralization means the alteration of notes based on their natural tendency within a certain key. See Schoenberg, *Preliminary Exercises*, 61–64.
203. Schoenberg also built on sketches he made in 1911 and 1926. *HHS*, 418–19.
204. *SR*, 194; and see his outline for this volume in Schoenberg, *Preliminary Exercises*, 224–25. Schoenberg mentioned this project to Richard Buhlig, to whom he said that the last part would be "an exhaustive treatment on dissonant counterpoint," and to some of his European students and friends in letters throughout the 1940s. See Richard Buhlig to Henry Cowell, 1 December 1936, Cowell Papers, NYPL; also Arnold Schoenberg to Erwin Stein, 22 November 1943, LC. Schoenberg also planned to write a book on Bach's counterpoint in 1948. See Jacob, *Grundbegriffe*, vol. 2, 909–10.
205. Langlie, "Arnold Schoenberg as Teacher," 84.
206. Neff, "Interview with Patricia Carpenter," 2.
207. Langlie, "Arnold Schoenberg as Teacher," 89.
208. Ibid., 83.
209. Ibid., 93; and Langlie, "Arnold Schoenberg as an Educator," 94.
210. Arnold Schoenberg, "Contrapuntal Composition" and "Fugue," in Jacob, *Grundbegriffe*, vol. 2, 926, 297–98.
211. Neff, "Interview with Patricia Carpenter," 2. Schoenberg termed the successive and simultaneous presentation of contrapuntal combinations in a piece "Abwicklung" or "unfolding": "The resulting piece simply rolls off like a film, picture by picture, gestalt by gestalt." See *MI*, 400.
212. Langlie, "Arnold Schoenberg as Teacher," 92–95.
213. Schoenberg, "Orchestration," in Jacob, *Grundbegriffe*, vol. 2, 952–53.
214. Ibid., vol. 2, 952.
215. Ibid., vol. 2, 951.
216. Knight, "Classes with Schoenberg," 152, 157; *SR*, 109.
217. *SR*, 305.
218. Maury quoted in *HHS*, 376–77. This suggestion did not prevent Schoenberg from challenging his performers in such works as his Violin Concerto.
219. Heylbut, "The Odyssey," 355.
220. Knight, "Classes with Schoenberg," 157; and Langlie, "Schoenberg as a Teacher," 117.
221. *SR*, 109, 126–27, 144, 227, 303–5; and see Schoenberg's schedules and course content in "UCLA Teaching II," ASC.
222. Knight, "Classes with Schoenberg," 157.
223. Ibid.
224. Ibid., 152.
225. Schoenberg considered French composers to be among the best orchestrators. See Langlie, "Arnold Schoenberg as a Teacher," 117.
226. Schoenberg, "Orchestration," in Jacob, *Grundbegriffe*, vol. 2, 951–69.
227. Langlie, "Arnold Schoenberg as an Educator," 93.

228. *SR*, 18, 23, 49, 129. See also Knight, "Classes with Schoenberg," 139, 145; and Arnold Schoenberg, *Models for Beginners in Composition*, 2nd rev. ed. (Pacific Palisades: Belmont Music Publishers, 1972), 4.
229. Knight, "Classes with Schoenberg," 143.
230. Schoenberg, *Models*, 3–4.
231. Knight, "Classes with Schoenberg," 140.
232. *SI*, 389.
233. Knight, "Classes with Schoenberg," 141.
234. Schoenberg, *Models*, 4.
235. Langlie, "Arnold Schoenberg as a Teacher," 96; and Arnold Schoenberg, *Fundamentals of Musical Composition*, ed. Gerald Strang and Leonard Stein (London: Faber, 1967), 95.
236. Knight, "Classes with Schoenberg," 141–42.
237. Perlis, "Interview with Gerald Strang," 29.
238. In 1942 Strang had copies of the manuscript printed at the Golden West Music Press in Los Angeles. A year later Schirmer published an enlarged edition. In 1972 Belmont Music Publishers printed a third revised edition. Gordon Root is currently preparing a new comprehensive critical edition of *Models* for Oxford University Press.
239. Schoenberg began *Fundamentals* in 1937. For more details see Strang, Editor's Preface to *Fundamentals*, xiii.
240. *ASGA*, 65. Translation by author.
241. Strang reported that many excerpts from Beethoven's Piano Sonatas can be traced back to Schoenberg's first "Composition I" course at USC in the summer of 1935. He recommended the first volume of Beethoven's Piano Sonatas as a necessary supplement to *Fundamentals*. Perlis, "Interview with Gerald Strang," 29–30; and Strang, Preface to *Fundamentals*, xiv.
242. *HHS*, 423.
243. Strang, Preface to *Fundamentals*, xiv.
244. Bestor, "Schoenberg Teaches," 3.
245. Plush, "Interview with Earl Kim."
246. *SI*, 377.
247. Schoenberg, "Wiesengrund," in Jacob, *Grundbegriffe*, vol. 2, 587. Translation by author.
248. Ibid., 586. See also *ASR*, 339.
249. Arnold Schoenberg to Ernst Krenek, 1 December 1939, in *ASL*, 210.
250. Interview with Dika Newlin, 26 May 2005.
251. Cage's Allemande is lost. Stein remembered this incident. See Perlis, "Interview with Leonard Stein," 4; and Cage to Schnebel, 11 December 1973.
252. Bruneau and Duke, *Jean Coulthard*, 61.
253. *SR*, 336–37.
254. Harrison's Suite comprises a "Prelude," "Aria," "Conductus," "Interlude" and "Rondo."
255. Lou Harrison, Preface to Suite for Piano (New York: C. F. Peters, 1964).
256. Richard Shaffer, "A Cross-Cultural Eclectic: Lou Harrison and His Music," *Percussive Notes* 29, no. 2 (December 1990): 45.
257. Vivian Perlis, "Interview with Lou Harrison."
258. Lautner, "Arnold Schoenberg in Kammern," 23.
259. Oscar Levant, *The Memoirs of an Amnesiac* (New York: Putnam's, 1965), 133. See also Levant quoted in Philip Scheuer, "Town Called Hollywood," *LAT*, 2 February 1941.
260. Oscar Levant, *The Unimportance of Being Oscar* (New York: Putnam, 1968), 147.
261. David Raksin, "Schoenberg as a Teacher," *Serial: Newsletter of the Friends of the Arnold Schoenberg Institute* 2, no. 1 (1988): 5.

262. Irene Kahn Atkins, "Interview with David Raksin" in *An Oral History*, vol. 1 (Los Angeles, 1976–78).
263. *SI*, 386.
264. Cage to Schnebel, 11 December 1973.
265. John Cage, "Mosaic," in *A Year from Monday* (Middletown: Wesleyan University Press, 1967), 49.
266. Castillo-Herreshoff, "Interview with Bernice Abrams Geiringer."
267. Perlis, "Interview with Gerald Strang," 39.
268. Ibid., 31.
269. Neff, "Interview with Patricia Carpenter," 7; and Castillo-Herreshoff, "Interview with Bernice Abrams Geiringer."
270. *SR*, 90.
271. Schoenberg wrote on behalf of Burkley, Carfagno, Coulthard, Estep, Harrison, Lautner, Levant, Newlin, Nixon, Rósza, Constance Shirley, Stein, and Strang, among others.
272. *HHS*, 377.
273. *SR*, 247.
274. Arnold Schoenberg, "Addendum," 254–56.
275. Heylbut, "The Odyssey," 355.
276. See Plush, "Interview with Earl Kim."
277. Russell, "Schoenberg the Teacher," 5–6.
278. Perlis, "Interview with Strang," 25.
279. Schoenberg quoted in Albert Goldberg, "Schoenberg Looks Backward – and Ahead," *LAT*, 26 September 1948.
280. Russell, "Schoenberg the Teacher," 5.
281. *SR*, 239, 243, 245, 257, 286.
282. Knight, "Classes with Schoenberg," 142.
283. Langlie, "Arnold Schoenberg as a Teacher," 118.
284. Perlis, "Interview with Gerald Strang," 69.
285. See, for instance, *SR*, 23.
286. Alderman, "Arnold Schoenberg at USC," 204.
287. Plush, "Interview with Earl Kim."
288. Ibid. *SR*, 307.
289. Knight, "Classes with Schoenberg," 156; *SR*, 45, 125; Plush, "Interview with Earl Kim"; and Harrison, Preface to *Suite*.
290. Arnold Schoenberg, "Vorschlag zur Errichtung eines zeitgemäßen Musikunterrichtsinstitutes," unpublished manuscript, ASC.
291. Arnold Schoenberg, "Arnold Schoenberg School of Composition," unpublished manuscript, ASC.
292. Arnold Schoenberg, "School for Soundmen," unpublished manuscript, ASC; and Arnold Schoenberg to Robert Hutchins, 2 June 1946, in *ASL*, 241. For more details see Sabine Feisst, "Arnold Schoenberg and the Cinematic Art," *MQ* 38, no. 1 (Spring 1999): 103–5.
293. Shoaf, "The Malkin-Schoenberg Correspondence," 218–20.
294. *ASLIB*, 323.
295. Arnold Schoenberg to Robert Sproul, 14 May 1936, LC.
296. *ASLIB*, 364.
297. Arnold Schoenberg, "Music Club" (n.d.), in "Memos and Letters concerning UCLA," unpublished manuscript, ASC.
298. Arnold Schoenberg, "Curriculum for Composers," in Scharenberg, *Überwinden*, 307.
299. *SR*, 203. Newlin, however, spoke of a "College of Composition."

300. *SR*, 40.
301. Arnold Schoenberg to Robert Sproul, 2 October 1937, in *ASL*, 203.
302. Arnold Schoenberg to Carl Engel, 12 December 1938, in Scharenberg, *Überwinden*, 304–5.
303. *SR*, 148, 164.
304. Several documents are included in *ASLIB*, 366.
305. *ASLIB*, 366. After Schoenberg's death many composers explored intersections between music and mathematics, and cross-disciplinary projects in the arts.
306. Stein quoted in Alderman, "I Remember Arnold Schoenberg," 57; and Arnold Schoenberg to Anton Webern, 8 July 1939, in *ASGA*, 66.
307. Knudsen quoted in Maurice Zam, "How Schoenberg Came to UCLA," *JASI* 3, no. 2 (October 1979): 224.
308. *Quellen zur Geschichte emigrierter Musiker 1933–1950*, ed. Horst Weber and Manuela Schwartz (Munich: Saur, 2003), vol. 1, 53.
309. Arnold Schoenberg to Robert Sproul, 14 May 1945. See *HHS*, 470–71.
310. Other speakers in the series were Virgil Thomson, Douglas Moore, Roger Sessions, Carlos Chávez, and Ernst Toch. Richard Hoffmann, "Schoenberg est vivant," *JASI* 1, no. 2 (February 1977): 65–67.
311. Arnold Schoenberg to Robert Sproul, 2 October 1937, in *ASL*, 202–3; Arnold Schoenberg to Josef Polnauer, 2 March 1939, WB. He never "directed the music department," as Stuckenschmidt claimed. See *HHS*, 469.
312. Roger Sessions, "Music in a Business Economy," in *Roger Sessions on Music*, ed. Edward Cone (Princeton: Princeton University Press, 1979), 164–65.
313. Perlis, "Interview with Leonard Stein," 6.
314. Arnold Schoenberg to Adolph Weiss, 30 April 1937, in George, "Adolph Weiss," 330; and Arnold Schoenberg to Anton Webern, 8 July 1939, in *ASGA*, 66.
315. Arnold Schoenberg to Fritz Stiedry, 25 August 1942, LC. Allen became the director of the UCLA Wind Band in 1935.
316. Arnold Schoenberg to H. H. Benedict, 1 June 1942, in *ASL*, 213–214.
317. Arnold Schoenberg, "Notes for an Autobiography," in *ASR*, 300. Schoenberg, however, officially taught at UCLA until February 1944 because UCLA owed him a sabbatical.
318. See Schoenberg's correspondence with Douglas Moore (Columbia), Robert Stuart (St. Louis Institute of Music), Robert Hutchins (University of Chicago), Archie Jones (University of Idaho), and Russell Miles (University of Illinois).
319. In 1941 Schoenberg became an honorary member of the MTNA.
320. *ASR*, 275–79.
321. *ASLIB*, 365.
322. "Eartraining Through Composing" and "How a Music Student Can Make a Living" were published in *Proceedings of the MTNA 1939* in 1940. The former article also appeared as "On the Appreciation of Music" in *Modern Music* in 1946,. See also *SI*, 377–82.
323. Compare Paul Pisk's articles on this subject: "Arnold Schoenberg as Teacher," in *American Society of University Composers: Proceedings of the Second Conference, April 1967*, ed. Hubert Howe (New York: ASUC/Columbia University, 1969), 51–53; "Arnold Schoenberg, the Teacher," *American Music Teacher* 24, no. 3 (January 1975): 12–13; "Memories of Schoenberg," *JASI* 1, no. 1 (October 1976): 39–44; Elliott Antokoletz, "A Survivor of the Vienna Schoenberg Circle: An Interview with Paul Pisk," *Tempo* 153 (1985): 15–21. See also Rosemary Hilmar, "Alban Berg's Studies with Schoenberg," *JASI* 8, no. 1 (June 1984): 7–30; and Ulrich Krämer, *Alban Berg als Schüler Arnold Schönbergs. Quellenstudien*

und Analysen zum Frühwerk (Vienna: Universal Edition, 1996); and "Schönbergs Kontrapunktlehre," *Bericht über den 3. Kongress der Internationalen Schönberg-Gesellschaft: "Arnold Schönberg – Neuerer der Musik." Duisburg, 24. bis 27. Februar 1993*, ed. Rudolf Stephan, Sigrid Wiesmann, and Matthias Schmidt (Vienna: Lafite, 1996), 147–61.

324. Arnold Schoenberg to Hugo Leichtentritt, 3 December 1938, in *ASL*, 207.
325. Virgil Thomson, "Atonality Today (I)," *New York Herald Tribune*, 29 January 1950.
326. Arnold Schoenberg to Ernst Krenek, 1 December 1939, in *ASL*, 210. See also Albert Goldberg, "Schoenberg Looks Backward and Ahead," *LAT*, 26 September 1948.
327. "I have to teach – beginners (!), as almost all are here, most of whom would be better off as quitters." Arnold Schoenberg to David Bach, 13 March 1935, in *ASR*, 258.
328. *SI*, 388.
329. Given how exorbitantly expensive Schoenberg's classes and lessons were, he was reliant upon the American equivalent of European aristocracy, just as composers had been in the eighteenth and nineteenth centuries. Leonard Stein suggested that "by American standards . . . he did all right. He bought the most elegant automobile he could get, a La Salle and wanted to have everything as nice as possible . . . they must have spent a lot of money on the kids, and the tennis business, and all the rest. But they never seemed to have denied themselves anything . . . they always had help in the house." Perlis, "Interview with Leonard Stein," 17. Considering that Schoenberg generously supported his relatives and friends in Europe before and after the war, his dissatisfaction with his monetary remuneration before 1944 has to be taken with caution.
330. Marc Blitzstein, "Forecast and Review: Talk – Music – Dance," *MM* 11, no. 1 (November–December 1933): 35.
331. Arnold Schoenberg, "Some Problems for the Educators," in *ASSG*, 330–36.
332. Allan Kozinn, "Guardian of the Schoenberg Flame," *NYT*, 10 May 1985.
333. *SI*, 226.
334. Rosenman's score for the *The Cobweb* (1955) uses dodecaphony and the instrumentation of Schoenberg's Piano Concerto. In 1965 Tremblay, who blended serial principles with jazz, founded the Los Angeles "School for the Discovery and Advancement of New Serial Techniques" and taught serialism to film and television composers. Cage gave Schoenberg credit for his novel rhythmic structures and utilization of chance operations. Eddie McGuire and Stephen Arnold, "John Cage in Conversation," *Cencrastus* 21 (Summer 1985): 7.

CHAPTER 7

1. See, for instance, "Arnold Schoenberg, 'Einstein of Music,' to Conduct San Diego Symphony Orchestra," *Sunday Union*, 24 July 1938. Nicolas Slonimsky endorsed Schoenberg as "the Einstein of music, whose rigorous technique of composition in 12 tones has profoundly influenced musical composition everywhere," in his article "Musical Emigrants," *CSM*, 23 September 1939. Dimitri Mitropoulos stated that Schoenberg "did for music in the twentieth century what Einstein did for science," and that "Schoenberg was absolutely necessary to our generation: for in synchronizing the Einstein Law of Relativity to the Art of Music, he fulfilled the basic function of art, which is to reproduce a contemporary image of our civilization." "From the Mail Pouch: Schoenberg," *NYT*, 19 August 1951. See also Ernst Krenek, "The Idiom and the Technic," *MM* 21, no. 3 (March–April 1944): 133.
2. Nicolas Slonimsky, "Modern Immortals," *Saturday Review of Literature*, 30 September 1950, 54.
3. Jennifer DeLapp, "Copland in the Fifties: Music and Ideology in the McCarthy Era" (Ph.D. diss., University of Michigan, 1997), 104–5.

4. Commissioned by the Alice M. Ditson Fund of Columbia University, Riegger's Third Symphony won the 1948 New York Music Critics' Circle Award and a Naumburg Foundation Recording Award. Babbitt's Composition for Four Instruments won the 1949 New York Music Critics' Circle Award.
5. Albert Goldberg, "The Sounding Board: Schoenberg Hall Dedicated at UCLA," *LAT*, 16 May 1956.
6. Raymond Ericson, "Schoenberg's Legacy," *NYT*, 10 February 1974.
7. Mitropoulos's 1958 Piano Concerto performance with the New York Philharmonic and Gould was recorded live, but only released in 1986 by Nuova Era.
8. All-Schoenberg concerts were more common in the realm of chamber music.
9. In Boulez's rug concerts the audience could listen to music "curled up on the carpet." Louis Snyder, "Boulez: Flooring the Music Lovers: N. Y. Philharmonic Plays to a Rug-Bound Audience in Seatless Avery Fisher Hall," *CSM*, 19 June 1974.
10. These include Wayne Barlow (Eastman); Mark Brunswick and Fritz Jahoda (City College, New York); Patricia Carpenter (Barnard and Columbia); Ingolf Dahl (USC);Emil Danenberg and Richard Hoffmann (Oberlin); Marcel Dick (Cleveland Institute); Frederick Dorian (Carnegie Institute); Felix Galimir (Juilliard and Mannes Schools); Hugh Hodgson (University of Georgia); Earl Kim and Leon Kirchner (Harvard); Rudolf Kolisch (University of Wisconsin and New England Conservatory); Ernst Krenek (Vassar and Hamline); Eugene Lehner (New England Conservatory); Dika Newlin (Drew, North Texas, and Virginia Commonwealth Universities); Paul Pisk (University of Redlands, and University of Texas, and Washington University, St. Louis); Rudolf Serkin (Curtis); Roger Sessions (University of California, Berkeley, and Princeton); Leonard Stein (USC, UCLA, and CalArts), Edward Steuermann and Jacob Lateiner (Juilliard); and Gerald Strang (Long Beach City College and UCLA).
11. The Juilliard Quartet made two sets of recordings for Columbia; the second set, dating from the 1970s, includes the D major Quartet. In the 1980s the LaSalle Quartet recorded for Deutsche Grammophon, in addition to all the quartets, *Verklärte Nacht*, *Ode*, and the String Trio.
12. Schoenberg students who performed his piano works in America include Patricia Carpenter, John Crown, Emil Danenberg, Hugh Hodgson, Warren Langlie, Oscar Levant, Natalie Limonick, Dika Newlin, Béla Rósza, Edward Steuermann, Leonard Stein, and James Sykes.
13. Gould recorded the Piano Concerto twice, the first time with the New York Philharmonic under Mitropoulos and the second with the CBC Symphony Orchestra under Robert Craft. He made premiere recordings of Two Songs, op. 1 (with Donald Gramm), and Two Ballads, op. 12 and "Am Strande" (both with Helen Vanni). In 1995 CBC reissued Gould's 1952 recordings of opp. 11 and 25, together with Berg's Sonata and Webern's Variations. In 1963 he delivered the University of Cincinnati's Corbett Music Lecture, entitled "Arnold Schoenberg: A Perspective," which was published a year later.
14. Emanuel Ax, "The Brahms-Schoenberg Connection," *Piano Today*, 15, no. 2 (1995): 66.
15. Olin Downes, "Ciccolini, Pianist, Heard at Concert," *NYT*, 3 November 1950; and "Schoenberg Work Presented Here," *NYT*, 14 April 1950; Harold Schonberg, "Krasner, with Philharmonic, Performs Difficult Violin Concerto by Schoenberg," *NYT*, 1 December 1952; and "Schoenberg – Was He Devil or Saint?" *NYT*, 3 February 1974; and Donal Henahan, "In Vienna They Neglect Schoenberg, at Tanglewood They Overlook Ives," *NYT*, 23 June 1974.
16. John Rockwell, "Signs of Vitality in New Music," *NYT*, 10 February 1980; Donal Henahan, "Schoenberg's Twelve-Tone Music Bothers Us No Longer," *NYT*, 4 April 1982; Richard Taruskin, "The Dark Side of Modern Music," *New Republic*, 5 September 1988; and John Rockwell, "Reactionary Musical Modernists," *NYT*, 11 September 1988.

17. Harold Schonberg, "Schoenberg – Was He Devil or Saint?"; Harold Blumenfeld, "A Controversial Look at a Controversial Genius," *LAT*, 22 September 1974; Bernard Holland, "Listen with the Ear, Not the Mind," *NYT*, 20 December 1998; and Edward Rothstein, "Hearing the Operatic Moses as Schoenberg's Alter Ego," *NYT*, 15 February 1999.
18. Donal Henahan, "A Detour That Led to Nowhere," *NYT*, 11 February 1990; see also Harold Schonberg, "Music: Boulez Specialty," *NYT*, 17 April 1971.
19. See, for instance, Paul Hume, "A Paradox of Total Achievement: A True Musical Revolutionary," *Washington Post*, 8 September 1974; Harold Schonberg, "Schoenberg – Was He Devil or Saint?"; Bernard Holland, "Schoenberg before and after Serialism," *NYT*, 29 January 1990; and "Fake Nudity with Real Angst," *NYT*, 10 February 1999; and David Schiff, "A New Measure for Heroes in Music's Valhalla," *NYT*, 28 February 1999.
20. Joan Peyser, "Two Masters Who Were in Conflict: Music at Dartmouth," *NYT*, 8 September 1968; see also Harold Schonberg, "Schoenberg – Was He Devil or Saint?"; and Harold Blumenfeld, "A Controversial Look at a Controversial Genius."
21. John Rockwell, "Signs of Vitality in New Music"; and "Serialism since Schoenberg's Death," *NYT*, 12 July 1981; see also Donal Henahan, "A Detour That Led to Nowhere."
22. Irving Fine, "Composers in France," *NYT*, 4 June 1950; Virgil Thomson, "Atonality Today (I)," *New York Herald Tribune*, 29 January 1950; Nicolas Nabokov, "Festivals of the Twelve-Tone Row," *Saturday Review of Literature*, 13 January1950; and Paul Hume, "A Paradox of Total Achievement: A True Musical Revolutionary," *Washington Post*, 8 September 1974.
23. René Leibowitz, "Two Composers: A Letter from Hollywood," *Partisan Review* 7, no. 1 (1948): 361–65; Carter Harman, "Hot, Cool, and Gone," *NYT*, 31 July 1949; Peter Yates, "Arnold Schoenberg: Apostle of Atonality," *NYT*, 11 September 1949; K. Robert Schwarz, "In Contemporary Music, a House Still Divided," *NYT*, 3 August 1997; and Paul Griffiths, "Surviving the Siege, But Barely," *NYT*, 17 August 1997.
24. Kurt List, "Schoenberg and Strauss," *Kenyon Review* 7, no. 1 (1945): 63; Peter Yates, "Arnold Schoenberg: Apostle of Atonality"; L. O. Symkins, "Arnold Schoenberg's New World of Dodecaphonic Music," *Etude* 68, no. 9 (September 1950): 14.
25. Thanks to Austin Clarkson for invaluable information on Wolpe.
26. Perle claimed to have stumbled upon his serial theories in the summer of 1939 without any prior knowledge about dodecaphony. His assertion, however, lacks credibility, as he studied with Wesley LaViolette (1934–38) and Krenek (1940), both of whom were friends of Schoenberg. As a music student in Chicago, he would have had access to twelve-tone scores in Cowell's New Music Edition and articles on Schoenberg in *Modern Music* and the *Musical Quarterly*, which in 1936 published Richard Hill's seminal essay "Schoenberg's Tone Rows and the Tonal System of the Future."
27. In 1984 ASUC comprised some 900 members, issued newsletters, and disseminated its members' music in the form of scores (*ASUC Journal of Music Scores*), recordings (ASUC Record Series on the Advance label), and radio festivals. In 1988 the organization changed its name to Society of Composers Inc. (SCI) to delete the word "University," which suggested that its members' music was academic, and to admit academically unaffiliated members. Thanks to Bruce Taub for this information.
28. However, Copland's "Poet's Song" (1927) and Piano Variations (1930) document an early interest in serialism.
29. Aaron Copland, *Music and Imagination* (Cambridge: Harvard University Press, 1952), 75.
30. Aaron Copland, "Fantasy for Piano," *NYT*, 27 October 1957; and "Conversation with Copland," in *Perspectives on American Composers*, ed. Benjamin Boretz and Edward Cone (New York: Norton, 1971), 141.

31. Olin Downes, "Students in Paris Hiss Fete Concert," *NYT*, 21 May 1952.
32. From the 1950s Stravinsky frequently socialized with Krenek in Los Angeles and was familiar with his music and writings.
33. Anne Shreffler, "Ideologies of Serialism: Stravinsky's *Threni* and the Congress for Cultural Freedom," in *Music and Aesthetics of Modernity*, ed. Karol Berger and Anthony Newcomb (Cambridge: Harvard University Press, 2005), 217–45.
34. Gilbert Chase, *America's Music: From the Pilgrims to the Present*, 2nd rev. ed. (New York: McGraw-Hill, 1966), 620.
35. Charles Wuorinen, "The Outlook for Young Composers," *PNM* 1, no. 2 (Spring 1963): 57; and *Simple Composition*, 3; Milton Babbitt, "Who Cares If You Listen? [original title: The Composer as Specialist]," *High Fidelity* 8, no. 2 (February 1958): 38.
36. Brown had been accepted for study with Schoenberg at the Aspen Music Festival in the summer of 1951. When Schoenberg canceled his participation in Aspen due to health problems, he agreed to teach Brown twice a week at his home. Nothing came of it because Schoenberg died soon thereafter. Arnold Schoenberg to Earle Brown, 27 June 1951, LC.
37. Wuorinen, "The Outlook," 54; and Gunther Schuller, "Schoenberg's Influence," in *TASC*, 260; see also Andrea Olmsted, *Conversations with Roger Sessions* (Boston: Northeastern University Press, 1987), 237.
38. Brown quoted in Amy Beal, *New Music, New Allies: American Experimental Music in West Germany from the Zero Hour to Reunification* (Berkeley: University of California Press, 2006), 140; on this issue see also *The Boulez-Cage Correspondence*, ed. Jean-Jacques Nattiez, trans. Robert Samuels (Cambridge: Cambridge University Press, 1993), 48.
39. Rochberg wrote a rebuttal to Boulez's polemical article "Schoenberg Is Dead," and wanted to found a Schoenberg Society in Philadelphia in 1955. See George Rochberg, *The Aesthetics of Survival: A Composer's View of Twentieth-Century Music*, ed. William Bolcom (Ann Arbor: University of Michigan Press, 1984), 29–45; George Rochberg to Edward Steuermann, 17 October and 12 December 1955, LC; and George Rochberg, "Reflections on Schoenberg," *PNM* 11, no. 2 (Spring–Summer 1973): 64.
40. Rochberg quoted in Allan Kozinn, "Concert Connects New with Newer," *NYT*, 28 April 2000.
41. American composers who have used dodecaphonic principles in their music in recent years include, among many others, Bruce Arnold, Babbitt, Robert Morris, Frank Oteri, Bruce Quaglia, Roger Reynolds, Bruce Taub, and Charles Wuorinen. For more information on this subject, see Joseph Straus, *Twelve-Tone Music in America* (Cambridge: Cambridge University Press, 2009), 157–73, 202–6.
42. I would like to thank Hayes Biggs, John Evans, Frank Oteri, Bruce Quaglia, Bruce Taub, and Marina Voyskun for information on this issue. See K. Robert Schwarz, "In Contemporary Music, a House Still Divided," *NYT*, 3 August 1997.
43. For more details see Sabine Feisst, "Echoes of Schoenberg's *Pierrot lunaire* in American Music," in *Schoenberg's Chamber Music, Schoenberg's World*, ed. James K. Wright and Alan Gilmor (Hillsdale: Pendragon, 2009), 173–92.
44. Symkins, "Arnold Schoenberg's New World," 13.
45. Schoenberg described this talk as a "superficial explanation" of the twelve-tone method, which he had written against his "'free' will." See Arnold Schoenberg, "Protest on Trademark," *NYT*, 15 January 1950.
46. Richard Hill, "Schoenberg's Tone-Rows and the Tonal System of the Future," *MQ* 22, no. 1 (January 1936): 30–31. See also Schoenberg's reaction to this article: "Schoenberg's Tone-Rows," in *SI*, 213.

47. Ernst Krenek, *Music Here and Now* (New York: Norton, 1939); and *Studies in Counterpoint Based on the Twelve-Tone Technique* (New York: Schirmer, 1940).
48. George Perle, "Evolution of the Tone Row: The Twelve-Tone Modal System," *Music Review* 2 (1942): 273–87; and "Twelve-Tone Tonality," *Monthly Musical Record* 43 (1943): 175–79.
49. Leibowitz's study was first issued in French in 1947 as *Schoenberg et son école* and was translated into English by Dika Newlin. Leibowitz, who published between 1945 and 1952 more than a dozen articles and five books on Schoenberg, Berg, and Webern, developed a friendship with Schoenberg, which, however, quickly ended over Leibowitz's plagiarism, alterations, and unauthorized performances and recordings of Schoenberg's works. See Sabine Meine, *Ein Zwölftöner in Paris. Studien zu Biographie und Wirkung von René Leibowitz (1913–1972)* (Augsburg: Wißner, 2000).
50. Aaron Copland, "The World of A-Tonality," *NYT*, 27 November 1949. Copland, however, declared the book to be one of the ten best books he had read in 1949. "The Best Books I Read This Year – Twelve Distinguished Opinions," *NYT*, 4 December 1949.
51. Milton Babbitt, "Review: René Leibowitz, *Schoenberg et son école* and *Qu'est-ce que la musique de douze sons?*" *JAMS* 3, no. 1 (Spring 1950): 57–60.
52. Between 1946, the year of *Modern Music*'s demise, and 1957, the inaugural year of the *Journal of Music Theory*, American music theorists often published their research in such British journals as *The Score, Music Review,* and *Tempo*. *Perspectives of New Music* was founded in 1962.
53. Thomson argued that music without a pitch center (atonal and dodecaphonic music) lacks meaning and coherence, and blamed Schoenberg for advancing theories that contaminated the course of music history. Thomson accused Schoenberg of not "fully comprehending tonality's nature, causes, and history." Primarily concerned with Schoenberg's theories, Thomson displays little knowledge of Schoenberg's compositions, which he sometimes confuses with each other. Aside from numerous unsubstantiated claims, the book contains many factual and typographical errors. William Thomson, *Schoenberg's Error* (Philadelphia: University of Pennsylvania Press, 1999), 50.
54. Fred Lerdahl, "Cognitive Constraints of Compositional Systems," in *Generative Processes in Music*, ed. John Sloboda (Oxford: Clarendon Press, 1988), 231–59.
55. Edward Cone, "Beyond Analysis," *PNM* 6, no. 1 (Fall–Winter 1967): 33–51; Joseph Kerman, "How We Got into Analysis, and How to Get Out," *Critical Inquiry* 7, no. 2 (Winter 1980): 311–31; Leo Treitler, "Structural and Critical Analysis," in *Musicology in the 1980s*, ed. D. Kern Holoman and Claude Palisca (New York: Da Capo, 1982), 67–77; Ernst Krenek, "Some Current Terms," *PNM* 4, no. 2 (Spring–Summer 1966): 84; George Perle, "Babbitt, Lewin, and Schoenberg: A Critique," *PNM* 2, no. 1 (Fall–Winter 1963): 120–27; and George Rochberg, "Reflections on Schoenberg," *PNM* 11, no. 2 (Spring–Summer 1973): 60. Rochberg's 1955 *The Hexachord and Its Relationship to the Twelve-Tone Row* was dismissed by Babbitt, Perle, and others for its dated information.
56. Treitler, "Structural and Critical Analysis," 71–75.
57. Schoenberg's 1932 analysis was translated into English and published by Claudio Spies as "Analysis of the Four Orchestral Songs [lecture of 1932]," in *PNM* 3, no. 2 (Spring–Summer 1965): 1–21.
58. George Perle, *Serial Composition and Atonality: An Introduction to the Music of Schoenberg, Berg and Webern* (Berkeley: University of California Press, 1962), 9–35; and David Lewin, "Re Intervallic Relations between Two Collections of Notes," *Journal of Music Theory* 3, no. 2 (1959): 298–301.

59. Ethan Haimo, "Atonality, Analysis, and the Intentional Fallacy," *Music Theory Spectrum* 18, no. 2 (Fall 1999): 167–99; George Perle, "Pitch-Class Set Analysis: An Evaluation," *Journal of Musicology* 8, no. 2 (Spring 1990): 151–72; and Richard Taruskin, "Reply to van den Toorn" *In Theory Only* 10, no. 3 (October 1987): 56.
60. Dika Newlin, *Bruckner, Mahler, Schoenberg* (New York: King's Crown Press, 1947), 10.
61. Joseph Auner, "Schoenberg's Compositional and Aesthetic Transformations, 1910–1913: The Genesis of *Die glückliche Hand*" (Ph.D. diss., University of Chicago, 1991); Elizabeth Keathley, "Revisioning Musical Modernism: Arnold Schoenberg, Marie Pappenheim, and *Erwartung*'s New Woman" (Ph.D. diss., State University of New York, Stony Brook, 1999); and Bryan Simms, *The Atonal Music of Arnold Schoenberg* (New York: Oxford University Press, 2000).
62. Schenker's theories gained popularity after World War II, as they were straightforward tools for the analysis of tonal music and successfully disseminated by Schenker's most prominent disciples who had immigrated to America before 1945. For more details see Nicolas Cook, *The Schenker Project: Culture, Race, and Music Theory in Fin-de-siècle Vienna* (New York: Oxford University Press, 2007).
63. Arnold Schoenberg, "New Music, Outmoded Music, Style and Idea," in *SI*, 122–23. See, for instance, Charlotte Cross, "Three Levels of 'Idea' in Schoenberg's Thought and Writings," *Current Musicology* 30 (1980): 24–36; and Patricia Carpenter and Severine Neff, "Schoenberg's Philosophy of Composition: Thoughts on the 'Musical Idea and Its Presentation,'" in *Constructive Dissonance: Arnold Schoenberg and the Transformation of Twentieth-Century Culture*, ed. Juliane Brand and Christopher Hailey (Berkeley: University of California Press, 1997), 146–59.
64. See, for instance, Patricia Carpenter, "*Grundgestalt* as Tonal Function," *Music Theory Spectrum* 5, no. 1 (April 1983): 15–38; and David Epstein, *Beyond Orpheus* (Cambridge: MIT Press, 1979), 17–33.
65. In 1939 Schoenberg stated: "What distinguishes art from science is: that here there should not be principles of the kind one has to use on principle: that the one 'narrowly' defines what must be left 'wide open' [in the other?]; that musical logic does not answer to 'if-, then-,' but enjoys making use of the possibilities excluded by if-then." See *ASL*, 210.
66. The Schoenberg Institute sponsored a journal, conferences, concerts, and exhibitions. In the 1990s USC incensed Schoenberg's children when it wanted to begin using the Schoenberg Institute for purposes unrelated to Schoenberg research and performance to get more "bang for the buck." The conflict led to a lawsuit, which Schoenberg's family won, and to the institute's relocation to Vienna in 1998. Mark Swed, "Now He's the Pride of Vienna: Composer Arnold Schoenberg's Nachlass Leaves L. A. for a City That Once Shunned Him," *LAT*, 21 June 1998; see also Therese Muxeneder, "Ethik des Bewahrens. Exil und Rückkehr des Schönberg-Nachlasses," in *Kulturelle Räume und ästhetische Universalität. Musik und Musiker im Exil*, ed. Claus-Dieter Krohn, Erwin Rotermund et al. (Munich: Edition Text + Kritik, 2008), 44–66. Following the Schoenberg family's vision of straightforward, technology-enhanced access to their father's legacy, the Viennese Schönberg Center made available numerous documents, including manuscripts, letters, recordings, and films, on its impressive website and on such other popular sites as YouTube.

Bibliography

Abel, Angelika. *Musikästhetik der klassischen Moderne: Thomas Mann, Theodor W. Adorno, Arnold Schönberg*. Munich: Fink, 2003.

Adorno, Theodor W. *Gesammelte Schriften*. Ed. Rolf Tiedemann. 23 vols. Darmstadt: Wissenschaftliche Buchgesellschaft, 1998.

———. *Essays on Music*. Ed. Richard Leppert, trans. Susan Gillespie. Berkeley: University of California Press, 2002.

Alderman, Pauline. "Schoenberg at USC." *JASI* 5 (November 1981): 203–11..

———. *We Build a School of Music*. Los Angeles: Alderman Book Committee, University of Southern California, 1989.

Angermann, Klaus, ed. *Paul Dessau: Von Geschichte gezeichnet*. Hofheim, Germany: Wolke, 1994.

Antokoletz, Elliott. "A Survivor of the Vienna Schoenberg Circle: An Interview with Paul Pisk." *Tempo* 153 (1985): 15–21.

Arendt, Hannah. *The Jew as Pariah: Jewish Identity and Politics in the Modern Age*. Ed. Ron H. Feldman. New York: Grove, 1978.

Armitage, Merle, ed. *Schoenberg*. New York: Schirmer, 1937.

Auner, Joseph. "Schoenberg's Handel Concerto and the Ruins of Tradition." *JAMS* 49, no. 2 (Summer 1996): 222–36.

———. "Schoenberg and His Public in 1930: The Six Pieces for Male Chorus, Op. 35." In *Schoenberg and His World*, ed. Walter Frisch, 85–125. Princeton: Princeton University Press, 1999.

Babbitt, Milton. "Who Cares If You Listen?" *High Fidelity* 8, no. 2 (February 1958): 38–40.

———. *Words about Music*. Ed. Stephen Dembski and Joseph N. Straus. Madison: University of Wisconsin Press, 1987.

———. "The Function of the Set Structure in the Twelve-Tone System." Ph.D. diss., Princeton University, 1992.

Bahr, Ehrhard. *Weimar on the Pacific: German Exile Culture in Los Angeles and the Crisis of Modernism*. Berkeley: University of California Press, 2007.

Bailey, Walter. *Programmatic Elements in the Works of Schoenberg*. Studies in Musicology 74. Ann Arbor: UMI Research Press, 1984.

———. "'Will Schoenberg be a New York Fad?' The 1914 American Premiere of Schoenberg's String Quartet in D Minor." *American Music* 26, no. 1 (Spring 2008): 37–73.

Bailey, Walter, ed. *The Arnold Schoenberg Companion*. Westport, CT: Greenwood, 1998.

Beal, Amy. *New Music, New Allies: American Experimental Music in West Germany from the Zero Hour to Reunification*. Berkeley: University of California Press, 2006.

Beller, Steven. *Vienna and the Jews, 1838–1938: A Cultural History*. Cambridge: Cambridge University Press, 1989.

Berman, Aaron. *Nazism, the Jews, and American Zionism: 1933–1948*. Detroit: Wayne State University Press, 1990.

Bernard, Jonathan. "The Legacy of the Second Viennese School." In *Schoenberg, Berg, and Webern: A Companion to the Second Viennese School*, ed. Bryan Simms, 315–83. Westport, CT: Greenwood, 1999.

Bernstein, David. "John Cage, Arnold Schoenberg, and the Musical Idea." In *John Cage: Music, Philosophy and Intention, 1933–1950*, ed. David Patterson, 15–45. New York: Routledge, 2002.

———. "Themes and Variations: John Cage's Studies with Arnold Schönberg." *JASC* 4 (2002): 325–38.

Bernstein, Martin. "On the Genesis of Schoenberg's Suite for School Orchestra." *JASI* 11, no. 2 (November 1988): 158–62.

Bestor, Dorothea N. "Schoenberg Teaches: An Interview with Arnold Schoenberg." *Musical Review* 3 (October 1934): 3, 6.

Bick, Sally. "Composers on the Cultural Front: Aaron Copland and Hanns Eisler in Hollywood." Ph.D. diss., Yale University, 2001.

Blake, David, ed. *Hanns Eisler: A Miscellany*. Edinburgh: Harwood, 1995.

Block, Geoffrey, and Peter Burkholder. *Charles Ives and the Classical Tradition*. New Haven: Yale University Press, 1996.

Bohlman, Philip. *Jewish Music and Modernity*. New York: Oxford University Press, 2008.

Bohlman, Philip, ed. *Jewish Musical Modernism, Old and New*. Chicago: University of Chicago Press, 2008.

Boretz, Benjamin, and Edward Cone, eds. *Perspectives on American Composers*. New York: Norton, 1972.

———. *Perspectives on Schoenberg and Stravinsky*. Rev. ed. New York: Norton, 1972.

Boulez, Pierre. *Notes of an Apprenticeship*. Trans. Herbert Weinstock. New York: Knopf, 1968.

Brand, Juliane, and Christopher Hailey, eds. *Constructive Dissonance: Arnold Schoenberg and the Transformation of Twentieth-Century Culture*. Berkeley: University of California Press, 1997.

Brand, Juliane, Christopher Hailey, and Donald Harris, eds. *The Berg-Schoenberg Correspondence: Selected Letters*. New York: Norton, 1988.

Brecht, Bertolt. *Journals*. Ed. John Willet, trans. Hugh Rorrison. New York: Routledge, 1993.

Brinkmann, Reinhold, and Christoph Wolff, eds. *Driven into Paradise: The Musical Migration from Nazi Germany to the United States*. Berkeley: University of California Press, 1999.

———. *Music of My Future: The Schoenberg Quartets and Trio*. Cambridge, Mass.: Harvard University Press, 2000.

Brody, Martin. "'Music for the Masses': Milton Babbitt's Cold War Music Theory." *MQ* 77, no. 2 (1993): 161–92.

———. "The Scheme of the Whole: Black Mountain and the Course of American Modern Music." In *Black Mountain College: Experiment in Art*, ed. Vincent Katz, 239–67. Cambridge, Mass.: MIT Press, 2003.

Brooks, William. "The Americas, 1945–70." In *Music and Society: Modern Times: From World War I to the Present*, ed. Robert Morgan, 309–48. Englewood Cliffs, NJ: Prentice Hall, 1994.

Bruneau, William, and David G. Duke. *Jean Coulthard: A Life in Music*. Vancouver: Ronsdale, 2005.

Brunswick, Mark. "Refugee Musicians in America." *Saturday Review of Literature*, 26 January 1946, 9, 50–51.

Buhrmann, Dirk. *Arnold Schönbergs "Ode to Napoleon Buonaparte" op. 41 (1942)*. Hildesheim, Germany: Georg Olms, 2002.

Byron, Avior. "Demystifying Schoenberg's Conducting." *Mid-Ad: Israel Studies in Musicology Online* 1 (2006): 1–15.

———. "Schoenberg as Performer: An Aesthetics in Practice." Ph.D. diss., Royal Holloway College, University of London, 2007.

Cage, John. "Mosaic." In *A Year from Monday*, 49. Middletown, CT: Wesleyan University Press, 1967.

Cahn, Steven J. "Variations in Manifold Time: Historical Consciousness in the Music and Writings of Arnold Schoenberg." Ph.D. diss., State University of New York at Stony Brook, 1996.

———. "Dépasser l'universalisme: Une écoute particulariste d'*Un survivant de Varsovie* op. 46 et du *Kol nidre* op. 39 de Schoenberg." *Ostinato rigore. Revue internationale d'études musicales* 17, no. 1 (2001): 221–34.

———. "'Kol nidre' in America." *JASC* 4 (2002): 203–18.

———. " *Kol nidre*, op. 39." In *Arnold Schönberg. Interpretationen seiner Werke*, ed. Gerold Gruber, 49–66. Laaber: Laaber, 2002.

———. "On the Representation of Jewish Identity and Historical Consciousness in Schönberg's Religious Thought." *JASC* 5 (2003): 93–108.

———. "Schoenberg, the Viennese-Jewish Experience and Its Aftermath." In *The Cambridge Companion to Schoenberg*, ed. Jennifer Shaw and Joseph Auner, 191–206. Cambridge: Cambridge University Press, 2010.

Calico, Joy. "Schoenberg's Symbolic Remigration: *A Survivor from Warsaw* in Postwar West Germany." *Journal of Musicology* 26, no. 1 (Winter 2009): 17–43.

———. "Schoenberg as Teacher." In *The Cambridge Companion to Schoenberg*, ed. Jennifer Shaw and Joseph Auner, 137–46. Cambridge: Cambridge University Press, 2010.

Campbell, Alan. "Roger Sessions' Adoption of the Twelve-Tone Method." Ph.D. diss., City University of New York, 1990.

Carroll, Brendan. *The Last Prodigy: A Biography of Erich Wolfgang Korngold*. Portland: Amadeus, 1997.

Carpenter, Patricia. "*Grundgestalt* as Tonal Function." *Music Theory Spectrum* 5, no. 1 (April 1983): 15–38.

———. "Musical Form and Musical Idea: Reflections on a Theme of Schoenberg, Hanslick, and Kant." In *Music and Civilization: Essays in Honor of Paul Henry Lang*, ed. Edmond Strainchamps and Maria Maniates with Christopher Hatch, 394–427. New York: Norton, 1984.

———. "Schoenberg's Theory of Composition." In *The Arnold Schoenberg Companion*, ed. Walter Bailey, 209–22. Westport, CT: Greenwood, 1998.

Cherlin, Michael. "Memory and Historical Trope in Schoenberg's String Trio." *JAMS* 51, no. 3 (Fall 1998): 559–602.

———. *Schoenberg's Musical Imagination*. Cambridge: Cambridge University Press, 2007.

Clarkson, Austin, ed. *On the Music of Stefan Wolpe*. Hillsdale, NY: Pendragon, 2003.

Clifford, James. "Diasporas." *Cultural Anthropology* 9, no. 9 (August 1994): 303–38.

Conlon, Colleen. "The Lessons of Arnold Schoenberg in Teaching the Musikalische Gedanke." Ph.D. diss., University of North Texas, 2009.

Copland, Aaron. *Our New Music: Leading Composers in Europe and America*. New York: McGraw-Hill, 1941.

———. *Music and Imagination*. Cambridge, Mass.: Harvard University Press, 1952.

Cowell, Henry. "Who Is the Greatest Living Composer?" *Northwest Musical Herald* 7, no. 5 (1933): 7.

Craft, Robert. *Down a Path of Wonder: Memoirs of Stravinsky, Schoenberg and Other Cultural Figures*. Norfolk: Naxos Books, 2006.

Crawford, Dorothy. "Peter Yates and the Performance of Schoenberg Chamber Music at 'Evenings on the Roof.'" *JASI* 22, no. 2 (November 1989): 175–201.

———. *Evenings On and Off the Roof: Pioneering Concerts in Los Angeles, 1939–1971*. Berkeley: University of California Press, 1995.

———. "Arnold Schoenberg in Los Angeles." *MQ* 86, no. 1 (Spring 2002): 6–48.

Cross, Charlotte. "Three Levels of 'Idea' in Schoenberg's Thought and Writings." *Current Musicology* 30 (Fall 1980): 24–36.

Cross, Charlotte, and Russell Berman, eds. *Political and Religious Ideas in the Works of Arnold Schoenberg*. New York: Garland, 2000.

———. *Schoenberg and Words: The Modernist Years*. New York: Garland, 2000.

Dahlhaus, Carl. *Schoenberg and the New Music*. Trans. Derrick Puffett and Alfred Clayton. Cambridge: Cambridge University Press, 1987.

Daniel, Oliver. *Stokowski: A Counterpoint of View*. New York: Dodd and Mead, 1982.

Danuser, Hermann. "Zu Schönbergs Vortragslehre." In *Die Wiener Schule in der Musikgeschichte des 20. Jahrhunderts*, ed. Rudolf Stephan, and Sigrid Wiesmann, 253–59. Vienna: Lafite, 1986.

Davis, Mike. *City of Quartz: Excavating the Future in Los Angeles*. New York: Vintage, 1992.

Dawidowicz, Lucy. *The Jewish Presence: Essays on Identity and History*. New York: Holt, Rinehart and Winston, 1977.

DeLapp, Jennifer. "Copland in the Fifties: Music and Ideology in the McCarthy Era." Ph.D. diss., University of Michigan, 1997.

———. "Aaron Copland and the Politics of Twelve-Tone Composition in the Early Cold War United States." *Journal of Musicological Research* 27, no. 1 (January 2008): 31–62.

Dibelius, Ulrich. *Herausforderung Schönberg – Was die Musik des Jahrhunderts veränderte*. Munich: Hanser, 1974.

Dudeque, Norton. *Theory and Analysis in the Writings of Arnold Schoenberg*. Aldershot: Ashgate, 2006.

Dümling, Albrecht, ed. *Verteidigung des musikalischen Fortschritts. Brahms und Schönberg*. Hamburg: Argument, 1990.

Edwards, Allen. *Flawed Words and Stubborn Sounds: A Conversation with Elliott Carter*. New York: Norton, 1971.

Eisenstadt, Shmuel. *Jewish Civilization: The Jewish Historical Experience in a Comparative Perspective*. Albany: State University of New York Press, 1992.

Eisler, Hanns. *Musik und Politik, 1924–1948*. Ed. Stephanie Eisler and Manfred Grabs. 3 vols. Leipzig: VEB Deutscher Verlag für Musik, 1973–83.

Ennulat, Egbert, ed. *Arnold Schoenberg Correspondence: A Collection of Translated and Annotated Letters Exchanged with Guido Adler, Pablo Casals, Emanuel Feuermann, and Olin Downes*. Metuchen, NJ: Scarecrow, 1991.

Epstein, David. *Beyond Orpheus: Studies in Musical Structure*. Cambridge, Mass.: MIT Press, 1979.

Feisst, Sabine. "Henry Cowell und Arnold Schönberg: Eine unbekannte Freundschaft." *AfMw* 55, no. 1 (1998): 57–71.

———. "Arnold Schoenberg and the Cinematic Art." *MQ* 38, no. 1 (Spring 1999): 93–113.

———. "Arnold Schoenberg and America." In *Schoenberg and His World*, ed. Walter Frisch, 285–336. Princeton: Princeton University Press, 1999.

———. "Dane Rudhyar on Arnold Schoenberg: About European Seeds in America." *20th-Century Music* 6, no. 2 (February 1999): 13–17.

———. "Zur Rezeption von Schönbergs Schaffen in Amerika vor 1933." *JASC* 4 (2002): 281–93.

———. "Arnold Schoenberg – Modernist or Romantic?" In *Engaged Romanticism: Romanticism as Praxis*, ed. Mark Lussier and Bruce Matsunaga, 196–207. Newcastle upon Tyne: Cambridge Scholars Press, 2008.

———. "Echoes of Schoenberg's *Pierrot lunaire* in America." In *I feel the Air of Another Planet: Schoenberg's Chamber Music, Schoenberg's World*, ed. James K. Wright and Alan Gillmor, 169–86. Hillsdale, NY: Pendragon, 2009.

———. "Schoenberg in America Reconsidered: A Historiographic Investigation." In *Music's Intellectual History*, ed. Zdravko Blažeković and Barbara Dobbs-Mackenzie, 409–25. New York: Rilm, 2009.

———. "Schoenberg Reception in America, 1933–1951." In *The Cambridge Companion to Schoenberg*, ed. Jennifer Shaw and Joseph Auner, 247–57. Cambridge: Cambridge University Press, 2010.

Fermi, Laura. *Illustrious Immigrants: The Intellectual Migration from Europe, 1930–41*. Chicago: University of Chicago Press, 1968.

Fetthauer, Sophie. *Musikverlage im "Dritten Reich" und im Exil*. Hamburg: von Bockel, 2004.

Finney, Ross Lee. *Thinking about Music: The Collected Writings of Ross Lee Finney*. Ed. Frederic Goossen. Tuscaloosa: University of Alabama Press, 1991.

———. *Profile of a Lifetime: A Musical Autobiography*. Ed. Don Gillespie. New York: C. F. Peters, 1992.

Föllmi, Beat. *Tradition als hermeneutische Kategorie bei Arnold Schönberg*. Bern: Haupt, 1996.

———. "'I cannot remember ev'rything.' Eine narratologische Analyse von Arnold Schönbergs Kantate *A Survivor from Warsaw*." *AfMw* 60, no. 1 (1998): 28–56.

———. "Intertextualität und Distanz als Mittel zur politischen Aussage. Arnold Schönbergs *Ode to Napoleon Buonaparte*." *JASC* 4 (2002): 93–103.

Folts, Martha. "Arnold Schoenberg's 'Variations on a Recitative' Opus 40 – An Analysis." *Diapason* 65 (September 1974): 4–9.

Forte, Allen. *The Structure of Atonal Music*. New Haven: Yale University Press, 1973.

Franklin, Peter. "Modernism, Deception, and Musical Others: Los Angeles circa 1940." In *Western Music and Its Others: Difference, Representation and Appropriation in Music*, ed. Georgina Born and David Hesmondhalgh, 143–62. Berkeley: University of California Press, 2000.

Friedrich, Otto. *City of Nets: A Portrait of Hollywood in the 1940s*. New York: Harper and Row, 1986.

Frisch, Walter. *Brahms and the Principle of Developing Variation*. Berkeley: University of California Press, 1984.

———. *The Early Works of Arnold Schoenberg, 1893–1908*. Berkeley: University of California Press, 1993.

Frisch, Walter, ed. *Schoenberg and His World*. Princeton: Princeton University Press, 1999.

Frühauf, Tina. *The Organ and Its Music in German-Jewish Culture*. New York: Oxford University Press, 2008.

Gallard, Jean-Claude. "Le dernier Schoenberg: synthèse et dépassement." Ph.D. diss., Université de Paris VIII, 2005.

Geiger, Friedrich, and Thomas Schäfer, eds. *Exilmusik. Komponisten während der NS- Zeit*. Hamburg: von Bockel, 1999.

George, William B. "Adolph Weiss." Ph.D. diss., University of Iowa, 1971.

Guilbaut, Serge. *How New York Stole the Idea of Modern Art: Abstract Expressionism, Freedom, and the Cold War.* Trans. Arthur Goldhammer. Chicago: University of Chicago Press, 1983.

Gillespie, Don. "William Russell: American Percussion Composer." *Southern Quarterly* 36, no. 2 (Winter 1998): 34–55.

Goehr, Lydia. "Music and Musicians in Exile: The Romantic Legacy of a Double Life." In *Driven into Paradise: The Musical Migration from Nazi Germany to the United States*, 66–91. Berkeley: University of California Press, 1999.

Goldman, Edwin Franko. *Band Betterment*. New York: Carl Fischer, 1934.

Goldmark, Daniel. *Tunes for 'Toons: Music and the Hollywood Cartoon*. Berkeley: University of California Press, 2005.

Grassl, Markus, and Reinhard Kapp, eds. *Die Lehre von der musikalischen Aufführung in der Wiener Schule. Verhandlungen des Internationalen Colloquiums Wien 1995*. Vienna: Böhlau, 2002.

Gruber, Gerold, ed. *Arnold Schönberg. Interpretationen seiner Werke*. 2 vols. Laaber: Laaber, 2002.

Gumprecht, Holger. *"New Weimar" unter Palmen: Deutsche Schriftsteller im Exil in Los Angeles*. Berlin: Aufbau Taschenbuch, 1998.

Haack, Helmut. "Ausdruck und Texttreue: Bemerkungen zur Aufführungspraxis der Musik Schönbergs und seiner Schüler." In *Die Wiener Schule in der Musikgeschichte des 20. Jahrhunderts*, ed. Rudolf Stephan and Sigrid Wiesmann, 202–12. Vienna: Lafite, 1986.

Haimo, Ethan. *Schoenberg's Serial Odyssey: The Evolution of His Twelve-Tone Method, 1914–1928*. Oxford: Clarendon, 1990.

———. "Atonality, Analysis, and the Intentional Fallacy." *Music Theory Spectrum* 18 (Fall 1996): 167–99.

———. *Schoenberg's Transformation of Musical Language*. Cambridge: Cambridge University Press, 2006.

———. "Schoenberg, Bach, and B-A-C-H." *JASC* 7 (2007): 85–98.

Harrison, Lou. "Schoenberg in Several Ways." *National Centre for the Performing Arts Bombay Quarterly Journal* 4 (1975): 9–34.

Haselböck, Lukas. *Zwölftonmusik und Tonalität. Zur Vieldeutigkeit dodekaphoner Harmonik*. Laaber: Laaber, 2005.

Heilbut, Anthony. *Exiled in Paradise: German Refugee Artists and Intellectuals in America, from the 1930s to the Present*. New York: Viking, 1983.

Heister, Hanns-Werner, Claudia Maurer-Zenck, and Peter Petersen, eds. *Musik und Exil. Folgen des Nazismus für die internationale Musikkultur*. Frankfurt am Main: Fischer, 1993.

Henke, Matthias. *Arnold Schönberg*. Hamburg: Deutscher Taschenbuch Verlag, 2001.

Hertzberg, Arthur. *The Jews in America: Four Centuries of an Uneasy Encounter: A History*. New York: Simon and Schuster, 1989.

Heskes, Irene. *Passport to Jewish Music: Its History Traditions, and Culture*. Westport, CT: Greenwood, 1994.

Hesselink, Paul. "Variations on a Recitative, Op. 40: Correspondence from the Schoenberg Legacy." *JASI* 7, no. 2 (November 1983): 140–96.

Heyworth, Peter. *Otto Klemperer: His Life and Times*. Vol. 2: *1933–1973*. Cambridge: Cambridge University Press, 1996.

Hiam, Jonathan. "Music at Black Mountain College: The European Years, 1939–46." Ph.D. diss., University of North Carolina, Chapel Hill, 2005.

Hicks, Michael. "John Cage's Studies with Schoenberg." *American Music* 8, no. 2 (Summer 1990): 125–40.

Hill, Richard. "Schoenberg's Tone Rows and the Tonal System of the Future." *MQ* 22, no. 1 (January 1936): 14–37.

Hilmar, Ernst, ed. *Arnold Schönberg Gedenkausstellung 1974*. Vienna: Universal Edition, 1974.

Hilmar, Rosemary. "Alban Berg's Studies with Schoenberg." *JASI* 8 (June 1984): 7–30.

Hines, Anna. "Music at Black Mountain College: A Study of Experimental Ideas in Music." DMA thesis, University of Missouri, Kansas City, 1973.

Hinton, Stephen. "Hindemith and Weill: Cases of 'Inner' and 'Other' Direction." In *Driven into Paradise: The Musical Migration from Nazi Germany to the United States*, ed. Reinhold Brinkmann and Christoph Wolff, 261–78. Berkeley: University of California Press, 1999.

Hitchcock, H. Wiley. *Music in the United States: A Historical Introduction*. Englewood Cliffs, NJ: Prentice Hall, 2000.

Hölbling, Walter, and Reinhold Wagnleitner, eds. *The European Emigrant Experience in the USA*. Tübingen, Germany: Narr, 1992.

Hoffmann, Richard. "A Schoenberg Centennial Symposium at Oberlin College (March 2, 1974)." *JASI* 8 (June 1984): 59–77.

———. "Schoenberg est vivant." *JASI* 1 (February 1977): 65–67.

Horowitz, Joseph. *Classical Music in America: A History of Its Rise and Fall*. New York: Norton, 2005.

———. *Artists in Exile: How Refugees from War and Revolution Transformed the American Performing Arts*. New York: HarperCollins, 2008.

Iggers, Georg. *Historiography in the Twentieth Century: From Scientific Objectivity to the Postmodern Challenge*. Middletown, CT: Wesleyan University Press, 1997.

Jacob, Andreas. *Grundbegriffe der Musiktheorie Arnold Schönbergs*. 2 vols. Hildesheim, Germany: Olms, 2005.

Jackman, Jarrell, and Carla M. Borden, eds. *The Muses Flee Hitler: Cultural Transfer and Adaptation 1930–1945*. Washington, D.C.: Smithsonian Institution Press, 1983.

Jackson, Ronald. "Schoenberg as Performer of His Own Music." *Journal of Musicological Research* 24, no. 1 (January–March 2005): 49–69.

Jacobson, Matthew. *Whiteness of a Different Color: European Immigrants and the Alchemy of Race*. Cambridge, Mass.: Harvard University Press, 1998.

Jalowetz, Heinrich. "On the Spontaneity of Schoenberg's Music." *MQ* 30, no. 4 (October 1944): 385–408.

Jay, Martin. "The German Migration: Is There a Figure in the Carpet?" In *Exiles and Emigrés: The Flight of European Artists from Hitler*, ed. Stephanie Barron and Sabine Eckmann, 326–37. New York: Harry Abrams, 1997.

John, Eckart, and Heidy Zimmermann, eds. *Jüdische Musik? Fremdbilder – Eigenbilder*. Cologne: Böhlau, 2004.

Kangas, William. "The Ethics and Aesthetics of (Self)Representation: Arnold Schoenberg and Jewish Identity." *Leo Baeck Institute Yearbook* 45 (2000): 135–69.

Kapp, Reinhard. "Die Stellung Schönbergs in der Geschichte der Aufführungslehre." In *Arnold Schönberg – Neuerer der Musik*, ed. Rudolf Stephan and Sigrid Wiesmann, 85–101. Vienna: Lafite, 1996.

Kashner, Sam, and Nancy Schoenberger. *A Talent for Genius: The Life and Times of Oscar Levant*. New York: Villard, 1994.

Kater, Michael. *Composers of the Nazi Era: Eight Portraits*. New York: Oxford University Press, 2000.

Keathley, Elizabeth. "'Dick, Dika, Dickest': Dika Newlin's 'Thick Description' of Schönberg in America." *JASC* 4 (2002): 309–24.

Kelley, Dorothea. "Arnold Schoenberg's Sixtieth Birthday in Chautauqua." *JASI* 11, no. 2 (November 1988): 154–57.

Kimmey, John A., Jr., ed. *The Arnold Schoenberg–Hans Nachod Collection*. Detroit: Information Coordinators, 1979.

Knight, Lovina M. "Classes with Schoenberg January through June 1934." *JASI* 13 (November 1990): 137–63.

Kolleritsch, Otto, ed. *Die Wiener Schule und das Hakenkreuz. Das Schicksal der Moderne im gesellschaftspolitischen Kontext des 20. Jahrhunderts.* Studien zur Wertungsforschung 22. Vienna: Universal Edition, 1990.

Kostelanetz, Richard. "Milton Babbitt and John Cage: The Two Extremes of Avant-Garde Music." In *On Innovative Music(ians)*, 21–30. New York: Limelight, 1989.

Kowalke, Kim. "I'm an American! Whitman, Weill, and Cultural Identity." In *Walt Whitman and Modern Music: War, Desire, and the Trials of Nationhood*, ed. Lawrence Kramer, 109–31. London: Routledge, 2000.

Krasner, Louis. "Schoenberg's Violin Concerto." *JASI* 2, no. 2 (February 1978): 84–98.

Krenek, Ernst. *Music Here and Now.* New York: Norton, 1939.

———. *Studies in Counterpoint Based on the Twelve-Tone Technique.* New York: Schirmer, 1940.

———. "New Developments of the 12-Tone Technique." *Music Review* 4, no. 2 (May 1943): 81–97.

———. "Schönberg's Idiom and Technic." *MM* 21, no. 3 (March–April 1944): 131–34.

———. *Musik im goldenen Westen.* Vienna: Hollinek, 1949.

———. "Is the Twelve-Tone Technique on the Decline?" *MQ* 39, no. 4 (October 1953): 513–27.

———. "The Extents and Limits of Serial Techniques." *MQ* 46, no. 2 (April 1960): 210–32.

———. "America's Influence on Its Emigré Composers." *PNM* 8 (Spring–Summer 1970): 112–17.

Krohn, Claus-Dieter, Erwin Rotermund, Lutz Winckler, Wulf Koepke, and Dörte Schmidt, eds. *Kulturelle Räume und ästhetische Universalität. Musik und Musiker im Exil.* Munich: Edition Text + Kritik, 2008.

Langlie, Warren. "Arnold Schoenberg as a Teacher." Ph.D. diss., University of California, Los Angeles, 1960.

———. "Arnold Schoenberg as an Educator." In *Arnold Schönberg. Gedenkausstellung 1974*, ed. Ernst Hilmar, 92–99. Vienna: Universal Edition, 1974.

Lautner, Lois. "Arnold Schoenberg in Kammern." *Michigan Quarterly Review* 16, no. 1 (Winter 1977): 21–27.

Lazar, Moshe. "Arnold Schoenberg and His Doubles: A Psychodramatic Journey to His Roots." *JASI* 17, nos. 1–2 (June–November 1994): 8–161.

Leibowitz, René. *Schoenberg and His School: The Contemporary Stage of the Language of Music.* Trans. Dika Newlin. New York: Philosophical Library, 1949.

———. *Schoenberg.* Paris: Editions du Seuil, 1969.

Lerdahl, Fred. "Cognitive Constraints on Compositional Systems." In *Cognitive Processes in Music*, ed. John Sloboda, 231–59. New York: Oxford University Press, 1988.

Lessem, Alan. "The Refugee Composer in America: A Topic for Twentieth-Century Music History." *Canadian University Music Review* 6 (1985): 222–38.

———. "Teaching Americans Music: Some Emigré Composer Viewpoints, ca. 1930–1955." *JASI* 11, no. 1 (June 1988): 4–22.

———. "The Emigré Experience: Schoenberg in America." In *Constructive Dissonance: Arnold Schoenberg and the Transformation of Twentieth-Century Culture*, ed. Juliane Brand and Christopher Hailey, 58–68. Berkeley: University of California Press, 1997.

Lester, Joel. "Analysis and Performance in Schoenberg's Phantasy, Op. 47." In *Pianist, Scholar, Connoisseur: Essays in Honor of Jacob Lateiner*, ed. Bruce Brubaker and Jane Gottlieb, 151–74. Stuyvesant, NY: Pendragon, 2000.

Levant, Oscar. *The Memoirs of an Amnesiac.* New York: Putnam, 1965.

———. *The Unimportance of Being Oscar.* New York: Putnam, 1968.

Lewin, David. "A Study of Hexachord Levels in Schoenberg's *Violin Fantasy*." *PNM* 6, no. 1 (Fall–Winter 1967): 18–32.

Litwin, Stefan. "Musik als Geschichte, Geschichte als Musik. Zu Arnold Schönbergs Klavierkonzert op. 42 (1942)." *Dissonanz* 59 (February 1999): 12–17.

Mäckelmann, Michael. *Arnold Schönberg und das Judentum*. Hamburg: Verlag der Musikalienhandlung Karl Dieter Wagner, 1984.

———. "*Israel exists again* – Anmerkungen zu Arnold Schönbergs Entwurf einer Israel-Hymne." *Musikforschung* 39, no. 1 (1986): 18–29.

———. "Ein Gebet für Israel, als die Synagogen brannten. Über Schönbergs *Kol nidre* – zum Gedenken an den Pogrom der Kristallnacht 1938." *Neue Zeitschrift für Musik* 11, no. 5 (May 1988): 3–8.

Maegaard, Jan. "Schoenberg's Late Tonal Works." In *The Arnold Schoenberg Companion*, ed. Walter Bailey, 177–206. Westport, CT: Greenwood, 1998.

Mäkela, Tomi. "Schönbergs Klavierkonzert Opus 42 – Ein romantisches Virtuosenkonzert?" *Musikforschung* 45, no. 1 (1992): 1–20.

———. "The Californian Refugee Situation as a Context of Musical Creativity: Towards Criteria for 'Exile Composition.'" In *Interdisciplinary Studies in Musicology: Report from the Third International Conference 1996*, ed. Jan Steszewski and Maciej Jablonski, 245–56. Poznań: University of Poznań, 1997.

Mahler, Alma. *Gustav Mahler: Memories and Letters*. Ed. Donald Mitchell. Trans. B. Creighton. Seattle: University of Washington Press, 1975.

Mann, Thomas. *The Story of a Novel; The Genesis of Doctor Faustus*. Trans. Richard and Clara Winston. New York: Knopf, 1961.

———. *Letters of Thomas Mann — 1889–1955*. Ed. and trans. Richard and Clara Winston. Berkeley: University of California Press, 1990.

———. *Dr. Faustus: The Life of the German Composer as Told by a Friend*. Trans. John E. Woods. New York: Knopf, 1997.

———. *Doktor Faustus. Das Leben des deutschen Tonsetzers Adrian Leverkühn, erzählt von einem Freunde und Kommentar*. Ed. Ruprecht Wimmer and Stephan Stachorski. 4 vols. Frankfurt am Main: Fischer, 2007.

Marcus, Kenneth. *Musical Metropolis: Los Angeles and the Creation of a Music Culture, 1880–1940*. New York: Palgrave Macmillan, 2004.

Martens, Frederick. *Schönberg*. Little Biographies, Series I, Musicians. New York: Breitkopf and Härtel, 1922.

Mary, Maureen. "Letters: The Brief Love of John Cage for Pauline Schindler 1934–35." *Ex Tempore* 8 (Summer 1996): 1–26.

Mason, Marilyn. "An Organist Plays for Mr. Schoenberg." *Organ Institute Quarterly* 6 (Spring 1956): 19–20.

Mattes, Arnulf. "Zur Konstellation von Ausdruck und Spiel in Schönbergs *Phantasy for Violin with Piano Accompaniment* op. 47." *JASI* 7 (2005): 227–42.

———. "Reflected Colours – Reflective Forms: On the Interpretation of Arnold Schoenberg's Late Chamber Music Works." Ph.D. diss., University of Oslo, 2007.

Maurer-Zenck, Claudia. "Arnold Schönbergs Klavierkonzert. Versuch, analytisch Exilforschung zu betreiben." In *Musik im Exil. Folgen des Nazismus für die internationale Musikkultur*, ed. Hanns-Werner Heister, Claudia Maurer-Zenck, and Peter Petersen, 357–83. Frankfurt am Main: Fischer, 1993.

Mayer, Hans. "Ein Briefwechsel zwischen Arnold Schönberg und Hermann Scherchen, 1950." In *Hermann Scherchen Musiker, 1891–1966*, ed. Hansjörg Pauli and Dagmar Wünsche, 62–67. Berlin: Edition Hentrich, 1986.

McClary, Susan. "Terminal Prestige: The Case of Avant-Garde Music Composition." *Cultural Critique* 12 (Spring 1989): 57–81.

McDonald, Malcolm. *Schoenberg*. London: Dent, 1976; New York: Oxford University Press, 2008.

McGeary, Thomas. "The Publishing History of *Style and Idea*." *JASI* 9, no. 2 (November 1986): 181–209.

Mead, Andrew. *The Music of Milton Babbitt*. Princeton: Princeton University Press, 1994.

———. "Twelve-Tone Composition and the Music of Elliott Carter." In *Concert, Music, Rock, and Jazz since 1945*, ed. Elizabeth West Marvin and Richard Herrmann, 67–102. Rochester: University of Rochester Press, 1995.

Mead, Rita. *Henry Cowell's New Music, 1925–1936: The Society, the Music Editions, and the Recordings*. Ann Arbor: UMI Editions, 1981.

———. "Henry Cowell's New Music Society." *Journal of Musicology* 1, no. 4 (October 1982): 449–63.

Meine, Sabine. *Ein Zwölftöner in Paris. Studien zu Biographie und Wirkung von René Leibowitz (1913–1972)*. Augsburg, Germany: Wißner, 2000.

Mendes-Flohr, Paul. *German Jews: A Dual Identity*. New Haven: Yale University Press, 1999.

Metzer, David. "The Ascendancy of Musical Modernism in New York City, 1915–1929." Ph.D. diss., Yale University, 1993.

———. "The New York Reception of *Pierrot lunaire*: The 1923 Premiere and Its Aftermath." *MQ* 78, no. 4 (Winter 1994): 669–699.

Metzger, Heinz-Klaus and Rainer Riehn, eds. *Arnold Schönberg. Musik-Konzepte, Sonderband*. Munich: Edition Text und Kritik, 1980.

Meyer, Christian, and Therese Muxeneder, eds. *Arnold Schönberg: Catalogue raisonné*. Vienna: Christian Brandstätter, 2005.

Miller, Leta, and Fredric Lieberman. *Lou Harrison: Composing a World*. New York: Oxford University Press, 1998.

Mittelmann, Hanni, and Armin A. Wallas, eds. *Österreich-Konzeptionen und jüdisches Selbstverständnis. Identitäts-Transfigurationen*. Tübingen: Max Niemeyer, 2001.

Monod, Jacques-Louis. "Interview: Patricia Carpenter and Her Studies with Arnold Schoenberg." *Gamut: Journal of the Georgia Association of Music Theorists* 7 (1997): 61–74.

Monson, Karen. *Alma Mahler, Muse to Genius: From Fin-de-Siècle Vienna to Hollywood's Heyday*. Boston: Houghton Mifflin, 1983.

Móricz, Klára. "Jewish Nationalism in Twentieth-Century Art Music." Ph.D. diss., University of California, Berkeley, 1999.

———. *Jewish Identities: Nationalism, Racism and Utopianism in Twentieth-Century Music*. Berkeley: University of California Press, 2008.

Morris, Robert. *Composition with Pitch Classes*. New Haven: Yale University Press, 1987.

Muxeneder, Therese. "Schönberg-Werkstätte und Patentrezepte." *JASI* 7 (2005): 42–59.

———. "Ethik des Bewahrens. Exil und Rückkehr des Schönberg-Nachlasses." In *Kulturelle Räume und ästhetische Universalität. Musik und Musiker im Exil*, ed. Claus-Dieter Krohn, Erwin Rotermund, et al., 44–66. Munich: Edition Text + Kritik, 2008.

Neff, Severine. "'This I Have Learned from My Students': The Teachings of Arnold Schoenberg." *Gamut: Journal of the Georgia Association of Music Theorists* 7 (1997): 3–30.

———. "An Unlikely Synergy: Lou Harrison and Arnold Schoenberg." *Journal of the Society for American Music* 3, no. 2 (May 2009): 155–93.

Neff, Severine, ed. "Two Unpublished Manuscripts: Excerpts from Arnold Schoenberg's Second Book on Harmony and His Text on Performance." *Gamut: Journal of the Georgia Association of Music Theorists* 8 (1998): 19–30.

———. *Schoenberg: The Second String Quartet in F-sharp minor, Opus 10: Authoritative Score, Background and Analysis, Commentary*. New York: Norton, 2006.

Neher, André. *They Made Their Souls Anew.* Trans. David Maisel. SUNY Series in Modern Jewish Literature and Culture, ed. Sarah B. Cohen. Albany: State University of New York Press, 1990.

Neimoyer, Susan. "Rhapsody in Blue: A Culmination of George Gershwin's Early Music Education." Ph.D. diss., University of Washington, 2003.

Nettl, Bruno. "Displaced Musics and Immigrant Musicologists: Ethnomusicological and Biographical Perspectives." In *Driven into Paradise: The Musical Migration from Nazi Germany to the United States,* ed. Reinhold Brinkmann and Christoph Wolff, 54–65. Berkeley: University of California Press, 1999.

Neumeyer, David, and Giselher Schubert. "Arnold Schoenberg and Paul Hindemith." *JASI* 13, no. 1 (June 1990): 3–46.

Newlin, Dika. "Schoenberg in America, 1933–1948." *Music Survey* 1, nos. 5–6 (1949): 128–31, 185–89.

———. "Self-Revelation and the Law: Arnold Schoenberg in His Religious Works." *Yuval* 1 (1968): 104–220.

———. "Secret Tonality in Schoenberg's Piano Concerto." *PNM* 13, no. 1 (Fall–Winter 1974): 137–39.

———. *Bruckner – Mahler – Schoenberg*. 2nd rev. ed. New York: Norton, 1978.

———. *Schoenberg Remembered: Diaries and Recollections, 1938–1976*. New York: Pendragon, 1980.

Nono-Schoenberg, Nuria. *Arnold Schönberg, 1874–1951: Lebensgeschichte in Begegnungen.* Klagenfurt, Austria: Ritter, 1992.

Oja, Carol. *Making Music Modern: New York in the 1920s.* New York: Oxford University Press, 2000.

Olmstead, Andrea. *Roger Sessions. A Biography*. New York: Routledge, 2008.

Olmstead, Andrea, ed. *Conversations with Roger Sessions*. Boston: Northeastern University Press, 1987.

———. "The Correspondence Between Arnold Schoenberg and Roger Sessions." *JASI* 13, no. 1 (June 1990): 47–62.

———. *The Correspondence of Roger Sessions.* Boston: Northeastern University Press, 1992.

Page, Tim, ed. *The Glenn Gould Reader.* New York: Knopf, 1984.

Palmier, Jean-Marie. *Weimar in Exile: The Antifascist Emigration in Europe and America.* London: Verso, 2006.

Pass, Walter, Gerhard Scheit, and Wilhelm Svoboda, eds. *Orpheus im Exil. Die Vertreibung der österreichischen Musik von 1938 bis 1945*. Vienna: Verlag für Gesellschaftskritik, 1995.

Peles, Stephen. "Serialism and Complexity." In *The Cambridge History of American Music,* ed. David Nicholls, 496–515. Cambridge: Cambridge University Press, 1998.

Perle, George. "Evolution of the Tone Row: The Twelve-Tone Modal System." *Music Review* 2, no. 4 (November 1941): 273–87.

———. "Twelve-Tone Tonality." *Monthly Musical Record* 43 (October 1943): 175–79.

———. "Schönberg's Late Style." *Music Review* 12, no. 4 (November 1952): 274–82.

———. "Babbitt, Lewin, and Schoenberg: A Critique." *PNM* 2, no. 1 (Fall–Winter 1963): 120–27.

———. *Serial Composition and Atonality: An Introduction to the Music of Schoenberg, Berg and Webern*. Berkeley: University of California Press, 1992.

———. *Twelve-Tone Tonality.* Berkeley: University of California Press, 1996.

Petersen, Peter. "'A grave situation was created.' Schönbergs Klavierkonzert von 1942." In *Die Wiener Schule und das Hakenkreuz. Das Schicksal der Moderne im gesellschaftspolitischen*

Kontext des 20. Jahrhunderts, Studien zur Wertungsforschung 22, ed. Otto Kolleritsch, 65–91. Vienna: Universal Edition, 1990.

Pisk, Paul. "Arnold Schoenberg as Teacher." *American Society of University Composers: Proceedings of the Annual Conference* 2 (1967): 51–53.

———. "Memories of Schoenberg." *JASI* 1 (October 1976): 39–44.

Pitt, Leonard, and Dale Pitt. *Los Angeles A–Z: An Encyclopedia of the City and County.* Berkeley: University of California Press, 1997.

Pollack, Howard. *Aaron Copland: The Life and Work of an Uncommon Man.* New York: Henry Holt, 1999.

———. *George Gershwin: His Life and Work.* Berkeley: University of California Press, 2006.

Rahn, John. *Basic Atonal Theory.* New York: Longman, 1980.

Raksin, David. "Schoenberg as Teacher." *Serial: Newsletter of the Friends of the Arnold Schoenberg Institute* 2, no. 1 (1988): 1, 5; 3, no. 1 (1989): 1, 5.

Ravenscroft, Brenda. "Re-construction: Cage and Schoenberg." *Tempo* 60, no. 235 (January 2006): 2–14.

Reich, Willi. *Schoenberg: A Critical Biography.* Trans. Leo Black. New York: Praeger, 1971.

Reif, Jo-Ann. "Adrian Leverkühn, Arnold Schoenberg, Theodor Adorno: Theorists Real and Fictitious in Thomas Mann's *Doctor Faustus.*" *JASI* 7, no. 1 (June 1983): 102–12.

Riesman, David. *The Lonely Crowd: A Study of the Changing American Character.* New Haven: Yale University Press, 1950.

Ringer, Alexander. *Arnold Schoenberg: The Composer as Jew.* New York: Oxford University Press, 1990.

———. *Arnold Schönberg. Das Leben im Werk.* Stuttgart: Metzler, 2002.

Rochberg, George. *The Hexachord and Its Relationship to the Twelve-Tone Row.* Bryn Mawr, PA: Theodore Presser, 1955.

———. "Reflections on Schoenberg." *PNM* 11, no. 2 (Spring–Summer 1973): 56–83.

———. *The Aesthetics of Survival: A Composer's View of Twentieth-Century Music.* Ed. William Bolcom. Ann Arbor: University of Michigan Press, 1984.

Rockwell, John. *All American Music: Composition in the Late Twentieth Century.* New York: Knopf, 1983.

Rodriguez, José, ed. *Music and Dance in California.* Hollywood: Bureau of Musical Research, 1940.

Rosen, Charles. *Arnold Schoenberg.* Chicago: University of Chicago Press, 1996.

Rosenfeld, Paul. *An Hour with American Music.* Philadelphia: Lippincott, 1929.

Ross, Andrew. "Containing Culture in the Cold War." In *No Respect: Intellectuals and Popular Culture,* 42–64. New York: Routledge, 1989.

Rubsamen, Walter. "Schoenberg in America." *MQ* 37, no. 4 (October 1951): 469–89.

Rufer, Josef. *Composition with Twelve Tones Related Only to One Another.* Trans. Humphrey Searle. London: Rockliff, 1954.

———. *The Works of Arnold Schoenberg: A Catalogue of His Compositions, Writings, and Paintings.* Trans. Dika Newlin. London: Faber and Faber, 1962.

Russell, William. "Schoenberg the Teacher." *Tempo* 8, no. 12 (1940): 6, 13.

Rutman, Neil C. "The Solo Piano Works of Lou Harrison." DMA thesis, Peabody Conservatory of Music, 1983.

Samet, Bruce. *Hearing Aggregates.* University Park: Pennsylvania State University Press, 1987.

Satz, David. "Rudolf Kolisch in Boston." In *Die Wiener Schule in der Musikgeschichte des 20. Jahrhunderts,* ed. Rudolf Stephan and Sigrid Wiesmann, 196–201. Vienna: Lafite, 1986.

Saunders, Richard Drake, ed. *Music and Dance in California and the West.* Hollywood: Bureau of Musical Research, 1948.

Scharenberg, Sointu. *Überwinden der Prinzipien. Betrachtungen zu Arnold Schönbergs unkonventioneller Lehrtätigkeit zwischen 1898–1951*. Saarbrücken, Germany: Pfau, 2002.

Scherbera, Jürgen, Nils Grosch, and Joachim Lucchesi, eds. *Emigrierte Komponisten in der Medienlandschaft des Exils 1933–1945*. Stuttgart: M & P, 1998.

Schiller, David. *Bloch, Schoenberg, Bernstein: Assimilating Jewish Music*. New York: Oxford University Press, 2003.

Schmidt, Christian Martin. "Arnold Schönberg, der Doyen der Wiener Schule in Amerika?" In *Innenleben–Ansichten aus dem Exil. Ein Berliner Symposium*, ed. Hermann Haarmann, 120–33. Berlin: Fannei und Walz, 1995.

Schmidt, James. "Mephistopheles in Hollywood: Adorno, Mann, and Schoenberg." In *The Cambridge Companion to Theodor W. Adorno*, ed. Thomas Huhn, 148–80. Cambridge: Cambridge University Press, 2004.

Schmidt, Matthias. "Experimente der Geschichte oder was Cage von Schönberg über Cage lernte." In *Jahrbuch des Staatlichen Instituts für Musikforschung Preußischer Kulturbesitz*, ed. Günther Wagner, 210–33. Stuttgart: Metzler, 2000.

Schoenberg, Anne. "Belmont Music." *Serial: Newsletter of the Arnold Schoenberg Institute* 1, no. 2 (1987): 1.

Schoenberg, Arnold. *Models for Beginners in Composition*. New York: Schirmer, 1943 and rev. 1972.

———. *Theory of Harmony: Harmonielehre*. Trans. Robert D. W. Adams. New York: Philosophical Library, 1948.

———. "Further to the Schoenberg-Mann Controversy." *Music Survey* 2, no. 2 (1949): 78–80.

———. *Style and Idea*. Ed. Dika Newlin. New York: Philosophical Library, 1950 and Rpt. 2010.

———. *Structural Functions of Harmony*. Ed. and rev. Leonard Stein. New York: Norton, 1954.

———. *Moderne Psalmen von Arnold Schönberg*. Ed. Rudolf Kolisch. Mainz: B. Schott's Söhne, 1956.

———. *Preliminary Exercises in Counterpoint*. Ed. Leonard Stein. London: Faber, 1963.

———. *Fundamentals of Musical Composition*. Ed. Gerald Strang and Leonard Stein. London: Faber, 1967.

———. *Letters*. Ed. Erwin Stein, trans. Eithne Wilkins and Ernst Kaiser. London: Faber, 1964.

———. *Sämtliche Werke*. Ed. Josef Rufer et al. Vienna, 1966–.

———. "Vortrag/12 TK/Princeton." Ed. and trans. Claudio Spies. *PNM* 13 (Fall–Winter 1974): 58–136.

———. *Stil und Gedanke: Aufsätze zur Musik, Gesammelte Schriften 1*. Ed. Ivan Vojtěch. Frankfurt am Main: Fischer, 1976.

———. *Theory of Harmony*. Trans. Roy E. Carter. Berkeley: University of California Press, 1978 and Rpt. 2010.

———. *Style and Idea: Selected Writings of Arnold Schoenberg*. Ed. Leonard Stein, trans. Leo Black. Berkeley: University of California Press, 1984 and rev. 2010.

———. *Coherence, Counterpoint, Instrumentation, Instruction in Form*. Ed. Severine Neff, trans. Charlotte Cross and Severine Neff. Lincoln: University of Nebraska Press, 1993.

———. "*The Biblical Way*." Trans. Moshe Lazar. *JASI* 17, nos. 1–2 (June–November 1994): 162–330.

———. *The Musical Idea and the Logic, Technique, and Art of Its Presentation*. Ed., trans. and annotated Patricia Carpenter and Severine Neff. New York: Columbia University Press, 1995.

———. *A Schoenberg Reader: Documents of a Life*. Ed. Joseph Auner. New Haven: Yale University Press, 2003.

———. *Die Prinzessin*. Ed. Matthias Henke. Munich: Hanser, 2006.

———. *Stile herrschen, Gedanken siegen. Ausgewählte Schriften*. Ed. Anna Maria Morazzoni. Mainz: Schott, 2007.

Schoenberg, E. Randol. "Arnold Schoenberg and Albert Einstein: Their Relationship and Views on Zionism." *JASI* 2, no. 3 (November 1987): 134–91.

Schoenberg, E. Randol, and Bernhold Schmid, eds. *Arnold Schoenberg – Thomas Mann. A propos du Docteur Faustus. Lettres 1930–1951*. Lausanne: La Bibliothèque des Arts, 2002.

———.*Apropos Doktor Faustus: Briefwechsel Arnold Schönberg–Thomas Mann 1930–1951*. Vienna: Czernin, 2008.

Schoenberg-Nono, Nuria. "The Role of Extra-Musical Pursuits in Arnold Schoenberg's Creative Life." In *Arnold Schoenberg: Playing Cards*, ed. Nuria Schoenberg-Nono and Ernst R. Ragg, 16–31. Vienna: Piatnik, 1981.

Schoenberg-Nono, Nuria, ed. *Arnold Schoenberg – Self-Portrait: A Collection of Articles, Program Notes and Letters by the Composer about His Own Works*. Pacific Palisades: Belmont Music, 1988.

Schreiner, Alexander. *Alexander Schreiner Reminisces*. Salt Lake City: Publishers Press, 1984.

Schuller, Gunther. *Musings: The Musical Worlds of Gunther Schuller*. New York: Oxford University Press, 1986.

Schwarzschild, Steven. "Adorno and Schoenberg as Jews Between Kant and Hegel." *Leo Baeck Institute Yearbook* 35 (1990): 443–78.

Sessions, Roger. "Some Notes on Schoenberg and the 'Method of Composing with Twelve Tones.'" *Score* 6 (May 1952): 7–10.

———. *The Correspondence of Roger Sessions*. Ed. Andrea Olmstead. Boston: Northeastern University Press, 1992.

Shaw, Jennifer. "Schoenberg's Choral Symphony, *Die Jakobsleiter*, and other Wartime Fragments." Ph.D. diss., State University of New York at Stony Brook, 2002.

Shaw, Jennifer, and Joseph Auner, eds. *The Cambridge Companion to Schoenberg*. Cambridge: Cambridge University Press, 2010.

Shawn, Allen. *Arnold Schoenberg's Journey*. New York: Farrar, Straus and Giroux, 2002.

Shoaf, R. Wayne. "The Schoenberg–Malkin Correspondence." *JASI* 13, no. 2 (November 1990): 164–257.

———. *The Schoenberg Discography*. 2nd ed. Berkeley: Fallen Leaf, 1999.

Shreffler, Anne C. "The Myth of Empirical Historiography: A Response to Joseph N. Straus." *MQ* 84, no. 1 (Winter 2000): 30–39.

———. "Ideologies of Serialism: Stravinsky's *Threni* and the Congress for Cultural Freedom." In *Music and the Aesthetics of Modernity*, ed. Karol Berger and Anthony Newcomb, 217–45. Cambridge, Mass.: Harvard University Press, 2005.

Sichardt, Martina. "Deutsche Kunst – jüdische Identität. Arnold Schönbergs Oper *Moses und Aron*." In *Deutsche Meister–böse Geister. Nationale Selbstfindung in der Musik*, ed. Hermann Danuser und Herfried Münkler, 367–83. Schliengen, Germany: Argus, 2001.

Simms, Bryan. "Arnold Schoenberg, *Theory of Harmony* – Commentary." *Music Theory Spectrum* 4 (Spring 1982): 155–62.

Simms, Bryan, ed. *Schoenberg, Berg, and Webern: A Companion to the Second Viennese School*. Westport, CT: Greenwood, 1999.

———. *The Atonal Music of Arnold Schoenberg, 1908–1923*. New York: Oxford University Press, 2000.

———. "Serialism in the Early Music of Aaron Copland." *MQ* 90, no. 2 (Summer 2007): 176–96.

Slonimsky, Nicolas. *Perfect Pitch: A Life Story*. New York: Coleman-Ross, 1947.

Smith, Catherine P. *Making Music in Los Angeles: Transforming the Popular*. Berkeley: University of California Press, 2007.

Smith, Joan Allen. *Schoenberg and His Circle – A Viennese Portrait*. New York: Schirmer, 1986.

Smyth, David. "Schoenberg and Dial Records: The Composer's Correspondence with Ross Russell." *JASI* 12, no. 1 (June 1989): 68–90.

———. "Stravinsky as Serialist: The Sketches for *Threni*." *Music Theory Spectrum* 22, no. 2 (Fall 2000): 205–24.

Stein, Leonard. "A Note on the Genesis of the *Ode to Napoleon*." *JASI* 2, no. 1 (March 1977): 52–53.

———. "Schoenberg's Jewish Identity: A Chronology of Source Materials." *JASI* 3, no. 1 (March 1979): 3–10.

———. "Stokowski and the *Gurrelieder* Fanfare." *JASI* 3, no. 2 (October 1979): 219–22.

Steiner, Fred. "A History of the First Complete Recording of the Schoenberg String Quartets." *JASI* 2, no. 2 (February 1978): 122–37.

Stephan, Alexander. *"Communazis": FBI Surveillance of German Emigré Writers*. Trans. Jan van Heurck. New Haven: Yale University Press, 2000.

Sterne, Colin. *Arnold Schoenberg: The Composer as Numerologist*. Lewiston: Edwin Mellen, 1993.

Steuermann, Clara, et al. *The Not Quite Innocent Bystander: Writings of Edward Steuermann*. Trans. Richard Cantwell and Charles Messner. Lincoln: University of Nebraska Press, 1989.

Stevens, Halsey. "A Conversation with Schoenberg about Painting." *JASI* 2, no. 3 (June 1978): 178–80.

Strasser, Michael. "*A Survivor from Warsaw* as Personal Parable." *Music & Letters* 76, no. 1 (February 1998): 52–63.

Straus, Joseph N. "The Myth of Serial Tyranny in the 1950s and 1960s." *MQ* 83, no. 3 (Fall 1999): 301–43.

———. *Stravinsky's Late Music*. Cambridge: Cambridge University Press, 2001.

———. "Stravinsky the Serialist." In *The Cambridge Companion to Stravinsky*, ed. Jonathan Cross, 149–74. Cambridge: Cambridge University Press, 2003.

———. "A Revisionist History of Twelve-Tone Serialism in American Music." *Journal of the Society for American Music* 2, no. 3 (August 2008): 355–95.

———. *Twelve-Tone Music in America*. Cambridge: Cambridge University Press, 2009.

Stuckenschmidt, Hans Heinz. *Arnold Schoenberg: His Life, World, and Work*. Trans. Humphrey Searle. New York: Schirmer, 1978.

Szmolyan, Walter. "Schönberg aus der Sicht seiner Schüler." *Österreichische Musikzeitschrift* 37, no. 10 (October 1982): 540–44.

Tallack, Douglas. *Twentieth-Century America: The Intellectual and Cultural Context*. Essex: Longman, 1991.

Taruskin, Richard. "The Dark Side of Modern Music: The Sins of Toscanini, Stravinsky, and Schoenberg." *New Republic*, 5 September 1988, 28–34.

———. "The Poietic Fallacy: Review of *Arnold Schoenberg's Journey*, by Allen Shawn." *Musical Times* 145, no. 1886 (Spring 2004): 7–34.

Thomson, Virgil. *Virgil Thomson*. New York: Knopf, 1966.

Tischler, Barbara. *An American Music: The Search for an American Musical Identity*. New York: Oxford University Press, 1986.

Toldi, Julius. *American Kaleidoscope*. New York: Philosophical Library, 1960.

Trenkamp, Anne, and John G. Suess, eds. *Studies in the Schoenbergian Movement in Vienna and the United States: Essays in Honor of Marcel Dick*. Lewiston: Mellen, 1990.

Trotter, William. *Priest of Music: The Life of Dimitri Mitropoulos*. Portland: Amadeus, 1995.

Türcke, Berthold. "Felix Greissle (1894–1982)." *JASI* 6, no. 1 (June 1982): 4–7.

Vilar-Payá, María Luisa. "Arnold Schoenberg's Fourth String Quartet and Milton Babbitt: Reconsidering an American Analytical Legacy." Ph.D. diss., University of California, Berkeley, 1999.

Velten, Klaus. "Werkidee und Kompositionsverfahren in Schönbergs Prelude zu einer Genesis-Suite (Opus 44)." *Zeitschrift für Musikpädagogik* 3, no. 6 (1978): 43–47.

Viertel, Salka. *The Kindness of Strangers*. New York: Holt, Rinehart, and Winston, 1969.

Walsh, Stephen. *Stravinsky: The Second Exile: France and America, 1934–1971*. New York: Knopf, 2006.

Waitzbauer, Harald. "Arnold Schönberg und das Mattsee-Ereignis. Sommerfrischen-Antisemitismus in Österreich und Salzburg." *JASC* 5 (2003): 14–26.

Watkins, Glenn. "Schoenberg and the Organ." *PNM* 4, no. 1 (Fall–Winter 1965): 119–35.

Ward, Keith. "Musical Idealism: A Study of the Aesthetics of Arnold Schoenberg and Charles Ives." Ph.D. diss., Northwestern University, 1986.

Weber, Horst, Manuela Schwartz, and Stefan Drees, eds. *Quellen zur Geschichte emigrierter Musiker 1933–1950*. Vol. 1: *California*. Vol. 2: *New York*. Berlin: de Gruyter, 2003.

Weiss, Adolph. "The Lyceum of Schönberg." *MM* 9, no. 3 (March–April 1932): 99–107.

Wellesz, Egon. *Arnold Schoenberg*. Trans. W. H. Kerridge. London: Dent, 1925.

Whitlock, E. Clyde, and Richard Drake Saunders, eds. *Music and Dance in Texas, Oklahoma and the Southwest*. Hollywood: Bureau of Musical Research, 1950.

Whittall, Arnold. *The Cambridge Introduction to Serialism*. Cambridge: Cambridge University Press, 2008.

Wistrich, Robert, ed. *Austrians and Jews in the Twentieth Century: From Franz Joseph to Waldheim*. New York: St. Martin's, 1992.

Wlodarski, Amy. "The Sounds of Memory: German Musical Representations of the Holocaust, 1945–1965." Ph.D. diss., University of Rochester, 2005.

———. "'An Idea Can Never Perish': Memory, the Musical Idea, and Schoenberg's *A Survivor from Warsaw*." *Journal of Musicology* 24, no. 4 (October 2007): 581–608.

Wolpe, Stefan. "Thinking Twice [1959]." In *Contemporary Composers on Contemporary Music*, ed. Elliott Schwartz and Barney Childs, 274–307. New York: Holt, Rinehart and Winston, 1965.

Wright, James K., and Alan Gillmor, eds. *Schoenberg's Chamber Music, Schoenberg's World*. Hillsdale, NY: Pendragon, 2009.

Wuorinen, Charles. *Simple Composition*. New York: C. F. Peters, 1979 and Rpt. 1994.

———. "The Outlook for Young Composers." *PNM* 1, no. 2 (Spring 1963): 54–61.

Yang, Mina. "New Directions in California Music: Construction of a Pacific Rim Cultural Identity, 1925–1945." Ph.D. diss., Yale University, 2001.

Zam, Maurice. "How Schoenberg Came to UCLA." *JASI* 3, no. 2 (October 1979): 223–27.

Zuck, Barbara. *A History of Musical Americanism*. Ann Arbor: UMI Research Press, 1980.

Index